Dec. 24, 2015

My Dearest,
May we have many
more happy miles.
Love &
Cin

Lupine and orange poppy, Washington

GUIDE TO
Scenic Highways & Byways

FOURTH EDITION

NATIONAL
GEOGRAPHIC

WASHINGTON, D.C.

CONTENTS

7   Call of the Road
8   America's Byways
10   About the Guide
11   Map Key

NEW ENGLAND
15   Maine
22   New Hampshire
31   Vermont
40   Massachusetts
48   Rhode Island
50   Connecticut

MIDDLE ATLANTIC
61   New York
73   New Jersey
75   Delaware
77   Pennsylvania
80   Maryland
90   West Virginia
97   Virginia

SOUTHEAST
109   North Carolina
115   Tennessee
121   Kentucky
127   Mississippi
132   Alabama
136   South Carolina
142   Georgia
146   Florida

GREAT LAKES
163   Michigan
169   Ohio
178   Indiana
185   Illinois
192   Wisconsin
199   Minnesota

CENTRAL PLAINS
213   North Dakota
219   South Dakota
227   Nebraska

229   Kansas
231   Missouri
237   Iowa

SOUTH CENTRAL
245   Louisiana
252   Texas
261   Oklahoma
267   Arkansas

SOUTHWEST
277   Utah
295   Arizona
310   New Mexico
323   Colorado

ROCKY MOUNTAINS
347   Montana
356   Wyoming
363   Idaho

NORTHWEST
381   Alaska
398   Washington
417   Oregon

FAR WEST
443   Nevada
449   California
475   Hawaii

484   State Tourism Offices
486   America's Byways
488   Illustrations Credits
489   Index
494   Acknowledgments

Cover: San Sebastian State Park,
Pacific Coast Scenic Byway, Oregon
pp. 2–3: Mount Rainier National Park,
Washington
Opposite: Former U.S. Coast Guard
Station, Old King's Highway,
Massachusetts

5

Call of the Road

D uring my many years as a travel writer, I moved across continents, oceans, and sometimes hemispheres. Yet my best moments—the kind that distill all the pleasure of being alive—have occurred on the back roads of America: booming past Wyoming buttes, with the west wind shoving at the car and a huge blue sky overhead; tunneling beneath a chromatic woodland of fall oaks and maples somewhere in the Virginia mountains; or winding along the California coast, with the sea stacks shimmering in the Pacific mist.

Roads web this country in a labyrinth of possibilities. As a nation of road builders, we have been hacking and cajoling trails, traces, country lanes, and superhighways out of the wilderness for some 400 years now. Happily, most of the old, slow-moving thoroughfares are still out there, weaving in and around the brash new ones. Ambling across the most scenic corners of the country, they are the thin meandering lines on the map that make you want to wander for the sheer sake of wandering. Just the names of some of these byways—Blue Ridge Parkway, Route 1, Great River Road, Going-to-the-Sun-Road, the Natchez Trace—are part of our national psyche.

"Great beautiful clouds floated overhead, valley clouds that made you feel the vastness of... America from mouth to mouth and from tip to tip."
—Jack Kerouac,
On the Road

More than 20 years ago, one social commentator remarked that we Americans had "become space-eaters, mile-consumers: Unless we can gulp distances down, we feel laggard as lizards." But in the current age of global living and virtual reality, many of us are ready to slow down and step backward a little in time. And nothing seems to bring the world back to a personal dimension better than a drive down these scenic highways and byways. Far from cyberspace, they still travel the true spaces of America, celebrating the regional diversity and hard-won histories that give this land its character.

In a place like Louisiana, for example, you can travel in a matter of miles from the robust high-spiritedness of Cajun swamp country to the manicured grace of an antebellum town. In the Northwest you can climb into mountains dense with fog-fed evergreens, then cascade down into the arid grandeur of the high desert. In New England you can wind through whitewashed villages as solid as Plymouth Rock or along coastlines whose ruggedness has inspired generations of painters and writers. In the Southwest you can explore adobe pueblos that haven't changed much in 200 years or deserted mining towns that lasted less than a decade. And in the Central Plains you can follow the bends of the Missouri River as it weaves through an exuberant wine country.

Each byway has its own character, its own promise. But all of them will give you back that sense of adventure that Walt Whitman proclaimed a century ago in his "Song of the Open Road": "Afoot, lighthearted, I take to the open road. Healthy, free, the world before me."

—*K. M. Kostyal*

South Dakota 240 through Badlands National Park

Dawn in Columbia National Wildlife Refuge, Coulee Corridor Scenic Byway, Washington

America's Byways.
Come CLOSER... AMERICA'S BYWAYS®

When you travel America's Byways, you encounter the familiar—small towns, large cities, historic structures, and beautiful scenery—but the stories behind the familiar are fascinating. In a small town on New Year's Eve, watch a 40-foot fiberglass walleye drop; in a fast-moving city, drive the same road as the first automobile test drive; visit the historic lighthouse where the first shot of the War of 1812 was fired; and travel a pristine byway that is totally on the water.

Follow the lure of undeveloped territory and the promise of wealth in logging, mining, hunting, and farming. Meet the explorers, conquistadores, Vikings, and voyagers; and understand the challenges and opportunities they found in this great country. Explore the byways that stretch across America—those that follow ancient trails, winding rivers, and historic roads. They tell the history of the Native Americans, westward pioneers, and wealthy industrialists.

Experience the byways and cross a "pig-tailed" bridge, a grand canyon, lush ranchland, or ancient path. Discover the byways where Judy Garland sang, Billy the Kid robbed, George Washington bathed, Martin Luther King, Jr., marched, and Sitting Bull rests. And learn the importance of protecting the land, honoring our history, and preserving our cultures for future generations.

America's Byways appeal to all your senses. Look up to catch a glimpse of rock climbers, snow skiers, and bald eagles. See war reenactments, alligators crawling, dinosaur footprints, and children playing. Listen to the locals share barbecue traditions and tall tale folklore; and hear the sounds of roaring rapids, banjo strumming, and moose calling. Smell pecan pie, wildflower fields, and pine forests. Touch a blue glacier or a newborn calf. And when you're hungry, taste fresh lobster, apple cider, cherry pie, or piñon cookies.

And, of course, the byways will take care of your sense of adventure! You can hike a "fourteener," explore a cave, spot a wildcat, and mine for gold. Get out and kayak, windsurf, ice fish, mountain bike, or ride a hot-air balloon.

When you drive America's Byways to a small town, big city, national wildlife refuge, or through a national forest, national park, or national heritage area, take some time and enjoy the byway experience. We invite you to learn about the culture and history of the byways, explore nature, watch the wildlife, and ride, hike, dive, climb, or soar!

Come CLOSER . . . America's Byways capture your imagination, satisfy your curiosity, and enliven your spirit every season of the year.

www.byways.org

America's Byways offer us the opportunity to explore our nation in a truly unique way. The U.S. Department of Transportation is committed to preserving these scenic routes to ensure travelers experience the best of U.S. history, culture, and nature. The beauty of these roadways helps tell our American story, whether traveling across the country or close to home.

—Ray LaHood,
U.S. Secretary of
Transportation

9

The U.S. Department of Transportation Federal Highway Administration National Scenic Byways Program began in 1991 to recognize roads having outstanding archaeological, cultural, historic, natural, recreational and scenic qualities. In 1996, the first roads were designated by the U.S. Secretary of Transportation as National Scenic Byways and All-American Roads—recognized today as America's Byways®.

Paddling Lake Pend Oreille, Pend Oreille Scenic Byway, Idaho

About the Guide

America has long been celebrated for its beauty and magic, and studies show that driving for pleasure is the nation's most popular outdoor pastime. This book combines the scenery with the activity and detailed regional maps to bring you a guide you'll use both in planning unforgettable trips and as an indispensable mile-by-mile companion.

To come up with 300 drives that reveal the scenic wonder and diversity of the 50 states, the staff considered many hundreds of possibilities—federal and state highways and parkways, county and local routes, National Park, National Forest Service, and Bureau of Land Management roads. We painfully winnowed the list to the selection before you, then sent writers out to explore every mile and report on what they saw. All states have scenic highway programs, and their travel offices can tell you about other excellent drives.

Some of the longest roads have been written in segments. For example, we treat Mississippi's Great River Road in ten drives. The Mississippi River Parkway Commission *(222 State St., Suite 400, Madison, WI 53703. 866-763-8310. www.experiencemississippiriver.com)* offers a map of the entire route.

> "I might have seen more of America when I was a child if I hadn't had to spend so much of my time protecting my half of the back seat from incursions by my sister."
>
> —Calvin Trillin,
> *Travels with Alice*

To the best of our knowledge, information about the sites is accurate as of press time, but call ahead when possible. In addition to the stated days of operation, many sites close on national holidays. Seasons in the headings are writers' recommendations of when best to go; unless otherwise stated, though, the roads are open year-round. All mileages are approximate, and drive times allow for little or no stopping. To savor the drives fully—to stop at sites and overlooks and to take side trips and hikes—leave considerably more time.

With this book and a good road map you're sure to enjoy your rambles across America's enthralling landscape.

Appalachian Trail, Great Smoky Mountains NP

MAP KEY and ABBREVIATIONS

National Battlefield	N.B.	
National Battlefield Park	N.B.P.	
National Conservation Area	N.C.A.	
National Historical Park	N.H.P.	
National Historic Site	N.H.S.	
National Lakeshore	N.L.	
National Memorial	NAT. MEM.	
National Monument	NAT. MON., N.M.	
National Park	N.P.	
National Preserve	NAT. PRES.	
National Recreation Area	N.R.A.	
National River		
National Scenic Riverways		
National Scientific Reserve		
National Seashore		
National Volcanic Monument	N.V.M.	

Forest Reserve	FOR. RES., F.R.
National Grassland	
National Forest	NAT. FOR., N.F.
State Forest	S.F.
Wilderness	

National Wildlife Refuge	N.W.R.
National Wildlife and Fish Refuge	
Wildlife Refuge	

State Historic Site	
State Historical Park	S.H.P.
State Natural Area	
State Park	S.P.
State Recreation Area	S.R.A.
State Reserve	S.R.

Indian Reservation	IND. RES., I.R.

Featured scenic drive — Divider between adjacent routes (on chapter opener maps only)

Interstate highway — (40)

U.S. federal highway — (17)

State road — (29)

County, local, or provincial road — (9)

Trail

Ferry

State or national border

Forest / wilderness boundary

POPULATION
● **San Antonio** — 500,000 and over
● **Lancaster** — 50,000 to under 500,000
● Williamsburg — under 50,000

(★) State capital   ) (Pass, Tunnel
! Dam   = Falls
■ Point of interest

11

Point Piños, Monterey Peninsula, California

0   50   100 miles
0   50   100   150 kilometers

CANADA

Smugglers
Notch
p. 34

Champlain Islands
p. 36

*Lake
Champlain*

Burlington

Montpelier

VERMONT

Vermont 22A
p. 38

Vermont 100
p. 31

Equinox Skyline Drive
p. 33

Lake Ontario

Rochester

Syracuse

NEW YORK

Albany

Mohawk Trail Drive
p. 40

MASSACH

Tyringham Valley
p. 42

Springfield

Binghamton

Litchfield Hills
p. 54

Hartford

CONNECTICU

Scranton

Merritt Parkway
p. 53

New Haven
Bridgeport

PENNSYLVANIA

Allentown

New York

**NEW
JERSEY**

Harrisburg

Trenton

Lower
Connecticut
River Valley
p. 52

New England

Maine, New Hampshire,
Vermont, Massachusetts,
Rhode Island, Connecticut

MAINE

Three Rivers
Scenic Drive
p. 22

Old Canada Road
Scenic Byway
p. 21

ctory
asin
rive
35

Rangeley Lakes
Scenic Byway
p. 20

Maine's
Big Sur
p. 15

Bangor

North Road
p. 23

Deer Isle
Drive
p. 19

Mt. Washington
Auto Road
p. 25

Augusta

Acadia
All-American Road
p. 18

White Mountain
Trail
p. 24

Kancamagus
Scenic Byway
p. 26

andwich
otch Road
p. 28

Portland

NEW
AMPSHIRE

New Hampshire 153
p. 29

Concord

Gulf of Maine

Connecticut River Byway
. 30

Cape Ann Ramble
p. 43

ETTS

Boston

Worcester

Old King's Highway
p. 45

ATLANTIC
OCEAN

Conn. State
te. 169
. 50

Providence

RHODE
ISLAND

Rhode Island 77
p. 48

Ocean Drive
p. 49

MAINE

Maine's Big Sur

Ellsworth to Calais on US 1 and Maine 186, 187, 189, and 190

- 197 miles • 1 day • Spring through fall. Road to Schoodic Point is one way.

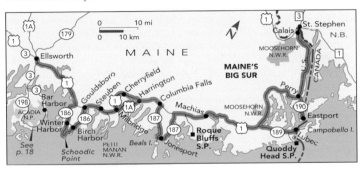

US 1 from Ellsworth to Calais is truly a road less traveled. Most tourists never get past Bar Harbor and miss the crashing surf at Acadia National Park's Schoodic Point, the tiny fishing villages, and the small cities near the Canadian border. This route includes the **Schoodic Scenic Byway** and much more.

Start at **Ellsworth** and head north on US 1 for 9 miles to the Hancock-Sullivan Bridge across **Taunton Bay.** Pull over after 1 mile at the **Frenchman Bay Scenic Turnout** for views of Cadillac Mountain and Mount Desert Island. Sixteen miles east of Ellsworth, turn right on Me. 186 for **Acadia National Park's Schoodic Point** *(207-288-3338. www.nps.gov/acad/. Adm. fee April-Oct.).* For the next 6 miles the road winds along the eastern shore of **Frenchman Bay** to Winter Harbor Village. Less than a mile from town, turn right for a side trip to **Schoodic Point,** a 2,266-acre preserve with a 6-mile drive along the windswept granite shores of **Schoodic Peninsula,** views of Mount Desert and Cadillac Mountain, hiking trails, and tidal pools full of life. The park road ends at the tiny fishing village of Wonsqueak Harbor.

Turn right on Me. 186 a few miles north at Birch Harbor. At the end of Me. 186, continue north again on US 1 and continue for 2 miles, turning right to visit **Bartlett Maine Estate Winery** *(207-546-2408. www.bartlettwinery .com. Tastings June–mid-Oct.),* where the Bartlett family has been making fruit wines since 1983. Follow US 1 for 3 miles to reach Washington County, the

Kennebec River and fall foliage

15

Corea, a coastal fishing village near Steuben

Sunrise County. Once the territory of the Passamaquoddy Indians, it is larger than Delaware and earned its sobriquet by being the first place in the United States to greet the rising sun each morning. It could as easily have been called the Blueberry County—about 30 million pounds are harvested each year.

Turn right onto Pigeon Hill Road in **Steuben** (Stoo-BEN) to visit the 8,100-acre **Maine Coastal Islands National Wildlife Refuge** *(207-594-0600. www.fws.gov/northeast/mainecoastal)*, where more than 300 bird species—including bald eagle, peregrine falcon, and roseate tern—have been sighted. A few miles farther, at the head of **Narraguagus Bay**, is **Milbridge,** a center for seafood landings and processing. Stay on US 1 at the junction of US 1A to visit **Cherryfield,** the "blueberry capital of the world." To skip Cherryfield and cut out several miles of driving, take 1A north for 8 miles to Harrington. Continue for 3.5 miles past Harrington to **Columbia Falls** and stop by the **Thomas Ruggles House** *(207-483-4637. www.ruggleshouse.org. June–mid-Oct.; adm. fee)*, built for a rich lumber dealer in 1818. Just past Columbia Falls is a right turn onto Me. 187 for a 10-mile side trip to the boatbuilding and fishing communities of **Jonesport** and **Beals.** In Jonesport, look for the puffin mailbox of Capt. Barna Norton to sign on for a cruise to **Machias Seal Island** or **Petit Manan Island** *(207-497-5933. June–Aug.; fares)*. Take Me. 187 back along the shore of **Chandler Bay** to US 1.

Once back on US 1, it's less than 2 miles to the turnoff for **Roque Bluffs State Park** *(207-255-3475. www.maine.gov/doc/parks. May–late-Oct.; adm. fee)*, with its sandy beach and freshwater swimming pond. The shire town of Machias is just 5 miles beyond the turnoff. Turn right on Me. 92 just south of town to visit the **Fort O'Brien State Historic Site** *(207-941-4014. www.maine.gov/doc/parks. Mem. Day–Labor Day; free to drive through, adm. fee to stay)*, near where the first naval battle of the Revolution was fought in 1775, and **Jasper Beach,** with its pebbles of jasper and rhyolite.

About 16 miles past Machias, turn right onto Me. 189 for Quoddy Head State Park, Lubec, and Campobello Island. Turn off Me. 189 after 9.5 miles to go to **Quoddy Head State Park** *(207-733-0911. www.maine.gov/doc/parks. May–mid-Oct.; adm. fee)*, with adjacent **West Quoddy Head Light** *(open for visits special dates only)*. The park's steep ledges offer a vantage point for the **Bay of Fundy** tides, which rise 20 to 30 feet. The lighthouse, perched atop a 90-foot cliff on the easternmost point of land in the United States, is visible from 20 miles at sea.

Once back on Me. 189, continue toward **Lubec**. This easternmost town in the United States was once home to 19 sardine factories. It's also the access point for the **International Bridge** to New Brunswick, Canada's **Campobello Island**, and the 2,800-acre **Roosevelt Campobello International Park** *(506-752-2922. www.nps.gov/roca. Late-May–mid-Oct.),* summer home of Franklin D. Roosevelt. As you climb the hill after clearing customs, turn around and look across the **Narrows**, where the strongest tidal currents on the East Coast flow at 15 miles an hour. **Friar's Head Picnic Area,** on the left just before the entrance to the international park, offers views of Lubec, Eastport, Cobscook Bay, and the mouth of **Passamaquoddy Bay.** If you're headed for Eastport and want to save about 40 miles of driving, consider taking the ferry. The Deer Isle ferry leaves just a few miles past the park entrance; from Deer Isle you can take another ferry to Eastport.

Retrace Me. 189 to the junction of US 1 and head north toward Calais. After 3 miles the road enters the southern boundary of the **Edmunds Unit** of the **Moosehorn National Wildlife Refuge** *(207-454-7161. www.fws.gov/northeast/moosehorn),* a breeding ground for migratory birds and other wildlife, including the reclusive American woodcock. Many of its 7,200 acres border **Cobscook Bay,** and when you watch the tide come in from the shores of **Cobscook Bay State Park** *(207-726-4412. www.maine .gov/doc/parks. Mid-May–Oct.; adm. fee),* it's easy to understand why Native Americans named the bay "boiling tides"—they average 24 feet in height.

A pet plan of FDR, the Passamaquoddy Tidal Project, begun in 1934, would have used the rise and fall of the bay tides for electricity—but it never got off the ground.

Seven miles past the state park entrance, watch for the turnoff to **Pembroke Falls,** one of the nation's largest reversing falls, a tidal phenomenon. The road to the falls is poorly marked: Turn right off US 1 onto Leighton Point Road; after 3.2 miles, turn right and continue for 1.2 miles past the Clarkside Cemetery. When the road forks, go left and continue 1.7 miles into the park. The tip of **Mahar Point** provides a fine view of the fierce white water created when **Dennys Bay** and **Whiting Bay** flow into Cobscook Bay. Watch for bald eagles, ospreys, and seals.

Halfway between the Equator and the North Pole lies the town of **Perry,** named for Commodore Oliver H. Perry, a hero of the War of 1812. Two miles from the Perry town line, at the junction of US 1 and Me. 190, turn right onto 190 for Eastport. For the first few miles the road passes by the **Pleasant Point Indian Reservation,** home to over 850 Passamaquoddy Indians. It's another 5 miles to downtown **Eastport.** To see **Old Sow Whirlpool,** one of the world's largest, turn left onto Water Street at the end of Me. 190, pass the entrance to the Deer Isle ferry, and continue to **Dog Island** at the end of the road. The whirlpool is best about two hours before high tide.

Back at the junction of US 1 and Me. 190, continue north on US 1 for 2 miles to the **45th Parallel Picnic Area.** The red granite stone marking the halfway point was erected in 1896 by the National Geographic Society.

About 5 miles from here, pull over at the next rest area to view the red granite cliffs of the **St. Croix River.** Between Robbinston and Calais look for 12 small, sequentially numbered granite markers on the river side of the road. Lumberman and journalist James S. Pike put them there in 1870 to time his racehorses. **St. Croix Island International Historic Site** *(207-454-3871. www.nps.gov/sacr),* at the Calais town line, is named for two long coves that meet to form a cross. Samuel de Champlain landed here in 1604, making this island in the middle of the St. Croix River the site of the country's first white settlement north of St. Augustine, Florida.

The city of **Calais** (CAL-lus), along the bank of the St. Croix River across from St. Stephen, New Brunswick, is one of the busiest ports of entry along the 3,000-mile U.S.-Canada border. Continue north on US 1 through town for 5 miles to the approximately 20,000-acre **Baring Unit** of the **Moosehorn Wildlife Refuge** *(207-454-7161. www.fws.gov/ northeast/moosehorn).* With the Edmunds Unit to the south, it's the northernmost in a chain of migratory bird refuges that extends from Maine to Florida. A fitting sentinel at the end of this road to the border, the American bald eagle has taken up residence here. Nesting areas line the entrance to the refuge at Charlotte Road.

Acadia All-American Road

Acadia National Park on Mount Desert Island

- 40 miles - 3 hours - Spring through fall. Expect traffic in July, August, and late September (for foliage). Not maintained in winter.

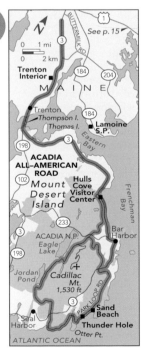

The **Park Loop Road** of **Acadia National Park** *(207-288-3338. www.nps.gov/acad. Adm. fee May-Oct.)* is a gently graded, two-lane blacktop winding through dense woodland and along rocky shoreline to the top of 1,530-foot Cadillac Mountain, with 360-degree views of the Atlantic Ocean and Maine coast. (If you're an early riser, drive to the summit before dawn for a spectacular sunrise.)

The drive begins about 10 miles north of Acadia on Route 3. South of Buttermilk Road in **Trenton,** watch for rare moose and other diverse wildlife inside the **Trenton Interior,** where seasonal deer hunting is permitted. On **Thomas** and **Thompson Islands** *(www .acadiamagic.com/thompson-island. Mid-May–mid-Oct.),* explore wildlife and tidal pools while watching for boats and planes launching from **Northeast Creek.** Continue east on Route 3 about 5 miles to **Hulls Cove.**

This loop begins at the **Hulls Cove Visitor Center** *(207-288-3338. Mid-April–Oct.)* near Frenchman Bay, first explored by Samuel de Champlain in 1604. After 5 miles, turn off for **Sieur De Monts** to visit the **Nature Center** *(207-288-3003. Mid-May–mid-Oct., call for hours)* and the **Abbe Museum** *(207-288-3519. www.abbemuseum.org. Mid-May–Nov.; adm. fee).*

Continue for 1 mile to the **Champlain Mountain Overlook,** offering a magnificent panorama of the Gouldsboro Hills, Frenchman Bay, and the tip of Schoodic Peninsula. As you leave, look back to the left toward **Thrumcap Island,** a rookery for gulls and cormorants. Four miles farther is **Sand Beach,** consisting mostly of crushed marine shells.

Stop a half mile past the beach at **Thunder Hole.** When seas run high, huge waves rush into a narrow slot in the rocks, forcing air trapped at the back of the chasm to compress and make a thundering sound. A mile past Thunder Hole, near the pink granite **Otter Cliffs,** explore the tidal pools an hour or two before low tide at **Otter Point.** Just beyond, the road enters a spruce-fir forest. **Wildwood Stables** *(877-276-3622. Mid-June–early Oct.; fare),* 4.5 miles

Mount Desert Island, Acadia National Park

past Otter Point, offers wagon rides on some of the 57 miles of wide, gravel **Carriage Roads** begun by John D. Rockefeller, Jr., in 1917; they're also open to horseback riders, hikers, bikers, and cross-country skiers.

A mile past the stables, stop at **Jordan Pond House** *(207-276-3316. www .thejordanpondhouse.com. Mid-May–late-Oct.)* for a meal or the century-old tradition of tea on the lawn. Four miles beyond, turn right off the main road to ascend the 3.5 miles to the top of **Cadillac Mountain,** the highest point on the eastern seaboard north of Brazil. To return to the visitor center, follow the signs.

Deer Isle Drive

Orland to Deer Isle on Maine 175, 166A, 166, 199, and 15

■ 82 miles round-trip ■ ½ day ■ Spring through fall. The roads here intersect constantly, looping back on one another and often sharing multiple designations. Pay close attention to directions.

This drive is a Down East sampler, circuiting a peninsula that juts into Penobscot Bay. You'll visit historic Castine and the fishing villages of Deer Isle and Stonington, then head back through the interior to Blue Hill.

Begin in **Orland** at the junction of US 1 and Me. 175, near where the **Penobscot River** meets **Penobscot Bay.** Follow Me. 175 south a short way to the junction of Me. 166A, then continue south on 166A for a few miles to **Castine,** home of the **Maine Maritime Academy** *(www.mainemaritime.edu).* Markers around town chronicle the 200-year-old history of this strategically located settlement. At the waterfront, you can tour the academy's training vessel, the **State of Maine** *(800-464-6565. Mid-July–Labor Day).* From here go north for a few miles on Me. 166 toward **Penobscot,** and then north on Me. 199 for 3 miles to Me. 175 south toward Brooksville. After about 6 miles, you'll come to the **Bagaduce River** bridge. Stop here to see the **Reversing Falls,** a phenomenon caused by the fast-flowing tides.

Six miles beyond the falls is the **Caterpillar Hill Rest Area,** where you can view Deer Isle, Penobscot Bay, Camden Hills, and the Bay Islands. About a half mile past the rest area, go south on Me. 15 and over the bridge to the island communities of **Deer Isle** and **Stonington.** On Deer Isle turn right and follow signs to Sunset, overlooking **Southwest Harbor.** Continue south 4 miles to **Stonington Harbor,** a charter-boat port, and the ferry for **Isle au Haut** *(www .isleauhaut.com. 207-367-5193. Fare),* about half of which is park.

To return to US 1, head north on Me. 15 for 20 miles to **Blue Hill,** which prospered during the late 1700s as a shipbuilding and trading center and is now known for its pottery. From there continue north on Me. 15 for another 12 miles to rejoin US 1 at Orland.

Rangeley Lakes Scenic Byway

Madrid to Houghton on Maine 4 and 17

▪ 35.6 miles ▪ 2½ hours ▪ All year. Watch for moose and logging trucks.

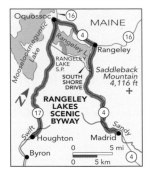

Waterfalls, lakes, mountains, gold deposits, great sunsets—this wishbone-shaped route offers the best of western Maine's Rangeley Lakes region.

Head north on Me. 4 at the **Madrid** town line. Following the **West Branch Sandy River,** the route climbs 3 miles to the beginning of a 20-mile state-designated scenic highway at the entrance to **Smalls Falls Picnic Area.** A path leads across the cataracts at the confluence of **Chandler Mill Stream** and Sandy River. Nearby the **Appalachian Trail** ascends the 4,116-foot **Saddleback Mountain.**

Eight miles past the picnic area, turn left for a 5-mile side trip on South Shore Drive to 869-acre **Rangeley Lake State Park** *(207-864-3858. www.maine.gov/doc/parks. May-Oct.; adm. fee),* a popular place to fish. Continue on Me. 4 for 1.5 miles past the state park turnoff to the **Rangeley Lakes** region, comprising numerous lakes, including Rangeley, Mooselookmeguntic, Richardson, Umbagog, Parmachenee, and Kennebago.

To visit **Saddleback Ski Area** *(207-864-5671. www.saddlebackmaine.com),* turn right on Dallas Hill Road, which climbs 7 miles to the base of Saddle-back Mountain. **Rangeley Center** on Rangeley Lake is on Me. 4 just a mile past this turnoff. The tiny town retains its frontierlike feeling, even though it has been the area's major service center since tourists started arriving more than a hundred years ago.

Continue on Me. 4 for 3.5 miles to **Orgonon** and the **Wilhelm Reich Museum** *(207-864-3443. www.wilhelmreichtrust.org. July-Aug. Wed.-Sun., Sun. only in Sept.; adm. fee)* to learn about the controversial physician-scientist who once lived and worked here. A nature study center and trails are open all year. Continue 3 miles past Orgonon to the junction of Me. 4 and 17. Turn left onto 17 to begin a 32-mile state-designated scenic highway. Just past the junction, an overlook offers a panorama of Rangeley Lake, Saddleback Mountain, and ranges to the east. Five miles on, stop at the rest area for a view

Dawn over Rangeley Lake

of **Mooselookmeguntic Lake**. The **Height of Land Overlook**, just half a mile past the lake turnoff, is spectacular at sunset. Keep an eye out for moose and an ear cocked for loons at **Beaver Pond**, 1 mile farther up on the right. The turnoff for 90-foot **Angel Falls** is 4.5 miles from Beaver Pond. Turn right immediately before the brown trailer, cross the bridge, and head down Bemis Road, an old railroad bed. From the road's end, it's an easy 45-minute hike to the falls.

Continue down Me. 17, through hardwood forest, watching for the bridge just 3.7 miles past the Angel Falls turnoff. If you want to try your luck at gold panning, continue 1 mile to **Coos Canyon Wilderness Campground** *(207-364-3880. www.cooscanyoncabins.com. Mid-April–mid-Nov. Fee for supplies)*, which offers demonstrations. At the **Coos Canyon Rest Area**, right across the way, the Swift River has carved a gorge into the bedrock. Staurolite crystals, jasper, garnets, and gold have been found here.

The drive ends a few miles short of Houghton.

Old Canada Road Scenic Byway

Solon to Canadian border on US 201

▪ 78 miles ▪ 3 hours ▪ All year. Watch for moose and logging trucks.

Woods, water, and wildlife are the watchwords of this appealing drive in western Maine. US 201 follows the valley of the Kennebec River for much of the way, before reaching the Moose River near the Canadian border.

Solon is typical of many small towns in Maine, its white Congregational church raising its bell tower over the community. (The town was named for a renowned ancient Greek lawmaker, which makes it appropriate that the next town to the east is Athens.) Turn west on Falls Road to reach the riverside spot where Revolutionary War Gen. Benedict Arnold camped in 1775, leading an army toward Quebec.

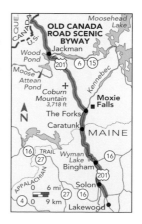

The byway borders the **Kennebec River,** past islands to Bingham, beyond which a dam backs up the Kennebec as Wyman Lake. Here the road skirts the edge of the water. At Caratunk, the famed **Appalachian Trail** crosses the byway, on its 2,174-mile way from Georgia to Maine's Mount Katahdin. A short section east to **Pleasant Pond** gives you a chance to stretch your legs.

Anglers are drawn to the Kennebec and its tributaries for trout, salmon, and smallmouth bass. In the area around **Caratunk** and **The Forks** *(www.forks area.com),* named for the confluence of the Kennebec and the Dead Rivers, you'll find opportunities for Class IV white-water rafting and kayaking, as well as canoeing on some of the gentler stretches of various streams.

Just before US 201 crosses the Kennebec north of The Forks, take Moxie Road east 2 miles to the parking area for **Moxie Falls.** A short trail leads to water plunging over a 90-foot ledge, the highest waterfall in the state.

Beyond The Forks, the byway climbs a flank of **Coburn Mountain.** Just before reaching **Jackman,** stop at a picnic area and make the climb up **Owls Head Mountain** for a vista of Attean Pond, Woods Pond, the Moose River, and beyond into Canada. Moose, loons, as well as black bears, ravens, and grouse help make northern Maine a rewarding place to visit.

NEW HAMPSHIRE
Three Rivers Scenic Drive

Wentworth Location to Glen on New Hampshire 16

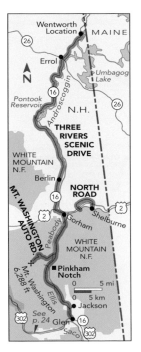

- 74 miles ▪ 2 hours ▪ All year. Especially beautiful in fall. Driving north to south offers most dramatic views of mountains and valleys. This is moose country; collisions can be disastrous, so watch out for the huge beasts on the road.

This drive follows the Androscoggin, Peabody, and Ellis Rivers, the water highway of the old-time log drivers who shuttled timber to the mills at Berlin. South of Berlin (BER-lin), the route winds along the floor of Pinkham Notch, in the shadow of mighty Mount Washington.

Begin on N.H. 16 in **Wentworth Location,** a speck on the map along the Maine border. For information on **Umbagog Lake,** partly in Maine and partly in New Hampshire, stop a short distance south at the **Lake Umbagog National Wildlife Refuge** *(603-482-3415. www.fws.gov/northeast/lakeumbagog .gov. Mon.-Fri.).* Umbagog, which means "clear water" in the local Abenaki dialect, teems with pickerel and salmon. The lake's outlet on its western shore is the headwaters of the **Androscoggin River.** Follow the Androscoggin to **Errol,** a lumber town settled in the late 1800s. N.H. 26 west out of Errol goes to **Dixville Notch,** famous as the first place to report results in national elections.

Continue south on N.H. 16 for about 16 miles to **Pontook Reservoir Recreation Area and Hydro Station,** where a diagram explains the workings of the hydroelectric dam. Shortly after the dam look to the south for a view of the **Presidential Range.**

As the smokestacks of **Berlin's** pulp and paper mills (no longer in operation) come into view, to the east the **Mahoosuc Range** stands out. Berlin sits on a flank of granite that is part of **Jefferson Dome.** Inside the city limits is **Nansen Wayside State Park** *(603-466-3860. www.nhstate parks.org),* known for its ski jump.

Continue south to **Gorham,** nestled in a sheltered valley at the junction of the Androscoggin and **Peabody Rivers.** When the Atlantic & St. Lawrence Railroad completed laying its track in the mid-1800s, Gorham became a gateway for tourists. *(Go east on US 2 for 3 miles to take the North Road scenic drive;* see sidebar at right.)

Proceeding south on N.H. 16, you follow the Peabody River through **Pinkham Notch.** Carved by stream and glacial action, it was named for Daniel Pinkham, who arrived from the coast in the late 1700s—on a sled pulled by a pig. At the entrance to the almost 800,000-acre **White Mountain National Forest** *(www.fs.usda .gov/whitemountain)* is a **Ranger Station** *(603-536-6100. Closed weekends in winter)* offering information. Continue into the forest, stopping a few miles from the entrance at the viewing area for the **Great Gulf**—a huge glacial cirque encompassed by the Great Gulf Wilderness.

North Road

Off US 2 near Gorham

- 8¹/₂ miles ▪ ¹/₂ hour or less
- Best as a fall foliage trip. The views along much of the route are obscured by trees. See map p. 22.

This forgotten byway of New Hampshire's North Country meanders along the Androscoggin River, passing family farms, old cemeteries, and a venerable country inn.

Turn left from US 2 onto North Road 3.5 miles east of Gorham at the 1884 stone house. Stop at the hydroelectric dam a short distance ahead for a view of the **Presidential Range** to the west.

Look to the right as you pass by thick stands of white birch for views of **Middle Moriah Mountain** and the **White Mountain National Forest.** The **Mahoosuc Range** to the left is mostly obscured. The surrounding forest has been heavily logged and is mostly new growth.

To visit the grave of Peter Poor, killed in 1781 by Native Americans working for the British, park at the Appalachian Trail's **Austin Brook Trailhead** about 3 miles past the dam and walk down the hill to the right. Just ahead, visit **Cobblestone Farm** *(603-466-2621),* where the Danforth family raises sheep, spins yarn, and makes apple cider.

Continue a short distance to **Philbrook Farm Inn** *(603-466-3831. Closed April & Nov.-Dec.).* Here the Philbrook family has put up travelers since 1861; nonlodgers can stop in for breakfast or dinner, if there's room.

Follow North Road 4 miles farther as it narrows before intersecting with Meadow Road back over the Androscoggin River to US 2 at Shelburne. Unpaved North Road continues into Bethel, Maine.

Peabody River, White Mountain NF

Go another mile for the entrance to the **Mount Washington Auto Road** (see sidebar opposite). The parking area of the **Glen House** *(603-466-3988)*, a former grand hotel at the base of the auto road, offers a magnificent view of **Tuckerman Ravine,** a glacial cirque formed by small glaciers during the last ice age.

The **Wildcat Mountain Ski Area** *(603-466-3326. www.skiwildcat.com)*, 2 miles past the Glen House, offers skiing and a gondola ride *(fare for nonskiers)*. From the ski area, continue for 0.75 mile to the Appalachian Mountain Club's **Pinkham Notch Visitor Center** *(603-466-2721)* and the trailhead for the short walk to the waterfall at **Crystal Cascade** and a longer climb into Tuckerman Ravine. A half mile farther south is the trailhead for the short walk to **Glen Ellis Falls.** As you proceed down N.H. 16, great views of the **Ellis River Valley** await you.

When you leave White Mountain National Forest, you enter the town of **Jackson** at the northernmost end of the **Mount Washington Valley.** The Three Rivers drive ends in Glen at the junction of US 302.

Mount Washington Auto Road

White Mountain Trail

North Woodstock to Conway on US 3 and 302

■ 65 miles plus side trips ■ 3 hours ■ Spring through fall. Reservations are recommended during fall foliage season.

Forest vistas, dramatic gorges, covered bridges, and the highest peak in the Northeast are found along the 100 miles of the White Mountain Trail. No matter which end of the route you start on, when you finish you can take the beautiful 34-mile **Kancamagus Scenic Byway** (see pp. 26–28) back to the beginning, for a loop trip.

For information on destinations in the area, check with **White Mountains Attractions** *(200 Kancamagus Hwy., North Woodstock, NH 03262. 603-745-8720 or 800-346-3687. www.visitwhitemountains.com)*. Much of the route passes through the 800,000-acre **White Mountain National Forest** *(603-536-6100. www.fs.usda.gov/whitemountain)*. The **White Mountain Visitor Center** *(I-93 at exit 32. 603-745-3816)*, near the western end of the trail in Lincoln, is a good place to get information on national forest activities.

Driving north from North Woodstock on US 3, you follow the Pemigewasset River into **Franconia Notch State Park** *(603-823-8800. www.nhstateparks.com/franconia.html)*, which encompasses a number of attractions. **Flume Gorge** *(603-745-8391. www.flumegorge.com. May-Oct; adm. fee)*

Mount Washington Auto Road

New Hampshire 16 at Glen House

- 16 miles round-trip ▪ 2 hours
- Spring through fall. Closed in winter. Toll road (603-466-3988). Trailers and RVs not permitted. No services. Temperatures from the bottom to the summit can vary as much as 30°F. See map p. 22.

P. T. Barnum is supposed to have called the view from the top of 6,288-foot **Mount Washington** *(www.mt-washington.com)*—extending into four states and Canada—the "second greatest show on Earth." The weather is equally impressive: Earth's highest wind speed of 231 miles an hour was recorded at the summit in 1934, and the climate above timberline is ecologically similar to that of northern Labrador.

Opened in 1861, the road climbs about 4,700 vertical feet at an average grade of 12 percent. The first 4 miles cut through dense forest, revealing the succession from hardwoods to evergreens. As you approach timberline at 4,500 feet, the trees become stunted and twisted. Above 4,000 feet there are views to the north of the **Great Gulf**—the White Mountains' largest glacial cirque—as well as **Mounts Adams, Jefferson,** and **Madison.** Beyond lie the **Androscoggin River Valley** and the peaks of the **Mahoosuc Range.**

Just past the 6-mile marker is the **Alpine Garden Trail;** look for diapensia, Lapland rosebay, alpine azalea, and mountain avens. Just past mile 7, where the road parallels the **Mount Washington Cog Railway** *(Bretton Woods. 603-278-5404. Reservations suggested; fare),* look down into two other glacial cirques. At the summit, visit the **Mount Washington Observatory Museum** *(603-356-2137. Mid-May–mid-Oct. weather permitting; adm. fee).*

extends 800 feet between granite walls up to 90 feet high.

Farther north, the **Cannon Mountain Aerial Tramway** *(603-823-8800. www.cannonmt.com. Mid-May–mid-Oct; fare)* ascends 2,022 feet in eight minutes to the top of 4,180-foot **Cannon Mountain,** where on a clear day you can see four states and Canada.

Beyond Franconia Notch, US 3 departs from I-93 and veers eastward; at Twin Mountain the trail follows US 302. As you continue, the spectacle of the **Presidential Range** lies to the east: an array of mountains, many named for presidents (such as Jefferson and Monroe), topped by 6,288-foot **Mount Washington,** the highest peak in the Northeast and the third highest in the country east of the Rockies. A 6-mile side road off US 302 leads to the **Mount Washington Cog Railway** *(603-278-5404 or 800-922-8825. www.thecog.com. Fare),* which has been taking passengers to the summit since 1869. At the top is 59-acre **Mount Washington State Park** *(603-466-3347. www.nhstateparks.org. May-Oct.).* On a clear day you might see the Atlantic Ocean, but Mount Washington's reputation for "the worst weather on Earth" is hardly exaggerated. It can be very cold and windy any time of year.

Train on Mount Washington Cog Railway

The main White Mountain Trail route runs south into the beautiful Saco River Valley though **Crawford Notch State Park** *(603-374-2272. www .nhstateparks.org. May-Oct.)*. The 4-mile hike to **Arethusa Falls** (the highest waterfall in the state) and **Frankenstein Cliff** yields great views.

As US 302 turns east it leaves the "notch." Four miles east of Bartlett, take a side road west to the 1851 **Bartlett covered bridge** over the Saco River. The route follows the meandering **Saco River** south to North Conway and Conway. The **Conway Scenic Railroad** *(603-356-5251 or 800-232-5251. www.conwayscenic.com. Fare)* takes passengers on sightseeing rides to various locations, including **Crawford Notch** over the Frankenstein trestle.

Kancamagus Scenic Byway

Lincoln to Conway on New Hampshire 112

▪ 34¹/₂ miles ▪ 1 hour ▪ May through October. Spectacular fall foliage.

Famous for its magnificent autumn color, the Kanc stretches from the Pemigewasset River at Lincoln to the junction of N.H. 16 in Conway and crosses several mountains, climbing nearly 3,000 feet as it traverses the flank of **Mount Kancamagus.** The views are breathtaking, the two-lane blacktop road is excellent, and numerous places offer camping, hiking, swimming, or fishing.

There is a **White Mountain Visitor Center** *(White Mountain Attractions. 603-745-3816. www.visitwhitemountains.com)* at the junction of I-93 and N.H. 112 in Lincoln. There are also two centers specifically for the

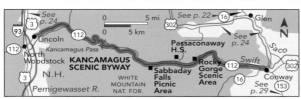

Kancamagus: **Lincoln Woods Visitor Center** *(603-630-5190. Mid-June–Labor Day & various times rest of year, depending on staff availability)* at the west end of the scenic highway and the White Mountain National Forest's **Saco Ranger District Office and Information Center** *(603-447-5448)* at the highway's east end.

The Kancamagus (Kan-kuh-MOG-us) highway took 20 years to build, starting in the late 1930s, partly on the bed of a narrow-gauge railroad that originally carried timber into Lincoln. The mountains along the Kanc are named after New Hampshire Indians. Kancamagus ("fearless one"), grandson of the great chief Passaconaway, served as the third and final ruler of the Penacook Confederacy and led a confederation of tribes in New Hampshire in the late 1600s. The Kanc's most scenic section begins 3 miles from Lincoln at the entrance sign to the **White Mountain National Forest.** The first parcels of this 770,000-acre woodland were set aside in 1911; today, 114,932 acres are officially designated as wilderness.

Approximately 184 species of birds have been sighted, including the green heron and the peregrine falcon. Moose, deer, foxes, and black bears are permanent residents. Trees along the Kanc include alder, spruce, pine, maple, white birch, black cherry, larch, and poplar.

For a few miles, the road follows the east branch of the **Pemigewasset River,** popular with trout fishermen. The Lincoln Woods Visitor Center is

26

a mile up on the left. The 8.9-mile **Wilderness Trail** begins at the parking lot just east of the highway bridge.

As the road begins to wind for 8 miles to the top of the 2,855-foot **Kancamagus Pass, Mounts Hancock, Hitchcock,** and **Huntington** rise up to the left; **Loon Mountain** and **Mount Osceola** are off to the right. The streams to the east empty into the **Saco River,** and those to the west feed the Pemigewasset. Pull in at the **C. L. Graham Wangan Ground** at the pass. You are now in the Saco River Valley section of the national forest.

To build the Kanc, Civilian Conservation Corps workers began hacking their way through the wilderness in the 1930s. Not until 1959 did the road open to through traffic.

Continue for 7 miles alongside the **Swift River** to **Sabbaday Falls Picnic Area,** trailhead for one of the most popular family hikes along the Kanc. It's an easy 0.4-mile walk on a graded path to the narrow flume and picturesque waterfalls. The falls owe their existence to the presence of a black basalt dike, which is beautifully exposed. Sand and gravel carved the potholes below the falls. Tradition says they were named by early explorers who discovered them on the Sabbath while searching for a mountain pass. There's excellent fishing along **Sabbaday Brook** *(license required).*

A few miles up at **Passaconaway Historic Site** *(information at Saco Ranger District),* you'll find a little bit of everything: romance, history, legend, and nature. The only historic house on the highway, the **Russell-Colbath Historic Homestead** *(July–Columbus Day; donation)* was built here about 1832. One day in 1891 Mr. Colbath left the house, telling his wife he'd be back soon. Every night for the next 39 years, Mrs. Colbath lit a lantern and placed it in a window to help him find his way. He finally did, but by then Mrs. Colbath had been dead for three years.

27

The house faces south, overlooking the **Albany Intervale** and **Mount Passaconaway,** the "monarch of the Sandwich Range" at 4,060 feet. Passaconaway, considered one of the greatest American Indian leaders, was head of the Penacook Confederacy when the first Europeans arrived.

In the small cemetery next to the Russell-Colbath house, look for the grave of Orren A. Chase, who died July 25, 1864. On leave from the Civil War, he was riding home by train for his wedding when he was robbed and killed. The half-mile **Rail 'n' River Trail,** which leaves from the parking lot at the house, is accessible to strollers and wheelchairs.

Just a half mile past the Passaconaway Historic Site is the turnoff for Bear Notch Road. This 9-mile route to Bartlett

The "Kanc" through White Mountain National Forest

Sandwich Notch Road

Center Sandwich to New Hampshire 49

- 9½ miles ▪ ½ hour ▪ May through October. Closed in winter. Narrow, hilly dirt road; not for RVs. No services.

In the early 1800s the town of **Sandwich** spent $300 to build a road one lane (16.5 feet) wide over **Sandwich Notch** to the town of Thornton, so that upcountry farmers could reach market towns to the south. In its heyday the Notch Road had a couple of dozen families, two mills, three schools, and a tavern.

Today, few traces of civilization remain along this bumpy dirt road that runs partly through the **White Mountain National Forest** *(603-536-6100).*

Before taking the drive, stop at **A. G. Burrows General Store** in the picturesque village of **Center Sandwich** to make sure the road is open. (For hikers, the **Town Hall,** open weekdays, offers an informative and free brochure, "Bearcamp River Trail Guide.")

Begin at Main and Grove Streets, following a sign for Sandwich Notch Mead Base, a Boy Scout camp.

Grove Street soon becomes Diamond Ledge Road, a country lane flanked by stone walls marking the boundaries of bygone farms.

At the fork about 2 miles ahead, bear left onto Sandwich Notch Road, which now narrows to one lane and then begins its climb up Sandwich Notch. Plants along the way range from balsam fir to wood sorrel to buttonbush. The 4.5-mile **Algonquin Trail,** about 4 miles ahead, ascends to the top of **Sandwich Mountain.**

The road ends at N.H. 49.

Swift River's rocky shore

passes by the 2,600-acre **Bartlett Experimental Forest,** where research on the growth, composition, and culture of a northern hardwood forest goes on. In winter the road is plowed for only a mile, up to the **Upper Nanamocomuck Ski Trail,** which runs alongside the Swift River.

Three miles past the Bear Notch Road turnoff, watch for the entrance to **Rocky Gorge Scenic Area,** between **Moat Mountain** and **Mount Chocorua,** designated a National Scenic Area in 1937. The gorge was once filled with basalt. Over the years, however, the waters of the Swift River have eroded the basalt, leaving the harder granite, waterfall, and narrow gorge. The rocks alongside are composed primarily of quartz and feldspar. The swimming is great along the river (not permitted in gorge), and the short **Lovequist Loop** circles trout-filled **Falls Pond,** formed during the Ice Age when a retreating glacier left a narrow ridge of gravel and sand.

Save energy for the popular **Boulder Loop Trail,** which begins near the covered bridge just a few miles from Rocky Gorge. You need only hike a short way up the 2.8-mile loop to see the effects of the glaciers that moved south from Canada and covered New Hampshire during successive Pleistocene ice ages.

The scenic section of the Kancamagus ends a few miles past the covered bridge, at the sign "Leaving White Mountain National Forest." Continue toward **Conway** for 2.5 miles to visit the Saco Ranger District information center.

New Hampshire 153

Conway to Sanbornville

- 35 miles ▪ 1 hour ▪ April through October. Spectacular fall foliage and less crowded than better known routes.

The two-lane country road that winds southeast from busy Conway through dense woods and past small, tree-lined lakes along central New Hampshire's border with Maine is quiet, yet filled with surprises—a vest-pocket ski area, two wildlife sanctuaries, and a historic village noted for its 18th- and 19th-century buildings.

Head south on N.H. 153 from its junction with N.H. 16 in **Conway.** Once a mountain retreat for writers and artists, Conway today is a mecca for shoppers. Slow down after about 5 miles, when you first see **Crystal Lake** ahead. It's worth turning left here for a short side trip to **Snowville,** a tiny village settled in the early 1800s. For a magnificent view of the **Presidential Range,** head a short distance up Stuart Road/Firelane 37 to **Snowvillage Inn** *(603-447-2818 or 800-447-4345. www.snowvillageinn .com)* or go 2.5 miles farther, up **Foss Mountain** to the blueberry barrens on top.

Returning to N.H. 153, turn left and follow Crystal Lake about a half mile to **Eaton Center** and **Inn at Crystal Lake** *(603-447-2120 or 800-343-7336. www.theinn atcrystallake.com),* where Irish bread is featured on the breakfast menu. The **Little White Church** up the road was built in 1879. Continue 2.5 miles to Purity Lake in East Madison, site of the **Purity Spring Resort** and **King Pine Ski Area** *(603 367 8896 or 800 373 3754. www.kingpine .com),* Mount Washington Valley's smallest ski area, named for its towering pine trees. A short distance past the resort, turn left onto Horseleg Road to visit the New Hampshire Audubon Society's 135-acre **Hoyt Wildlife Sanctuary** *(603-224-9909. www.nhaudubon.org).* This wetland is a haven for birds such as the great blue heron and the black-throated blue warbler; flora includes the insect-eating pitcher plant.

Should you miss Hoyt, there's another sanctuary just 7 miles farther south—New Hampshire Audubon's **Charles Henry & Mabel Lamborn Watts Wildlife Sanctuary** *(603-224-9909. www.nhaudubon.org).* This 380-acre preserve on the **Ossipee River** is composed of mixed forest and wooded swamp, and provides a diversity of habitats for creatures such as river otter and waterfowl. There are trail maps in the parking lot mailbox.

A stone marker in **Effingham,** 2 miles past the sanctuary, marks the site of the first normal school in New Hampshire. Continue for about 6 miles to **Province Lake,** where ancient Indian hearths have been found on the western shore. It's only 10 miles from the lake to **Wakefield,** the self-described "center of New England." Turn right off N.H. 153 to visit the **Wakefield Corner National Historic Area** *(Town Hall. 603-522-6205. www.historicwake fieldnh.com).* The town was developed 200 years ago at the intersection of two stagecoach routes. Twenty-six of its 18th- and 19th-century buildings are on the National Register of Historic Places. Though most are private residences, some are open to the public on special days throughout the year.

Finish the drive by continuing roughly 1 mile past the Wakefield Corner turn to reach the junction of N.H. 153 and 109 in **Sanbornville.**

Connecticut River Byway

From mid-Massachusetts north through Vermont and New Hampshire, paralleling Connecticut River on both sides to Canadian border

- 530 miles - 3 to 4 days - Spring through fall. Increased congestion and crowds can be expected during fall foliage season.

The Connecticut River, a center of regional life since the days when Native Americans called it the Quenticut, provided livelihoods, transportation, and recreation. This byway follows roads on both sides of it.

The drive begins at South Hadley in western Massachusetts. About 5.5 miles north of South Hadley on Mass. 47, enter **Skinner State Park** *(www .mass.gov/dcr/parks/skinner)* for a drive to the summit of 889-foot **Mount Holyoke.** Back on 47, pass three historic districts north to **Millers Falls** before crossing into Vermont.

Brattleboro, Vermont *(Chamber of Commerce, 180 Main St. 802-254-4565 or 877-254-4565. www.brattle borochamber.org),* lies at the joining of the West and Connecticut Rivers.

Take US 5 until a few miles north of Bellows Falls, then turn west on Vt. 103 to reach **Rockingham Meeting House** *(802-463-3694. May-Oct.; donation),* an early building used for religious and civil meetings. Cross the river into New Hampshire and drive north on N.H. 12 through Charlestown to The **Fort at No. 4** *(N.H. 11. 603-826-5700. www.fortat4.com. May-Oct. Wed.-Sun.; adm. fee),* a museum of life in the mid-18th century. Return to the Vermont side and go north on US 5 alongside 3,144-foot Mount Ascutney. In Windsor, the **American Precision Museum** *(196 Main St. 802-674-5781. www.americanprecision.org. May-Oct.; adm. fee)* holds a collection of machine tools. Cross the Connecticut again on the **Cornish-Windsor Bridge** (the longest wooden covered bridge in the United States) and take N.H. 12A 2 miles north to **Saint-Gaudens National Historic Site** *(603-675-2175. www .nps.gov/saga. May-Oct.; adm. fee),* home and studios of sculptor Augustus Saint-Gaudens.

30

N.H. 11 will take you to White River Junction and the **New England Transportation Institute and Museum** *(100 Railroad Row. 802-291-9838).* Three miles west of town via US 4 is **Quechee Gorge,** a nearly 200-foot chasm with the Ottauquechee River at the bottom. For trails, visit **Quechee State Park** *(802-295-2990. www.vtstateparks.com/htm/quechee.htm).* A short drive north on N.H. 10 are Hanover and Dartmouth College and the **Hood Museum of Art** *(603-646-2808. http://hoodmuseum.dartmouth.edu. Closed Mon.).* Next is Haverhill, known for its **Haverhill Corner Historic District.**

Episcopal Church in Lancaster, N.H.

In St. Johnsbury, Vermont, the **Fairbanks Museum and Planetarium** *(1302 Main St. 802-748-2372. www.fairbanksmuseum.org. Adm. fee)* houses collections in natural science, history, and world cultures in a striking 1891 building. Continue north in Vermont on US 2 and Vt. 102, or cross the river to New Hampshire and drive north on N.H. 135 and US 3.

31

VERMONT
Vermont 100

Wilmington to Newport

- 188 miles ▪ 5 hours ▪ Late spring through mid-fall. In the north, fall foliage peaks earlier; display is usually over by mid-October. Traffic can be heavy in high summer and fall foliage season. Road is well maintained in winter.

Vt. 100 is the Main Street of Vermont's Green Mountains, running alongside the state's rugged spine from Massachusetts almost to Quebec. The road passes through many villages typical of this Yankee heartland.

Begin at **Wilmington,** where Vt. 100 crosses Vt. 9. Wilmington is a lodging and service center for several nearby ski areas and amply supplied with comfortable inns.

Follow Vt. 100 north out of Wilmington; soon the north branch of the **Deerfield River** will be on your right. Rising on your left is 3,400-foot **Haystack Mountain,** one of the southernmost peaks of the **Green Mountains.** A northern extension of the Appalachians, the Green Mountains were formed some 450 million years ago by the folding and faulting of sedimentary rock. Erosion and the action of Ice Age glaciers have since rounded them.

Vt. 100 climbs toward **West Dover,** at 1,720 feet one of the loftiest villages in Vermont. Roughly 8 miles north of Wilmington, near the access road for the **Mount Snow Ski Area** *(802-464-3333. www.mountsnow.com),*

you can see the slopes to the left. Vt. 100 soon cuts through a southern portion of the **Green Mountain National Forest** *(802-747-6700. www.fs.usda.gov/green mountain).* Land acquisition for the forest began during the 1930s; today it encompasses well over 350,000 acres greened by hardwoods.

Continue north on Vt. 100 as it descends through densely forested country to **West Wardsboro,** where a left turn would take you to 3,936-foot **Stratton Mountain** and its giant ski resort. **North Wardsboro** itself, 4.5 miles past the Stratton turnoff, is a 0.25-mile-long string of small restaurants, general stores, and craft shops. From here, follow Vt. 100 for 4.5 miles to East Jamaica, then bear left for the 3-mile drive up the **West River Valley** to Jamaica.

To stay on Vt. 100, bear right at Rawsonville, 5 miles northwest of Jamaica, then left at South Londonderry toward Londonderry, where you take another left to reach **Weston.** Weston sums up so much of what outsiders find captivating about Vermont villages—the fenced green with its bandstand, the white steeples and cradling hills. It is home to two durable attractions: the **Weston Playhouse** *(802-824-5288. www.westonplayhouse.org. Summer)* and the **Vermont Country Store** *(802-362-4667),* a tribute to Yankee shopkeeping around the potbellied stove.

Bear right 3.5 miles north of Weston and follow Vt. 100 for 7 hilly miles into **Ludlow,** a former factory town that wears a cheerful new look now that the factory has been turned into a lively agglomeration of shops and restaurants.

Continue on Vt. 100 back into rural Vermont. On your right, **Lake Rescue** soon comes into view, followed by **Echo** and **Amherst Lakes**—strung together by the **Black River,** a tributary of the Connecticut. Three miles past the northern end of Amherst Lake turn right onto Vt. 100A for a 2-mile side trip into history. It was in tiny **Plymouth Notch** that Calvin Coolidge became President of the U.S. on August 3, 1923. Vice President Coolidge was visiting his boyhood home when word of President Harding's death arrived, and he was sworn in by his father, a notary public. The hamlet's houses, barns, and old Coolidge store are now part of the **President Calvin Coolidge State Historic Site** *(802-672-3773. www.historicsites .vermont.gov/Coolidge. Late May–mid-Oct.; adm. fee).*

Return to Vt. 100 and continue north along the floor of the **Black River Valley,** reaching US 4, central Vermont's principal east-west highway, at **West Bridgewater.** The **Otauquechee River** here once turned the wheels of Bridgewater's woolen mills.

In 1934 a group of skiing enthusiasts pooled $500 to build Vermont's first ski tow. It was put together out of 1,800 feet of rope and an old Model T, but it was the start of a revolution in the Green Mountains.

As Vt. 100 and US 4 follow the river, they are the same highway, climbing in elevation as they pass the **Killington Ski Area** *(802-422-3333. www .killington.com),* Vermont's largest. The summit of **Killington Peak,** part of

Equinox Skyline Dr.

Off Vermont 7A, south of Manchester Center

- 12 miles round-trip ■ 45 minutes
- Toll road. Generally open May to November. Fall foliage peaks around first week of October, earlier at high elevations. See map p. 32.

The **Taconic Range** dominates the southwestern portion of Vermont, and highest among the slate-and marble-bearing hills is 3,852-foot **Mount Equinox.**

The **Equinox Skyline Drive** (802-362-1115. *www.equinoxmountain.com*), which takes you to the summit, offers spectacular views of—and from—a mountain remarkably free of development. The new Saint Bruno Scenic Viewing Center opened in fall 2012 and is a refreshing rest stop with 360° of promontory vistas. Three decades ago, businessman J. G. Davidson donated 8,000 Mount Equinox acres to the Carthusians, a Catholic monastic order committed to silence and self-sufficiency. The Carthusians currently make their home in a secluded granite monastery *(closed to public)* on the southwest slope.

Along the route, you can look out across the countryside from three parking areas, but the stellar vistas are from the summit. Immediately below are **Manchester** and the southern reaches of the **Valley of Vermont,** separating the Taconics from the Green Mountains. The **Berkshire Hills** in Massachusetts and New York's **Adirondacks** range to the south and west, and summit markers boast of clear-weather views of New Hampshire peaks and even Montreal's **Mount Royal.**

Plan to sample the summit hiking trails, ranging from a half mile to 2 miles in length.

the 4,235-foot massif on your left, is visible ahead nearly 6 miles beyond the junction of Vt. 100 and US 4.

In about 1.5 miles the routes diverge. Bear right to stay on Vt. 100, which enters a heavily wooded stretch of rolling, mountainous terrain, with the northern section of the Green Mountain National Forest on the left.

The village of **Pittsfield,** 7.5 miles from US 4, is marked by a bandstand on the common. The road here follows the deep valley of the **Tweed River,** which empties into the White River, a tributary of the Connecticut, just ahead at Stockbridge. The waters on this side of the Green Mountains divide ultimately empty into Long Island Sound; west of the divide, the rivers drain into Lake Champlain.

Bear left to stay on Vt. 100 at the intersection with Vt. 107 at Stockbridge, then left again just after crossing the White River bridge. Ahead is

33

Aerial view of Stowe

Smugglers Notch

Stowe to Jeffersonville on Vermont 108 and Mount Mansfield Toll Road

- 17½ miles (plus 9-mile round-trip on toll road) ■ 1 hour ■ Summer and early fall. Road is plowed only to ski areas on either side of Smugglers Notch. Summit is usually snowed in between November and early May. See map p. 32.

At 4,393 feet, **Mount Mansfield** is Vermont's highest mountain. It's accessible via a summit road and a highway that skirts its eastern flanks and traverses the rocky fastness called Smugglers Notch.

Start at the beginning of Vt. 108 in the ski capital of Stowe. The first few miles are thick with businesses serving the ski and summer trades; at mile 2 is the left turn for the famous **Trapp Family Lodge** *(802-253-8511. www.trappfamily .com)*. Just beyond is a view of the profile of Mount Mansfield—the forehead, nose, and chin of what is said to resemble a reclining man's face. Follow Vt. 108 for 5 miles to reach the 4.5-mile **Mount Mansfield Toll Road** *(802-253-3000. Late-May–late-Oct. Toll)*, which leads to the 4,062 foot "nose."

Views take in the northern **Lake Champlain Valley**, New York's **Adirondacks**, New Hampshire's **White Mountains**, and—on a clear day—the **Montreal** skyline.

Return to Vt. 108 and climb into the **Mount Mansfield State Forest**. The road twists through switchbacks; the height of land at Smugglers Notch, a pass allegedly used for contraband during the War of 1812, is 2.5 miles past the entrance to **Smugglers Notch State Park** *(802-253-4014. www.vt stateparks.com/htm/smugglers.htm. Mem. Day–Columbus Day; adm. fee)*.

Enjoy vistas of the **Lamoille River Valley** as you descend 8 miles to the village of **Jeffersonville**.

Talcville, named after the former talc mines here. **Rochester,** less than a mile ahead, is the prettiest of the towns along this stretch of Vt. 100. The bandstand on its village green looks ready for a summer concert.

Head north beyond Rochester, skirting pastures and cornfields crowded along the floor of the steep-sided **White River Valley**. Once you pass Granville, the valley narrows beyond the possibilities of agriculture as Vt. 100 enters the **Granville Gulf Reservation,** where jutting escarpments and a heavy canopy of foliage in season cast the road in shade. Look to your left for lovely **Moss Glen Falls,** cascading down a sheer rock wall 1.4 miles into the reservation. The roadside vistas won't broaden for 3 miles, by which point Vt. 100 enters the **Mad River Valley**.

Now you're once again in ski country, as you can tell from the inns and restaurants as you drive through **Warren** and approach the regional commercial center of **Waitsfield**. A left turn on Vt. 17 at Irasville, about a mile south of Waitsfield, offers access to the **Sugarbush** and **Mad River Glen Ski Areas**.

The 12-mile stretch of Vt. 100 between Waitsfield and Waterbury is largely farmland, with fine mountain views. The highest peak you see here is 4,083-foot **Camels Hump,** fourth highest in Vermont.

Four and a half miles north of Waitsfield, bear left to stay on Vt. 100 and continue for another 7 miles to **Waterbury,** where the highway crosses the **Winooski River** and I-89. Just a mile past the interstate is one of Vermont's most popular attractions, **Ben & Jerry's** *(802-882-1240 or 866-258-6877. www.benjerry.com. Fee for tours)* ice-cream factory. At the **Cold Hollow Cider Mill** *(800-327-7537. www .coldhollow.com),* 2.5 miles past Ben & Jerry's, you can watch cider being made.

Ten miles north of Waterbury is **Stowe,** a town long synonymous with skiing and, for many, with Vermont itself. If you've never been to Stowe, the tininess of the village may surprise you—it's barely more than a couple of blocks clustered around the needlelike spire of its **Community Church** and the 1833 **Green Mountain Inn** *(802-253-7301. www.greenmountaininn.com).* Most of Stowe's businesses, and its ski area, are spread along the Mountain Road (Vt. 108), which leads out of town toward Mount Mansfield (see sidebar opposite).

Hiker on Mount Mansfield

Follow Vt. 100 north out of Stowe, but to avoid the traffic around the market town of Morrisville, bear left 1.8 miles past Stowe and take an 8.5-mile shortcut to Hyde Park on the Stagecoach Road (Vt. 108). On the left will be excellent views of **Mount Mansfield;** on the right, **Mount Elmore** rises beyond the Stowe Valley. At Hyde Park you can pick up Vt. 100 at Vt. 15.

Now Vt. 100's character changes. The terrain is wilder, more like the forested fastnesses of the nearby Northeast Kingdom. Up here, logging looms larger than agriculture, and moose and bear abound.

Go north through Eden and Lowell, beyond which the mountains give way to broader vistas. The last great sentinel of the Green Mountains, 3,861-foot **Jay Peak,** stands just south of the Canadian border. You can see the summit poking above the mountains to the left at the junction of Vt. 100 and 105, just outside little **Newport.** And that is where Vt. 100 ends, some 200 miles from the Massachusetts border.

35

Victory Basin Drive

US 5 and Vermont 114 to US 2 from St. Johnsbury

▪ 46 miles ▪ 1¹/₄ hours ▪ Late spring through early fall. Blackflies are a problem in May and June. Fall foliage season arrives early in northern Vermont, usually by mid-September.

In this far northeastern corner of Vermont, a gravel road leads through remote and unspoiled **Victory Basin,** a hauntingly beautiful wetlands area surrounded by 13,000-acre Victory State Forest.

Begin in **St. Johnsbury,** which boasts an excellent art gallery at its 1871 **Athenaeum** *(1171 Main St. 802-748-8291. www.stjathenaeum.org. Mon.-Sat.),* with paintings by artists of the Hudson River school, and the eclectic **Fairbanks Museum and Planetarium** *(1302 Main St. 802-748-2372. www.fairbanksmuseum.org. Adm. fees).* Follow US 5 north to Lyndonville, and bear right onto Vt. 114 for East Burke. North of town is **Burke Mountain Ski Resort** *(802-626-7300. www.skiburke .com),* where many U.S. Olympians train.

About 2.5 miles north of East Burke, turn right onto an unnumbered road, following signs for **Gallup Mills,** 7.5 miles away; along the way the road becomes gravel. This is the center of **Victory,** one of the last Vermont towns to receive electricity (1961). Turn right and follow the **Moose River** into the 5,000-acre **Victory Basin Wildlife Management Area.**

The wetlands, prized by naturalists for their vegetation and wildlife, are made up of swamps, marshes, and hard-to-reach bogs. Highly acidic and low in nutrients, bogs are characterized by a floating mat of vegetation over still water. Trees along the wetlands route include red and black spruce, speckled alder, willow, black cherry, and aspen. Mink, otter, moose, and bear are among the animal residents. The area is an important breeding ground for the unusual black-backed woodpecker.

As you continue south, the terrain's flat, subtly colored expanse makes a fine visual foil for ranks of spruce and fir in the middle distance and for the lonely peaks of **Umpire** and **Burke Mountains** off to the right. Eleven miles south of Gallup Mills, the Victory road meets US 2 at North Concord. Turn right and drive another 11 miles back to St. Johnsbury.

Champlain Islands

Colchester to Alburg on US 2

■ 33 miles ■ 1 hour ■ Late spring to mid-fall. Lake Champlain is ice covered into April. Fall lingers here due to moderating lake influence; fall foliage peaks in early October.

When Vermonters talk about "the islands," chances are they're referring to the archipelago in northern Lake Champlain. This drive follows the main route through the chain, with lake and mountain views on either side. Start where US 2 leads west from I-89 at **Colchester,** 9 miles north of Burlington. After 2 miles you will cross the **Lamoille River** near its mouth at **Lake Champlain.** Beyond the river, the mainland is low and marshy, prime waterfowl habitat.

On your right at 4.7 miles is the entrance to **Sand Bar State Park** (*802-893-2825. www.vtstateparks.com/htm/sandbar.htm. Mem. Day–Labor Day; adm. fee*), with a fine bathing beach on a shallow lake cove. Just past the park, US 2 crosses a causeway to **South Hero Island.** Look to the left for magnificent views of the broadest portion of the lake and of New York's **Adirondack Mountains.**

The islands and towns of North and South Hero were named after Vermont's two Revolutionary leaders, Ethan and Ira Allen; legend has it that the proud brothers themselves did the naming. South Hero is becoming a bedroom community for Burlington, but if you turn left onto South Street, 2.5 miles after reaching the island, you'll soon see acres of apple trees. Several orchards here run pick-your-own operations in early autumn, and during the first weekend in October, South Street is the setting for an annual **Applefest.**

Continue north on US 2 for 2 miles past the South Street crossroads, with Lake Champlain's **Keeler Bay** on your right, to reach the intersection with Vt. 314. Turn left here and drive 3 miles if you have time for a scenic, 12-minute ferry ride to **Plattsburgh, New York** *(ferry information 802-864-9804. www.ferries.com).* Opposite the ferry dock on the Vermont side is the **Ed Weed Fish Culture Station** *(802-372-3171),* which offers free self-guided tours.

Back on US 2, you soon enter the town of **Grand Isle.** Here is the **Hyde Log Cabin** *(802-828-3051. www .historicsites.vermont.gov. July-Sept. Thurs.-Mon.; adm. fee),* built in 1783 and believed to be one of the oldest U.S. log cabins in its original state.

Hay- and cornfields line the road north of the cabin, while off to the southeast are clear views of the northern **Green Mountains,** including the handsome profile of **Mount Mansfield.** Soon a drawbridge carries US 2 across a Lake Champlain passage called **The Gut** to **North Hero Island.** The lake and Adirondack views to the left are especially fine. In summer Austria's famous Royal Lipizzan Stallions perform here *(Lake Champlain Islands Chamber of Commerce. 802-372-8400. www.champlainislands.com).*

The opening of the Lake Champlain Canal in 1823 connected this relatively isolated lake region to the Hudson River, creating not only fresh access to untapped resources but also a line of commerce between New York City and Montreal.

As you drive along US 2 just north of the drawbridge, look ahead and to the right to see the northernmost outrider of the Green Mountain chain, **Jay Peak.** The town center of **North Hero** rambles along **City Bay,** with none of its buildings more than a few yards from the water. Structures include the 1824 Greek Revival **Grand Isle County Courthouse,** in locally quarried stone.

Your next 2 miles on US 2 take you along the narrow neck of land called the **Carrying Place,** a portage point used by Native Americans and early settlers crossing Lake Champlain. Beyond, North Hero Island widens into a landscape of cornfields and pastures, with the lake always on your right. Soon a road branches off to the right for **North Hero State Park** *(802-372-8727. www .vtstateparks.com. Mem. Day–Labor Day; adm. fee),* where lean-to campsites offer splendid lake and mountain views.

37

Drawbridge connecting Grand Isle and North Hero Island, Lake Champlain

Cabins along US 2 in the Champlain Islands

Continue 2 miles past the park road to the bridge across **Alburg Passage.** You are now in **Alburg,** which occupies a peninsula reaching down from Canada and separated from the rest of the U.S. by Lake Champlain. At the intersection with Vt. 129, turn left for a side trip onto **Isle La Motte,** smallest and least developed of the three main lake islands. In 1666 the French established Vermont's first white settlement here; the spot is marked by the outdoor **St. Anne's Shrine** *(802-928-3362. www.saintannesshrine.org. Mid-May–mid-Oct.).*

Continue north on US 2 for 6 miles past the Alburg Passage bridge to the intersection with Vt. 78. Unless you are heading north to Canada, turn right here to reach I-89 *(11 miles east)* by way of the **Missisquoi National Wildlife Refuge** *(802-868-4781. www.fws.gov/northeast/missisquoi),* a birder's paradise centered upon the delta of the **Missisquoi River** at Lake Champlain.

Vermont 22A

Vergennes to Fair Haven

▪ 41 miles ▪ 1 hour ▪ Late spring to mid-fall. Fall foliage is spectacular, and warming influence of Lake Champlain often extends peak season well into October.

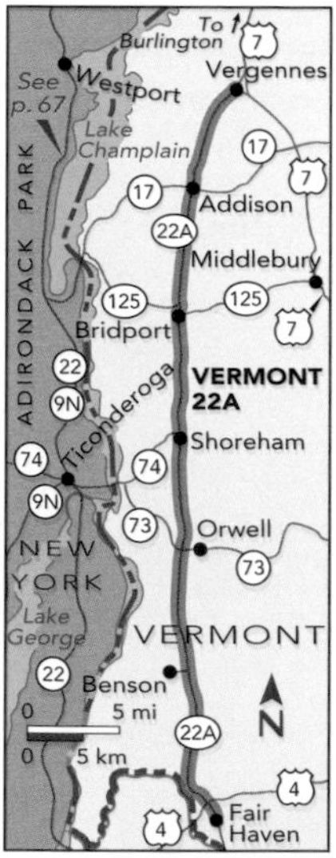

Travel south along the rich bottomlands of the Lake Champlain Valley, where views of New York's majestic Adirondack Mountains rise above some of Vermont's choicest dairy lands.

Start at the northern end of Vt. 22A in **Vergennes.** At 1 square mile, it claims to be the smallest chartered city in the country—and you'll notice that the tidy 19th-century downtown quickly gives way to pastures.

Continue south on Vt. 22A into the predominantly agricultural community of **Addison.** The marshy lowlands that lie off to your right, starting about 5 miles south of Vergennes, are part of the **Dead Creek Wildlife Management Area,** a stopover for waterfowl using the Lake Champlain migration corridor. In the background in New York stand the high peaks of the **Adirondacks,** dominated by 5,344-foot **Mount Marcy.** Less imposing, though far more accessible, is 1,287-foot **Snake Mountain,** which rises in a long ridge to the left of Vt. 22A, just beyond the intersection with Vt. 17. (Turn right here if you want to take the **Lake Champlain Bridge** to New York State.) To reach the trail to the top of Snake Mountain, turn left onto Vt. 17, then right after a mile, and left after another 3.3 miles.

Mountains, high or low, do not figure in the immediate landscape as you drive south along Vt. 22A. Traditionally a dairy state, Vermont has been steadily losing individual farms over the past few decades. But in the gently rolling lowlands of the southern **Champlain Valley,** dairying is still king.

Unlike the rocky Green Mountain foothills, this fertile terrain encourages the consolidation of smaller farms into large operations and the maintenance of economically viable herds of cows numbering in the hundreds. Head down Vt. 22A through Addison and Bridport, and you'll see pasture after pasture dotted with black-and-white holstein-friesians, Vermont's most popular dairy cow, as well as the occasional herd of fawn-colored jerseys or fawn-and-white guernseys.

As you enter the village of Bridport, 10 miles south of Vergennes, you will pass the right turn onto Vt. 125 west, an alternative way to the Lake Champlain Bridge. Just ahead on the left is Vt. 125 east to the college town of **Middlebury,** 8 miles away. Drive another 10 miles through the dairy country south of Bridport to reach **Shoreham,** whose antique shops, inn, and country store lie just to the right of Vt. 22A on Vt. 74. Shoreham looms large in Vermont agriculture: Here, as in the Champlain island communities to the north, the temperature-moderating influence of the lake encourages apple growing. Late summer marks the opening of numerous roadside stands and pick-your-own orchards.

A right turn onto Vt. 74 at Shoreham leads you, in 5 miles, to the little ferry *(802-897-7999. www.forttiferry.com. Mid-April–mid-Sept.; fare)* for **Ticonderoga** in New York State. **Fort Ticonderoga** *(518-585-2821. www .fortticonderoga.org. Early May–mid-Oct.; adm. fee),* now restored to its Revolutionary-era appearance, was the British stronghold captured on May 10, 1775, by Benedict Arnold and Ethan Allen, legendary leader of Vermont's Green Mountain Boys. If you take the ferry from Larrabees Point near Shoreham to the New York side, you will be following in the wake of Allen's wooden boats.

Back on Vt. 22A, continue 6 miles south past Shoreham to reach Vt. 73 at **Orwell.** A left turn here leads directly into the village, with its handsome green and 1810 Town Hall; a right will bring you, in 6 miles, to another Revolutionary War site, **Mount Independence** *(802-948-2000 in season. www.historicsites.vermont .gov. May–Oct.; adm. fee).* Interpretive trails here connect remnants of a 1776 fort built to block a southward British drive. The lake and mountain views alone are worth a ramble along the trails.

Just 1.5 miles south of Orwell on Vt. 22A, look to your left for **Historic Brookside Farms** *(802-948-2727),* a 1789 farmhouse with a stately 1843 Greek Revival front and a beautiful freestanding curved staircase. Not a working farm at this time, Brookside serves as a B&B with miles of trails for nature hikes and cross-country skiing.

Barn along Vermont 22A

As you drive south of Orwell, notice how the terrain becomes increasingly hilly, and the ubiquitous Champlain Valley dairy farms begin to give way to woodland. Roughly 5.5 miles past the Vt. 73 intersection, you can stop at a pleasant picnic area on the left. A mile and a half farther is a right turn for **Benson,** a tiny village from which a network of gravel roads spreads out toward the narrow southern tip of Lake Champlain. Continue south for little more than 6 miles to where Vt. 22A meets US 4. Head east from here to Rutland on US 4 or west into New York State; just ahead is the town of **Fair Haven,** where brick storefronts face the green in a scene little changed over the past century.

MASSACHUSETTS
Mohawk Trail Drive

Greenfield to Williamstown on Massachusetts 2

▪ 41 miles ▪ 1 hour ▪ Late spring to mid-fall. Massachusetts 2 can be very busy in summer and at peak fall foliage season (early to mid-October), but fall colors are magnificent and worth braving traffic.

Named after a route followed by Mohawk Indians traveling between what are now Massachusetts and New York State, the Mohawk Trail Drive has been a favorite scenic byway since it was first opened to automobile traffic in 1914. To follow this route across the **Hoosac Range** of wooded hills, head west from **Greenfield** on Mass. 2. (The actual **Mohawk Trail** begins at Orange, about 20 miles east.)

The road soon begins to climb out of the Connecticut River Valley. After 1 mile, stop at the Long View Observation Tower to enjoy a view reaching northward into New Hampshire and Vermont.

Continue west past the sort of roadside attractions that vanished from much of America with the coming of the interstate highways. Just 4.5 miles

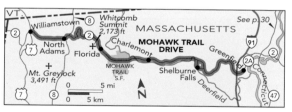

west of I-91 is the eye-catching **Mohawk Trading Post** *(413-625-2412. www.mohawk-trading-post.com. Closed Wed.-Thurs. Jan.-March, closed Tues. all year),* complete with tepee and totem pole. This is the first of several establishments along the drive specializing in Native American crafts in a region that has not had an appreciable Indian population for centuries. Within the first 7 or 8 miles west of Greenfield, two maple-sugar houses offer demonstrations in early spring of how maple sap is boiled down into syrup. They sell the finished product all year.

Three miles past the Mohawk Trading Post, detour left onto Mass. 2A for a half-mile side trip to **Shelburne Falls.** This snug mini-city, its tidy downtown mostly unchanged since early in the 20th century, is graced by the **Bridge of Flowers** *(April-Oct.),* a 400-foot span across the **Deerfield River** built for a trolley line that stopped running in 1928. Ever since, the women's club has cultivated a garden along the bridge's pedestrian walkway.

Continue along Mass. 2 past the Shelburne Falls turnoff. Cross the Deerfield River and follow its path through the town of Charlemont. A half

40

Autumn in Massachusetts' Berkshires

mile beyond Charlemont, you can rent a canoe at **Zoar Outdoor** (413-339-4010. www.zoaroutdoor.com. Daily May–mid-Oct., Wed.-Sun. March-April & mid-Oct.–mid-Nov., Tues.-Fri. mid-Nov.–Feb. Reservations recommended) and enjoy a water-level view of the Deerfield Valley.

Roughly 4 miles past Charlemont, Mass. 2 enters the **Mohawk Trail State Forest** (413-339-5504. www.mass.gov/dcr/parks/western/mhwk.htm. Adm. fee). The Mohawk Trail's commercial aspect abruptly ends here. The road follows a deep ravine, appearing almost to tunnel through trees whose crowns tower above: In autumn the effect is kaleidoscopic. You will find summer attractions as well—on your right, just over a half mile into the state forest, there's a picnic area with swimming in the river (Parking fee Mem. Day–Columbus Day).

Coming out of the state forest, Mass. 2 winds to the highest point along the Mohawk Trail at **Whitcomb Summit** (2,173 feet), reached just after you pass, on the right, the bronze "Elk on the Trail," dedicated by Massachusetts Elks to honor their World War I dead. The view from Whitcomb Summit takes in Vermont's **Green Mountains** to the north, New Hampshire's **Monadnock Mountain** to the northeast, the **Berkshire Hills** to the south, and, west, **Mount Greylock** (3,491 feet), the highest point in Massachusetts.

The Hoosac Tunnel, near the town of Florida, was one of the greatest engineering accomplishments of the railway age. Completed in 1875, the 25,000-foot tunnel cost 20 million dollars and 195 lives.

Mount Greylock dominates the western horizon as you descend through the Mohawk Trail's famous **Hairpin Turn,** 3.5 miles beyond Whitcomb Summit. The turn is situated on the shoulder of a ledge, with views of the valley. If you'd rather enjoy the scenery while sitting still, there's the roadside **Golden Eagle Restaurant** (413-663-9834. www.thegoldeneaglerestaurant.com. Daily in summer, Fri.-Sun. rest of year) at the head of the turn.

Head downhill for 3 miles past the hairpin turn to enter **North Adams,** a classic small New England factory city. For a glimpse of North Adams's industrial and railroad history, visit the **Western Gateway Heritage State Park** (413-663-6312. www.mass.gov/dcr/parks/western/wghp.htm. Donation), downtown on

41

Deerfield River at Charlemont

Mass. 8, just south of Mass. 2. The park is the northern gateway to the Mount Greylock Scenic Byway, which traverses the state's highest mountain. Climb the historic tower for long-range views of the area.

Drive west on Mass. 2 for 4 miles past North Adams to reach **Williamstown.** If North Adams is the factory city from central casting, Williamstown is the archetypal New England college town. **Williams College** *(413-597-3131. www.williams.edu)* has dominated the local landscape since its founding in 1793; its main buildings, many in Georgian and federal styles, surround the lovely village green that marks the end of this drive. Just off Mass. 2 and US 7, a mile south of the town center, is one of the area's principal cultural attractions, the **Sterling and Francine Clark Art Institute** *(413-458-2303. www.clarkart.edu. Closed Mon. Sept.-June; summer adm. fee, free for students or under 18),* with magnificent collections of old master, French Impressionist, and 19th-century American paintings.

42

Tyringham Valley

Great Barrington to Lee on Massachusetts 23 and Tyringham and Main Roads

- 17 miles ▪ ½ hour ▪ Late spring to mid-fall. Foliage is spectacular from late September to early October.

No matter how well beaten the Berkshire paths have become, it's easy to wander onto roads less traveled. This route through Tyringham Valley combines forests and farms with a sculptor's storybook retreat.

Begin in **Great Barrington** at US 7 and Mass. 23, heading east on Mass. 23. The road soon enters a hardwood forest filled with maples and a few elms that survived the Dutch elm disease.

Continue along Mass. 23 for 8 miles to the village of **Monterey,** named for an American victory in the Mexican War. Monterey today is an arts and crafts center; in the village and along local byways are a number of galleries and potters' studios.

At Monterey turn left onto the unmarked Tyringham Road at the big white church on the left. The road climbs through shady woods, with **Lake Garfield** on the right within the first mile. About 2.5 miles out of town, expansive views of the northern Berkshires open up ahead.

Turn left at a T-intersection onto Main Road, 4 miles north of Monterey, to continue toward **Tyringham.** The town lies in the deep **Tyringham Valley** along Hop Brook, so named because of the wild hops early settlers found growing. The valley today is almost entirely agricultural—all pastures, barns, and fences, culminating in a town "center" with no more than a toylike stone post office, a tidy flower bed, and **Tyringham Cobble** *(off Jerusalem Rd. 413-298-3239. www.berkshireweb.com/trustees/cobble.html. Donation),* a little hill with a view of the valley.

Continue north 1 mile past the Tyringham post office to **Santarella,** also known as Tyringham's gingerbread house *(413-243-2819. www.santarella.us. Tours by appt.),* a building straight out of J. R. R. Tolkien's *The Hobbit.* The British sculptor Sir Henry Kitson, creator of "The Minute Man" statue in Lexington, Massachusetts, built this medieval hideaway as a studio in the 1920s. The structure has chestnut beams, a layered shingle roof that suggests thatching, and great stone buttresses that seem to rise naturally out of the ground.

Leaving Santarella, drive north along the remaining 4 miles of Tyringham Road. The road ends in Lee at US 20, which, as it travels east, becomes Jacob's Ladder Trail Scenic Byway. Follow signs.

Along Massachusetts 23

Cape Ann Ramble

Essex to Salem on Massachusetts 133, 127, 127A, and 1A

43

■ 30 miles ■ 1½ hours ■ Spring to late fall. Ocean views are usually fine. Roads can be crowded in high summer.

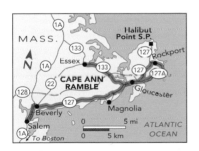

Cape Ann is Massachusetts' "other cape"—not as well known as Cape Cod, but suffused with the traditions of New England seafaring and the tang of Atlantic breezes.

Start a Cape Ann circuit at Mass. 22 and 133 in **Essex,** a village built along broad salt marshes. Essex was a shipbuilding center as early as the 17th century, and today is the home of the **Essex Shipbuilding Museum** *(978-768-7541. www.essexshipbuildingmuseum.org. May-Oct. Wed.-Sun., Nov.–mid-May weekends; adm. fee).* Just south of Essex center, at an intersection surrounded by antiques shops, bear left to follow Mass. 133 onto Cape Ann proper. Seven miles beyond the intersection is **Gloucester Harbor,** home of the country's oldest commercial fishing fleet. Turn left onto Mass. 127 at its intersection with Mass. 133 and look to the right for the famous **Fishermen's Memorial Statue,** a bronze helmsman hunched over his wheel. "They that go down to the sea in ships 1623-1923," the inscription reads, and Gloucestermen still, in the rest of the words of that biblical passage, do business in great waters.

Follow Mass. 127 along Gloucester's waterfront; a mile past the statue, bear left (Mass. 127A goes to the right) and follow signs for **Rockport.** In 3 miles you will come to the second intersection with Mass. 127A.

Turn left here for a side trip to **Halibut Point State Park** *(978-546-2997. www.mass.gov/dcr/parks/northeast/halb.htm. Parking fee Mem. Day–Labor Day),* where foot trails follow the cape's granite bound northern tip. To stay on the scenic drive, veer right at the intersection onto Mass. 127A (Broadway), which leads to Rockport's quaint downtown.

Geese in a pond off Mass. 127

Parking in central Rockport is often difficult *(peripheral parking offered in summer, with shuttle buses to downtown),* but it's worth the extra effort to get out of the car and stroll along **Bearskin Neck,** a narrow strip of land projecting into the harbor and lined with craft shops and art galleries. Nearby, **Motif #1** is a little red fishing shack jutting into the harbor that earned its name because of its countless depictions by painters. Destroyed in the blizzard of February 1978, the beloved structure was immediately rebuilt.

Continue south on Mass. 127A as it reenters Gloucester, along that city's oceanside residential district, past **Long Beach** *(adm. fee)* and **Good Harbor Beach** *(adm. fee).* If you stop for a swim, you'll find the Atlantic cold even in late summer. Follow Mass. 127A through the **Bass Rocks** area, where views of the rockbound coast are interspersed with textbook examples of the turn-of-the-20th-century shingle style of New England seaside architecture—all turrets, wraparound porches, and weathered cedar siding.

Head back along the coast toward the Gloucester business district, watching for two roads on the left. The first leads to **Eastern Point,** where Henry Davis Sleeper's mansion **Beauport,** the Sleeper-McCann House *(75 Eastern Point Blvd. 978-283-0800. www.historicnewengland.org. June–mid-Oct.; adm. fee),* built between 1907 and 1934, is a mélange of styles. The

44

Gloucester's rocky Atlantic coast

second road, a half mile past the Eastern Point road, leads to **Rocky Neck Art Colony,** filled with artists' studios, galleries, and shops.

Head back into downtown Gloucester and pick up Mass. 127 again, going west out of town. Mass. 127 next takes you through North Shore, the coastal region between Boston and New Hampshire. Along the route you find—**Magnolia, Manchester-by-the-sea, Beverly Farms,** and **Prides Crossing**—towns and villages developed for summer use by Boston's upper crust over a century ago. Most of the surviving mansions are set back from the road with ocean views. Just off Mass. 127 on Hesperus Avenue in Magnolia, the medieval stone pile of **Hammond Castle** *(978-283-2080. www.hammondcastle.org. Summer; adm. fee)* belongs to the post–World War I era. Its flamboyant builder, electronics innovator John Hays Hammond, installed a massive organ still used for concerts.

> The first fried clam is said to have been served about 80 years ago at Woodman's on Main Street, Essex, where they're still frying up the tender bivalves.

Mass. 127 ends at Mass. 1A in **Beverly,** where the first American privateer was commissioned; hence the city's claim as the "birthplace of the American Navy." Continue through downtown and cross the harbor bridge to reach the port city of **Salem,** with its many reminders of the 17th-century witch trials and its days as a late 18th- to early 19th-century maritime trading center. The **Salem Witch Museum** *(Washington Square N. 978-744-1692. www.salemwitchmuseum.com. Adm. fee)* evokes the witch hysteria. Native son Nathaniel Hawthorne often visited a 1668 house, now the **House of the Seven Gables** *(Derby St. 978-744-0991. www.7gables.org. Adm. fee).* The National Park Service's tall ship, *Friendship,* is part of the **Salem Maritime National Historic Site** *(Derby St. 978-740-1650. www.nps.gov/sama).* Nearby is the **Peabody Essex Museum** *(Essex St. 978-745-9500. www.pem.org. Adm. fee)* one of the country's oldest museums.

45

Old King's Highway

Sagamore to Provincetown on Massachusetts 6A and US 6

- 59 miles ▪ 1½ hours ▪ All year. Cape Cod is best known as a summer resort, but spring and fall are lovely and less crowded. Winter seas and skies are cast in somber grays and blues.

The most picturesque of the three routes on the shoulder-to-elbow portion of Cape Cod's crooked arm is along Mass. 6A and US 6, known as the King's Road of colonial times. Beyond, US 6 follows the majestic, lonely dunelands of Cape Cod National Seashore.

After crossing **Sagamore Bridge** over the Cape Cod Canal, follow the signs for Mass. 6A. About 1.5 miles ahead turn right into **Sandwich,** the oldest town on the cape (settled 1637). The town is famous for its beautiful

colored 19th-century glass, a craft celebrated at the **Sandwich Glass Museum** *(Main St. 508-888-0251. www.sandwichglassmuseum.org. Closed Jan. & Mon.-Tues. Feb.-March; adm. fee).*

At Cape Cod National Seashore you can see the site of the station from which in 1903 Guglielmo Marconi sent and received the first transoceanic radio messages between world leaders—Theodore Roosevelt and Britain's King Edward VII.

Driving in and around Sandwich offers a quick introduction to the cape's potpourri of history and architecture—somber 17th-century saltboxes, classically proportioned Georgians, federal-style houses, and of course the region's signature Cape Cod cottages. As you reconnect with Mass. 6A and continue east toward Barnstable, note the attention Cape Codders pay to their gardens. Everywhere you look, you'll see the white snowball bushes and bright blue hydrangeas that thrive in season.

Continue on Mass. 6A for 12 miles past the Sandwich turnoff to the center of **Barnstable,** the seat of Barnstable County, which encompasses all of Cape Cod. The grand Greek Revival **Court House,** a relic of New England's early 19th-century "granite age," dominates this tree-shaded village. Three miles down the road in **Yarmouth Port,** a domestic version of the Greek Revival style executed in wood can be seen at the **Capt. Bangs Hallet House** *(508-362-3021. www.hsoy.org. June–mid-Oct. Thurs.-Sun.; adm. fee),* filled with treasures garnered during the captain's career in the Asia trade.

Follow Mass. 6A east out of Yarmouth Port into **Dennis.** Turn right onto Old Bass River Road at the Dennis village green, then left on Scargo Hill Road for a half-mile side trip to **Scargo Hill,** at 160 feet one of Cape Cod's highest points. Topped by an observation tower, the hill affords fine views of the cape terrain along the bay side as far north as Provincetown.

Brewster, about 6 miles east of Dennis via Mass. 6A, is a town of 19th-century sea captains' houses, many serving today as inns and restaurants. The main street is also lined with an eclectic assortment of antique shops.

Continue on Mass. 6A for 3 miles past Brewster to reach the entrance to **Nickerson State Park** *(508-896-3491. www.mass.gov/dcr/parks/southeast/nick.htm. Camping mid-April–mid-Oct.; adm. fee),* nearly 2,000 acres of pond-studded scrub-conifer forest. The park is an access point for the **Cape Cod Rail Trail,** open to cyclists and walkers, which extends north to Wellfleet and south to Dennis on a former paved railbed.

On the beach at Provincetown

Mass. 6A meets US 6, the Mid-Cape Highway, near Orleans, 2 miles past the state park. You can continue directly north on US 6 to Provincetown or stay on Mass. 6A for the 1-mile drive into the town center of **Orleans,**

Cape Cod National Seashore

commercial hub of the Outer (or Lower) Cape. Beyond Orleans, US 6 heads along the middle of the narrow forearm of Cape Cod, flanked on the right by the 43,500-acre **Cape Cod National Seashore** *(508-771-2144. www.nps .gov/caco. Parking fee in summer),* which encompasses much of the Outer Cape. Stop at the **Salt Pond Visitor Center** *(508-255-3421),* 4 miles past the junction with US 6, for information on the historic attractions, lighthouses, and ocean beaches that lie within this federal property.

For a marked contrast with the Outer Cape's oceanside environment of high dunes and white-capped breakers, head north for 3.5 miles past the visitor center to the Massachusetts Audubon Society's **Wellfleet Bay Wildlife Sanctuary** *(508-349-2615. www.massaudubon.org/wellfleet. Adm. fee),* a secluded tract of woods and salt marshes along the bay side.

The town of **Wellfleet** itself is just off US 6 to the left 5 miles past the sanctuary. Stay on US 6 beyond Wellfleet to enter **Truro,** which offers what many visitors consider the purest distillation of the Cape Cod landscape: heather-blanketed moors, high dunes, and the sense that you are never far from the sea—as indeed you are not.

At North Truro, 7.5 miles north of Wellfleet, the road forks and Mass. 6A reappears. Bear right and continue on US 6 past brackish **Pilgrim Lake** for access to the **Province Lands** *(Province Lands Visitor Center. 508-487-1256)* section of the national seashore. Its paths wind through dunelands fragrant with beach plum and bayberry, and its excellent beach overlooks Herring Cove.

Or bear left to hug the bay shore for the final few miles to **Provincetown,** that peerless amalgam of beach resort, colonial village, Portuguese fishing port, and flamboyant art colony—all at the very tip of Cape Cod.

RHODE ISLAND
Rhode Island 77

Tiverton to Sakonnet Point

■ 14 miles ■ ¹/₂ hour ■ Late spring to mid-fall. Harvest season from late summer to early autumn is especially recommended, when roadside stands sell local produce.

Rhode Island's easternmost corner is separated from the rest of the state by Narragansett Bay and the Sakonnet River and by the Fall River area of Massachusetts. Worlds away from busy Newport and Providence, this often overlooked part of "little Rhody" offers tranquil vistas of farmlands, vineyards, and the sea.

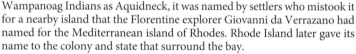

Start this short tour in the town of **Tiverton,** at the intersection of R.I. 138 and 77, and head south on R.I. 77. Immediately to your right, as you drive out of Tiverton, is the narrow head of the **Sakonnet River;** opposite is the northeasternmost tip of **Rhode Island,** largest of the Narragansett Bay islands. Known by the Wampanoag Indians as Aquidneck, it was named by settlers who mistook it for a nearby island that the Florentine explorer Giovanni da Verrazano had named for the Mediterranean island of Rhodes. Rhode Island later gave its name to the colony and state that surround the bay.

Within the first mile south of Tiverton, the Sakonnet River—not a true river but a tidal channel—widens to reveal broad views of **Portsmouth** on the opposite shore and of tiny, rocky **Gould Island.** The protected waters of the Sakonnet are popular with boaters, and in summer this stretch of the "river" is flecked with white sails.

Continue on R.I. 77 as it veers eastward and farther inland along the shores of **Nannaquaket Pond** and across **Sin and Flesh Brook.** We can only guess whether this little stream was named by the Puritans as a general warning against the ways of the world, or because of some local reputation for misbehavior. R.I. 77 next passes through a patchwork of small farms, their fields marked off by old stone walls. Blueberries and corn are among the local crops available at roadside stands in midsummer. Also along here is the **Emilie Ruecker Wildlife Refuge** (*right on Seapowet Ave., follow signs. 401-949-5454. www.asri.org/refuges/emilie-ruecker-wildlife-refuge.html*) with three salt marsh trails.

Turn left at a point slightly more than 7 miles south of Tiverton to enjoy another

Tiverton salt marsh in fall

local crop. **Sakonnet Vineyards** *(401-635-8486. www.sakonnetwine .com)* has been a leader among New England wineries since 1975; the vines here benefit from the moderating climatic influence of the ocean, and cultivation of Chardonnay grapes has been particularly successful. Tours highlight various aspects of winemaking, and a tasting and sales room is open daily.

Along with Sakonnet's grapes, crops such as peaches and strawberries also benefit from the mild local climate, as evidenced by the farm stands that dot the roadsides around here. Proximity to the ocean, of course, also means fog.

Head south for another 1.8 miles beyond the Sakonnet Vineyards turnoff and turn left for the mile drive to **Little Compton Commons**, a secluded gem of a New England village. Little more than a crossroads with a restaurant (specializing in johnnycakes, a

Sailboats at a Newport dock

cornmeal-based Rhode Island tradition) and a century-old general store, Little Compton is clustered about the magnificently steepled 1832 **United Congregational Church**. Take a few moments to walk through the churchyard; the church was founded in 1704, and there are many 18th-century gravestones. Little Compton, which comprises not only the village of Little Compton Commons and its environs

Ocean Drive

Newport Loop

■ 10 miles ■ ¹/₂ hour ■ All year.
Road can be crowded in summer.
See map p. 48.

The colonial seaport of **Newport**, at the entrance to Narragansett Bay, is perhaps best known for its extravagant turn-of-the-20th-century "cottages" *(Preservation Society of Newport County. 401-847-1000. www.newportmansions .org. Call for schedule; adm. fee)*. This drive takes them in as well as the city's rugged shoreline.

From downtown Newport, follow Memorial Boulevard to the corner of Bellevue Avenue and turn right into the heart of mansion territory. Directly on your right is the 1839 Gothic Revival **Kingscote**, followed by **The Elms**, a 1901 château.

Turn left from Bellevue onto Narragansett Avenue, then right onto Ochre Point Avenue to reach **The Breakers**, the 1895 extravaganza designed for Cornelius Vanderbilt II.

Head back up to Bellevue Avenue by turning right onto Ruggles Avenue, then left onto Bellevue. Over the next mile you will pass **Rosecliff** (1902), where *The Great Gatsby* was filmed in 1974. You will also enjoy seeing **Marble House** (1892), incorporating 500,000 cubic feet of marble. Next is the 1894 **Belcourt Castle** *(401-846-0669. www.belcourt castle.com. Adm. fee)*.

At the end of Bellevue Avenue follow signs for Ocean Drive. The route affords vistas of Rhode Island Sound and the rocky coast, passing **Brenton Point State Park** and **Hammersmith Farm** *(private)*, site of John and Jacqueline Kennedy's wedding reception in 1953.

Continue past **Fort Adams State Park** *(401-847-2400. www.riparks.com/fort adams.htm)*, where there is a **Museum of Yachting** *(401-847-1018. www.moy.org. May-Oct.; adm. fee)*, and finish at the downtown waterfront.

49

but the entire southern tip of this corner of the state, was where the famous Rhode Island Red breed of chicken was developed in the 1850s. There is a monument to the bird in the community of **Adamsville**, near the Massachusetts border.

> This part of the coast has long had the name Fogland, and the mist can badly hamper visibility any time of year, especially in the morning.

Return to R.I. 77 and turn left for **Sakonnet Point**. On the left, a mile past the Little Compton Commons turnoff, stands a 1690 structure housing the small museum of the **Little Compton Historical Society** *(401-635-4035. www.littlecompton.org. Late-June–Labor Day, Sept. weekends, call for other dates; adm. fee).* From here, the 2.5-mile drive that remains before land's end at Sakonnet Point takes you through rolling meadows and small farms, with occasional views of the 4-mile-wide Sakonnet River near its mouth at Rhode Island Sound. If wine, peaches, and berries haven't filled your picnic basket, you can still stock up at a roadside stand along the way back north. The end of the line, Sakonnet Point, comes at a little anchorage for fishing boats and pleasure craft, where a stone jetty is usually lined with anglers. There is a place to buy lobsters—and not much else, unless you count spectacular sunsets over Newport, just 6 miles across the sound.

CONNECTICUT

Connecticut State Route 169

Lisbon to North Woodstock

- 22 miles ▪ ½ hour ▪ Spring to mid-autumn. Fall foliage peaks in early to mid-October.

Although the roads of Connecticut's northeastern Quiet Corner were traveled by colonial settlers as far back as the 1680s, this unsung nook of the Nutmeg State still affords the pleasures of discovery. The secret is to stay off I-395, the area's main north-south artery, and follow the byways through a skein of unspoiled villages.

Begin by picking up Conn. 169 in Lisbon, just 4 miles west of I-395 at exit 83A. Travel north to the intersection with Conn. 14 in Canterbury where the 1805 **Prudence Crandall Museum** *(860-546-7800. May-Nov. Wed.-Sun; adm. fee)* stands. The house was where Prudence Crandall set out to educate black girls in the early 1830s; she was hounded out of town for it. Fifty years later a penitent Connecticut voted the aged Crandall a pension.

Continue north on Conn. 169, past late 18th-century farmhouses and fields that were here before the Revolution. Along the way, you'll see examples of classic New England stone walls. The low walls are remarkably durable monuments to early farmers' determination to find a practical use for the curse of Yankee agriculture—the rocks and boulders deposited by glaciers. In some places, the walls have outlasted

Trinity Church, Brooklyn, Connecticut

the fields: Areas once completely cleared for agriculture have long since reverted to forest, with the enduring stone fences surviving amid the trees. A little over 5 miles north of Canterbury, you'll pass through a thick stand of maple and pine, along a shady allée canopied by foliage in summer.

Follow Conn. 169 to **Brooklyn,** 6 miles north of Canterbury. Since 1852, the **Brooklyn Fair** has been held here the week before Labor Day. The fairgrounds are on your left, along Conn. 169 just south of town.

A half mile past the fairgrounds, also on the left, stands the handsome **Israel Putnam Monument** to Brooklyn's most famous resident, a Revolutionary War major general. Born in Salem Village, now Danvers, Massachusetts, Putnam spent much of his life here and is buried beneath this monument. The command "Don't fire until you see the white of their eyes" was allegedly given by Putnam at the Battle of Bunker Hill.

Just past the Putnam monument is the Brooklyn town center, dominated by the lovely white spire of the 1771 Congregational **Meeting House,** which, in 1816, became Connecticut's first Unitarian church. Stay on Conn. 169 past its intersection with US 6 at Brooklyn and continue 7 miles into the town of **Pomfret,** clustered, like Brooklyn, around the antique spire of a Congregational church. This one was built in 1832 in the Greek Revival style. (The Congregationalists, so called because of the autonomy of their individual congregations, stem from England's original Puritan churches.)

As you drive through Pomfret, you'll notice that along with stone walls and churches, this corner of Connecticut is steeped in another New England tradition— private boarding schools. The campuses of the **Pomfret School** (1894) and the **Rectory School** (original building dates from 1792) both line Conn. 169 within a short distance of each other. **Woodstock,** 4 miles ahead, lies along the route of the Connecticut Path, the wilderness link between the Massachusetts and Connecticut colonies, and it is possible that Thomas Hooker and his party passed near the present-day site of Woodstock en route to Hartford in 1636.

In 1674 the Reverend John Eliot, "apostle to the Indians," preached to the local tribes near Woodstock, and 12 years later the first white settlers arrived.

51

You won't be able to drive past the Woodstock town green without taking notice of the vividly painted house across the street. This is **Roseland Cottage** *(860-928-4074. www.historicnewengland.org. Early June–mid-Oct. Wed.-Sun.; adm. fee),* the summer home of abolitionist publisher Henry Bowen. The 1846 cottage is a masterpiece of the Gothic Revival style. Bowen hosted several U.S. Presidents here during his July 4th celebrations; his barn houses perhaps the oldest indoor bowling alley in the United States.

Head on to **North Woodstock,** a village that does as much as any place to help the Quiet Corner earn its sobriquet. Here, you can choose to continue north toward Southbridge and Sturbridge (home of Old Sturbridge Village) just over the Massachusetts line, or follow the tranquil east-west byways of northeastern Connecticut.

Forest stream, Woodstock

Lower Connecticut River Valley

Loop from Middletown on Connecticut 66, 151, 149, 82, 156, I-95, and Connecticut 9 and 154

▪ 56 miles ▪ 2 hours ▪ May through October

The towns and harbors along the lower reaches of the Connecticut River have hummed with activity for over 300 years. This route explores the natural and man-made environments that inspired The Nature Conservancy to designate this area one of forty "Last Great Places" in the hemisphere. Start in **Middletown,** home of **Wesleyan University** *(860-685-7871. www.wesleyan.edu),* at the junction of Conn. 9 and 66. Main Street parallels the **Connecticut River,** which stretches some 400 miles from near the Canadian border to Long Island Sound.

Head east on Conn. 66 across the river into **Portland,** settled in 1690 and once a brownstone quarrying center. Five miles farther, at the junction of 66 and 151 in the village of **Cobalt**—named for an early mining venture—turn right and head south for 8 miles on Conn. 151 and then south on Conn. 149. Continue 3 miles into **East Haddam,** home of the restored **Victorian Goodspeed Opera House** *(860-873-8668. www.goodspeed.org. April-Dec. Wed.-Sun.; adm. fee),* where musicals are performed.

From the junction of Conn. 149 and 82 in East Haddam, go west on Conn. 82 and follow signs for **Gillette Castle State Park** *(via River Rd. 860-526-2336. www.stateparks.com.*

Grounds open all year, castle open Mem.
Day–Columbus Day; adm. fee). The
fieldstone castle, on a hill overlooking
the Connecticut River, was built in
1919 by actor William Gillette, famed
for his portrayal of Sherlock Holmes.

Leaving the park, turn left on
Conn. 148 through the town of Had-
lyme, then pick up Conn. 82 and continue east for 4 miles to the intersection
with Conn. 156. Turn right and head
south. The road crosses **Eightmile
River**, site of **Joshua's Rock**, where the
first Englishmen to sail up the Connecticut River were killed by Native
Americans, through Hamburg, and
into the township of **Old Lyme**. To visit
the town, which is filled with the mansions of 18th- and early 19th-century
sea captains, take a left on Halls Road,
then a right on Lyme Street. Otherwise, continue the drive south on I-95,
cross over the Connecticut River, and
take the first exit to Conn. 9. Take the
second exit off Conn. 9 to Conn. 154.

One mile north on Conn. 154 is
Essex, settled in 1690. The first Connecticut warship, the *Oliver Cromwell,*
was built here in 1775. **Ivoryton,** a part
of Essex, once manufactured ivory
piano keys. Turn off onto Conn. 9
and follow signs for the historic waterfront to visit the **Connecticut River
Museum** (*foot of Main St. 860-767
8269. www.ctrivermuseum.org. Closed
Mon.; adm. fee*). Stop for lunch or
dinner at the **Griswold Inn** (*860-767-
1776. www.griswoldinn.com*), open
since 1776.

North on Conn. 154, past the junction with Conn. 9, is the **Essex Steam
Train & Riverboat Ride** (*860-767-0103.
www.essexsteamtrain.com. Early May–
Dec., call for schedule; fare*). The **E. E.
Dickinson Company**, a witch hazel distillery, is also here. Continue north for
3 miles to **Deep River**, settled in 1635.
On the third Saturday of July the town
hosts the country's largest **Ancient Fife
and Drum Muster.**

Five miles north, you can turn west
on Conn. 148 for about 5 miles, then

Merritt Parkway

*New York state line to Housatonic River
on Connecticut 15*

■ 37 miles ■ 1 hour ■ All year. Avoid
weekday rush hours.

At the 1934 ground breaking for the
Merritt Parkway, Representative Schuyler Merritt said the route was designed
so the driver could "enjoy as you go."
Merritt was right about the features of
the road: It remains one of America's
outstanding achievements in public
engineering and architecture. The Merritt Parkway was placed on the National
Register of Historic Places in 1991.

Entering the parkway from New
York, on the right is **Tollgate Pond**, actually a quarry from which fill was taken in
construction. Road cuts and fill helped
smooth the road's ups and downs.
When the parkway was completed in
1940, each of its 69 bridges had a unique
design. The **Lake Avenue Bridge** (*exit 29*),
for example, has arches covered in intricate cast-iron vines. A few miles eastward, the **Guinea Road Bridge** is one of
only three original bridges faced with
stone. The others are concrete, a material that caused controversy at the time
of construction, since few thought it
could be made attractive.

The next bridge, **Riverbank Road,** was
criticized as
"elaborate fool-
ishness" for its
art deco design.
**Merwins Lane
Bridge** (*3 miles
east of exit 42*)
features spi-
ders and butter-
flies, while **Burr
Street Bridge**
has bas-reliefs
of workers who
surveyed and
built this now
busy parkway.

53

Haddam Meadows State Park on the Connecticut River

right on Cedar Lake Road, and follow signs to Pattaconk Reservoir for a side trip to 16,000-acre **Cockaponset State Forest** *(860-345-8521. www.stateparks.com),* with some of New England's few tulip trees.

Drive north along the river 4 miles past Conn. 82 to **Haddam,** once an important salmon and shad fisheries center. According to the indigenous Wangunk Indians, each year the Shad Spirit would lead the fish from the ocean to spawn in the Connecticut River. Turn left onto Walkley Hill Road to visit the 1794 **Thankful Arnold House** *(860-345-2400. www .haddamhistory.org/arnold_house.htm. Daily Mem. Day–Columbus Day, Wed.-Fri. & Sun. rest of year).* Return to Conn. 154; on the right is the entrance to **Haddam Meadows State Park** *(860-663-2030. www.stateparks .com),* a meadow in the river's floodplain.

The scenic portion of Conn. 154 ends some 4 miles ahead, at a waterfall in **Seven Falls State Highway Park.** Just past the falls, the stone slabs of **Bible Rock** stand on edge like an open book. Across from Bible Rock is **Shopboard Rock,** a freestanding boulder with a flat top, brought here by a glacier some 25,000 years ago. About 1 mile from the park is an entrance to Conn. 9 back toward Middletown.

Litchfield Hills

Loop on US 202, 7, 44, Connecticut 63, 109, 47, 45, 341, and 8

■ 87 miles ■ ¹/₂ day ■ May through October

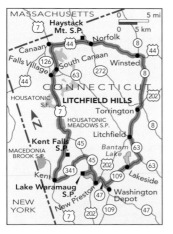

Connecticut's gently rolling Litchfield Hills are often called the "foothills of the Berkshires," but they have a character all their own—which could be described as country squire manners with just the right amount of rustic Yankee charm.

Begin this drive in **Torrington** by the Civil War statue at the junction of South Main Street and US 202. Once one of the "brass towns" of the **Naugatuck River Valley,** Torrington has a rich industrial history. The source of waterpower for these early industries was the scenic **Naugatuck River,** which flows through town. Follow US 202 for about 5 miles southwest as it climbs a plateau to the quintessential New England town of **Litchfield,** whose lovely town green is edged with stately colonial houses and elm trees. The **West Street Grill** *(43 West St. 860-567-3885. www.weststreetgrill.com)* on the green serves an excellent lunch and dinner. The **Tapping Reeve House and Law School** (*South St. 860-567-4501. www.litchfieldhistoricalsociety .org/lawschool.html. Mid-April–late-Nov.; adm. fee*) was America's first law school. Among the school's graduates were Vice President Aaron Burr— Reeve's first student—and Vice President John C. Calhoun.

For a side trip to the state's largest nature center, wildlife sanctuary, and natural lake, bear right and head west on US 202 for a few miles to **White Memorial Foundation** (*860-567-0857. www.whitememorialcc.org. Museum adm. fee*). This 4,000-acre sanctuary on **Bantam Lake** has a museum, hiking and cross-country ski trails, and bird observation platforms.

The **Bantam River,** flowing through the grounds, is a spawning ground for the state's largest freshwater game fish, the northern pike, and offers some of the best flat-water canoeing in Connecticut. The scenic drive continues its climb south on Conn. 63. A few miles past the junction is **White Flower Farm** (*800-503-9624. www.whiteflowerfarm.com. April-Oct.*), with 5 acres of perennial display gardens and 30 acres of pastures. Less than a mile past the farm, at the junction of Conn. 63 and 109, turn right and go west on Conn. 109 toward Washington Depot.

About 3.5 miles west on Conn. 109, in **Lakeside,** glass sculptor Larry LiVolsi welcomes visitors to his **Lorenz Studio and Gallery** (*226 Lakeside Rd. 860-567-4280*). The farmland and rolling hills that Conn. 109

Before sunrise on Lake Waramaug

55

traverses farther west typify the New England uplands. At the junction of Conn. 109 and 47 in tiny **Washington Depot,** turn right and head north on 47 toward Lake Waramaug State Park. If you're hungry, detour a few miles south on Conn. 47 to the elegant 1890 **Mayflower Inn** (*860-868-9466. www .mayflowerinn.com*).

Continue on Conn. 47 for 3 miles, then turn left onto US 202. Much of this area is marshy—in the summer, look for ferns and cattails. Turn right at the light onto Conn. 45 toward the **Connecticut Wine Trail,** which winds past local wineries between Brookfield and Clinton on the coast. In **New Preston,** the **Aspetuck River** once powered mills that manufactured wagons and sleighs. Today the tiny town is a mecca for antiques collectors.

Lake Waramaug, a short distance from New Preston, lies in heavily forested country and is one of the state's largest natural lakes. Its Native American name, "good fishing place," is still apt: Large- and smallmouth bass, chain pickerel, and yellow perch swim its waters. A few miles up Conn. 45, turn off onto Lake Road to visit **Lake Waramaug State Park** *(860-868-0220. www.lakewaramaug .com. Adm. fee weekends & holidays)*. The park offers a bathing beach, hiking trails, and paddleboat rentals. On the way to the park, stop at the tasting room of **Hopkins Vineyard** *(860-868-7954. Daily May-Dec., Fri.-Sun. Jan.-Feb., Wed.-Sun. March-April)*. The soil is favorable for growing vinifera and French-American hybrid grapes; the Seyval Blanc is excellent. In season, the 19th-

Main Street, Winsted

century **Hopkins Inn** *(860-868-7295. www.thehopkinsinn.com. Restaurant open April–New Year's, closed Mon. except holidays)* serves lunch and dinner on a terrace overlooking the lake.

Continue north on Conn. 45 for 3 miles past the turnoff for the state park to Conn. 341. Turn left and continue for about 10 miles to Kent. At the junction of Conn. 341 and US 7, continue west on 341, then turn right on Macedonia Brook Road for a 4-mile detour to **Macedonia Brook State Park** *(860-927-3238. www.stateparks.com. Camping fee April-Sept.)*. Trails offer excellent views reaching far into New York State to the west.

Or you can turn right from Conn. 341 onto US 7 and head into **Kent,** on the banks of the **Housatonic River.** The Housatonic, whose Mohican name means "place beyond the mountains," has its source in the Berkshire Hills of Massachusetts and makes its way for 148 miles through Connecticut to Long Island Sound. Kent's Main Street is lined with well-preserved old houses, art galleries, and antiques shops. But in the mid-1800s this was a workaday town, with three stone blast furnaces busy turning ore into iron. The discovery of iron ore in marble bedrock led to a massive deforestation of western Connecticut, as vast amounts of charcoal were needed to keep the furnaces in blast. The last furnace—Beckley Furnace in East Canaan—quit in 1923, and the woods are beginning to recover as second-growth replaces the vanished forest.

Stop about 1.5 miles north of Kent at the **Sloane-Stanley Museum & Kent Iron Furnace** *(860-927-3849. May-Oct. Wed.-Sun.; adm. fee)* to visit the ruins of a blast furnace and to see works by Eric Sloane, author, artist, and celebrator of American folk technology. Just past the museum is **Flanders Historic District,** buildings that were part of early Kent.

Continue north on US 7 for 4 miles to **Kent Falls State Park** *(860-927-3238. www.stateparks.com. Adm. fee weekends & holidays, parking fee May–end of fall foliage season. Temp. trail construction)*. For most of its way through Connecticut, the Housatonic River flows through marble lowlands called the **Marble Valley.** In the park, a tributary of the river has

In colonial times 95 percent of the citizens of Connecticut, then known as the Provisions State, worked on farms; today less than one percent do.

56

eroded the marble bedrock, creating a spectacular waterfall that drops 200 feet in 0.25 mile. You can see the waterfall from the road. North of Kent Falls, US 7 follows the Housatonic through a mixed deciduous forest to **Housatonic Meadows State Park** *(860-672-6772. www.stateparks.com. Camping fee)*. The river here is shallow, and only fly-fishing is permitted in the park. The **Pine Knob Loop Trail,** which joins the **Appalachian Trail,** begins on the left less than 1 mile north of the junction with Conn. 4. Watch for the right turn onto Conn. 128 for the covered bridge built about 1864 that links West Cornwall with Sharon. There are several buildings on the other side of the bridge, including a Shaker woodworking showroom, a bookstore, and a restaurant.

Continue north on US 7 for 5 miles to reach the turnoff for **Music Mountain** *(860-824-7126. www.musicmountain.org. June-Sept.; adm. fee for concerts),* site of the oldest chamber music series of its kind in the country. Along the way, you'll pass through **Housatonic State Forest.** One and a half miles past the Music Mountain turnoff, turn left on Conn. 126 and drive a half mile to **Falls Village** and the falls of the Housatonic.

Beyond the Falls Village turnoff, US 7 passes through South Canaan, then sidles along **Canaan Mountain.** The views here of **Mount Riga** and **Bear Mountain** are fine, particularly in fall foliage. Up the road lies **Canaan Village** that once served as the hub for the Connecticut Western Railroad.

At the junction of US 7 and 44, turn right and head east on US 44. At Norfolk, turn left onto Conn. 272 for a 0.25-mile side trip to **Haystack Mountain State Park** *(860-482-1817. www.stateparks.com).* A 36-foot stone tower atop the 1,680-foot peak provides wonderful views.

In the late 1800s many rich families built summer homes in **Norfolk.** Today, music lovers are drawn here by the artists performing each summer at the **Norfolk Chamber Music Festival** *(860-542-3000 in summer, 203-432-1966. www.yale.edu/norfolk. June-Aug.; adm. fee, some free performances).*

The fountain on the green was designed by architect Stanford White; the fountain at the southern corner of the green was designed by sculptor Augustus Saint-Gaudens and executed by White.

Travel past 10 commercialized miles of US 44 to Conn. 8. In **Winsted** turn right and head south for 9 miles on Conn. 8 to return to Torrington.

Litchfield Hills

Lake Huron

CANADA

Lake Ontar

MICHIGAN

Flint

Detroit

Toledo

Cleveland

Akron

Lake Erie

Erie

Rochester

Buffalo

Great Lakes
Seaway Trail
p. 63

Longhouse
Scenic Byway
p. 79

Timber, Oil, and
Coal Country Driv
p. 78

PENNSYLV

OHIO

Columbus

Dayton

Wheeling

Pittsburgh

Historic
National Road
p. 83

Laurel
Highlands
p. 80

Gettysbu

Staunton-
Parkersburg
Turnpike
p. 93

Canaan
Valley
Byway
p. 91

Washington
Heritage Trail
p. 90

WEST
VIRGINIA

Ohio

Charleston

Highland
Scenic Highway
p. 94

Skyline
Drive
p. 100

Georg
Washing
Mem. Pl
p. 99

Midland Trail
p. 95

Coal Heritage
Trail
p. 96

Journey through
Hallowed Grou
p. 80

Charlottesville

Richmond

KENTUCKY

Roanoke

Blue Ridge
Parkway
p. 102

VIRGINIA

TENNESSEE

NORTH CAROLINA

37
Whiteface Mountain
Memorial Highway
p. 62

11

*Lake
Champlain*

91

Burlington

Great Lakes
Seaway Trail
p. 63

86   9N

Montpelier

30

89

3

87

81

The Adirondacks
p. 61

VERMONT

93

**NEW
HAMPSHIRE**

Lakes
to Locks
Passage
p. 67

30

Concord

90

Mohawk Towpath
Scenic Byway
p. 68

Syracuse

Manchester

95

93

NEW YORK

Cayuga Lake p. 70

Albany

495

88

MASS. Boston

Ithaca

81

28

Catskill
Mountains
p. 71

90

Worcester

90

inghamton

Springfield

17

87

9

Hudson

River Road
p. 69

84

Providence

Grand Army of the
Republic Highway
p. 78

17

Hartford

CONN.

395

R. I.

6

95

Scranton

George W. Perkins
Memorial Drive
p. 72

380

84

91

6

New Haven

Delaware

95

Bridgeport

80

476

80

495

A

81

Allentown

**NEW
JERSEY**

New York

78

Millstone Valley
p. 74

Lancaster
County
Drive
p. 77

arrisburg

Trenton

Delaware River Scenic Byway
p. 73

30

76

Philadelphia

Brandywine Valley Scenic Byway
p. 76

ltimore's Hist.
harles Street
p. 87

Wilmington

95

Mouth of the
Delaware
p. 75

Baltimore

1

Dover

97

50

Chesapeake Country
p. 88

ools

DELAWARE

13

shington

MARYLAND

50

Harriet Tubman
Underground Railroad
Byway
p. 89

eligious Freedom
yway
. 85

Chesapeake Bay

EASTERN SHORE

*ATLANTIC
OCEAN*

olonial
arkway
. 97

13

64

Norfolk

Chesapeake Bay
Bridge-Tunnel
p. 98

Virginia Beach

0   50   100 miles
0   50   100   150 kilometers

New York, New Jersey, Delaware,
Pennsylvania, Maryland,
West Virginia, Virginia

NEW YORK
The Adirondacks

*Speculator to Saranac Lake through Adirondack Park on
New York 30 and 3*

■ 92 miles ■ 2¹/₂ hours ■ Late spring to early fall. Fall colors occur
early, about mid-September. Roads are well plowed, but snow is
frequent and heavy in winter.

Lofty heart of a 6-million-acre state parkland, the Adirondack Mountains
constitute one of the Northeast's last great wildernesses, with 42 peaks rising
higher than 4,000 feet. Scoured by Ice Age glaciers, the area is now densely
forested and pocked with countless lakes and ponds.

A choice Adirondack drive begins at the intersection of N.Y. 8 and 30 in
the village of **Speculator,** a hunting, fishing, and skiing center. The mountains rise gradually as you follow N.Y. 30 north through forests of maple,
beech, and birch that explode with color in the fall.

After 12 miles, you come to **Lewey Lake** and the
entrance to Lewey Lake Campground. *(For information on campgrounds, contact Dept. of Environmental
Conservation 518-648-5266. www.dec.ny.gov.)* Just
beyond, the road crosses a stream linking Lewey
Lake with larger **Indian Lake,** which forms part of the
Hudson River's headwaters. Following Indian Lake
for the next 8 miles, you'll crest a hill and views of
the distant peaks of the northern Adirondacks will
open up. After several miles, a scenic turnoff takes
in 3,353-foot Bullhead Mountain and surrounding
peaks in the area.

One mile past the turnout, take a left at the
T-junction in the hamlet of Indian Lake and continue on N.Y. 30 across the **Cedar River,** another
Hudson River tributary. After 10 miles, you'll cross
the divide between the Hudson and St. Lawrence
drainage systems. Beyond that point Adirondack
lakes and streams do not drain into the Hudson but
rather into the distant St. Lawrence River.

Thirteen miles past Indian Lake, the small resort
town of **Blue Mountain Lake** offers outfitting services

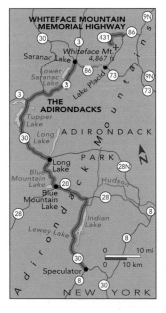

61

Amish country, Lancaster County, Pennsylvania

Franklin Lake and Whiteface Mountain

and a shop that sells the Adirondack's famous wooden slat chairs. Turn right to stay on N.Y. 30. Ahead is the lake from which the town takes its name and on the right rises **Blue Mountain.** Its 3,759-foot summit is crowned by a fire tower and accessible by a 2.2-mile trail that begins about a mile north of town. Just before you reach the trailhead, you'll see the excellent **Adirondack Museum** *(518-352-7311. www.adkmuseum.org. Mid-May–Oct.; adm. fee).* Its collection includes such regional classics as antique guide boats, furniture, mementos of early resort life, and an opulent private railroad car.

From the museum, the road descends through forests to **Long Lake.** These larger Adirondack lakes continue to harbor trout and other fish, but the smaller ponds, particularly on the west side of the park, were the first bellwethers of acid rain, and some no longer support fish.

Whiteface Mountain Memorial Highway

New York 86 to the summit of Whiteface Mountain on New York 431

■ 12 miles ■ ³/₄ hour ■ Late spring to late fall only. Toll booth halfway up mountain; elevator to summit from end of roadway. See map p. 61.

Whiteface Mountain isn't the loftiest of the Adirondacks—that distinction belongs to 5,344-foot Mount Marcy. But this 4,867-foot peak stands well enough apart from the rest of the range to offer the region's finest views. It's also the only Adirondack mountain whose summit can be reached by road.

The Whiteface Mountain Memorial Highway (N.Y. 431) begins off N.Y. 86, 9 miles east of Lake Placid, where the 1932 and 1980 Winter Olympics were held.

Climbing along the sides of **Esther Mountain,** this road offers broad views of the **Saranac River Valley.** After 1.5 miles, you pass the community of **North Pole,** home to **Santa's Workshop** *(518-946-2211. www.northpoleny.com. Mid-June–mid-Oct. & 5 weekends before Christmas; adm. fee).* The toll booth for the summit drive is 1.5 miles beyond.

For the next 3 miles, the road hugs the mountain's north and west faces and makes the final ascent by a pair of sharp switchbacks. From road's end, you can hike to the summit or go up by elevator whose shaft was cut into the mountain rock when the road was built in 1932.

The summit offers striking views: east to Vermont's **Mount Mansfield** and adjacent peaks and north to the skyscrapers of **Montreal;** to the west and south, the **Adirondack Mountains** and much of northern New York State is visible, with **Lake Placid** shimmering in the foreground.

Split Rock Falls in the Adirondacks

Turn left at the town of Long Lake, 11 miles from Blue Mountain Lake, to stay on N.Y. 30. After a 20-mile forest drive, cross an arm of **Tupper Lake** and follow N.Y. 3/30 signs through the town of the same name, notable for its early 20th-century facades. As the road crests a hill on the east side of town, look ahead for a view of 4,867-foot **Whiteface Mountain,** one of the highest peaks in the Adirondacks.

Bear right onto N.Y. 3 about 5 miles past Tupper Lake. This forested, mountainous road leads 15 miles to the town of **Saranac Lake.** As you approach town, spectacular views of glistening **Lower Saranac Lake** open up. Famous a century ago for its tuberculosis sanatorium, the town itself is now the largest community in Adirondack Park and a hub for outdoor recreation. The drive ends at the intersection of N.Y. 3 and 86.

Great Lakes Seaway Trail

Ohio-Pennsylvania state line to Rooseveltown, New York, on Pennsylvania 5 and 5A, New York 5, 265, 18, 104, 3, 12E, 12, 37, 131, and local roads

- 518 miles ▪ 3 days ▪ All year

The Great Lakes Seaway Trail guides travelers along truly legendary waterways: Lake Erie, Niagara Falls, Lake Ontario, and the St. Lawrence River. Water is in view for much of the route, yet the vistas vary by location and season. The Great Lakes can be placid or tumultuous—Niagara Falls roars with the power that has thrilled millions of people from around the world, and the beauty of the Thousand Islands region has enticed the wealthy to build magnificent houses. Recreational opportunities abound, and the historical legacy of the trail is just as rewarding. Look for green-and-white Seaway Trail road signs that indicate the route. Watch, too, for brown signs with a white ship; these point out sites related to the War of 1812.

The westernmost 54 miles of the trail lie within Pennsylvania, with Pa. 5 and 5A running through woods, fields, and small towns to reach the geological oddity of **Presque Isle.** This "almost island" is a narrow, curving spit of land reaching about 7 miles into Lake Erie, creating a protected harbor that made **Erie** *(Convention & Visitors Bureau, 208 E. Bayfront Pkwy. 814-454-1000 or 800-524-3743. www.visiteriepa.com)* an important shipping port. **Presque Isle State Park** *(Pa. 832. 814-833-7424. www.presqueisle.org)* offers a number of ways to explore, including hiking trails, boat rentals and tours, swimming at the state's best sandy beaches, and natural history exhibits at **Tom Ridge Environmental Center** *(814-833-7424. www.trecpi.org).*

Located on Erie's waterfront, the 187-foot **Bicentennial Tower** *(814-455-6055. www.porterie.org/bicentennial. Nov.-March weekends; adm. fee)* offers a panoramic view of Lake Erie, Presque Isle Bay, and downtown. The

Erie Maritime Museum *(150 E. Front St. 814-452-2744. www.flagshipniagara .org. Closed Mon.-Wed. Jan.-March; adm. fee)* features a variety of exhibits on Lake Erie and the War of 1812, but its main attraction is U.S. Brig *Niagara*. A reconstruction of the warship Oliver Hazard Perry used to win the Battle of Lake Erie during the War of 1812, the *Niagara* is docked September through May but sails sporadically during the summer. About 1.5 miles east, the sandstone 1867 **Erie Land Lighthouse** *(end of Lighthouse St.)* is one of 28 lighthouses found along the Seaway Trail; two others are on Presque Isle.

As you continue into New York, you're traveling through a region renowned for its grapes. Most of the crop goes into juice, jellies, or table grapes, but several wineries offer tours and tastings.

Lighthouse buffs should turn north off N.Y. 5 in Dunkirk on Point Drive to see the 1875 **Dunkirk Lighthouse**.

The highway often hugs the shore of Lake Erie as it continues to **Buffalo** *(Buffalo Niagara Convention & Visitors Bureau, 617 Main St. 888-228-3369. www.visitbuffaloniagara.com)*, a city that ought to be as famous for architecture as it is for its "lake effect" winter snows.

Admire the 1896 **Ellicott Square Building** *(295 Main St.)*, the 1895 **Guaranty Building** *(28 Church St.)*, or the mansions along **Delaware Street** *(Millionaire's Row)*. Some of Frank Lloyd Wright's best work can be seen at the **Darwin D. Martin House Complex** *(125 Jewett Pkwy. 716-856-3858. www .darwinmartinhouse.org. Closed Mon.; fee for tours)*, which Wright himself called "a well-nigh perfect composition."

The most spectacular sight of the Seaway Trail lies just a few minutes north at **Niagara Falls,** one of the most famous geological features on Earth. Made up of three more-or-less separate waterfalls—**Horseshoe Falls, American Falls,** and **Bridal Veil Falls**—Niagara has been a tourist attraction since the mid-19th century.

Today's visitors have several choices to view the falls, including land observation decks, observation towers on both the American and Canadian sides of the Niagara River, tunnels, and the *Maid of the Mist* boats *(fare)*. **Niagara Falls State Park** *(716-278-1796. www.niagarafallsstatepark .com)* is the place to start, including the **Niagara Gorge Discovery Center**

Sackets Harbor on Lake Ontario, New York

(716-278-1070. Adm. fee), where you can learn about the geological forces that created the falls.

Eighteen miles north, where the Niagara River flows into Lake Ontario, **Old Fort Niagara State Historic Site** *(716-745-7611. www.old fortniagara.org. Adm. fee)* preserves several buildings at this strategic location, which has seen military forces of France, Britain, and the United States. The oldest structure here is the **French Castle**, dating from 1726. Living-history interpreters provide regular programs at the park, which also includes history exhibits.

N.Y. 18 now runs through farm fields along the south shore of Lake Ontario, with the occasional park providing access to the water. Lake Ontario State Parkway leads to **Rochester** *(Greater Rochester Visitors Association, 45 East Ave. 800-677-7282. www.visitrochester.com)*, home to several worthwhile museums.

Niagara Falls

At the **George Eastman House** *(900 East Ave. 585-271-3361 or 585-279-8300. www.eastmanhouse.org. Closed Mon.; adm. fee)*, once home of the man who made Kodak a household name, you can tour the fabulous 37-room mansion and visit the **International Museum of Photography and Film,** which displays photographs, photographic equipment, books, and motion pictures. The **Strong–National Museum of Play** *(1 Manhattan Square. 585-263-2700. www.museumofplay.com. Adm. fee)* includes all sorts of fun-related stuff, including a Reading Adventureland, a butterfly garden, a Sesame Street exhibit, and—perhaps most fun for adults—the National Toy Hall of Fame, honoring Barbie, Crayolas, Mr. Potato Head, Slinky, Tinkertoys, and other childhood icons. At the **Susan B. Anthony House** *(17 Madison St. 585-235-6124. www.susanbanthonyhouse.org. Closed Mon.; adm. fee)* you'll learn about the famed crusader for women's rights, with exhibits set in the house where she was arrested in 1872—for voting.

About 30 miles east of Rochester, **Sodus Bay** is known for the 1870 **Sodus Bay Lighthouse** *(N.Y. 14. 315-483-4936. www.soduspointlighthouse .org. May-Oct.; adm. fee)* on the west side, and, on the east, **Chimney Bluffs State Park** *(Bluff Rd. 315-947-5205. www.nysparks.com/parks)*. The former includes a museum with exhibits on Lake Ontario and lighthouse lore, and the latter features terrain of strikingly sculpted spires (which can be seen from the lighthouse).

The tidy little town of **Sackets Harbor** is located where the Lake Ontario shore becomes more irregular, with bays, peninsulas, and islands giving a preview of things to come. The town is home to the **Seaway Trail Discovery Center** *(401 W. Main St. 315-646-1000 or 800-732-9298. www.seawaytrail .com)*, the official visitor center for the Seaway Trail. Located in a stone 1817 hotel building, the center includes exhibits on maritime history, the War of 1812, lighthouses, and Great Lakes natural history.

Sodus Bay Lighthouse, Lake Ontario, New York

N.Y. 12E reaches the shore of the mighty **St. Lawrence River** at Cape Vincent, where the **Tibbetts Point Lighthouse** *(315-654-2700. www .capevincent.org/light house. Daily in summer, Fri.-Mon. in spring & fall, closed in winter)* offers views of the huge seagoing ships that travel from the Great Lakes through the St. Lawrence. Across the water, Wolfe and Carleton Islands are among the legendary **Thousand Islands** that dot the river downstream from here. Fifteen miles east, the harbor town of **Clayton** is an appropriate place for the **Antique Boat Museum** *(750 Mary St. 315-686-4104. www.abm.org. Mid-May–Oct.; adm. fee),* which displays more than 200 pleasure craft, from skiffs to fancy houseboats.

Continuing on N.Y. 12 now, you'll pass the I-81 bridge to Ontario, and beyond that the tourist town of **Alexandria Bay.** Boats leave from here for tours of **Boldt Castle** *(800-847-5263. www.boldtcastle.com. Mid-May–Sept.; adm. fee),* a turn-of-the-20th-century millionaire's extravaganza on Heart Island. The builder was the owner of the Waldorf-Astoria Hotel in New York City, and when his wife died he stopped construction and never returned; the "castle" went almost to ruins before being rehabilitated.

N.Y. 12 has intermittent views of the St. Lawrence, particularly at a scenic turnoff 14.5 miles east. Here, you can see **Chippewa Bay,** the Canadian shore, and the easternmost Thousand Islands, which are composed of the same rock as the Adirondacks. Several state parks offer access to the riverbank along this stretch.

The famed Western artist Frederic Remington grew up in part in **Ogdensburg,** and at the age of 39 brought a summer home on an island in the St. Lawrence. Today Ogdensburg is home to the **Frederic Remington Art Museum** *(303 Washington St. 315-393-2425. www.fredericremington.org. Closed Mon.-Tues. Nov.-April; adm. fee),* which displays Remington paintings, sketches, and sculptures, as well as personal memorabilia. The works include not just Old West themes but also scenes from the St. Lawrence area and other locales.

Another bridge to Canada crosses the river just downstream from Ogdensburg, and 10 miles farther is the **Iroquois Lock and Dam,** one of seven structures in the St. Lawrence River that regulate flow in the **Saint Lawrence Seaway,** the river-canal system that lets ships travel from the Great Lakes to the Atlantic. At Massena, learn about the seaway at the **Saint Lawrence– FDR Project Visitor Center** *(Barnhart Island Rd. off N.Y. 131. 315-764-0226. www.nypa.gov/vc/stlaw.htm. Mon.-Fri. in winter),* which has displays on the waterway's role in transportation and power generation.

Lakes to Locks Passage

Waterford to Rouses Point on US 4, New York 22, and US 9

- 234 miles ▪ 1 day ▪ Spring through fall

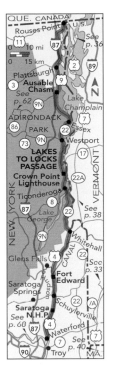

History, commerce, recreation, and dramatic landscapes come together in this rewarding byway, which connects the Hudson River Valley to Lake Champlain in upstate New York. Events here during the Revolutionary War determined the fate of the United States; later, New York's canal system made vital contributions to the young nation's economic growth.

The route's southern terminus, **Waterford,** is situated on the Hudson River where the Erie and Champlain Canals meet. Visit the downtown **Waterford Harbor Visitor Center** *(1 Tugboat Alley. 518-233-9123. www.town .waterford.ny.us),* on the Erie Canal, for travel advice. To learn more about attractions here, including the **Waterford Flight of Locks** and **Peebles Island State Park** see the **Mohawk Towpath Scenic Byway** (sidebar p. 68).

The Lakes to Locks Passage follows the Upper Hudson River and the Champlain Canal northward, passing through farmland and small towns. In about 20 miles you'll reach **Saratoga National Historical Park** *(518-664-9821. www.nps.gov/sara. Adm. fee),* the site where American troops defeated an advancing British army in October 1777. This "turning point of the American Revolution" quite literally changed the course of world history. See the orientation film at the **visitor center** before taking a self-guided tour of the battlefield. Seven miles north in Schuylerville, you can tour the **Schuyler House** *(518-664-9821. www.nps.gov/sara. Mem. Day Labor Day Wed.-Sun.),* the restored country house of American Gen. Philip Schuyler. George Washington, Alexander Hamilton, and the Marquis de Lafayette were among

67

those who visited the house, which after the war became the center of Schuyler's farm and mill businesses.

Also part of the national historical park is the nearby 155-foot-tall **Saratoga Monument** *(Burgoyne Rd.),* commemorating the battle.

Just north of the locks at Schuylerville, US 4 crosses to the east side of the Hudson to reach **Fort Edward,** the site of a large and important British outpost during the French and Indian War.

Saratoga National Historical Park

Mohawk Towpath Scenic Byway

Waterford to Schenectady on local roads

■ 28 miles ■ 2 hours ■ Late spring through fall

Paralleling New York's Mohawk River and the Erie Canal, this drive goes from the Hudson River to Schenectady.

Waterford occupies a strategic location where the Erie Canal enters the Hudson River. To bypass **Cohoes Falls,** a series of locks was built on the canal north of the river. Near the **Waterford Harbor Visitor Center** (*1 Tugboat Alley. 518-233-9123*) you can see today's Lock No. 2 at work, part of the **Waterford Flight of Locks,** raising watercraft 165 feet.

Just across one of the Hudson River channels from Waterford, you'll find good views in **Peebles Island State Park** (*Delaware Ave. in Cohoes. 518-237-8643. www.nysparks.com/parks*). Also located on this side is the **Erie Canalway National Heritage Corridor Visitor Center** (*518-237-7000. www.eriecanalway.org. May–mid-Nov.*).

Upstream on the north side of the Mohawk River, **Vischer Ferry Nature and Historic Preserve** (*Riverview Rd.*) offers trails for hiking or wildlife observation.

To reach the area, cross an 1862 truss bridge over the Erie Canal and towpath.

In **Schenectady,** the riverfront **Stockade District** (*around Front & Green Sts. www.historicstockade.com*) ranks among the region's most historic neighborhoods. Here, more than a hundred notable structures date back to the late 17th century.

Here you cross the southern end of the original route of the Champlain Canal connecting Lake Champlain with the Hudson. Stop at the **Rogers Island Visitor Center** (*11 Rogers Island Dr. 518-747-3693. www.rogers island.org. Tues.-Sun. mid-May–Oct.*) to learn not only about the military tactics of "Rogers' rangers" but also about archaeological investigations into the Native American presence on the island.

In Glens Falls you can explore the 7-mile towpath along the **Feeder Canal,** built in 1832 to move water from the Hudson to the Champlain Canal. The **Old Fort House Museum** (*29 Broadway St. 518-747-9600. Daily June-Aug., Mon.-Fri. Sept.–mid-Oct.; adm. fee*) is located in a 1772 house built with timbers taken from the ruins of Fort Edward. It was used as headquarters by both British and American generals in the Revolutionary War. (George Washington dined here twice.) It features authentic furnishings depicting the lives of occupants from the 1770s through the 1940s.

The route occasionally approaches the canal closely on its way to **Whitehall,** which became "the birthplace of the U.S. Navy" when in 1776 Gen. Benedict Arnold took possession of a ship and sailed it into Lake Champlain. Situated on the canal in a 1917 terminal building, the **Skenesborough Museum** (*Skenesborough Dr. 518-499-1155. Daily mid-June–Labor Day, weekends Sept.-June; adm. fee*) interprets naval history and provides local travel information. Drive up to the Gothic-style stone 1874 **Skene Manor** (*off US 4. 518-499-1906. www .skenemanor.org. Fri.-Sun.*) for great views of the Champlain Valley and the Champlain Canal.

The byway switches to N.Y. 22 and crosses the lower end of 133-mile-long **Lake Champlain,** in a glacially shaped valley stretching north into Canada. Roadsides are more forested as you travel toward **Ticonderoga** (*Lake Champlain Visitor Center, 94 Montcalm St. 518-585-6619 or 866-843-5253. www.lakechamplainregion .com*), situated on a strategic neck of land between Lakes Champlain and George. Drive to the top of **Mount Defiance** for a panorama of the surroundings before visiting **Fort Ticonderoga** (*N.Y. 74. 518-585-7450. www .fortticonderoga.org. Mid-May–mid-Oct.; adm. fee*) to learn about local history during the French and Indian and Revolutionary Wars. A restored fort, gardens, battlefield, and costumed interpreters are among the attractions at this national historic landmark.

Farther north, where Bridge Road crosses the lake, **Crown Point State Historic Site** (*518-597-4666. www.nysparks .com/historic-sites. May–Oct.; adm. fee*) preserves the ruins of a fort on a site that was occupied at various times by French, British, and American troops. A museum tells the story of this much fought-over piece of land.

Be sure to stop at the impressive **Crown Point Lighthouse**, which also serves as a memorial to French explorer Samuel de Champlain. This memorial features a Rodin bust that was a gift from France.

North of Westport, N.Y. 22 turns inland to follow the Boquet River through farmland before returning to the lake at Essex.

Off US 9 north of Keeseville, **Ausable Chasm** (*518-834-7454. www.ausable chasm.com. Adm. fee*), a commercial attraction since 1870, encompasses a striking sandstone gorge, waterfalls, caves, and extensive trails to explore them, as well as rafting and kayaking on the Ausable River.

After passing **Valcour Island** and a now-closed Air Force base, you reach **Plattsburgh**, where the Saranac River flows into Lake Champlain. A monument here remembers Commodore Thomas Macdonough, whose 1814 naval victory over the British in the Battle of Plattsburgh was one of the

River Road

Rhinebeck to New York 9G on West Market Street and New York 103

- 9 miles ▪ 20 minutes ▪ Spring to mid-fall. Fine fall foliage. See map p. 71.

One of the earliest settled regions in the country, the Hudson River Valley was home to Dutch colonists long before the Pilgrims landed at Plymouth. Sought out later by 19th-century barons of the gilded age, the valley wears the look of a well-used landscape that still possesses much of its natural charm.

Begin this drive in **Rhinebeck,** settled in 1686. The **Old Rhinebeck Aerodrome** (*9 Nornton Rd. 845-752-3200. www .oldrhinebeck.org. Mid-May–Oct.; adm. fee*) displays a collection of antique planes. The **Beekman Arms and Delamater Inn** (*6387 Mill St. 845-876-7077. www.beekmandelamaterinn.com*), an 18th-century inn, was the spot where Franklin Roosevelt held his election-night rallies.

Follow West Market Street, which becomes Rhinecliff Road. As you crest a hill, you'll see the distant **Catskill Mountains** across the **Hudson River.** About a mile from town, turn right onto N.Y. 103, the River Road. Along this winding, tree-canopied road, low stone walls and handsome gatehouses mark estates that date from the 19th century.

Turn left 6 miles down to enter **Montgomery Place** (*845-758-1036. House under renovation but still open to public. May-Oct. Thurs-Sun, closed Jan.-March; adm. fee*), a 434-acre estate and 1805 mansion with splendid views of the Hudson and Catskills. In early autumn you can pick and purchase the estate's apples.

The River Road soon takes you through the campus of **Bard College** in the village of **Annandale.** End the drive at the intersection with N.Y. 9G.

decisive battles of the War of 1812. Nine miles north, **Point Au Roche State Park** *(518-563-0369. www.nysparks.com/parks)* offers access to the lake, hiking trails, and a nature center where visitors can learn about the environment around Champlain.

From the park, continue on Lake Shore Road northward to its junction with N.Y. 9B, following the latter to the northern end of the byway at Roches Point, on the border with Canada.

Cayuga Lake

Ithaca to Seneca Falls on New York 89

- 39 miles ▪ 1 hour ▪ All year. Summer and early fall are best for winery visits; winter, with lack of foliage, allows good views of lake.

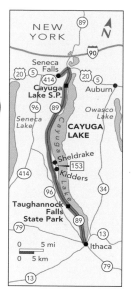

Few geographical features are more aptly named than New York State's Finger Lakes, which fan across the Allegheny Plateau like outstretched digits of a hand. This drive winds along the shoreline of the longest of them, 40-mile-long Cayuga Lake, where the countryside is flavored by pleasant towns and fine wineries.

The drive begins in **Ithaca** at the southern end of **Cayuga Lake.** A **visitor center** *(904 E. Shore Dr. 607-272-1313)* has information on sites in the area.

As N.Y. 89 heads north, it first winds past Ithaca's outlying suburbs before cutting through **Taughannock Falls State Park** *(607-387-6739. www.nysparks .com/parks. Vehicle fee mid-May–mid-Oct.)*, 10 miles outside town. Here, you'll find boat launches and rentals, a beach, and the falls themselves. At 215 feet high, Taughannock is higher than Niagara—but don't expect a roaring cascade. Changing seasonally, the narrow white ribbon of water needles down into a cold green pool at the center of a vast natural amphitheater of shale.

North past the falls, N.Y. 89 passes through tranquil lakeside farmland, with occasional views of Cayuga Lake and its eastern shore. This is wine country; you'll find almost a dozen wineries located just off the road. Most offer tours and on-site purchasing. Several roadside apiaries also sell honey along the way.

New York's Finger Lakes region ranks as the largest wine-producing area in the East.

For a pleasant side trip with outstanding lake views, turn right 8 or 9 miles north of Taughannock Falls on Deerlick Springs Road, then left on Cty. Rd. 153, which winds through the little towns of Kidders and Sheldrake. Restaurants in **Kidders** serve local wines, and there are two B&Bs in **Sheldrake**. Otherwise, this route is uncommercialized, passing gracious Victorian homes framed by big weeping willows that drape their branches out across the water. The shore road, called Weyers Point Road, loops up and rejoins N.Y. 89 after 4.5 miles, but the panoramas of the lake continue to the east. To the west, farmlands, orchards, and the occasional

70

Cayuga Lake countryside

small town occupy the gently rising pillow of land that reaches across to the shores of **Seneca Lake.** Two of the communities here, Ovid and Romulus, typify the penchant in the early 1800s for naming towns after people and places of classical antiquity.

You'll follow Cayuga Lake quite closely along much of the northern half of the route, with little to interrupt views of the water and of the patchwork of meadows and woods on the opposite shore. As recently as the 1920s, steam ferries plied the lake, some running its entire length.

The drive ends in **Seneca Falls,** just west of Cayuga Lake on US 20. Here, in the mid-19th century, Elizabeth Cady Stanton and Susan B. Anthony laid the groundwork for the modern women's movement. The small city is now home to the **National Women's Hall of Fame** *(76 Fall St. 315-568-8060. www .greatwomen.org. Closed Sun.-Tues. Nov.-May; adm. fee),* whose portraits and photographs tell the stories of distinguished American women.

71

Catskill Mountains

Kingston to Margaretville on New York 28

▪ 43 miles ▪ 1½ hours ▪ Spring to fall. Foliage peaks in mid-October. In winter, ski resorts dot snow-covered mountains, and small towns take on a festive alpine air.

Hudson River school painters, beginning in the 1820s with Thomas Cole, celebrated the scenery of the Catskill Mountains, whose gentle slopes are laced with trout streams.

Start just west of **Kingston,** where N.Y. 28 begins. After 6 miles—

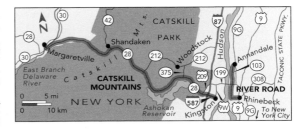

some of them heavily commercialized—turn right onto N.Y. 375, and you'll soon reach the artist colony of **Woodstock,** made famous by the 1969 music festival that actually was held 50 miles southwest of here.

Eagle Lake in the Catskills

Returning to N.Y. 28, you pass **Kenozia Lake** after several miles. To the left, though not visible from the road, is the **Ashokan Reservoir,** built in 1915 as part of New York City's water supply system. The reservoir was formed by damming **Esopus Creek,** the Hudson River tributary that N.Y. 28 follows for a portion of its length.

The creek valley deepens as you drive along, with rising hills crowding in on both sides. The early Dutch settlers here called such deep ravines "cloves." The word survives in many local designations, describing the shady, sometimes almost somber defiles that give the region so much of its scenic flavor. A good example can be found along N.Y. 42, a right turn off N.Y. 28 near the village of Shandaken. Roughly half a mile past the town of Pine Hill, take a left turn for **Belleayre Mountain Ski Center** (845-254-5600. www.belleayre.com), a state-run facility that is open to hikers in the off-season (lifts operate only in winter). Mountain views are spectacular from the base lodge at 2,541 feet, and even better if you hike to the 3,375-foot summit of **Belleayre Mountain.**

End the drive with a right turn onto N.Y. 30 at **Margaretville.** The bridge here crosses the **East Branch Delaware River,** a parent stream of the great river that flows into Delaware Bay some 200 miles to the south.

George W. Perkins Memorial Drive

Seven Lakes Drive to the summit of Bear Mountain

▪ 5 miles ▪ 20 minutes ▪ Spring through fall. Fine fall foliage. Weekends crowded mid-spring through late fall. Winter weather often causes closings. Open daily 8 a.m. to dusk.

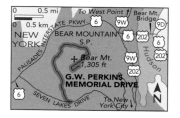

This drive climbs 1,305-foot Bear Mountain, second highest of the granite Hudson Highlands peaks (1,355-foot Storm King is first). The summit has commanding views of the lower Hudson Valley.

The drive begins off Seven Lakes Drive, the main route through **Bear Mountain State Park** (845-786-2701. www.nysparks.com/parks. Parking fee except winter weekends). The lower portion of the drive winds through deep woods and past exposed rock ledges characteristic of the region's upthrust Precambrian granite. Broad vistas of the **Hudson Valley** open up as you ascend.

The summit offers spectacular views. To the east is **Bear Mountain Bridge;** on the Hudson's opposite shore is a rocky promontory called **Anthony's**

Nose. The northern view takes in the river valley toward **West Point** and **Storm King.** To the west the **Hudson Highlands** recede toward the lake-studded landscape of **Harriman State Park** *(845-786-2701. www.nysparks .com/parks).* And to the south the broad swath of the Hudson River called the **Tappan Zee** is spanned by the **Tappan Zee Bridge.** On the clearest days, you can see the gleaming steel towers of the **George Washington Bridge** at the threshold of Manhattan Island.

NEW JERSEY
Delaware River Scenic Byway

Trenton to Frenchtown on New Jersey 29

■ 30 miles ■ 1 hour ■ Fine fall foliage

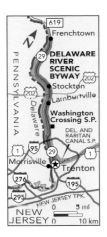

The small towns and green parklands that characterize New Jersey's Delaware River shoreline belie the state's popular image as a place of densely packed cities. Just over an hour from both New York and Philadelphia, this part of New Jersey is a world apart from urban bustle.

The excursion begins in **Trenton,** in the shadow of the golden-domed **State House** *(W. State St. 609-292-7065. www.njleg.state.nj.us).* Drive a block north on State Street, turn left, and follow signs for N.J. 29 north. At 8 miles, turn right on Cty. Rd. 546 to visit 841-acre **Washington Crossing State Park** *(609-737-0623. Adm. fee Mem. Day–Labor Day weekends),* site of George Washington's tactically brilliant crossing of the Delaware River on Christmas night 1776.

The waterway visible on the left as you drive through the park—and along much of this route—is a 22-mile feeder channel of the 1834 canal, now preserved in the **Delaware and Raritan Canal State Park** *(609-924-5705. www.dandrcanal.com).* The canal was built to route barges around stretches of the river.

After 14 miles on N.J. 29, bear left to see the neatly painted brick facades of **Lambertville.** George Washington visited here in 1777, at the **Holcombe House** *(private)* at 260 N. Main St.

Go north for 3.5 miles to Stockton, where the **Stockton Inn** *(1 Main St. 609-397-1250. www.stocktoninn.com)* has been in business since 1796 (the building dates from 1710). The inn is believed to have inspired the Rodgers and Hart song, "There's a Small Hotel." At nearby **Prallsville Mills Historic District,** canalside mill buildings stand amid oaks and willows.

From here, the road heads through an oak and maple forest for 3 miles to the **Bull's Island Recreation Area** *(609-397-2949. www.state.nj.us/dep/parks andforests).* Part of the Delaware and Raritan Canal State Park, it welcomes canoeists, cyclists, and hikers. Past this northern end of the canal, N.J. 29 follows the Delaware to **Frenchtown,** whose streets are lined with 19th-century homes, antique shops, trim B&Bs, and the restored 1851 **National Hotel** *(31 Race St. 908-996-3200. www.thenationalhotelnj.com).*

Millstone Valley Scenic Byway

A loop around the Delaware and Raritan Canal on local roads from Princeton, New Jersey

- 28 miles ▪ 45 minutes ▪ Spring through fall. Fine foliage; occasional flooding.

Meandering through the Millstone River Valley in central New Jersey, this bucolic loop encircles a wildlife haven within the **Delaware and Raritan Canal State Park** *(609-924-5705. www.state.nj.us/dep/parksandforests/parks/drcanal.html)* and offers rich vistas of waterways and farmland. Echoes of the canal era, the Revolutionary War, and the early Dutch settlers resonate throughout this vibrant valley.

From **Princeton,** follow N.J. 27 (Nassau Street/Lincoln Highway) north into **Kingston.** Turn left onto Laurel Avenue (Cty. Rd. 603), which becomes Kingston–Rocky Hill Road. **Rockingham Historic Site** is one mile on the left. Here you can tour the Berrien Mansion *(609-683-7132. www.rockingham.net. Closed Mon.-Tues.),* which served as George Washington's Revolutionary War headquarters in 1783. The house now also hosts a **children's museum** and **colonial kitchen garden.**

Continue north on Kingston–Rocky Hill Road and cross Cty. Rd. 518 onto Canal Road. The blacktop is narrow and potholed in places; as you follow the **Delaware and Raritan Canal** on your left, watch for steep ditches to your right.

The D&R Canal transported coal via the Delaware River to Bordentown and the Raritan River to **New Brunswick,** and it shuttled Union troops and cargo throughout the Civil War. The 74-mile waterway, opened in 1834, was dug by Irish immigrant laborers.

Watch for horses crossing near **Little Valley Stables** *(1345 Canal Rd. www.littlevalleystables.com).* Other traffic will likely include vintage tractors, as well as cyclists and hikers heading for local trails and picnic sites.

Continue on Canal Road, past Copper Mine Road. Turn right onto the stony lane up to **Griggstown Native Grassland Preserve** *(1091 Canal Rd.)* for a peek at the Suri alpacas and llamas of **Belle Mere Farm** *(1079 Canal Rd. 908-359-9387).*

Five miles north of **Kingston,** you'll pass the **Griggstown Causeway,** which crosses the canal. Just past the bridge, **Griggstown Canoe and Kayak Rental** *(908-359-5970. www.canoenj.com/griggs1.htm)* offers aquatic adventure.

About 2.3 miles farther along Canal Road, turn left onto Suydam Road, which swings right, becoming Canal Road again. Another 1.3 miles on, **Blackwells Mills Canal House** *(732-828-7418. www.themeadowsfoundation.org/blackwell-mills.html)* stands at the intersection of Blackwells Mills Road. The house, built in 1835, was home to generations of bridge tenders and now hosts music festivals and art exhibits.

At the top of the byway is **East Millstone,** where some of the area's earliest settlers, dating to the 18th century, rest in the graveyard of the **Dutch Reformed Church.** As Canal Road becomes Elm Street, make a left onto Market Street.

Stop into **East Millstone Antiques and Café** *(732-220-0042. Closed Mon.-Wed.)* on Market Street for refreshments. The hallway displays old photos and news clippings about this sleepy village. Ask the owners to activate the 1930s Christmas fantasia that once enchanted yuletide shoppers in a Manhattan department store.

Turning left onto Amwell Road, cross the bridge and make a sharp right onto North River Street and round the corner to the **Old Millstone Forge museum** *(www.oldmillstoneforge.org. Open Sun. 1-4 p.m. April-June, Sept.-Nov.).* This forge operated from 1832 to 1959. The Indian millstone out front was excavated at the site of a nearby Native American village.

A walk along the canal's leafy **towpath** is highly recommended. These waterways teem with warblers, loons, ducks, egrets, ospreys, and hawks. Red-bellied turtles and hognose snakes frequently cross the roads; watch, too, for deer darting from woodlands of oak, maple, and horse chestnut.

A left onto Main Street/Millstone River Road (Cty. Rd. 533) takes you back down the valley on much improved roads. At the end of Millstone River Road, cross Bridgeport Road and go south on US 206. After ¼ mile, make a left onto Montgomery Avenue, which becomes River Road (Cty. Rd. 605). Follow this for 3½ miles and turn south onto N.J. 27 to return to **Princeton.**

Autumn foliage on the Millstone Valley canal

75

DELAWARE
Mouth of the Delaware

New Castle to Dover on Delaware 9 and 8

■ 45 miles ■ 1½ hours ■ Spring and fall. Summer is hot, humid, and bug-ridden along marshes.

The Delaware River, navigable from Delaware Bay to Trenton, New Jersey, has long been an important highway of commerce for tankers and freighters, but this drive explores a different aspect of the river. Ambling through the northern end of the Delmarva (Delaware, Maryland, Virginia) Peninsula, it passes through small towns and salt marshes where herons and egrets wade.

Begin at **New Castle.** Founded in 1651 as a Dutch outpost, the town went on to become the capital of the colony. New Castle's **Old Court House** *(211 Delaware St. 302-323-4453. www.history.delaware.gov/museums/ncch/visitors.shtml. Closed Mon.; donation)* is one of the nation's oldest public buildings, dating from 1732. Heading west, Del. 9 twists through several miles of industrial and residential neighborhoods. In vacant lots you'll see *Phragmites communis,* the tall feathery-topped marsh reed characteristic of wetland environments.

See p. 76

Phragmites quickly takes over when pollution has extirpated more delicate marsh plants.

Ten miles down the road, a bridge carries Del. 9 across the **Chesapeake & Delaware Canal,** which links the upper reaches of Chesapeake Bay with the lower Delaware River. On the left is the **Delaware River;** ahead lies the New Jersey shore and the massive cooling tower of the Salem nuclear power plant; to the west, the canal and marshes spread toward Maryland.

Three miles past the bridge, the road enters the small town of **Port Penn,** named for William Penn, founder of the Pennsylvania Colony. In 1682 a British land grant also awarded him what is now Delaware. The **Port Penn Interpretive Center** *(302-836-2533. www.destateparks.com. Mem. Day–Labor Day Fri.-Sun.)* focuses on the interplay between the region's natural environment and its human uses.

Beyond Port Penn, the countryside is dominated by farmland. The fields alternate with stretches of salt marsh, protected at the **Augustine, Cedar Swamp,** and **Woodland Beach Wildlife Areas;** all three lie along Del. 9.

The Woodland Beach Wildlife Area is worth a detour. At an intersection roughly 20.5 miles south of Port Penn, turn left and drive 3 miles through the wildlife area's pristine tidal marshes— prime feeding grounds for great blue herons and snowy egrets. Cross Duck Creek to enter the tiny Delaware River hamlet of Woodland Beach.

Continue roughly 3 miles past the Woodland Beach turnoff to the **Bombay Hook National Wildlife Refuge** *(302-653-9345. www.fws.gov/northeast/ bombayhook. Adm. fee).* This is one in a string of preserves along **Delaware Bay,** a major stopover for birds migrating along the Atlantic flyway.

After the village of Leipsic, the road continues 6 miles south through more farmland to the intersection with Del. 8. This road leads 4 miles west to **Dover,** Delaware's small but pleasant capital.

Brandywine Valley Scenic Byway

Wilmington into Pennsylvania on Delaware 52 and 100

■ 12 miles ■ 1 day to explore ■ Spring through fall. Avoid weekday rush hours in and around Wilmington.

In 1802 a French immigrant named du Pont began manufacturing gunpowder in the **Brandywine River Valley.** This byway is dominated by the houses, gardens, and museums of his legacy.

Beginning in **Wilmington** *(Convention & Visitors Bureau, 100 W. 10th St. 800-489-6664. www.visitwilmingtonde.com),* the byway's two routes head north to such showplaces as **Winterthur** *(6 miles north on Del. 52. 800-448-3883. www .winterthur.org. Closed Mon.; adm. fee),* Henry F. du Pont's 175-room mansion set on 979 acres, with naturalistically landscaped gardens.

Another du Pont built **Nemours Mansion and Gardens** *(850 Alapocas Dr. 800-651-6912. www.nemoursmansion .org).* This Louis XVI–style mansion also boasts formal gardens.

Continuing into Pennsylvania, the byway reaches the du Pont–created 1,050-acre **Longwood Gardens** *(US 1. 610-388-1000. www.long woodgardens.com. Adm. fee).*

Just 4 miles east at Chadds Ford, the du Ponts founded **Brandywine River Museum** *(US 1. 610-388-2700. www.brandy winemuseum.org. Adm. fee).* Known for its works by the Wyeth family, the museum also administers the nearby **N. C. Wyeth House and Studio** *(adm. fee).*

PENNSYLVANIA
Lancaster County Drive

Gap to Marietta on Pennsylvania 772

■ 35 miles ■ 1 hour ■ All year. Summers are crowded; all shops and facilities closed Sunday. Horse-drawn buggies have right-of-way.

This drive traverses the center of Amish life in the East and one of the nation's most productive agricultural communities. As you drive past the farm fields, small towns, and developing suburbs of southeastern Pennsylvania, you'll be sharing the road with the horse-drawn buggies of the Amish.

Begin your tour at **Gap** and head northwest on Pa. 772. In about 5 miles the road hits the center of **Intercourse**, located at the intersection of two roads. The buildings, shops, and galleries at the **People's Place** *(3513 Old Philadelphia Pike. 717-768-7171. Closed Sun.)* is a must-see. Here, the documentary "Who Are the Amish?" *(adm. fee)* explains that today's bearded, black-coated Amish men and plainly dressed Amish women are members of a Protestant sect that developed in Switzerland in the 16th century.

About 19,000 Amish now live in Lancaster County, working their family farms with draft horses instead of tractors, which gives the landscape a distinctive look. In part due to the presence of the Amish, the county now draws about five million visitors a year.

Outside Intercourse, stop at one of the many farm stands for fresh fruits, vegetables, cider, and wonderful butter and cheese. After about 12 miles, you'll come to **Lititz**. The handsome square in the middle of town is dominated by the **Moravian Church** *(717-626-8515. www.lititzmoravian .org)*, built in 1787, and by **Linden Hall**. Begun in 1746, it's the oldest girls' boarding school in the country. Across the street, the **Lititz Historical Foundation** *(717-627-4636. www.lititzhistoricalfoundation.com. Mem. Day–Oct. Mon.-Sat.; donation for museum, fee for tours)* features exhibits and old photographs of the Moravian community in this area.

The nearby **Sturgis Pretzel House** *(219 E. Main St. 717-626-4354. Tours Mon.-Sat.; fee for tours)* claims to be the oldest commercial pretzel bakery in the nation. If you have a longing for chocolate, stop at the **Candy Americana Museum and Wilbur's Chocolate Factory** *(48 N. Broad St. 717-626-3249. www.wilburbuds.com. Closed Sun.)*.

For 12 miles past Lititz, Pa. 772 dips through farm country. When it crosses Pa. 283, the scenery becomes more developed and suburban.

Pa. 772 ends in the town of **Marietta**, on the **Susquehanna River**, where the streets are lined with restored 19th-century homes.

Amish buggy and farms of Lancaster County

77

Grand Army of the Republic Highway

Clarks Summit to Towanda on US 6

- 68 miles ▪ 2 hours ▪ Spring through fall. Fine fall foliage

As US 6 crosses northern Pennsylvania, it follows the Susquehanna River past rolling hills, forested mountains, and historic small towns. One of the nation's first transcontinental highways, US 6 has linked the East and West Coasts since 1927. In 1948 Pennsylvania's portion of US 6 was dubbed the Grand Army of the Republic Highway, in honor of Union Civil War veterans.

From I-81 or I-84 near Scranton, pick up US 6/11 to **Clarks Summit.** This small town is in Pennsylvania coal country, and not long ago the reforested hills you're traveling past were barren, the streams polluted from a mining industry that dated back to the 1840s.

Near **Tunkhannock,** about 17 miles from Clarks Summit, you start seeing the **North Branch Susquehanna River.** For the rest of the drive, you have occasional grand vistas of the rock-strewn river in its narrow valley, a natural pathway cut through the mountains that has been used by American Indians, wagoners, the railroad, and now US 6.

Beyond Wyalusing, stop at the **Marie Antoinette Lookout** and gaze down on the site of the **French Azilum** (*570-265-3376. www.frenchazilum.com. Mid-May–Aug. Wed.-Sun., Sept.–mid-Oct. Fri.-Mon.; adm. fee*). In 1793 a band of aristocrats fleeing the French Revolution began building a mini-Paris out of log cabins arranged on broad avenues here. To visit the Azilum, turn left in Wysox onto Pa. 187, then follow the signs for 7 miles.

Back on US 6, the drive ends 2 miles farther on in **Towanda,** where local memorabilia are displayed at the **Bradford County Historical Society Museum** (*Pine St. 570-265-2240. www.bradfordhistory.com. May-Nov. Wed.-Sat.; adm. fee*)

Timber, Oil, and Coal Country Drive

Wellsboro to Warren on US 6

- 129 miles ▪ 5 hours ▪ Spring through fall

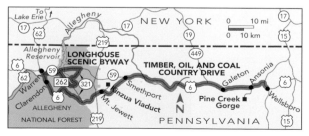

This portion of the **Grand Army of the Republic Highway** takes you through Pennsylvania Wilds, pristine hills and mountains. This is a land that gave up its wealth of coal, oil, and timber to make Pennsylvania and much of the nation into an industrial powerhouse. The drive begins in **Wellsboro.** Head 12 miles west to the town of Ansonia and turn left on Colton Road to visit **Pine Creek Gorge,** locally known as the Grand Canyon of Pennsylvania. The road leads 6 miles to **Colton Point State Park** *(570-724-3061. www.dcnr.state .pa.us),* where overlooks and walkways offer views of the 830-foot-deep gorge.

Return to US 6, which follows **Pine Creek** to the town of **Galeton,** formerly home to one of the world's largest sawmills. The **Allegheny Mountains** surrounding the town were stripped by 19th-century timbermen greedy for their hemlock and white pine. For 13 miles beyond Galeton trundle through these forests before reaching the **Pennsylvania Lumber Museum** *(814-435-2652. www.lumbermuseum .org. Closed weekends Dec.-March; adm. fee),* featuring exhibits on the life of 19th-century lumberjacks.

From here, follow the **Allegheny River** as forests give way to farmlands interspersed with towns. After 35 miles you reach Smethport; for the next 15 miles the road curves through forests along a stream loved by anglers: trout-laden **Marvin Creek.** Just before you enter Mount Jewett, a turnoff on the right leads 2.5 miles to the 301-foot-high **Kinzua Viaduct,** highest railroad viaduct in the world when built in 1882. Views from the park are still breathtaking.

Back on US 6, you enter the 513,325-acre **Allegheny National Forest** *(814-723-5150. www.fs.usda.gov/allegheny).* Between Kane and Ludlow, look for a sign for the **North Country National Scenic Trail,** a segment of the 3,200-mile trail being built between New York and North Dakota. Around **Clarendon** you'll begin to see scattered oil wells—reminders that the modern oil industry started southwest of here in Titusville.

Stay on US 6 to the drive's end in **Warren,** where well-appointed mansions built from timber, oil, and coal money line the boulevards.

Longhouse Scenic Byway

Loop around Allegheny Reservoir on Pennsylvania 59 and 321 and Forest Road 262

■ 29 miles ■ 1 hour ■ Spring to fall. See map p. 78.

Looping through the **Allegheny National Forest** *(814-723-5150),* the byway encircles the Allegheny Reservoir, offering vistas of the Allegheny Mountains.

Start the tour 3 miles southeast of Warren, where Pa. 59 branches east off US 6. Along the way here, you can view the **Kinzua Dam,** which formed the reservoir, and hike the half-mile **Little Boulder Nature Trail** that begins at the **Big Bend Access Area.**

For thousands of years, this area was inhabited by Native Americans. The large, communal longhouses of the Seneca tribe give the drive its name. Completion of the Kinzua Dam in 1965 flooded the Allegheny reservation and forced the relocation of the 482 bottom-land Seneca who lived there.

Back on Pa. 59, you cross the reservoir on **Casey Bridge** and climb a forested plateau. At its top, stop at the **Rimrock Overlook** for a spectacular view of the reservoir. Make a hard right at Pa. 321 and follow **North Fork Creek,** then **Chappel Creek** to dramatic views of **Chappel Bay.** Complete the loop by making another hard right onto FR 262. Follow its twisting course along the reservoir.

Longhouse Scenic Byway in fall

Laurel Highlands

Farmington to Normalville on Pennsylvania 381

- 17 miles • ½ hour • All year. Fine fall foliage. *See map page 83.*

Frank Lloyd Wright's Fallingwater

Tucked between ridges of the Alleghenies, this road through the picturesque Laurel Highlands is a short drive, but you could spend days exploring its attractions.

From **Farmington** follow Pa. 381 north for about 8 miles to **Ohiopyle State Park** *(724-329-8591. www.dcnr .state.pa.us)*. At the **Ohiopyle Falls** day-use area, stop for a look at these 20-foot falls tumbling down sandstone ledges. They are part of the **Youghiogheny River Gorge,** about 14 miles of which cut through the park. The "Yock" offers some of the best white-water rafting in the East. For an easy hike, sample the 4 miles of trails across the river on the **Ferncliff Peninsula,** famous for its wildflowers and other flora and for its excellent overlooks of the gorge.

Continue up Pa. 381 a couple of miles, where a left turn leads to **Falling-water** *(724-329-8501. www.fallingwater.org. Mid-March–Nov. Closed Wed., mid-Nov.–March Sat.-Sun.; adm. fee)*. Designed by Frank Lloyd Wright in 1935, this dramatic house is cantilevered over a waterfall on Bear Run. It was rated the "best all-time work of American architecture" in a poll taken of the American Institute of Architects.

Back on Pa. 381, you come almost immediately to the turnoff for **Bear Run Nature Reserve,** where there are more than 20 miles of marked trails through forests rich in rhododendron and mountain laurel.

The drive ends about 6 miles beyond in the small town of **Normalville.**

MARYLAND
Journey through Hallowed Ground

Gettysburg, Pennsylvania, to Charlottesville, Virginia, on US 15 and Virginia 20

- 175 miles • 2 days • Spring through fall

It can safely be said that few routes in the United States touch on so much history in such a short distance as does the Journey through Hallowed Ground. Taking its name from Abraham Lincoln's Gettysburg Address, this drive passes presidential homes, significant Civil War battlefields, and a host of other historic places in Pennsylvania, Maryland, and Virginia.

At **Gettysburg National Military Park** *(97 Taneytown Rd. 717-334-1124. www.nps.gov/gett),* where the bloodiest battle of the Civil War was fought in early July 1863, a wide variety of programs, living history presentations, battlefield walks, auto tours, and other offerings allow visitors to learn about the war's causes, the battle (where the Union victory ended Confederate hopes for an independent South), and the aftermath. (The new visitor center opened in 2008.)

Nearly a century after the battle at Gettysburg, World War II Gen. Dwight D. Eisenhower bought a farm adjacent to the battlefield. During his later presidency, the house and surroundings of today's **Eisenhower National Historic Site** *(1195 Baltimore Pike. 717-338-9114. www .nps.gov/eise. Adm. fee)* were a place of retreat and relaxation, where "Ike" often met with national and foreign leaders. Visitors can tour the home and see programs on Eisenhower's military and political career.

US 15 crosses the Mason-Dixon Line into Maryland and follows the **Catoctin Mountain Scenic Byway.** It skirts **Catoctin Mountain Park** *(301-663-9330. www.nps.gov/ cato),* developed in the New Deal days of the 1930s and the site of **Camp David** presidential retreat. Camp David is closed to the public, but hiking trails, trout fishing, camping, and scenic drives are available.

Among the attractions in **Frederick** *(Tourism Council of Frederick County, 151 S. East St. 301-600-2888 or 800-999-3613. www.fredericktourism.org)* is **Rose Hill Manor Park and Children's Museum** *(1611 N. Market St. 301-600-1650. www.rosehillmuseum .com. Daily April-Oct., weekends Nov. Fee for tours),* which includes a 1790s house, a farm museum, a carriage museum, and garden, with living history interpreters. Frederick attracts travelers to its 50-block **downtown historic district,** full of 18th- and 19th-century architecture, including the **Barbara Fritchie House** *(154 W. Patrick St.),* home of the Civil War Union heroine immortalized in a poem by John Greenleaf Whittier. Fritchie is buried in **Mount Olivet Cemetery** *(515 S. Market St.),* as is Francis Scott Key, who wrote America's national anthem. Contact the tourism council for a driving map of county Civil War sites, including **Monocacy National Battlefield** *(5201 Urbana Pike. 301-662-3515. www.nps.gov/mono),* preserving the site of the July 9, 1864, battle, that saved Washington, D.C., from advancing Confederates.

The route continues south to reach the Potomac River at **Point of Rocks,** named for a

81

Rocket larkspurs and Shasta daisies along the route

geologic feature visible from the river. On the north side of town, note the 1843 **St. Paul's Church** *(1914 Ballenger Creek Pike),* used by Union troops in the Civil War (and later awarded $1,000 by Congress for damages). The striking 1876 **Point of Rocks railroad station** is still in use. Here Maryland's America's Byway ends.

Travelers interested in Civil War history will want to make a northwestward side trip from the route to **Antietam National Battlefield** *(5831 Dunker Church Rd. 301-432-5124. www.nps.gov/anti. Adm. fee).* Ranger programs and tours recall "the bloodiest one-day battle in American history," when 23,000 soldiers were killed, wounded, or missing after combat on September 17, 1862.

In Virginia, just north of Leesburg, you'll reach the turn to **Ball's Bluff Battlefield Regional Park** *(703-737-7800. www.nvrpa.org/park/ball_s_bluff. Tours May-Oct. weekends),* with interpretive trails telling of a disastrous Union defeat in the early part of the Civil War. In Leesburg, visit the **General George C. Marshall House** *(217 Edwards Ferry Rd. 703-777-1880. www.georgecmarshall.org. Adm. fee),* also called "Dodona Manor," where the famous soldier and architect of the post–World War II Marshall Plan lived from 1941 to 1959. On US 15 a few miles south of town stands the majestic **Oatlands** *(703-777-3174. www.oatlands.org. April-Dec.; adm. fee),* a restored 1804 house and associated gardens that compose a national historic landmark. A side trip east on Va. 234 will take you to **Manassas National Battlefield** *(703-361-1339. www.nps.gov/mana. Adm. fee),* site of two Civil War battles. In one of them, Confederate general Thomas Jackson received the nickname "Stonewall." After the orientation film *(adm. fee)* in the **visitor center,** you can take an auto tour or walk one of several interpretive trails.

The next major stop lies on Va. 20, 4 miles south of Orange (where the 1858 **Orange County Courthouse** on Main Street is worth a drive-by look for its odd Italian Villa design). James Madison, fourth U.S. President, lived his entire life at **Montpelier** *(540-672-2728. http://montpelier.org. Adm. fee),* which today remains the heart of a 2,700-acre estate administered by the National Trust for Historic Preservation. The estate includes farmland, racecourses, a garden, archaeological sites, and more than 130 buildings, including the main house, which dates from about 1760.

Few Americans can think of **Charlottesville** *(Charlottesville/Albemarle Co. Convention & Visitors Bureau, Va. 20. 434-293-6789 or 877-386-1103. www .charlottesville.org)* without thinking of Thomas Jefferson: third President and author of the Declaration of Independence, who chose the countryside where

he played as a boy to build his dream house, **Monticello** *(2 miles southeast on Va. 53. 434-984-9800. www .monticello.org. Adm. fee for house & grounds tours).*

At the **Monticello Visitor Center** *(adm. fee)* you can see and study more than 400 Jefferson objects, artifacts discovered during archaeological excavations, and architectural models and drawings.

Catoctin furnace near Thurmont, Maryland

Historic National Road
(Maryland, Pennsylvania, and West Virginia)

Baltimore, Maryland, to Ohio state line on Maryland 144 and US 40 and 40A

- 275 miles ▪ 2 days ▪ Spring through fall

The National Road, the nation's first federally funded highway, originally linked Cumberland, Maryland, with Vandalia, Illinois. The route expanded to become a vital artery in America's westward expansion. This byway takes you from Baltimore, Maryland, to Wheeling, West Virginia.

Baltimore *(Visitor Center, 401 Light St. 877-225-8466. www.baltimore.org)* has revitalized its Inner Harbor area with sporting venues, recreational sites, museums, and the city's most popular destination, the **National Aquarium in Baltimore** *(Pier 3, 501 E. Pratt St. 410-576-3800. www.aqua.org. Adm. fee)*, home to more than 11,000 aquatic animals. Among many nearby maritime-related attractions is the 1854 **U.S.S. Constellation** *(Pier 1, 301 E. Pratt St. 410-539-1797 www.historicships.org. Adm. fee)*, the last all-sail warship built by the U.S. Navy.

Follow Lombard Street a short distance west to the **Baltimore & Ohio Railroad Museum** *(901 W. Pratt St. 410-752-2490. www.borail.org. Adm. fee)*, which ranks with the city's must-visit sites. Its 40 acres of exhibits, historic rail cars and locomotives, the roundhouse, and other features compose the most significant railroading display in the country.

Less than a mile west, take Frederick Street (Md. 144), a direct descendant of the Old National Pike, and cross the Patapsco River to **Ellicott City.** The **B&O Railroad Museum** *(2711 Maryland Ave. 410-461-1945 www.borail .org. Closed Mon.-Tues.; adm. fee)* features railroad exhibits in the oldest surviving railroad station in America.

The route briefly joins US 40 before returning to Md. 144. Soon you're driving through farmland just south of I-70, the modern-day equivalent of the National Road. Md. 144 crosses and recrosses the interstate to reach the Monocacy River, site of the locally renowned **Jug Bridge Monument,** an oddly shaped ten-ton stone jug that dates from the time of the original 1809 stone bridge just outside of **Frederick.** (For attractions in Frederick, see Journey through Hallowed Ground drive, pp. 80–82.) West of Frederick, take US 40A through Braddock Heights and Middletown, and then up South Mountain via Turner's Gap, a route blazed by British troops in 1755 and later followed by the National Pike. Just north of the highway is **Washington Monument State Park** *(301-791-4767. www.dnr.state.md.us)*, featuring the first monument dedicated to George Washington, erected by Boonsboro citizens in 1827.

Past the urban area of Hagerstown and I-81, the route follows US 40, weaving through rolling countryside. You join I-70 before exiting west onto Scenic 40. At **Hancock,** the state of Maryland is only about 1.5 miles wide, squeezed between the Potomac River and the Pennsylvania state line.

You soon reach **Cumberland,** site of the Cumberland Narrows, a path through the **Allegheny Mountains.** To visit the town's historic area, turn off US 40/I-68 and follow the tourist information signs to the **Western Maryland Station Center** *(13 Canal St.).* From this restored 1913 railroad station, you can take an excursion on Maryland's only coal-fired train, **Western Maryland Scenic Railroad** *(800-872-4650. www.wmsr.com. Call for trips; fare),* between Cumberland and Frostburg. The station also serves as a visitor center for the **Chesapeake & Ohio Canal National Historical Park** *(301-722-8226. www.nps.gov/choh),* preserving the historic 184-mile canal along the Potomac River. The **Lavale Toll Gate House,** the National Road's only remaining tollhouse in Maryland, stands on Cumberland's western edge.

Just east of Grantsville you'll pass the 1813 **Casselman River Bridge,** the longest single-arch stone bridge in the country when it was built. After Grantsville, at Keysers Ridge, US 40A merges into US 40 and you soon cross into Pennsylvania. As you enter Addison, take Main Street (the original National Road route) and you'll pass the **Petersburg Toll House,** made of hand-cut stone and one of only two original National Road tollhouses extant in Pennsylvania. Just past Farmington, **Fort Necessity National Battlefield** *(724-329-5512. www.nps.gov/fone. Adm. fee)* commemorates the 1754 battle in which 22-year-old George Washington led British troops against French forces in the French and Indian War. Don't miss the park's 1828 **Mount Washington Tavern;** among the numerous taverns on the National Road, this was one of the most elegant.

Beyond Uniontown you reach the other of the state's two remaining toll-houses, the brick 1835 **Searights Toll House.** The byway reaches the **Monongahela River** at Brownsville. About 2 miles past Centerville, you pass a true icon of the National Road: a **Madonna of the Trail Monument,** one of many from Maryland to California to honor the spirit of American pioneer women.

The National Road passes through West Virginia for only 15 miles. Where US 40, Md. 88, and I-70 meet, note the 1817 **Elm Grove stone bridge,** originally limestone but topped with concrete in 1958. Less than a mile farther along is West Virginia's own **Madonna of the Trail** statue.

In **Wheeling** *(Convention & Visitors Bureau, 1401 Main St. 800-828-3097. www.wheelingcvb .com),* the 1,010-foot **Wheeling Suspension Bridge** over the main channel of the Ohio River is among the greatest engineering feats in American history. Opened in 1849 and updated several times, it's the oldest operating suspension bridge in the world. Displays in **West Virginia Independence Hall** *(1528 Market St. 304-238-1300. www.wvculture.org/museum/wvihmod.html. Closed Sun.)* explain why this 1859 structure is called "the birthplace of West Virginia." It was here that debates led to Union sympathizers splitting their region from Confederate Virginia during the Civil War. (See western segment of Historic National Road pp. 174–177.)

Wheeling Suspension Bridge

Religious Freedom Byway

A branching route through southern Maryland that includes the Nanjemoy Loop Maryland 6, 234, and 5 and local roads

- 195 miles ■ 5 hours ■ All year

Persecuted for their religion in Anglican England, the Catholic Calvert family founded the colony of Maryland in 1634 upon the principle of religious tolerance. The towns, churches, and plantations started by the settlers who followed the Calverts are stitched together by this rural scenic byway, which begins about an hour's drive south of Washington, D.C., and follows the Potomac River toward the Chesapeake Bay.

Head south on Md. 210 from Washington to enter the byway on the **Nanjemoy Loop** at Md. 225, which edges a broad peninsula on the Potomac. Then follow Md. 224 about five miles to where it curves past the 628-acre **Smallwood State Park** *(2750 Sweden Point Rd. 301-743-7613)* and **Smallwood's Retreat**, built in 1760, the home of Revolutionary War general and Maryland governor William Smallwood.

South of the park, Md. 224 becomes a narrow country lane. At **Douglas Point**, nature trails lead to the remains of the **Chiles Homesite** *(703-339-8009)*, built in 1790 and situated on a plantation dating to 1653.

Continuing around the loop, turn down Friendship Landing Road to reach **Friendship Farm Park** *(4705 Friendship Landing Rd. www.charlescountyparks.com)* for serene views of Nanjemoy Creek. Return to Ironsides Road to visit the Episcopal **Old Durham Church** *(8685 Ironsides Rd. 301-743-7099)*, on the site of one of the original 30 churches chartered in Maryland in 1692. The redbrick building, surrounded by gravestones, dates to 1732.

Continue northeast to Port Tobacco. Stop in at the **Thomas Stone National Historic Site** *(6655 Rose Hill Rd. 301-392-1776)*, about two miles north of town, home to one of the signers of the Declaration of Independence. Then backtrack to historic **Port Tobacco** *(8730 Commerce St. 301-934-4313)*, established in 1634. During the Civil War, John Wilkes Booth and his co-conspirators

Christ Episcopal Church, Chaptico, MD

85

met here to plot against Abraham Lincoln. Costumed docents at the court-house museum give tours and discuss the town's history from 1620 on.

Detour up Valley Road to **Mount Carmel Monastery** *(5678 Mount Carmel Rd. www.carmelofporttobacco.com)*, established in 1790 as the first Carmelite monastery in the U.S. Then continue south from Port Tobacco on Chapel Point Road for four miles to **St. Ignatius Catholic Church** *(8855 Chapel Point Rd. 301-934-8245. www.chapelpoint .org)*, founded in 1641. Wander among the age-darkened gravestones of its cemetery, situated on a 120-foot bluff with magnificent views over the Potomac River. The present church was built in 1798.

Continue on Md. 234 to Chaptico and **Christ Episcopal Church** *(25390 Maddox Rd. 301-884-3451. www .christepiscopalchaptico.org)*. Built in 1736, the Georgian church has fine symmetrical arched windows and detailed cornices. Turn south down Md. 238 and follow Colton Point Road to its end near **St. Clement's Island Museum** *(38370 Point Breeze Rd. 301-769-2222. Adm. fee)*. With a view across the water to St. Clement's Island State Park, the museum's exhibits recount Maryland's founding and the region's rich oystering and crabbing history.

Return to Md. 234 and continue southeast to **Leonardtown** *(www.leonard town.somd.com)*, established in 1708, which was a hub of commerce for the area's tidewater plantations in the 18th century. Drive past the welcoming shops, cafés, and galleries in the historic downtown to **Tudor Hall** *(41680 Tudor Pl. 301-475-2467)*, where the Historical Society offers guided tours.

Eight miles southeast of Leonardtown, turn down Md. 249 and follow the byway past pebbly beaches to **Piney Point Lighthouse and Museum** *(44701 Lighthouse Rd. 301-994-1471. Adm. fee.)*. Built in 1836, the conical white lighthouse is the oldest on the Potomac. The Potomac River Maritime Exhibit displays historic Chesapeake Bay sailing craft, and signs around the six-acre beachfront park describe the living and working conditions of the lighthouse's keepers. Piney Point Road continues south across narrow cause-ways to low-lying **St. George's Island,** where elegant vacation homes and small crabbers' houses alike rise from stilts planted in the marshy ground.

> Elements of Chaptico's Christ Episcopal Church were inspired by the work of renowned English architect Sir Christopher Wren.

Thomas Stone National Historic Site, Port Tobacco, MD

Backtrack to Md. 5 and follow the byway southeast to historic **St. Mary's City** *(23115 Leonard Hall Dr. 800-762-1634. www.stmaryscity.org)*, established in 1634 as Maryland's first capital and a testing ground for the new colony's ideal of religious freedom. Researchers have painstakingly re-created many of the city's 17th-century streets, houses, and public buildings to form a remarkable living history museum. Costumed interpreters share details on life in the 1600s at such rebuilt spots as Smith's Ordinary, Cordea's Hope, and the Godiah Spray Tobacco Plantation.

The byway ends as the Potomac meets the Chesapeake at **Point Lookout State Park** *(11175 Point Lookout Rd. 301-872-5688. www.dnr.state.md.us)*, where visitors can hike, fish, and camp amid soaring pines and dazzling water views.

Baltimore's Historic Charles Street

Charles Street from Federal Hill to the Baltimore Beltway (I-695)

- 12 miles ▪ 1 hour ▪ All year

Although only 12 miles long, this byway traverses hundreds of years of history as it strikes through the heart of downtown Baltimore.

Begin in venerable **Federal Hill,** crowded with stone churches and cheery taverns. Beyond is the **Inner Harbor,** a vibrant commercial center whose attractions include the **National Aquarium** *(501 E. Pratt St. 410-576-3800. www.aqua.org. Adm. fee).*

Baltimore's elegant skyscrapers take center stage as Charles Street continues inland. Mies van der Rohe designed **One Charles Center** *(100 N. Charles St. 410-244-7200. www.onecharlescenter.com),* completed in 1962. The **Basilica of the National Shrine of the Assumption of the Blessed Virgin Mary** *(409 Cathedral St. 410-727-3565. www.baltimorebasilica.org),* built between 1806 and 1821, was the first metropolitan cathedral erected in the U.S. after the adoption of the Constitution.

Continue north past the **Walters Art Museum,** whose diverse collection includes more than 30,000 objects *(600 N. Charles St. 410-547-9000. http://thewalters.org).* **Mount Vernon Place** encloses the 178-foot **Washington Monument** *(699 N. Charles St. Adm. fee),* built in 1809 to honor George Washington. Visitors can climb the column's 228 steps for splendid city views.

On the square, the **Peabody Institute** *(1 E. Mount Vernon Pl. 410-659-8100. www.peabody.jhu.edu)* houses a renowned music conservatory and art gallery endowed in 1857 by "father of modern philanthropy" George Peabody. The **Garrett-Jacobs Mansion** *(11 W. Mount Vernon Pl. 410-539-6914. www.garrettjacobsmansion.org)* is Baltimore's grandest Gilded Age home.

Detour a few blocks west to the **Eubie Blake National Jazz Institute and Cultural Center** *(847 N. Howard St. 410-225-3130. www.eubieblake.org)* before continuing north on Charles Street to the **Station North Arts and Entertainment District** *(1800 N. Charles St. 410-962-7075. www.stationnorth .org),* a lively community of art galleries and studios. Architect Stanford White designed the 1887 **Lovely Lane United Methodist Church** *(2200 St. Paul St. 410-889-1512. http://lovelylane.net),* located just north of the district.

Charles Street becomes a tree-lined avenue toward **Johns Hopkins University.** Stop in at the **Homewood Museum** *(3400 N. Charles St. 410-516-5589. www .museums.jhu.edu)* and the **Baltimore Museum of Art** *(10 Art Museum Dr. 443-573-1700. www.artbma.org)* before the drive ends at the Baltimore Beltway.

BALTIMORE'S HISTORIC CHARLES STREET

87

Chesapeake Country

Chesapeake City to Tilghman Island on Maryland 213, 20, 445, 18, 662, 33, and US 50

▪ 100 miles ▪ 4 hours ▪ Spring and fall. Winter brings a brooding charm to Tilghman Island.

Although close to the fast-paced world of the Eastern megalopolis, this peninsular portion of Maryland still remains a place apart. Here, broad tidal rivers drain tranquil farmlands, and watermen in wooden skipjacks sail out to harvest the Chesapeake Bay's abundance.

The first half of this route, which follows the **Chesapeake Country Scenic Byway,** begins in **Chesapeake City,** a handsomely restored 19th-century town. Sitting near the western end of the Chesapeake & Delaware Canal, it's dotted with pleasant inns, cafés, and marinas.

Driving south along Md. 213, you'll pass fields green in summer with corn and soybeans, two Delmarva (Delaware, Maryland, Virginia) Peninsula staples. Within the first 15 miles, the highway crosses the **Bohemia** and **Sassafras Rivers,** the latter thought to have been explored by Capt. John Smith during his 1608 reconnoiter of Chesapeake Bay.

Continue on to **Chestertown,** on the banks of the Chester River since 1706. The **Historical Society of Kent County** *(101 Church Alley. 410-778-3499. www.kentcountyhistory .org. Wed.-Fri. all year, also Sat. May-Oct.; donation)* functions as a colonial house museum, and you can take afternoon tea at the 18th-century **White Swan Tavern B&B** *(410-778-2300. www.whiteswantavern.com)* on High Street. Or just ramble past stately Georgian and gaily painted Victorian homes.

A side trip follows Md. 20 and 445 west and south to **Eastern Neck National Wildlife Refuge** *(410-639-7056. www.fws.gov/northeast/eastern neck),* known for migrant swans, tens of thousands of geese and ducks, bald eagles, and the endangered Delmarva fox squirrel. Once set to be a massive housing development, this area was acquired as a wildlife refuge in the 1960s. A former hunting lodge is now the visitor center.

Back on Md. 213, you'll drive through **Centreville,** named county seat in 1792 because it was in the center of Queen Annes County. You can take another detour on Md. 18 to follow the officially designated Chesapeake Country Scenic Drive America's Byway toward the **Chesapeake Bay Environmental Center** *(Discovery Ln. 410-827-6694. www.bayrestoration.org),* a 500-acre preserve with trails, exhibits, and ecology-oriented programs.

Or continue south just past the Md. 213 intersection with US 50, to reach **Wye Mills** *(410-827-6909. Donation),* the last in a line of gristmills built on this site. The mill is preserved in its 19th-century state, its massive granite millstones still using water power to grind grain into flour. South of the mill on Md. 662, another landmark stood for more than 400 years: the enormous **Wye Oak,** Maryland's state symbol, was toppled by a storm in June 2002.

To continue the drive, head south on US 50 toward Easton. Nearby, at the mouth of the Wye, stands **Wye House** *(private),* once the seat of a vast

88

plantation where the great abolitionist leader Frederick Douglass spent his boyhood as a slave.

Near Easton, turn right onto Md. 322, then right again onto Md. 33 east. Eleven miles down the road is **St. Michaels**, an old harbor town graced by a tidy inn and good restaurants—both the elegant and the casual. The excellent **Chesapeake Bay Maritime Museum** *(410-745-2916. www.cbmm.org. Adm. fee)* is dedicated to the history and the workaday lore of the bay. Crossing the little bridge over **Knapps Narrows,** 13 miles beyond

Skipjack at Hooper Strait Light

St. Michaels, you leave the mainland and are on **Tilghman Island,** home for centuries to the hardy individuals who harvest the bay's bounty. Less than half a mile from the bridge, turn left on Dogwood Harbor Road to see the famed Chesapeake Bay skipjacks, wooden sailing vessels ranging from 25 to 60 feet in length. Several are usually docked here.

At the fork 2.5 miles farther on, bear right onto Black Walnut Point Road. The road ends in half a mile at the gate of **Black Walnut Point Inn** *(410-886-2452. www.blackwalnutpointinn.com),* perhaps the most secluded B&B on the Eastern Shore.

89

Harriet Tubman
Underground Railroad Byway

Cambridge, Maryland, to the Mason-Dixon Line on Maryland 16, 335, 404, 313, and 287 and local roads

- 125 miles - 3 to 4 hours - All year

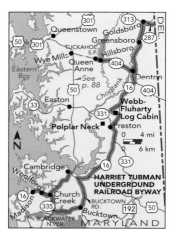

This byway leads through rolling farm fields, reed-lined marshland, and quiet country towns on Maryland's Eastern Shore as it traces major events in the life of 19th-century abolitionist Harriet Tubman. Having escaped slavery herself as a child, Tubman later guided hundreds of slaves to freedom on the Underground Railroad.

Start your drive in **Cambridge,** a regional center for the slave trade in the 18th and 19th centuries. Ships from Africa and the West Indies brought slaves to the **Long Wharf** at the end of High Street. In the nearby brick-paved historic district, slave auctions were held in front of the **Dorchester County Courthouse** *(206 High St.*

410-228-0480). In 1850, Tubman orchestrated the rescue of three relatives from the courthouse auction block.

Stop in at the **Harriet Tubman Museum and Educational Center** *(424 Race St. 410-228-0401. Closed Sun.-Mon.),* then head south on Md. 16 to **Woolford,** Tubman's likely birthplace in 1822.

Backtrack to **Church Creek** and turn south down Md. 335. The tidewater wetlands and forests of **Blackwater National Wildlife Refuge** *(2145 Key Wallace Dr. www.fws.gov/blackwater)* once offered shelter to escaping slaves. Continue east to the crossroads at **Bucktown,** where Tubman defied an overseer and refused to help subdue another slave in 1835.

Take Greenbriar Road, which turns into Bucktown Road, and turn east on Md. 16 to **Preston.** Tubman returned to the **Poplar Neck** farmstead *(privately owned)* here in the 1850s to lead her brothers and parents to freedom.

Detour down Grove Road past the circa 1852 **Webb-Fluharty Log Cabin** *(23459 Grove Rd. 410-479-0655),* the area's only remaining log home built by a pre-Emancipation free black man. Then rejoin Md. 16 north to historic Denton. Captured Underground Railroad "conductors" were jailed here at **Courthouse Square** *(Museum of Rural Life, 16 N. 2nd St. 410-479-2055).* Cross the Choptank River and head west on Md. 404 to **Adkins Arboretum** *(13070 Crouse Mill Rd. www.adkinsarboretum.org)* and **Tuckahoe State Park,** set among terrain that fleeing slaves passed through on their way north.

The byway continues north on Md. 313 to Goldsboro before turning east on Md. 287 and ending at the Mason-Dixon Line on the Delaware border.

WEST VIRGINIA
Washington Heritage Trail

Loop through West Virginia's Eastern Panhandle on US 340 and 522, West Virginia 9, 51, and other local roads

- 136 miles ▪ 1 day ▪ Spring through fall

As its name indicates, this byway encounters reminders of George Washington as it travels West Virginia's Eastern Panhandle.

Start the loop at **Harpers Ferry National Historical Park** *(304-535-2627 or 888-435-5689. www.wveasterngateway.com. Adm. fee).* Restored buildings, exhibits, and programs tell the site's story: its beginning as a ferry operated by Robert Harper in the mid-18th century, visits by Jefferson and Washington, John Brown's raid, and Civil War battles.

Stop for local information at the **Harpers Ferry Welcome Center** *(37 Washington Ct. 304-535-2627 or 866-435-5698. www.wveasterngateway.com).* The byway continues through **Shepherdstown,** charmingly nestled beside the Potomac River, the oldest incorporated town (1762) in West Virginia and home to Shepherd University. Next is **Martinsburg** *(Martinsburg-Berkeley County Convention & Visitors Bureau, 115 N. Queen St. 304-264-8801. www .travelwv.com),* founded in 1773 by Gen. Adam Stephen, George Washington's second in command during the French and Indian War. Named for a Confederate spy, the 1853 **Belle Boyd House** *(126 E. Race St. 304-267-4713. www.bchs .org. Open Thurs.-Sat. or by appointment)* is a museum and information center.

George Washington came to relax in the warm natural spring water that still flows in **Berkeley Springs** *(Travel Berkeley Springs, 127 Fairfax St. 304-258-9147 or 800-447-8797. www.berkeleysprings.com),* officially Bath—its original name. You can take the waters at **Berkeley Springs State Park** *(2 S. Washington St. 304-258-2711. www.berkeleyspringssp.com),* one of several spas in town.

On US 522 9 miles south of Berkeley Springs, **Cacapon Resort State Park**

(304-258-1022. www.cacaponresort.com) occupies 6,000 acres on the side of Cacapon Mountain where George Washington is said to have enjoyed riding. Modern visitors can ride, hike, or play golf.

The main part of the route heads back eastward through the village of Gerrardstown to **Charles Town,** laid out in 1786 by Charles Washington, a brother of George. You can visit the **Jefferson County Courthouse** *(100 E. Washington St. 304-728-3240. Closed weekends),* where abolitionist John Brown was sentenced to be hanged, or—on a lighter note—take in the **Charles Town Races & Slots** *(US 340. 800-795 7001. www.hollywood casinocharlestown.com)* for horse racing, gaming, and enjoying the fabulous buffet offered there.

Shepherdstown residence

91

Canaan Valley Byway

Blackwater Falls State Park to Virginia state line on West Virginia 32 and 55

■ 99 miles ■ 3 hours ■ Spring through fall. Fall foliage peaks in mid-October. Watch for fast-moving trucks.

This scenic byway will take you from beautiful Blackwater Falls to Seneca Rocks, through parts of both the Monongahela and the George Washington National Forests.

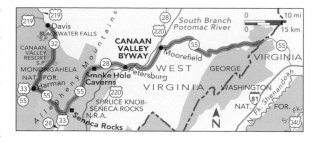

Begin at **Blackwater Falls State Park** *(304-259-5216. www .blackwaterfalls.com),* a mile off W. Va. 32 near Davis. From the parking lot, stairs and a gently sloping trail lead down to a view of the 60-foot falls plunging into an 8-mile-long gorge. Leached tannic acid from fallen hemlock and red spruce needles makes the water look black.

Follow W. Va. 32 south 10 miles from Blackwater Falls to the **Canaan Valley Resort State Park** *(304-866-4121 or 800-622-4121. canaanresort.com),* popular with hikers and skiers. The park also operates a chairlift in summer

Moonrise above Seneca Rocks

for panoramic views of the mountains and valleys of the Potomac Highlands.

Continue along this winding, wooded road to the intersection of W. Va. 32 and W. Va. 55, in the town of **Harman.** From here, head east on W. Va. 55. After 3 miles you'll begin to climb **Allegheny Mountain,** cresting it at 3,293 feet. The road curves down the far side of the mountain, and you pass through the small town of Onego (ONE-go).

White churches steeple the landscape as you follow **Seneca Creek** to the **Spruce Knob–Seneca Rocks National Recreation Area** *(304-567-2827. www.stateparks.com. Visitor center closed Dec.-April),* 3 miles beyond Onego. Seneca Rocks is a spectacular 900-foot sandstone formation created over millions of years by erosion. A trail leads to an observation deck with a view of the valley and the river; the **visitor center** has exhibits on the geology and history of the area. The **Sites Homestead** has a reconstruction of the single-room log cabin built in 1839 by Jacob Sites, one of the early settlers in the Potomac Highlands.

For the next 6 miles the road follows the **South Branch Potomac River** past fields and farms to **Champe Rocks.** Similar to Seneca Rocks, the formation was named for John Champe, who lived nearby. A sergeant in the Revolutionary War, he was sent by Gen. George Washington on an unsuccessful mission to kidnap the traitor Benedict Arnold from behind British lines.

Rocky meadows, almost alpine in appearance, open up on either side of the road, and flocks of sheep graze on distant hillsides.

Continuing beyond the town of Hopeville, you'll find **Smoke Hole Caverns** *(304-257-4442 or 800-828-8478. www.smokehole.com. Adm. fee),* a commercialized but nonetheless unique natural formation. Nearly 225 million years old, the caverns feature the world's longest ribbon stalactite, as well as an underground lake filled with golden and rainbow trout.

At **Petersburg Gap,** 1.5 miles farther on, the **North Fork South Branch Potomac River** breaks through **North Fork Mountain,** forming a cleft 800 feet deep as it does.

Continue through the city of Petersburg, and 7 miles on the other side you'll find the **West-Whitehill Winery** *(304-538-2605. April-Dec. Sat.-Sun., Jan.-March Sat.).* This region is ideal for growing wine grapes, and you can stop here for tastings and for information on the local wine industry.

About 5 miles farther on, in **Moorefield,** charming antebellum houses and public buildings line the main street of town. Beyond Moorefield, W. Va. 55 climbs into the mountains through a series of hairpin turns. You will observe some lovely mountain views along this stretch of roadway.

As you continue, the road cruises through farmland, then winds up a steep grade to a mountain crest. For its final 9 miles the byway weaves amid hardwoods of the **George Washington and Jefferson National Forest** *(540-265-5100. www.fs.usda.gov/gwj)* before ending at the Virginia border.

Staunton-Parkersburg Turnpike

Virginia state line to Parkersburg on US 250 and 33 and West Virginia 47

- 180 miles ▪ 1 day ▪ Late spring through fall

Before the Civil War, what is now West Virginia was part of Virginia. The state built a turnpike across the Allegheny Mountains to the Ohio River. Both Union and Confederate forces fought for its control. Today's Staunton-Parkersburg Turnpike national byway follows that route.

US 250 enters West Virginia in the **Monongahela National Forest** *(304-636-1800. www.fs.usda.gov/mnf).* The first byway site is the Civil War's **Camp Allegheny,** where Confederate troops spent the winter of 1861 to 1862. Trenches and stones mark former camp structures. Follow **Camp Allegheny Backway** (Cty. Rd. 3) to the valley of the Greenbrier River. In Bartow a **Forest Service office** *(304-456-3335)* can supply maps and travel advice.

Four miles west of Durbin, turn north on FR 27 to reach 140-acre **Gaudineer Scenic Area** and its virgin forest of red spruce, yellow birch, beech, red maple, and sugar maple. Next, descend to the **Tygart Valley,** where in Valley Bend and Dailey you'll note houses built for a New Deal project to aid families during the Great Depression.

In Elkins, on the grounds of **Davis and Elkins College** *(304-637-1900. www.dewv.edu),* stand two historic mansions: 1893 **Graceland,** now an inn, and 1890 **Halliehurst Hall,** now an administrative building. Both can be visited during office hours. Take US 33 west, exiting at Norton to follow Cty. Rd. 151 to Buckhannon. Continue on US 33 to **Weston** *(Lewis County Convention & Visitors Bureau, 499 US 33 E. 304-269-7328. www.stonewallcountry.com)* where **Jackson's Mill Historic Area** *(Jackson Mill Rd. 304-269-5100 or 800-287-8206. www.jacksonsmill.ext.wvu.edu)* protects the boyhood home of Confederate general Thomas J. "Stonewall" Jackson.

After the village of Pickle Street, take W. Va. 47 west through Troy and on past Racket, Burnt House, and Thursday.

The byway ends in **Parkersburg** *(Parkersburg/Wood County Convention & Visitors Bureau, 350 7th St. 304-428-1130 or 800-752-4982. www.greaterparkersburg.com).* Attractions include **Blennerhassett Museum of Regional History** *(137 Juliana St. 304-420-4800. www.blennerhassettislandstatepark.com. Adm. fee),* displaying artifacts dating back to prehistoric Native Americans.

Cass Scenic Railroad in West Virginia

93

Highland Scenic Highway

Richwood to US 219 on West Virginia 55 and 150

▪ 43 miles ▪ 2 hours ▪ Spring through fall. Fine spring wildflower bloom and fall foliage

Winding through the Monongahela National Forest, this national forest scenic byway traverses a narrow valley and passes a unique bog wilderness where cranberries grow, then climbs into the forests of the Appalachian Plateau.

Take W. Va. 55 north out of **Richwood**, the gateway to the **Monongahela National Forest** *(304-636-1800. www.fs.usda.gov/mnf)*. At the head of the Cranberry, Williams, Gauley, and Cherry Rivers, Richwood supports a thriving timber industry.

The **Gauley District Ranger Station** *(304-846-2695)* is 2 miles northeast of Richwood. From here, the road meanders through a dense forest of oak, poplar, maple, beech, hemlock, and red spruce. Be on the lookout for wildlife. While the area's black bear and wild turkey will not generally appear on the side of the road, you may well spot white-tailed deer, fox, or see a hawk soaring overhead.

About 4 miles past the ranger station, you arrive at the North Bend Picnic Area; just beyond, a 2-mile access road leads to **Summit Lake.** This man-made lake, rimmed by forests, is stocked with trout from April to early June.

One of this drive's highlights is the **Falls of Hills Creek,** about 15 miles southeast of Richwood. A steep trail leads past two of the waterfalls; the lower of these, at 65 feet, ranks as one of the highest waterfalls in West Virginia.

Back on the road 5.5 miles beyond the falls, turn left onto Public Road 102 and drive 2 miles to the **Cranberry Glades Botanical Area.** Similar to Arctic tundra, it features plants not generally found this far south. A half-mile boardwalk takes you into the bogs. For information, stop at the **Cranberry Mountain Nature Center** *(304-653-4826. April-Nov.)* at the junction of W. Va. 39 and W. Va. 150. From here, take W. Va. 150 north, skirting the edge of the **Cranberry Wilderness** and moving onto the **Appalachian Plateau** with elevations over 4,000 feet. Here, the road runs through hardwood forests, broken by open areas speckled with mountain ash. Views of the valleys are spectacular. After a few miles you'll come to the **Cranberry Glades Overlook,** where a short path leads to a view of the Cranberry Glades.

Monongahela National Forest in the Allegheny Mountains

As this hilly, curving road winds toward its end at the junction with US 219, be sure to enjoy the vistas from several scenic overlooks, including **Little Laurel,** about 17 miles from Cranberry Mountain, and **Red Lick,** 3 miles farther on.

Midland Trail

Charleston to White Sulphur Springs on US 60

- 117 miles ▪ 2 hours ▪ All year

This national scenic route follows the Kanawha River out of Charleston, then snakes along the New River Gorge before veering through rolling farmlands. Along the way, you'll find a dozen waterfalls, historic towns, and a resort hotel that has catered to Presidents.

Begin in **Charleston** either at the **Midland Trail Visitors Information Center** *(2504 Kanawha Blvd. 304-343-6001 or 800-768-8360. www.midlandtrail .com)* or at the **State Capitol** *(Kanawha Blvd. E. 304-558-4839. Tours Mon.- Sat.),* a majestic, golden-domed Greek Revival structure completed in 1932. Continue east on US 60 a mile to **Daniel Boone Park.** Frontiersman Daniel Boone lived across the Kanawha River in the late 1700s.

Four miles ahead, US 60 enters the small town of **Malden,** which developed as a center of salt production in the early 19th century. The African American educator Booker T. Washington worked at the salt licks when he was young. Today a park honors him on the site of his sister's home.

As you drive east through the **Kanawha River Valley,** you'll see barges and pleasure boats plying the river. In the town of **Belle,** you'll find **Shrewsbury House** *(304-949-3289. Spring-fall 3rd Sat., closed in winter; adm. fee).* Built about 1800, this homestead is one of the older structures to have survived the region's industrialization.

Tunneling through woods, the road passes Cedar Grove and the small redbrick **Virginia's Chapel,** built in 1853 as a graduation present for Virginia Tompkins, the daughter of a prominent pioneer citizen.

For the next 17 miles, the Midland Trail follows the **Kanawha River** through small towns, with wildflowers growing in abundance along the roadsides. At **Kanawha Falls** you can picnic or fish while enjoying the 10-foot-high falls. Two miles farther on, the **New** and **Gauley Rivers** join to form the Kanawha. Soon thereafter, take a sharp left turn into the pull-off for **Cathedral Falls;** a short but steep trail leads to the top of the falls.

From here, the drive climbs high above the New River, with overlooks of the mountains and the river. At **Hawks Nest State Park** *(304-658-5212. www.hawksnestsp.com),* walk just beyond the parking area for a particularly

New River Gorge

dramatic view of the New River and the sheer sandstone cliffs of its gorge. A half mile farther, a park tram will take you down into the gorge itself, where there is a marina with paddle-boats for rent.

After leaving the park, US 60 continues to weave through more rural countryside, past small farms, rolling green hills, and forests that flame with color in October. You may want to take a detour about 5 miles south on US 19 to the **New River Gorge National River.** The **Canyon Rim Visitor Center** *(304-574-2115. www.nps.gov/neri)* here features a local history and natural resource museum, as well as a stunning view of white water riffling through the gorge. To get a closer look, take the boardwalk and staircase that wind down into the gorge.

Back on US 60, you meander for the next 50 miles through country dotted with cattle, sheep, and horses. As you climb **Sewell Mountain,** you may pass logging trucks. The nearby town of Rainelle was once home to the world's largest hardwood mill.

Lovely old farmhouses punctuate the landscape from Sam Black Church to historic **Lewisburg,** a Southern outpost during the Civil War and the site of an 1862 engagement between Union and Confederate forces and now the county seat. Graced with many beautiful 18th- and 19th-century houses and a number of shops, the old part of town is now a national historic district. Stop at the **visitor center** *(200 W. Washington St. 304-645-1000 or 800-833-2068. www.greenbrierwv.com. Daily Mem. Day–Nov., closed Sun. rest of year)* for information on the self-guided walking tour of this charming town.

Ten miles past Lewisburg, the Midland Trail ends beyond the town of **White Sulphur Springs,** whose mineral springs have lured visitors since the 1700s. The town's luxurious **Greenbrier Resort** *(304-536-1110 or 800-624-6070. www.greenbrier.com)* has hosted Presidents and other luminaries. The Greenbrier Bunker, once a secret hideaway for government officials in case of nuclear attack during the Cold War, is now open to resort guests.

Coal Heritage Trail

Fayetteville to Bluefield on US 19, US 60, West Virginia 16, and US 52

▪ 127 miles ▪ 5 to 6 hours ▪ Spring through fall. Watch for slow-moving coal trucks.

West Virginia coal has fueled industry, heated homes, and made millionaires, as well as given impetus to the American labor union movement.

The byway begins at outdoor-sport hot spot **Fayetteville,** home to the **New River Gorge Bridge,** one of the world's longest single-span arch bridges *(304-465-0508. www.nps.gov/neri)*. From Fayetteville, US 19 heads northeast out of town.

In Hico, turn west onto US 60 for the baro-
nial **Page Vawter House** *(304-658-3335. http://page-
vawterhouse.com)* in **Ansted** and **Chimney Corner,**
the trail's only switchback, engineered for mountain rail.

Turn south at Chimney Corner onto W. Va.
16. Take 16 past Fayetteville 22 miles to Beckley,
stopping in Oak Hill en route for a photo op of the
nonoperating, 1909 **Bank of Glen Jean** *(1 Main St.).*

In Beckley, the **Beckley Exhibition Coal Mine
and Youth Museum of Southern West Virginia** *(513
Ewart Ave. 304-256-1747. www.beckley.org. April-
Nov.; adm. fee)* takes visitors 1,500 feet beneath
the surface to travel in "man cars" through former
working tunnels to get a feel for coal miners' lives.

W. Va. 16 winds through the mountains to
reach the valley of the **Guyandotte River.** Along
the way you'll see mining's damage to the environment, as well as attempts to heal the scars.

The byway joins US 52 at **Welch,** where in 1921 two murders on the
steps of the McDowell County Courthouse constituted a defining moment
in the "West Virginia mine wars" over union activities. A reconstructed
train depot is the **Southern Interpretive Center** *(304-248-8687)* of the Coal
Heritage Trail, where visitors can get information.

In **Bluefield** *(304-327-2401. www.visitwv.com),* take W. Va. 598 to **East
River Mountain Scenic Overlook** for a view of the highest elevation city
(2,655 feet) in the Mountain State.

VIRGINIA

Colonial Parkway

Jamestown to Yorktown through Colonial National Historical Park

- 23 miles - 1 hour - All year. Spring bloom and fall foliage

Crossing the Virginia Peninsula from the James to the York Rivers, this
parkway leads through pristine tidewater countryside and 175 years of
colonial history.

For a chronological orientation, begin at **Jamestown Island** *(757-856-
1200. www.nps.gov/jame. Adm. fee),*
where excavated foundations of the
17th-century settlement overlooking the **James River** are preserved.
Take the Island Loop Drive to see
the wilderness as the colonists
found it, then leave via the causeway across Sandy Bay.

On the mainland, the **Glass-
house** features craftspeople in

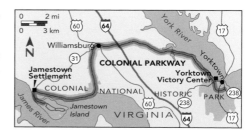

Chesapeake Bay Bridge-Tunnel

Virginia Beach to the Eastern Shore

- 17.6 miles - ¹/₂ hour - All year. Toll. Obey security restrictions.

The longest bridge-tunnel complex ever built, this stretch of US 13 links Virginia Beach and Norfolk with Virginia's Eastern Shore. Completed in 1964, the structure is a unique combination of trestles, tunnels, bridges, man-made islands, and a causeway. In 1987 the complex was officially renamed the Lucius J. Kellam, Jr. Bridge-Tunnel to honor the project's visionary chairman.

From the south, you pass through the toll plaza onto the first section of trestled roadway and are suddenly flanked by open sea: the **Atlantic Ocean** on the right and on the left the **Chesapeake Bay,** the largest estuary in the country. After 3.5 miles you come to **Sea Gull Island,** the first of four man-made islands and the only stopping point.

From the 625-foot bayside fishing pier here, you can watch ships plying busy **Hampton Roads** harbor.

Leaving the island, the road enters 5,734-foot-long **Thimble Shoal Tunnel,** one of two tunnels underlying shipping channels.

More trestled roadways lead to the 5,423-foot-long **Chesapeake Channel Tunnel,** then across **Fisherman Island** *(757-331-2760. www.fws .gov/northeast/easternshore).* This is a natural island that is preserved as a national wildlife refuge.

A bridge across the Inland Waterway brings you to the end of the Chesapeake Bay Bridge-Tunnel Drive at the southernmost tip of Virginia's pastorally peaceful **Eastern Shore.**

period costumes demonstrating 17th-century glassblowing—one of America's earliest industries. The nearby **Jamestown Settlement** *(757-253-4838. www.historyisfun.org. Adm. fee),* a gallery and living history museum, holds reproductions of a fort, a Powhatan Indian village, and the three ships that brought the colonists from England in 1607.

For the next 5 miles or so, the parkway wends along the James River, passing marshes frequented by egrets, herons, and other birds. Approaching Williamsburg, woodlands of oak, white-barked American sycamore, and poplar predominate.

Colonial Williamsburg *(757-253-2277 or 800-447-8679. www.history.org. Adm. fee)* is the country's largest living history museum, with more than 500 original and reconstructed buildings and 90 acres of gardens and greens. Costumed interpreters throughout the village re-create life here in the 18th century, when this was the capital of Virginia.

As you exit the tunnel at Colonial Williamsburg, bear right toward Yorktown. The parkway winds 5 or 6 miles through the woods until it picks up the **York River.**

Soon you'll see the **Yorktown Victory Center** *(200 Water St. 757-253-4838. www.historyisfun.org. Adm. fee)* off to the left. This museum of the American Revolution features a re-created farmstead, a Continental Army camp, and military demonstrations.

The parkway ends in the small colonial seaport of **Yorktown,** where American Revolutionaries scored their decisive victory against the British in 1781. In **Colonial National Historical Park** *(757-898-2410. www.nps.gov/colo),* exhibits at the park **visitor center** *(757-898-3400)* detail the siege, and a driving tour of the battlefield leads past redoubts to **Surrender Field.** You can also view the **Moore House,** a private home where officers drafted surrender documents under a two-hour truce.

98

George Washington Memorial Parkway

Mount Vernon to I-495

- 25 miles ▪ 1 hour ▪ All year. Rush-hour traffic can be heavy.

This sinuous roadway parkscape traces the Virginia shoreline of the Potomac River, linking historic sites and showcasing the skyline of the nation's capital.

The route begins at **Mount Vernon** *(703-780-2000. www.mountvernon.org. Adm. fee)*, the Potomac River plantation that was George Washington's home from 1754 to 1799. Now a national icon and the site of the first President's grave, Mount Vernon enshrines Washington's private life as a Virginia planter.

From here, the parkway winds past stands of maple, oak, beech, and tulip poplar. Influenced by New York's Bronx River Parkway, the first 15.5 miles of this road were completed in the 1930s and carefully landscaped to capture the look of the Virginia countryside.

About a mile past Mount Vernon, the first in a series of low-slung concrete spans arches across the roadway. Soon the woods clear and the wide **Potomac River** comes into view at **Riverside Park.**

A mile farther on, 208-acre **Fort Hunt Park** preserves the batteries that, from 1898 to 1918, guarded the river approach to the city of Washington. Across the Potomac stands the masonry ramparts of **Fort Washington** (1824), an example of a 19th-century coastal fortification.

A turnoff to the right, as the road veers briefly away from the river, leads to **River Farm** *(703-768-5700. www.ahs.org/river_farm. Mon.-Sat.; donation)*. Once part of George Washington's estate and now headquarters of the American Horticultural Society, it features gardens and the original 18th-century house.

As the parkway passes Belle Haven Park, you have a great view downriver. Bird-watchers will want to check adjacent **Dyke Marsh Wildlife Preserve** with 380 acres protected, of which 327 are marsh. These wetlands attract nearly 300 different bird species. The parkway becomes Washington Street as it enters **Old Town Alexandria.** Founded in 1749 as a colonial port, Old Town holds many historical high points. For information on the town, visit **Ramsay House**

99

George Washington's Mount Vernon

Visitor Center *(221 King St. 703-838-4200. www.visit alexandriava.com).*

Beyond Old Town, the parkway passes 106-acre **Daingerfield Island,** a great spot to stroll or bird-watch. After you curve past **Reagan National Airport,** the Washington skyline looms into view. Continue under **Memorial Bridge,** built as a symbolic link between hilltop **Arlington House** *(703-235-1530. www.nps .gov/arho),* Robert E. Lee's home as an adult, and the **Lincoln Memorial.** Beyond Roosevelt Bridge, there's a turnout for 88-acre **Theodore Roosevelt Island** *(703-289-2550. www.nps .gov/this),* a nature preserve commemorating our 26th President. Past the island, as you dip below **Key Bridge,** the spires of **Georgetown University** come into view.

George Washington Memorial Parkway

As the drive climbs above the Potomac, overlooks afford views of the increasingly wild and rocky river. The parkway ends at its junction with I-495.

Skyline Drive

Front Royal to Rockfish Gap through Shenandoah National Park

▪ 105 miles ▪ 6 to 8 hours ▪ Spectacular spring bloom and fall foliage. Fall weekends are crowded; in winter road occasionally closes due to weather. Distances designated by mileposts. Admission fee to park.

Teetering atop the narrow spine of the Blue Ridge, the Skyline Drive gazes down on the fertile Shenandoah Valley to the west and rolling foothills to the east. Inhabited by Native Americans, then mountaineers, this wild backcountry became Shenandoah National Park in the 1930s.

From Front Royal, follow US 340 south 1 mile to the entrance to **Shenandoah National Park** *(540-999-3500. www.nps.gov/shen. Adm. fee).* As the road climbs forested **Dickey Ridge,** patterned lowlands appear to the east through the hickories and oaks. Below the **Shenandoah Valley Overlook** *(mile 2.8)* stretches the fabled valley that Native Americans purportedly called "Daughter of the Stars"—Shenandoah. Through it the **Shenandoah River** wanders amid farm fields studded with barns. Bisecting the valley is the long rampart of **Massanutten Mountain.** The nearby **Dickey Ridge Visitor Center** *(mile 4.6. April–mid-Nov.)* offers park information.

Six miles beyond, the road runs into the **Blue Ridge** at **Compton Gap**, and from here follows the mountain crest. In spring the Blue Ridge is vibrant with blossoming redbud, dogwood, azalea, and mountain laurel, and in fall its forested ridges are painted in rich autumnal hues.

At **Hogback Overlook** *(mile 21)* stop to look down on the looping course of the Shenandoah River. From here, the road snakes down to **Thornton Gap**, then enters **Marys Rock Tunnel** *(mile 32.4)*. At its southern portal, the **Tunnel Parking Overlook** peers into a hollow where more than 20 families lived when the park was established.

The park's third highest peak is **Hazel Mountain**, whose 3,815-foot summit may be seen at **Hazel Mountain Overlook** *(mile 33)*. Hikes into the area called Hazel Country, along rocky streams and through forests of hemlock and mountain laurel, begin a half mile ahead. Relics of former inhabitants are visible everywhere: rock walls, split-rail fences, abandoned orchards.

Moseying south, the road winds around **The Pinnacle**, then **Stony Man Peak**. Keep a lookout for white-tailed deer, prominent throughout the park, as well as less visible denizens—skunks, barred owls, and the occasional black bear. At mile 41.7, the parkway reaches its highest point—3,680 feet at **Skyland** *(540-999-2211. www.nationalparkreservations.com/shenandoah_skyland .php. April-Nov.)*. Now a hub of park facilities, this historic mountain resort was founded in the 1890s.

At the **Old Rag View Overlook** *(mile 46.5)*, note the ancient Old Rag granite visible on this venerable mountain's upper peaks. Two fine hikes can be accessed along the next several miles. From **Upper Hawksbill Parking** *(mile 46.7)* a mile-long trail leads to the top of 4,050-foot **Hawksbill Mountain**, the park's highest peak.

Farther on, a steep trail descends less than a mile past ferns and liverworts to **Dark Hollow Falls**. Thomas Jefferson once stood below this 70-foot cascade, admiring its beauty.

Beyond, the road enters an open area called **Big Meadows** *(mile 51)*, remnant of an ancient plain that once extended over the entire region. Blueberries and strawberries grow here, and deer like to browse along the edges. At the **Byrd Visitor Center** *(540-999-3283. April-Nov.)*, a movie depicts the history of the park.

A wonderful view of the Blue Ridge's classic smoky peaks appears at **Hazeltop Ridge Overlook** *(mile 54.4)*. As you continue along the ridgetop,

101

Autumn along the Skyline Drive

watch for **Bearfence Mountain Parking** *(mile 56.4)*, where you can scramble up a short, boulder-strewn trail leading to one of the few 360-degree vistas in the park.

After that the road curves in long, lazy turns to **Swift Run Gap** *(mile 65.7)*, an important Blue Ridge crossing for decades. Beyond here, the views overlook a sea of undulating blue ridges, especially striking at the **Big Run Overlook** *(mile 81.2).*

Crescent Rock on Hawksbill Mtn., Shenandoah

After passing through the park's southern boundary, the parkway ends at **Rockfish Gap,** where a buffalo path, then a colonial road, once ran.

Blue Ridge Parkway

Rockfish Gap, Virginia, to Great Smoky Mountains National Park, North Carolina

▪ 469 miles ▪ 2 days ▪ Spring through fall. Fine fall foliage and spring bloom. Higher elevations occasionally close in winter.
Distances designated by mileposts.

Showcasing the age-old beauty of the southern Appalachians, the Blue Ridge Parkway is one of America's most popular scenic drives. Connecting Shenandoah and Great Smoky Mountains National Parks, the two-lane drive rides the crest of the Blue Ridge and other ranges, occasionally dipping into hollows or climbing above timberline to heights more than 6,000 feet.

The road begins where Skyline Drive leaves off (see above), at **Rockfish Gap** near Waynesboro. After a brief heavenward climb—perhaps the most dramatic stretch in Virginia—the road gracefully rises and falls along the narrow, forested spine of the **Blue Ridge.** The mountain drops off sharply on both sides, leaving the parkway to soar above foothills to the east and the Great Valley of Virginia, the Shenandoah, to the west.

Until the road was built in the 1930s, some mountaineers, mostly of Scotch-Irish and German descent, led hardscrabble lives in these timbered hollows. Some restored rock-and-timber farm buildings can be visited at **Humpback Rocks Pioneer Exhibit** *(mile 5.8. 540-943-4716. www.blueridge parkway.org. April–late-Oct.).*

Beyond, the forested parkway winds alongside sprightly Dancing Creek, then Otter Creek. **Otter Lake** is one of the parkway's man-made embellishments.

Midway to Roanoke, the road dips to its lowest elevation, 649 feet, at the **James River** *(mile 65).* The **James River Visitor Center** *(mile 63.6. 828-298-0398. www.nps.gov/blri. Late April–Nov. Wed.-Sun.)* tells the story of this river, its 7-mile gorge through the Blue Ridge, and the adjacent Kanawha Canal, a Civil War supply route.

Winding sharply up to the crest line again—about 3,300 feet in 13 miles—the Blue Ridge Parkway reaches **Apple Orchard Mountain,** its highest point in Virginia (3,950 feet). Whipping winter winds punish and twist the northern red oaks that predominate between here and the Arnold Valley Overlook into spindly shapes resembling apple trees.

At mile 85.6, the parkway reaches rustic **Peaks of Otter Lodge** *(540-586-1081. www.peaksofotter.com),* surrounded by Sharp Top, Flat Top, and Harkening Hill—the three Peaks of Otter. A **visitor center** *(mile 86. 540-586-4496. May-Oct.)* has information on the area.

Entering the **Roanoke River Basin,** the parkway cruises for about 30 miles in the shadow of a discontinuous series of freestanding peaks. Then, south of Roanoke, the scenery turns exceedingly pastoral as the road climbs onto the **Blue Ridge Plateau.** Distant views alternate with close-ups of small highland farms, where tobacco, hay, and vegetables grow in neat fields and Herefords graze behind split-rail fences.

At mile 176.2, **Mabry Mill** *(276-952-2947. May-Oct.)* and other exhibits portray some elements of turn-of-the 20th-century life. Local farmers relied on the ingenuity of men like Ed Mabry, who built this gristmill, along with a sawmill and a blacksmith shop.

To learn to identify the kinds of split-rail fences that divide the farmlands and edge the roadsides, stop at **Groundhog Mountain** *(mile 188.8),* where an exhibit identifies snake rail, buck rail, and post-and-rail. A fire tower here yields sweeping views of the high country.

The road continues south, with the distinct outline of **Pilot Mountain** on the eastern horizon. At mile 216.9, it crosses the state line into North Carolina and the rolling plateau begins to build into the soaring mountains and deep valleys of **Pisgah National Forest** *(828-257-4200).*

With its array of regional crafts, antiques, and homemade pastries, the **Northwest Trading Post** at mile 258.6 adds local color. Beyond, the solitary bulk of **Mount Jefferson** looms over the town of Jefferson as the road drops down into **Deep Gap.** This wild, rugged area was known only to the Cherokee and buffalo in the late 1700s when Daniel Boone, a nearby resident, forged a path through here to Kentucky. Look for **Boone's Trace** at mile 285.1.

The road continues past **Blowing Rock,** a pleasant mountain resort, and **Moses H. Cone Memorial Park** *(mile 294. 828-295-7938.*

See p. 100
See p. 95
See p. 96
See p. 120
See p. 137
See p. 113
See p. 114
See p. 138

103

View from Craggy Gardens Overlook, North Carolina

March-Nov.). Built as a mountain retreat by Cone, a textile magnate, the manor houses a visitor center and the **Parkway Craft Center.**

Just down the road hulks 5,964-foot **Grandfather Mountain** *(www.grand father.com),* the highest mountain in the Blue Ridge and one of the oldest in the world. (Geologists say its quartzite is more than a billion years old.) Head

west 1 mile on US 221, then take the 2-mile entrance road that twists up to a **visitor center** *(800-468-7325).* Here, you'll find spectacular views and a pedestrian swing bridge crossing to **Linville Peak.**

Back on the parkway, the drive now encounters the "missing link," the last 7.5-mile section of the road, completed in 1987. To preserve Grandfather Mountain's fragile environment, 153 precast segments specifically fitting the mountain's contours were used to build the S-shaped **Linn Cove Viaduct,** which snakes along its rocky slopes.

At the **Linn Cove Parking Area** *(mile 304.4.*
Spring rhododendron bloom, *828-733-1354. May-Oct.),* a trail leads to a view
Blue Ridge Parkway of the elevated roadway.

The terrain's ruggedness persists at **Linville Falls Recreation Area** *(mile 316.5. Follow spur road 1.4 miles along Linville River. 828-765-1045. May-Oct.).* Here, the river drops over rock ledges, then flows between 2,000-foot-high walls—the deepest cleft this side of the Grand Canyon. The mile-long trail to the falls passes through one of the few remaining virgin stands of eastern hemlocks.

As you continue, the parkway enters the mining district of **Spruce Pine,** where 57 different types of minerals are found, including emeralds and rubies. To learn more, stop at the **Museum of North Carolina Minerals** *(mile 331. 828-765-2761).*

Farther south, the parkway explores beautiful forests. The big bold **Black Mountains,** named for the black-green Fraser fir and red spruce that carpet their slopes, rise darkly in the distance.

Beyond **Crabtree Meadows Recreation Area** *(mile 339.5. 828-675-4236. May-Oct.),* the road begins its last climb on the Blue Ridge. Views widen of surrounding blue peaks and the vegetation changes from that of southern forests to northern spruces and firs.

After about 15 miles, the highway leaves the Blue Ridge at **Ridge Junction** and begins its traverse across a jumble of colliding ranges. It briefly skirts the southern edge of the Black Mountains, then at Balsam Gap begins a tipsy ride across the **Great Craggy Mountains.** At **Black Mountain Gap,** a 5-mile detour on N.C. 128 climbs **Mount Mitchell** *(828-675-4611. www.ncparks.gov. May-Oct.),* at 6,684 feet the highest peak in the East. A short walk leads to the summit, where a sweater is needed for the Canada-like climate (snow in July is not impossible).

Back on the parkway just past mile 361, look for views of **Glassmine Falls** tumbling down Horse Range Ridge, and of **Graybeard Mountain,** a prominent Blue Ridge peak that, if surrounded by clouds, indicates rain.

In mid-June, the slopes of **Craggy Dome** are carpeted with the red-purple blossoms of catawba rhododendron. The **Craggy Gardens Visitor Center** *(mile 364.6. May-Oct.)* has exhibits on heath gardens.

104

Leaving the Great Craggies, the road begins its gradual descent into the **French Broad River Valley** and Asheville. The **Folk Art Center** *(mile 382. 828-298-7928)* displays traditional Appalachian crafts—quilts, woven baskets, furniture—and sells them in the outlet run by the Southern Highlands Handicraft Guild. Here you can detour to the highlands city of **Asheville** and palatial **Biltmore Estate** *(3.5 miles north of parkway on US 25. 828-225-1333 or 800-411-3812. www.biltmore.com. Adm. fee),* a château built by George Vanderbilt at the turn of the 20th century.

Crossing the **French Broad River** beyond Asheville, the tree-framed road plays hide-and-seek with a series of tunnels, climbing onto the rocky, rugged back of **Pisgah Ledge.** Soon you see **Mount Pisgah** looming to the right. When Vanderbilt came to the area in 1884, he became so enraptured with Mount Pisgah that he bought it. His lands became the nucleus of Pisgah National Forest and site of the first U.S. Forestry School. The **Pisgah Inn** *(mile 408.6. 828-235-8228. www.pisgahinn.com. April-Nov.)* has a panoramic mile-high view of this rugged land.

At Tanassee Bald the parkway swings westward along the Great Balsams, sharply climbing and dropping on a winding road. Intermingled with dense forests are increasingly breathtaking panoramas of bold mountain peaks: **Cold Mountain, Looking Glass Rock,** and **Devil's Courthouse,** which the Cherokee believed to be the dancing chamber of their devil. The parkway reaches its highest point (6,047 feet) at **Richland Balsam** *(mile 431).* Below, the ranges of the southern Appalachians ripple to the horizon. For its last 10 miles, the parkway passes through these beautiful ranges, once home to the Cherokee Nation and now part of the Cherokee Indian Reservation.

105

The parkway ends in a valley on the **Oconaluftee River.** To the right, on US 441, lies **Great Smoky Mountains National Park** (see Newfound Gap Road, pp. 115–117). To the left is **Cherokee** and the **Museum of the Cherokee Indian** *(589 Tsali Blvd. 828-497-3481. www.cherokeemuseum.org. Adm. fee).*

Sunset over the Great Smokies

Kentucky Heartland
Drive
p. 124

Country Mu
Highw
p. 1

Lincoln Heritage
Scenic Highway
p. 125

Red River
Gorge Sc
Byway
p. 122

Woodlands
Trace
p. 126

Wilderness Road
Heritage Highway
p. 123

Newfound Gap Road
p. 115

Cades Cove
Loop Drive
p. 117

Great River Road
p. 118

Cherohala
Skyway
p. 118

Great River Road
p. 127

Cullasaja River Gorge
p. 114

Natchez Trace
Parkway
p. 127

Russell-Brasstown
National Scenic Byway
p. 142

Talladega
Scenic Drive
p. 133

Selma to
Montgomery
March Byway
p. 132

Lower Mississippi
Great River Road
p. 129

Hospitality
Highway
p. 131

Alabama's
Coastal
Connection
p. 134

Panhandle
Scenic Drive
p. 146

Big Bend
Scenic Byway
p. 147

Gulf of Mexico

| 0 | | 100 | | 200 miles |
| 0 | 100 | | 200 | 300 kilometers |

MARYLAND

Charleston

WEST VIRGINIA

Richmond

VIRGINIA

Roanoke

Blue Ridge Parkway
p. 102

Norfolk

Virginia Beach

The Tidewater
p. 111

Winston-Salem

Durham

Raleigh

Outer Banks Scenic Byway
p. 109

rest Heritage enic Byway 113

NORTH CAROLINA

Charlotte

Fayetteville

Cherokee Foothills Scenic Highway
p. 137

enville

Wilmington

annah River ic Byway . 141

Columbia

SOUTH CAROLINA

Augusta

Ashley River Road
p. 136

Charleston

Edisto Island National Scenic Byway
p. 139

Savannah

ATLANTIC OCEAN

Sea Islands
p. 143

Jacksonville

A1A Scenic and Historic Coastal Byway
p. 149

Ormond Scenic Loop and Trail
p. 152

Black Bear Scenic Byway
p. 151

FLORIDA

Orlando

Indian River Lagoon Scenic Highway
p. 153

Tampa

St. Petersburg

Lake Okeechobee

BAHAMAS

Tamiami Trail
p. 156

Miami

Southern Everglades
p. 155

Florida Keys
p. 157

Key West

NORTH CAROLINA
Outer Banks Scenic Byway

Kill Devil Hills to Harkers Island or Otway on US 158, North Carolina 12, the Hatteras Inlet ferry, the Ocracoke–Cedar Island ferry, and US 70

■ 138 miles ■ 5 to 6 hours ■ Spring through fall

109

North Carolina's Outer Banks—a 200-mile-long chain of low, slim barrier islands—arc out from the mainland, protecting the coast and shallow sounds from the battering Atlantic. This drive takes in the Cape Hatteras National Seashore, established in 1953.

From the mainland, US 158 crosses **Albemarle Sound** to the Outer Banks. Several miles down, the road passes through **Kill Devil Hills,** where you'll find the **Wright Brothers National Memorial** *(252-473-2111. www.nps.gov/wrbr. Adm. fee),* site of the first mechanically driven flight in 1903. A few miles beyond, the **Jockey's Ridge State Park** *(252-441-7132. www.jockeys ridgestatepark.com)* boasts the East Coast's highest dune (130 feet); prevailing winds across the dune attract hang gliders. From Jockey's Ridge, turn east on one of the numerous side roads that connect US 158 with N.C. 12, which hugs the coastline.

N.C. 12 plows south past the beach houses of Nags Head to Whalebone Junction, where an **information center** has maps and brochures on **Cape Hatteras National Seashore** *(252-473-2111. www.nps.gov/caha. Camping fee).*

After crossing the grassy marshlands of **Bodie** (pronounced BO-dy) **Island** for about 6 miles, you reach the dunes near **Coquina Beach,** and, just beyond, the 1872 **Bodie Island Lighthouse** *(252-441-5711).*

Beyond Bodie, you cross **Oregon Inlet** and have a sweeping vista of the **Atlantic Ocean** and **Pamlico Sound.** On the far side of the bridge lies the 5,834-acre **Pea Island National Wildlife Refuge.** Located on the Atlantic flyway, it attracts more than a million migratory birds in spring and fall. It's also one of the northernmost nesting grounds for threatened loggerhead sea turtles.

Here, the route is flanked by salt flats stretching into Pamlico Sound and man-made barrier dunes edging the Atlantic, stabilized by beach grasses

Bodie Island Lighthouse near Nags Head

and sea oats. Continuing south, you pass **North Pond**, site of a 5-mile interpretive trail and the **Pea Island National Wildlife Visitor Center** *(252-987-2394)*. For the next 2 miles or so, a wall of sandbags replaces seaside dunes flattened by a storm in 1991. Coastal processes—waves, winds, tides, currents, storms—are pushing the islands ever westward, constantly challenging attempts to maintain permanent structures.

On **Hatteras Island**, you'll pass historic **Chicamacomico Life Saving Station** *(252-987-1552. www.chicamacomico.net. April–late-Nov. Mon.-Fri.; adm. fee)*. Built in 1874 as a U.S. Life Saving Service Station, it's now a museum displaying maritime rescue equipment and early Coast Guard memorabilia.

For the next 20 miles the road passes through the beach communities of Rodanthe, Waves, Salvo, and Avon. Pockets of coastal forest once dotted this area, but in the 1800s the trees were felled to build clipper ships. Along this stretch are fine views of **Pamlico Sound**. Covering more than 1,800 square miles, Pamlico is the largest sound on the East Coast, and the steady winds here draw hundreds of windsurfers.

The next town, **Buxton**, features the **Cape Hatteras Light Station** and **Hatteras Island Visitor Center** *(252-995-4474. Visitor center open all year; lighthouse closed Columbus Day–Good Fri.; adm. fee to climb light)*. The 210-foot lighthouse, built in 1870, is the nation's tallest brick lighthouse. You'll also find the north end of **Buxton Woods** here, as well as a beach where you can see the tip of **Cape Hatteras** jutting into the Atlantic. The notorious **Diamond Shoals** offshore have caused hundreds of ships to run aground.

From Buxton the road burrows through the woods about 5 miles to **Frisco**, where you hit a touristy strip for the final 5 miles to the resort town of **Hatteras**. Once there, follow the sign for the **Hatteras Inlet Ferry** *(252-928-1665 or 800-368-8949. www.ncferry.org)*, a delightful 40-minute, free ferry trip across **Hatteras Inlet** to **Ocracoke Island**. Once on the island, N.C. 12 leads 14 miles to the village of Ocracoke, the island's only settlement. Along the way, you'll pass pristine seacoast and marshland, where you may spot some of the island's legendary Banker horses, popularly believed to be descended from purebred Spanish mustangs.

Hugging the tidal harbor of **Silver Lake, Ocracoke** was settled by ship pilots—and haunted by Blackbeard. The notorious pirate was captured and beheaded here in 1718. The historic town features the state's oldest operating lighthouse (1823) and a national seashore **visitor center** *(end of N.C. 12. 252-928-4531. www.ocracokeisland.com)*.

The **North Carolina State Ferry Route** *(800-293-3779. www.ncdot.gov/ferry)* and many local private ferry operators *(www.nps.gov/calo/planyourvisit/ferry .htm)* will take you from the mainland to the islands along this byway.

You can ferry from **Ocracoke Island** to the abandoned **Portsmouth Village** *(252-728-2250. www.nps.gov/calo/historyculture),* which survived the Civil War, hurricanes, and shipping competition until its last two inhabitants left in 1971. Sleep over by renting a cabin or pitching a tent—but bring your own food, drinks, bug spray, and trash bags.

Portsmouth Village sits at the northern tip of the sandy **Cape Lookout National Seashore** *(252-728-2250. www.nps.gov/calo),* where fishing and ATV excursions *(252-928-4484. www.portsmouthislandatvs.com)* are available.

Ferries also cross Pamlico Sound from Ocracoke to connect to **Cedar Island National Wildlife Refuge** *(252-225-2511. www.fws.gov/cedarisland).* Watch for alligators, pelicans, and an array of waterfowl.

Continue south on US 70, where the small shoreside towns of **Sea Level** and **Marshallberg** mark an entrance into **Cedar Island's** tourist-friendly **Crystal Coast,** full of seafood restaurants and shops.

Just past **Marshallberg,** drive the bridge over to **Harkers Island** for fresh clam chowder and a seafaring exhibit at the **Core Sound Waterfowl Museum and Heritage Center** *(252-728-1500. http://coresound.com. Donation).* Carved seabirds are available for purchase from **Core Sound Decoy Guild** *(252-838-8818. www.decoyguild.com).*

Another ferry ride away, the **Cape Lookout Lighthouse** *(252-728-2250. www.carolinalights.com. Adm. fee)* stands 163 feet tall. This lighthouse flashes four times per minute, day and night. While there, don't miss the wild horses at **Shackleford Banks** *(www.shacklefordhorses.org),* and bring supplies for shelling, fishing, birding, and camping.

111

The Tidewater

Portsmouth, Virginia, to New Bern, North Carolina, on US 17

■ 173 miles ■ 4 hours ■ Fall through spring

Part of the old Ocean Highway linking New York and Florida, this section of US 17 meanders through the lush lowlands and historic tidewater towns of Virginia and North Carolina.

From **Portsmouth,** head south past several miles of strip centers and suburbs. In the adjacent city of **Chesapeake,** signs lead to **Deep Creek Lock,** one of the two remaining locks of the **Dismal Swamp Canal.** Cross the bridge over the canal—now part of the **Atlantic Intracoastal Waterway** that runs between Boston and Key West—and turn right onto an open stretch of road.

Once in the countryside, the drive begins running parallel to the 200-year-old canal, which links Virginia's Chesapeake Bay and North Carolina's Albemarle Sound. Built by slaves, it ranks as the country's oldest continually operating artificial waterway and is now used by recreational boaters. Off to the right sprawls the dense

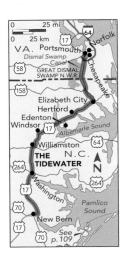

vegetation of the 111,000-acre **Great Dismal Swamp National Wildlife Refuge** *(757-986-3705. www.fws.gov/northeast/greatdismalswamp)*, a fine example of freshwater swampland. Forested mostly by red maple and juniper, the refuge centers around 3,100-acre **Lake Drummond.**

After about 4 miles the road enters a wooded stretch, then emerges into fields cultivated in corn, wheat, and potatoes. Continue across the North Carolina border, and in about 3 miles you'll see the **Dismal Swamp Canal Welcome Center** *(252-771-8333. www.dismalswamp.com. Closed Sun.-Mon. Nov.–Mem. Day).* Here, you can get a close-up look at the canal's black waters, the result of juniper and cypress tannins.

The roadside becomes cluttered for several miles as you approach **Elizabeth City.** A commercial center at the narrows of the **Pasquotank River,** it was incorporated in 1793. Stop at the **Museum of the Albemarle** *(501 S. Water St. 252-335-1453. www.museumofthealbemarle.com. Closed Mon.)* for regional history and culture, then take a turn through the historic district and waterfront.

Great Dismal Swamp

Leaving town, you have to bear with several more miles of strip centers before crossing the wide and lovely **Perquimans River,** where knobby cypress knees poke from the water. Continue through the town of **Hertford,** and 3 miles south of it, you'll see signs for the 1730 **Newbold-White House** *(151 Newbold-White Rd. 252-426-7567. www.perquimansrestoration.org. April-Oct. Tues.-Sun.; adm. fee),* the state's oldest house.

The landscape now becomes rural again, edged by fields of corn, soybeans, peanuts, and cotton. The elegant colonial town of **Edenton** *(Historic Edenton Visitor Center, 108 N. Broad St. 252-482-2637. www.visitedenton.com),* beautifully set at the junction of the **Chowan River** and **Albemarle Sound,** is worth a short detour on N.C. 32. Leaving Edenton, you soon rejoin US 17 south, which crosses over the Chowan River. For the next 30 miles the landscape is coastal plain, consisting of sandy soil. Coming into **Windsor,** you'll see signs for historic **Hope Plantation** *(132 Hope House Rd. 252-794-3140. www.hope plantation.org. Adm. fee).* This 19th-century federal-style home of Governor David Stone is furnished with 18th- and 19th-century Carolina antiques.

NORTH CAROLINA

At Windsor, US 17 takes a turn south and for the next 6 miles passes more farmland before the landscape turns lush and dense as you drive through the 21,000-acre **Roanoke River National Wildlife Refuge** *(252-794-3808. www.fws .gov/roanokeriver)*—a wetlands preserve on the river's floodplain.

After crossing the Roanoke River, the road enters Williamston before returning to farmland, some 10 miles south in Beaufort County. These once boggy lands now support fields of soybean, tobacco, and corn cultivated by families whose ancestors have farmed here for generations.

George Washington, the great canal developer, had an early hand in planning the Dismal Swamp Canal.

The town of **Washington** *(Chamber of Commerce, 102 Stewart Pkwy. 252-946-9168. www.wbcchamber .com),* the "original Washington," was incorporated in 1782 and is the country's first community named for George Washington. Where the **Tar** and the **Pamlico Rivers** come together, the town was destroyed by fire during the Civil War and rebuilt. Then in 1900 its downtown burned once again. A walking tour here takes you along the riverfront and through the town's historic district.

From Washington, the road weaves through suburbs for 7 miles and then reenters endless fields. If you're here during harvesttime, you may share the road with carts packed with big-leaf tobacco.

Dense brush and forest flank the roadside as you near the bridge over the **Neuse River** to the drive's terminus in **New Bern** *(Convention & Visitors Bureau, 203 S. Front St. 252-637-9400. www.visitnewbern.com).*

Set at the confluence of the Neuse and the **Trent River,** the former colonial and state capital—and the state's second oldest town—was founded in 1710 by German and Swiss settlers, who named it after Bern, Switzerland. Along with its federal-style buildings, New Bern's main attraction is **Tryon Palace Historic Sites and Gardens** *(610 Pollock St. 252-639-3500. www.tryonpalace .org. Adm. fee),* the restored estate of colonial governor William Tryon.

Forest Heritage Scenic Byway

Loop from Brevard on US 64 and 276 and North Carolina 215

■ 80 miles ■ 2 hours ■ All year. Blue Ridge Parkway occasionally is closed due to weather. Fine fall color.

Passing the waterfalls, streams, and pastures that sprinkle the forested foothills and upper slopes of North Carolina's Blue Ridge Mountains, the byway loops through the sylvan lands that gave birth to America's forestry program.

Charming **Brevard,** dating from the 1860s, is known for the summer concert season at its **Music Center** *(349 Andante La. 828-862-2100. www .brevardmusic.org).* From Brevard, the drive heads northeast on US 64, then northwest on US 276, soon passing through the stone entrance gate of **Pisgah**

Forest Heritage Scenic Byway in autumn

National Forest. The road twists beneath oaks, poplars, balsam firs, and birches along the **Davidson River.** Stock up on information at the **Pisgah Visitor Center** *(828-877-3265. Closed weekends in winter),* 1.5 miles inside the entrance.

Nearby **Looking Glass Falls** thunders 60 feet into a dark pool by the roadside, and 2 miles farther on, **Sliding Rock** creates a natural, 60-foot water slide. After this, the road begins its heavenward ascent up **Pisgah Ledge,** a long, wooded ridge topped by Mount Pisgah. In the woodlands ahead is the **Cradle of Forestry in America** *(828-877-3130. www.cradleofforestry.com. Mid-April–early Nov.; adm. fee),* where a modern visitor center and restored dwellings celebrate the birthplace of American forestry in 1889. The idea is attributed to wealthy conservationist George Vanderbilt, who once owned the lands now composing the nucleus of Pisgah National Forest.

Past **Pink Beds,** where massive beds of rhododendron, azalea, and mountain laurel bloom in early summer, US 276 curves up the mountainside toward **Wagon Road Gap** (elevation 4,533 feet). Here, you'll find a junction with the **Blue Ridge Parkway** (see pp. 102-105). For soaring views, head to **Mount Pisgah,** about 3 miles north on the parkway.

Back on US 276, you drop precipitously off the northern side of Pisgah Ledge and twist between the steep slopes of **Mount Pisgah** and **Cold Mountain.** At the parking lot by the **East Fork Pigeon River,** trails lead into 18,500-acre **Shining Rock Wilderness.**

The road continues through mountain-ringed **Cruso Valley,** dotted with grazing cows, green pastures, and leaning barns. Development marks the approach to Cruso, but when you reach N.C. 215 and turn south, you're back in more pastoral countryside.

About 8 miles farther on, the byway climbs back up Pisgah Ledge again, with long views of roadside waterfalls and the glorious backcountry of Shining Rock and **Middle Prong Wildernesses.** Cresting at **Beech Gap,** the drive passes back under the Blue Ridge Parkway and plummets off Pisgah Ledge's southern slope, offering views of tree-carpeted foothills.

Continuing to descend, you thread through mountain pastures and pass under the open jaws of **Alligator Rock.** N.C. 215 ends at its junction with busy US 64, which leads 6 miles back to Brevard.

Cullasaja River Gorge

Franklin to Highlands on US 64

- 18 miles ▪ ½ hour ▪ Spring through fall. *See map p. 113.*

Clinging to a mountainside high above the Cullasaja River, this steep mountain road showcases a number of breathtaking waterfalls.

Start in the town of **Franklin,** which calls itself the "gem capital of the world," due to a score of nearby ruby, garnet, and sapphire mines. Head south on US 64 through genteel countryside that gives no sense of the road ahead.

After 7 miles the pastures disappear, and the road swings onto **Higdon Mountain,** a towering hulk of granite gneiss flanked by **Cullasaja Gorge.** The narrow, curving ribbon of pavement passes **Lower Cullasaja Falls,** an unmarked but obvious cascade plummeting 150 feet beside the road. Winding between towering cliffs, the road follows the **Cullasaja River** through forests of pine, hemlock, and maple.

Dry Falls, about 6 miles ahead, is found at the end of a short trail; a path tunnels under the 75-foot falls.

A mile farther on, the drive reaches **Bridal Veil Falls.** While the current road skirts around the falls, a portion of the old road passes under it, and you can still drive on it, conditions permitting.

Dry Falls, Cullasaja Gorge

The route ends in a town appropriately named **Highlands.** Sitting at an altitude of 4,118 feet, it is the highest and wettest town in North Carolina. Some 80 inches of precipitation a year explains the lushness of the flora in this resort, popular in both summer and fall.

115

TENNESSEE
Newfound Gap Road

Sugarlands Visitor Center, Tennessee, to Oconaluftee Visitor Center, North Carolina, through Great Smoky Mountains National Park

- 40 miles ▪ 2 hours ▪ Spring through fall. Bloom for dogwood and wildflowers best mid-March into July. Fall foliage peaks mid-October. Traffic is heaviest in summer and fall.

Traversing the East's most massive mountain uplift, Newfound Gap Road in **Great Smoky Mountains National Park** *(865-436-1200. www.nps.gov/grsm)* climbs through a botanical paradise, where vegetation ranges from southern hardwood forests to alpine spruce and fir forests. Constructed in the 1930s, the road through this gap in the Appalachian Mountains features such artful touches as stone bridges, sweeping curves, and stone guardrails.

Begin at the park's **Sugarlands Visitor Center,** located in a valley rich in sugar maples and pioneer history. As you head east, the road wanders through a gorge carved by the **West Prong Little Pigeon River,** through a cove hardwood forest of red maples, white oaks, tulip trees, basswoods, and magnolias. Several trails, designated **Quiet Walkways,** amble through the woodlands, offering a chance to escape the often crowded road in this, the nation's most visited national park.

About 2 miles from the visitor center, the first sweeping views appear, showcasing **Mount LeConte**—at 6,593 feet the highest peak, from base to summit, east of the Mississippi. For a closer look, stop at **Campbell Overlook.** From here, the road begins its ascent, gentle at first, winding along the West Prong. After about 2 miles, the jagged **Chimney Tops** appear. Three pullouts give slightly different perspectives of these 4,700-foot twin peaks of quartzite and slate.

Snow in Great Smoky Mountains NP

Just beyond, the road curves more dramatically and soon enters the forest transition zone, where northern hardwood forests begin to dominate the slopes. Lush rainfall (averaging more than 85 inches annually) and mild temperatures contribute to the park's diverse flora, which includes more than 1,500 species of flowering plants. You get an idea of the terrain's increasing complexity less than a mile ahead. To negotiate the steep, crowding mountains, the road passes through a tunnel, then loops up, around, and over itself.

Beyond this, several pullouts along the river allow contemplation of the Smokies' lifeblood. The 900 billion gallons of water pulsing through the park each year nourish abundant plant life and feed rivers that eventually drain into the Gulf of Mexico.

Farther on, the road passes the parking area for the 2.5-mile-long **Alum Bluffs Trail** to the summit of Mount LeConte. Still climbing, you pass **Anakeesta** (Cherokee for "place of balsam") **Ridge,** covered with spruce and fir, then sidle alongside its base. You are now in a harsh vegetation zone, characterized by steep slopes and rocky outcrops and dominated by Fraser fir and red spruce.

> The Cherokee gave the Smokies their name, calling them Shaconage, "the place of blue smoke."

At sky-high **Morton Overlook** you can look down on the **Sugarlands Valley** or up to the notch in State Line Range, where **Newfound Gap** joins Tennessee to North Carolina.

The views are even better just around the corner at the **Newfound Gap Overlook** (elevation 5,048 feet), the road's highest point. From here, you can peer into Tennessee or into North Carolina's **Oconaluftee Valley.**

It's downhill from here, unless you opt to visit 6,643-foot **Clingmans Dome,** the park's highest

Cades Cove

116

peak. A 7-mile spur road *(closed in winter)* climbs along the ridge of the dome. From the parking area at road's end, a steep but short half-mile hike leads to a lookout tower with 360-degree panoramas of the hazy, undulating peaks and rounded summits that are this park's signature. Whether mist veils the mountains or clear skies illuminate the endless ridges, the view is beautiful.

Back on Newfound Gap Road, the drive soon passes **Ocolonee Valley Overlook,** perched atop the long ridge of **Thomas Divide.** A Tennessee mountainman who made one of the first trips on the road reacted this way to the view: "If the world's as big back that aways as it is out yonder, then she's a whopper."

As the road switchbacks down the divide, the views of the Smoky Mountains backcountry are breathtaking. At **Webb Overlook,** you can gaze up at Clingmans Dome. Beyond here, you enter a deciduous forest. Soon, the road picks up the **Oconaluftee River** and follows its curves and bends to **Mingus Mill** *(www.nps.gov/grsm. March-Nov. weather permitting).* Built in 1886, it is now one of two working mills in the national park.

At the end of the road the **Oconaluftee Visitor Center** features a mountain farmstead of historic log buildings transplanted here to demonstrate pioneer life.

Cades Cove Loop Drive

Loop road off Laurel Creek Road in Great Smoky Mountains National Park

■ 11 miles ■ 1 hour one way. Spring through fall. Allow ample time to reach loop road. Speed limit is 20 mph. See map p. 115.

Hidden from the world by big, rumpled mountains, Cades Cove retains the pastoral beauty of the early 19th century, when settlers first cleared the land. At its peak in the 1850s, the picturesque valley was the remote home of 680 mountaineers. Today, a loop road through the cove passes the restored remains of their farms and villages.

From the **Sugarlands Visitor Center** *(865-436-1200)* in Great Smoky Mountains National Park, follow Little River and Laurel Creek Roads 25 miles to the Cades Cove Loop.

The drive leads through a nostalgic landscape, where weathered fence posts, bounding deer, majestic oak trees, and bales of hay recall a different era.

Along the way, you can visit 18 marked sites. Although various in kind, they all evoke a time in the history of the United States when folks could live neighborly, yet fiercely independent, lives, close to the natural world that sustained and nourished—even as it challenged—them.

The sites include the **John Oliver Place,** a small cabin with split-wood shingles and hand-hewn logs; the plain white-frame **Primitive Baptist Church,** organized in 1827; the **Elijah Oliver Place,** a rustic farmstead with a smokehouse, springhouse, and corn crib; and the **John Cable Mill,** where corn was ground into meal.

Midway is the **Cades Cove Visitor Center,** with exhibits illustrating turn-of-the-20th-century rural life.

117

Cherohala Skyway

Tellico Plains, Tennessee, to Robbinsville, North Carolina, on County Road 165 and North Carolina 143

■ 43 miles ■ 2 to 3 hours ■ Spring through fall

Crossing the Tennessee–North Carolina border and the crest of the Great Smoky Mountains, this byway climbs to a mile above sea level as it winds through forests of hardwoods and evergreens. The only services are Forest Service campgrounds.

In Tellico Plains, stop at the **Cherohala Skyway Visitor Center** *(225 Cherohala Skyway. 423-258-8010. www.cherohala.org. Daily)* for information. You'll be passing through **Cherokee National Forest** *(423-476-9000. www.fs.usda.gov/cherokee),* which offers several recreational sites.

At the start you'll be following the **Tellico River** through mixed forest. In 5 miles, take a 6-mile side trip on FR 210 to see 80-foot **Bald River Falls.** This section of the Tellico is popular with white-water enthusiasts.

On Cty. Rd. 165 the vistas get better every mile. Thirteen miles from Tellico Plains is the turn to the national forest's **Indian Boundary Campground,** on a small lake. Not far beyond that, you enter North Carolina, where the highway name changes to N.C. 143 and you're in **Nantahala National Forest** *(828-524-6441. www.fs.usda.gov/nfsnc).* The road continues to rise, with panoramas of the **Great Smokies** from scenic overlooks along the way. The high point is the picnic spot at 5,390-foot **Santeetlah Overlook.**

The most famous spot along the skyway is **Joyce Kilmer Memorial Forest,** reached by turning north of the main road on N.C. 134 and driving 2 miles. This magnificent woodland honors the poet who wrote the well-known line "I think that I shall never see a poem lovely as a tree."

Great River Road (Tennessee)

Phillippy to Memphis, Tennessee, on Tennessee 78, 181, 88, and 388 and local roads

■ 185 miles ■ 1 to 2 days ■ All year

From old riverport cotton hubs to the "home of the blues" and beyond, Tennessee's section of the Great River Road Scenic Byway travels through a region that has contributed more than its fair share to the national sense of identity. The route itself is a bit fractured, though, with several spurs and significant gaps. Before setting out, check out the detailed turn-by-turn directions on *http://byways.org.*

Begin on Tenn. 78 at the Kentucky border, which also marks the continuation of the Kentucky leg of the Great River Road (see p. 127).

After passing through **Phillippy** on your way to **Tiptonville,** you'll find the 15,000-acre lake formed by the New Madrid earthquakes in 1811-12 at **Reelfoot Lake State Park** *(731-253-9652. www.tn.gov/ environment/parks/ReelfootLake).* Today the lakeshores are known for varied botanical species, especially soaring stands of old-growth cypress and other tree species where bald and golden eagles nest. "Eagle tours" take place daily from early January through the end of February, as do other tours that help visitors appreciate the spectacular numbers of waterfowl; advance reservations are required.

Consider a visit to the park's **R. C. Donaldson Memorial Museum** to see exhibits on the natural and human history of the area and to take a stroll on the shoreline boardwalk through a handsome cypress grove.

You might want to detour to **Fishgap Hill Overlook,** where on a clear day the view can take in three states (Missouri, Kentucky, and Tennessee).

From Tiptonville, there's a nine-mile gap in the byway. Continue south on Tenn. 78; the official route picks up again just south of **Ridgely.** As you drive south on Tenn. 181 toward **Hales Point,** you'll come upon **Heloise Landing,** a historic Mississippi riverport.

Continue winding south about 15 miles through **Hales Point** and **Halls** to the **Arp Overlook,** more than 200 feet above the river, for views of the 25,000-acre **Chickasaw National Wildlife Refuge** *(731-635-7621. www .fws.gov/chickasaw).*

Next, press on to **Henning** and *Roots* author Alex Haley's boyhood home, now the **Alex Haley Museum and Interpretive Center** *(200 S. Church St. 731-738-2240. www.alexhaleymuseum.com. Closed Mon.; adm. fee).* Then follow the spur to nearby **Fort Pillow State Historic Park** *(3122 Park Rd. 731-738-5581. www.tn.gov/environment/ parks/FortPillow),* site of a massacre of Union troops during an 1864 Civil War battle.

Return to the byway and head south. When you reach **Covington,** you can detour 15 miles west on Tenn. 59 to the tiny riverside farming community of **Randolph.** Located on what's known as the second Chickasaw Bluff, this formerly bustling port once shipped more cotton than Memphis did and was also the site of Fort Wright, one of the Confederacy's main training camps.

The *Island Queen* paddleboat on the Mississippi River in Memphis

Backtrack to Covington and take US 51 south. After another gap in the byway, the route begins again just north of **Memphis** *(888-633-9099. www.memphistravel.com).* In the city, attractions include the nightclubs of **Beale Street** *(901-526-0115. www .bealestreet.com),* known as the "home of the blues," and the meandering scale model of the Mississippi at the **Mud Island Park and Museum** *(125 N. Front St. 901-576-7241. www.mudisland.com. April-Oct. Closed Mon.; adm. fee).*

Not to be missed, the **National Civil Rights Museum** *(450 Mulberry St. 901-521-9699. www.civilrightsmuseum.org. Closed Tues.; adm. fee)* features exhibits detailing the long history of the movement and preserves the site of the **Lorraine Motel**, one of the few hotels where African Americans could find lodging in the segregated South as late as the 1960s. Martin Luther King, Jr., while in Memphis to support striking sanitation workers, was fatally shot there in April 1968.

East Tennessee Crossing

Cumberland Gap to Del Rio, Tennessee, on US 25 and US 25E

▪ 83 miles ▪ 1 day ▪ April to October

Originally a game trail through the Cumberland Gap, the East Tennessee Crossing was traveled by Cherokee warriors centuries before the United States was even an idea. In 1775, frontiersman Daniel Boone led a work party that turned this Appalachian footpath into what came to be called the Wilderness Road. More than 300,000 pioneers traveled the improved route on their way to settle the trans-Appalachian frontier.

Begin your East Tennessee Crossing explorations near the Kentucky border by following US 25E to **Cumberland Gap National Historical Park** *(606-248-2817. www.nps.gov/cuga)*. Stop by the visitor center to learn more about the significant role the area played in American history, then drive up to the 2,440-foot Pinnacle Overlook for expansive views that encompass three states.

Back in the car, detour 12 miles via US 58 east to **Wilderness Road State Park** *(8051 Wilderness Rd. 276-445-3065. www.dcr.virginia.gov)*, where you can poke around a faithful reproduction of Martin's Station, a fort and trading post that Boone himself likely frequented. The visitor center here also shows an award-winning docudrama, *Spirit of a Nation*, and rents bikes you can use to pedal eight miles of the original route.

If that exercise has left you feeling a bit parched, head south on US 25E and turn right onto Bullen Valley Road, where you'll find the **Clinch Mountain Winery** *(1335 Bullen Valley Rd. 865-767-3600. www.clinchmountain winery.com)*. Inside the rustic wooden tasting room, you can sample some of the winery's 20 different varietals and blends, including the signature Hound Dog Red, and take home a variety of locally produced foodstuffs.

Once you find your way back to US 25E, continue south a couple of miles to enjoy sweeping views from **Clinch Mountain Overlook.** Next up is **Bean Station** *(www.beanstationtn.com)*, which traces its history all the way back to 1776, when the area was still part of North Carolina. Then it's on to **Morristown,** the byway's largest town and home to a number of interesting diversions, including the **Crockett Tavern Museum** *(2002 Morningside Dr. 423-587-9900. www.discoveret.org/crockett. Closed Sun.-Mon; adm. fee),* the boyhood home of Davy Crockett.

Continue on through rolling hills and farm fields on your way to the town of **Newport,** located on the banks of the Pigeon River. Before you continue on to the end of this scenic byway at the North Carolina border, Newport may tempt you to take away a reminder of its moonshine-making past by picking up a jar of modern—and entirely legal—white lightning from any of the local "likker" stores.

Kentucky

Country Music Highway

Southshore to Whitesburg on US 23 and 119

■ 144 miles ■ 2 days ■ Spring through fall. Music venues are more active during summer months.

Paralleling the eastern border of Kentucky, this Appalachian route takes its theme from the many stars of country music who hail from the region. Loretta Lynn, Dwight Yoakum, Wynonna and Naomi Judd, Billy Ray Cyrus, Tom T. Hall, Ricky Skaggs, and Patty Loveless are the most prominent of the performers born in the seven counties crossed by this drive.

The route begins at Southshore and continues along the **Ohio River** to **Ashland** *(Convention & Visitors Bureau, 1509 Winchester Ave. 606-329-1007 or 800-377-6249. www.visitashlandky.com),* where music fans will enjoy the **Paramount Arts Center** *(1300 Winchester Ave. 606-324-3175. www .paramountartscenter.com),* a 1931 art deco movie theater now offering concerts of a range of talent.

Just before passing a major oil refinery at I-64, US 23 leaves the Ohio River to follow the **Big Sandy River,** here forming the state line with West Virginia. Beyond Louisa, the drive winds through Appalachian foothills. Where Ky. 80 leaves the Country Music Highway to the southeast, it's only about a half-hour side trip to **Breaks Interstate Park** *(276-865-4413. www.breakspark.com. Adm. fee),* centered on a sandstone gorge often called the "Grand Canyon of the South" for the 5-mile-long, 0.25-mile-deep chasm cut by the **Russell Fork.**

Back on US 23, the route continues past Jenkins, then follows US 119 to Whitesburg, home of the arts and education center called **Appalshop** *(91 Madison St. 606-633-0108. www.appalshop.org).* The center produces films, music, theater, radio programs, books, and other media with the goal of documenting and enriching life in Appalachia.

Red River Gorge Scenic Byway

Stanton to Zachariah on Kentucky 15, 77, 715, and 11

▪ 46 miles ▪ 3 hours ▪ Spring through fall

Forested hills and sandstone bluffs surround travelers as they follow this winding route through the Appalachian Mountains southeast of Lexington. More than 160 natural rock arches are found in the area, as well as waterfalls and the deep gorge through which the Red River flows.

Most of the drive lies within **Daniel Boone National Forest** *(859-745-3100. www.fs.usda.gov/dbnf)*, which administers picnic areas, campgrounds, trails, and other recreation sites. The ranger office in **Stanton** *(705 W. College Ave. 606-663-2852)* can provide information as you begin the drive.

Ky. 15 meanders eastward past farmland to Ky. 77, which heads north into the forest, passing through 900-foot-long **Nada Tunnel,** completed in 1911 using steam drills, hand tools, and dynamite. Originally a rail tunnel, it's now open to one-way auto traffic.

After crossing the Red River on the Iron Bridge on Ky. 77, turn east on Ky. 715 to reach the **Red River Gorge Geological Area,** centered on the **Red River,** a national wild and scenic river popular with canoeing enthusiasts. Spectacular sandstone cliffs in the region challenge rock climbers. Learn about the area's history and current recreational opportunities at the Forest Service's **Gladie Cultural-Environmental Learning Center** *(Ky. 715. 606-663-8100. www.fs.usda.gov/dbnf. Mon.-Fri March-Nov., daily Nov.-March).* Nearby **Gladie Cabin** is a reconstructed log structure illustrating life in the late 1800s.

When Ky. 715 turns south and crosses the Red River, watch for the turn to the **Sky Bridge Picnic Area,** where a loop trail passes under one of the largest rock arches in the area, offering excellent views of the gorge and the **Clifty Wilderness Area** to the east. A short distance south, a walk at **Angel Windows** provides close looks at several smaller arches.

Creation Falls, Daniel Boone NF

At Pine Ridge, the byway follows Ky. 15 back to the west. Along the way, Tunnel Ridge Road leads north to other trails, including the one at **Grays Arch Picnic Area.** At Slade, turn south on Ky. 11 to reach **Natural Bridge State Resort Park** *(606-663-2214 or 800-325-1710. www.parks .ky.gov/parks/resortparks/natural-bridge),* named for a 65-foot-high sandstone arch. Ten trails let hikers explore the park and adjacent nature preserve. The privately operated **Sky Lift** *(606-663-2922. April-Oct; fare),* something like a chair lift at a ski area, lets visitors bypass most of the climb to see the natural bridge, although some up-and-down walking is still required for the best views of the massive formation.

Wilderness Road Heritage Highway

Middlesboro to Berea on US 25E, Kentucky 229, and US 25

■ 94 miles ■ 3 hours ■ Spring through fall

Meandering through Kentucky's Cumberland Plateau, the Wilderness Road Heritage Highway leads today's traveler into the Appalachians and the mountain people's heritage.

The route begins near Middlesboro at **Cumberland Gap National Historical Park** *(606-248-2817. www.nps.gov/cuga)* on the Kentucky-Virginia border. Used by Native Americans for centuries for travel and trade, the gap is associated with Daniel Boone, who was hired in 1775 to blaze a trail for westward-moving pioneers.

Visitors today can drive Skyland Road to 2,440-foot **Pinnacle Overlook** for a panorama of hills in Kentucky, Virginia, and Tennessee.

US 25E winds north beside Rocky Face Mountain to **Pine Mountain State Resort Park** *(606-337-3066 or 800-325-1712. www.parks.ky.gov)*, which has 14 miles of hiking trails, a highly regarded golf course, a lodge and cabins, and an 868-acre nature preserve. After meeting the Cumberland River near Pineville, follow the river briefly on the way north to Barbourville. Here you can detour 5 miles west on Ky. 459 to **Dr. Thomas Walker State Historical Site** *(606-546-4400. www.parks.ky.gov)* and see a copy of the first cabin built in what is now Kentucky. Walker (not Daniel Boone) in 1750 was the first white explorer to find Cumberland Gap. Five miles north of Barbourville you'll reach **Kentucky Communities Crafts** *(US 25E. 606-546-3152 or 800-880-3152. www.ky-crafts.com)*, where local artists and craftspeople sell pottery, baskets, textiles, dolls, and musical instruments. Leave US 25E now for Ky. 229, which leads to **Levi Jackson Wilderness Road State Park** *(606-330-2130. www.parks.ky.gov)*. This park preserves portions of two historic 18th-century trails, the **Wilderness Road** and **Boone's Trace** and includes the **Mountain Life Museum** *(April-Oct.; adm. fee)*, in seven buildings.

Near London the byway follows US 25 and soon enters **Daniel Boone National Forest** *(859-745-3100. www.fs.usda.gov/dbnf)*.

Crossing I-75 twice, US 25 parallels I-75 north to **Berea** *(Tourism Center, 201 N. Broadway. 859-986-2540 or 800-598-5263. www.berea.com)*, which calls itself "the folk arts and crafts capital of Kentucky." Woodworkers, potters, jewelers, painters, weavers, and others create their art here.

Dulcimer making in Berea

Kentucky Heartland Drive

Lexington to Harrodsburg on US 68

▪ 30 miles ▪ 1 hour ▪ All year

Following a former buffalo trace and an early 19th-century Shaker toll road, this rolling rural drive takes you into central Kentucky's famed Bluegrass region and through the rugged Kentucky River Gorge.

The drive begins in **Lexington,** center of the state's lucrative tobacco and horse industries. Head south from downtown on busy South Broadway (US 68). Soon after passing **South Elkhorn Creek,** the road begins sweeping around precipitous curves as urban development gives way to plots of burley tobacco and lush pastures dotted with dairy cows and bales of hay.

The most prominent feature of this region is its black or white plank fences, behind which statuesque Thoroughbreds graze in lush pastures. Here in the heart of Kentucky's Bluegrass country, the world's finest racing stock is bred, born, and raised. Perhaps the most famous horse farm along the route is the old **Almahurst Farm,** 10 miles outside Lexington. Dating from land grant days, it boasts cream-colored barns trimmed in green and burgundy.

Several miles after entering Jessamine County, the drive begins its descent into a narrow side valley of the **Kentucky River Gorge.** After 1.5 miles of tricky driving, you cross **Kentucky River,** with a view of its 300-foot-high palisades. The road follows the river, then, suddenly begins climbing up the sloped southern wall.

After 2 miles you'll see rough, rolling farmland. Note the native limestone fences bordering much of this section of road. These mortarless fences were built by Irish stonemasons, who came to build roads in the mid-1800s.

Soon the **Shaker Village of Pleasant Hill** *(800-734-5611. www.shaker villageky.org. Adm. fee)* appears on the right. A religious sect known for industriousness and celibacy that spread down from New England, Shakers came here in 1805. This colony disbanded in 1910, leaving many buildings, many of which are now restored and available for touring.

The drive continues another 7 miles before ending in **Harrodsburg.** Kentucky's oldest permanent settlement, it began as a palisaded village in 1775, built to protect settlers from Native Americans. A reproduction of the fort can be seen at **Old Fort Harrod State Park** *(859-734-3314. www.parks .ky.gov. Adm. fee),* situated near the original site. The **Lincoln Marriage Cabin,** where the parents of Abraham Lincoln were married in 1806, was moved to the park from its original location a few miles west.

Mares and foals in Bluegrass country

Lincoln Heritage Scenic Highway

Hodgenville to Danville, Kentucky, on Kentucky 61 and US 31E and 150

- 71 miles ▪ 3 hours ▪ April to October

Abraham Lincoln's birthplace and boyhood home are prime draws along the Kentucky scenic byway named for him. History also pervades other sites along the route: an abbey, an inn,

a composer's home, a Civil War battlefield, and even a number of distilleries.

You can gather insights into the 16th President's beginnings by starting at **Abraham Lincoln's Birthplace National Historical Park** *(270-358-3137. www.nps.gov/abli)*, just south of Hodgenville. In addition to seeing the sinking spring that gave the Lincolns' farm its name, you can explore visitor center exhibits that show how these humble frontier surroundings influenced the man young Abe would ultimately become. Down the road, you can dig deeper into the story at **Abraham Lincoln's Boyhood Home at Knob Creek** *(270-358-3137. www.nps.gov/abli)*, a place Lincoln mentioned often when, as President, he spoke about his childhood.

Next you'll come upon the **Abbey of Gethsemani** *(3642 Monks Rd. 502-549-3117. www.monks.org)*, whose monks have been welcoming travelers since 1848. The abbey was also home to mid-20th-century monk, poet, and author Thomas Merton; a selection of his more than 70 books are sold in the gift shop—along with the abbey's famous bourbon-flavored fudge.

In **Bardstown** *(www.visitbardstown.com)* sample the homey fare at the Old Talbott Tavern *(107 W. Stephen Foster Ave. 502-348-3494. www.talbotts.com)*, which has been serving guests—including Daniel Boone and Jesse James—since 1799.

> **Abraham Lincoln first saw enslaved Africans when they were being brought south past his childhood home at Knob Creek.**

Bardstown is also home to many of the state's largest distilleries, and you can learn everything you ever wanted to know about bourbon at the **Heaven Hill Distillery and Bourbon Heritage Center** *(1311 Gilkey Run Rd. 502-337-1000. www.bourbon heritagecenter.com)*. While free tours are available, aficionados should spring for the three-hour Behind the Scenes Tour, which includes a taste of two of the distillery's premium bourbons. Further research can be conducted at the nearby **Oscar Getz Museum of Whiskey History** *(114 N. 5th St. 502-348-2999. www.whiskeymuseum.com)*, which chronicles the development of strong drink all the way back to the colonial era.

From Bardstown, the byway turns east onto US 150 toward **My Old Kentucky Home State Park** *(501 E. Stephen Foster Ave. 502-348-3502. www.parks .ky.gov/parks/recreationparks. Adm. fee)*, where you can tour Federal Hill; the mansion and its grounds are said to have inspired Stephen Foster to pen the tune that has preceded the running of every Kentucky Derby since 1930.

125

Twenty-three miles farther east on US 150, the **Perryville Battlefield State Historic Site** *(1825 Battlefield Rd. 859-332-8631. www.perryvillebattlefield.org)* commemorates the bloodiest Civil War engagement in Kentucky.

From there, it's just another dozen miles to the end of the Lincoln Heritage Scenic Highway in **Danville.**

Woodlands Trace

Barkley Canal, Kentucky, to South Welcome Station, Tennessee, on the Trace

■ 40 miles ■ 1 hour ■ All year

Called the Trace, the drive meanders the length of a long, narrow wooded peninsula jutting between Kentucky Lake and Lake Barkley and straddling the Kentucky-Tennessee border. Ravaged by floods, wars, and poverty, the region—originally known as the "Land Twixt the Rivers"—was converted to a recreation area by the Tennessee Valley Authority in the 1960s. This natural wonderland is rich in wildlife, including a variety of fish that delights anglers.

The drive begins in Kentucky just south of the bridge over **Barkley Canal,** which connects the two lakes. For vistas of the canal and **Kentucky Lake,** detour onto Kentucky Lake Drive, a pretty, 3.2-mile loop-tour. Back on the Trace, you can pick up maps and brochures at the **North Welcome Station.**

From here, the Trace proceeds 17 miles through a genteel corridor of white oaks, sugar maples, black walnuts, and dogwoods. The **Golden Pond Visitor Center and Planetarium** *(270-924-2233. www.lbl.org/plgate.html. March.–mid-Dec.; adm. fee to planetarium)* has information and regional exhibits explaining, among other things, the area's moonshining past. During Prohibition this isolated pocket was home to one of the nation's most notorious moonshining operations, which capitalized on the limestone-rich mineral water and the abundant corn of this area.

About 8 miles farther, just across the Tennessee border, lies **Cedar Pond,** a picnic spot and prime wildlife-viewing area. Continue 1.5 miles to the **Homeplace–1850** *(931-232-6457. www.lbl.org/hpgate.html. Closed Dec.-Feb.; adm. fee),* a farm worked by costumed interpreters. Across the road American bison roam a 200-acre pasture.

Deterred from farming by flooding and poor soil, many early settlers turned to iron. By the 1830s Kentucky ranked third in the nation in iron-ore production. The remains of this industry can be found at the nearby **Great Western Iron Furnace.**

The drive ends at the **South Welcome Station** 9 miles ahead, but don't leave the area before exploring its many recreational opportunities.

The Homeplace–1850

Great River Road (Kentucky)

Wickliffe, Kentucky, to the Tennessee border on
US 51 and Kentucky 1203, 123, 239, and 94

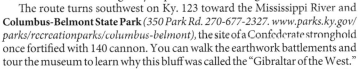

- 63 miles ▪ 1 day ▪ All year

Prehistoric Native American civilizations and an old
Confederate fort await exploration on the Kentucky leg
of the Great River Road Scenic Byway. This leg starts
north of the Tennessee section of the Great River Road
(see pp. 118–120) and connects to it at Reelfoot Lake on
the two states' border.

Begin your drive by following US 51 south to **Wickliffe
Mounds State Historic Site** *(94 Green St. 270-335-3681.
www.parks.ky.gov/parks/historicsites/wickliffe-mounds).*
Here you'll find intriguing remnants of Native American village life that have been dated back to 1100.

Continue south about a mile to **Fort Jefferson Memorial.** Though the actual 1780s fort is long gone, this hilltop
still offers the sweeping views of the confluence of the Mississippi and Ohio
Rivers that made it strategically important in defending the western frontier.

The route turns southwest on Ky. 123 toward the Mississippi River and
Columbus-Belmont State Park *(350 Park Rd. 270-677-2327. www.parks.ky.gov/
parks/recreationparks/columbus-belmont),* the site of a Confederate stronghold
once fortified with 140 cannon. You can walk the earthwork battlements and
tour the museum to learn why this bluff was called the "Gibraltar of the West."

Continue south through tiny **Columbus,** which missed becoming the
new U.S. capital by a single Senate vote during Thomas Jefferson's presidency. About 20 miles on head west on Ky. 94 to **Hickman,** where you
can walk or drive onto the **Dorena-Hickman Ferry** *(731-693-0210. www
.dorena-hickmanferryboat.com)* for an inexpensive ride across the Mississippi.

MISSISSIPPI

Natchez Trace Parkway

*Nashville, Tennessee, to Natchez, Mississippi, on Tennessee 96 and
the Trace Parkway via Alabama*

- 444 miles ▪ 2 days ▪ Spring and fall. Wildlife sightings are more
likely in early morning and late afternoon. Only one service station
on parkway at mile 193; otherwise you must exit for gas, food,
and lodging. Speed limit of 50 mph strictly enforced. Mileposts
record mileages in reverse, from Natchez to Nashville.

Stretching from the Tennessee Valley to the Mississippi River, the richly
scenic Natchez Trace Parkway is one of America's most famous frontier
trails. From buffalo paths used by prehistoric hunters, the Trace became a
series of Native American trails later trod by French and Spanish trappers,

traders, missionaries, and soldiers. The current two-lane parkway, administered by the National Park Service, meanders through forest, farmland, marshland, and prairie, more or less paralleling the original Trace.

The parkway begins at Tenn. 100 in the outskirts of Nashville. Continue on to **Franklin** *(Franklin Visitor Center, 209 E. Main St. 615-591-8514. www.visitfranklin.com),* site of a bloody Civil War battle in 1864. The town now boasts a restored, 19th-century downtown and antebellum landmarks including graceful **Carnton Plantation** *(1345 Carnton La. 615-794-0903. www.carnton.org. Adm. fee).* From here, drive west 8 miles on Tenn. 96 to enter the parkway.

The Trace gets off to a slow (40 miles per hour) start, sweeping in great, elegant curves through the woods. Emerging into open fields, it rolls along for the next 20-some miles through idyllic Tennessee horse and farm country. At mile 407.7 **Gordon House** survives as one of the few structures from the old Trace.

Three miles beyond, a paved path leads to a pool at the base of **Jacksons Falls,** and a little farther on lies a **Tobacco Farm** featuring farm buildings with exhibits on tobacco growing. A 2-mile drive along the original **Old Trace** begins here.

At the park dedicated to **Meriwether Lewis** *(mile 385.9),* you'll find a reconstruction of the old log inn, or "stand," where he died in 1809 of gunshot wounds. The building now holds a ranger station and history exhibit. Lewis's grave and a symbolic broken obelisk are also here.

Continue through the woods and across the **Buffalo River.** About 10 miles down, turn left on Old Trace Drive, which loops along a scenic ridge (one-way northbound) on a section of the old road.

South of here, you leave the woods behind for a breather of open farmland. Then the trees return, and you soon see **Sweetwater Branch** *(mile 363);* in spring, wildflowers garnish the nature trail here. After about 20 miles of moving in and out of forests of oak and hickory, the Trace then crosses

Mississippi River at Natchez

into Alabama and the land becomes noticeably flatter, marked by red-clay plains and cotton fields.

At mile 327.3 you cross the wide **Tennessee River** at **Colbert Ferry**, where in the mid-19th century itinerant preacher George Colbert ran a stand and a ferry "over the worst natural obstacle on the trace." Cultivated fields and low hills dominate for the next 10 miles. At **Freedom Hills Overlook** *(mile 317)* a 0.25-mile trail leads to the 800-foot hilltop, the highest point on the Alabama portion of the Natchez Trace.

Continuing south into Mississippi, you start to see more wetlands. About 9 miles across the state line, you reach the **Jamie L. Whitten Bridge** over the **Tennessee-Tombigbee Waterway.** Finally completed in 1985 (the idea was first proposed in the mid-1700s), the Tenn-Tom, as it's called, provides a 459-mile-long navigable link between the Tennessee River and the Gulf of Mexico.

After a few miles, watch for **Pharr Mounds** *(mile 286.7)*—the largest and most important archaeological site in northern Mississippi. The ancient Mound Builder culture constructed eight great, dome-shaped burial mounds here, across 90 acres, about 2,000 years ago.

Crossing a boggy area that is habitat for great blue herons, egrets, and other birds, the road winds past **Donivan Slough.** An interpretive trail leads through a hardwood swamp.

Continue on past fields of cotton, soybean, and milo (used for making sorghum and cattle fodder) to **Dogwood Valley** *(mile 275.2)*. The stand of large old dogwoods blooms profusely in the early spring.

If you pull off at the next **Old Trace** marker about 5 miles beyond, you can follow a short trail to a clearing in the woods that is believed to hold the graves of 13 unknown Confederate soldiers.

The **Natchez Trace Parkway Visitor Center** *(mile 266. 800-305-7417. www.nps.gov/natr)* serves as park

Lower Mississippi Great River Road

Vicksburg to Woodville on US 61

■ 101 miles ■ 3 hours ■ All year

Impressive antebellum houses and Civil War battlefields are among the destinations to be discovered, along with two of the South's most historic cities, as US 61 meanders through rolling hills on the east bank of the **Mississippi River.**

Situated on bluffs above the Mississippi, **Vicksburg** *(Convention & Visitors Bureau. 601-636-9421 or 800-221-3536. www.visitvicksburg.com)* was an important port during the Civil War. **Vicksburg National Military Park** *(601-636-0583. www.nps.gov/vick. Adm. fee)* comprises 20 miles of reconstructed trenches and earthworks, a 16-mile tour road, 144 cannon, and a restored Union gunboat. Vicksburg's historic houses include **McRaven** *(1445 Harrison St. 601-636-1663. www.mcraventourhome.com. Adm. fee)*, with sections dating back to 1797.

South 23 miles, **Grand Gulf Military Park** *(601-437-5911. www.grandgulfpark.state.ms.us. Adm. fee)* preserves a Civil War battle site. Eight miles south, **Port Gibson** *(Chamber of Commerce, 1601 Church 601-437-4351. www.portgibsononthemississippi.com)* boasts many historic buildings and churches.

The byway continues to **Natchez** *(Convention & Visitors Bureau, 640 S. Canal St. 601-446-6345 or 800-647-6724. www.visitnatchez.org)*, famed for

its antebellum structures. Start at **Natchez National Historical Park** *(601-442-7047. www.nps.gov/natc. Tour fee)*.

129

headquarters and offers exhibits and an audiovisual presentation about the Trace. From here, a 5-mile detour off the Trace on US 45 will bring you to **Tupelo.** Birthplace of legendary Elvis Presley, the small town celebrates its favorite son in several museums.

Back on the Trace, the **Chickasaw Village** at mile 261.8 marks the site of a former Native American settlement and interprets Chickasaw life. The glorious, open country you're now in—called the **Black Belt** for its black soil, in which cedar and oak thrive—is the remnant of a vast prairie.

You reenter an oak, hickory, and pine forest that is part of the **Tombigbee National Forest** *(662-285-3264)*. Before you leave the forest, take a stretch under the fragrant pines at magical **Witch Dance;** then head south, past the twin **Bynum Mounds,** where there are more Mound Builder remains.

The next 40 miles offer a constantly changing picture of pretty farmscapes, pastures, and forests. **Jeff Busby Site** *(mile 193.1)* has the only services along the Trace and offers a view from 603-foot **Little Mountain.** From here, the Trace soon crosses a bottomland, where shrubs replace trees. Down the road is the site of a former inn that became **French Camp Academy** *(662-547-6482)*. The name refers to the inn's original French-Canadian proprietor. Now a Christian boarding school, the grounds contain a visitor center, B&B, and historic buildings.

The landscape turns swampy over the next few miles, and the trail at **Cole Creek** leads through this fecund, fragrant bottomland hardwood forest. At mile 160 **Kosciusko,** pronounced koz-ee-ES-ko *(Chamber of Commerce, 124 N. Jackson St. 662-289-2981)*, was named for the Polish soldier who became a hero during the American Revolution. The town is also the birthplace of talk-show star Oprah Winfrey. Aside from the new **Kosciusko Visitor Center,** this Victorian village boasts a charming town square and some fine historic homes.

Continuing through more swamp and bottomland for 30-some miles, the Trace passes **River Bend** *(mile 122.6)*, where you have a splendid

view up the **Pearl River.** Just beyond, a boardwalk trail penetrates the eerie forest of bald cypress and tupelo at **Cypress Swamp.**

Picking up the shoreline of the scenic **Ross Barnett Reservoir,** the parkway follows it for 8 miles before reaching the **Mississippi Crafts Center at Ridgeland** *(950 Rice Rd. 601-856-7546. www.mscrafts.org. Mon.-Sun.)*, which sells traditional Choctaw baskets, pottery, quilts, and other crafts. South of here, in 2005 the final segments of the Natchez Trace were finished 67 years after work began as a New Deal project.

Along the original Trace

Mississippi's gracious capital, **Jackson** *(Jackson Convention and Visitors Bureau, 111 E. Capitol St. 601-960-1891 or 800-354-7695. www.visitjackson.com)*, offers such attractions as museums, gardens, and a walking tour of the historic downtown.

From here you soon enter some of the most productive farmland in the state. Rolling through this pastoral countryside for about 25 miles, the Trace passes the silent site of a 19th-century cotton town. Now, only an old church and cemetery survive, and the trees are draped in Spanish moss.

Crossing **Big Bayou Pierre** four times, you get a view of its cultivated floodplain before reaching peaceful Mangum Site and Grindstone Ford. Now the parkway sweeps south past farms and wetlands, passing at mile 41.5 the **Sunken Trace,** a short trail along a deeply eroded portion of the old Trace.

Leaving the gently rolling countryside, the road begins to climb an upland ridge forested with hardwoods and pines. At **Mount Locust** *(mile 15.5)* you can visit the only inn still remaining on the Trace. It ranks as one of the oldest structures in the state.

And at **Emerald Mound** *(mile 10.3)* you can see the second largest Indian mound in the country: an 8-acre, earthen temple built about 600 years ago by ancestors of the present-day Natchez Indians.

Cypress Swamp along the Natchez Trace

The parkway winds to its current southern terminus 2 miles farther on when it intersects US 61. Seven miles southwest lies **Natchez** *(Convention & Visitor Bureau, 640 S. Canal St. 601-446-6345 or 800-647-6724),* an elegant vestige of the Old South containing a wealth of historic homes.

131

Hospitality Highway

Clermont Harbor to Ocean Springs on South Beach Boulevard and US 90

▪ 32 miles ▪ 1 hour ▪ Fall through spring

This drive along Mississippi's Gulf Coast traces a section of the Old Spanish Trail. It passes shorelines, a profusion of subtropical flora, and charming towns recovering from the damage inflicted on them by Hurricane Katrina.

From **Clermont Harbor,** follow South Beach Boulevard east along **Mississippi Sound,** where the bird-watching is superb. The drive passes **Buccaneer State Park,** a 400-acre shoreline park *(1150 South Beach Blvd. 228-467-3822 or 800-467-2757. www.home.mdwfp.com),* then continues through the small town of Waveland, into the heart of historic **Bay St. Louis.** Long a favorite getaway, this colorful resort community was seriously damaged by Hurricane Katrina but is recovering slowly, reopening galleries and antique shops and repairing vintage architecture, including Spanish and old classical revival buildings.

Hurricane Katrina Memorial at Biloxi, Mississippi

Beach Boulevard brings you to US 90 at the bridge over **St. Louis Bay.** Less than half a mile east of the bridge, severely damaged by the storm, you suddenly have a view of **Mississippi Beach**—the longest man-made strand in the world—at a bend in the road leading toward **Pass Christian** (pronounced Chris-CHAN). The designated scenic drive, once a look at the antebellum mansions that Southern planters and New Orleanian aristocrats occupied, is now a journey of destruction and reconstruction.

The drive feeds back into Beach Boulevard, and you continue east through **Long Beach.** Here you see the **Port of Gulfport** ahead, and some 4 miles farther you enter the city of **Gulfport.**

The 12 miles from Gulfport to Biloxi are dotted with reopening casinos and commercial strips. In **Biloxi** *(Visitor Center, 1050 Beach Blvd. 228-374-3105 or 800-245-6943. www.biloxi.ms.us)* the Old South is returning but slowly. The once gracious veranda-fronted **Beauvoir** *(2244 Beach Blvd. 228-388-4400. www.beauvoir.org)* and Jefferson Davis's presidential library are being restored, but the task is overwhelming and slow. The bridge over **Biloxi Bay** puts you in the lovely artist community of **Ocean Springs,** known for the **Walter Anderson Museum of Art** *(510 Washington Ave. 228-872-3164. http://walterandersonmuseum.org. Adm. fee),* and **Shearwater Pottery** *(102 Shearwater Dr. 228-875-7320. www.shearwaterpottery.com. Call for schedule),* featuring works by Anderson family members.

ALABAMA
Selma to Montgomery March Byway

Selma to Montgomery on US 80

■ 54 miles ■ 4 hours ■ All year

This short but historic drive retraces the path of one of the most important events in the American civil rights movement, during which African Americans worked toward equality in education, economic opportunity, voting, housing, and other aspects of citizenship.

On March 7, 1965 (a day that came to be known as Bloody Sunday), marchers protesting racial discrimination and violence tried to walk from Selma to the State Capitol in Montgomery, only to be attacked by police at the Edmund Pettus Bridge. On March 21, more than 3,000 marchers,

led by Martin Luther King, Jr., walked the 54 miles from Selma to Montgomery, at which point their numbers had grown to 25,000 people from around the world.

In **Selma** *(Selma Welcome Center, 132 Broad St. 334-875-7241. www.selmaalabama.com)* take the Martin Luther King Jr. Street Walking Tour past such historic spots as **Brown Chapel A.M.E. Church** *(410 Martin Luther King Jr. St. www.nps.gov/nr/travel/civilrights/al2.htm)*, site of meetings during the civil rights movement, now with a memorial to King outside. The **National Voting Rights Museum and Institute** *(6 US Hwy. 80 E. 334-418-0800)* has exhibits on the long struggle to extend the right to vote to all people.

The drive begins by crossing the **Edmund Pettus Bridge** over the Alabama River, where police brutally attacked peaceful marchers on Bloody Sunday. US 80 continues eastward to **Montgomery** *(Convention & Visitors Bureau, 300 Water St. 334-261-1100 or 800-240-9452. www.visitingmontgomery.com)*. Be sure to see the moving **Civil Rights Memorial** *(400 Washington Ave. 334-956-8200)*, a monument with water flowing over a table inscribed with the names of those who died during the civil rights movement.

The Rev. Martin Luther King, Jr. preached at **Dexter Avenue King Memorial Baptist Church** *(454 Dexter Ave. 334-263-3970. www.dexterkingmemorial.org. No tours Sun.-Mon., adm. fee)*, now a national historic landmark. At the conclusion of the Selma to Montgomery march, King gave his famed "How Long, Not Long" speech at the 1846 **Alabama State Capitol** *(600 Dexter Ave. 334-242-3935. www.preserveala.org/capitol.aspx)*, which served as the first capitol of the Confederacy. Within months of the march, President Lyndon Johnson signed the Voting Rights Act of 1965.

Talladega Scenic Drive

US 78 to Pinhoti Trailhead at Adams Gap on Alabama 281

▪ 26 miles ▪ 1 hour ▪ Spring and fall

Winding atop the long, narrow spine of Horseblock Mountain then scaling Alabama's highest peak—Cheaha Mountain—this drive offers dreamy views of the southern Appalachian's wooded valleys and ridges.

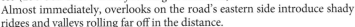

The byway begins 3 miles west of Heflin, where you head south on Ala. 281 through a wooded corridor in **Talladega National Forest** *(256-362-2909. www.fs.usda.gov/alabama)*. Almost immediately, overlooks on the road's eastern side introduce shady ridges and valleys rolling far off in the distance.

About a mile ahead a sign emblazoned with a hiker marks the **Pinhoti Trail** *(accessible from several points along byway)*. The 80-mile-long path winds through forested coves and past rocky streams. Wander down the trail and

Along the Talladega Scenic Drive

you might spot a wild turkey or a white-tailed deer.

Beyond I-20 and US 431, the byway climbs the long slender ridge of **Horseblock Mountain.** Through pine forests, you have views of the rugged **Coosa River Valley,** whose gentle ridges mark the southern reaches of the Appalachians. Continuing south, the undulating byway passes Ala. 24, which leads west to **Morgan Lake** and east to sinewy **Ivory Mountain.** Past the Ala. 24 turnoff, the drive tackles the steep slopes of **Cheaha Mountain,** Alabama's highest peak (2,407 feet). On the mountain's wooded crest you'll find **Cheaha State Park** *(256-488-5115 or 800-252-7275. www.alapark.com/cheaharesort. Adm. fee),* a rustic haven with a restaurant, lodge, and rental cottages. From **Bunker Tower,** a 1930s stone observation tower at the summit, you can see peaks and valleys 60-some miles away on clear days.

Beyond the park, the road plummets 1,200 feet through the mountainous backcountry of the 7,275-acre **Cheaha Wilderness.** For 7 miles, continue on Ala. 281 past signs for the turnoff for **Lake Chinnabee Recreation Area** *(256-362-2909. Closed Dec.–mid-April; parking & camping fees),* where the 2-mile **Lakeshore Trail** circles the lake toward Turnipseed Camp. The drive ends at the parking area for the Pinhoti Trailhead at Adams Gap. A dirt road continues, but it is best driven with a four-wheel-drive vehicle.

Alabama's Coastal Connection

Grand Bay to Spanish Fort, Alabama, on I-10 Alabama 188, 193, and 180 and US 98

- 130 miles ▪ 4 hours ▪ All year

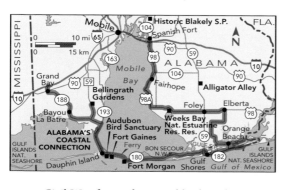

Over the course of its 130-mile run, Alabama's Coastal Connection Scenic Byway abounds with contrasts: The byway passes through peaceful wildlife sanctuaries and hopping beachside resort towns. You'll be transported back in time as you walk through a massive Civil War fort and snapped back to the present as you hold a squirming baby alligator.

You'll find the start of the route just off I-10, about 30 minutes southwest of Mobile in Grand Bay. From here you'll head southeast on Ala. 188 toward **Bayou La Batre.** Made famous as the home of Forrest Gump's slow-talking Army buddy, Bubba.

Continuing on Ala. 188, turn north on Bellingrath Road for a stop at **Bellingrath Gardens** *(12401 Bellingrath Gardens Rd. 251-973-2217. www .bellingrath.org. Adm. fee).* Once the Bellingrath family's humble fishing camp on the Fowl River, the 65-acre attraction you see today can best be described as a home improvement project that got way out of hand, with a 10,500-square-foot brick mansion surrounded by eclectic gardens filled with a seemingly endless array of blooming plants.

Back on 188, the route then crosses the bridge to **Dauphin Island,** a 14-mile-long barrier island that offers much more than sun and sand—such as the hundreds of species that come to call at the 164-acre **Audubon Bird Sanctuary** *(109 Bienville Blvd. 251-861-3607. www.dauphinisland.org/bird .htm),* making this one of the top birding destinations in the country. To get a look at wildlife of a different sort, stop at the **Dauphin Island Sea Lab's Estuarium** *(101 Bienville Blvd. 251-861-2141. www.sealabestuarium.org. Adm. fee),* which features exhibits on the broad range of critters that call these waters home. History buffs will also want to check out the island's remarkably well-preserved **Fort Gaines** *(51 Bienville Blvd. 251-861-6992. www.dauphinisland.org/fort.htm),* which has been standing watch over Mobile Bay since before the Civil War.

The thriving port town of Bayou La Batre boasts of being the "Seafood Capital of Alabama," a believable claim considering the number of commercial fishing and shrimp boats tied up in its quaint harbor.

Now you've come to one of the more unique aspects of this scenic byway, namely, the **Mobile Bay Ferry** *(1606 Bienville Blvd. 251-861-3000. www .mobilebayferry.com).* During the summer, boats generally run every 45 minutes and are a fun and scenic way of crossing the mouth of the bay.

You'll make landfall in the shadow of the 1830s-vintage **Fort Morgan** *(110 Hwy. 180 W. 251-540-5257. www.fortmorgan.org),* which many historians regard as a world-class example of military architecture. When you've had enough history, head east on Ala. 180 through the coastal dunes and marshes of the **Bon Secour National Wildlife Refuge** *(251-540-7720. www.fws .gov/bonsecour),* where miles of trails make a good place to stretch your legs.

Several miles east of the refuge, turn south onto Ala. 135 and follow it to Ala. 182 and **Gulf State Park** *(251-948-7275. www.alapark.com/gulfstate),* which offers a 1,540-foot pier—the longest on the Gulf—that is a favorite of local fishermen.

Two stops along Ala. 182 are the bustling resort centers of **Gulf Shores** *(Welcome Center, 3150 Gulf Shores Pkwy./Hwy. 59. 251-968-7511. www.gulf shores.com),* west of Gulf State Park, and **Orange Beach** *(Welcome Center, 23685 Perdido Beach Blvd./Hwy. 182. 251-974-1510. www.gulfshores.com).* Suffice it to say you'll find just about every form of amusement known to man here, from casino gambling and biplane rides to kayaking and horseback riding.

As the route turns north from here, you'll reach the tiny farming community of Elberta before turning west on US 98 toward Foley. Railroading enthusiasts—and kids of all ages—will enjoy a stop at the

135

town's former railroad depot, now home to the **Foley Railroad Museum** *(125 E. Laurel Ave. 251-943-1818. www.foleyrailroadmuseum.com. Closed Sun.)* and one of the largest and most elaborate model railroad setups you'll ever lay eyes on.

After you've had your fill of these big-boy toys, continue west on US 98 and you'll come upon the **Weeks Bay National Estuarine Research Reserve** *(11300 US Hwy. 98. 251-928-9792. www.weeksbay.org. Closed Sun.),* where you can take a short stroll through lush bogs full of ferns and wildflowers to a pavilion with peaceful views of the broad Fish River in the distance.

Now turn north on US 98A along the shores of Mobile Bay. Entering Fairhope, you'll want to make a detour to see what locals call simply the **Fairhope Castle** *(www.fairhopecastle.com).* While this whimsical work of architecture built in the 1940s is a private home and not open for tours, it makes for a memorable photo op. Detouring 15 miles east of Fairhope on Alabama 104 takes you to **Alligator Alley** *(19500 Hwy. 71, Summerdale. 251-946-2483. www.gatoralleyfarm.com. Adm. fee),* where you can see hundreds of the toothy beasts in action during daily feeding times.

Backtrack to the main route, and it's a short drive to the end of the byway at **Spanish Fort,** home to **Historic Blakeley State Park** *(34745 Hwy. 225. 251-626-0798. www.blakeleypark.com. Adm. fee),* site of the Civil War's last major battle.

SOUTH CAROLINA
Ashley River Road

South Carolina 61 just northwest of Charleston

■ 11 miles ■ 1 hour ■ All year. Azaleas, camellias, and other flowers make spring the most popular time to visit.

History and lush gardens combine to make this drive a small jewel, set in the region called the South Carolina Lowcountry. The Ashley River area is a tranquil place where travelers can experience the diverse attractions of the Old South.

Although the byway officially begins a few miles outside **Charleston** *(Convention & Visitors Bureau, 375 Meeting St. 800-774-0006. www.charlestoncvb.com)* it's really a must to visit this city. The **Charleston Museum** *(360 Meeting St. 843-722-2996. www.charleston museum.org. Adm. fee)* is an excellent first stop to learn about local history. One of the most interesting things to do is simply to stroll the streets in the **Old City Market** area or the area "SOB" (south of Broad) and enjoy the buildings, gardens, and iron gates that are Charleston trademarks.

Cross the Ashley River on the US 17 bridge and turn north on S.C. 61; the byway officially begins about 2 miles north of I-526. **Old St. Andrew's Parish Church** *(2604 Ashley River Rd. 843-766-1541. www.oldstandrews.org)*

was founded in 1706 and rebuilt in 1764 after a fire. **Springfield Baptist Church** *(2619 Ashley River Rd. 843-766-9971)* was established by African Americans freed from enslavement.

The major attractions on Ashley River Road are three plantations. Red brick **Drayton Hall** *(3380 Ashley River Rd. 843-769-2600. www.draytonhall .org. Adm. fee),* the oldest (dating from 1738-1742) unrestored plantation house in America, is open to the public.

The original house at **Magnolia Plantation** *(3550 Ashley River Rd. 843-571-1266 or 800-367-3517. www.magnoliaplantation.com. Adm. fee)* burned in the Civil War (the present house dates from the 1870s), but the gardens were started in the 1860s. On a bluff over the Ashley River, **Middleton Place** *(4300 Ashley River Rd. 843-556-6020 or 800-782-3608. www.middletonplace.org. Adm. fee)* also burned during the Civil War (one original building is a museum) and has survived earthquakes and hurricanes.

Drayton Hall plantation

Cherokee Foothills Scenic Highway

137

Gaffney to Lake Hartwell State Park on South Carolina 11

■ 112 miles ■ 3 hours ■ All year. Peach bloom peaks in May, fall foliage in mid-October.

Following a path trodden by Cherokee Indians, frontier traders, and bootleggers, the drive ambles through Blue Ridge foothills, past peach orchards, soaring mountain peaks, lakes, and fish-filled streams.

Begin in **Gaffney,** one of the world's largest peach-shipping centers. At **Cowpens National Battlefield** *(864-461-2828. www.nps .gov/cowp),* about 9.5 miles from Gaffney, a quiet green meadow commemorates one of the most strategic battles of the American Revolution, where in 1781 American colonists scored a triumph in their fight for independence.

From Cowpens, S.C. 11 begins to roll gently, undulating more as the rumpled mountains ahead grow closer. About 9 miles beyond Campobello, the road passes just south of **Hogback Mountain,** then along the base of **Glassy Mountain.** You are now in the Blue Ridge foothills.

Crossing the **North** and **Middle Saluda Rivers,** the byway enters Cleveland, where a 6-mile detour on River Falls Road leads to **Jones Gap State Park** *(303 Jones Gap Rd. 864-836-3647. www.southcarolinaparks.com. Day-use fee).*

Here, in a pleasant wooded glen, picnic tables sit beside the clear, murmuring Middle Saluda River.

As the byway continues beside the **South Saluda River,** you'll pass the cars of anglers who try their luck on the river, stocked with rainbow and brown trout. The 1,200-foot rock precipice protruding from a forested mountainside is **Caesars Head.** If you take a 7.5-mile detour up precipitous US 276, you can walk out to its edge at **Caesars Head State Park** *(8115 Geer Hwy. 864-836-6115. www .southcarolinaparks.com. Trail fees).* The sudden drop in elevation here provides a soaring view of the Blue Ridge and three states—South Carolina, North Carolina, and Georgia.

Back on S.C. 11, roadside stands sell hot boiled peanuts and quilts. **Table Rock,** revered by the Cherokee as the dining spot of the Great Spirit, hulks over the rolling landscape.

In the shadow of Table Rock stands **Aunt Sue's Country Corner** *(107A Country Creek Rd. 864-878-4366. Tues.-Sun.),* a quirky, old-time village of craft and food shops, where the employees call each other "Cousin."

Table Rock State Park *(158 E. Ellison Ln. 864-878-9813. www.south carolinaparks.com. Vehicle & adm. fees),* 2 miles down the road, is the halfway point of the drive. The east gate leads to historic **Table Rock Lodge** *(864-878-9813),* famous for its spectacular views and country-style Sunday buffets. The west gate accesses **Pinnacle Lake,** with trails up the slopes of **Pinnacle** and **Table Rock Mountains.**

Forested ridges soon envelop the road, and the state's highest peak, **Sassafras Mountain,** towers 3,554 feet above the hills. Shortly after the junction with US 178, **Keowee-Toxaway State Natural Area** *(108 Residence Dr. 864-868-2605. www.southcarolinaparks.com. Adm. fee)* straddles the road. To the left, a museum and trail with

South Carolina 107

Oconee State Park to the North Carolina border on South Carolina 107

■ 12 miles ■ ¹/₂ hour ■ Spring through fall. Fine spring bloom and fall foliage. See map p. 137.

Rustic and remote, S.C. 107 heads into the Blue Ridge foothills, climbing 1,122 feet in 12 miles. Along the way, side roads lead to a rich variety of recreational opportunities.

Begin at **Oconee State Park** *(864-638-5353. www.southcarolinaparks.com. Adm. fee)* on the wooded shores of a 20-acre lake. A mantle of loblolly and white pine, hickory, and oak drapes the road as it winds northward through **Sumter National Forest** *(803-561-4000. www.fs.usda.gov/scnfs).* In spring, mountain laurel, dogwood, and rhododendron color the understory.

Lake Cherokee, a mile-long lake surrounded by hills, lies 4.5 miles east on Tamassee Road (FR 710), an old Cherokee trail. The 43-mile-long **Foothills Trail** passes by the lake on its way through some of the most rugged terrain in the Carolinas.

Back on S.C. 107, you'll soon pass a pleasant picnicking and camping spot at **Moody Springs Recreation Area.** A mile beyond, a 3-mile side trip on Burrells Ford Road (FR 708) leads to the **Chattooga River.** The rapids-filled river, a national wild and scenic river, drops almost 2,500 feet in 50 miles. It's especially popular with anglers fishing for trout.

Ahead on the left, the road to the **Walhalla State Fish Hatchery** *(198 Fish Hatchery Rd. 864-638-2866. www.dnr .sc.gov)* twists 2 miles down the mountain, following the **East Fork Chattooga River.** You can also take a walk here in the **Ellicott Rock Wilderness,** rich in old-growth white pines and eastern hemlocks. The drive ends at the North Carolina border, but the road continues into that state's rugged mountains.

Caesars Head State Park

exhibits explore the history and culture of the Upper Cherokee, who were forced out in the late 18th century.

Soaring across the **Keowee River,** the byway is soon intersected by Rte. 25, which leads 5 miles to **Devils Fork State Park** *(161 Holcombe Cir. 864-944-2639. www.south carolinaparks.com. Adm. fee).* Nestled on the shores of **Lake Jocassee** against a backdrop of mountain slopes, the park is popular with anglers and boaters.

The road dips and rises beyond Devils Fork through a secluded region, setting the scene for historic **Oconee Station** *(500 Oconee Station Rd. 864-638-0079. www .southcarolinaparks.com. April-Nov. daily, Dec.-March weekends. Adm. fee),* one of several outposts erected in the early 1790s to protect frontier families. The oldest building in Oconee County, it is also a state park. Not far ahead is the small town of **Walhalla,** its Main Street lined with majestic antebellum homes. As the road veers south, soon you're back in the "down country," the same flat, rural landscape in which the drive began. The final stop on the drive is **Lake Hartwell State Recreation Area** *(19138-A Hwy. 11 S. 864-972-3352. www.southcarolinaparks .com. Adm. fee).* On the shady banks of **Lake Hartwell,** the park features shoreline picnic tables, boating, and a nature trail.

Edisto Island National Scenic Byway

Intracoastal Waterway to Edisto Beach State Park on South Carolina 174

- 17 miles - ¹/₂ to 1 day - All year

Settled by a progression of Native Americans, wealthy plantation owners, and freed slaves, among others, South Carolina's coastal "lowcountry" has more than two dozen sites listed on the National Register of Historic Places. There's abundant natural beauty here, too, from blue herons gliding along the fringes of salt marshes to stately live oaks softened with curtains of Spanish moss.

To begin your explorations along the scenic byway that stitches it all together, cross the McKinley Washington, Jr., Bridge on S.C. 174 for impressive views of the Intracoastal Waterway. There's room to pull over at the top of the bridge so you can safely spend a few minutes ogling the resident bald eagles above and the passing yachts below.

Coastal tide flats on Edisto Island

Once you reach the Edisto Island side of the bridge, watch for the right turn onto Rosa Scott Road, leading to **Dawhoo Landing.** In addition to giving you a different perspective on the broad Intracoastal, Dawhoo Landing is a peaceful place to while away a little time with fishing pole in hand (nearby gas stations sell bait and tackle).

Continuing on S.C. 174, you'll want to stop to lay in picnic provisions at **King's Farm Market** *(2559 Hwy. 174. 843-869-3600. www.kingsfarmmarket edisto.com).* This seasonal operation also stocks local specialties such as rice, honey, and barbecue sauce to take back to those foodie friends at home.

Back on the road, make your next stop the **Edisto Island Museum** *(8123 Chisolm Plantation Rd. 843-869-1954. www.edistomuseum.org. Closed Sun.-Mon; adm. fee),* where you'll find displayed objects ranging from prehistoric sharks' teeth to an original copy of South Carolina's Civil War–spurring Ordinance of Secession. For a uniquely local gift, stop at the **Sweetgrass Basket Stand** just down the road. The handmade works of art on offer are crafted using techniques that African slaves brought here with them four centuries ago.

For a glimpse at a slightly wilder side of the area, plan to stop at the **Edisto Island Serpentarium** *(1374 Hwy. 174. 843-869-1171. www.edisto serpentarium.com. Adm. fee),* home to a menagerie of alligators, snapping turtles, lizards, and snakes, including local favorites like the water moccasin and the copperhead. You can also learn more about the unique estuarine ecosystem

Spanish moss covers oak trees on Edisto Island

you've been traveling through at the **Edisto Beach State Park Interpretive Center** *(8377 State Cabin Rd. 843-869-2756. www.southcarolinaparks.com).* Among the exhibits here are touch tanks full of sea creatures that will appeal especially to children.

From there, all that's left is to hit the sand at **Edisto Beach State Park.** Aside from beachcombing (the area is popular with shell collectors), you can explore nearby highlights, including a huge shell midden dating back to 2000 B.C., via the park's extensive trail system.

Savannah River Scenic Byway

Clarks Hill to Oakway on South Carolina 28, 81, 187, and 24

- 110 miles - 4 hours - All year

Recreational opportunities abound along this pine-lined byway in northwestern South Carolina, from three large reservoirs to state parks to national forest campgrounds and picnic areas.

The drive begins at 71,000-acre **J. Strom Thurmond Lake,** one of the most popular Corps of Engineers reservoirs in the nation. Visitors enjoy waterskiing, boating, and fishing for white, striped, hybrid, and largemouth bass; crappie; bluegill; and catfish. The lake **visitor center** *(US 221 just east of dam. 864-333-1100. www.sas.usace.army.mil/lakes/thurmond)* features exhibits on wildlife and local history. The nearby **Clarks Hill Park Recreation Area** is one of several swimming and picnicking areas scattered along the lakeshore.

Much of the southern part of the byway passes through **Sumter National Forest** *(803-561-4000 www.fs.usda.gov/scnfs),* which offers campgrounds, hiking trails, and other recreation sites just minutes off the route. Further opportunities for outdoor activities can be found at state parks on the shore of Thurmond Lake, including **Hamilton Branch State Recreation Area** *(111 Campground Rd. 864-333-2223. www.south carolinaparks.com. Adm. fee),* which sits on a peninsula jutting into the lake, **Baker Creek State Park** *(863 Baker Creek Rd. 864-443-2457. www.southcarolinaparks.com. Adm. fee),* with a 10-mile mountain-bike trail along the lakeshore, and **Hickory Knob State Resort Park** *(1591 Resort Dr. 864-391-2450 or 800-491-1764. www.southcarolinaparks.com. Adm. fee),* with cabins, a restaurant, and a lakeside golf course.

The old brick buildings in **McCormick** *(Chamber of Commerce, 100 S. Main St. 864-852-2835)* are the legacy of the discovery of gold here in 1850; many are listed on the National Register of Historic Places. The community itself was named for inventor Cyrus McCormick, whose mechanical grain reaper revolutionized

141

agriculture and who donated land for the town when the mines he had invested in were unprofitable.

Leaving national forest land, the byway skirts Richard B. Russell Lake, which you can visit at **Calhoun Falls State Recreation Area** *(46 Maintenance Shop Rd. 864-447-8267. www.southcarolinaparks.com. Adm. fee)*. The 1.7-mile **Cedar Bluff Nature Trail** offers good vistas of the lake as it loops through mixed pine-hardwood forest.

Beyond Lowndesville the byway meanders through woods and pastures before reaching sprawling **Hartwell Lake,** where 395-acre **Sadlers Creek State Recreation Area** *(940 Sadlers Creek Rd. 864-226-8950. www.southcarolina parks.com. Adm. fee)* offers picnicking, camping, and hiking.

The byway follows S.C. 24 across an arm of the lake to end at Oakway. Here it intersects **Cherokee Foothills Scenic Highway** (see pp. 137-139).

Georgia
Russell–Brasstown
National Scenic Byway

Loop drive from Helen on Georgia 17/75, 180, 348, and 75A

■ 41 miles ■ 1 hour ■ Spring through fall. Fine fall foliage

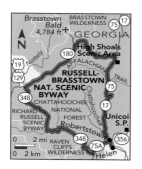

This drive travels through the forested foothills, mountains, and valleys of Chattahoochee National Forest, climbing to the top of Georgia's highest peak.

Begin in charming **Helen,** a former sawmill town with a Bavarian motif and bustling with German-style biergartens, inns, and shops. From Helen head north on Ga. 17/75 as it follows the headwaters of the **Chattahoochee River** through the southern end of the **Chattahoochee National Forest** *(770-297-3000. www.fs.fed.us/conf. Parking fee)*, one of the most productive hardwood forests in the world.

A mile ahead in Robertstown, you can detour 3 miles on Ga. 356 to the wilderness haven of **Unicoi State Park** *(706-878-2201 or 800-573-9659. www.gastateparks.org/info/unicoi. Vehicle fee)*. The park's 7 miles of hiking trails wind into the surrounding hills. If you continue 1.5 miles farther on Smith Creek Road, you'll come to **Anna Ruby Falls** *(706-878-3574. www.fs.fed.us/conf. Vehicle fee)*, where a half-mile paved trail through the forest leads to a twin waterfall. Back on Ga. 17/75, the road now moves alongside crystal-clear **Andrews Creek,** wending through pines, poplars, hemlocks, and oaks. After 3 miles it ascends the slopes of the mountains; along this stretch you'll find a shady picnic spot by **Andrews Creek.**

The precipitous road crests at 2,949-foot **Unicoi Gap,** where the **Appalachian Trail** crosses on its 2,100-mile journey from Georgia to Maine. Just beyond, **High Shoals Scenic Area** has a 1.2-mile trail past Blue Hole and High Shoals Falls. Back on the road, turn left onto Ga. 180. This quiet country road climbs the lower slopes of **Brasstown Bald,** Georgia's highest mountain. You'll get a closer look at the actual bald—the treeless area on the mountain's summit—by following the Ga. 180 spur. From the parking area, you can either be shuttled or you can hike the last half mile to the 4,784-foot summit, with a modern, exhibit-filled **visitor center** *(706-896-2556. May-Nov.)* and a 360-degree view of misty mountain peaks reaching into Tennessee and the Carolinas.

Back on Ga. 180, the drive continues through some of Georgia's most spectacular Blue Ridge country, then enters a rolling, mountain-fringed valley. At Ga. 348 turn left on the Richard Russell Scenic Byway, which follows the headwaters of the **Nottely River.**

The countryside gives way to hills, then steep mountains, as the road climbs to 3,137-foot **Tesnatee Gap,** then to 3,480-

Russell-Brasstown Scenic Byway

foot **Hogpen Gap.** The steep, rugged drainage on the left is, appropriately, **Lordamercy Cove.** You are now on top of the Blue Ridge Divide; water flowing west from here drains into the Tennessee River, and east, into the Chattahoochee. As you descend, stop at the overlook perched on the divide for a view of the wild backcountry of the **Raven Cliffs Wilderness.** Descending along **Piney Ridge,** with views of the wilds to the right, the road comes to **Dukes Creek Falls** about 4.5 miles ahead, where a short trail wanders to an observation platform. Soon after, you turn left onto busy Ga. 75A, which leads back to Helen.

143

Sea Islands

Jekyll Island to Savannah on Georgia 520, 99, and US 17

▪ 81 miles ▪ 2 hours ▪ All year

Savannah residential architecture

So interlaced with sea marshes, swamps, mudflats, and sloughs is Georgia's shoreline that no coastal road exists to showcase its quiet beauty. The closest thing is US 17, which, though it lies a few miles from the sea, swings to and fro through grassy tidal estuaries, pine thickets, and quaint shrimping villages.

Along the way, causeways and bridges meander off to explore a few of Georgia's splendid "golden isles," a string of subtropical barrier islands that hold everything from posh resorts to the tangled wilds of coastal salt marshes.

The drive takes off from **Jekyll Island,** purchased in 1886 as the exclusive winter playground of 50 business magnates, including William Rockefeller, William Vanderbilt, and J. P. Morgan. Their luxurious "cottages" may now be seen in the **Jekyll Island Historic District** *(912-635-3636. www.jekyllisland.com. Vehicle & tour fees).*

From the island, follow the Jekyll Island Causeway (Ga. 520) to US 17 and head north across the **Brunswick River** to **Brunswick,** founded in 1771 and one of Georgia's largest shrimping and oystering ports. Brunswick's **Old Town** is lined with restored turn-of-the-century homes.

To the north and east of Brunswick lie the **Marshes of Glynn.** Beneath the marshes' soft facade of cordgrass hides one of the most biologically productive environments on Earth, teeming with microscopic creatures, as well as crabs, shrimp, oysters, fish, alligators, and even bobcats. A short boardwalk at the marshes' **Overlook Park** *(Jct. of US 17 & Ga. 25)* provides a good vantage on marsh life.

Three of Georgia's barrier islands cluster together just east of Brunswick. **Little St. Simons** is accessible only by boat, but St. Simons and Sea Island are a quick jaunt across the marshes via the F. J. Torras Causeway. Before crossing, load up on information at the **Brunswick–Golden Isles Welcome Center** *(912-264-5337 or 800-933-2627).*

On oak-shaded **St. Simons Island,** you can explore **Fort Frederica National Monument** *(912-638-3639. www.nps.gov/fofr. Vehicle & adm. fees),* a fortified town built in the mid-1700s to protect against Spanish invasion; **St. Simons Lighthouse** and **Museum of Coastal History** *(101 12th St. 912-638-4666. www.saintsimonslighthouse.org. Tues.-Sun.; adm. fee);* and miles and miles of shell-strewn beaches.

Exclusive, manicured **Sea Island,** the next island over, boasts the **Cloister** *(912-638-3611. www.seaisland.com),* a Mediterranean-style resort dating from the 1920s, as well as Sea Island Drive, called Millionaires' Row.

Back on US 17 you drive through a mixed stretch of urban development, backwater towns, marshlands, and woodlands full of loblolly pines and moss-draped oaks. Ten miles ahead, at **Hofwyl-Broadfield Plantation State Historic Site** *(912-264-7333. www.gastateparks.org/info/hofwyl. Thurs.-Sat.; adm. fee),* rice fields crossed with dikes and floodgates testify to the area's rice culture that flourished along the coastline throughout the 1800s.

The drive continues across the mazelike flood delta of the **Altamaha River.** Part of the 27,078-acre **Altamaha State Waterfowl Management Area,** the delta attracts herons, egrets, ducks, and other birds.

As you cross **Butler Island,** look on the left for the white house and crumbling brick rice-mill chimneys of **Butler Island Plantation,** a former rice plantation that is now a private home. On the river's north bank is **Darien.** A quiet town founded as a military outpost in 1736, it has gained renown for its annual April blessing of the shrimp fleet. If you follow the road

Low-tide waders on Jekyll Island

immediately to the right, past the **Darien Welcome Center** *(912-437-4837. Closed Sun.)*, you'll come to **Fort King George State Historic Site** *(912-437-4770. www.gastateparks.org/fortkinggeorge. Tues.-Sun.; adm. fee)*. This site is a reconstruction of the British Empire's southernmost outpost, occupied by its troops from 1721 to 1736.

From Darien, US 17 continues through the same coastal-plain scenery. Or you can take Ga. 99 *(just north of McIntosh County Courthouse)*, a country road leading off to places like the **Thicket** *(5 miles north of Darien)*, with its ruins of a sugar mill and rum distillery, and the shrimping community of **Valona.**

Ga. 99 rejoins US 17 at Eulonia. Eight miles farther, another detour will take you to **Harris Neck National Wildlife Refuge** *(7 miles east on Ga. 131. 912-832-4608. www.fws.gov/harrisneck)*. As many as 30,000 wading birds congregate here in late summer and fall.

Back on US 17, the drive passes under I-95, and the scenery begins to fluctuate between interstate commercialism and timeworn towns like **Midway.** At the **Midway Museum** *(US 17. 912-884-5837. Tues.-Sat.; adm. fee)*, you'll find colonial furnishings and documents. Next door, the white clapboard **Midway Congregational Church** *(key available at museum)* has stood since Massachusetts Puritans built it in 1792.

The Marshes of Glynn stretch in a serene landscape of swaying cordgrass and mirror-smooth ponds.

The drive ends 30 miles farther in **Savannah.** With its open squares, live oaks, historic inns, and flowering gardens, this city embodies classic Southern charm. Along the restored **Savannah Riverfront,** visit the **Savannah History Museum** *(303 Martin Luther King Blvd. 912-651-6840. Adm. fee)* or tour the city's historic districts, dating from the 18th-century era of the cotton barons.

FLORIDA
Panhandle Scenic Drive

Pensacola to Panama City on US 98 and Florida 30A

- 103 miles - 3¹/₂ hours - All year

Never straying far from the Gulf of Mexico, the Panhandle Scenic Drive wanders by lucid blue-green waters and sugar white beaches, through live oak thickets and ubiquitous tourist strips.

The drive begins in **Pensacola**, best known for its nearby naval air station. The **Pensacola Historical Museum** *(115 E. Zaragossa St. 850-595-1559. www.historicpensacola.org. Tues.-Sat., call for schedule)* has exhibits that explain why this town has flown five different flags. A bit of the rural charm of the Old South can be found at bougainvillea-draped **Seville Square** *(Between E. Government & S. Alcaniz Sts.),* one of three historic districts.

Head east on Main Street (Bayfront Pkwy./US 98) past Pensacola Harbor. Here, **Pensacola Bay** will shimmer on your right, and the road soon crosses 3-mile-long **Pensacola Bay Bridge** to Gulf Breeze. As the road forks you can continue east on US 98, through the **Naval Live Oaks Area,** a trail-laced thicket of live oak trees that is part of the 150-mile-long **Gulf Islands National Seashore** *(1801 Gulf Breeze Pkwy./US 98. 850-934-2600. www.nps.gov/guis).*

Or you can pick up Fla. 399 to **Santa Rosa Island,** whose eastern end is known as Okaloosa Island. A barrier island that is also part of the national seashore, it offers unspoiled miles of live oaks, sea oats, and billowing sand dunes topped by miniature magnolias. The two roads reconvene in the town of **Navarre.** From here, neon-lit hotels, roller coasters, beach boardwalks, and condominiums line much of the rest of the way to Panama City, relieved only by a few undeveloped beaches.

Beach at Seaside

Beyond the town of Fort Walton Beach, US 98 returns to Santa Rosa Island, where a recreation area on **Choctawhatchee Bay** offers swimming and boating. The road cuts through a pretty stretch of pine-dotted dunes with Gulf vistas before crossing the mouth of the Choctawhatchee Bay and entering **Destin,** a town that is a well known destination for charter-fishing enthusiasts.

As you continue to head east through pine thickets and urban development, small side streets wander down to lovely sand beaches.

Sunset over the Gulf lowlands

Three miles west of Sandestin, you can detour onto Fla. 30A, a secondary road that angles 20 miles past lily-dotted lakes, pine thickets, and backwater towns. Highlights include **Grayton Beach State Recreation Area** (*850-267-8300. www.floridastateparks.org/graytonbeach. Vehicle fee*) and **Seaside,** a resort village with small pastel villas bordered by white picket fences.

About 9 miles beyond Seaside, Fla. 30A joins US 98 for the last brassy stretch to **Panama City,** known for its 27 miles of beaches.

147

Big Bend Scenic Byway

The Coastal and Forest Trails on US 98, Florida 267, 300, and 65, and local roads

■ 220 miles ■ 2 to 3 days ■ Spring and fall are ideal

Named for the crescent of Florida coastline where peninsula meets panhandle, this 220-mile-long scenic byway boasts bald cypress swamps, shimmering beaches, nine state parks, and a slow-paced, "Old Florida" feel not to be found in the Sunshine State's high-profile tourist destinations.

Practically speaking, the Big Bend Scenic Byway combines two distinct sections. The southern route, called the Coastal Trail, follows the Gulf of Mexico shoreline, while the more northerly Forest Trail travels inland, amid stands of slash pine, lazy blackwater rivers, and spring-fed sinkholes. Connect the two sections, and you have a leisurely two- or three-day drive.

A good starting point is the laid-back port town of **Apalachicola** (*Chamber of Commerce Visitor Center, 122 Commerce St. 850-653-9419. www.apalachicolabay.org*). Begin the day with a kayak tour on the Apalachicola Paddling Trail, a 100-mile waterway system; then, spend a leisurely afternoon admiring the town's hundreds of historic homes—many dating back to the 1830s—on a self-guided walking tour.

Heading east out of town along US 98, detour south on Fla. 300 and cross the bridge to St. George Island, a 28-mile-long barrier island. Join other sun worshipers on the unspoiled beaches of **St. George Island State Park** *(1900 E. Gulf Beach Dr. 850-927-2111. www.floridastateparks .org/stgeorgeisland)*. You can also rent a stand-up paddleboard or take a seashell-hunting boat tour from the folks at **Journeys** *(240 E. Third St. 850-927-3259. www.sgislandjourneys.com)*.

Back on the mainland, head east again on US 98 and continue toward **Carrabelle** *(http://carrabelle.org)*. Here, **Camp Gordon Johnston Museum** *(1001 Gray Ave. 850-697-8575. www.camp gordonjohnston.com)* houses artifacts recalling the countless soldiers and sailors who received amphibious assault training on nearby beaches during World War II. While there's no shortage of fishing charter operations in town, for something deliciously different consider spending a few hours in search of Apalachicola Bay's most famous delicacy with **Captain Don Davis's Oyster Charters** *(411 River Rd. 850-566-4177)*.

A docked sailboat in Apalachicola, FL

Continuing northeast, you'll find the town of **Panacea,** named for the supposedly curative spring waters that drew 19th-century visitors here by the thousands. Saltwater flora and fauna draw present-day visitors to the **Gulf Specimen Marine Lab and Aquarium** *(222 Clark Dr. 850-984-5297. www.gulfspecimen.org)*.

From Panacea, continue northeastward toward **St. Marks,** one of the oldest communities in Florida and gateway to the 68,000-acre **St. Marks National Wildlife Refuge,** established in 1931 as a winter habitat for migratory birds. While you're in the neighborhood, you'll want to follow Cty. Rd. 59 south for a visit to the historic 82-foot **St. Marks Lighthouse** *(Visitor Center, 1255 Lighthouse Rd. 850-925-6121. www.fws.gov/ saintmarks)*; built in 1832, it's the second oldest lighthouse—and one of the most picturesque—in Florida.

> Apalachicola National Forest is home to the largest population of Red-cockaded Woodpeckers, an endangered species unique to the southeastern United States.

From there, backtrack toward Newport. Civil War buffs will want to detour north on Fla. 363 toward Woodville, where signs indicate the way east to the **Natural Bridge Battlefield Historic Site** *(7502 Natural Bridge Rd. 850-922-6007. www.floridastateparks.org/naturalbridge)*. It was here that Confederate forces repelled Union attackers intent on capturing Tallahassee in the closing days of the war.

Return to Newport and turn northwest on Fla. 267. After a stop at the roadside tupelo honey stand for a taste of what singer-songwriter Van Morrison (a native of distant Northern Ireland) celebrated in his song of the same name, you'll be ready for the northern section of the Big Bend Scenic Byway known as the **Forest Trail.**

A don't-miss stop west along this pleasantly wooded route is **Edward Ball Wakulla Springs State Park** *(465 Wakulla Park Dr. 850-561-7276. www .floridastateparks.org/wakullasprings).* Set amid bald cypress swamps and pine forests, this one-time private estate holds one of the world's largest freshwater springs and makes a great place for a refreshing dip on a hot day.

Follow the tour route through the **Apalachicola National Forest** *(850-643-2282. www.fs.usda.gov/apalachicola).* Beyond it, past Tallahassee's outskirts, the road turns southwest to follow the shoreline of 14-mile-long **Lake Talquin.** Take time to get out and stretch your legs with a short hike at any of the trailheads you'll pass in the lake's namesake state park *(14850 Jack Vause Landing Rd. 850-922-6007. www.floridastateparks.org/laketalquin).*

Continue on and you'll end up in the turn-of-the-20th-century railroad town of Sopchoppy. Aside from its small-town charm, Sopchoppy's claim to fame is its **Worm Gruntin' Festival** *(www.wormgruntinfestival.com),* held annually in April, when contestants compete to lure earthworms (aka bait) to the surface by rubbing a piece of wood over a metal stake driven into the ground. Spring brings the town a profusion of blooming azaleas. At any time of year, you may want to rent a kayak to explore the **Sopchoppy River Paddling Trail** *(Wilderness Way. 850-877-7200. www.thewildernessway.net)* for a closer look at the region's untamed, cypress-filled swamps.

As you head south out of town, keep an eye peeled for the locally famous white squirrels. As you approach the coast, turn west on US 98 and then north on Fla. 65 to follow the Apalachicola River into the naturally diverse **Tate's Hell State Forest** *(850-697-3734. www.floridaforestservice.com/ state_forests/tates_hell.html)* to enjoy the final stretch of the Forest Trail.

A1A Scenic and Historic Coastal Byway

Ponte Vedra Beach to Flagler-Volusia county line on Florida A1A

- 72 miles - 2 hours - All year

Much of what makes Florida a favorite destination can be found right along the roadside on this Atlantic Coast drive: inviting beaches, warm water, golf courses, seafood, and recreation areas. Those who look closer will find historical sites and traces of the "old Florida": towns that predate the tourist boom.

Where the byway begins at Ponte Vedra Beach, golfers know the town as the headquarters of the PGA Tour, and the hub of dozens of world-class courses. The **World Golf Hall of Fame** *(1 World Golf Pl. 904-940-4123. www.wgv.com. Adm. fee)* is located just a few minutes south.

After passing through a bevy of golf courses, the byway enters 60,000-acre **Guana Tolomato Matanzas National Estuarine Research Reserve** *(904-823-4500.*

See p. 152

Castillo de San Marcos, St. Augustine

www.dep.state.fl.us/coastal/sites/gtm), a combined federal-state entity that protects salt marsh, oyster bars, estuarine lagoons, upland habitat, and ocean, and includes the northernmost mangroves on the East Coast.

The route crosses the **Tolomato River** (with a fine panorama from the bridge) to reach **St. Augustine** *(Convention & Visitors Bureau, 29 Old Mission Ave. 800-653-2489. www .floridashistoriccoast.com)*, the oldest continuously occupied community in the United States. This town lays claim to literally hundreds of significant structures and sites, including **Castillo de San Marcos National Monument** *(904-829-6506. www.nps .gov/casa. Adm. fee)*, a star-shaped masonry fort built by Spain in the late 17th century. The **Oldest House** complex *(271 Charlotte St. 904-824-2872. www.staugustinehistoricalsociety.org. Adm. fee)* includes a Spanish colonial house dating from the 1700s, two museums, an art gallery, and a garden, telling the story of four centuries of Florida.

A1A passes near two imposing Spanish Renaissance buildings: the former Ponce de Leon Hall, an 1887 grand hotel that's now Flagler College, and the former Hotel Alcazar, also from 1887 and now the **Lightner Museum** *(75 King St. 904-824-2874. www.lightnermuseum.org. Adm. fee)*, with 19th-century paintings, furnishings, art glass, and decorative objects.

Cross the Matanzas River on the 1927 **Bridge of Lions,** on the National Register of Historic Places. As you reach Anastasia Island, the 1876 **St. Augustine Lighthouse** *(904-829-0745. www.staugustinelighthouse.com. Adm. fee)* stands out with its black and white stripes. Visit the museum or climb the 219 steps to the top for a view of the old town. Adjacent **Anastasia State Park** *(904-461-2033. www.floridastateparks.org/anastasia. Adm. fee)* has miles of trails through hardwood hammocks. The byway continues south through beach communities to **Fort Matanzas National Monument** *(904-471-0116. www.nps.gov/foma)*, the remains of a Spanish fort completed in 1742.

Crossing Matanzas Inlet, you'll soon reach **Marineland** *(9600 Oceanshore Blvd. 904-471-1111 or 877-933-3402. www.marineland.net. Adm. fee)*. Built in the 1930s as the world's first oceanarium, it offers visitors close encounters with dolphins and other sea creatures. Nearby **River to Sea Preserve** *(386-313-4020. www.flaglerparks.com/riversea/preserve)* protects 90 acres of beach, oak woods, and marsh. Farther south, **Washington Oaks Gardens State Park** *(386-446-6780. www.floridastateparks.org/washingtonoaks. Adm. fee)* is known for its native and exotic plants. Passing through the towns of Beverly Beach and Flagler Beach, you'll see opportunities for beach access. The byway ends at **Gamble Rogers Memorial State Recreation Area** *(386-517-2086. www.floridastateparks.org/gamblerogers. Adm. fee)*, a 144-acre beach park with nesting sea turtles, a nature trail, and a boat launch for canoes and kayaks.

Florida Black Bear Scenic Byway

Ormond Beach to Silver Springs and Umatilla to Palatka, Florida, on Florida 40 and 19

■ 123 miles ■ 4 hours ■ October to April

Located a one-hour drive west of the Sunshine State's famous Atlantic beaches, the Black Bear Scenic Byway offers access to impossibly blue freshwater springs, secluded hiking and horseback trails, and long stretches that feel little changed from the late 1800s, when hardscrabble pioneers scratched out a living here.

From the outskirts of Ormond Beach, head inland on Fla. 40, the east–west leg of this cross-shaped byway, toward Barberville. Here you'll discover the **Pioneer Settlement for the Creative Arts** *(1776 Lightfoot Ln. 386-749-2959. www.pioneersettlement.org),* where you can get a feel for what life was like for those early settlers and the native Timucuan and Seminole peoples.

Continue west and you'll enter the Ocala National Forest as you cross the St. Johns River—the state's longest—at the small town of **Astor.** This is a good place to pick up the supplies (including insect repellent) you'll want when you discover some of the prime alfresco dining spots ahead.

Press on a few miles and you'll cross Fla. 19, which forms the north–south leg of this byway, before you come to the **Juniper Springs Recreation Area** *(26701 E. Hwy. 40. 352-625-3147. www.fs.usda.gov/florida. Adm. fee).* The park has hundreds of freshwater springs, including its namesake, a large pale-blue pool filled with crystal-clear 72-degree water that invites a plunge. To see one of the largest freshwater springs in the world, continue west on Fla. 40 to **Silver Springs Nature Park** *(5656 E. Silver Springs Blvd. 352-236-2121. www.silversprings.com),* where you can take one of the glass-bottom boat tours that have been luring visitors here since the 1870s. This long-time tourist attraction also features wild animals on exhibit, including a "lucky" white alligator, and all the usual theme park trappings.

Backtrack on Fla. 40 toward its intersection with Fla. 19. Head north on Fla. 19 eight miles to the shores of **Lake George,** the second largest lake in Florida, where you'll also find **Silver Glen Springs** *(5271 N. Hwy. 19. 352-685-2799),* another beautiful blue-green natural swimming hole.

Continuing north on Fla. 19 for 11.5 miles toward Palatka, you'll reach the **Salt Springs Recreation Area,** which takes its name from the trace salinity the water picks up as it courses upward through

151

Silver Springs Nature Park, Ocala, FL

underground salt deposits. For an unusual experience, turn east on Forest Service Road (FR) 43 (unpaved, but passable in good weather) to reach the **Ft. Gates Ferry** *(386-467-2411. Wed.-Mon., 7 a.m.-5:30 p.m.),* a tiny two-car transporter that's been giving travelers a lift across this placid stretch of the St. Johns River for more than 150 years.

While you're exploring the southern stretch of the byway on Fla. 19, take Cty. Rd. 445 (about eight miles south of Fla. 40) east to get to **Alexander Springs,** located within Ocala National Forest. With the largest output of any spring on federal land (the swimming area is more than an acre in size), this natural spring also features a sandy beach that slopes gently into the water, making it especially family friendly.

This north–south section of the byway also offers several opportunities to explore Ocala National Forest. North of Fla. 40 on FR-10, across Fla. 19 from the entrance to Silver Glen Springs, you'll find the trailhead for the 5.5-mile **Yearling Trail,** which leads hikers to the old homestead of the early settlers whose story inspired *The Yearling,* a classic book and film about a young boy who adopts an abandoned fawn.

If hiking is not your thing, **ATV Off-Road Adventure Tours** *(352-546-5514. www.atvoffroadadventuretours.com)* offers small-group outings during which you might encounter a variety of local wildlife species, including the black bears that give the byway its name. If you prefer four legs to four wheels, **Fiddler's Green Ranch** *(42725 W. Altoona Rd., Altoona. 352-669-7111. www.fiddlersgreenranch.com),* on the southern leg of Fla. 19 just south of Lake Dorr, offers one- and two-hour horseback rides on forest trails north of Umatilla.

Ormond Scenic Loop and Trail

Flagler Beach to Ormond Beach, Florida, via Florida A1A and local roads

■ 36 miles ■ 1 hour ■ All year

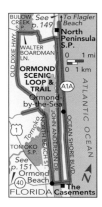

Start your exploration of the short Ormond Scenic Loop and Trail along Fla. A1A just south of the town of Flagler Beach. On the Atlantic shores of **North Peninsula State Park** *(386-517-2086. www.floridastateparks.org/northpeninsula),* about 3.5 miles south of Flagler Beach, you can surf, hunt for seashells, or plan your drive along the figure-eight-shaped byway.

Follow A1A south toward Ormond-by-the-Sea and Ormond Beach as it leaves the park and turns into Ocean Shores Boulevard. The firm white sands around Ormond Beach, 5.5 miles south of the state park, once hosted car races that resulted in more than a dozen world land speed records.

Turn west at Ormond Beach onto Granada Boulevard for a tour of the 9,000-square-foot mansion known as **The Casements** *(25 Riverside Dr. 386-676-3216. www.thecasements.net. Closed Sun.).* Located on the shores of the Halifax River (part of the Intracoastal Waterway), this grand house was the winter digs in the 1920s and '30s of oil baron John D. Rockefeller, who was known simply as "Neighbor John" at weekly sing-alongs in the lobby of the Ormond Hotel.

Walk along the adjacent Granada Street Bridge for broad views of the Intracoastal Waterway. Or just continue driving, heading north about ten miles on John Anderson Drive from the Casements until the pavement dead-ends at High Bridge Road.

Turn west and cross the Halifax River on the drawbridge that gives the road its name. Turn left onto Walter Boardman Lane and then left onto Old Dixie Highway—on your left you'll soon reach 5,600-acre **Bulow Creek State Park** *(3351 Old Dixie Hwy. 386-676-4050. www.floridastateparks .org/bulowcreek)*, where you can lay out a picnic spread beneath the 400-year-old Fairchild Oak.

Next, follow Old Dixie Highway south about six miles through **Tomoka State Park** *(2099 N. Beach St. 386-676-4050. www.florida stateparks.org/tomoka)*. A half-mile nature trail yields views of ospreys flying above the slow-moving Tomoka River, which can also be explored in canoes rented at the park's store.

From here, the route continues south about three miles along North Beach Street to the end of the byway at the Granada Boulevard bridge in Ormond Beach.

The original cupola of Ormond Beach's Ormond Hotel

153

Indian River Lagoon Scenic Highway

Loop from Titusville in the north to Sebastian in the south on US 1 and Florida A1A, 3, 402, and 520, and County Routes 405 and 510

- 150 miles ■ 2 days ■ All year. Summers are very hot and attractions are more crowded in winter.

Indian River Lagoon is a long, narrow series of estu-aries (coastal bodies of water where fresh- and salt-water meet) between Florida's central Atlantic Coast mainland and bordering barrier islands. Biologists say it has the highest diversity of any estuary in the country, providing a home for manatees, sea turtles, dolphins, oysters, clams, shrimp, crabs, and hundreds of species of birds and fish.

Indian River Lagoon Scenic Highway offers trav-elers several ways to experience this abundance of wildlife, especially at national wildlife refuges and state and local parks. Beach lovers, bird-watchers, and anglers will find nearly limitless opportunities here.

The most famous attraction, though, is the Ken-nedy Space Center at Cape Canaveral, where U.S. space shuttles were launched into orbit.

Great egrets, North Fork Saint Lucie River

At the north end of the drive, **Merritt Island National Wildlife Refuge** *(321-861-0667. www.fws.gov/merrittisland)* ranks high among Florida's best wildlife-viewing areas. Birders enjoy waterbirds, bald eagles, ospreys, and endangered Florida scrub-jays; manatees are regularly seen at the designated viewing area on Fla. 3. Stop at the **visitor center** on Fla. 402 to learn about the refuge's four hiking trails and the 7-mile wildlife auto tour.

Continuing east on Fla. 402 will take you to an Atlantic Ocean barrier island and **Canaveral National Seashore** *(321-267-1110. www.nps.gov/cana. Adm. fee),* which offers visitors great beaches (with seasonal lifeguards), kayaking, and guided sea-turtle walks.

Take Fla. 406 westward across Indian River Lagoon to the mainland, drive south 6 miles on US 1, and take Cty. Rd. 405 to the **Kennedy Space Center Visitor Complex** *(866-737-5235. www.kennedyspacecenter.com. Adm. fee)* where you can see the **Astronaut Hall of Fame,** watch giant-screen space films, take a ride in an interactive flight simulator, meet an astronaut, see launch pads and the **Vehicle Assembly Building,** and walk through the **Rocket Garden** display of historic space vehicles.

Continue on Fla. 3 south and Fla. A1A east across the Banana River to the town of Cape Canaveral, where you'll pass a major cruise-ship port. Heading south to Cocoa Beach, you can't miss a retail establishment that's become a tourist attraction in its own right: **Ron Jon Surf Shop** *(4151 N. Atlantic Ave. 321-799-8888. www.ronjons.com)* gets more than two million visitors a year, shopping for surfboards, dive gear, and beach clothes.

A1A passes through intensive residential development on a narrow spit of land before passing Patrick Air Force Base. Then it's more of the same, with the highway only a block from the beach, lined with houses, condominiums, and hotels. Eventually you reach **Sebastian Inlet State Park** *(321-984-4852. www.floridastateparks.org/sebastianinlet. Adm. fee),* famed for saltwater fishing (snook, redfish, bluefish, and Spanish mackerel), swimming, and surfing. Manatees and dolphins can be seen offshore, and in June and July rangers lead walks to see nesting loggerhead sea turtles. Within the park, **McLarty Treasure Museum** tells the story of the ill-fated 1715 Spanish treasure fleet (11 galleons sank along the Florida coast), and the **Sebastian Fishing Museum** recounts the history of the local fishing industry.

South across Sebastian Inlet, **Pelican Island National Wildlife Refuge** *(772-469-4275. www.fws.gov/pelicanisland),* America's first refuge set aside to protect nesting birds, is home to brown pelican, wood stork, anhinga, American oystercatcher, and various herons and egrets. Trails and observation towers allow viewing, and local operators offer boat tours *(fee).* To continue the route, take Cty. Rd. 510 west toward the mainland.

At the foot of the bridge, stop to visit the **Environmental Learning Center** *(255 Live Oak Dr. 772-589-5050. www.discoverelc.org.),* where you can walk trails, visit a butterfly garden, and experience the Indian River Lagoon's upland hammocks, mangroves, and marsh.

The drive heads north on US 1 on the west side of the lagoon, mostly through residential areas. In Palm Bay, **Lagoon House** *(3275 US 1. 321-952-3443. www.palmbayflorida.org/parks/city_parks/)* serves as an information center for the region and the scenic highway.

In Melbourne, the **Brevard Zoo** *(8225 N. Wickham Rd. 321-254-9453. www.brevardzoo.org. Adm. fee)* is home to more than 550 animals representing 165 different species. It offers guided kayak trips and scheduled feedings of alligators, crocodiles, and otters. Its **Wild Florida area** houses deer, red wolves, bobcats, and other regional species.

Southern Everglades

Ernest F. Coe Visitor Center to Flamingo on main park road

■ 38 miles ■ 1 hour ■ All year. Dry winter months preferable for sighting animals and for relatively fewer mosquitoes, but insect repellent and long clothing advised year-round. Bird-watching is best at dawn and dusk.

A slow-moving, freshwater river measuring 50 miles wide and 6 inches to 2 feet deep, the Everglades crawls seaward through a horizon-wide landscape of pale green saw grass. The only place on Earth where such a vast wetland exists, this is one of the best wildlife-viewing areas in the country.

The drive begins at the entrance gate to 1.5-million-acre **Everglades National Park** *(305-242-7700. www.nps .gov/ever. Adm. fee).* Established in 1947, it now ranks as the third largest park in the contiguous United States. Just inside the entrance, the **Ernest F. Coe Visitor Center** offers park information, exhibits, and films on the natural history of the area. Heading southwest, the flat road arrows through the endless river of grass, where regal egrets poise stone still to catch fish, and black-and-white anhingas perch in trees with their great wings spread out to dry.

After crossing over marshy **Taylor Slough**, one of many drainages in the Everglades, detour 2 miles to **Royal Palm Visitor Center** *(305-242-7700),* which is named for the palms that dominate the area. Here you'll find two trails that, despite their proximity, couldn't be more different. The half-mile-long **Anhinga Trail** wanders on boardwalks over Taylor Slough, promising glimpses of turtles, garfish, and an American alligator or two. Nearby is the **Gumbo Limbo Trail.** Also a half mile long, it leads through one of the Everglades' many hardwood hammocks. Raised just a few feet in elevation, the hammock provides a dry environment for a luxuriant forest of gumbo-limbo, strangler fig, poisonwood, and other tropical trees.

Back on the road, you'll soon notice slash pines dotting the saw-grass prairie. Once covering much of southern Florida's higher, drier ground, the vast pine forests have been lost to loggers. But you can detour 1.7 miles

Tamiami Trail

Miami to Naples on US 41

▪ 50 miles ▪ 3 hours ▪ All year

The Tamiami Trail cuts through the heart of the Everglades. (It got its name because it connects Tampa and Miami.) Alligators, bald eagles, snail kites, and wading birds will be your companions.

Soon after leaving Miami, US 41 reaches the northern border of **Everglades National Park** *(305-242-7700. www.nps.gov/ever. Adm. fee)*, protecting part of the famed "river of grass" that includes saw-grass prairie, marsh, and swamps. At **Shark Valley**, a 15-mile loop into the marsh is accessible only by ranger-led tram ride *(305-221-8776. Fare)*, on bicycle, or on foot.

On the north side of the highway at the **Miccosukee Indian Village** *(305-552-8365. www.miccosukee.com/indian_village)*, a museum and activities show visitors the tribe's traditional way of life.

Shortly afterward, the byway enters **Big Cypress National Preserve** *(239-695-1201. www.nps.gov/bicy)*, which protects forest and wetlands that supply freshwater for estuaries on the Gulf Coast. Wood storks, black bears, and endangered Florida panthers live here. Driving the Loop Road, a 26-mile route south of US 41, is a more intimate preserve experience. Check road conditions at the visitor center on US 41 before proceeding.

After passing Ochopee, you'll reach **Fakahatchee Strand Preserve State Park** *(239-695-4593. www.floridastateparks.org/fakahatcheestrand)*, known for its diversity of tropical plants. The "Amazon of North America," Fakahatchee boasts impressive wildlife, too.

Slash pines and palmettos

to **Long Pine Key,** an island of pines, saw palmettos, and hardwood hammocks, where a 7-mile network of trails weave beneath the tall, skinny trees. Or take the half-mile loop in **Pinelands,** farther up the road, where interpretive signs explain the pines' dependence on fire. Without fire, hardwoods would shade out the more fire-resistant pines and predominate.

Soon you reach **Rock Reef Pass,** a 3-foot-high limestone ridge that is one of the highest spots in the southern Everglades. Beyond it you'll spot a forest of dwarf cypress, a variety of bald cypress stunted by the area's poor soil. A half mile farther on at **Pa-hay-okee Overlook** (pa-hay-okee is a Native American term meaning "grassy waters"), a boardwalk provides a popular perch from which to study wildlife; an observation tower offers a perspective on the vastness of the swaying saw grass, which covers nearly 8 million acres.

From here, the road turns due south to **Mahogany Hammock,** where a boardwalk penetrates a cluster of mahogany trees that includes the largest living mahogany in the country. As you near the coast, saltwater mixes with the Everglades' freshwater, and salt-tolerant mangroves replace the saw grass, palms, and mahoganies. The mangrove-filled estuaries produce a nutrient-rich soup, the food base for a vast variety of marine life.

The best way to travel the tangled, mangrove wilderness is by canoe, and several access points are found along the roadside between here and Flamingo. Along the way, too, are ponds that attract majestic wading birds in winter. Good places to watch for egrets, roseate spoonbills, ibis, and herons are brackish **Nine Mile Pond, West Lake** (which has a boardwalk trail leading through mangroves), **Mrazek Pond,** and **Coot Bay Pond.**

The road dead-ends in **Flamingo** on **Florida Bay.** Settled in the late 1800s, this small community is now the southern hub of the park. It has a **visitor center** *(239-695-2945),* ranger station, motel, restaurant, and marina *(lodge, cabins, restaurant, & boat tours to Florida Bay closed due to hurricanes; canoe & small motorboat rentals available; Thurs.-Mon. pelican backcountry boat tour; fare).* If you haven't spotted a roseate spoonbill on your way through the park, stop at lovely **Eco Pond**, just past the motel on the main park road.

Florida Keys

Florida City to Key West on US 1

▪ 126 miles ▪ ½ day ▪ Fall to spring. Summers can be hot, bug-ridden, and subject to thunderstorms. The crowded tourist season runs from October through March.

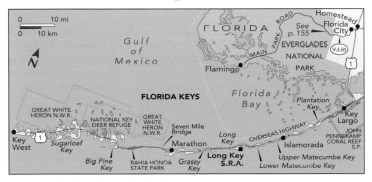

Mangrove-fringed and waterbound, the Overseas Highway (US 1) links a chain of subtropical isles that arc off the tip of Florida. Delving ever deeper into a tropical terrain, the route reveals a land of hammocks and reefs, miniature deer, and, at last, the fanciful, idiosyncratic town of Key West.

The drive begins a mile below Florida City on the mainland, where mile marker 126 starts counting down the miles to Key West. Following the former roadbeds and bridges of the Florida East Coast Railway, which was completed from the mainland to Key West in 1912, the highway shoots across the southern edge of the Everglades.

Southernmost house, Key West

A mile beyond **Lake Surprise,** named by early railroad explorers who weren't expecting to find it, the highway enters **Key Largo,** the largest and northernmost Key along US 1. Bustling with activity, Key Largo contains all aspects of the Keys, from their tropical vegetation and opalescent waters to their billboards, dive shops, great food choices, and mom-and-pop motels.

At **John Pennekamp Coral Reef State Park** *(mile 102.5. 305-451-1202. www .floridastateparks.org/pennekamp. Adm. fee),* the first underwater state park in the United States, you can take snorkeling, diving, or glass-bottomed boats out to the lacy coral reef that parallels the Keys' Atlantic shoreline from here all the way to the Dry Tortugas.

Continuing through **Plantation Key,** where pineapple and banana plantations flourished at the turn of the 20th century, US 1 crosses **Snake Creek** on one of the 42 bridges that connect the Keys. At Windley Key the **Theater of the Sea** *(mile 84.5. 305-664-2431. www.theaterofthe sea.com. Adm. fee)* features sea lions, sharks, and dolphins.

Islamorada (Spanish for "purple isle"), the only settlement on Upper Matecumbe Key, marks the beginning of the Middle Keys. The island's **Hurricane Memorial** *(mile 82)* honors victims of the Labor Day hurricane in 1935, which washed out much of the railroad and was one of the most powerful ever in the United States.

Two sites can be visited off Lower Matecumbe Key. **Lignumvitae Key State Botanical Site** *(Accessible via boat tours from Robbie's Marina. 305-664-2540. www.floridastateparks.org/lignumvitaekey. Thurs.-Mon.; fee),* an uninhabited

Little Palm Key

280-acre island, contains a rare virgin tropical forest that includes gumbo-limbo, pigeon plum, poisonwood, and the namesake lignumvitae. At the **Indian Key State Historic Site** *(305-664-2540. www.florida stateparks.org/indian key. Accessible by boat, kayak, & canoe),* the foundations of structures from an 1830s village, established to salvage ships grounded on the reef, are visible amid the tropical undergrowth.

At the **Long Key State Recreation Area** *(mile 67.5. 305-664-4815. www.florida stateparks.org/longkey. Adm. fee),* swimming is poor, but beachcombers may find the rubbery egg cases left by sea turtles. The **Golden Orb Trail** here leads through a delightful mangrove-edged lagoon.

The **Long Key Viaduct** sweeps toward tiny **Conch Key,** then US 1 angles across **Grassy Key** and into **Marathon,** the heavily developed commercial center of the Middle Keys. Amid the sprawl is **Crane Point Hammock,** where you'll find a thatch-palm hammock with the combined **Crane Point Museum and Nature Center** *(mile 50. 305-743-9100. www.cranepoint.net. Adm. fee).*

South of Marathon, US 1 crosses **Seven Mile Bridge.** One of the world's longest bridges, it offers sweeping views of the open Atlantic on the left and the Gulf of Mexico to the right. On the other side of the bridge, **Bahia Honda State Park** *(mile 37. 305-872-2353. www.floridastateparks.org/bahia honda. Adm. fee)* has white-sand beaches, rare in the keys. Satinwood, key spider lily, and other West Indian plants can be found along the **Silver Palm Trail.**

As the road pushes southwest, the Keys seem more isolated and less populated. Bridges become shorter, and islands begin to merge. Eagles, falcons, and red-tailed hawks like this area, and it's not uncommon to see a large osprey nest perched atop a telephone pole.

Big Pine Key, unusual for its large slash pines, is the only place in the world where endangered Key deer live. Standing only 2.5 feet tall, the dainty subspecies of the Virginia white-tailed deer might be spotted if you take a 2.5-mile detour onto Key Deer Boulevard through the **National Key Deer Refuge** *(305-872-2239. www.fws.gov/nationalkeydeer).*

For its final 30 miles, US 1 crosses one small tropical key after another until it reaches **Key West,** an eccentric tropical town whose atmosphere is more Caribbean than American. Here, you can poke through the shops on **Duval Street;** see the southernmost point and the southernmost house at 1400 Duval St. *(private)* in the continental United States; wander streets lined with fine Victorian homes and quaint white-frame "conch" cottages; visit the **Ernest Hemingway Home and Museum** *(907 Whitehead St. 305-294-1136. www.hemingway home.com. Adm. fee);* or simply soak up the town's distinctive ambience.

> Long a gathering place for writers, entertainers, and other members of the glitterati, Key West also boasts the country's largest historic district.

159

Sunset fishing in the Florida Keys

Whitefish Bay
Scenic Byway
p. 164

Cherry Orchards
Drive
p. 166

River Road
Scenic Byway
p. 168

Pierce
Stocking
Scenic
Drive
p. 167

Lake Huron

CANADA

MICHIGAN

Grand Rapids

Flint

Lansing

Detroit

Woodward
Avenue
p. 169

Lake Erie
Coastal
Ohio Trail
p. 169

Buffalo

Lake Erie

Erie

N.Y.

Cleveland

Toledo

Akron

Amish Culture
Crafts Route
p. 178

Fort Wayne

Amish Country
Byway
p. 172

Ohio and
Erie Canalway
p. 171

PA.

Pittsburgh

Historic
National
Road
p. 174

OHIO

INDIANA

Indianapolis

Dayton

Columbus

Covered Bridge
Scenic Byway
p. 173

Indiana's Historic
Pathways
p. 183

Cincinnati

Ohio River
Scenic Byway
p. 180

Ohio

WEST
VIRGINIA

Charleston

Louisville

Frankfort

Lexington

Lincoln Hills
Scenic Drive
p. 179

KENTUCKY

VIRGINIA

MICHIGAN
Copper Country Trail

Houghton to Copper Harbor on US 41

■ 47 miles ■ 6 hours ■ Summer through early fall.
Though US 41 is plowed throughout winter, many
attractions close from late fall through spring.

Michigan's Keweenaw Peninsula curves into Lake Superior at the state's
northernmost point. American Indians knew of copper's presence here
and used it for tools and trade. In the mid-19th century, the world's largest
copper deposit brought thousands of Irish, German, English, Scandinavian,
and Italian immigrants to work in the mines. From the 1840s to the 1960s,
more than 11 billion pounds were extracted.

163

The trail begins at the **Portage Lake Lift Bridge,** the world's widest and
heaviest double-deck lift bridge, providing 100 feet of clearance for ships.
It connects the towns of Houghton and Hancock via a canal dredged across
the peninsula in the 19th century.

Preserving and interpreting the legacy of the area, **Keweenaw National
Historical Park** *(906-337-
3168. www.nps.gov/kewe)*
administers a range of
facilities. In addition, the
park has public and pri-
vate partners known as
Keweenaw Heritage Sites.
The **Quincy Unit** *(906-482-
3101)* of the park, on US
41 in Hancock, includes
mine shafts, hoist houses,

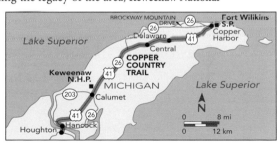

and a copper-smelting complex *(not all open to public).* The **Quincy Mine
Hoist Association** *(906-482-3101. www.quincymine.com. Limited hours fall-
spring. Fee for tours)* has a museum and offers tours of mine shafts.

Eleven miles north, in Calumet, the park's **Calumet Unit** *(25970 Red Jacket
Rd. 906-337-3168)* concentrates on copper heritage in the communities,
commerce, and lifestyles of the era. Heritage sites include the 1889 **Calumet
Theatre** *(340 6th St. 906-337-2610. www.calumettheatre.com. June-Aug.; adm.
fee)* and the **Coppertown Mining Museum** *(25815 Red Jacket Rd. 906-337-4354.
www.uppermichigan.com/coppertown. Adm. fee),* interpreting the history of

Palisade Head overlooking Lake Superior, North Shore Scenic Drive, Minnesota the Calumet & Hecla copper-mining firm. In the town of **Central,** note the miners' houses and the Methodist Episcopal church. At the **Delaware Mine** *(7804 Delaware Mine Rd. 906-289-4688. www.delawarecopperminetours.com. May-Oct.; fee for tours)* you can descend 110 feet to see copper veins.

At the tip of the peninsula, **Fort Wilkins State Park** *(906-289-4215. www .michigandnr.com/parksandtrails)* preserves several military-post buildings dating to the 1840s. Exhibits interpret frontier life, and you can take a boat tour to the nearby 1866 **Copper Harbor Lighthouse** *(906-289-4966. www .copperharborlighthouse.com. May-Oct.; fare).*

Take Mich. 26 west of Copper Harbor to reach **Brockway Mountain Drive,** a 9-mile byway atop Brockway Mountain. Constructed in the 1930s, it offers views of Lake Superior and the Keweenaw Peninsula shore.

Whitefish Bay Scenic Byway

Brimley to Whitefish Point on Lakeshore Drive, Curley Lewis Road, Michigan 123, and Whitefish Point Road

■ 54 miles ■ 2 hours ■ Spring through fall

Tracing the shoreline of Lake Superior's Whitefish Bay, this lonely byway on Michigan's Upper Peninsula delves deep into the North Woods, where the air is fresh and wildflowers and white birch trees abound. Leaving **Brimley,** a commercial fishing and agricultural community, the drive enters pristine hardwood forest—mainly birch, maple, and oak, scattered with pine. Watch for black bears and, more likely, white-tailed deer. Periodically, St. Marys River appears to the right through the trees.

The drive passes through the community of **Bay Mills,** within the Bay Mills Indian Reservation, and arcs around placid South Pond. Just beyond town, look for Tower Road on the left. This 1-mile, partly paved detour leads

to **Spectacle Lake Overlook.** And what a sight: glimmering Spectacle Lake, St. Marys River, and the distant Canadian shore.

Back on the road, the drive enters **Hiawatha National Forest** *(906-428-5800. www.fs.usda.gov/hiawatha),* an 894,654-acre preserve named after Longfellow's poem. A shady, mile-long side road about a mile ahead takes you to secluded **Monocle Lake.** The drive continues through the woods, framed by a constant profusion of wildflowers: white trilliums in spring, bunchberries and gaywings in summer, and blue asters and chickories in fall. A mile beyond the lake, **Point Iroquois Light Station** *(12942 W. Lakeshore Dr. 906-437-5272. Mid-May–mid-Oct.; donation)* comes into view. For 107 years, the light guided ships through the channel between shallow Point Iroquois and the rocky shore of Canada's Gros Cap. You can climb to the top of the 65-foot tower to view the headwaters of St. Marys River—the only passage between Lake Superior and the other Great Lakes. Down below, two rooms of a keeper's residence are preserved, and a small museum explains the light's history.

The road continues west through the town of **Dollar Settlement,** and a mile beyond, **Big Pines Picnic Area** offers a choice spot along a section of **Whitefish Bay's** 19 miles of accessible beach. The white sand is lovely, but **Lake Superior**—coldest of the Great Lakes—seldom warms to 60°F.

The road reenters the forest, now dominated by white birches. At **Pendills Creek National Fish Hatchery** *(21990 W. Trout Ln. 906-437-5231. www.fws.gov/midwest/pendillscreek. Closed weekends),* 3 miles beyond the picnic area, lake trout are raised to restock

Whitefish Point Lighthouse, Lake Superior

the Great Lakes. A half mile farther is **Salt Point** turnout, where the bay's turquoise waters lap against a gorgeous stretch of sandy beach. On calm days you can see the ribs of a sunken salt barge that washed ashore during a storm.

Farther west, occasional waysides permit closer inspection of the bay. The road then climbs away from the shoreline along the base of Naomikong Point, then returns to the bay. Near Naomikong Creek the **North Country National Scenic Trail** *(www.nps.gov/noco)* crosses the road, then follows it for about 4 miles. (When completed, the trail will extend from New York to North Dakota.) About 5.5 miles beyond, the drive leaves the water through a pretty stretch of trees to the junction with Mich. 123.

As you veer north on Mich. 123, the drive is straighter, faster, and edged with development. Beelining back to the bay's western shore, it crosses over the marshy, cattail-filled mouth of the **Tahquamenon River** beyond the fishing hamlet of **Emerson,** once a wild lumbering town. A picnic area here overlooks the river's confluence with Whitefish Bay.

The drive continues through stands of pine, cedar, birch, and maple, crossing Black Creek, passing through the village of Clarks, then to the resort town of **Paradise.** A 10-mile detour west on Mich. 123 leads to **Tahquamenon Falls State Park** *(906-492-3415. www.michigandnr.com/parksandtrails. Vehicle fee),* which boasts one of the largest falls east of the Mississippi.

Continue the drive north on Whitefish Point Road, along the bay's northwestern shore. The road is a bit cluttered with vacation cabins, but stretches of forest and water views remain pristine. About 10.5 miles north of Paradise, the road becomes twisty, and soon **Whitefish Point Lighthouse** peeks through the trees. Believed to be the oldest active lighthouse on Lake Superior, dating from 1849, the steel light replaced a brick tower in 1861. Fateful lake journeys are detailed at the **Great Lakes Shipwreck Museum** *(18335 N. Whitefish Point Rd. 906-635-1742. www.shipwreckmuseum.com. May–late-Oct.; adm. fee).* The nearby **Whitefish Point Bird Observatory** *(16914 N. Whitefish Point Rd. 906-492-3596. www.wpbo.org. Mid-April–mid-Oct.),* only a few miles from the Canadian shore, is an excellent place to view hawks, waterfowl, and songbirds on their spring and fall migrations.

Cherry Orchards Drive

Cross Village to Traverse City on Michigan 119 and US 31

▪ 96 miles ▪ 3 hours (plus 36 miles and 1 hour for round-trip to Old Mission Peninsula) ▪ Spring through fall

Prolific cherry trees, handsome summer resort towns, stunning fall foliage, and Lake Michigan vistas highlight this eastern lakeshore drive—a route used by Native Americans, fur traders, and Jesuit missionaries.

From **Cross Village**, a historical center of Catholic missionary work, Mich. 119 begins a lovely 27-mile drive through oaks, maples, birches, and cedars, along an old Ottawa Indian trail sprinkled with secluded summer dwellings. It traces a hump of Michigan's rugged shoreline through an area known as *l'arbre croche*—the crooked tree, named by early voyageurs who used a lone gnarled fir on the lakeshore as a landmark. Only sometimes can you catch glimmers of **Lake Michigan** through the trees, but the dense foliage lends beauty to the winding road. Scattered pullouts permit longer looks at the lake.

You know you're nearing **Harbor Springs** when the road passes a golf course and opulent houses. The small downtown is a pleasant cluster of boutiques, ice-cream parlors, and fine restaurants. Nearby **Thorne Swift Nature Preserve** *(Lower Shore Dr. 231-526-6401. www.landtrust.org/Nature Preserves/ThorneSwiftInfo.htm. Mem. Day–Labor Day, May & Sept. weekends; vehicle fee)* offers a sampling of pre-resort Michigan, with dunes, wetlands, and woods of birch, cedar, balsam, willow, and quaking aspen. Mich. 119 wends southeast around Little Traverse Bay (you can't see it) and past **Petoskey State Park** *(231-347-2311. May-Oct.; vehicle fee).* About 1.5 miles farther south, the road ends, and the drive continues west on US 31, past a fast-food stretch, to **Bay View.** Perched atop limestone bluffs overlooking **Little Traverse Bay,** the charming town was founded by Methodists in 1876 as a summer retreat. Leafy, winding streets harbor more than 500 Victorian "cottages" decorated with ornamental cornices and high gables.

On Petoskey's beach, look for Petoskey stones— 300-million-year-old coral fossils.

Among early vacationers to **Petoskey,** west of Bay View, was Ernest Hemingway, who spent 20 summers in a nearby cottage and set many of his stories in the area. An exhibit at the **Little Traverse History Museum** *(100 Depot Ct. 231-347-2620. May–late Sept. Mon.-Sat.; donation)* honors him. Try to catch one of the famous sunsets from **Sunset Park Scenic Overlook,** down by the waterfront. Beyond Petoskey, US 31 follows the shoreline of Little Traverse Bay, then veers south where the coast dips into **Grand Traverse Bay.** A scattered forest of birch and pine fringes the highway, and in spring wildflowers carpet the roadside meadows. An **M-DOT Roadside Park,** 9.5 miles west of town, has a lovely picnic spot on a sandy cove, one of many along the lakeshore.

When you see the tip of **Lake Charlevoix** through the trees to the left, you'll know **Charlevoix** is only a mile or so ahead. Straddling a strip of land between Lake Michigan and Lake Charlevoix (the third largest inland lake in the state), the resort community—with its boutiques, restaurants, yacht-dotted harbor, and bluff-top cottages—has been luring wealthy families for six generations. You can catch a 2.25-hour ferry ride to **Beaver Island** *(Beaver Island Boat Co. 103 Bridge Park Dr. 231-547-2311. www.bibco.com. Limited hours April–Dec., full-time May–Sept.; fare)*, the largest in a group of islands in the northern part of Lake Michigan, inhabited by Mormons in the mid-1800s. You'll find sandy beaches, hiking trails, and the **Marine Museum** *(Main St. 231-448-2476. Mem. Day–Labor Day, by appt. rest of year; donation)*.

As US 31 continues south, the woods give way to rolling farmland. Every now and then, the road crests a high hill, providing panoramas of shimmering Grand Traverse Bay to the west, with the forested hills of the Leelanau Peninsula beyond. Just before **Atwood**, you begin to see rows and rows of cherry trees. Temperate weather from the nearby lake and deep alluvial soil help this region produce more than 100 million pounds of cherries a year. The trees blossom beautifully but only briefly in spring; in summer you can sample the harvest from a roadside stand.

Just north of the town of **Torch Lake**, look for **Barnes County Park**, located west on Barnes Park Road. Here you'll find a secluded beach on Grand Traverse Bay. You can get a close-up view of Torch Lake—a spring-fed lake once fished at night by Native Americans with torches—by detouring east from US 31 onto Barnes Road, about 3 miles south of town. Ranging from pale aqua to deep violet, the lake is part of a chain of lakes created when glacial meltwater filled in the valleys. From here, veer right on West Torch Lake Drive, and follow it to Campbell Road, which takes you back to US 31.

Back on US 31, an **M-DOT Roadside Park** just 2.5 miles south offers a picnic spot next to serene **Birch Lake.** The road continues for 12 miles past

Pierce Stocking Scenic Drive

Loop Road off Michigan 109

■ 7 miles ■ ¹/₂ hour ■ Closed mid-November through April. See map p. 166.

Winding atop sand dunes with views of Lake Michigan, the Pierce Stocking Scenic Drive is an interpretive (and often crowded) drive. The centerpiece is **Sleeping Bear Dunes**, a 4-square-mile expanse of sand between **Glen Lake** and **Lake Michigan.** Created about 10,000 years ago, the dunes are the sand-covered remains of hills and ridges left behind when sheets of glacial ice melted. Some are as high as 500 feet. Trees and beach grass have since grown to stabilize them.

Plaques at the drive's 12 overlooks and pullouts describe the region's ecology. Highlights include views of Glen Lake and the Cottonwood Trail, a 1.5-mile loop through the dunes with a first-hand look at "ghost" forests—clusters of trees buried by sand for a century or more, then uncovered by wind.

Pierce Stocking, a lumberman awed by the beauty of the dunes, in the 1960s built the road in order to share them with visitors. Today, the drive is part of **Sleeping Bear Dunes National Lakeshore** *(www.nps.gov/slbe)*. Driving tour maps and other information are available in Empire at the **visitor center** *(9922 Front St./Mich. 72. 231-326-5134)*.

Sleeping Bear Dunes National Lakeshore

167

Sailing on Little Traverse Bay

more cherry orchards and farmland, through the former lumber towns of **Elk Rapids** and **Acme.** At this point, you hit the congested stretch, alongside beautiful Grand Traverse Bay, that leads into **Traverse City.**

From this lakeside resort town and host of the National Cherry Festival in July, you can drive out to **Old Mission Peninsula** on Mich. 37, a narrow ridge road overlooking the west and east arms of Grand Traverse Bay. The road meanders north through vineyards and the nation's greatest concentration of cherry trees, breathtaking in mid-May. At the end stands the 1870 **Old Mission Lighthouse,** located just south of the 45th parallel—halfway between the Equator and the North Pole.

River Road Scenic Byway

Michigan 65 to Oscoda on River Road

▪ 22 miles ▪ 1 hour ▪ Late spring through fall

French fur traders named this waterway *Rivière Aux Sable*, or "River of Sand," when they used it for access to the forests. Today's travelers can enjoy recreational activities on the Au Sable River or simply take in the views from roads and scenic overlooks.

About six miles north of Hale, Mich. 65 enters **Huron National Forest** *(231-775-2421 or 800-821-6263. www.fs.usda.gov/hmnf)* on its way to Oscoda, on Lake Huron. The **Westgate Welcome Center** has maps. After following the south shore of Loud Dam Pond, the byway leaves Mich. 65 for River Road. At **Largo Springs Interpretive Site** enjoy another fine vista of the river.

Three miles farther east, **Lumberman's Monument Visitor Center** overlooks the river. Trails feature historic artifacts of the lumberjack era.

At **Foote Pond Overlook,** you're atop a sand dune informally called Champagne Hill. **Footesite Park** is the docking area for the **Au Sable River Queen** *(989-739-7351. www.ausableriverqueen.net. Late-May–Sept. Fee)*, a paddlewheel river boat offering narrated cruises on the river.

Woodward Avenue

Downtown Detroit to Pontiac on Woodward Avenue (Michigan 1)

■ 27 miles ■ 2 hours ■ All year. Avoid rush hours.

Just as "Hollywood" means movies, **Detroit** *(Convention & Visitors Bureau, 211 W. Fort St., Suite 1000. 313-202-1800 or 800-338-7648. www.visitdetroit.com)* means cars. Starting at the Detroit River downtown near the **Renaissance Center,** Woodward Avenue abounds with names and landmarks connected with Ford, Chrysler, Cadillac, and Pontiac.

The **Detroit Historical Museum** *(5401 Woodward Ave. 313-833-7935. www.detroithistorical.org. Closed Mon.-Tues.; adm. fee)* features exhibits on the industry. Two blocks off Woodward, the **Model T Automotive Heritage Complex** *(461 Piquette Ave. 313-872-8759. www.tplex.org. April-Oct. Closed Mon.-Tues. Call for hours; adm. fee)*, the birthplace of the Ford Model T, is the only early Detroit auto factory open to visitors.

A little more than 4 miles from downtown, you reach the **Boston-Edison District**, where grand houses testify to the wealth created by the automobile industry. A mile farther, you pass the **Ford Highland Park Plant,** a mammoth office-factory complex designed by famed Detroit architect Albert Kahn and built between 1909 and 1920.

The ultimate avenue experience is the **Woodward Dream Cruise** *(www.woodwarddreamcruise.com)*, billed as "the world's largest one-day celebration of car culture." Held in August, it attracts both classic and custom cars.

169

OHIO
Lake Erie Coastal Ohio Trail

Pennsylvania state line to Toledo on US 20, Ohio 531, 534, 283, and 2, US 6, Ohio 269, 163, and 53, and city and county roads

■ 293 miles ■ 2 to 3 days ■ Spring through fall

Ohio's Lake Erie shoreline bears the marks of a long heritage as one of the country's most important industrial and transportation centers. Raw materials, finished goods, armaments for two world wars, midwestern grain, and countless other items have left ports here to be shipped around the

Marblehead Lighthouse

world. Historic lighthouses dot the shore, reminders of days before high-tech navigational tools. Museums along this route recount Lake Erie's history and interpret its ecology.

From the Pennsylvania state line, Ohio 531 follows the somewhat sparsely developed lakeshore to reach **Ashtabula** and its **Hubbard House Underground Railroad Museum** *(Walnut Blvd. & Lake Ave. 440-964-8168. www.hubbardhouseugrrmuseum .org. Mem. Day–Sept. Fri.-Sun.; adm. fee),* an important stop on the Underground Railroad, which helped southern slaves escape to Canada in the early and mid-19th century. Nearby, the **Ashtabula Maritime and Surface Transportation Museum** *(1071 Walnut Blvd. 440-964-6847. www .ashtabulamarinemuseum.org. Mem. Day–Sept. Fri.-Sun.; adm. fee)* displays its historical exhibits in an 1898 former lighthouse keeper's home, and provides a viewing spot for the 1895 **Ashtabula Harbor Lighthouse**.

The drive continues west to **Fairport Harbor** and the **Fairport Harbor Marine Museum and Lighthouse** *(129 2nd St. 440-354-4825. www.ncweb.com/ org/fhlh. Summer Wed.& Sat.-Sun.; adm. fee),* where you can climb a spiral staircase to the top of an 1871 lighthouse. The mile-long natural sand beach just west at **Headlands Beach State Park** *(216-881-8141. www.stateparks.com)* is the longest in Ohio. Nature lovers enjoy three adjacent preserves totaling more than 1,000 acres.

Eight miles south, in Mentor, is **James A. Garfield National Historic Site** *(8095 Mentor Ave. 440-255-8722. www.nps.gov/jaga. Adm. fee),* home of the man who was president for six months before being assassinated in 1881.

The drive becomes increasingly suburbanized as it approaches **Cleveland** *(Convention & Visitors Bureau, 334 Euclid Ave. 216-875-6680 or 800-321-1001. www.positivelycleveland.com),* where the revitalized lakefront is home to a great many attractions. One excellent stop is the **Great Lakes Science Center** *(601 Erieside Ave. 216-694-2000. www.glsc.org. Adm. fee),* with a large exhibit area devoted to the geology, environment, history, and economy of Lake Erie and the other Great Lakes. A short walk away at the **Steamship William G. Mather Museum** *(601 Erieside Ave. 216-694-2000. www.glsc.org/ mather_museum.php. Daily June-Aug., Fri.-Sun. May & Sept.-Oct.; adm. fee),* you can tour a huge 1925 Great Lakes freighter.

On the western outskirts of Cleveland, in **Vermillion,** visit the **Inland Seas Maritime Museum** *(480 Main St. 440-967-3467 or 800-893-1485. www .inlandseas.org. Adm. fee)* to learn about Great Lakes ships, the shipping industry, shipwrecks, and lighthouses. About 20 miles west as the gull flies, **Marblehead Lighthouse State Park** *(419-734-4424. www.stateparks.com)* protects a limestone light built in 1822. Marblehead can be climbed for views of the bay and Lake Erie islands to the north.

About a half-hour west off Ohio 2, **Crane Creek State Park** *(419-836-7758. www.stateparks.com. Tours in summer Mon.-Fri. p.m.)* and adjacent **Magee Marsh Wildlife Area** are among the top sites in the country to see various species, especially in spring migration. Birds pause to rest and feed here on their northward flight, gathering energy to cross Lake Erie into Canada.

Ohio & Erie Canalway

Cleveland to Dover, following Cuyahoga and Tuscarawas Rivers on local roads

- 110 miles ■ 6 hours ■ Spring through fall

The Ohio & Erie Canalway, built between 1825 and 1832 to connect Lake Erie with the Ohio River, enabled faster shipment of grain and other goods from the Midwest to eastern cities. Before its construction, 30 days were required for land travel between Akron and New York City; by canal, it took ten days. Congress has designated the Ohio & Erie Canalway as a National Heritage Area. Parks, trails, and museums dot its northern stretches, and the driving route links attractions along the **Cuyahoga and Tuscarawas Rivers.**

Cleveland *(Convention & Visitors Bureau, 334 Euclid Ave. 216-875-6680 or 800-321-1001. www.positively cleveland.com)* is the northern terminus of the canalway, where the Cuyahoga empties into Lake Erie (see Lake Erie Coastal Ohio Trail drive, pp. 169-170). In the suburbs of Valley View and Cuyahoga Heights, the **Ohio & Erie Canal Reservation** *(4524 E. 49th St. 216-635-3200. www.clemetparks.com)* encompasses the northernmost remaining 4.4 miles of canal still holding water, as well as hiking trails and interpretive displays on the canal and the Cuyahoga River.

The river is the heart of **Cuyahoga Valley National Park** *(Boston Store Visitor Center. 15610 Vaughn Rd., Brecksville. 330-657-2752 or 800-257-9477. www.nps.gov/ cuva)*, the real gem of the canalway. The park's 33,000 acres hold quiet paths, beautiful streams, waterfalls, and wildlife. In the northern part of the park, the **Canal Visitor Center** *(216-524-1497)* is the best place to learn about the canal and the Cuyahoga River environment.

The **Towpath Trail,** where mules once plodded, towing boats through the canal, has been converted into a hiking and biking trail, running 20 miles and connecting with other trails north and south for a total of more than 60 miles.

Be sure, too, to visit **Tinkers Creek Gorge, Brandywine Falls,** and the area called the **Ledges.** An excellent way to see the area is the **Cuyahoga Valley Scenic Railroad** *(330-657-2000 or 800-468-4070. www.cvsr.com. Fare),* providing scenic tours through the national park.

Akron *(Convention & Visitors Bureau. 330-374-7560 or 800-245-4254. www.visitakron-summit.org)* grew as a result of the Ohio & Erie

The Joseph Bimelek Log Haus in Zoar

171

Canal, and later called itself the "rubber capital of the world" for its tire industry. **Stan Hywet Hall and Gardens** (*714 N. Portage Path. 330-836-5533 or 888-836-5533. www.stanhywet.org. April-Dec.; adm. fee),* a 65-room English Tudor Revival mansion, was built in 1915 by a cofounder of the Goodyear Tire & Rubber Company. It sits amid 70 acres and includes nationally renowned gardens. Downtown, **Cascade Locks Park** and the **Mustill Store** (*248 Ferndale St. 330-374-5625. www.cascadelocks.org*) feature locks that helped carry the canal between the Cuyahoga and Tuscarawas Rivers and a restored store.

Continuing through the quaint towns of Massillon and Navarre to **Zoar** (*www.ohiohistory.org/places/zoar. Fee for tours),* a community founded in 1817 by German immigrants, the canalway ends in **Dover,** where you can tour the **J. E. Reeves Victorian Home and Carriage House Museum** (*325 E. Iron Ave. 330-343-7040 or 800-815-2794. www.doverhistory.org. Daily mid-Nov.- late-Dec., Thurs.-Sun. June-Oct.; adm. fee),* a 17-room mansion full of original furnishings of a 19th-century English immigrant who became a prominent local industrialist.

Amish Country Byway

Loudonville and Brinkhaven on the west to Wilmot and Sugarcreek on the east on US 62 and Ohio 39, 60, and 515

■ 76 miles ■ 4 hours ■ Spring through fall. Use caution in sharing roads with slow-moving horse-drawn buggies, and watch for bicycles. Do not take photographs of Amish people. Many attractions are closed on Sunday.

Ohio's population of Amish and Mennonites is centered in Holmes County, in the northeastern section of the state. With Swiss-German origins dating from the 16th century, these Christian sects do not use certain modern devices, such as telephones and automobiles.

Their seemingly simple life emphasizes self-sufficiency—which to outside visitors means excellent agricultural products and crafts, from cheese and breads to quilts and fine handmade furniture. (*Ask locally about produce auctions held weekly in season in various towns.*) Visiting Amish country is like traveling back in time, when close-knit families lived off the land.

Entering **Holmes County** from the east on Ohio 39, you'll reach **Walnut Creek** and the **German Culture Museum** (*330-893-2571. www.german culturemuseum.com. Sat. only),* which houses artifacts that include antique furniture and tools. Nearby, **Yoder's Amish Home** (*Ohio 515. 330-893-2541. www.yodersamishhome.com. Mid-April–Oct. Mon.-Sat.; adm. fee*) offers tours of two houses and a barn, with guides who explain Amish beliefs and customs.

Northeast of Berlin, the **Amish and Mennonite Heritage Center** (*5798 Cty. Rd. 77. 877-858-4634. www.behalt.com. Closed Sun.*) features a cyclorama 265 by 10 feet depicting the history of the Amish and Mennonites

Amish farm in Holmes County

from 1525 to the present. Tour guides are available to interpret the lifestyle still seen in the countryside today.

In **Millersburg** *(Holmes County Tourism Bureau, 35 N. Monroe St. 330-674-3975. www.visitamishcountry.com),* the **Victorian House Museum** *(484 Wooster Rd. 330-674-0022 or 888-201-0022. www.victorianhouse.org. Closed Mon. May-Oct., limited hours April & Nov.-Dec.; adm. fee)* displays period furnishings and exhibits on Holmes County history in a 28-room Queen Anne house built in 1900.

If you've eaten too much of the good local food, take a walk on the **Holmes County Trail** *(330-674-0475. www.holmestrail.org),* a rails-to-trail conversion that runs 12 miles from Millersburg to Fredericksburg (with more sections under development).

Bird-watchers and other wildlife enthusiasts will want to take the time to make a side trip north on Ohio 83. Just past Holmesville you'll find the **Killbuck Marsh Wildlife Area** *(330-567-3390).* In the 5,492 acres preserved here, the marsh, woods, and fields make it one of the best spots in Ohio to see birds of many species, particularly bald eagles, sandhill cranes, waterfowl, rails, and shorebirds.

Southwest of Millersburg in Killbuck, the **Killbuck Valley Museum** *(Front St. 330-264-2839. www.killbuckmuseum.org. May-Oct. Sat.-Sun.; adm. fee)* has exhibits on archaeology, geology, and natural history.

173

Covered Bridge Scenic Byway

Marietta to Woodsfield on Ohio 26

- 48 miles ▪ 2 hours ▪ Spring through fall. Heavy snows may close road in winter.

The Covered Bridge Scenic Byway traverses southeastern Ohio through Wayne National Forest, either snaking along Little Muskingum River or climbing onto forested bluffs. Along the way, tiny towns, century-old covered bridges, and weathered barns recall quieter days. But the starting point, **Marietta,** has bustled since beginning in 1788 as the first permanent organized settlement in the Northwest Territory. After boning up on outpost history at the **Campus Martius Museum** *(601 2d St. 740-373-3750. www.campusmartiusmuseum.org. March-Oct. Wed.-Sun.; adm. fee),* take Ohio 26 north through Marietta's outskirts. About 4 miles ahead, the road twists along a wooded ridgetop that overlooks hilly fields, deep hollows, and tree-covered ridges, then descends to the river valley.

Rinard covered bridge in Marietta

Here, some of the nation's oldest oil wells produce a few barrels a month.

Detour half a mile east on Cty. Rd. 333 to **Hills Covered Bridge.** Built in 1878, it's one of the more than 2,000 bridges, covered to protect the main structural timbers from inclement weather, that once spanned Ohio's rivers.

Back on the byway, the **Little Muskingum River** soon appears on the right. The river's name is Indian for "muddy river." Popular in spring and fall with canoeists, the Little Muskingum also draws anglers with more than 40 species of fish, including spotted and rock bass and sunfish. Continue along the valley, meandering onto bluffs and through towns. Watch for **Hune Covered Bridge,** built in 1879. Cross it to hike part of the **North Country National Scenic Trail,** which one day will link New York and North Dakota.

The byway leaves the river beyond Rinard Mills, but you have two more chances to enjoy it: at **Knowlton Covered Bridge,** built in 1887, and at **Ring Mill** (*follow gravel Cty. Rd. 68 east for 3 miles*), a historical house and a mill in use between 1846 and 1921. Back on the byway, continue through hilly farmland; at the junction with Ohio 800, head north 3 miles to **Woodsfield.**

Historic National Road
(Ohio, Indiana, and Illinois)

Bridgeport, Ohio, to East St. Louis, Illinois, on US 40 and others

▪ 548 miles ▪ 3 to 4 days ▪ Late spring through fall. Be sure to follow marked roads as they change frequently.

In the early 19th century, Thomas Jefferson was one of many in the federal government who came to believe that the country needed a land route over the Appalachians to facilitate travel, trade, and immigration, all of which would help national expansion and promote unity in the youthful United States. In 1806, Congress authorized the construction of a road from

Maryland to the Ohio River—America's first federally funded interstate highway. In the succeeding decades, the "National Road" would be lengthened westward to the Mississippi River. The importance of the road diminished with railroad travel, but as automobiles became common the old route was transformed into US Highway 40. Later, I-70 took away most of the traffic. Along the old highway traces of history remain, from inns and taverns to bridges and museums. Today's traveler, passing farmland, forest, and cities, can imagine following in the paths of pioneers seeking new homes, mail carriers braving bad weather, or traders with wagonloads of goods. (See eastern segment Historic National Road pp. 83-84.)

Just 6 miles west of the Ohio River, you can see one of the finest extant legacies of the old National Road: the 1828 **Blaine Hill Bridge** over Wheeling Creek. One of a number of S-curve bridges built where the road crossed streams at a non-90-degree angle, this sandstone structure has been restored after being saved from demolition in 1999.

West of St. Clairsville, look for the redbrick **Lentz Tavern** along US 40. Built in 1830, it's a reminder of days when a warm fire was a welcome comfort to tired, hungry travelers. To see an example of the woodland traversed by the early National Road travelers, take a short side trip to **Dysart Woods Laboratory** *(5 miles south of Belmont on Ohio 147. www.plantbio.ohiou.edu/ index.php/facilities/dysart)*, the largest known remnant of the region's original old-growth oak forest. You can see another S-bridge (Ohio's longest) by exiting I-70/US 40 at Ohio 513 and following Bridgewater Road on the north side of the interstate 3 miles west to the **Salt Fork S-bridge**.

In **Old Washington,** founded in 1805, you'll see some of the National Road's best traditional architecture as well as segments of early highway.

175

Driving on National Road in a 1931 Ford Cabriolet

In New Concord, the **John and Annie Glenn Historic Site** *(72 W. Main St. 740-826-3305 or 800-752-2602. www.johnglennhome.org. Wed.-Sun.; adm. fee)* contains exhibits and memorabilia of the man who in 1962 became the first American to orbit the Earth (and in 1998 became the oldest person to travel into space). Near Norwich, the **National Road/Zane Grey Museum** *(8850 E. Pike. 740-872-3143 or 800-752-2602. www.ohiohistory.org/ places/natlroad. Mem. Day–Labor Day; adm. fee)* features exhibits on the National Road including a 136-foot diorama, as well as on famed Western writer Zane Grey, an Ohio native.

Rohe family members shucking corn

Five miles west of Zanesville, with its notable **Y Bridge,** the 1830s **Headley Inn** dates from the early days of travel on the National Road. At Brownsville, a short side trip north leads to **Flint Ridge State Memorial** *(7091 Brownsville Rd. 740-787-2476 or 800-283-8707. www.ohiohistory.org/flint ridge. Mem. Day–Labor Day; adm. fee)*, which preserves a quarry important to Native Americans for its beautiful flint, used for tools and weapons.

US 40 passes through increasingly intensive agricultural land before traversing downtown **Columbus** *(800-354-2657. www.experiencecolumbus .com)* and crossing the Scioto River on Broad Street. More farmland waits on the nearly ruler-straight way to Springfield, where the **Pennsylvania House Museum** *(1311 W. Main St. 937-322-7668. www.pennsylvaniahousemuseum .info. Call for tour times. Adm. fee)*, set on the old National Road, dates from the 1830s. On the west side of the city you'll pass the **Madonna of the Trail Monument,** depicting a pioneer woman with two small children. Twelve identical monuments were placed along historic routes in the 1920s to honor the spirit of women in America's westward migration.

Just beyond the Dayton airport, visit **Aullwood Audubon Center and Farm** *(1000 Aullwood Rd. 937-890-7360. http://web4.audubon.org/local/sanctuary/ aullwood. Adm. fee)* to learn about the local environment, with exhibits on geology, flora, and fauna; trails meander through woods and meadows.

The original National Road was built across Indiana from 1827 to 1834. As you enter the state in Richmond, you'll pass another **Madonna of the Trail Monument**. In **Whitewater Gorge Park** you can see the foundation ruins of an 1834 National Road bridge over the Whitewater River, the first covered bridge in Indiana. Look for **original mile markers** from the National Road along US 40 as you cross the flat farm country near Centerville. Here, the **Lantz House Inn** *(214 W. Main St. 765-855-2936 or 800-495-2689. www .lantzhouseinn.com)*, dating from the 1830s, has been nicely restored. Ten miles west, the 1841 **Huddleston Farmhouse Inn Museum** *(838 National Road. 765-478-3172. www.indianalandmarks.org. Jan.-March by appt., Fri. rest of year; adm. fee)* once hosted many travelers on the National Road. Visitors can tour the house, barn, and other buildings.

At the community of Dunreith, you can leave US 40 to follow a 5-mile stretch of the original National Road just south of the modern highway. In

Greenfield, the **James Whitcomb Riley Old Home and Museum** *(250 W. Main St. 317-462-8539. April-Oct. Tues.-Sat.)* contains memorabilia of the "Hoosier poet," as well as 19th-century household items.

When the National Road reached **Indianapolis** *(Convention & Visitors Assoc. 800-323-4639. www.visitindy.com)* in 1827 it followed Washington Street, just as US 40 does today—passing through downtown's **Washington Street–Monument Circle Historic District.** One block north the **Soldiers' and Sailors' Monument** rises 284 feet and offers a view of the city center from its observation deck. West of the State Capitol, you'll pass **White River State Park** *(800-665-9056. http://inwhiteriver.wrsp.in.gov),* home to the Indianapolis Zoo, several museums, and a baseball park, as well as a 1916 National Road bridge over the river (now a pedestrian walkway).

Plainfield is noted for its old-fashioned **Plainfield Diner** *(3122 E Main St.),* a reminder of 1950s-style road trips. It's also the site of the **Van Buren elm** *(US 40 & Wabash St.),* where in 1842 President Martin Van Buren's coach was overturned by tree roots in the road—an accident arranged, so it's said, by local people upset that he refused to support road repairs.

US 40 continues through farms and woods, to **Terre Haute,** called "the crossroads of America" in the pre-interstate days for its location at US 40 and US 41.

A few miles into Illinois (where the drive is clearly marked with National Road signs), the 1841 **Archer House** *(717 Archer Ave. 217 826 8023)* in **Marshall** is the oldest lodging establishment in Illinois. West of town, note the limestone arch bridge, which dates from the 1830s. Near Martinsville follow a National Road spur to the **Lincoln School Museum** *(Cleone Rd. 217-382-4765. June-Aug. Sun.)* a restored 1880s one-room school. **Greenup,** named for a National Road supervisor, is known for its downtown overhanging porches and a reproduction of an 1830s covered bridge.

The route continues through farm country to **Vandalia,** the state capital from 1819 to 1839 and once the terminus of the National Road. The **Vandalia State House** *(315 W. Gallatin St. 618-283-1161. www.illinoishistory.gov/hs/vandalia_state house.htm. Closed Sun.-Mon. Sept.-May)* served as State Capitol from 1836-1839; Abraham Lincoln served here in the House of Representatives. On the grounds, you'll find another **Madonna of the Trail.**

Follow the National Road signs to one of the most significant sites along the entire route. **Cahokia Mounds State Historic Site** *(30 Ramey St., Collinsville. 618-346-5160. www.cahokiamounds.com. Donations)* preserves remnants of the largest known prehistoric Native American community north of Mexico. At its peak, it covered 4,000 acres with approximately 20,000 inhabitants. **Monks Mound,** rising to 100 feet high, is the largest prehistoric earthen mound in North America. The archaeological importance of Cahokia has merited its listing as a World Heritage site.

Madonna statue on the Indiana National Road

INDIANA
Amish Culture and Crafts Route

Elkhart to Lagrange on US 20 and County Roads 16, 250N, and 200N

■ 28 miles ■ 1 hour ■ Spring through fall

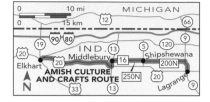

This rambling drive across northern Indiana's Amish country features well-groomed farms and quaint villages, offering an intimate look at a religious community that still thrives on centuries-old traditions.

From **Elkhart,** a manufacturing center with a Norman Rockwell collection at the **Midwest Museum of American Art** *(429 S. Main St. 574-293-6660. Closed Mon.; adm. fee),* head east for 10 miles on busy US 20. At Ind. 13, veer north into **Middlebury,** a town on the edge of Crystal Valley, the heart of Amish country. Amish families from Pennsylvania first arrived in this region in the 1840s, attracted by the rich glacial-till soil. Following the tenets of a 17th-century Mennonite elder, the Amish live, without modern conveniences, as productive farmers.

At East Warren Street (which begins as Cty. Rd. 16, then turns into 250N) turn right. Immediately you'll sense the change of scene. **Forks County Line Store** *(closed Sun.)* on the left, has hitching posts for horses. Lining the roadside are barns with gambrel roofs and trim, white frame houses. Horses graze in lush pastures, and corn, rye, oats, and hay grow in manicured fields. Be careful on this narrow road when passing horse-and-buggies. Three miles east of Middlebury at **Deutsch Käse Haus** *(574-825-9511. Cheesemaking: Mon.-Fri.),* watch Colby and Colby Jack cheeses being made.

About 3 miles farther, you enter **Shipshewana,** the Amish market center with home-style restaurants and craft shops. At Van Buren Street (Ind. 5), turn right and head south. To learn more about the Amish and Mennonites, stop by the **Menno-Hof Mennonite-Amish Visitor Center** *(510 S. Van Buren St. 260-768-4117. www.mennohof.org. Closed Sun.; adm. fee),* just ahead on the right.

At the stoplight, turn left onto Farver Street (Cty. Rd. 200N) and head

Amish wash day

east, back into farm country. The road leads past **Wana Cabinets and Furniture** *(7245 W. 200N. 260-768-4640. Closed Sun.),* custom builders of oak furniture. (More than half of the area's Amish heads of household work in factories.) **Babers Blacksmith Shop** and **M&M Harness Shop,** a mile on the right, are typical cottage industries.

Three miles down the road you'll reach Ind. 9. Turn right into **Lagrange,** where the drive ends. Consider touring the **Lagrange County Courthouse** *(105 N. Detroit St. 260-499-6300. www.lagrangecounty.org. Closed weekends, tours by appt.),* a marvelous redbrick structure built in 1878.

Lincoln Hills Scenic Drive

Corydon to Dale on Indiana 62

- 62 miles - 2 hours - Spring through fall

A scenic alternative to I-64, Ind. 62 bisects a portion of southern Indiana that Ice Age glaciers never reached. Instead, their torrential meltwaters carved out a hilly landscape of limestone caverns, deep woods, disappearing rivers, steep meadows, and broad lakes.

Snuggled in the Blue River Valley, **Corydon** is your starting point. The town's restored 19th-century buildings recall its place in history as the state's first capital. On High Street you can see the stunted trunk of the **Constitutional Elm,** beneath which the first state constitution was drafted in 1816. The drive leaves town through a mixed stretch of farmland, houses, and forested hills.

Soon you cross the **Blue River** and enter Appalachian-like woodlands, thick with black walnut, oak, hickory, flowering dogwood, and sassafras. You might spot white-tailed deer and wild turkey. Limestone walls rise above the road as it winds among the hills. Near the Crawford County line, detour to the **Wyandotte Caves State Recreation Area** *(812-738-2782 or 812-738-8232. Check www.in.gov/dnr to see if open. March-Sept.),* which showcases **Wyandotte Cave** *(Closed Mon. in winter; fee for tours),* Indiana's largest commercial cave with multiple levels and over 8 miles of explored passages.

About 350 million years ago, a warm, shallow inland sea deposited layers of limestone, which eroded over time, creating southern Indiana's extensive cave systems.

About 4 miles ahead in the hilltop town of **Leavenworth,** the road curves, revealing a splendid horseshoe bend in the **Ohio River.** Leavenworth was down by the river until 1937, when a flood forced it to relocate. Beyond town, the drive enters the approximately 200,000-acre **Hoosier National Forest** *(812-275-5987. www.fs.usda.gov/hoosier),* a favorite camping, boating, and hiking place known for undulating hills and sharp ridges. Once stripped of trees, the forest has been restored to its previous glory by the Forest Service. The road continues up, down, and around the hills, passing through the little towns of **Sulphur** (named for nearby sulfur springs), **West Fork, St. Croix,** and **Uniontown.** Far removed from large cities, locals live quiet, hard lives as cattle and pig farmers.

Just beyond the junction with Ind. 145, the road crosses the **Anderson River,** then continues through patches of cornfields and soybean fields squeezed into any available space between the hills. Upon rounding a curve into **St. Meinrad,** you sight the spires of the Benedictine **St. Meinrad Archabbey**

179

(812-357-6585 or 800-581-6905. www.saintmeinrad.org. Tours Sat.), a Romanesque structure built in the mid-19th century. Its community became self-sufficient through farming and quarrying. The road continues through barn-dotted fields, and gradually the terrain flattens out. Coal and petroleum reserves are rich here—you can see oil pumps rising above the soybean fields.

The drive ends in the town of **Dale,** with several historical sites nearby, including a living history farm at the **Lincoln Boyhood National Memorial** *(2 miles east of Gentryville on Ind. 162. 812-937-4541. www.nps.gov/libo. Adm. fee)*, which celebrates Lincoln's 14 years in Indiana, and the **Lincoln State Park** *(812-937-4710. www.in.gov/dnr. Park open all year, camping: April-Oct.; adm. fee)*, where his sister, Sarah, is buried.

Ohio River Scenic Byway

East Liverpool, Ohio, to Cairo, Illinois, on marked roads

▪ 967 miles ▪ 3 to 4 days ▪ Spring through fall

Prehistoric Native Americans, early explorers, pioneer immigrants, flatboats, steamboats, heavy industry, modern recreation—all these and much more have played a part in the legacy of the Ohio River. This byway runs nearly 1,000 miles along the Ohio's north bank, a journey through history as well as a recreational and scenic delight.

The byway's eastern terminus is **East Liverpool,** Ohio, where the **Museum of Ceramics** *(400 E. 5th St. 330-386-6001 or 800-600-7180. www.themuseumof ceramics.org. Closed Sun.-Mon.; adm. fee)*, in a 1909 former post office, celebrates the town's long association with ceramics. From 1840 to 1930, East Liverpool produced more than half of America's ceramics output.

There's more history downstream in **Steubenville,** where **Old Fort Steuben** *(120 S. 3rd St. 740-283-1787. www.oldfortsteuben.com. May-Oct.; donation)* is a reconstructed 1786 fort, including blockhouses, officers' quarters, quartermaster shop, and hospital. Authentic artifacts are displayed in a museum on the grounds. In mid-June, the **Fort Steuben Festival** brings reenactors and Native Americans to re-create 18th-century frontier life.

Ohio 7 continues downstream, rarely straying far from the Ohio and passing small towns squeezed against the riverbank. Towns get fewer and smaller as the byway reaches **Wayne National Forest** *(740-753-0101. www .fs.usda.gov/wayne)*, which offers recreation areas such as **Leith Run,** along the byway near Newport.

In **Marietta** *(Convention & Visitors Bureau, 121 Putnam St. 740-373-5178 or 800-288-2577. www.mariettaohio.org)*, the major attraction for river travelers is the **Ohio River Museum** *(601 Front St. 740-373-3750 or 800-860-0145.*

www.ohiohistory.org/places/ohriver. Late-April–Oct. weekends; adm. fee). It displays exhibits on the river's natural history and steamboat days, as well as the **W. P. Snyder Jr.,** a historic steam-powered, stern-wheeled towboat. The nearby **Campus Martius Museum** *(601 2nd St. 740-373-3750 or 800-860-0145. www.campusmartiusmuseum.org. March-Oct. Wed.-Sun.; adm. fee)* recalls early settlement days. (See also Covered Bridge Scenic Byway, pp. 173-174.)

In Gallipolis, **Our House** *(1st Ave. 740-446-0586. www.ohiohistory.org/ourhouse. Mem. Day–Oct. Wed.-Sun.; adm. fee)* is a restored 1819 three-story brick tavern, once the social center of town; it hosted Lafayette in 1825. Continuing downstream, you reach **Portsmouth,** which boasts 50 colorful murals on its Front Street flood wall.

Leaving Portsmouth and crossing the Scioto River, US 52 runs between wooded bluffs on the north and fields along the river. Hills on both banks rise 700 feet or more above the Ohio. Just after passing the large power plant at Moscow, reach tiny **Point Pleasant,** site of the **Ulysses S. Grant Birthplace** *(614-297-2300 or 800-686-6124. www.ohiohistory.org/grant. April-Oct. Wed.-Sun.; adm. fee).* This three-room cottage once toured the nation on a railroad car, but now resides in its original setting beside Big Indian Creek. The byway quickly reaches the outskirts of **Cincinnati** *(Convention & Visitors Bureau, 525 Vine St., Ste. 1500. 513-621-2142 or 800-543-2613. www.cincyusa .com),* with its series of bridges across the Ohio and its riverfront stadiums. Set between these sports palaces is the **National Underground Railroad Freedom Center** *(50 E. Freedom Way. 513-333-7500 or 877-648-4838. www .freedomcenter.org. Closed Mon.; adm. fee).* Cincinnati was a major destination for southern slaves seeking freedom in the northern states. Seven galleries of interactive exhibits include an authentic slave pen.

You will enjoy, among many other Cincinnati museums and attractions, the **William Howard Taft National Historic Site** *(2038 Auburn Ave. 513-684-3262. www.nps.gov/wiho),* dedicated to the man who was the 27th President

Hune covered bridge in Wayne National Forest

as well as chief justice of the Supreme Court. Exhibits focus on the way young Will Taft's family and social environment shaped his character. The **Harriet Beecher Stowe House** *(2950 Gilbert Ave. 513-751-0651. www.ohiohistory.org/places/stowe. Call for hours)* preserves the house occupied from 1832 to the 1850s by the Beecher family, active in education, abolition, and women's

Phlox in Wayne NF

rights movements. Her experiences in the Cincinnati area inspired Harriet Beecher Stowe to write *Uncle Tom's Cabin,* the antislavery novel that ranks among the most influential books of all time.

Over the Indiana state line, in **Aurora,** you'll reach imposing **Hillforest** *(213 5th St. 812-926-0087. www.hillforest.org. April-Dec. Tues.-Sun.; adm. fee),* an 1855 Italian Renaissance mansion overlooking the Ohio. Owner Thomas Gaff established more than 30 businesses, including a brewery and a fleet of steamboats. Downstream, you pass Big Cedar Cliffs and reach picturesque **Madison** *(Visitor Center, 601W. First St. 812-265-2956 or 800-559-2956. www.visitmadison.org),* with the largest historic district in Indiana. The Greek Revival **Lanier Mansion State Historic Site** *(601 W. 1st St. 812-265-3526. Open daily)* was built in 1855 by a financier who at one point lent Indiana the money needed to keep it from bankruptcy.

Byway environs become increasingly agricultural until the route reaches the adjacent cities of **Jeffersonville, Clarksville,** and **New Albany** *(Clark-Floyd Counties Convention & Tourism Bureau. 812-282-6654 or 800-552-3842. www.sunnysideoflouisville.org),* part of the Louisville, Kentucky, metropolitan area. The riverside **Falls of the Ohio State Park** *(201 Riverside Dr., Clarksville. 812-280-9970. www.fallsoftheohio.org. Adm. fee)* protects the largest exposed fossil bed of its era (386 million years old) in the world. The original falls here were a series of rapids that made the area a natural stopping point for river travelers. The **Howard Steamboat Museum** *(1101 E. Market St., Jeffersonville. 812-283-3728. www.steamboatmuseum.org. Closed Mon.; adm. fee)* recalls riverboat days with exhibits in an 1894 Victorian mansion constructed by a family of steamboat builders.

From 1813 to 1825, the small town of Corydon served as Indiana's capital. At **Corydon Capitol State Historic Site** *(126 E. Walnut St. 812-738-4890. www.indianamuseum.org. Closed Mon.)* tour the limestone Federal-style old capitol and a brick house built in 1817 by an early governor. The byway follows Ind. 66 south through **Hoosier National Forest** *(812-275-5987. www.fs.usda.gov/ hoosier).* You'll have close views of the river at tiny communities like Derby and Rocky Point and larger ones like Tell City. Farm fields take over before you reach the outskirts of **Evansville** *(Convention & Visitors Bureau, 401 S.E. Riverside Dr. 812-421-2200 or 800-433-3025. www.evansvillecvb.org)* and **Angel Mounds State Historic Site** *(8215 Pollack Ave. 812-853-3956.*

Visitors at Camel Rock in the Garden of the Gods

www.angelmounds.org. Closed Mon.; adm. fee), the well-preserved site of a Middle Mississippian Native American town occupied A.D. 1100 to 1450.

Crossing the Wabash River into Illinois, the route turns south to **Old Shawneetown** on the Ohio. The **Shawneetown Bank** *(280 Washington St.),* an imposing three-story Greek Revival structure, is a reminder of the town's legacy. The byway now enters **Shawnee National Forest** *(618-253-7114 or 800-699-6637. www.fs.usda.gov/shawnee),* Illinois's only national forest. A loop west leads to **Garden of the Gods** *(off Karber's Ridge Rd. 618-658-2111)* and noted formations Camel Rock, Anvil Rock, and Devils Smoke Stack.

The byway continues south to **Cave-In-Rock State Park** *(618-289-4325. http://dnr.state.il.us/lands/landmgt/parks),* centered on a massive cavern that long served as a landmark for Ohio River travelers. Once a notorious outlaw lair, the site today welcomes travelers.

Another hour or so brings you to **Metropolis** *(Chamber of Commerce, 607 Market St. 618-524-2714 or 800-949-5740. www.metropolischamber.com),* which shares its name with that of Superman's fictional hometown and displays a 15-foot-high statue of the superhero *(6th & Market Sts.).* The annual June Superman Celebration *(contact Chamber of Commerce)* features celebrities, games, music, and contests. The **Super Museum** *(517 Market St. 618-524-5518. Adm. fee)* has the world's largest collection of Superman-related memorabilia; only a fraction of them is on display at one time.

Adjacent **Fort Massac State Park** *(1308 E. 5th St. 618-524-4712. http://dnr .state.il.us/lands/landmgt/parks/r5/frmindex.htm)* occupies the site of military posts from French occupation through the Civil War. Today's park includes a reproduction of an 1802 fort with barracks, blockhouses, officers' quarters, and stockade. Trails wind in woods and along the Ohio.

The Illinois segment of the Ohio River Scenic Byway runs downstream to the town of **Cairo** *(Chamber of Commerce, 220 8th St. 618-734-2737),* located at the confluence of the Ohio and Mississippi Rivers. Here it meets Illinois's section of the Great River Road (see pp. 186-188).

183

Indiana's Historic Pathways

South-central Indiana from Vincennes to Clarksville/Aurora on US 50 and US 150

■ 110 to 162 miles ■ 4 hours ■ Spring through fall

In the decades following independence, south-central Indiana was America's great northwest. Settlers followed the wide tracks of the bison herds west from Kentucky at the Falls of the Ohio River. The Indiana Territory's old Buffalo Trace became US Highways 50 and 150, two forks of a pastoral route through limestone hills, forests, and a handful of proud county seats. Branching south from US 50, US 150 connects Vincennes to New Albany, 110 miles east, across the Ohio River from Louisville. Route 50 continues 95 miles northeast to **Aurora.**

Vincennes, capital of the territory from 1800 to 1813, commands the eastern bank of the Wabash River. The grand brick mansion here is **Grouseland** *(812-882-2096. www.grouseland.org. Adm. fee),* home of governor and later U.S. President William Henry Harrison. The estate now borders the Vincennes University campus. The **Vincennes State Historic Sites** *(812-882-7422. www.spiritofvincennes.org. Adm. fee)* interpret the town's pioneer culture in five preserved buildings. Begin at the Visitors Center, an 1840s log cabin a short walk from Grouseland.

Follow First Street south to the Doric columns of the **George Rogers Clark Memorial** *(812-882-1776. www.nps.gov/gero. Adm. fee).* The monument honors the Revolutionary War hero who defeated the British here in 1779, opening the frontier.

US 50 traces 23 level, wooded miles east to the Daviess County seat of **Washington.** The **Robert C. Graham House** *(101 W. Maple St.)* is a handsome example of prairie architecture, listed on the National Register of Historic Places. Continue across the East Fork of the White River for another 23 miles.

East on Route 150

At **Shoals,** US 50 bears north toward Aurora (see p. 185). Bear south instead onto US 150 for 13 miles, turning right on Ind. 56 to **French Lick Resort** *(888-936-9360. www.frenchlick.com).* Look for the unusual brick-red dome and Moorish towers of the West Baden Springs Hotel. It and the French Lick Springs Hotel share rolling parkland and a 19th-century pedigree. West

The George Rogers Clark Memorial

Baden's spectacular rotunda was the largest in the world when it was added in 1902. Both hotels maintain the traditional mineral baths and popular golf courses, and the old **French Lick Scenic Railway** *(800-748-7246. www.indiana railwaymuseum.org)* still offers a ten-mile excursion to the village of Cuzco. From French Lick's town square, follow Ind. 56/US 150 11 miles to **Paoli.**

The creamy, restored cupola of the Greek Revival–style courthouse marks Paoli, where Ind. 56 and US 150 meet on the edge of **Hoosier National Forest** *(812-275-5987. www.fs.usda.gov/hoosier).* Drive three more miles on US 150 to a rare old grove of virgin hardwood preserved in **Pioneer Mothers Memorial Forest.** To experience the lush canopy that covered Indiana 200 years ago, enter the one-mile hiking trail that leads from the parking area off Ind. 37.

Continue past the intersection of I-64 through New Albany to **Clarksville.** The exposed limestone outcroppings along the shoreline of the **Falls of the Ohio State Park** *(201 W. Riverside Dr. www.fallsoftheohio.org)* are the world's largest Devonian fossil beds. You can learn the site's 390-million-year history in the park's **Interpretive Center.**

East on Route 50

If you choose to continue from Shoals on Route 50, you'll cross the East Fork of the White River once again, approximately one mile before **Bedford.** The durable white oolith limestone of the region—used to build national icons like the Empire State Building, the Pentagon, and the National Cathedral—is beautifully evident in the unusual monuments of **Green Hill Cemetery** (turn right to enter from US 50). Local stonecutters crafted these memorials, including ornate tree stones detailed with the deceased person's hobbies and interests, to honor their fellow workers. A block from the town square is the **Lawrence County Museum of History** *(812-278-8575. www.lawrence countyhistory.org),* in a 100-year-old building on 15th Street.

Mansion Row, New Albany, IN

Forty miles east, continue through the interchange of I-65 three miles to the **Muscatatuck National Wildlife Refuge** *(812-522-4352. www.fws.gov/refuge/ muscatatuck).* This is birdland—a well-known waterfowl sanctuary that annually attracts trumpeter and tundra swans, whooping and sandhill cranes, and nesting eagles. Reintroduced river otters thrive here, too, you may sight them along the four-mile driving tour past the wetlands.

Returning to US 50, head into the Ohio River Valley past North Vernon. The mix of Greek Revival, Italianate, and Romanesque structures in **Aurora,** 55 miles from Muscatatuck, suggests the town's history as a riverboat boom town. **Hillforest** *(213 5th St. 812-926-1075. www.hillforest.org. Adm. fee),* the vast estate of a steamboat magnate, is the grandest example.

ILLINOIS

Shawnee Hills

Mitchellsville to Cave-in-Rock on Illinois 34, Karbers Ridge Road, and Illinois 1

- 33 miles ▪ 1 hour ▪ Spring through fall

From Mitchellsville, take Ill. 34. Within 5 miles, the road becomes curvy, and the farmland gives way to forest. These are the Shawnee Hills, also known as the Illinois Ozarks, part of the 277,831-acre **Shawnee National Forest** *(618-253-7114. www.fs.usda.gov/shawnee).* The hills, sediments from an ancient inland sea, started forming some 70 million years ago when the continent's crust uplifted.

Illinois 34 near Herod

A few miles south of Herod, turn left onto Karbers Ridge Road; drive 3 miles and make a detour to the **Garden of the Gods** *(2 miles north, follow signs. 618-658-2111).* A trail with boardwalks and rock steps winds around sandstone towers, overhangs, and boulders eroded into strange shapes over the last 200 million years. Signs explain the geology. For other rock formations and spectacular forest vistas, take the 2.5-mile gravel detour to **High Knob,** about 2 miles farther east on Karbers Ridge Road. Trails lead from the picnic area to the bottom of the bluffs.

Back on the byway, you continue through the tiny town of Karbers Ridge, with views of the Shawnee Hills. **Rim Rock National Recreation Trail** *(618-658-2111),* just west of Pounds Hollow, wanders 3 miles through woodlands. The first mile has interpretive signs about the area's history and geology. At **Pounds Hollow Recreation Area** *(618-658-2111),* visit 25-acre Pounds Hollow Lake.

The drive continues on Karbers Ridge Road to the junction with Ill. 1; turn south. At the end of Ill. 1, about 13 miles ahead, lies **Cave-in-Rock,** an Ohio River village with the river's only car and passenger ferry. Follow the signs to **Cave-in-Rock State Park** *(618-289-4325. http://dnr.state.il.us/lands/landmgt/parks),* on the eastern edge of town, where a short trail leads to a 200-foot-deep cavern overlooking the Ohio. A skylight carved in the cave's roof gives you a bird's-eye view of the hideout used as early as 1797 by river pirates, who preyed upon passing flatboats and keelboats.

Great River Road (Illinois)

Galena to Cairo on Illinois 84 and 92, County Road 11, Illinois 96, 57, and 3, and local roads

▪ 557 miles ▪ 2 to 3 days ▪ Late spring through fall

Illinois's segment of the Great River Road spans the length of the state's long western border, from the tall bluffs along the Mississippi River in the north to the Kentucky state line.

Set in Illinois's northwestern corner, **Galena** *(Convention & Visitors Bureau, 101 Bouthillier St. 877-464-2536. www.galena.org)* was named for the lead ore that brought miners here in the early 19th century. The **Galena–Jo Daviess County History Museum** *(211 S. Bench St. 815-777-9129. www.galena historymuseum.org. Adm. fee)* exhibits the town's history.

The route follows a ridgeline south from Galena. A mile before Ill. 84 splits from US 20, the **Long Hollow Scenic Overlook** offers excellent vistas from a 100-foot-tall tower. After descending to pass through farmland, Ill. 84 reaches **Mississippi Palisades State Park** *(815-273-2731. http://dnr.state*

.il.us/lands/landmgt/parks/r1/palisade.htm), where 15 miles of trails wind among the steep limestone cliffs that gave the park its name.

The Great River Road generally hugs the river south to **Fulton** (see Lincoln Highway, pp. 191-192) and on to **Moline** *(Convention & Visitors Bureau, 1601 River Dr., Ste. 110. 309-277-0937 or 800-747-7800. www.visitquad cities.com),* part of the Quad Cities area of Davenport and Bettendorf, Iowa; and Moline and Rock Island, Illinois. Moline's **John Deere Pavilion** *(1400 River Dr. 309-765-1000. www.johndeereattractions.com)* recalls the history of agriculture in the Midwest. The pavilion is the heart of **John Deere Commons,** a riverfront area of shops and restaurants. On **Arsenal Island,** the **Mississippi River Visitor Center** *(309-794-5338. www.mvr .usace.army.mil/missriver)* has displays on the river. In Rock Island, **Black Hawk State Historic Site** *(1510 46th Ave. 309-788-0177. www.blackhawkpark.org)* includes **Hauberg Museum** *(Closed Mon.-Tues.),* which interprets the culture of the Sauk and Mesquakie Indians who lived in the area in the 18th and 19th centuries.

The Great River Road follows Ill. 92 out of the Quad Cities and follows the Mississippi downstream. The small town of **Oquawka** boasts one of the route's oddest and most poignant sites: the **grave of Norma Jean the elephant,** a small-time circus performer who was struck by lightning in 1972 and buried where she fell—in the town square.

At its height as a Mormon center in the 1840s, **Nauvoo** *(Tourism Office, 1295 Mulholland St. 217-453-6648 or 877-628-8661. www.beautifulnauvoo.com)* had a population of 20,000, but opponents murdered leader Joseph Smith and forced members of the faith to leave the area. The **Historic Nauvoo Visitors Center** *(350 N. Main St. 888-453-6434)* and the **Joseph Smith Historic Visitors Center** *(865 Water St. 217-453-2246. Adm. fee)* can provide information.

Ill. 96 hugs the Mississippi beside bluffs, veers from the river, crosses more farmland, then returns to the riverbank at **Quincy** *(Convention & Visitors Bureau, 532 Gardener Expressway. 800-978-4748. www.seequincy.com).* The **Quincy Museum** *(1601 Maine St. 217-224-7669. www.thequincymuseum.com. Closed Mon.; adm. fee)* provides an overview of the city's history.

The byway continues south, and abruptly Ill. 95 jogs east and Ill. 100 follows limestone bluffs on the western edge of the **Illinois River Valley.** For information on this region, see **Meeting of the Great Rivers Scenic Route** (below) and the **Historic National Road** in Illinois (see pp. 174-177). The officially marked byway picks up again in Granite City on Ill. 3.

Reminders of the days of French exploration of the Mississippi River are found just south of the town of

187

Mississippi River at Nauvoo

Ellis Grove at **Fort Kaskaskia State Historic Site** *(618-859-3741. www.illinois history.gov)*, which includes the remains of earthworks.

Ill. 3 closely approaches the Mississippi southward. After **Thebes,** the route continues south to pass alongside **Horseshoe Lake State Fish and Wildlife Area** *(618-776-5689)*. Bald cypresses, tupelos, and cottonwoods ring the 2,400-acre Mississippi River oxbow lake, open to bird-watching, fishing, camping, and picnicking.

The Illinois segment of the Great River Road ends at the southernmost tip of the state, in **Cairo** *(Chamber of Commerce, 220 8th St. 618-734-2737)*, which sits on a spit of land where the Ohio and Mississippi Rivers meet, protected by a levee.

Meeting of the
Great Rivers Scenic Route

Kampsville to Alton on Illinois 100

■ 45 miles ■ 1 hour ■ All year

Following the course of the Illinois River to where it joins the Mississippi, this drive ends along wonderful white limestone palisades.

Begin in **Kampsville,** a tiny Illinois River town with exhibits on the region's prehistoric Indians at the **Center for American Archeology** *(618-653-4316. www.caa-archeology.org. May-Nov. Tues.-Sun.)*. Leaving town, Ill. 100 wends along steep limestone bluffs on the western edge of the **Illinois River Valley.** After about 9 miles the road enters **Hardin,** the Calhoun County seat.

Cross the river on Joe Page Bridge. The road jogs to the other side of the valley; a row of cottonwoods and birches down the middle of the valley is the only sign of the river now. Soon the road reaches the valley's eastern edge and veers south along its bluffs. About 10 miles ahead, you'll find **Pere Marquette State Park** *(618-786-3323. http://dnr.state.il.us/lands/landmgt/parks)*, where the Meeting of the Great Rivers Scenic Byway (an official America's Byway) starts. The drive up the flank of **McAdams Peak** offers views of the valley. The rustic **Pere Marquette State Park Lodge** *(618-786-2331)*, built in the 1930s, is listed on the National Register of Historic Places. Near the park's east entrance stands a stone cross marking the spot where, in 1673, French explorers Jacques Marquette and Louis Jolliet began their journey up the Illinois River to the Great Lakes.

Five miles south of the park at **Grafton,** the Illinois and Mississippi Rivers meet but don't mingle. One clear and the other muddy, they flow side by side for several miles. Here the road squeezes between steep bluffs and the Mississippi. Turnouts along the 14-mile stretch offer good views of the river. On sunny days, barges share the waterway with smaller boats.

Chautauqua, about half a mile south of Grafton, is a national historic district dating from the 19th century, when it was a cultural center. Take time to meander through **Elsah,** just 2 miles farther. Tucked between bluffs, the entire Victorian village seems to have been forgotten by time.

A modern rendition of a fearsome Piasa bird, an Illini Indian legendary creature, now decorates Piasa Park in **Alton,** near Norman's Landing. A similar Indian painting impressed Marquette in 1673. In Alton, visit the **Alton Museum of History and Art** *(2809 College Ave. 618-462-2763. www.alton museum.com. Closed Sun.- Tues.; adm. fee).*

Clark Bridge at Alton

Continue to Ill. 3 and the **Lewis and Clark Historic Site** *(1 Lewis & Clark Trail, Hartford. 618-251-5811. www.campdubois.com)* for an orientation to the mission undertaken by the Corps of Discovery.

Historic Route 66 (Illinois)

Chicago to Mississippi River on I-55, US 34 and 66, Illinois 53, 4, 157, and city streets and secondary highways

- 436 miles ■ 2 to 3 days ■ Spring through fall

Legendary Route 66, running 2,440 miles between Chicago and Los Angeles, was commissioned in 1926 to create a major east-west national highway, linking cities and small towns in eight states to facilitate both personal and business travel in the new mobility of America's automobile culture.

Illinois's segment of Route 66 was the first to be completely paved. As time passed and the highway was widened to four lanes, there are different "old Route 66" corridors through the state. Heading south, Historic Route 66 begins in **Chicago** *(Convention & Tourism Bureau, 301 E. Cermak Rd. 312-567-8500. www.choose chicago.com)* where Jackson Boulevard leaves Lake Shore Drive, then follows Adams Street west, passing such landmarks as the **Art Institute of Chicago,** the **Willis Tower,** and **Union Station** before taking Ogden Avenue to join Joliet Road and I-55.

Along the way you'll spot a great number of old-fashioned motels, drive-ins, and colorful 1950s-style signs. To see one of the most famous, exit at Ill. 83 in Willowbrook and take the north frontage road (the original 66) to **Dell Rhea's Chicken Basket** *(645 Joliet Rd. 630-325-0780.*

www.chickenbasket.com). In **Odell,** don't miss the 1932 **Standard Oil Station** *(400 S. West St. 815-998-2133)* or the **Old Log Cabin Restaurant** *(18700 Old Ill. 66. 815-842-2908)* in **Pontiac,** which was jacked up and turned 180 degrees when Route 66 was realigned in the 1940s. The next destination, south of Bloomington, is where the Funk family has produced maple "sirup" since 1824: **Funks Grove** *(5257 Old Ill. 66. 309-874-3360. www .funksmaplesirup.com),*

The attractions in **Springfield** *(Convention & Visitors Bureau, 109 N. 7th St. 217-789-2360 or 800-545-7300. www.visit-springfieldillinois.com)* include **Shea's Gas Station Museum** *(2075 Peoria Rd. 217-522-0475),* full of gas-station artifacts. Beyond Springfield, one historic Route 66 alignment essentially follows Ill. 4; another mostly follows frontage roads beside I-55.

Illinois River Road: Route of the Voyageurs

Ottawa to Havana on US 6 and 24, Illinois 29, 26, 71, and local roads

■ 291 miles ■ 1 to 2 days ■ Late spring through fall

The significance of the Illinois River takes many forms: French explorers (voyageurs) used it as an early travel route. Canals and locks connected the Great Lakes to the Mississippi River via the Illinois and made Chicago a world-class commercial center. This byway parallels the Illinois River on both sides, linking parks, wildlife areas, and historic sites.

On the north riverbank a few miles west of Ottawa, exhibits in the **Illinois Waterway Visitor Center** *(950 N. 27th Rd. 815-667-4054)* tell the history of water transportation in the region, from American Indian canoes to modern barges. Perhaps the most important development in that history was the Illinois & Michigan Canal. A 61-mile segment of the canal towpath is now the **Illinois & Michigan Canal State Trail** *(http://dnr.state.il.us/lands/ landmgt/parks),* a hiking-biking trail that can be accessed at several nearby spots, including Ottawa, Utica, and Buffalo Rock State Park.

Across the river, **Starved Rock State Park** *(Ill. 178. 815-667-4726. http://dnr.state.il.us/lands/landmgt/parks)* is known for 18 canyons carved into sandstone bluffs, formed by glacial action and erosion.

In pioneer times, the Illinois River was flanked by shallow backwater areas, home to a wide array of animals, especially waterbirds. Drainage for agriculture eliminated most of these, but restoration projects have succeeded in bringing back much of the former diversity. To see one such area, take Ill. 71 west to Ill. 26, drive south 2.5 miles, and turn west on Hennepin Farms Road. The **Hennepin and Hopper Lakes Restoration** *(www.wetlands-initiative.org/what-we-do)* has revitalized 2,600 acres of wetlands, bringing back birds, amphibians, and plants not seen in the area for decades.

Ill. 26 and 29 run down the east and west sides, respectively, of the Illinois River. The byway travels mostly through cropland but passes several wetlands, some of which have been protected as state wildlife areas. Ill. 29 runs along wooded hillsides to reach downtown **Peoria** *(Convention & Visitors Bureau, 456 Fulton St., Ste. 300. 800-747-0302. www .peoria.org),* where the **River Front** *(309-671-5555. www.peoriariverfront.com)* features shops, restaurants, museums, and a Saturday morning market *(June-Sept.).*

Wildlife along the river

The southern section of the byway traverses a major complex of wetlands important as breeding, feeding, and wintering areas for waterfowl. Some are protected within 4,488-acre **Chautauqua National Wildlife Refuge** *(19031 E. County Rd. 2110N. 309-535-2290. www.fws.gov/refuges),* where visitors can walk a nature trail to see waterfowl and bald eagles. One of the byway's most important and rewarding historic sites is located 6 miles northwest of Havana off Cty. Rd. 31. **Dickson Mounds Museum** *(10956 N. Dickson Mounds Rd. 309-547-3721. www.museum.state.il.us)* occupies a location where people have lived and hunted since Ice Age times. Exhibits here follow 12,000 years of interaction between Native Americans and the Illinois River environment. The excavated ruins of buildings dating back 800 years are available for viewing on the museum's 230 acres.

191

Lincoln Highway

Indiana state line to Fulton on US 30, Illinois 31, 38, and 2, and city streets and minor roads

- 179 miles ▪ 1 day ▪ Spring through fall

Conceived in 1913 when nearly all highways were dirt, the Lincoln Highway became the first paved coast-to-coast road. Illinois was the first state to completely pave its section of the route, which crossed the state roughly parallel to today's I-80.

From the Indiana state line and Lynwood, US 30 runs through suburbs and fields to Chicago Heights, where the old Lincoln and Dixie (now Ill. 1) Highways intersected. Here, the **Arche Fountain,** with a bust of Abraham Lincoln, was a favorite stopping place for early motorists. On the opposite corner stands a life-size statue of Lincoln called "On the Road to Greatness."

Blacksmith shop at the John Deere Historic Site near Dixon

Westward through the rapidly expanding Chicago suburbs, you reach New Lenox, where an **original Lincoln Highway marker** stands on the grounds of Lincoln-Way High School *(corner of Schoolhouse Rd.)*. Boy Scouts placed 3,000 of these milestones in 1928; in Illinois only a few still exist.

The route follows US 30 through Joliet to Aurora, where Ill. 31 heads north along the west side of the Fox River. At Geneva, you'll pass **Fabyan Villa Museum and Japanese Gardens** *(630-377-6424. www.ppfv.org/fabyan .htm. May-Oct. Wed. & Sat.-Sun.; donation),* featuring extensively landscaped gardens and a house redesigned by Frank Lloyd Wright in 1907.

West of Geneva, Ill. 38 leads on to **DeKalb,** possibly best known as the place where barbed wire was perfected and patented in 1874. **Rochelle** is a pilgrimage site for rail buffs, who visit a viewing platform at **Railroad Park** *(1 block south on 9th St.),* where more than 100 trains pass each day. A 1918 **Standard Oil station,** the first gas station built on the original Lincoln Highway, has been restored as the town **visitor center** *(500 Lincoln Ave. 815-562-7031. Closed Tues.-Wed.).* In Dixon, the **Victory Memorial Arch** over the highway was built in 1919 to welcome soldiers home from World War I. The **Ronald Reagan Boyhood Home** *(816 S. Hennepin Ave. 815-288-5176. www.reaganhome.org. April-Nov. daily; adm. fee)* has been restored to its condition in 1920 when the Reagan family moved here.

The route crosses the Rock River at Dixon, then makes a northern loop on Palmyra Road through Prairieville before joining Ill. 2. In Sterling, take Emerson Road to US 30 and continue westward to Morrison, where you can see another **original Lincoln Highway marker.**

Follow US 30 and Ill. 136 to **Fulton,** named for steamboat inventor Robert Fulton, on the Mississippi. In a once-abandoned limestone quarry, **Heritage Canyon** *(515 N. 4th St. 815-589-4545. www.cityoffulton.us/canyon .php)* is a collection of historic buildings dating back to the 1800s.

WISCONSIN
Kettle Moraine Scenic Drive

Greenbush to County Route H on county routes

▪ 33 miles ▪ 1 hour ▪ Spring through fall. Open in winter, but icy conditions can make driving the many sharp turns tricky.

This northern portion of the Kettle Moraine Scenic Drive—part of a marked 120-mile route through southeastern Wisconsin—winds through wooded hills, ridges, and valleys that reveal a landscape that was sculptured by glaciers. More than 20,000 years ago, during the Wisconsin era of glaciation, two great wedges of ice—the Green Bay Lobe from the west and the Lake Michigan Lobe from the east—collided in this area. Eventually the mass melted, leaving jumbles of rock and debris as high as 300 feet. The drive traverses one of nine units of the **Ice Age National Scientific Reserve,** the northern portion of **Kettle Moraine State Forest** *(262-626-2116).* These units preserve glacial deposits and offer a dramatic roadside geology lesson.

From Glenbeulah, the drive wends south on Cty. Rd. A through farmland to **Greenbush,** a pleasant rural town. Here, the **Old Wade House State Park** *(Jct. of Kettle Moraine Scenic Dr. & Cty. Rd. T. 920-526-3271. Closed Nov.-April; adm. fee)* features an 1850s stagecoach inn. Take Kettle Moraine Scenic Drive out of town. The road suddenly climbs steeply onto the **Green Bay Terminal Moraine,** looping around the ridges that mark the farthest advance of the Green Bay Lobe. Covered with oaks, sumacs, and sugar maples, the enclave shelters deer, weasels, red foxes, and more than 230 bird species.

About 2 miles ahead, the **Ice Age National Scenic Trail** *(www.nps .gov/iatr)* crosses the road. When completed, this statewide hiking path will follow the end moraines of the most recent glaciation. The **Greenbush Kettle Geological Marker,** a mile farther on the right, showcases one of the area's deep ground depressions, formed when thick layers of glacier-deposited sediment settled over a melting ice block.

Beyond the marker, head east on Wis. 67, then south on Cty. Rd. A. The drive descends off the moraine into a glacial outwash area, a plain of sand and gravel (now covered with cornfields) deposited by glacial meltwater. These fine silts nourish some of Wisconsin's best farmland. The drive jogs across the flat plain then, after about a mile, enters the steep, wooded hills of the **Lake Michigan Terminal Moraine**—the farthest advance of the Lake Michigan Lobe.

193

White-tailed bucks sizing up the competition

Aerial view of Kettle Moraine State Forest

At Cty. Rd. U, turn west. A quarter mile ahead, the **Parnell Observation Tower** yields an above tree line view of the region. From here, the drive continues southwest on Woodside Road, Shamrock Road, and Scenic Drive, descending into another glacial outwash plain. On the left and right are examples of kames—steep-sided conical hills formed as debris flowed through holes in the ice, much like inverted funnels. Where Scenic Drive veers south, the road climbs through a stretch of maples and oaks, back into the hilly Lake Michigan Terminal Moraine, which it traverses for 2 miles or so.

At Butler Lake Road, head south, then west. The road climbs onto **Parnell Esker,** a serpentine, grass-covered ridge of gravel formed by a subglacial stream. The drive returns to the glacial outwash, passing Butler Lake and, where **Butler Lake** and Division Roads meet, **Long Lake Recreation Area.** The state forest service has worked to make this area a recreationist's paradise. Lakes, some glacial, offer swimming and canoeing; and woodsy trails through the moraines attract hikers, bikers, and cross-country skiers.

Follow Division Road south, then turn west on Cty. Rd. F. The massive hill to your right is **Dundee Mountain,** an example of a kame. Beyond the town of Dundee, pick up Wis. 67, which climbs onto the Green Bay Terminal Moraine. To gain a better understanding of the region's geology, go straight at the junction with Cty. Rd. G to the **Henry S. Reuss Ice Age Visitor Center** *(920-533-8322. Call for hours during winter).*

As you head south on Cty. Rd. G, the drive descends into the **Jersey Flats,** extremely fertile farmland dotted with barns and cornfields. Turn east on Cty. Rd. SS to **New Prospect,** which lies on the edge of the Lake Michigan Terminal Moraine, then follow the moraine's spine south via Cty. Rd. GGG. Just before Tower Drive, the road crosses the Ice Age National Scenic Trail again, then touches an outwash plain. Beyond **New Fane,** continue south to Cty. Rd. H, the end of the drive.

Though the northern unit of the forest features the most dramatic glacial formations, the official Kettle Moraine Scenic Drive continues for some 90 miles south through populated towns, ending in the Kettle Moraine State Forest, Southern Unit.

Wisconsin River Scenic Drive

Sauk City to Prairie du Chien on Wisconsin 60

▪ 96 miles ▪ 2 hours ▪ All year

This farm-to-market road in southwestern Wisconsin follows the Wisconsin River—the state's longest river, running 430 miles from Lac Vieux Desert in the north to its confluence with the Mississippi—through a region of rugged limestone bluffs and rich farmland. Beyond **Sauk City,** take Wis. 60 into **Fair Valley,** a narrow, steep-walled coulee carpeted with cornfields. The road descends past several sloughs, typical offshoots of the river's main channel formed by high water full of frogs, turtles, and snakes. Where the sloughs widen and join the **Wisconsin River,** you see the vast alluvial plain of the "river of a thousand isles."

In the valley's heart is **Spring Green,** best known as the home of Frank Lloyd Wright, whose architectural philosophy—to meld the structure with its landscape— was partially inspired by the surrounding countryside. You can visit nearby **Taliesin East** (*3 miles south of Wis. 60 on Wis. 23. 608-588-7900. www.taliesin preservation.org. Tours May-Oct., by appt. in winter; adm. fee),* Wright's residence and studio.

Beyond town, the drive shoots 10 miles across fertile fields of corn and hay interspersed with copses of pine. Ridges stippled with oaks, maples, basswoods, and hickories edge both sides of the wide riverbed, marking the level of the land before the river carved the valley. This region of limestone-capped bluffs, sandstone outcroppings, and narrow valleys—known as the **Driftless Area**—is the only part of Wisconsin left untouched by the last glaciers.

Just beyond **Gotham,** the road curves onto the lower slope of protruding **Bogus Bluff,** where local legend says counterfeiters operated in a cave before and during the Civil War. Soon, the Wisconsin River comes into view.

With over 40,000 acres of public land preserved for hunting and recreation and another 40,000 acres protected scenically, the river's lower reaches look much as they did when French explorers Jacques Marquette and Louis Jolliet paddled the route in 1673, searching for the Mississippi. Herons and kingfishers nest on wooded islands. Marshlands and timber stands shelter woodcock and grouse.

On the Wisconsin River

For 2 miles or so, the road twists along steep limestone bluffs with river views, then ducks into rich dairy land. The river appears again as the road enters **Port Andrew,** once the busiest port along the lower Wisconsin. You can picnic at a river wayside near the town's entrance.

From here, the road alternates between farmland and river-edged bluffs. West of **Wauzeka,** where the **Kickapoo River** spills into the Wisconsin, cornfields cover the floodplain, now vast and fanlike. In the olden days, the smoke of stern-wheelers might be visible ahead, beyond the Mississippi River's hazy bluffs.

At Bridgeport, Wis. 60 joins US 18, which leads to **Prairie du Chien,** an 18th-century river town 3 miles north of the confluence of the Wisconsin and Mississippi.

Great River Road (Wisconsin)

Prescott to the Illinois line on Wisconsin 35 and 133 and local roads

■ 249 miles ■ 1 to 2 days ■ Late spring through fall

For much of its length, the Wisconsin segment of the Great River Road squeezes between steep, verdant bluffs and the wide Mississippi River, passing through river towns dating from the days of fur traders and explorers.

The northern terminus of the route lies in **Prescott,** which is home to the new **Great River Road Visitor Center** *(Freedom Park. 715-262-0104. www .freedomparkwi.org).* The site sits on a sandstone bluff overlooking where the clear St. Croix River flows into the muddy Mississippi. Wis. 35 heads south, paralleling the railroad tracks that it will shadow nearly the entire way. After briefly wandering from the river, you return at **Diamond Bluff.** Pause at the historical marker here to learn the macabre story of the 1890 *Sea Wing* disaster: 98 people died when a storm overturned a steamship making a pleasure cruise on the river.

For the next 20 miles or so the road runs alongside **Lake Pepin,** formed by sediment deposited into the Mississippi by the Chippewa River. **Stockholm** is noted for its arts community, and **Pepin** is home to several attractions revolving around Laura Ingalls Wilder, the author of the *Little House* books, who was born 7 miles away.

The highway crosses wetlands at the mouth of the Chippewa, then again runs beneath tall riverside bluffs. At **Alma,** drive up to **Buena Vista Park** for

wonderful views of the Mississippi. The tallest of the bluffs is **Eagle Bluff** at **Fountain City;** at 550 feet, it's the highest point alongside the upper Mississippi River.

Crossing the Trempealeau River, Wis. 35 borders **Trempealeau National Wildlife Refuge** *(608-539-2311. www.fws.gov/ midwest/Trempealeau),* where the 5-mile wildlife drive is an excellent place to see waterfowl, eagles, and other birds. Nearby **Perrot State Park** *(608-534-6409. http://dnr.wi.gov/topic/parks. Adm. fee)* offers good views of **Trempealeau Mountain,** oddly situated in the river.

La Crosse *(Convention & Visitors Bureau, 410 Veterans Memorial Dr. 608-782-2366 or 800-658-9424. www.explorelacrosse.com)* is the largest town along the Mississippi in Wisconsin. Take Main Street east to Grandad Bluff for a panorama over the Mississippi River Valley into Minnesota and Iowa, voted "most scenic view in the state" by a regional magazine. The Italianate 1860 **Hixon House** *(429 N. 7th St. 608-782-1980. www.lchsweb.org/ hixon-house. Mem. Day–Labor Day. Tues.-Sun., by appt. Mon. & in winter; adm. fee)* has the original furnishings.

Wis. 35 continues south through a series of small towns, alongside reservoirs formed by locks and dams on the Mississippi. In other spots, the river is choked by islands. Little **Ferryville** claims to be "the longest one-street village in the world."

The drive reaches **Prairie du Chien** *(Chamber of Commerce, 211 S. Main St. 800-732-1673. www.prairieduchien.org),* a former outpost for French voyageurs. The town's **Villa Louis** *(521 Villa Louis Rd. 608-326-2721. http://villalouis.wisconsinhistory.org.*

196

May-Oct., call for hours in Dec.; adm. fee), a fur trader's Victorian country house, dates from 1870 and contains many original furnishings and family items.

Passing through cornfields and cow pastures, Cty. Rd. X leads to **Wyalusing State Park** (*608-996-2261. http://dnr.wi.gov/topic/parks*), a pretty spot perched on bluffs above the confluence of the Wisconsin and Mississippi Rivers. Bird-

Lock and Dam No. 9 on the Mississippi

watchers consider Wyalusing State Park one of the state's best sites, because several southern bird species reach their range limits here.

The Wisconsin Great River Road follows Cty. Rd. W and Wis. 133 and 35 to reach its end at the Illinois state line. Along the way, in **Potosi,** an ambitious project is restoring a once-crumbling old brewery building into a brewery museum and visitor center.

Apostle Islands Country

Ashland to Superior on Wisconsin 13

■ 95 miles ■ 2 hours ■ Spring through fall. In winter, when average temperature is 17°F, you can walk to the islands on the frozen lake.

Wis. 13 traces Lake Superior's southern shore, a remote North Woods landscape of windswept fishing villages and vistas of the low-lying Apostle Islands. Just west of **Ashland**—where the Soo Line Iron Ore Dock serves as a reminder of the area's mining and shipping legacy—the route follows Lake Superior's **Chequamegon Bay** north, its shimmering water visible through the trees.

Washburn, about 10 miles ahead, has an old bank building, courthouse, and other edifices made of brownstone originally quarried nearby and on Basswood Island, near Bayfield. In the 19th century Basswood stone was used in building construction all over the country.

The road moves on past farms cut out of the forest, their individualism expressed in the art painted on their barns—a rainbow stretches across one. Where the road returns to the bay shore, you can see forested **Van Tassells Point** ahead, a great hogback protruding lakeward onto which the road soon climbs. The drive continues through the hilly woods, with glimpses of the water and islands, then twists and turns back down the bluff to sheltered Pikes Bay. Across

Amnicon Falls State Park, Wisconsin

Pikes Creek, the **Les Voigt State Fish Hatchery** *(715-779-4021. http://dnr.wi.gov/topic/fishing/hatcheries/lesvoigtbayfield.html)* explains how lake trout, chinook salmon, and other fish are raised for lake stocking.

Victorian-style inns and shops signal the approach to **Bayfield**, a fishing and tourist village with fairytale mansions once owned by lumber magnates. Stroll along the deepwater harbor, where the **Apostle Islands** appear to float offshore. Most prominent are **Madeline** and **Basswood**, resembling green gems. For maps and information on boat tours, drop by the **Apostle Islands National Lakeshore Bayfield Visitor Center** *(415 Washington Ave. 715-779-3397. www.nps.gov/apis. Daily May-Oct., closed weekends Nov.-April).* **Red Cliff Indian Reservation** encircles the tip of Bayfield Peninsula, north of where Wis. 13 heads west. La Pointe Chippewa Indians have lived here since 1854, when a treaty giving them 14,142 acres was negotiated by Chief Buffalo. Beyond the town of **Red Cliff,** turn right on Cty. Rd. K and right on Little Sand Bay Road to reach the **Little Sand Bay Visitor Center** *(715-779-7007. May–Labor Day).* Stroll along the sandy crescent overlooking the lake.

Back on Wis. 13, zigzag across the peninsula, then descend to Siskiwit Bay and tiny **Cornucopia.** Here, a 19th-century fishing village has been reborn with craft shops and a café. **St. Mary's Greek Orthodox Church** belies the town's Scandinavian roots.

Wetlands border the road west of Cornucopia, where **Lost Creek No. 1, Lost Creek No. 2,** and **Lost Creek No. 3** wander through a wide floodplain cut by a postglacial river and now drained by a river and a creek. Tiny **Herbster,** down the road, has a nice beach at the end of Lake Avenue.

West of the small fishing village of **Port Wing,** Wis. 13 enters dense newgrowth forest similar to what the first settlers encountered more than a century ago. The road crosses the **Iron River** and, soon after entering **Brule River State Forest** *(715-372-4866),* veers south. Watch for Brule River Road, which leads 4 miles to the mouth of the **Bois Brule River** at Lake Superior. Wisconsin's premier trout stream, the Bois Brule has been fished by five U.S. Presidents.

Beyond the river, the road dips into stream-filled valleys and climbs over high glacial hills covered with trees and wildflowers. After crossing the **Amnicon River,** look to the left for the green-roofed Davidson windmill, built in 1885 by a Finnish settler who hand-carved the gears. The last stop before Superior is **Amnicon Falls State Park** *(3 miles south on Cty. Rd. U. 715-398-3000. http://dnr.wi.gov/topic/parks. Adm. fee),* where the Amnicon River tumbles through a red sandstone and basaltic lava escarpment. Ancient volcanic activity and thick Ice Age glaciers created this lovely landscape.

About 3 miles ahead, on the world's largest freshwater lake, **Superior** has the world's largest grain elevators, iron ore docks, and coal-shipping terminal. You can see them from **Barkers Island** or **Connors Point.**

MINNESOTA
Gunflint Trail Scenic Byway

Grand Marais to Gull Lake, Minnesota, on Cook County Highway 12

- 57 miles ▪ 3 hours ▪ April to October

Tucked away in the northeast corner of Minnesota, this 57-mile scenic byway is the perfect antidote to life in the big city. As Cty. Hwy. 12 arcs northwest toward the Canadian border, you'll find the roadsides lined with pine forests and dotted with cold mountain lakes where the thing most likely to assault your senses is the call of a loon echoing across the water.

Along the way, you'll also find rustic lodges and homey cafés, along with a number of outfitters who can set you up with everything you'll need to explore the adjacent **Boundary Waters Canoe Area Wilderness** *(www.bwca.cc)*.

Start your trip at the small lakeside hamlet of **Grand Marais** *(www.grand marais.com)*. As the road begins to climb, you'll come to the 1,000-foot-high rocky outcropping known as the **Pincushion Overlook,** where you can take in views stretching from Lake Superior to Minnesota's Sawtooth Mountain Ridgeline to the west.

Pressing on into the Superior National Forest, keep in mind that this is moose country; the abundance of rivers, marshes, and ponds attracts the animals, so use caution when driving. Along the way, the byway crests the hills of the Giant's Range at the **Laurentian Divide,** a ridge at 1,837 feet that separates the region's watersheds. Rain and snow that falls on one side of the ridge runs southeast to Lake Superior; from the other side, water flows north to the Arctic Ocean and Hudson Bay.

In the late 1800s, dog-sledding was essential for communications between northern Minnesota's small villages during the dangerous winter months.

At mile 44.2, you'll come to the **Gunflint Lake and Magnetic Lake Overlook** (1,545 feet), which offers sweeping views into Canada. Just ahead, the land bears the scars of an unusual 1999 weather event known as the Boundary Waters Blowdown, during which winds estimated at up to 100 mph leveled tens of millions of trees in a single night.

As you near the end of the byway, turn right on Cty. Rd. 81 toward the **Chik-Wauk Museum and Nature Center** *(28 Moose Pond Dr. 218-388-9915. www.chikwauk.com. Adm. fee)*. This former resort, which is on the National Register of Historic Places, sits on the shore of Saganaga Lake and features exhibits on the history of the Gunflint Trail and surrounding lands.

The byway ends at the appropriately named **Trail's End Campground** *(12582 Gunflint Trail. 218-388-2212)* where you can follow a short trail along the Gull River to view picturesque rapids and a small waterfall.

199

North Shore Scenic Drive

Duluth to international border on Minnesota 61

■ 154 miles ■ 3 hours ■ All year

Skirting the jagged, glacier-worn Sawtooth Mountains, this winding road follows the rocky shoreline of Lake Superior, passing lighthouses and cascading streams and penetrating the only part of the continental United States where the northern boreal landscape thrives.

The drive begins in **Duluth,** where you can obtain a free guide from **Visit Duluth** *(21 W. Superior St. 218-722-4011 or 800-438-5884. www.visitduluth .com).* After viewing the **Aerial Lift Bridge** and visiting the group of museums known as **The Depot** *(506 W. Mich. St. 218-727-8025. www.duluthdepot .org. Adm. fee),* pick up Minn. 61—the old meandering route, not the new four-lane expressway—and go northeast. Resort development sprinkles the first 30 miles, relieved by stands selling wild rice and smoked fish. About 4 miles beyond downtown Duluth at **Lester River**—the traditional beginning of the North Shore—walks, overlooks, and stairways reveal Lake Superior's immensity. In surface area, it is the world's largest freshwater lake.

Beyond Two Harbors the road climbs and twists among steep headlands, passing through tunnels bored through **Silver Cliff** and **Lafayette Bluff** to avoid the precipitous outer edge. Ancient volcanoes created the North Shore's bedrock, which was then sculptured by the same glaciers that carved out the Great Lakes. A remnant of virgin white pine forest is visible as you cross the **Encampment River.**

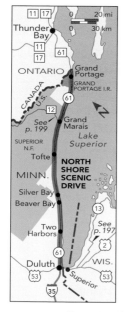

From the **Gooseberry River** highway bridge, you can see the Gooseberry River drop 100 feet into the lake. This series of three cataracts, the centerpiece of **Gooseberry Falls State Park** *(218-834-3855. www.dnr.state.mn.us/state_parks. Adm. fee),* is the first of eight extraordinary state parks along the drive.

The road continues east, crossing over Split Rock River to **Split Rock Lighthouse State Park** *(218-226-6377. www.dnr .state.mn.us/state_parks. Lighthouse tours in summer; adm. fee),* where a restored lighthouse sits atop a 130-foot cliff that juts into rocky shoals. First lit in 1910 after 215 men drowned during a disastrous shipping season, it now serves only visitors. The **Split Rock History Center** *(218-226-6372. Closed Mon.-Thurs. mid-Oct.–mid-May; adm. fee)* has exhibits on shipwrecks and commercial lake fishing.

Between Split Rock and **Beaver Bay**—one of the oldest continuous European settlements along the North Shore, platted in 1856—the terrain becomes more precipitous. But beyond the planned community of **Silver Bay,** the landscape softens. Just ahead is **Tettegouche State Park** *(218-226-6365. www.dnr.state.mn.us/state_parks. Adm. fee),* with 22 miles of trails through mountainous hardwood forest dotted with lakes. **Palisade Head** rises 214 feet above the lake, with a spectacular view of the far-off Apostle Islands (see pp. 197-198). Peregrine falcons nest nearby.

The drive continues across several rivers to **Taconite Harbor Observation Area,** where you can watch the action on the lake. Just beyond Cross River, a road winds down a bluff to a peninsula, where you find a reproduction of **Father Baraga's Cross.** The missionary erected it in the mid-1840s in thanks for his safe passage across the lake in a storm. About 3 miles beyond Cross River you'll find **Temperance River State Park** *(218-663-7476. www.dnr.state.mn.us/ state_parks);* thus named because there is no "bar" at the river's mouth.

Soon the drive enters **Superior National Forest** *(218-626-4300. www .fs.usda.gov/superior),* the heart of the boreal forest. Its inhabitants include

Kayaker on Beaver Bay, Lake Superior

moose, wolves, black bears, and loons. Near **Tofte,** outcroppings such as 1,526-foot **Carlton Peak** break the gentle terrain. For a sweeping view of Lake Superior, hike to the peak top from a Superior Hiking Trail parking lot *(look for Sawbill Trail).* From up there you can also see how jagged the Sawtooth Mountains have become.

The drive continues through Lutsen to **Cascade River State Park** *(218-387-3053. www.dnr.state.mn.us/state_parks. Adm. fee).* If you take a short walk upstream, you'll see the river dropping off a cliff. Go a bit farther and you'll find a rain forest setting, with water spilling over mossy ledges. Beyond, the road passes **Cutface Wayside,** which features a massive lava wall with red sandstone deposits.

About 5 miles ahead is **Grand Marais,** a resort town and artist colony at the base of a hill with a picturesque natural harbor and lighthouse, fine restaurants, and shops. But if you don't go on, you'll miss the most spectacular stretch of the drive.

A sense of remoteness envelops the road as it continues deeper into the realm of the early fur trappers and missionaries. Breaks in the trees frame **Lake Superior** to the right. The lake can appear to be calm and serene but may quickly release its legendary fury, thrashing icy waves against the shore. Just past the second intersection with Cty. Rd. 14, look for the "Moose Area" sign, a good spot to see a moose. Mile-long **Paradise Beach** *(no signs, but look for pull-off near the small pond)* is a wonderful place to experience the area's solitude. Turn off the car motor and listen to the wind in the forest and to the lake's surf.

The road continues through Hovland and enters the **Grand Portage Indian Reservation,** an area where Ojibwa Indians have lived for generations. Beyond this point, geologic processes have created spectacular mountains, ridges, and peninsulas. **Grand Portage Bay,** surrounded by jagged peaks, was the start of the historic Grand Portage between Lake Superior and Fort Charlotte, an 8.5-mile trail trudged by voyageurs and American Indians to avoid the rapids-filled Pigeon River. Their story is retold and preserved at **Grand Portage National Monument** *(218-475-0123. www.nps.gov/grpo. Mid-May–mid-Oct.; adm. fee),* a reproduction of the stockade of the North West Company.

Beyond Grand Portage, the road climbs several hundred feet to a crest near 1,348-foot **Mount Josephine,** which juts at a right angle into Lake Superior. From a scenic overlook you can see the rugged escarpment, Lake Superior, Wauswaugoning Bay, the Susie Islands, and, on a clear day, Michigan's Isle Royale.

As you've come this far, you might want to follow the North Shore Drive across the international border to Thunder Bay, Ontario.

201

Great River Road (Minnesota)

Itasca State Park to Iowa state line on local county and state roads, US 61, and Minnesota 26

- 575 miles ■ 3 days ■ All year. Some roads are unpaved; use caution in poor weather.

From Minnesota to Louisiana, the Great River Road parallels the Mississippi River. It continues for 2,552 miles from the North Woods to the warm waters of the Gulf of Mexico.

This byway begins where the river does: in **Itasca State Park** *(218-699-7251. www.dnr.state.mn.us/state_parks/itasca. Adm. fee)*, Minnesota's oldest, with more than 100 lakes, 32,000 acres, and dozens of miles of trails to explore. The park's most famous activity is stepping across the river as it issues as an ankle-deep brook from Lake Itasca. Visit the **Mary Gibbs Mississippi Headwaters Center** for exhibits on the river.

The route heads north briefly, past large boulders—glacial erratics, left at the end of the last ice age. The Mississippi in these parts seems no different than other streams crisscrossing Minnesota. The first city of any size on the river is **Bemidji** *(Tourist Information Center, 300 Bemidji Ave. 800-458-2223. www.bemidji.org)*, where the river flows into Lake Bemidji. Some claim the lake is the footprint of the legendary giant lumberjack Paul Bunyan, though geologists say it, too, is the result of glacial activity. Statues of Paul Bunyan and his companion, Babe the Blue Ox, stand beside the lake.

The Mississippi near La Crescent

Many towns in this area began as logging camps, and timber is still a local mainstay. Today, sportfishing ranks as an important business catering to fishermen. As you follow the Great River Road east past some of Minnesota's 12,000 lakes, you'll pass resorts catering to anglers. The route crosses **Chippewa National Forest** *(218-335-8600. www.fs .fed.us/r9/forests/chippewa)* and reaches **Grand Rapids** (see sidebar right) before turning south.

Beyond Grand Rapids the route follows a series of county roads through an area where the Mississippi wriggles constantly. Cropland becomes more prevalent as the river enters the **Cuyuna Iron Range,** which produced vast amounts of high manganese ore and is being reborn as a state recreation area.

The coming of the railroad in the 1870s transformed this region, and **Brainerd** *(Brainerd Lakes Area Chambers of Commerce. 218-829-2838 or 800-450-2838. www.explorebrainerdlakes .com)* began when the Northern Pacific built a bridge over the Mississippi here.

In the town of Little Falls (once the site of a Mississippi River waterfall, now replaced by a dam), **Charles A. Lindbergh Historic Site** *(1620 Lindbergh Dr. S. 320-616-5421. www.mnhs.org/ places/sites/lh. Closed Mon. in summer, weekdays Sept.-Oct.; and Nov.-May. Adm. fee)* preserves the house where Lindbergh grew up. Artifacts and a copy of the cockpit of the *Spirit of St. Louis,* tell the story of his long life.

Downstream toward **St. Cloud** *(Convention & Visitors Bureau, 525 Minn. 10 S. 320-251-4170 or 800-264-2940. www.granite country.com),* known for its high-quality granite deposits, fields and

Edge of the Wilderness

Grand Rapids to Effie on Minnesota 38

■ 47 miles ■ 2 hours ■ Summer and fall

Forests, lakes, and wildlife attract travelers to this short but scenic byway in north-central Minnesota. Begin in **Grand Rapids** *(Experience Grand Rapids, 171 Monroe Ave. NW, Ste. 700. 616-459-8287 or 800-678-9859. www.experiencegr .com),* where the **Forest History Center** *(2609 Cty. Rd. 76. 218-327-4482. www .mnhs.org/places/sites/fhc. Closed weekends Sept.-June; adm. fee)* re-creates a logging camp of a century ago. Here, also, trails and exhibits recount timber industry heritage.

Winding through stands of pine, spruce, white cedar, and hardwoods, you'll enter **Chippewa National Forest** *(218-335-8600. www.fs.fed.us/r9/forests/ chippewa),* noted for its high density of nesting bald eagles. Look for them along rivers and at large lakes such as **North Star Lake.** A good place to scan this lake is from a scenic overlook on the west side of the byway.

In this area you'll pass a kiosk marking the **Laurentian Divide.** Streams to the north of this spot flow toward Hudson Bay; streams to the south of here flow toward the Gulf of Mexico.

The logging town of **Marcell** moved when the railroad tracks moved in 1911. Ask locally about how the Minneapolis & Rainey River Railroad got the name "the Gut and Liver Line." No one seems to know for sure how the name came about, but all the stories are good.

The **Chippewa National Forest office** *(218-335-8600)* can provide information about recreational opportunities.

EDGE OF THE WILDERNESS

Effie

0   10 mi

0   15 km

CHIPPEWA N.F.

Marcell

North Star Lake

N

MINN.

See p. 202

Grand Rapids

CHIPPEWA N.F.

203

Grand Rounds Scenic Byway

Near-loop around Minneapolis on city parkways and streets

■ 52 miles ■ 3 hours ■ Late spring through early fall

While nearly encircling downtown **Minneapolis** *(Meet Minneapolis, 250 Marquette Ave. 612-767-8000 or 888-676-6757. www.minneapolis.org)*, this byway makes "rounds" along the banks of several lakes and a section of the Mississippi River. The route follows landscaped parkways for much of its length.

One place to start is **Minnehaha Park,** famed for 53-foot-tall **Minnehaha Falls** in Longfellow's poem "Song of Hiawatha." Here, 1906 **Longfellow House** *(4800 Minnehaha Ave. S. 612 230-6400. www .minneapolisparks.org. Closed weekends),* a reproduction of Longfellow's house in Cambridge, Mass., provides information for city parks and the scenic byway.

West of Minnehaha Park, the byway circles **Lake Nokonis** and follows Minnehaha Parkway to the **Chain of Lakes** area. Just north, **Theodore Wirth Park** is home to **Eloise Butler Wildflower Garden and Bird Sanctuary** *(612-370-4903. April–mid-Oct.).* In downtown Minneapolis, the byway follows West River Parkway past 1883 **Stone Arch Bridge,** a rail bridge now used by walkers and bikers.

pastures have largely replaced forest. The Mississippi, occasionally dotted with islands, has swollen. Located on the east bank of the Mississippi, **Munsinger and Clemens Gardens** *(Kilian Blvd. SE. 320-255-7216. www.munsinger clemens.com. Closed in winter)* are delightful places to walk—the former natural in design, the second more formal with rose gardens.

The **Twin Cities** of **Minneapolis** *(Meet Minneapolis, 250 Marquette Ave. 612-767-8000 or 888-676-6757. www .minneapolis.org)* and the Minnesota capital, **St. Paul** *(Convention & Visitors Authority, 75 W. 5th St. 651-292-3225. www.visitsaintpaul.com),* offer many attractions. Those on a river-themed journey, though, will especially appreciate the **Mississippi National River and Recreation Area** *(651-290-4160. www .nps.gov/miss),* which administers a variety of sites. Start your exploration at the **visitor center,** located inside downtown St. Paul's **Science Museum of Minnesota** *(120 W. Kellogg Blvd. 651-221-9444. www.smm.org. Adm. fee).* The Minneapolis Parks Department's **Carl W. Kroening Interpretive Center** *(4900 Mississippi Ct. 763-694-7693. www .minneapolisparks.org)* also focuses on the Mississippi River. For information on the river, the **Stone Arch Bridge,** and **St. Anthony Falls,** see the **Grand Rounds Scenic Byway** (sidebar left).

Beyond Hastings the route passes a riverside area and joins US 61. The road now offers panoramas of the Mississippi between steep headlands.

The highway winds among bluffs rising several hundred feet over the Mississippi. At **Frontenac State Park** *(Cty. Rd. 28 651-345-3401. www.dnr .state.mn.us/state_parks. Adm. fee),* trails offer sweeping vistas of **Lake Pepin,** popular with boaters; the large marina at **Lake City** is used to launch motorboats, sailboats, and Jet Skis.

Near Reads Landing, watch for a roadside sign marking **Bald Eagle Bluff Scientific and Natural Area;** as many as 70 eagles roost here from late fall to early spring. In **Wabasha,** which sits on a 12-square-mile area of forests, sloughs, islands, and marshlands, check out the **National Eagle Center** *(www.nationaleaglecenter.org)* and the 1856 **Anderson House** *(333 Main St. 651-565-3509),* Minnesota's oldest hotel, known for its food and bedtime cat companions.

At the 19th-century lumber town of **Winona,** on a giant sandbar of the Mississippi, about half of North America's canvasback ducks stop in

Mississippi River near Lake Itasca

their southbound migration. Winona's summer **Great River Shakespeare Festival** *(507-474-7900. www.grsf.org)* has become a major theater event in the region.

The Great River Road hugs the Mississippi below, soaring along bluffs to **LaMoille** for a view of **Trempealeau Mountain,** then crosses I-90 to **La Crescent.** For the last 20 miles to the Iowa line, the byway follows Minn. 26, past backwaters where the Mississippi widens and is choked with islands.

Paul Bunyan Scenic Byway

205

Pine River to Pequot Lakes on County Roads 1, 15, 16, 66, 3, and 11

■ 54 miles ■ 3 hours ■ Late spring through fall

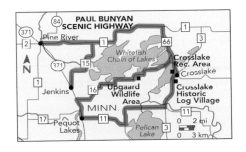

A day spent wandering the peaceful backroads of Minnesota's Crow Wing County will show why this area has been a resort destination for decades. Fishing has long been one of the popular recreational activities. But now new trails beckon hikers and bikers, and nature lovers find birds and other wildlife to enjoy. Shopping and dining are always pleasurable experiences that intrigue others.

Begin at the **visitor center** in **Pine River** *(US 371. 218-587-4000 or 800-728-6926. www.pinerivermn.com),* where you can pick up area maps and learn a few of the tall tales of legendary North Woods lumberjack Paul Bunyan, for whom the route was named. Cty. Rd. 1 heads east through forests of pine, spruce, aspen, and birch, through fields and past rivers and lakes to intersect with Cty. Rd. 66. These roads, along with Cty. Rds. 15 and 16, encircle the **Whitefish Chain of Lakes,** 14 interconnected lakes totaling more than 13,000 acres in surface area. Anglers fish local waters for walleye, large- and smallmouth bass, northern pike, crappie, sunfish, and trout.

Where Cty. Rds. 3 and 66 meet, the **Cross Lake Corps of Engineers Recreation Area** *(218-692-2025)* attracts campers, swimmers, and picnickers. The original dam here was a wooden structure built in 1884. Also, in the small

Boardwalk on Pelican Lake

town of Crosslake, the **Crosslake Historical Society Log Village and Museum** *(218-692-5400. Summer only, call for hours)* comprises seven restored structures from the 1800s.

Backtracking and taking Cty. Rd. 16 west to US 371 will lead you past many resorts and fishing lodges, several of which offer the chance to taste the bounty of nearby waters. **Uppgaard Wildlife Management Area** *(218-828-2228)* is a 110-acre tract comprising Minnesota's first "landscaping for wildlife demonstration area," with trails running through different habitat types excellent for bird-watching and other nature observation.

From Pequot Lakes, complete the route by taking Cty. Rd. 11 east, past one of the few remaining fire towers in the state, to link with Cty. Rds. 3 and 66. Along the way, look for loons, ospreys, bald eagles, deer, and beavers.

Historic Bluff Country Scenic Byway

La Crescent to Dexter on Minnesota 16

■ 88 miles ■ 3 hours ■ Late spring through fall

Gently rolling farmland and prairie, limestone bluffs, winding rivers, and peaceful small towns are the main elements of southeastern Minnesota's Bluff Country. Travelers along this byway have opportunities to explore natural areas (both above and below ground), visit historic sites, hike well-developed trails, or simply enjoy a relaxing drive through a part of the world that lives at a slower pace than most. The carriages of Amish people are seen around some of the communities, adding to the feeling that a visitor here has gone back in time a ways.

The Historic Bluff Country Scenic Byway begins in **La Crescent** on the **Mississippi River,** in an area where it flows under bluffs and past islands, across the river from La Crosse, Wisconsin. (See Great River Road—Minnesota, pp. 202-205, and Great River Road—Wisconsin, pp. 196-197). La Crescent, Minnesota's apple center, holds an **Applefest** in mid-September.

On Minn. 16, 4 miles west of the small village of Hokah, **Mound Prairie Scientific and Natural Area** encompasses oak forests and the type of thin-soiled grassland locally called "goat prairie." Goat prairie is home to several rare plants. Hike to the top of one of the bluffs here for an overview of the surrounding countryside. The natural area is adjacent to one unit of **Richard J. Dorer Memorial Hardwood State Forest,** which includes scattered tracts of walnut, oak, elm, birch, basswood, black cherry, and other hardwoods in a state that is usually associated with conifers.

Houston is the eastern end of **Root River State Trail** *(www.rootrivertrail .org)*, a 42-mile path that connects six communities and offers vistas of the **Root River Valley.** In summer it's used by hikers and bikers; in winter, by cross-country skiers. The **Houston Nature Center** *(215 W. Plum St. 507-896-4668. www.houstonmn.com. Call for hours),* located on the trail, has a wetland area and Saturday-evening nature programs in summer.

Just west of Rushford, nature lovers should make another stop at **Rushford Sand Barrens Scientific and Natural Area,** where a short walk leads to Minnesota's southernmost population of jack pine as well as a chance to see other plants such as silky aster, leadplant, blue-eyed grass, and witch hazel.

In **Peterson,** note the 1877 railroad depot, now a small museum of local items. The byway winds constantly for a while, paralleling the Root River past wooded bluffs to **Lanesboro** *(Chamber of Commerce. 507-467-2696 or 800-944-2670. www.lanesboro.com),* a town with a vibrant arts community and several companies that offer tours of surrounding Amish country. You can also rent a bike here to explore another part of the Root River State Trail.

From Lanesboro, the byway quickly climbs 400 feet before descending a bit to Preston. Here you can access the **Harmony–Preston Valley State Trail** *(www.dnr.state.mn.us/state_trails/blufflands/harmony_preston.html),* an 18-mile hiking-biking path that connects with the Root River State Trail.

South of Minn. 16, about 7 miles west of Preston, **Forestville/Mystery Cave State Park** *(Cty. Rd. 118, Forestville. Park: 507-352-5111, Mystery Cave: 507-937-3251. www.dnr.state.mn.us/state_parks/forestville_mystery_cave. Closed winter, limited hours spring & fall. Separate adm. fees)* offers two very different experiences. Forestville is a restored 19th-century village operated by the Minnesota Historical Society, with tours of a store, house, kitchen, garden, granary, carriage barn, and barn. This was a thriving farm community until the railroad bypassed it in 1868, at which point it gradually lost population until one man owned the entire town. Mystery Cave is a series

Hikers in Richard J. Dorer Memorial Hardwood State Forest

of underground passages sculpted by water flowing through limestone, explored by ranger-led tours. The park attracts hikers and horseback riders, who enjoy traversing the steep bluffs and valleys carved by glacial meltwater. Park streams are popular with trout anglers, as well.

Fans of Laura Ingalls Wilder, author of the acclaimed *Little House* books, should stop in Spring Valley at the **Methodist Church Laura Ingalls Wilder**

Site *(221 W. Courtland St. 507-346-7659. www.springvalleymnmuseum.org. Daily June-Aug., weekends Sept.-Oct.; adm. fee),* an 1876 church she attended in the 1890s. Exhibits include Wilder memorabilia and other local artifacts.

For its last 16 miles to I-90, the byway crosses flat farmland with fields and farm roads as regular as a checkerboard—part of the nation's breadbasket of corn, soybeans, and other crops, with the bluffs of Minnesota's Bluff Country left in the rearview mirror.

Minnesota River Valley Scenic Byway

Belle Plaine to Browns Valley on Minnesota 93, 169, 68, 67, 59, and 7, US 212 and 75, and county roads

■ 287 miles ■ 2 days ■ Summer and fall. Some sections of route are unpaved; drive with caution.

Traversing the Minnesota River Valley, this byway leads travelers to parks and natural areas, Native American sites, historic places, and rolling farm fields. Several small cities and one college town lie along the route. A massive glacial river carved today's landscape more than 10,000 years ago, leaving a valley up to 5 miles wide with a smaller stream at its bottom.

The byway officially begins just north of **Belle Plaine,** where Cty. Rd. 6 parallels the winding **Minnesota River** and its old meander oxbows. Byway signs depicting an eagle help drivers follow the route as it changes roads and highways and repeatedly crosses the river.

You'll cross the river on Minn. 93 to **Le Sueur** *(Chamber of Commerce, 500 N. Main St. 507 665-2501. www.lesueurchamber.org),* which really is in "the valley of the Jolly Green Giant." The Green Giant Company began here in 1903 as the Minnesota Valley Canning Company (the name changed in 1950), and the giant's image is seen all over town. The **Le Sueur Museum** *(709 N. 2nd St. 507-665-2050. www .lesueurchamber.org/area-attractions. Labor Day-Mem. Day Tues.-Thurs.)* has exhibits on the firm and other local history. The **W. W. Mayo House** *(118 N. Main St. 507-665-3250. www.mayohouse.org. June-Aug. Tues.-Sat., May & Sept.-Nov. Sat.; adm. fee)* was built in 1859 by the doctor who founded the famed Mayo Clinic and later occupied by the owners of Green Giant. Restored to its 1860s appearance, it has exhibits on Le Sueur's early days.

To get a feel for the local environment, visit **Chamberlain Woods Scientific and Natural Area,** a 254-acre tract 3 miles south of Le Sueur. Cottonwood, basswood, elm, and oak cloak this site, where you can walk more than a mile along the riverbank. Not far south, The Nature Conservancy's **Ottawa Bluffs Preserve** protects 63 acres of oak savanna, a rare ecosystem.

Two sites in St. Peter recall days of the Dakota Indians, who signed a treaty opening their land to settlement in 1851. A thriving town called Traverse des Sioux grew up along the river, only to die when St. Peter was named county seat. **Traverse des Sioux Historic Site** *(US 169. 507-934-2160. http:// sites.mnhs.org/historic-sites/traverse-des-sioux)* offers a self-guided trail of the townsite, with displays on Dakota culture, the fur trade, and the 1851 treaty. The **Treaty Site History Center** *(1851 N. Minnesota Ave. 507-934-2160. www .nchsmn.org/sites.html. Closed Mon; adm. fee)* provides more information.

Mankato *(Chamber of Commerce, 1 Civic Center Plaza, Ste. 200. 507-385-6660 or 800-657-4733. www.greatermankato.com)* has several historic buildings that are particularly striking, including the 1889 **Blue Earth County Courthouse** *(204 S. 5th St.),* the 1896 **Union Depot** *(112 N. Riverfront Dr.),* the 1871 **R. D. Hubbard House** *(606 S. Broad St.),* and the 1898 **Cray Mansion** *(603 S. 2nd St.).* Five miles west, **Minneopa State Park** *(507-389-5464. www.dnr.state.mn.us/state_parks/minneopa)* is known for the **Seppmann windmill,** built in 1864.

Continue upstream along the Minnesota to **New Ulm** *(Chamber of Commerce, 1 N. Minnesota St. 507-233-4300 or 888-463-9856. www.newulm .com),* a decidedly German town known for its 45-foot-tall **glockenspiel bell tower** *(4th & Minnesota Sts.)* with animated figures depicting local history. The **Brown County Historical Museum** *(2 N. Broadway. 507-233-2616. www .browncountyhistorymn.org. Closed Sun.; adm. fee),* housed in a 1910 post office, features exhibits on local history.

New Ulm was one of several towns affected during the 1862 Dakota war, which arose from tensions between settlers and Dakota Indians after the 1851 treaty. **Fort Ridgely State Park** *(Cty. Rd. 30, 7 miles south of Fairfax. 507-426-7840. www.dnr.state.mn.us/state_parks/fort_ridgely)* preserves the site of a U.S. Army fort, active 1855-1872, which came under siege during the conflict. A few minutes farther upstream, near Morton, the **Lower Sioux Agency Historic Site** *(507-697-6321. www.mnhs.org/places/sites/lsa. Mem. Day–Labor Day Fri.-Sun.; adm. fee)* provides another perspective, with interpretive trails at the location of the war's first organized attack.

The Dakota Indians gave a name to a lake on the Minnesota River that the French translated as **Lac qui Parle,** or "lake that speaks," because of the creaking of the ice when it broke up. **Lac qui Parle State Park** *(320-734-4450. www.dnr.state .mn.us/state_parks/lac_qui_parle)* and the nearby **wildlife management area** *(320-734-4451)* offer noise of a different kind as flocks pass through on their spring and fall migrations. On **Big Stone National Wildlife Refuge's** *(320-273-2191. www.fws .gov/refuge/big_stone)* 5-mile **Prairie Drive** auto tour, you may see pelicans, pheasants, and shorebirds, as well as white-tailed deer, beavers, and muskrat.

Oxcart in Red River Valley

CANADA

Great Falls

MONTANA

North Dakota 22
p. 217

Oxbow Overlook
Scenic Drive
p. 218

NORTH DAKOTA

Grand F

Sakakawea Trail
p. 215

Billings

Bismarck

Sheyenne
River Valley
Scenic Byway
p. 213

Native American
Scenic Byway
p. 214

Aberdeen

Water

Black Hills
p. 219

Gillette

Rapid
City

Badlands
p. 208

Pierre

SOUTH DAKOTA

Peter Norbeck
Scenic Byway
p. 222

Custer

Custer
Scenic Byway
p. 224

South
Dakota 44
p. 225

WYOMING

Casper

Missouri

Nebraska 29
p. 228

Pine Ridge
Country
p. 227

Rock Springs

NEBRASKA

Laramie

Cheyenne

Kearney

UTAH

Fort Collins

Denver

COLORADO

Colorado Springs

KANSAS

Salina

Wetlands
and Wildlife
Scenic Byway
p. 230

Wich

Santa Fe

Albuquerque

OKLAHOMA

Oklahoma Cit

Amarillo

NEW
MEXICO

TEXAS

Lawton

Lake Superior

MINNESOTA

Duluth

MICHIGAN

go

94

35

Wausau

St. Paul

Minneapolis

94

Green Bay

43

Lake
Michigan

Milwaukee

WISCONSIN

39

ux Falls

90

26

Madison

94

Kenosha

Great River Road
(Iowa)
p. 239

Sioux
City

Loess Hills
Scenic Byway
p. 238

20

Waterloo

Dubuque

Rockford

90

88

Chicago

Gary

Des Moines

380

61

Davenport

80

39

55

65

IOWA

Cedar Rapids

Iowa City

aha

80

218

74

Peoria

Bloomington

lcoln

35

34

Woodlands
Scenic Byway
p. 237

61

Champaign

74

Springfield

Decatur

IND.

St.
Joseph

Little Dixie Highway
of the Great River Road
p. 235

72

ILLINOIS

79

Kansas City

Kansas City

Columbia

70

St. Louis

70

7

335

Topeka

70

Jefferson City

64

35

Flint Hills
p. 229

Missouri Valley
Wine Country
p. 234

44

57

67

Missouri
Ozarks
p. 233

55

Ohio

MISSOURI

Joplin

Springfield

63

KENTUCKY

Glade Top
Trail
p. 232

160

19

44

Fayetteville

Crowley's
Ridge
Parkway
p. 231

55

TENNESSEE

40

Tulsa

ARKANSAS

40

Memphis

Little Rock

49

Helena

55

MISS.

Mississippi

North Dakota

Sheyenne River Valley Scenic Byway

Baldhill Dam to Lisbon on County Roads 17, 19, 21, 38, 13, and township roads

■ 63 miles ■ 3 hours ■ Spring through fall

Through the rolling farmland and prairies of southeastern North Dakota, this relaxing drive follows the narrow Sheyenne River past Norwegian settlements established in the 19th century.

At the route's northern point, Baldhill Dam (named for the hills around it) impounds 27-mile-long **Lake Ashtabula.** From a Native American word for "fish river," Ashtabula indeed offers excellent fishing for walleye, white bass, northern pike, and yellow perch.

Valley City *(Rosebud Visitor Center, 250 W. Main St. 701-845-1891. www .hellovalley.com)* is known for eight attractive bridges crossing the Sheyenne River; self-guided tour information is available at the Rosebud Visitor Center. At 3,860 feet long and 162 feet above the riverbed, the 1908 **Highline Bridge** is one of the longest and highest single-track railroad bridges in the nation.

The first several miles south on Cty. Rd. 21 quickly immerse you in a landscape of farms and grainfields. At various times of year wildflowers put on a colorful display, and in late summer cultivated sunflowers turn large areas brilliant yellow.

Just a few miles south of I-94, stop at the **Riparian Restoration Interpretive Site,** on the bank of the Sheyenne, a combination of native plant arboretum, picnic area, and canoe landing. Continuing southward, a side trip west will take you to popular **Clausen Springs** *(6 miles),* a park offering picnicking, fishing, hiking paths, and a dock.

Back on the main route, a little over a mile past the tiny town of Kathryn, you'll pass **Wadeson's Cabin,** built of hand-hewn oak logs on the east bank of the Sheyenne River in 1878. It's now a state historic site. A bit farther along the route, **Standing Rock State Historic Site** preserves a rock marker sacred to the Sioux that stands on a complex of burial mounds dating from the Woodland period (A.D. 0–1400).

View from Chadron State Park in northwestern Nebraska's Pine Ridge country

213

Farm in North Dakota

Fort Ransom State Park *(701-973-4331. www.parkrec.nd .gov)* straddles the Sheyenne and features a dramatic overlook of low wooded hills, upland prairies, and farmlands stretching into the distance. The bur oak, green ash, and elm that grow here are among the reasons this byway is noted for fall foliage color.

The town of **Fort Ransom,** established in 1878, contains the **T. J. Walker Historic District,** listed on the National Register of Historic Places in recognition of the Ransom County Historical Society Museum (in a 1908 building that once was a general store), the T. J. Walker Mill building, the Mill Dam, and the town's former ice house. The settlement took its name from the outpost that is now **Fort Ransom Historic Site,** where a military post was established in 1867 to protect frontier villages. The fort is gone, but earthworks are visible.

Nearby, **Sheyenne State Forest** encompasses part of the Sheyenne River floodplain, including deep draws and steep banks wooded with oak, ash, elm, ironwood, and basswood. Hiking trails and river access for fishing and canoeing are among the forest's attractions, along with bird-watching and other wildlife viewing.

214

Native American Scenic Byway

Cannonball River, North Dakota, to Chamberlain, South Dakota, on North Dakota 1806, 24, South Dakota 1806, 63, 50, Bureau of Indian Affairs (BIA) Routes 3, 7, 10, 4 and US 12, 212, and 14

■ 357 miles ■ 2 days ■ Spring through fall. Learn and respect laws and customs of tribal nations through whose land this route passes; do not take photographs without permission.

This landscape of stark beauty in North and South Dakota, crossing the reservations of four Sioux tribes—Standing Rock, Cheyenne River, Lower Brule, and Crow Creek—is secondary to experiencing the history and culture of the Sioux people. All four tribes welcome tourism, but understand that these societies have their own traditions and conventions. Be respectful!

The byway begins in North Dakota where N. Dak. 1806 crosses south over the Cannonball River into the 2.3-million-acre reservation of the **Standing Rock Sioux Nation** *(701-854-7201. www.standingrocktourism.com).* The terrain has hills and buttes, ravines, and rolling ridges. At the marina 11 miles south, the **Standing Rock Lewis and Clark Legacy Trail** comprises three connecting mile-long trails that wind through ravines and up hilltops overlooking the Missouri River, here part of 231-mile-long **Lake Oahe.**

At the town of Fort Yates, established as a military post in 1874, only a stockade remains of the original fort. Here you'll find **Sitting Bull Burial State Historic Site** and the **Standing Rock Monument.** Just south of Fort Yates, visit **Four Mile Creek,** where Lewis and Clark camped on October 14, 1804.

Seven miles after crossing into South Dakota, you pass **Fort Manuel Lisa** *(closed Nov.-April; adm. fee),* a reconstruction of an 1811 fort; its museum describes the fur trade's impact on Native Americans. Sacagawea, Lewis and Clark's guide and interpreter, is believed to be buried nearby. Shortly after the route crosses Lake Oahe and turns west on US 12, look for a turnoff south to two monuments: a spire honoring **Sacagawea** and a bust of **Sitting Bull** *(701-854-8500. www.nps .gov/libi/historyculture).*

Ring-necked pheasant

Traveling now through the land of the Cheyenne River Sioux, turn south on S. Dak. 63 from Eagle Butte toward the Cheyenne River. Signs tell the story of the Sioux, including Chief Big Foot (Spotted Elk) and the 1890 massacre at Wounded Knee.

At the confluence of the Bad River and the Missouri (now in Fort Pierre's Fischers Lilly Park), Lewis and Clark encountered the Sioux people for the first time in September 1804. In South Dakota's capital, **Pierre** *(Pierre Area Chamber of Commerce, 800 W. Dakota Ave. 605-224-7361 or 800-962 2034. www.pierre.org),* visit the **South Dakota Cultural Heritage Center** *(900 Governors Dr. 605-773-6346. www.sdhsf.org/society. Adm. fee).* Next, the route passes through the lands of the Lower Brule Nation and, after crossing the Missouri, those of the Crow Creek Nation.

One of the most rewarding sites along the byway comes at the southern terminus in Chamberlain: The **Akta Lakota Museum and Cultural Center** *(N. Main St. 605-234-3452 or 800-798-3452. www.aktalakota.org)* displays artifacts as well as art by Native Americans, including pictographs (paintings on rawhide, buffalo, and other animal hides), pottery, jewelry, and quilts.

Sakakawea Trail

Washburn to Grassy Butte on North Dakota 200A and 200

■ 109 miles ■ 2 hours ■ Spring through fall

This east-west drive traverses the open ranges and rolling grainfields between US 83 and US 85, south of Lake Sakakawea. From the unspoiled banks of the Missouri River to the striking mesas and buttes

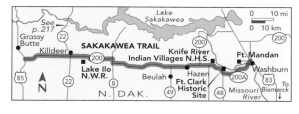

of the badlands, the road runs traffic-free through scenic western North Dakota. En route, a handful of historic forts and Native American sites attract motorists hypnotized by the highway. Anchoring the drive's east end, the agricultural town of **Washburn** occupies a bluff on the Missouri, an ideal site for riverboat trade in the late 1800s. Two later arteries—the railroad and US 83—have kept the town vigorous into the 21st century.

Head 3 miles west of town on Cty. Rd. 17 to **Fort Mandan** *(701-462-8535 or 877-462-8535. www.fortmandan.com. Adm. fee),* which commemorates the 1804-05 winter quarters of Lewis and Clark. The site has a reproduction of the fort the explorers stayed in on their way up the Missouri. Here, Sakakawea, the "bird woman" who helped guide the expedition to the Pacific coast, gave birth to a son, Jean-Baptiste, nicknamed "Pomp" by Clark.

The Lake Ilo area has produced an astounding cache of prehistoric human artifacts, especially stone tools.

Back in Washburn on N. Dak. 200A, take the bridge across the broad Missouri. The picture is not so different from what Lewis and Clark saw. Sandbars may have shifted over the years, but the tree-lined shores remain undeveloped in this area of long, severe winters. Summers carpet the lumpy hills in shades of brown and green.

Continue west on N. Dak. 200A for 10 miles, past rolling ranchland and fields of corn, wheat, and hay. Soon you begin to see the kinds of mesas and buttes that become more and more prominent as you travel west. Along here, too, you get glimpses of the scenic Missouri out your right window. About 3 miles after the Arroda Lakes, turn right to the **Fort Clark Historic Site** *(701-328-2666. www.history.nd.gov).* Nothing remains of the fort on this deserted, windswept prairie. On-site brochures and plaques detail the history of the fur-trading post that operated on the river here from 1831 to 1860. Passengers on one steamboat brought smallpox, nearly wiping out the local Mandan Indians.

Lake Sakakawea

To learn more about the area's Native Americans, travel 8 miles west to the **Knife River Indian Villages National Historic Site** *(701-745-3300. www.nps.gov/knri).* An **interpretive center** traces the life of the Hidatsa through artifacts, exhibits, and a full-size reproduction of an earth lodge. Ground depressions offer evidence of the Mandan and Hidatsa villages that thrived here from the early 16th century to the late 19th century.

Over the next 40 miles the drive, now N. Dak. 200, opens up to huge panoramas of rolling farmlands. And small towns such as **Hazen** and **Beulah** stoke the fires of local industry. Miners extract lignite coal from the hills, which is then turned into gas or burned in one of six area electric power plants.

The western part of the drive takes you past beautiful gulches and buttes that become deeper and taller the farther west you go. Late afternoon light etches these landforms into striking relief, and breezes make the tall prairie grass shimmer like swells on an ocean.

Though the ocean is far away, drive 1.5 miles west of Dunn Center to see flocks of waterfowl on their semiannual layovers at the **Lake Ilo National Wildlife Refuge** *(701-548-8110. www.fws.gov/lakeilo. Headquarters closed weekends).* The 4,043-acre refuge provides feeding and nesting grounds for up to 20,000 birds each spring, including herons and Canada geese. A few miles beyond, in the mining town of **Killdeer,** is the start of another scenic drive, N. Dak. 22 (see below). Or follow N. Dak. 200 20 miles to the intersection with US 85, near Grassy Butte.

North Dakota 22

Killdeer to New Town

▪ 64 miles ▪ 1½ hours ▪ Spring through fall

A road noticed by few outsiders, N. Dak. 22 dips and curves over the hills of the western part of the state. Several highlights make the excursion worth your while, and in between you'll feast on vistas that seem to go on forever.

Start out from **Killdeer,** home to cowboys and coal miners. Oil wells used to dot the nearby landscape, but many have recently been played out. Be sure to gas up in town since there's not another drop to be found until Mandaree, 37 miles north.

217

Two miles north you can take a 14-mile round-trip to the **Killdeer Battlefield State Historic Site,** but you'll find only a marker. Better to drive on, observing the **Killdeer Mountains** to the west and noting that here, on July 28, 1864, Gen. Alfred Sully with 2,200 troops dispersed a Sioux encampment of some 6,000 warriors in retaliation for an uprising in Minnesota.

Drive northward 12 miles or so past dun hayfields, and suddenly you approach the badlands. For a closer look, turn right 15 miles after Killdeer Battlefield turnoff and drive 2 miles on a gravel road to **Little Missouri State Park** *(701-764-5256. www.parkrec.nd.gov. May-Oct.; vehicle fee).* The knobs and pinnacles and the beehive-shaped stone masses resulted from the erosion of crumbly sedimentary rock deposited millions of years ago by streams flowing from the young Rocky Mountains. This 5,749-acre park offers horseback riding, hiking trails, and camping.

A bridge across the **Little Missouri River,** a few miles north, replaces the **Lost Bridge,** which provided passage to ranchers on their way from winter camps in the bottomlands to their ranches around the mountains.

After crossing the Little Missouri, you are on the **Fort Berthold Reservation,** inhabited by the Hidatsa, Arikara, and Mandan. The 450,000-acre reservation was partially flooded by the creation of Lake Sakakawea in the early 1950s. Cattle and horses graze the wide pastures on this beautiful, rugged land.

Continue north through the reservation about 25 miles until the highway ends at N. Dak. 23. Head east on N. Dak. 23 about 7 miles to **Four Bears Memorial Park,** which was

Little Missouri State Park

named for a Mandan chief and honors local Native Americans who died in conflicts from World War I to Vietnam. An A-frame houses the **Three Tribes Museum** *(701-627-4477. www.lewisandclarktrail.com/section2/nd cities/newtown/museum.htm. Mid-April–Nov.; adm. fee),* a good introduction to tribal history and culture. Next door, the **Four Bears Casino and Lodge** offers slot machines, video poker, and blackjack tables.

Cross **Four Bears Bridge** and turn left at the historical site marker for **Crow Flies High Butte.** This spectacular panorama of sparkling water and rolling hills came about in 1955 when the Garrison Dam backed up the Missouri and made 178-mile-long **Lake Sakakawea.** The dam protects downstream states from flooding and provides water for irrigation, navigation, and electricity. Buildings from the town of Old Sanish (now a bay) were moved east to what is now known as **New Town,** which has motels, restaurants, and gas stations.

Oxbow Overlook Scenic Drive

Theodore Roosevelt National Park (North Unit)

- 14 miles ■ 1½ hours ■ Spring through fall

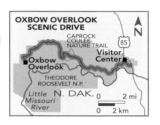

Meandering through the magnificent badlands of western North Dakota so beloved by Theodore Roosevelt, this park road traverses the length of the 24,000-acre **North Unit** of the **Theodore Roosevelt National Park** *(701-842-2333. www.nps .gov/thro. Adm fee).* Traffic tends to be light for a national park, and you have ample opportunities for viewing wide prairies, wildlife, and the wonderful badlands rock formations. Pullouts en route have interpretive plaques and hiking trails.

The drive begins at the **visitor center,** a worthwhile stop with good displays and films and a friendly staff. The park was named for the man whose experiences in North Dakota helped mold him into a world leader. Roosevelt first visited the badlands in 1883 to hunt bison and other big game. A vigorous conservationist, he set aside a tremendous amount of land for parks, forests, and wildlife refuges during his terms as President (1901-1909).

The **Longhorn Pullout** *(mile 2)* is situated on the edge of a prairie where a small herd of longhorn steers graze. Longhorn in the area date from an 1884 Texas trail drive that pushed 4,000 head into an open range vacated by dwindling bison. Thousands of longhorn followed in subsequent drives, but in 20 years they, too, had gone, victims of overgrazing and hard winters.

The scenery that captured Roosevelt's imagination is evident at every bend in the road. Climbing through hills laced with juniper trees, the road soars above the canyons and draws characteristic of the badlands. Watch for wildlife, often not far from the road—mule deer, bighorn sheep, bison, and more. The **Caprock Coulee Nature Trail** *(mile 6)* takes about an hour (or longer if you make a loop) and offers an up-close examination of the local geology. Interpretive brochures are available at the trailhead.

River Bend Overlook *(about mile 8)* affords splendid views of peaks and rounded buttes and the cottonwood-lined Little Missouri far below.

The multicolored rock formations are layers of sandstone, clay, shale, and petrified wood deposited millions of years ago. Easily eroded by the elements, the rocks have become infinitely varied in shape—from drip castles to capped pillars and buttes. In 1864 Gen. Alfred Sully described the region as "hell with the fires out." The fires sometimes still burn when seams of lignite coal catch fire from lightning and bake the surrounding clay into a sienna red substance.

The road ends at **Oxbow Overlook,** another breathtaking vantage point. Here you can see where the Little Missouri once flowed north toward Hudson Bay. Forced by a glacier to find a new course, the river turned east and began running to the Mississippi during the last ice age.

Little Missouri River from River Bend Overlook

SOUTH DAKOTA

Black Hills

Devils Tower Junction, Wyoming, to Custer, South Dakota, on US 385, 85, 14A; Wyoming 24; and South Dakota 34

- 155 miles ▪ 4 hours ▪ All year

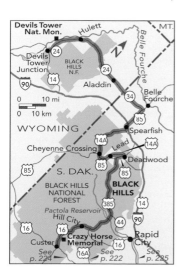

A crescent-shaped drive around the famous Black Hills of western South Dakota, this route connects five different highways in two states. Highlights include natural landmarks, historic mining towns, and views varying from immense rolling ranches to the pine-covered mountains and upthrust granite of the Black Hills.

From **Devils Tower Junction,** Wyoming, travel north on Wyo. 24 through rugged rangeland toward **Devils Tower National Monument** *(307-467-5283. www.nps.gov/deto. Adm. fee).* Winding through this first section of the drive, you see big red capstones and beautifully exposed red clay hills. After about 3 miles you also glimpse **Devils Tower** sprouting from the landscape. This stone monolith, a 60-million-year-old fountain of magma

Black Hills National Forest

that cooled and fractured into long columns, rises 867 feet from its base. Indian legend maintains the tower was the stump of a great tree clawed by a bear.

The entrance to the monument lies 6 miles from US 14. A road through the monument grounds passes a prairie dog community and ends at the **Visitor Center** *(closed late-Nov.–April),* where a 1.3-mile trail circles the tower and provides views of rock climbers scaling the heights. Bring binoculars.

Continue north on Wyo. 24 past ranchlands that open out to a backdrop of rocky hills stippled with pines. Sheep and cattle graze the abundant grasslands. In 10 miles you go through the cowboy and logging town of **Hulett,** where the road begins to climb to an upland forest of tall pines and hardwoods. The signature dark green ponderosa pines cover the landscape so thickly that from a distance the hills look black—hence the area's name. The jagged schist and granite outcroppings that punctuate the hills were exposed millions of years ago when overlying sedimentary layers began eroding away.

The whole Black Hills area roughly describes an oval—120 miles north to south and 50 miles west to east—with the highest, and oldest, rocks in the center. To Native Americans, the Paha Sapa, or Black Hills, were a sacred place. By the 1840s trappers and traders had infiltrated the region, and the discovery of gold brought a wave of white settlers. Today, though altered, the Black Hills continue to give of their richness and beauty.

After Hulett, Wyo. 24 veers east through forests and meadows. In about 20 miles watch for a sign that marks Lt. Col. George A. Custer's 1874 expedition into the Black Hills. With 1,000 men, 110 wagons, and 200 animals, Custer's survey team marched through here to verify rumors of gold. Ruts from the expedition remain just off the highway.

Not much remains of **Aladdin,** 4 miles farther on, other than a saloon and a century-old general store. Just east of town, the **Aladdin Tipple**

Historical Park *(Information at Aladdin Store 307-896-6432)* recounts the coal-mining heyday of the area, which at its peak supported 500 people. The site preserves a turn-of-the-20th-century mine shaft and wooden coal chute.

Crossing the South Dakota state line, Wyo. 24 becomes S. Dak. 34. In 10 miles you'll be near **Belle Fourche,** a sheep and cattle shipping center. The fertile valley of the **Belle Fourche** ("beautiful fork") **River,** named by French trappers, has long supported the area's large farms.

Head 10 miles south on US 85 to **Spearfish,** home of the popular Black Hills Passion Play. While in town, visit the **High Plains Heritage Center Museum** *(825 Heritage Dr. 605-642-9378. www.westernheritagecenter.com. Adm. fee),* with Western art and artifacts. The **Spearfish Canyon Scenic Byway** (US 14A) leads you southward out of town, following lovely **Spearfish Creek,** which flows north. Modern fishermen find this stream burgeoning with trout. Waterfalls and high rock walls make this a picturesque drive.

At Cheyenne Crossing take US 85 northeast up out of the canyon to the little mining town of **Lead** (pronounced LEED). Perched on a steep hill, Lead owes its existence to the 1876 gold rush. The **Homestake Gold Mine** *(605-584-3110. www.homestakevisitorcenter.com. Visitor center open all year, surface tours May-Sept.; fee for tours),* operated for some 120 years up until 2001, yielding more than 350,000 ounces of gold a year.

The road now descends 4 miles down into shadowy **Deadwood Gulch.** The town of **Deadwood** sprang to life soon after the discovery of gold nearby, when hundreds of people flooded into the area and began panning and sluicing the creek and then dynamiting the hills. By 1877 the government had imposed a treaty that forced the Sioux to sell the Black Hills.

Deadwood's downtown buildings of brick and stone maintain a solidly western flavor with their flat facades and ornate rooflines. Wild Bill Hickok was shot dead in a saloon here in 1876.

The **History and Information Center** *(3 Siever St. 605-578-2507),* in the old railroad depot, has exhibits and a brochure for a walking tour that takes you along three blocks of Main Street, where the clinks and beeps of more than 40 casinos keep Deadwood alive at all hours. Legalized in 1989, gambling has turned the town again into a frenzy of small-time speculation.

Backtrack on US 85 up the forested hills from Deadwood and veer south on US 385. After about 30 miles, just after the turnoff for S. Dak. 44, you'll see **Pactola Reservoir,** created by a dam on Rapid Creek. The **Black Hills National Forest** *(605-673-9200. www.fs.usda.gov/blackhills)* maintains a **visitor center** here *(Mem. Day–Labor Day).*

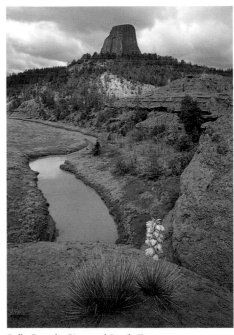

Belle Fourche River and Devils Tower

221

Back on the road, travel southward through a long stretch of dips and rises offering yet more beautiful views of the pine-covered hills and the exposed peaks looking like whitecaps on a dark sea. The highway passes towering stone cliffs near the small town of **Hill City** (4,980 feet), which has camping areas, motels, and a menu of trailheads.

Visitors gravitate to Devils Tower much the way the aliens did in Steven Spielberg's *Close Encounters of the Third Kind.*

About 8 miles later you pass **Crazy Horse Memorial** (605-673-4681. www.crazyhorsememorial.org. Adm. fee), where the sculpture of the Sioux leader on horseback continues to emerge. For the best views of the Crazy Horse project, you must pay to enter the grounds. Work remains to be done. Begun in 1948 by the late Korczak Ziolkowski, a noted sculptor, the tribute is being chiseled from the mountain under the direction of Ziolkowski's family.

Continue south about 6 miles to the town of **Custer,** where George Custer's 1874 expedition found gold nearby and precipitated a rush. The population quickly rose, then plunged as more gold was discovered in the northern Black Hills. But enough people stayed to establish a town. Today tourism, lumbering, ranching, and mining support the economy.

Peter Norbeck Scenic Byway

Loop from Custer past Mount Rushmore on US 16A, Iron Mountain Road, and South Dakota 244, 87, and 89

- 68 miles (add 18 miles for Custer State Park Wildlife Loop Road)
- 3 hours ■ Iron Mountain Road is closed in winter.

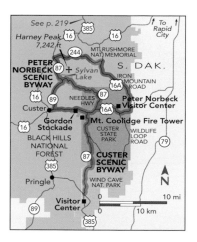

This loop through the Black Hills offers an ever changing backdrop of close-up and distant views. It takes in the gentle prairie and diverse wildlife of Custer State Park, climbs Iron Mountain Road for spectacular views of Mount Rushmore, passes mountain lakes, and descends back to the historic town of Custer. Named after Peter Norbeck, a South Dakota governor and senator who guided the building of the road in the 1920s, the byway offers some of the best touring in the Black Hills.

Heading east from **Custer** on US 16A, you'll pass forested hills and RV parks alternating with open meadows and ranchlands. In a few miles you enter **Custer State Park** (605-255-4515. www.gfp.sd.gov/state-parks. Adm. fee). Two jewel-like lakes near the entrance—**Bismark** (Black Hills NF) and **Stockade**—offer swimming, fishing, boating, and camping; more camping is available a little farther down the road at **Legion Lake.** Beside Stockade Lake stands a reproduction of **Gordon Stockade,** where a party of 27 gold prospectors spent the winter of 1874-1875 in defiance of the U.S. Cavalry, which was trying to maintain the Fort Laramie Treaty by keeping the area free of white settlers. Though the Gordon party was removed, more

Granite Presidents' heads, Mount Rushmore

whites soon slipped in, and the Sioux were forced to give up their sacred hills.

In Custer State Park glimpses of wildlife are almost guaranteed. Bison, elk, pronghorn, and burros are some of the animals that make their homes here, while fields of coneflowers, wild roses, bluebells, and other wildflowers brighten the grasslands and hills.

Continue east on US 16A about 6 miles past the Needles Highway (S. Dak. 87) turnoff and stop in at the **Peter Norbeck Visitor Center** *(605-255-4464. May-Nov.),* which will help satisfy your curiosity about area history, geology, and flora and fauna. Just after the visitor center, you can turn right and take the 18-mile **Wildlife Loop Road** through the park's grassy prairies, then head up S. Dak. 87 to rejoin US 16A. Or continue past the Wildlife Loop and follow US 16A as it turns left onto the fabulous **Iron Mountain Road** and enters the Black Hills National Forest.

A winding highway to the monumental sculptures on Mount Rushmore, this 17-mile stretch goes up and down, loops around hairpin curves, and threads through tunnels that frame the four Presidents' heads on the opposite mountain. Peter Norbeck tramped and rode horseback through these woods to help lay out the byway and also is largely responsible for founding Custer State Park. The **Norbeck Memorial Overlook,** at 5,445 feet the highest point on the drive, gives you one of the best views of **Mount Rushmore** (from 3 miles south). Seeing these American icons staring out from a range

223

Stockade Lake, Custer State Park

Custer Scenic Byway

Junction of US 385 and South Dakota 87 in Wind Cave National Park to Sylvan Lake

■ 33 miles ■ 1¹/₂ hours ■ Spring through fall. Needles Highway closed in winter. Adm. fee to park. See map p. 222.

This Black Hills drive follows S. Dak. 87 north from Wind Cave, through Custer State Park, to the junction with S. Dak. 89 at Sylvan Lake. (The 14.5-mile part of S. Dak. 87 north of US 16A is known as the **Needles Highway.**)

At **Wind Cave National Park** *(605-745-4600. www.nps.gov/wica. Fee for tours)*, you'll see subterranean architecture sculpted over eons. Begin the drive at the junction of US 385 and S. Dak. 87 and stop at the **Prairie Dog Pullout.** If you stay in the car, you won't spook the rodents. Continue north on S. Dak. 87 into **Custer State Park** *(605-255-4515. Adm. fee)*, contiguous with the national park.

The road soon begins winding up through dense pine forest. Near **Mount Coolidge** you'll see vast tracts charred by the fires of 1988 and 1990. For a 360-degree panorama of the Black Hills, take the 1.3-mile gravel road *(on the left)* to the **Mount Coolidge Fire Tower.**

As you cruise the needles (upthrust pylons of granite) in the heart of Sioux holy land, amazing views appear before you. The drive ends at **Sylvan Lake.**

Hikers on Harney Peak, Black Hills

of ragged peaks, you get a sense of the boldness of a colossal project.

The first tunnel occurs about 5 miles from Mount Rushmore. The second tunnel provides a good rear-view shot of the monument. Just afterward, you cross the first of three rustic bridges supported by logs from the surrounding woods. Feats of engineering, these bridges are neither straight nor level. You now take a one-way right around a grove of shimmering aspen and birch, and head into the last and longest tunnel. The second bridge follows, curling gently down. After the third bridge you drop into a valley and cross **Grizzly Bear Creek.**

The road delivers you to the **Mount Rushmore National Memorial** *(605-574-2523. www.nps.gov/moru. Adm. fee)*, where the 60-foot-high heads of (from left to right) Washington, Jefferson, Theodore Roosevelt, and Lincoln emerge from a wall of granite. Begun in 1927, the carving took 14 years. Though more was planned, chief sculptor Gutzon Borglum died in 1941. His son continued the project until funds dried up.

Traveling down from Mount Rushmore on S. Dak. 244, you continue to see rock ledges sprouting from dense forest. Road cuts reveal granite, feldspar, and quartz. Lighter tones of aspen and paper birch accent the dark green of ponderosa pine and spruce.

Much of the area outside Custer State Park is part of the 35,000-acre **Norbeck Wildlife Preserve,** established by Congress in 1920. **Harney Peak** (7,242 feet), on your left as you descend Mount Rushmore, is the highest mountain east of the Rockies. Take S. Dak. 87 and 89 south to Custer, named for the army officer who in 1874 opened the area to a flood of settlers by publicizing his expedition's discovery of gold. Though George A. Custer died two years later at age 37 in the infamous Battle of the Little Bighorn, his legend lives in the Black Hills, visited by more than 3.5 million people a year.

South Dakota 44

Rapid City to Badlands National Park

■ 65 miles ■ 1½ hours ■ All year

A scenic alternative to I-90, S. Dak. 44 travels between the Black Hills and Badlands National Park, passing farms and ranches, Wild West towns, and open prairies. Going east from Rapid City, the highway follows the Rapid Creek Valley for about 30 miles, then enters the White River badlands area, crosses Buffalo Gap National Grassland, skirts the Pine Ridge Indian Reservation, and ends at the Cedar Pass entrance to Badlands National Park.

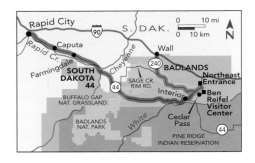

Situated on the eastern edge of the Black Hills, **Rapid City** dates back to 1876, two years after Custer's noisy expedition infected the region with gold fever. South Dakota's second largest city with 62,000 people, Rapid City functions as a tourism center, while mining, agriculture, and lumber also add to the economy. A powwow takes place here in July.

Driving east from Rapid City, you follow the hardwood-lined valley of **Rapid Creek** through the tiny agricultural communities of **Caputa** and tumbledown **Farmingdale**. The elms and cottonwoods along the creek make a river of green through an otherwise monochromatic prairie. After about 30 miles the creek joins the Cheyenne River and heads north, while the road continues southeast, gradually heading up to a vast plateau.

Sweet clover in bloom, Badlands NP

About halfway into the drive, you find yourself engulfed in a shallow bowl of long, rolling, brown-carpeted prairie creased with gullies. To a non-native, the immensity of space is almost overwhelming: You can see buttes and tablelands 30 miles away, with no sign of civilization anywhere.

Scattered throughout this area are the expanses of **Buffalo Gap National Grassland** *(308-432-0300. www.fs.fed.us/grasslands),* one of 20 such areas in the Great Plains. In the 1930s the federal government started buying up land that had been overplanted or overgrazed, then drought stricken, to try to stabilize the soil and restore the grass. Some 4 million acres of this land became national grasslands in 1960 under the Forest Service. Ranchers graze cattle by permit, and anyone can hike or pitch a tent for free on Buffalo Gap's 591,000 acres. Contact the **National Grasslands Visitor Center** *(708 Main St. 605-279-2125. Daily in summer, Mon.-Fri. Sept.-May)* in **Wall** for information.

Nearing **Badlands National Park,** you see to your left the magnificent saw-toothed wall of stone pyramids and castles stretching 60 miles east to west. South of here is the **Pine Ridge Indian Reservation,** site of the 1890 massacre at Wounded Knee. The last major conflict between Indians and the U.S. Army, the battle ended the ghost dances that the Sioux thought would banish the whites and bring back the buffalo. Today 23,000 Oglala live on the reservation, and many old traditions survive. To hear the sound of Lakota (a Sioux dialect), tune your radio to 90.1 FM, *Voice of the Lakota Nation,* which broadcasts music and cultural programs. **Interior** and **Cedar Pass** have lodging, food, and gas. **Cedar Pass Lodge** *(Inside park. 605-433-5460. www.cedarpasslodge.com. April-Oct.),* run by the Oglala tribe, sells Lakota arts and crafts.

Badlands

Northeast entrance of Badlands National Park to Wall on South Dakota 240

■ 30 miles ■ 2 hours ■ All year but spring and fall are best. Adm. fee to park mid-March through November. *See map p. 225.*

This tour takes you through the starkly beautiful scenery of Badlands National Park, traversing the 300-foot-high escarpment that divides the upper from the lower prairie.

Heading south from the northeast entrance to **Badlands National Park** *(605-433-5361. www.nps.gov/badl. Adm. fee)* on S. Dak. 240, pull over at the **Big Badlands Overlook** for an outstanding view. You stand atop the **Badlands Wall;** prairie stretches both behind you and in the far distance ahead. In the middle lie the odd spires and knobs, steep gulches and ravines of the bad-lands. From here you can appreciate why French fur trappers in the early 1800s called the area *les mauvaises terres à traverser*—bad lands to cross.

Stop at the next pullout and take one of the short trails. The **Door** (0.75 mile), **Windows** (0.25 mile), and **Notch** (1.5 miles) **Trails** lead through a wonderland of high buttes and pinnacles, eroded from clay stone and volcanic ash deposits up to 38 million years old. The rugged **Castle Trail** (5 miles one way) starts across the road and joins the **Saddle Pass Trail.** A little farther down the road, the **Cliff Shelf Nature Trail** makes a delightful half-mile loop through an island of juniper and features good views of the spreading prairie.

Badlands under stormy skies

Stop at the **Ben Reifel Visitor Center** for a film, exhibits, and literature. Continuing west, you arrive in 4.5 miles at the **Fossil Exhibit Trail,** with its fossil reproductions displayed under clear plastic domes. Though the reproductions are hard to see, the trail offers proof that the badlands rank as one of the world's richest beds of prehistoric mammal fossils.

A little farther on, facing the less dramatic side of the road, **Prairie Winds Overlook** draws few motorists. But standing here at the edge of a prairie sea listening to the wind, you start to understand the homesteaders' attraction to the lonely prairie. Of the many overlooks, perhaps the most jaw-dropping is the **Pinnacles Overlook.** Here, almost surrounded by a badlands panorama, you can study the various landforms or just absorb the beauty. The rich interplay of light and shadow in the early morning or late afternoon adds another photogenic dimension.

Continue on the gravel Sage Creek Rim Road, which overlooks the 64,250-acre **Sage Creek Wilderness Area** and offers likely sightings of bison, prairie dogs, and other animals, or travel north 8.5 miles to the town of **Wall,** which has the **National Grasslands Visitor Center** *(708 Main St. 605-279-2125. Mon.-Thurs. year-round),* featuring excellent exhibits.

Nebraska
Pine Ridge Country

Gordon to Crawford on US 20

■ 67 miles ■ 1½ hours ■ Spring through fall

Starting at the western edge of the Sand Hills, US 20 travels west through hilly farm and ranch country into the rugged Pine Ridge area of northwestern Nebraska. Ranging through a diverse geographical region, the highway passes near picturesque state parks and connects several small agricultural towns noted for their pioneer history. **Gordon** prides

itself as the childhood home of writer Mari Sandoz (1896-1966), whose novels and nonfiction books about Native Americans, pioneers, and homesteaders gained her wide fame. The **Tourist Information center** *(300 S. Main St. 308-282-0730. www.gordonchamber.com. Mon.-Fri.)* contains first editions, letters, manuscripts, and memorabilia.

A block south of the tall, white grain elevator, Gordon's most prominent building, head west on US 20. Ten miles to the south and east lie the western reaches of the **Sand Hills,** dunes stabilized by a layer of grass. In front of you, to the west, spread the flat plains, where cattle are common and trees scarce. With little annual rainfall, the main crops are wheat, alfalfa, and hay. Spring to fall wildflowers color the roadsides. Though the small towns of **Rushville**

Near Fort Robinson State Park

and **Hay Springs** each hold a historical museum, wayfarers will especially appreciate their oasislike parks.

On to the **Pine Ridge**, this is a country of high buttes and ridges, small streams, and steep gullies. This narrow, 100-mile-long escarpment crosses the state's northwestern corner, defining the edge of the Nebraska High Plains. Prairie intermingles with pine-covered hills, and the landscape seems to change from mile to mile.

Three miles east of Chadron, the **Museum of the Fur Trade** *(308-432-3843. www.furtrade.org. May-Oct., by appt. in winter; adm. fee)* tells the history of North American fur trading, with a collection of flintlock guns, a reconstructed trading post, and a garden of Native American crops.

Main Street in **Chadron** shows off a handsome row of Western-style, two-story buildings. About 10 miles south of town is the lovely 974-acre **Chadron State Park** *(308-432-6167. www.outdoor nebraska.ne.gov/parks. Adm. fee),* which offers swimming, horseback riding, and hiking. Forest trails lead to good views at elevations of nearly 5,000 feet.

From Chadron, continue west along the **White River.** To the north lie rolling hills, the result of the erosion of ancient clay and clay-shale beds. To the south, you begin to see the buttes of the badlands. In 24 miles you reach the town of **Crawford,** known chiefly for **Fort Robinson State Park** *(308-665-2900. www.outdoornebraska.ne.gov/*

Nebraska 29

Harrison to Agate Fossil Beds National Monument

■ 23 miles ■ ½ hour ■ Spring through fall. See map p. 227.

A short ride south from Harrison takes you through high ridges and grassy ranchlands to an area rich in Miocene mammal fossils.

Offering motels and other visitor services, **Harrison** is the county seat, and the only town, of Sioux County. It reached its peak population of 500 in 1940, but nothing could reverse the trend toward large, mechanized farms and ranches. Now it is home to only about 280 citizens.

Travel south on Nebr. 29 along brown pastureland, relieved by sharp-edged buttes and ridges and broken up by deep gullies. After 23 miles you arrive at **Agate Fossil Beds National Monument** *(308-668-2211. www.nps.gov/agfo. Adm. fee).* Situated along the **Niobrara River,** this 2,770-acre park contains fossilized mammals that roamed here from 25 to 13 million years ago. Named for nearby agate-rich rock formations, these fossil beds preserve the bones of such odd creatures as the Moropus, an animal with the head of a horse, neck of a giraffe, and body of a tapir. The most common grazer was the Menoceras, a two-horned rhinoceros that ran in herds. A 2-mile interpretive walk explores the sites.

Agate Fossil Beds NM

parks.), the largest state park in Nebraska. Centerpiece of the 22,000-acre park, **Fort Robinson** dates from the Indian battles of the 1870s. Chief Crazy Horse died here in 1877. During World War II German prisoners were held here. The complex includes a parade ground and twin rows of stately barracks and elegant officers' quarters (used as visitor accommodations in the summer). Trails explore the rocky bluffs and pine-clad slopes.

Within the park, the **Fort Robinson Museum** *(308-665-2919. www .nebraskahistory.org/sites. Daily April-Oct., weekends Nov.-March; adm. fee)* showcases memorabilia in the old post headquarters. The **Trailside Museum** *(308-665-2929. www.trailside.unl.edu. May-Sept., call for winter schedule; adm. fee)* interprets area geologic and natural history. North about 15 miles on Nebr. 2 is the 95,000-acre **Oglala National Grassland** *(308-432-0300. www .fs.fed.us/grasslands),* popular for camping and hunting, and **Toadstool Park** *(308-432-0300),* noted for its mushroom-shaped rock outcroppings.

Kansas
Flint Hills

Manhattan to Cassoday on Kansas 177

- 84 miles - 2 hours - Spring and fall

This eastern Kansas route arrows through the heart of the lovely Flint Hills, a region of rounded limestone hills covered by bluestem prairie. Along the way, it dips into the largest remaining tracts of tallgrass prairie in the United States.

Start out in **Manhattan,** home of Kansas State University. The present town dates from 1855, when a steamboat full of settlers from Cincinnati ran aground nearby. With other area settlers they formed Manhattan. Its population drawn mostly from the North, the town remained abolitionist during the Bleeding Kansas and Civil War years.

Head south on Kans. 177 through uplands pierced by limestone outcroppings. In about 8 miles, you pass the **Konza Prairie Biological Station** *(785-587-0441. www.konza.ksu.edu).* Turn right on Cty. Rd. 901 and drive 5 miles to the entrance. Owned by The Nature Conservancy and run by Kansas State University, this 8,616-acre parcel is one of the country's largest remaining tracts of virgin tallgrass prairie. Self-guided tour brochures are available.

After you cross I-70, the landscape unfurls in pastures of green grass and delicate wildflowers. Much of the land in this 30- to 40-mile-wide band has remained unchanged for thousands of years. Native Americans used pieces of chert, or flint, found here for tools and weapons. Many pioneers, doubting such rocky ground would make for good farmsteads, moved on.

Continue south past tree-lined valleys and rocky ledges and pick up the officially designated **Flint Hills Scenic Byway** in **Council Grove,** where Osage

chiefs opened the Santa Fe Trail in 1825, when they sold the right-of-way through their land for $800. The trunk of the **Council Oak,** where the agreement was penned, stands under a gazebo at 210 East Main Street. The popular **Hays House** restaurant *(Main St. between Neosho St. & Wood St. 620-767-5911. www.hayshouse.com)* dates from 1857. For a good overview of area history, visit the **Kaw Mission State Historic Site** *(Mission St. north of US 56. 620-767-5410. www .kawmission.org. Wed.-Sat.; adm. fee),* which houses Native American artifacts.

Continue south into Chase County. North of Strong City looms the historic **Z-Bar/Spring Hill Ranch Headquarters Area** *(620-273-8494)* just off the highway on your right with a three-story ranch house built by cattle baron S. F. Jones in 1881. In 1996 the 10,861-acre ranch became the **Tallgrass Prairie National Preserve** *(www.nps.gov/tapr).*

A few minutes south is **Cottonwood Falls** (pop. 966) where a French Renaissance-style building rears up from the prairie: the native limestone and walnut **Chase County**

Through the Flint Hills of Kansas

Courthouse *(620-273-8469 or 800-431-6344. Call for tour schedule; donation),* the state's oldest courthouse still in use. Visit the **Chase County Historical Society and Museum** *(301 Broadway. 620-273-8469 or 800-431-6344. Tues.-Sat.; donation)* to see the boots of author William Least Heat-Moon. Then continue about 25 miles south through the **Flint Hills** to **Cassoday,** the prairie-chicken capital of the world.

Wetlands and Wildlife Scenic Byway

From US 281 near Hoisington to US 281 near St. John on Kansas 4, NE 100 Avenue, Kansas 156, NE 30 Road, RS 980, RS 1484, RS 554, RS 506, and RS 636

▪ 77 miles ▪ 3 hours ▪ Spring and fall are best for bird-watching. Watch for slow-moving farm vehicles in harvest season.

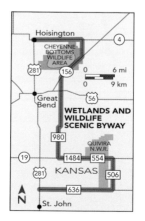

The rolling hills of rural central Kansas are home to some of the most important wetlands in the Midwest, vitally important to tens of thousands of resident and migratory birds. This route offers excellent opportunities to experience the best of the area's wildlife viewing.

About 2 miles east of Hoisington, stop at the kiosk on Kans. 4 for an introduction to The Nature Conservancy's 7,300-acre **Cheyenne Bottoms Preserve** *(www.nature.org),* where secondary roads lead to lakes and marshes. Geese, ducks, and shorebirds throng these wetlands at various times of the year. About 6 miles farther east, enjoy the view from the Cheyenne Bottoms overlook.

Take NE 100 Avenue and Kans. 156 to **Cheyenne Bottoms Wildlife Area** *(www.visitgreatbend.com),* a 19,857-acre wetland that is home to bald eagles, pelicans, and many more species. Then follow NE 30 Rd., RS 980, RS 1484, RS 554, RS 506, and Fourth Avenue (RS 636) to **Quivira National Wildlife Refuge** *(620-486-2393. www.fws.gov/refuge/quivira),* where 7,000 acres of prairie wetlands and native grasslands interspersed with shrubs and trees attract a diversity of birds and mammals such as coyotes, bobcats, white-tailed deer, and prairie dogs. Displays in the refuge **visitor center** explain the importance of wetlands, and a driving tour is available. In April, you may see endangered whooping cranes at **Big Salt Marsh.**

MISSOURI
Crowley's Ridge Parkway

Malden, Missouri, to Helena, Arkansas, on US 62, 49, 412, 64B, 79, County Roads J and WW, Arkansas 141, 135, 168, 351, 1B, 163, 14, 284, 1, 44, 242, and minor connecting roads

■ 212 miles ■ 1 day ■ All year. Final segment of byway overlaps Arkansas section of Great River Road.

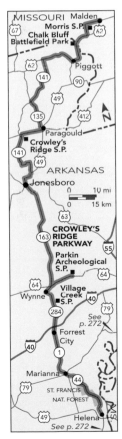

So distinctive, both geologically and ecologically, that it comprises its own natural division, Crowley's Ridge runs from extreme southeastern Missouri into eastern Arkansas, ending at the historic river port of Helena.

What created this geological oddity—this thin strip of upland averaging 150 to 200 feet higher than the surrounding flat delta landscape? Once, geologists say, the Mississippi River flowed west of its current course, while the Ohio occupied what is now the Mississippi's path. As these two great rivers meandered, they left a long ribbon of uneroded land between them. In a dry period after the last ice age about 15,000 years ago, prevailing westerly winds carried fine soil called loess and deposited it in a thick layer on this strip.

Today's byway follows the top of Crowley's Ridge, exploring its natural and human history. Long popular with settlers (it's named for Benjamin Crowley, an early resident), the ridge has an agricultural heritage that's still apparent in roadside stands along the way selling watermelons, peaches, and other produce.

Only 14 miles of this byway lie in Missouri, but during the brief journey here you can get a close look at the geology of Crowley's Ridge at **Morris State Park** *(off Cty. Rd. WW. 573-748-5340. www.mostateparks.com).* A 2-mile loop trail takes hikers past areas interpreting the formation of Crowley's Ridge and some of its unusual plants, including trees such as tulip-poplar, American holly, American beech, and cucumber tree.

The byway crosses the St. Francis River into Arkansas near **Chalk Bluff Battlefield Park** *(3 miles northwest*

231

Glade Top Trail

Forest Road 147, Mark Twain National Forest

■ 23 miles ■ 1 hour ■ Spring through fall. Gravel road

Built by the Civilian Conservation Corps in the 1930s, this two-lane gravel road traverses the gentle hills of Missouri's Ozark Plateau. Heading south from the northern boundary of the **Mark Twain National Forest's Ava Ranger District** *(417-683-4428)*, you come in about a mile to **Haden Bald,** an area managed by a controlled burn every four to six years. Just across the road lies the **Smoke Tree Scene** interpretive site. Locals call smoke trees "yellowwoods" for the color beneath the bark. Come autumn, the trees blaze with brilliant reds and golds.

The forest opens up to vistas 1.5 miles farther on, with **Arkansas View** offering on a clear day a look at the **St. François Mountains,** 40 miles to the southeast. This stop has a shady picnic area, strategically positioned for a panoramic view.

Continue south 1 mile to **Watershed Divide,** which splits the Little North Fork of the White River watershed on the east from the Beaver Creek watershed on the west. From here you can see an abundance of hardwoods and also observe your next stop, **Caney Lookout Tower,** 3 miles south.

A few miles beyond the tower, the forest road forks. FR 147 heads southeast toward **Longrun,** the trail's end, and FR 149 wanders southwest to Mo. 125. Take your pick: From both, peaceful hills and farms slip by your window like a dream.

of St. Francis via Cty. Rds. 341 & 347), site of a series of Civil War battles in 1863 that ended Confederate Gen. John Marmaduke's incursion into Missouri. The bluffs here, by the way, are not really chalk but light-colored clays, silts, and sands that are easily eroded into steep slopes.

The small town of **Piggott** seems an unlikely birthplace for a classic work of American literature, but Ernest Hemingway spent much time here after marrying Arkansas native Pauline Pfeiffer in 1927. His in-laws' house and adjacent "studio" (a converted red barn) where much of *A Farewell to Arms* was written now compose the **Hemingway-Pfeiffer Museum and Educational Center** *(1021 W. Cherry St. 870-598-3487. http://hemingway .astate.edu. Closed Sun.; donation)*. The relationship among Hemingway, the Pfeiffers, and Piggott wasn't always the best, but fans of "Papa" will enjoy seeing his desk and poker table and imagining how the great writer passed time in these environs.

The route continues through cropland and pastures, past the town of Paragould to **Crowley's Ridge State Park** *(Ark. 168. 870-573-6751. www .arkansasstateparks.com/crowleysridge)*, with cabins, hiking trails, and lakes.

Jonesboro *(Jonesboro Regional Chamber of Commerce, 1709 E. Nettleton St. 870-932-6691. http://jonesboro chamber.org)* is the largest city along the byway. The **Arkansas State University Museum** *(322 University Loop W. Circle. 870-972-2074. www.astate.edu/museum)* is well worth a visit for its exhibits on American Indian and pioneer history, paleontology, and a regionally renowned glassware and ceramics collection. The **Forrest Wood Crowley's Ridge Nature Center** *(600 E. Lawson Rd. 870-933-6787. www.crowleysridge.org. Closed Mon.)* ranks as one of the best spots to learn about the natural history of Crowley's Ridge, with exhibits, interpretive trails, and a 30-foot-long satellite photo of the region.

Where Ark. 163 crosses US 64, consider an 8-mile side trip east on the latter highway to **Parkin Archeological State Park** *(870-755-2500. www.arkansasstateparks.com. Closed Mon.; adm. fee)*, which preserves the site where a Mississippi-period Native American village was located from A.D. 1000 to 1550. Many scholars believe the Parkin site is the village of Casqui visited by the expedition of Hernando de Soto in 1541. Visitors can observe archaeological excavations when such research is in progress.

Probably the most rewarding place to experience the natural history of Crowley's Ridge is **Village Creek State Park** *(off Ark. 284. 870-238-9406. www.arkansasstateparks .com)*, where hiking and horse trails wind through woodlands, streams, and lakes. The park's **Military Road Trail** follows the most dramatic remaining portion of an 1829 route between Memphis and Little Rock, which

Watermelon stand

became part of the Trail of Tears when Native Americans of the Creek, Chickasaw, and Cherokee Nations were forcibly removed from their homelands in the East.

Crowley's Ridge Parkway continues south to Marianna and Helena, overlapping part of Arkansas's **Great River Road** byway (see pp. 272-273.)

233

Missouri Ozarks

Salem to Eminence on Missouri 19

▪ 44 miles ▪ 1 hour ▪ Spring through fall

Coursing through the peaceful farm country and upland forests of southeastern Missouri, this winding road passes near a large section of the Mark Twain National Forest and crosses the Ozark National Scenic Riverways wilderness area. Most popular in spring and fall, the highway boasts redbud and dogwood in pink and white and a palette of brilliant autumn colors. Wildflowers from last frost to first frost enhance the beauty of the roadsides.

From **Salem,** seat of Dent County, head south past the courthouse *(on left)* on Mo. 19. The first several miles envelop you in the big, undulant pastures typical of the region. Roads at 4 and 7 miles lead east to the Salem and Potosi Districts of the 1.5-million-acre **Mark Twain National Forest** *(573-364-4621. www.fs.usda.gov/mtnf)*. After about 10 miles (from Salem), the wide

Early morning fog along Missouri 19

fields begin yielding to thick forests. Cross Gladden Creek and continue on the windy road through shadowed glens and grassy meadows. A brief stretch of mobile homes and shacks gives way to woods and long views of the misty blue-green Ozarks.

Traveling up now through the hardwood forest, Mo. 19 ascends the **Ozark Plateau,** an eroded tableland spreading from northern Arkansas to southern Missouri and west to northeastern Oklahoma. Continue south into the **Ozark National Scenic Riverways** *(573-323-4236. www .nps.gov/ozar),* a National Park Service unit protecting more than 134 miles of the **Current** and **Jacks Fork Rivers.**

Cross the sparkling Current River and make a left into the **Round Spring Campground and Picnic Area.** Here you can explore one of the area's many caves, tucked into the high limestone bluff. Continue south as the road begins climbing again to views of the valley and hills. In about 3 miles you pass a tract of virgin pine. About 9 miles farther, a pull-off lets you savor the southern panorama of forested mountains before you begin a steep descent to the Jacks Fork River. Just beyond, the town of **Eminence** has outfitters for river expeditions, trail rides, and other activities.

Missouri Valley Wine Country

US 61 to Hermann on Missouri 94

▪ 56 miles ▪ 1½ hours ▪ Spring through fall

Tracing the broad bends of the Missouri River, Mo. 94 ambles over sweeping green hills, past picturesque farmhouses, and into the heart of Missouri wine country just west of St. Louis. The drive ends at Hermann, a town of German architecture and heritage situated near several award-winning wineries.

Take Mo. 94 west from US 61 and turn right in about 1 mile for the **August A. Busch Memorial Conservation Area** *(2 miles west on Cty. Rd. D. 636-441-4554. www.mdc.mo.gov),* which, combined with two adjacent areas, offers 16,900 acres for fishing, hiking, hunting,

Missouri Valley Old World scene

biking, and picnicking. Back on Mo. 94, drive toward Defiance. The road soon becomes extremely twisty as it goes up and down the forested hills and past many small houses. After 6 miles, take Cty. Rd. F west for 5 miles to see the **Daniel Boone House** *(636-798-2005. Call for hours; adm. fee),* a four-story, Georgian-style house that the pioneer built with his son and lived in during his last years in the early 1800s.

Back on the highway, you'll see on the right the **Katy Trail State Park** *(www .mostateparks.com),* a 225-mile biking and hiking trail that follows abandoned railroad rights-of-way along the Missouri. A few miles west of Defiance, you encounter a stretch of wineries around **Augusta.** As soon as you pass one, you begin seeing signs for the next. **Montelle Winery** *(636-228-4464. www .montelle.com),* perched 400 feet above the river valley, provides a scenic view of the bluffs and farmland below. All the wineries offer tours and tastings.

Proceed cautiously along the vertiginous highway. Detour, if you wish, 4 miles south of Dutzow to the riverfront town of **Washington,** a charming collection of restaurants, B&Bs, shops, and 19th-century houses built in the Missouri-German style. Washington also has the world's only corncob pipe factory.

Again on Mo. 94, drive a mile or so west of Dutzow to a side road leading to the **Daniel Boone Grave and Monument,** though no one knows for sure if Boone is buried there. Continue west through Marthasville and

Little Dixie Highway of the Great River Road

AMERICA'S BYWAYS

Clarksville to the northern Pike County line on Missouri 79

■ 30 miles ■ 2 hours ■ Spring through fall

This byway is in a part of Missouri known as "Little Dixie," for the population of southerners who settled here in the early, and mid-19th century.

In recent years artists have established studios along Mo. 79. You'll note some of them (metalworkers, furniture makers, etc.) in **Clarksville,** where the byway begins. Enjoy views of the Mississippi from the Riverfront Park or from the observation point at **Lock and Dam No. 24,** 2 miles north. From late fall through winter, you'll see bald eagles.

Ten miles to the north, **Louisiana** is famed for its **Georgia Street Historic District,** with more than 60 buildings dating from 1850 to 1935 that exhibit striking architectural details. The **Henry Lay Sculpture Park** *(573-754-4726. www.greatriverroad .com/hannibal/laypark.htm. April-Dec. Thurs.-Sun.),* just a few miles west via US 54 and Mo. UU, features the excellent work of contemporary artists.

The artworks are situated in nature, in natural meadows and woodlands, or along lakeshores and streams.

North of Louisiana *(turn east on Mo. TT)* is the 6,700-acre **Ted Shanks Conservation Area** *(573-248-2530. www.mdc.mo.gov),* a wildlife paradise of bottomland hardwoods, marsh, fields, and Mississippi River frontage.

See p. 186

235

Missouri River's 1869 Poeschel-Harrison House, built in typical German style

Treloar along the fertile **Missouri River Valley.** To your left lie flat fields of grain stretching to the Missouri, and beyond rises a ridge of bluffs several hundred feet high paralleling the river's course. On your right side loom the cliffs that define the north edge of the valley. Just over 3 miles after Treloar, you pass the lovely **St. Johns of Pinckney United Church of Christ** (1870) and its cemetery.

For the next 15 miles, a rich tableau unrolls—cornfields and cow pastures, one-lane bridges over small creeks, dips into shady vales, and rises to views of the river and the ranks of green hills.

The sweet wines of previous years are giving way to drier vintages made from more desirable French hybrids, resulting in a 15-million-dollar industry for the state.

At Mo. 19 take the truss bridge across the **Missouri River** into **Hermann.** From the bridge you can see the steeples and old brick buildings emerging from the limestone bluff on the south side of the river. German immigrants founded the town of Hermann in 1837 to preserve their language and customs. They also set about making Missouri the nation's second largest wine producer. Then Prohibition dried up the area. Missouri Valley winemaking geared up again in the 1960s, and tourists now flock to Hermann to visit its German architecture, B&Bs, museums, and historic wineries.

Driving along the steep streets, you see charming houses with wide porches and hanging flowerpots, neatly groomed lots, clean sidewalks, and attractive shops. **Stone Hill Winery** (*1110 Stone Hill Hwy. 573-486-2221 or 800-909-9643. www.stonehillwinery.com. Fee for tours*), established in 1847, commands a fine view of the town and nearby countryside, and showcases an impressive array of vaulted cellars. Just east of the Missouri River bridge, the **Hermann-hof Winery** (*330 E. 1st St. 800-393-0100. www.hermannhof .com. Free self-guided tours*) dates from 1852 and features a smokehouse and brick wine cellars. The **Historic Hermann Museum** (*4th & Schiller Sts. 573-486-2389. www.historichermann.com. April–late-Oct. Tues-Sun., call for* *schedule in Dec.; adm. fee)*, housed in the 1871 German School Building, has displays on area shipbuilding, winemaking, and early furniture.

If you continue on Mo. 94 west of Hermann to Jefferson City (43 miles) you won't find any more wineries, but you'll travel through a similar stretch of gentle farmland with excellent views of valleys and bluffs interspersed with woodlands and a handful of tiny villages.

IOWA
Woodlands Scenic Byway

US 34 near Ottumwa to Farmington on County Roads T61, T7J, J40, and W40, Iowa 273 and 2, and US 63

■ 74 miles ■ 2 hours ■ Spring through fall. Some gravel roads.

Along the back roads of southeastern Iowa, this peaceful route takes travelers by Amish farmsteads and historic riverfront hamlets. The tour connects several roads, varying from hard top to gravel.

Start 12 miles west of Ottumwa and take Cty. Rd. T61 south from US 34, following the "Scenic Byway" signs. Rolling farmlands and narrow valleys beckon. In about 4 miles you reach the small farming community of **Blakesburg.** Pass a row of clapboard houses along a shady main street, then turn right when the pavement ends, veer past the white-washed Christian Church, and continue south. After 5 more miles, turn left onto gravel Cty. Rd. T7J and travel along cornfields and feathery meadows. After about 9 miles the hard top starts up again and takes you through **Drakesville.** Be on the lookout

for slow-moving, horse-drawn Amish vehicles. Take Iowa 273 for 4 miles past Drakesville, turn right on US 63, and go about 3 miles to **Bloomfield.** Stop in at the **Iowa Welcome Center** *(301 N. Washington St. 641-664-1104. www.visitdavis county.com)* for information, then continue past the French Renaissance-style courthouse. Take a left at the square onto Cty. Rd. J40.

The next several miles feature fields of crops. Stands of oak and hickory break the steady rhythm of the fields. In 11 miles, pass through the crossroads town of Troy and continue another 13 miles to the village of **Keosauqua,** where the steamboat Gothic Manning Hotel sits by the **Des Moines River.**

Cross the river on the steel truss bridge and turn right for **Lacey-Keosauqua State Park** *(319-293-3502. www.iowa dnr.gov. Camping fee),* a detour that offers picnicking, hiking, and camping.

Keosauqua Bridge, Bentonsport

237

Back on the road, travel about 6 miles to another historic port town, **Bentonsport.** You cross the river again to enter this tiny, tranquil mid-19th-century town. Cruise along the gravel riverside road by B&Bs, a blacksmith shop, general store, and arts and antiques shops. Then head back to Cty. Rd. J40 and up a bluff to an overlook of the river.

In 4 more miles you arrive in the third erstwhile port town, **Bonaparte.** On the gentle Des Moines, this town preserves many buildings from the mid-1800s. Head south on Cty. Rd. W40 and then east on Iowa 2 through pastoral landscapes to the pleasant town of **Farmington,** also on the river.

Loess Hills Scenic Byway

Akron to Hamburg on Iowa 12, 292, 141, 175, 37, 183, 127, 191, 192, 184, US 30, 275, I-29, I-680, and county roads

▪ 220 miles ▪ 1 day ▪ Spring through fall. Drive carefully on gravel roads.

There's plenty of enjoyment in simply driving the rural roads that weave through picturesque farmlands and bluffs along this route, which roughly parallels the Missouri River in western Iowa. Signs mark the main route, with several loops along the way offered for alternatives.

You'll appreciate the trip more, though, if you know something of the geology that shaped the landscape. The Loess Hills stretch in a band about 200 miles long and up to 15 miles wide, from north of Sioux City southward into Missouri. They're built of fine, wind-deposited soil called loess (pronounced LUSS) produced by glacial abrasion 15,000 to 12,000 years ago. Winds carried this powdery soil to the eastern side of the Missouri River floodplain, where it built up bluffs, fairly steep on the west-facing slopes and gentler on the east. Only in China are there loess deposits as deep as these.

Leaving **Akron** on Iowa 12 (you might want to walk the town's **Big Sioux River** or **Prairie Trails** before beginning), you don't start seeing the true Loess Hills until you reach Westfield, where the route lies between the bluffs and the Big Sioux River. A few miles south of Westfield, an east turn on Butcher Road leads to The Nature Conservancy's **Broken Kettle Grasslands Preserve** and adjacent **Five Ridge Prairie** *(712-947-4270. www.nature.org or www .plymouthcountyparks.com),* 3,000 acres of prairie ridgetops with plants and animals typically found farther west in the Great Plains, as well as critical habitat for many species of prairie butterflies such as regal fritillary and Ottoe skipper.

As you approach **Sioux City** *(Sioux City Tourism Bureau, 801 4th St. 712-279-4800 or 800-593-2228. www .visitsiouxcity.org),* you'll find one of the best places to learn about the Loess Hills: the **Dorothy Pecaut Nature Center** *(4500 Sioux River Rd. 712-258-0838.*

IOWA

http://woodburyparks.com. Closed Mon.). Located within **Stone State Park,** the center offers Loess Hills natural history exhibits on prairies, wetlands, and woodlands, but-terfly and wildflower gardens, and miles of trails to forest and prairie viewpoints.

South of Sioux City the route passes through rich farmland, while always keep-ing fairly close to the loess hills that give this drive its name. Yuccas along the roadside give this area a western feeling. South of Moorhead off Iowa 183, **Preparation Can-yon State Park** *(712-423-2829. www.iowadnr .gov)* is a peaceful, 344-acre tract with dra-matic hills all around and fine vistas of the farmlands below. Bur oaks are the most

Yucca blooms at sunset, Loess Hills

prominent of the tree species. At Pisgah, a short side trip west on Cty. Rd. F20 leads to **Murray Hill Scenic Overlook.**

On US 30 a few miles past Logan, watch for the **Harrison County Histori-cal Village** and **Iowa Welcome Center** *(712-642-2114. www.harrisoncounty parks.org/welcome. Historical village closed Dec.–mid-April; adm. fee),* where you can tour an old general store, schoolhouse, and log cabin; the site also offers travel information for Iowa and the Loess Hills region.

Among the attractions of **Council Bluffs** *(Council Bluffs Convention & Visitors Bureau 712-325-1000 or 800-228-6878. www.councilbluffsiowa.com)* are the **General Dodge House** *(605 3rd St. 712-322-2406. www.dodgehouse .org. Closed Mon. & Jan.; adm. fee),* a Victorian mansion built in 1869 by Gen. Grenville M. Dodge, a Civil War general called "the greatest railroad builder of all times," and the **Western Historic Trails Center** *(3434 Richard Downing Ave. 712-366-4900. www.iowahistory.org/historic-sites)* with exhibits on life along the Lewis and Clark, Mormon, California, and Oregon Trails.

On US 275 south of Council Bluffs, the drive occasionally climbs high enough for views of the **Missouri River Valley.** The highlight of the final leg of the byway is **Waubonsie State Park** *(712-382-2786. www.iowadnr.gov/ parks/state_park_list/waubonsie),* a place of rugged ravines.

239

Great River Road (Iowa)

New Albin to Keokuk on US 52, 18, 67, 61, Iowa 26, 76, 340, 22, 38, 92, 99, and county roads

■ 326 miles ■ 2 to 3 days ■ Spring through fall

Expansive views of the Mississippi River reward travelers on this route hugging Iowa's eastern border. The roller-coaster ride winds up, down, and around the limestone bluffs on the northern section of the route, stretching southward to a gentler landscape as the drive nears the Missouri border. Along the way you'll find great wildlife viewing, historically significant American Indian sites, and attractive river towns.

In Lansing, stop at **Mount Hosmer City Park,** set on a bluff 450 feet above the town, for splendid views of the Mississippi, here dotted with islands.

Southwest of Harpers Ferry, explore the environment of northeastern Iowa at beautiful **Yellow River State Forest** *(563-586-2254. www.iowadnr.gov)*, 8,500 acres of rugged terrain with rock outcrops, bluffs, and woods of sugar maple, basswood, ash, oak, elm, and cottonwood.

From about 500 B.C. until Europeans arrived in the region, a unique Effigy Mound culture of American Indians developed in the upper Midwest. **Effigy Mounds National Monument** *(563-873-3491. www .nps.gov/efmo. Adm. fee)* preserves 206 such mounds, 31 of them in shapes of birds and bears. The Marching Bear Group stretches along a bluff overlooking the Mississippi.

Southward from Marquette, the road wriggles between tall, steep slopes and the wide Mississippi, with an eye-level view of barges, towboats, and pleasure craft. After passing through McGregor, with its brick streets and bluffs, you'll once again ascend slopes wooded with oaks and maples as you climb to **Pikes Peak State Park** *(563-873-2341. www.iowa dnr.gov)*, within which lies the highest bluff on the Mississippi River—and one of the most spectacular views in Iowa. Named for Zebulon Pike (the famed Colorado mountain also bears his name), the site has remained largely untouched since the explorer came here in 1805 to scout fort locations.

The route winds its way down through cornfields to riverside **Guttenberg,** settled in 1845 by German immigrants and named for the inventor of the movable-type press (the extra *t* was a mistake). Pretty **River Front Park** stretches for a mile along the Mississippi, offering views of the passing scene, as does an overlook at **Lock and Dam No. 10.** Guttenberg's downtown is filled with German-style limestone buildings from the 1840s and 1850s.

Just beyond town, stop at a bluff-top scenic overlook for a good view of the river's deep-sided valley, etched with limestone strata and containing rich deposits of lead ore. The route continues past barns, dairy cows, and farmland, rising and falling until it reaches **Dubuque.** In Iowa's oldest city, plan a stop at the **National Mississippi River Museum and Aquarium** *(350 E. 3rd St. 563-557-9545. www.mississippirivermuseum.com. Adm. fee),* with interactive exhibits on river life, river craft from canoes to steamboats and tugboats, and wildlife. A hall of fame commemorates Mississippi River pioneers, explorers, and artists, including such notables as Lewis and Clark and Mark Twain.

South on US 52, Bellevue lives up to its name with fine views of the river. Just south of town, **Bellevue State Park** *(563-872-4019. www.iowadnr .gov)* features Iowa's largest butterfly garden, with walking paths through more than a hundred flower plots. The river road switches to US 67, and the lookout at **Eagle Point Park,** just north of Clinton, offers a view of the widest point on the Mississippi.

The striking stretch of road south of Princeton leads to **LeClaire,** birthplace of William F. "Buffalo Bill" Cody. The cabin where he was born no longer exists, but the **Buffalo Bill Cody Museum** *(199 N. Front St. 563-289-5580.*

www.buffalobillmuseumleclaire.com. Adm. fee) shows memorabilia from his life, local artifacts, and a historic steamboat.

Davenport *(Quad Cities Convention & Visitors Bureau, 102 S. Harrison St. 563-322-3911. www.visitquadcities.com)* is one of the Quad Cities, along with Bettendorf, Iowa, and Moline and Rock Island, Illinois. Because Davenport has no floodwall or levee, construction codes mean all new buildings in the floodplain must be elevated or otherwise protected from high water. The **1834 Colonel Davenport House** *(Hillman Ave. on Arsenal Island. 309-786-7336. www.davenporthouse.org. May-Oct. Thurs.-Sun.; adm. fee)* preserves the residence of the man who came here with the U.S. Army in 1816, became a prosperous trader, and established what is now a thriving urban area. (Davenport was murdered in his house by robbers on July 4, 1845.)

> The Mississippi River Valley was created over thousands of years—from the time it lay under Paleozoic seas to the most recent ice age, when glacial meltwaters scoured the river's course.

As the Mississippi and this route wind west and south through farmland and pastures, elevations decrease but bluffs still offer good lookout points. Mark Twain praised the town of **Muscatine** for its sunsets (he lived here for a while in 1854), and a lookout bearing his name near the town provides a fine view of the great river he loved so much. A bit farther south, just east of Wapello, you'll find the headquarters for a division of **Mark Twain National Wildlife Refuge Complex** *(217-224-8580. www.fws.gov/midwest/marktwain)*, where you can explore trails, observation areas, and roads excellent for viewing a variety of wildlife.

Toolesboro Indian Mounds National Historic Landmark *(319-523-8381. www.iowahistory.org. Weekends, closed Nov.–late-May)*, on Iowa 99, presents the well-preserved legacy of an ancient American Indian culture flourishing from 200 B.C. to A.D. 300. The 5-acre site includes several large mounds, an education center, and a prairie demonstration plot.

Burlington *(Burlington Area Convention & Tourism Bureau, 610 N. 4th St. 319-752-6365. www.growburlington.com)* may be best known for **Snake Alley** *(north of the 600 block of Washington St.)*, which locals call "the crookedest street in the world." Constructed in 1894 as an experimental street design by three German immigrants, the stretch consists of five half-curves and two quarter-curves and drops 58 feet over a distance of 275 feet.

241

Along Iowa's Great River Road

Views from the Great River Road are widening by the time you reach Fort Madison; the landscape flattens, and the river seems lazier as it broadens. Bald eagles are common in winter along much of the Mississippi River, but the winter concentrations at **Keokuk** can be astounding at times, totaling several hundred. Among many good observation points are the downtown riverfront and **Lock and Dam No. 19,** the highest of all the locks on the Mississippi.

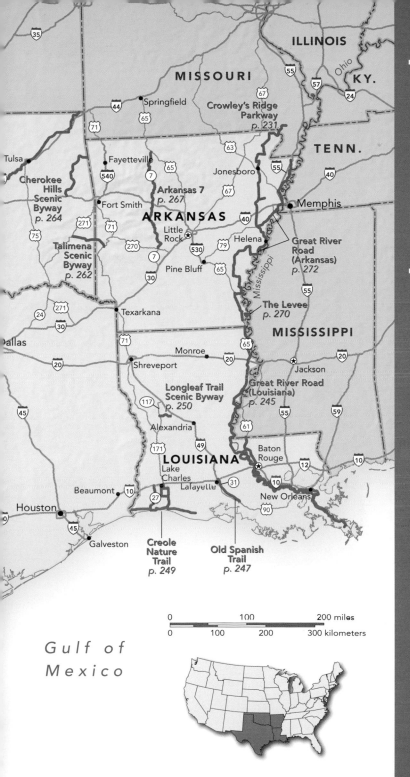

ILLINOIS

Ohio

MISSOURI

KY.

35

55

57

24

Springfield

Crowley's Ridge
Parkway
p. 231

44

65

67

71

63

TENN.

Tulsa

Fayetteville

Jonesboro

55

40

Memphis

540

7

65

67

Cherokee
Hills
Scenic
Byway
p. 264

Fort Smith

ARKANSAS

Arkansas 7
p. 267

271

71

Little
Rock

40

Helena

Great River
Road
(Arkansas)
p. 272

75

71

530

79

55

Talimena
Scenic
Byway
p. 262

270

7

Pine Bluff

65

Mississippi

The Levee
p. 270

30

MISSISSIPPI

271

Texarkana

65

24

30

Monroe

20

Jackson

20

59

Dallas

20

71

Shreveport

Great River
Road
(Louisiana)
p. 245

45

117

Longleaf Trail
Scenic Byway
p. 250

55

Alexandria

61

49

LOUISIANA

Baton
Rouge

12

10

171

Lake
Charles

10

Beaumont

10

Lafayette

31

New Orleans

Houston

27

90

45

Galveston

Creole
Nature
Trail
p. 249

Old Spanish
Trail
p. 247

Gulf of
Mexico

0   100   200 miles
0   100   200   300 kilometers

LOUISIANA

Great River Road (Louisiana)

Arkansas/Mississippi state lines to Venice, Louisiana, via US 65 and 61, Louisiana 15, 415, 991, 75, 405, 44, and 18 and local roads

▪ 717 miles ▪ 2 to 4 days ▪ All year

The grand old mansions along Louisiana's Great River Road Scenic Byway call to mind both the gentility of the antebellum planter class and the inexcusable slave labor system that made that gentility possible. Today the 717 miles of this byway mix that conflicted history with pockets of small-town charm to create a savory gumbo. As with most of the Great River Road, the Louisiana portion of the route often simultaneously follows separate roads on both sides of the big river. You'll find detailed driving directions at www.byways.org.

Following US 65 south from the Arkansas state line, travel along the shore of a natural oxbow lake before coming to the small riverfront farming town of **Lake Providence.** Take a few minutes here to visit the **Louisiana State Cotton Museum** *(7162 Hwy. 65 N. 318-559-2041),* whose exhibits detail the crop's influence on the economy and culture of the River Road.

Continuing south, you'll come to Tallulah, where you can detour across the river to explore the historic city of **Vicksburg,** Mississippi *(www.visitvicksburg .com),* and its famous Civil War battlefield. Or press south on US 65 toward Ferriday and the **Natchez-Vidalia Bridge,** twin cantilever bridges leading to the antebellum landmarks of **Natchez** *(www.visitnatchez .com)* on the east side of the Mississippi.

From Natchez, backtrack to the west bank of the Mississippi and continue south about 100 miles, where you'll eventually cross back over to the east bank on the impressive new John James Audubon Bridge to the quaint town of **St. Francisville,** Louisiana *(www .stfrancisville.us).* Visit **The Myrtles** *(7747 US Hwy. 61. 225-635-6277. www .myrtlesplantation.com),* a restored 1796 plantation home in St. Francisville,

Moss-draped live oaks along the Old Spanish Trail

St. Louis Cathedral, New Orleans

for a tour that includes some hair-raising stories of ghostly happenings here.

Via either the east or west bank of the river, the byway then takes you south through the state capital of **Baton Rouge** *(www.visit batonrouge.com).* Following the River Road south out of town, you can take the **Plaquemine Ferry** *(www.dotd.la.gov/ferry)* across to the west side of the river for a visit to the **Plaquemine Lock State Historic Site** *(57730 Main St. 225-687-7158. www.crt.state.la.us/parks/ iplaqlock.aspx).* The lock, built in 1909, provided access to a series of waterways in the Louisiana interior. Then cross back to the east bank again.

Along with cane fields and petrochemical factories, the stretch between Baton Rouge and New Orleans holds some of the most impressive antebellum homes along Louisiana's portion of the Great River Road. High points include the 53,000-square-foot **Nottoway Plantation** *(31025 Hwy. 1. 225-545-2730. www.nottoway.com)* in White Castle and **Houmas House** *(40136 Hwy. 942. 225-473-9380. www.houmashouse.com)* in Darrow. **Evergreen Plantation** *(4677 Hwy. 18. 985-497-3837. www.evergreenplantation.org),* located in Edgard, is worthy of special mention as it's the most complete surviving plantation home. Its three dozen historic buildings include 22 original slave cabins.

If you only have the stamina to tour a couple of plantation homes, however, start with **Oak Alley** *(3645 Hwy. 18. 225-265-2151. www.oakalley plantation.com)* in Vacherie, a photogenic manor house with an approach framed by 300-year-old moss-draped live oaks. The other must-see is the distinctive **San Francisco Plantation** *(2646 Hwy. 44. 985-535-2341. www.sanfranciscoplantation.org)* in Garyville, an ornately decorated Creole-style home. **Destrehan Plantation** *(13034 River Rd. 985-764-9315. www.destrehanplantation.org)* in Destrehan, about 20 miles west of New Orleans, dates back to 1787 and is the oldest home in the area.

"Swamp Pop," a uniquely Louisianan mix of Cajun, Creole, blues, and rock-and-roll, still rings out in Baton Rouge today.

Continuing east from Destrehan, the byway skirts **New Orleans** *(www.neworleanscvb.com).* Spending some time cruising through the Garden District and the French Quarter is highly recommended. On the water, a two-hour tour on the authentic **Steamboat** *Natchez (400 N. Peters St. #203. 504-586-8777. www.steamboatnatchez.com)* gives a hint of the days when the Mississippi was thick with paddle wheelers.

From here, the byway heads south through **Belle Chasse, Pointe à La Hache,** and **Port Sulphur** and on into the wetlands of the Mississippi Delta. When you come to the tiny sport-fishing center of **Venice**—which was largely wiped out by Hurricane Katrina and continues struggling to recover after that disaster and the 2010 BP oil spill—you'll want to stop and take a photo of the marker that declares this the southernmost point in Louisiana. You've reached, quite literally, the end of the road.

Old Spanish Trail

Houma to Breaux Bridge on US 90 and Louisiana 182 and 31

- 108 miles ▪ 3 hours ▪ Spring and fall. Summers are hot and humid.

Originally a section of a 19th-century Spanish frontier trail and trading route, the drive wends through southern Louisiana's Cajun country. This low, flat land of bayous, moss-draped live oaks, sugarcane fields, and old plantation manors also sustains a burgeoning oil industry.

Begin in **Houma,** the seat of Terrebonne Parish and a center of Cajun culture. Before leaving town try a spicy étouffée dish or a rich gumbo. From town head west on Bayou Black Drive (US 90), which hugs the bayou. Roadside signs advertise swamp tours, some run by the area's colorful Cajun entrepreneurs. The tours explore parts of the **Atchafalaya Basin,** which covers several hundred thousand acres and ranks as the continent's largest river-basin swamp.

A few miles outside Houma, the drive cuts through the first fields of sugarcane. After another 10 miles or so, it reaches the turnoff for **Wildlife Gardens** *(right at Greenwood School, then left 2 miles to 5306 N. Black Bayou Dr. 985 575 3676. www.wild lifegardens.com. Closed Sun.-Mon.; adm. fee).* Featuring an alligator farm and trapper's cabin, the gardens also offer nature and swamp tours.

Back on US 90, you see evidence of the region's rampant oil industry around **Gibson.** For the next 15 miles or so the drive passes oil-platform fabricators and other heavy equipment used by the inshore oil industry.

As you cross the bridge into St. Mary Parish along **Bayou Boeuf,** you can literally smell the industry generated by the enormous **McDermott Shipyard** on your left. Soon you enter **Morgan City,** a major port on the **Intracoastal Waterway.**

From Morgan City, follow signs for Berwick/La. 182, which will take you across **Berwick Bay** and the **Atchafalaya River** on the **Long-Allen Bridge,** then into the tiny towns of Berwick and Patterson. Paralleling the course of **Bayou Teche,** the drive now passes through one of the most fertile parts of the state's "sugar bowl," where plantations—each with its own sugar mill—flourished prior to the Civil War.

On the outskirts of Patterson, La. 182 jogs left and feeds into US 90 for about a mile before veering off again into flats and cane fields. After a couple of miles you enter **Centerville,** one of St. Mary Parish's oldest communities and a former sugar hub, with fine Victorian homes and antebellum planters' mansions.

Passing through the small town of Garden City, the road soon arrives in **Franklin,** the seat of St. Mary Parish and an official Main Street, U.S.A., town. La. 182 now becomes a stately boulevard running through the restored downtown and the elegant historic district, where you'll find **Oaklawn Manor** *(3296 E. Oaklawn Dr. 337-828-0434. www.oaklawnmanor.com. Closed Mon.; adm. fee)* and **Grevemberg House** *(407 Sterling Rd./Hwy 322. 337-828-2092. www.grevemberghouse.com. Adm. fee).*

247

Continuing west on La. 182, you'll pass through more cane-field country. In **Jeanerette,** one of the state's 18 active sugar mills still processes cane into raw sugar. There's also the **Jeanerette Bicentennial Museum** *(500 E. Main St. 337-276-4408. www.jeanerettemuseum.com. Closed Wed., Sat.-Sun.; adm. fee),* with exhibits on the sugar industry and bayou life. As you pass **LeJeune's Bakery** *(1510 W. Main St. 337-276-5690. www.lejeunes bakery.com. Closed weekends),* look for a blinking red light; this indicates the bakery has its famous French bread for sale, a town staple since 1884.

For the next 8 miles, the drive wanders through more flat cane country before entering **New Iberia** *(Tourist Commission, 2513 La. 14. 337-365-1540),* another town that sugar built. Main Street leads through the handsome historic district. The crown jewel here is **Shadows-on-the-Teche** *(317 E. Main St. 337-369-6446. www.shadowsontheteche.org. Adm. fee),* a restored 1834 plantation home with gardens. Other sights include the **Conrad Rice Mill** *(307 Ann St. 337-367-6163. Closed Sun.; adm. fee),* the oldest rice mill in the country, and the stunning **Rip Van Winkle Gardens** *(5505 Rip Van Winkle Rd. 337-359-8525. Adm. fee).*

From here, you can detour 20 miles on La. 182 to **Lafayette,** a colorful hub of Cajun country and a fine place to enjoy zydeco music. Or you can continue on the drive by turning right on La. 31. After 10 more miles of cane fields, you enter **St. Martinville** *(La Remise Visitor Information Center, Evangeline Oak Park, Evangeline Blvd. 337-394-2273),* the seat of St. Martin Parish. Known as "Petit Paris," this elegant, French-style town was made famous by Henry Wadsworth Longfellow's poem *Evangeline;* it recounts the story of two Acadian exiles who fled from Nova Scotia in 1755 to escape British rule. You can see the **Evangeline Oak** in **Evangeline Town Park** *(E. Port St.).* On St. Martin Square you'll find the **Evangeline Monument.**

A mile north on La. 31 is 135-acre **Longfellow-Evangeline Historic Site** *(1200 N. Main St. 337-394-3754. www.crt.state.la.us/parks/ilongfell.aspx. Adm. fee),* with a plantation home, visitor center, and recreation area. Continuing on La. 31, you follow Bayou Teche to the town of Parks. Seven miles farther, the drive ends in the town of **Breaux Bridge.**

Antebellum mansion, New Iberia

Creole Nature Trail

Sulphur to Lake Charles on Louisiana 27, 82, 14, and 384

■ 180 miles ■ 5 hours ■ Fall through spring. Summers are hot and humid; bring insect repellent. Excellent birding area.

It's called "Louisiana's Outback," and while it may not be quite as remote as Australia's backcountry, this area of southwestern Louisiana offers visitors lots of wide-open, unpeopled spaces. The southern part of the drive passes through the marshes and prairies of Cameron Parish, which is both the state's largest and least populous parish (Louisiana's equivalent to a county).

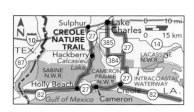

In September 2005, Hurricane Rita came ashore along Louisiana's southwestern coastline with devastating effect. Thousands of buildings—indeed, entire towns—were seriously damaged or completely destroyed. The area will be recovering for years to come, but the resilient spirit of the people (they also rebuilt after 1957's massive Hurricane Audrey) has led them to return to their homes, and to a way of life dominated by seafood production, oil and gas exploration, hunting, and fishing.

The drive begins in **Sulphur**, 5 miles west of Lake Charles on I-10. The town's name derives from the huge mineral deposits found in a nearby salt dome. Visit the **Brimstone Historical Museum and Tourist Information Center** (*900 S. Huntington St. 337 527 0357. www.brimstonemuseum.org. Closed Sun.*) for an overview of local history and mining.

As the drive heads south on La. 27, it soon crosses the **Intracoastal Waterway**, a shipping route that runs from Texas to the Atlantic coast. On the left is **Calcasieu Lake**, 19 miles long and 8 miles wide, linked by a separate shipping channel to the Gulf of Mexico.

On the other side of the bridge, the landscape changes dramatically to brackish marsh with few trees. The small town of **Hackberry** also suffered damage from Hurricane Rita, but has rebounded along with its shrimping and crabbing industries.

La. 27 passes through 124,000-acre **Sabine National Wildlife Refuge** (*3000 Holly Beach Hwy. 337-762-3816. www.fws.gov/swlarefugecomplex/sabine*), where most visitor facilities were destroyed by Hurricane Rita. Nonetheless, alligators and dozens of species of waterbirds still can be seen along roadsides.

The town of **Holly Beach** was wiped off the map by Rita, but

Louisiana has 5,000 miles of ice-free navigable rivers, bayous, and canals—the most extensive water transportation network in the country.

249

Alligators in a Louisiana marsh

the beaches that attracted people here are still inviting.

A side trip on La. 82 leads west along the Gulf to Texas. Along the way, the **Peveto Woods Sanctuary** *(8.5 miles west of Holly Beach. www .braudubon.org/peveto-woods-sanctuary.php)* ranks among the region's most popular birding locations during spring migration. Surf-fishing can produce flounder, redfish, drum, and speckled trout.

Back on La. 27/82, a ferry *(fare)* crosses the Calcasieu Ship Channel to Cameron, another town seriously damaged by Rita and quickly rebuilt and reoccupied by its residents. At Creole, La. 27 heads north. Note the cheniers; these are sandy beach ridges, often topped with oaks, that were once sandbars in the Gulf. Two miles after

Sunset at Sabine National Wildlife Refuge

again crossing the Intracoastal Waterway is the right turn onto the **Pintail Wildlife Drive** of **Cameron Prairie National Wildlife Refuge** *(337-598-2216. www.fws.gov/swlarefugecomplex)*, another excellent birding spot. The refuge visitor center is 2 miles farther north.

You can take either La. 384 or continue on La. 27 to La. 14 to reach **Lake Charles** *(Southwest Louisiana Convention & Visitors Bureau, 1205 N. Lakeshore Dr. 337-436-9588 or 800-456-7952. www.visitlakecharles.org)*.

The city's **Charpentier District** preserves about 20 square blocks of historic Victorian architecture. The **Mardi Gras Museum of Imperial Calcasieu** *(809 Kirby St. 337-430-0043. www.swlamardigras.com/year-round/mardi-gras-museum.cfm. Tues.-Fri.; adm. fee)* features a display of Mardi Gras memorabilia from the Imperial Calcasieu area, including the largest costume display in the state.

Longleaf Trail Scenic Byway

Louisiana 117 to Louisiana 119 on Forest Road 59 in Kisatchie National Forest

■ 17 miles ■ ½ hour ■ Spring and fall. Summers are hot and humid.

Winding through Louisiana's 600,000-acre Kisatchie National Forest, the drive traces a high ridge through beautiful pine forests.

Before starting at the western end of the marked byway, head south 3 miles on La. 117 to FR 350. Follow it east 1.9 miles to **Kisatchie Overlook** for views of **Kisatchie Bayou,** a state-designated natural and scenic stream. Return to La. 117 and head north to the beginning of the byway on FR 59.

After winding through a mixed pine forest for 3.5 miles, you cross Kisatchie Bayou. Unlike Louisiana's usually languid bayous, this one follows a steeper course, creating falls and rapids.

The drive ascends from here, past pastures and farms and through the community of Lotus Hill. Just beyond you enter the 38,450-acre **National Red Dirt Wildlife Management Preserve** *(Kisatchie National Forest. 318-472-1840),* established in 1941 to protect game animals.

After passing the preserve's Cane Campground, you'll see a stand of longleaf pines, as well as taller, straighter "superior pines" that have been genetically engineered.

Farther on, the drive passes through a forest of longleaf, loblolly, and shortleaf pines. It's worth a detour to **Kisatchie Bayou Campground** *(4 miles south on FR 321, then west 2 miles on FR 366).* From the campground's bluffs, you have great views of the bayou's white-sand beaches, rapids, and forested bottomland flats.

Back on FR 59 east, you soon come to a stand of nursery pines on the right. Another half mile down on the left, look for white-banded "nest trees" set aside throughout the forest as habitat for the endangered red-cockaded woodpecker.

After about 3 miles the drive reaches the boundary of the **Kisatchie Hills Wilderness,** an 8,700-acre preserve featuring rugged sandstone bluffs,

251

Passing through the pines, Longleaf Trail Scenic Byway

outcrops, and mesas. For the drive's remaining 7 miles, this wilderness monopolizes the view to the northeast.

At **Longleaf Vista** a short, paved interpretive walk offers superb views of the wilderness and the longleaf pine forest; the walk connects with a 1.5-mile nature trail that circles through these glorious pinelands.

The byway's final 2 miles follow a section of the old Opelousas–Fort Jesup Military Road, a major Civil War route. At **Bayou Cypre Overlook** stop for more views of the Kisatchie Hills Wilderness. The drive ends at the intersection with La. 119.

TEXAS
Texas Hill Country

Oak Hill to New Braunfels on US 290, Texas 16, 27, 39, 46, and Farm Road 187 and 337

▪ 280 miles ▪ 2 days ▪ All year. Wildflower bloom peaks in April. Area is subject to flash floods.

This lofty oasis is rife with rolling hills, plunging gorges, limestone bluffs, diverse wildlife, and charming villages that reflect the region's Old World heritage.

From **Oak Hill,** US 290 west heads for the Texas Hills. You won't see much for the first 10 or 11 miles, aside from glimpses of the plains as you ascend the 100-million-year-old geologic region called the **Edwards Plateau.** After about 18 miles, you cross the margin of the plateau, a landscape strewn with limestone rubble and stands of gnarled oaks set off by shrubby hills and ridges. The deep limestone bedrock here was formed by the shells and skeletons of tiny creatures that lived in ancient, shallow seas covering much of present-day Texas. Later, massive shifts inside the Earth caused a giant surface bulge. When part of the bulge fell toward the Gulf of Mexico, it left the great ragged Balcones Fault and this uplifted plateau, since carved by erosion.

About 3 miles west of the hamlet of Henly is a right turnoff to 5,212-acre **Pedernales** (pronounced the LBJ way: perd'n-AL-es) **Falls State Park** *(6 miles north on FR 3232. 830-868-7304. www.tpwd.state.tx.us/state-parks/ pedernales-falls. Adm. fee),* flanking the wooded **Pedernales River.** Pedernales Falls drops 50 feet over tilted limestone stair steps.

Continuing west on US 290, you reach the junction with US 281, leading 9 miles south to the Devil's Backbone drive (see p. 254).

Six miles north, you enter **Johnson City** *(Visitor & Tourism Bureau, 100 E. Main St. 830-868-7684.).* Lyndon Johnson was born nearby in 1908, and the town is named for his ancestors. The **Lyndon B. Johnson National Historical Park** *(100 Ladybird Ln. 830-868-7128. www.nps.gov/lyjo)* contains the frame house that was **Johnson's Boyhood Home,** and the **Johnson Settlement,** the ranch complex where President Johnson's forebears first settled.

Watch for deer as you drive west on US 290; grazing buffalo on the right some 13 miles along mark a second unit in the national historical park. Here, bus tours depart for the **LBJ Ranch** *(830-868-7128),* which preserves Johnson's birthplace and the one-room Junction School he attended. Nearby, the **Lyndon B. Johnson State Park and Historic Site** *(830-644-2252. www.tpwd .state.tx.us/state-parks/lyndon-b-johnson)* features a living history farm, a nature trail, and wildlife.

The hills are barely visible as you enter the peach country of Gillespie County. The fruit of the vine also flourishes here, resulting in several wineries. The nearby town of **Fredericksburg** *(Chamber of Commerce,*

Chuckwagon at LBJ National Historical Park

302 E. Austin St. 830-997-6523) is 19th century in character and German in custom. The **Admiral Nimitz State Historic Site and National Museum of the Pacific War** (*340 E. Main St. 830-997-4379. www.pacificwarmuseum.org. Adm. fee*) is housed in the 1850s Nimitz Hotel established by the admiral's grandfather.

From here, take an 18-mile detour north on Farm Rd. 965 to **Enchanted Rock State Natural Area** (*830-685-3636. www.tpwd.state.tx.us/state-parks/enchanted-rock. Adm. fee*). Centerpiece of the 1,643-acre park is a massive 440-foot-high dome of pink granite—the second largest batholith on the continent.

Back in Fredericksburg, head south on Tex. 16, crossing through the rich, fertile country of the Pedernales River watershed. Gradually, the hills dissolve and the landscape flattens. After about 18 miles, the road begins twisting steeply down into the **Guadalupe River Valley**.

Another couple of miles puts you into the summer playground of **Kerrville,** home of the **Museum of Western Art** (*1550 Bandera Hwy. 830-896-2553. www.museumofwesternart.com. Closed Sun.-Mon.; adm. fee*) and the historical **Schreiner Mansion** (*226 Earl Garrett St. 830-896-8633. http://mansion.schreiner.edu. Tues.-Sat. by appt.; adm. fee*), set in a stone Romanesque-Victorian mansion.

At this point, you can proceed south on Tex. 16 toward Medina through a breathtaking 35 miles, promising hairpin turns, lofty vistas, craggy canyons, and crystal streams. Or you can detour west to explore some of the Texas Hills' most remote and spectacular country. If you choose this second option, take Tex. 27 west to Ingram, where you pick up Tex. 39. At the junction of the two routes, historical murals on a lumber company

253

Cattle roundup in Texas Hill Country

Texas bluebonnets and Indian paintbrush

Devil's Backbone

Loop from Blanco on US 281 and Farm Road 32, 12, 2325, and 165

■ 56 miles ■ 2 hours ■ Fall through spring. See map p. 252.

This twisting, razor-backed ridge offers dramatic views of the Balcones Fault Zone, a 400-mile-long break in the Earth's crust. The road tops a broken, crumpled remnant of the Edwards Plateau.

From Blanco, named for the clear waters of the pretty Blanco River that runs through it, drive 3 miles south on US 281 to Farm Rd. 32. For the first 7 miles, the road rolls through limestone hills, past pasturelands scattered with oak and juniper. As you begin to climb, feast your eyes on the rugged stair step hills on the northern skyline.

The next 10 miles or so offer ample opportunities to see how erosion has carved the layer cake of sedimentary deposits typical of Texas Hill Country.

After 18 miles on Farm Rd. 32, stop at the picnic area on the left for a view of these colorful hills and incised valleys. The drive continues another 6 miles through karst terrain dotted with sinkholes before intersecting Farm Rd. 12. Take Farm Rd. 12 north for 5 miles through the Hill Country to arty **Wimberley**, then follow Farm Rds. 2325 and 165 west 24 miles back to Blanco.

building are evidence of the area's vigorous artist colony.

Roller-coasting through dipping ranchlands, the road hugs the serpentine **South Fork Guadalupe River**. At Farm Rd. 187 turn south toward Vanderpool and continue about 11 miles to a picnic area with a fabulous panorama of rugged hills and canyons. Descending steeply, the road pitches into **Sabinal River Canyon** and weaves past its towering limestone walls and buttes for 4 miles. At Farm Rd. 337, a designated state scenic highway, turn west toward Leakey. For the next 17 miles, the drive skirts the sheer cliffs and deep gorges of the **Frio** and **Sabinal Rivers** before reaching **Leakey** *(tube and kayak rentals are available at Josh's Frio River Outfitters. 830-232-6292).*

From here, head east again on Farm Rd. 337. It will return you to Vanderpool, then back into rugged high country with more panoramic views.

Rolling through the pastoral valley of the **West Prong of the Medina River**, the road enters **Medina**, "apple capital of Texas." Turn southeast on Tex. 16, and

Armadillo along Devil's Backbone

continue 14 miles through the flat prosperous ranchland of Bandera County. The town of **Bandera** itself, a ranching center, has a real cowboy flavor with a frontier-style Main Street—and one of the oldest Polish communities in the country. Stop by the **Frontier Times Museum** *(510 13th St. 830-796-3864. www.frontiertimesmuseum.org. Closed Sun.; adm. fee)* to see exhibits on the Old West and the town's founding in 1852.

Continue east on Tex. 16 for about 12 miles across the southern end of the Edwards Plateau, with Hill Country now out of sight. At the intersection with Tex. 46, turn left and dip through low hills for about 12 miles to the restored Main Street, U.S.A., town of **Boerne** (pronounced BUR-nee). Settled by Germans in the 19th century, the town proudly preserves its Old World heritage and serves as an antiques hub. Its **Cibolo Wilderness Trail** *(830-249-4616)* is a 100-acre greenbelt with trails through four ecosystems.

About 13 miles east of Boerne, Tex. 46 passes PR 31, which leads 3 miles to the rugged and scenic **Guadalupe River State Park** *(830-438-2656. www.tpwd.state.tx.us/state-parks/guadalupe-river. Adm. fee).*

Back on Tex. 46, continue for 30 miles through rolling green hills edged in oak and cedar to **New Braunfels** *(Chamber of Commerce, 390 S. Seguin Ave. 830-625-2385 or 800-572-2626. www.nbcham.org).* Texas' oldest community, it features the historic district of **Gruene** *(Gruene Rd.),* a restored, turn-of-the-20th-century German-style town with half-timbered houses and shops.

Ross Maxwell Scenic Drive

255

Santa Elena Junction to Santa Elena Canyon Overlook in Big Bend National Park

▪ 32 miles ▪ 1 hour ▪ All year. Unless you have a four-wheel-drive vehicle, route requires backtracking. Adm. fee to park

Within the big bend of the Rio Grande, which forms the U.S. border with Mexico, 801,163-acre Big Bend National Park contains deserts, canyons, mesas, and mountains. The drive—designed by Ross Maxwell, a geologist and the national park's first superintendent—gives you a look at the remarkably varied terrain.

From **Santa Elena Junction** in **Big Bend National Park** *(432-477-2251. www.nps.gov/bibe. Adm. fee),* the drive heads south. Mountains command the left view, with **Burro Mesa** on the right. After about 2 miles, you can make out angular and domed formations in the mountain rock that indicate ancient volcanism. Fortress-like outcroppings called dikes are also common here.

For the next few miles you ascend steadily past boulder-strewn slopes. **Sotol Vista,** one of the best views in the park, offers a stunning perspective on **Santa Elena Canyon** and the floodplain of the **Rio Grande.** From here, the drive descends through a series of switchbacks, past views of the unmistakable **Mule Ears Peaks** formation; **Tuff Canyon,** named for its gray, volcanic ash rock; and **Cerro Castellan,** a pile of volcanic rock that towers 1,000 feet. As you continue down, the **Chihuahuan Desert** benchland opens before you.

Don't bypass the old Army compound of **Castolon**, a frontier trading post still open for business. Paralleling the Rio Grande, the road crosses a

Santa Elena Canyon

fertile floodplain. The scattered remains of old adobe buildings along this stretch mark former farms.

About 8 miles from Castolon, the **Santa Elena Canyon Overlook** offers a view down on the narrow Rio Grande flowing through a chasm with 1,500-foot limestone walls. The road ends half a mile farther, where a 1.5-mile trail leads into the mouth of the canyon.

El Camino del Rio

Lajitas to Presidio on Farm Road 170

■ 50 miles ■ 1½ hours ■ Fall through spring. Summers are extremely hot. Be aware of steep grades, sharp curves, and poor shoulders along this route.

One of the most spectacular routes in Texas, El Camino del Rio—the River Road—plunges over mountains and into steep canyons, following the sinuous Rio Grande through the desolate but beautiful Chihuahuan Desert.

Begin by orienting yourself with a stop at the **Barton Warnock Environmental Education Center** *(1 mile east of Lajitas on Farm Rd. 170. 432-424-3327. www.tpwd.state.tx.us/state-parks/barton-warnock. Adm. fee for toy exhibits),* where you can pick up information on the **Big Bend Ranch State Park** *(432-358-4444. www.tpwd.state.tx.us/state-parks/big-bend-ranch. Adm. fee),* a 438-square-mile preserve—over 300,000 acres—encompassing the River Road.

Continue on to the town of **Lajitas** (la-HEE-tahs), an Army post established in 1915 to protect settlers from Pancho Villa, the famed Mexican renegade.

Farm Rd. 170 begins its roller-coaster course before you even leave town, following the **Rio Grande** west. A couple of miles out of town, the volcanism that shaped this region is obvious in dark lava flows topped by white tuff, or hardened volcanic ash.

After another couple of miles, the road swings away from the river, dips to cross spring-fed **Fresno Creek,** which is flanked by layered beds of buff-colored limestone, and returns to the river. After 2 to 3 miles you'll see a cluster of weathered volcanic ash formations called hoodoos along the river. Not far from here, colorful tepees mark a dramatic picnic spot overlooking the river at **Madera Canyon.**

Writer James Michener called the dusty little adobe town of Presidio his "favorite place in all Texas."

The drive now starts a steady, 5-mile climb up the "big hill" of **Santana Mesa.** A major engineering feat, this portion of the road ascends at a 15 percent grade. At the summit, an overlook affords superlative views of the canyon below and the rugged, rather forbidding volcanic landscape that sweeps to the horizon.

As you make your serpentine descent off the mesa, the Rio Grande winds below, a green path through the wild **Chihuahuan Desert.** The **Rio Grande Valley** continues to widen, filled with a sculptural array of eroded lava hills and mesas. You cross **Panther Creek** about 1.5 miles down, then pass a narrow fissure known as **Closed Canyon,** the first in a series of canyons along this undulating stretch.

Continuing on, you have expansive scenic views of the arid valley below. After crossing **Tapado Canyon,** well watered for this dry region, watch for traces of a former smugglers' path that is now a ranch trail in the bare

Main Street, Lajitas

mountain slopes to the north. About 10 miles farther on, the drive enters windblown **Redford,** an old farming community.

Pressing on through open range, the road finds the river again and passes through a couple of refreshingly green oases before entering **Presidio.** A former Spanish mission village, the small adobe border town now functions as a U.S. port of entry. Nearby **Fort Leaton State Historic Site** *(432-229-3613. www.tpwd.state.tx.us/state-park/fort-leaton. Adm. fee),* built to protect settlers from hostile Indians and Mexican banditos, serves as the western information center for visitors traveling the River Road.

Davis Mountains Loop

Loop from Fort Davis on Texas 118, 166, and 17

■ 74 miles ■ 2 hours ■ All year

This drive weaves through the ragged Davis Mountains—the "Texas Alps"—and around 8,382-foot Mount Livermore, the state's second highest peak. But you'll also see desert, rolling hills, fantastic volcanic formations—and lots of stars.

Start in the frontier village of **Fort Davis** *(Chamber of Commerce, 4 Memorial Square. 432-426-3015 or 800-524-3015. www.fortdavis.com. Closed weekends)*—at 4,900 feet the state's most elevated town. Its main attraction is the 1854 **Fort Davis National Historic Site** *(432-426-3224. www.nps.gov/foda. Adm. fee),* the first military post on the San Antonio–El Paso Road and a home of the famed African-American buffalo soldiers.

Just past the fort, bear left on Tex. 118. Winding up **Limpia Canyon,** past walls of jointed lava columns, the drive parallels the cottonwood-lined banks of **Limpia** (Spanish for "clear" or "clean") **Creek.** For the next 8 miles through the canyon, you dip along foothills covered with oak woodlands, passing 2,800-acre **Davis Mountains State Park** *(432-426-3337. www.tpwd.state.tx.us/ state-parks/davis-mountains. Adm. fee).* Vistas of hills and valleys, intruded by volcanic outcroppings and weathered, rounded slopes, predominate for a few more miles.

Beyond Prude Ranch, you drive out onto an expanse of Texas grassland. In this open country, you have views of **Mount Livermore** and the dome that tops 6,809-foot **Mount Locke.** This is the University of Texas' **McDonald Observatory** *(432-426-3640. www.mcdonaldobservatory.org. Visitor center daily, scheduled observatory tours, and Star Parties Tues., Fri., & Sat. evenings),* which boasts a 432-inch telescope, the world's third largest.

Inspiring mountain views continue as the drive hugs the rim of **Elbow Canyon** for several miles before winding steadily down past sylvan **Madera Canyon,** greened by oak, juniper, and pinyon woodlands, toward the high desert. At the Y-junction, turn left on Tex. 166 into a typically arid desertscape. Straight ahead looms landmark **Sawtooth Mountain,** a worn volcanic cone. Opposite its base stands the **Rock Pile,** a fine example

of jointed lava blocks. A couple of miles beyond this site, you enter a chaos of volcanism: precipitous slopes, jagged outcroppings, and towering rock peaks. The **Davis Mountains,** 35 million to 39 million years old, represent one of the largest volcanic centers in the geologic belt stretching from Montana to Mexico.

Along the Davis Mountains Loop

The peaks subside during the next few miles, yielding to flat, Big Sky country for about 17 miles. Off to the southwest you can see miles into Mexico. The road swings eastward, and as you start to climb again through dun-colored hills, the trees gradually reappear.

Pass a dozen miles of green pastureland before reaching Tex. 17, which leads about 3 miles north to Fort Davis.

Officers Row, Fort Davis National Historic Site

Canyon Sweep

Silverton to Claude on Texas 86 and 207

■ 53 miles ■ 1 hour ■ All year. Most scenic in light of early morning and late afternoon.

Traversing the vast, windswept High Plains that occupy the middle of the Texas Panhandle, this drive reaches its scenic height when it descends into splendid Palo Duro Canyon.

The drive begins in **Silverton,** commercial center for the area's farms and ranches and the Briscoe County seat. From here, you follow Tex. 86 west for 5 miles, then head north on Tex. 207 through several miles of unbroken flatness, where rows of milo and wheat alternate with pastureland. This region is part of the High Plains, the southernmost reach of the continent's Great Plains.

About 11 miles beyond Silverton, the road drops into **Tule Canyon,** a beautiful gorge worn by **Tule Creek.** Winding through a geologic jumble, the drive passes colorful rock strata and dramatic, sheer-faced buttes. After crossing Tule Creek, you begin to ascend, soon passing 896-acre **MacKenzie Reservoir,** which offers a variety of recreational opportunities, including boating, swimming, fishing, and picnicking.

For the next 15 miles the road stretches through tableland ranch country dotted with shrubby mesquite and juniper. Suddenly the plains part, revealing the spectacular, 9-mile-wide, 120-mile-long **Palo Duro Canyon.** In Spanish the name means "hard wood," a reference to the junipers growing from the canyon walls. As you approach the southern rim, a picnic area offers a sweeping view of the nearly 1,000-foot-deep canyon, whose colorful sedimentary layers span 250 million years. When you begin to descend, notice the distinctive color bands in the canyon rock; they represent five major geologic periods. Here and there in the lowest level,

Palo Duro Canyon

you'll see red formations veined by white gypsum. Sixteenth-century conquistador Francisco Coronado called these "Spanish skirts," as they look like the ruffles on a hoop skirt.

When you reach the floor of the canyon, the road crosses the languid **Prairie Dog Town Fork of the Red River,** which carved most of the gorge during the Pleistocene epoch. After climbing the other side of the canyon for about a mile, you have a view of the winding stream below. The ascent grows steeper until you attain the tableland again.

After crossing the grainfields of agricultural Armstrong County, the drive ends about 15 miles farther on in **Claude,** the county seat. From here, you can continue about 40 miles to **Palo Duro Canyon State Park** (*806-488-2227. www.tpwd.state .tx.us/state-parks/palo-duro-canyon. Adm. fee*) by taking Ranch Rd. 1151 west 29 miles to Ranch Rd. 1541. Then head south 8 miles to Tex. 217, which leads to the park. The park **visitor center** has exhibits on the area's history; a road plunges 600 feet to the canyon floor, where you'll find hiking and horse trails.

Oklahoma's Quartz Mountains

Blair to Lone Wolf on Oklahoma 44

■ 16 miles ■ ¹/₂ hour ■ All year

This short spin takes you through an outcrop of the Wichita Mountains in southwestern Oklahoma, detouring for wonderful bird's-eye views of Lake Altus-Lugert.

From **Blair,** a small farm town and bedroom community for Altus Air Force Base, drive north on Okla. 44. Cotton fields stretch away on both sides of the road, with the bumpy Quartz Mountains rising on the horizon ahead of you.

After 7 miles you cross the North Fork Red River. The Quartz Mountains, peppered with huge sienna boulders, suddenly loom up beside the road.

Once sacred ground and a winter camp for Kiowa and Comanche Indians, the area now attracts vacationers, who come to **Quartz Mountain Resort Arts & Conference Center** (*580-563-2424. www .quartzmountainresort.com*).

Turn left at the state park entrance for an enchanting 4-mile round-trip detour through the 4,300-acre park. Passing a small amusement park, the

road ascends to a steep pass that falls away on the right, affording gorgeous views of 6,300-acre **Lake Altus-Lugert.**

Back on Okla. 44, head north along the lake. If the water is low, you can glimpse foundations of the former town of **Lugert,** flooded in the 1920s to create the lake. After 6 miles the drive ends in the small agricultural community of **Lone Wolf.**

OKLAHOMA
Wichita Mountains Byway

A loop with extensions on Oklahoma 49, 115, 9, 58, and 19

- 93 miles ▪ 3 hour ▪ All year

Just off I-44, this route traverses the Wichita Mountains Wildlife Refuge in southwestern Oklahoma, providing exquisite views of the rocky Wichitas, the refuge's many lakes, and such prairie grazers as buffalo, Texas longhorn, and elk.

From I-44 follow Okla. 49 west through a small residential area near the town of Medicine Park and out past cattle ranches and stands of cottonwood and oak. In just over 6 miles you enter the 59,020-acre **Wichita Mountains Wildlife Refuge** *(580-429-3222. www.fws.gov/southwest/ refuges/oklahoma/wichita.html).* You can see close up the rugged, boulder-strewn peaks that arose about 250 million years ago when enormous pressure within the Earth fractured blocks of granite and gabbro (cooled magma), forcing them up 1,000 feet and more above the plain.

Continue about 2 miles through mixed-grass prairie interspersed with oak forests to the turnoff for **Mount Scott.** This 2.5-mile spur road winds up the mountain, with views of the Wichitas to the west and flat plains all around. From the lookout on top, you can see **Fort Sill Military Reservation** to the south. Dating from 1869, it holds the grave of Apache leader Geronimo.

Back on Okla. 49, go west through open rangeland with a backdrop of red-rock hills. A herd of 550 bison grazes along here, as well as 300 Texas longhorn. Just beyond the turnoff for Okla. 115, the **Quanah Parker Visitor Center** *(closed Tues.)* has good exhibits on local geology, flora, and fauna.

The road now passes several small lakes and picnic sites. In about 7 miles you'll spot a prairie dog town, with **Elk Mountain** rearing up to the south. Okla. 49 ends 6 miles west of the refuge at the junction with Okla. 54.

Instead of following Okla. 49 to its end, veer right onto Okla. 115 (4.4 miles into the refuge) for an adventurous 70-mile loop back to Okla. 49. Going north, view 17 miles of scenic mountains before passing Saddle Mountain on the right, where settlers first noticed two peaks forming a saddle seatlike dip.

To see **Mount Zodletone** and the **Mount Zodletone Spring Microbial Observatory** *(www.zodletone.org/Zodletone_Splash/*

Wichita Mountains

261

Zodletone_Spring.html), operated by **Oklahoma State University** researchers, turn right after 8.5 miles (E. 1400 Rd.) and then left after 2.3 miles (unnamed road).

Back on Okla. 115, the road dead-ends soon, but a right-hand turn onto Okla. 9 begins a 7.5-mile stretch of the byway east to **Carnegie** *(Chamber of Commerce. 580-654-2121. www.carnegieok.com).* In this small town of 1,723 sits Oklahoma's oldest continually operating cinema, the **Liberty Theatre** *(9 W. Main St. 580-654-1776. www.libertytheatres.com).*

Pick up Okla. 58 in Carnegie and follow the byway south until a left turn reveals the **Blue Canyon I Wind Farm.** This clean-energy powerhouse supports 20,000 Oklahoma homes and stands on the **Slick Hills,** a span of ancient limestone foothills made of shell, plankton, and coral fossils left by a Mesozoic sea.

Continuing south, Okla. 58 merges with Okla. 19 a mile before turning left. Three miles after the left turn, branch south on 58 (while 19 continues east). **Chief Stumbling Bear Pass** soon overlaps part of Okla. 58. Bison and other animals stomped out the path millennia ago, and later Native Americans started using it. Named for a Kiowa leader who negotiated treaties for his tribe in Washington, D.C., this tree-lined pass today welcomes cars and motorcycles.

In **Lawton** *(302 W. Gore Blvd. 580-355-3541. www.lawtonfortsillchamber .com),* overnight on the **Slick Hills** at Slick Hills RV Park *(9 Kirk Ave. 580-248-2806 or 580-678-2703. www.slickhillsrvpark.com).* Or stay for a day or night at **Lake Lawtonka** *(580-529-2663. www.cityoflawton.ok.us/parksnrec/lawtonka .htm),* which completes the loop with camping, fishing, beach swimming, boating, and hiking within view of **Mount Scott.**

For a larger lake, stay on Okla. 19 (instead of turning south on 58) for an eastbound spur of the byway, which heads toward **Apache** *(Chamber of Commerce. 580-588-3361),* named for multiple tribes of Apache bison hunters from the 1800s. With fewer amenities than **Lake Lawtonka** but more boat ramps and landings for fishing, **Lake Ellsworth** *(580-529-2663. www .cityoflawton.ok.us/parksnrec/ellsworth.htm)* lies 5 miles south of Apache, just beyond the end of the byway.

Talimena Scenic Drive

Talihina, Oklahoma, to Mena, Arkansas, on Oklahoma 1 and Arkansas 88

■ 54 miles ■ 2 hours ■ Spring through fall. Spring bloom occurs in April and May; fall foliage peaks from mid-October to early November.

Built in the late 1960s expressly for grand views, this two-lane highway ripples over the gentle Ouachita Mountains along the border of Oklahoma and Arkansas. Evergreen and deciduous trees shoulder the road, the latter making for gorgeous floral displays in spring and brilliant color in autumn.

Catering to Choctaw Indians and cattle ranchers, **Talihina** (Choctaw for "iron road") was founded by missionaries in the late 1880s, when the Frisco

View from Rich Mountain, Talimena Scenic Drive

Railway came through the mountains. The byway's name derives from a combination of the towns that form its end points—Talihina and Mena. It lies within the 1.7-million-acre **Ouachita National Forest** *(501-321-5202. www.fs.usda.gov/ouachita)*, the South's oldest (established in 1907) and largest national forest. Ouachita is an Indian word meaning either "good hunting grounds" or "hunting trip," and these woods still hold plentiful deer, squirrel, and other wildlife.

263

A visitor information station about 7 miles northeast of Talihina, at the junction of US 271 and Okla. 1, marks the start of the designated byway. Just 0.3 mile past the information station you come to **Choctaw Vista,** on the west end of **Winding Stair Mountain,** part of the **Ouachita Mountains.** From here you can look out on the beautiful dark blue hills and valleys through which the Choctaw traveled on their way west from Mississippi, in compliance with the 1830 Indian Removal Act.

For the next several miles the road cuts through a forest of shortleaf pine and scrub oak. Along here, too, grow prairie grasses such as little bluestem. The east-west lay of the Ouachita Mountains has caused separate plant communities to develop on either side: Post oak, blackjack, and serviceberry predominate on southern slopes, while the rich soil of the northern slopes supports white oak, hickory, dogwood, and papaw.

About 5 miles past the forest entrance, stop at **Panorama Vista** for wonderful, sweeping views of the mountains and the small farming villages tucked into the **Holson Valley.** Hang-glider enthusiasts often launch from here on weekend days with easterly winds. Golden eagles, vultures, and hawks also soar on the updrafts.

Continue on to **Horse Thief Springs** *(mile 16).* In the late 1800s, horse thieves in transit between Texas and Missouri often rested from their labors here. The road now swoops back and forth down Winding Stair Mountain, giving you constantly shifting views. The Ouachita Mountains once extended to the Appalachians, before the Mississippi separated the ranges. The 300-million-year-old sandstones and shales of the Ouachitas were thrust up, folded, and faulted. Fault lines are visible in places along the drive, including the area around **Robert S. Kerr Arboretum and Nature Center** *(mile 23. 918-653-2991).* Three short trails here interpret the environment.

For several miles past the nature center, the byway follows the crest of **Rich Mountain** through a forest of dwarf oak stunted by severe ice storms and southerly winds. At about mile 40, the **Old Pioneer Cemetery** holds the graves of 23 people who homesteaded here between the mid-19th and the mid-20th centuries.

Two miles beyond, the **Queen Wilhelmina State Park** *(479-394-2863. www .queenwilhelmina.com)* features dramatic southerly views from the crest of Rich Mountain. The park centers around a rustic stone lodge. Originally constructed at the turn of the century and since rebuilt, the lodge was named for the queen of Holland, whose country held a substantial stake in the local railroad.

Three miles east of the park stands the highest point on the drive, **Rich Mountain Fire Tower** (2,681 feet). From this vantage, you have fine views of the forested mountains and of the ribbon of road snaking over the ridges.

The drive ends at the **visitor information station** *(479-394-2382)* in **Mena.** A timber and cattle town, Mena sprang to life in 1896 when the first train of the Kansas City Southern Railroad came chugging through the mountains.

Cherokee Hills Byway

West Siloam Springs to Gore, Oklahoma, on US 59 and 62, Oklahoma 10, 82, 100, and 10a/100 and I-40

■ 84 miles ■ 2 hours ■ All year. April to October is peak season.

When it comes to terrain, the 84-mile Cherokee Hills Scenic Byway in northeastern Oklahoma offers exceptional variety in a state not well known for it. Along the way, the road passes through native grasslands, parallels gently flowing rivers, and runs in the shadow of rugged cliffs that mark the beginning of the Ozarks' foothills.

The historical, cultural, and recreational attractions scattered along the byway's length are even more striking. This is the land of the Cherokee Nation, whose 1838 forced march along the Trail of Tears from its ancestral homelands brought it to a wilderness referred to at the time simply as the "Indian Territories."

Starting at the Arkansas state line, the Cherokee Hills Scenic Byway ambles westward along US 59 toward the small town of Kansas. Along the way it passes by **Natural Falls State Park** *(918-422-5802. www.travelok.com/state_parks),* whose 77-foot waterfall—the state's highest—creates a cool glade that makes it an ideal respite from summertime's midday heat.

On the outskirts of Kansas, the route turns south onto Okla. 10. To get the lay of the land, consider stopping at the **Cherokee Nation Welcome Center** *(59914 US Hwy. 59. 918-422-8130).* In addition to area maps, brochures for local attractions, and general visitor information, you can find authentic Native American crafts, including pottery and jewelry, at the facility's gift shop.

From here, continue south on Okla. 10 along the **Illinois River.** While you're in the area, consider renting a canoe, raft, or inner tube from a local outfitter to enjoy a leisurely float trip.

After about 20 miles, the route turns west again at US 62 toward **Tahlequah** *(Tahlequah Area Chamber of Commerce. 918-456-3742. www.tourtahlequah.com)*, the modern-day capital of two tribes: the Cherokee Nation and the United Keetowah Band. Continue south toward the town of Park Hill for a visit to the **Cherokee Heritage Center** *(21192 S. Keeler Dr. 918-456-6007. www.cherokeeheritage.org)*, which includes a fascinating exhibit about the Trail of Tears. There are living history displays here, too, including the Tsa-La-Gi Ancient Village, which shows what life

A reconstructed store at the Cherokee Heritage Center

was like for the Cherokee before European contact. From there, you can fast-forward to the 1890s at the center's Adams Corner Rural Village, whose period-correct structures include a general store, schoolhouse, church, and log cabin. Taken as a whole, the village gives a sense of the tribe's efforts to rebuild itself after the devastation wrought by the Civil War.

A couple of blocks farther south stands the **George Murrell Home** *(19479 E. Murrell Home Rd. 918-456-2751. www.okhistory.org/sites/georgemurrell. Donation)*, the only surviving antebellum mansion in Oklahoma. Filled with original furnishings, the Greek Revival–style residence is surrounded by parklike grounds that make a great spot for a picnic.

From Park Hill, follow Okla. 82 south by southeast until it turns into Okla. 100 along the shores of **Lake Tenkiller** *(918-457-4403. www.laketenkiller.com)*. Created by the damming of the Illinois River by Tenkiller Dam, the lake boasts several marinas, campgrounds, and water clear enough to make it a favorite destination for scuba enthusiasts. Continue south toward the town of **Gore** *(www.townofgore.com)*, a fisherman's paradise on the banks of the Arkansas River that bills itself as the Trout Capital of Oklahoma.

265

Historic Route 66 (Oklahoma)

Quapaw to Texola, Oklahoma, on Route 66 (comprising US 69 and US 59, I-44 and I-40, and local roads)

■ 400 miles ■ 2 to 3 days ■ All year

Though America's famous "Mother Road" runs from Chicago to Los Angeles, many of its highlights lie within Oklahoma's borders. In fact, Route 66 owes its existence to Tulsa businessman Cyrus Avery, the state's first

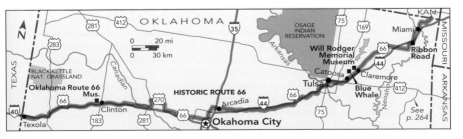

highway commissioner. Appointed to membership on the new federal board designated to forge a national highway system in 1925, Avery was instrumental in both creating Route 66 and then bucking competing interests to get it routed through his state. It was here, too, that later champions fought to preserve the historic route, resulting in Oklahoma having more drivable miles of the original alignment than does any other state.

Oklahoma's
Route 66

The tricky part is following the somewhat convoluted route as it winds through dozens of small towns (and a couple of big cities). Fortunately, the **National Scenic Byways** website *(www.byways.org/explore/states/ OK)* offers detailed turn-by-turn directions designed to keep you pointed in the right direction.

Begin at the Kansas state line and head southwest on US 69/Okla. 66 to **Miami**—"My-am-uh" in local-speak—where you can tour the 1929 **Coleman Theatre Beautiful** *(103 N. Main St. 918-540-2425. www .colemantheatre.org),* a 1,600-seat vaudeville palace with an ornate interior and a massive pipe organ that once accompanied silent films. Back on Main Street, follow the signs directing you to a nine-foot-wide stretch of old Route 66 six miles long known as the **Ribbon Road** that dates back to the early 1920s.

Continue on and you'll come to **Claremore** *(Convention and Visitors Bureau, 400 Veterans Pkwy. 877-341-8688. www.visitclaremore.com),* birthplace of humorist Will Rogers and home to the **Will Rogers Memorial Museum** *(1720 W. Will Rogers Blvd. 918-341-0719. www.willrogers.com. Adm. fee).* The museum has an extensive collection of Western art, along with thousands of photographs and other memorabilia chronicling the life of the vaudeville trick-roper turned movie star.

Route 66 is known for its slightly quirky attractions, and none fit that bill quite as well as Catoosa's landmark **Blue Whale** *(2600 N. Hwy. 66. 918-694-7390. www.bluewhaleroute66.com).* Perched at the edge of a roadside pond, the 80-foot-long beast with the irrepressible grin is a reminder of a pleasantly low-tech era when summertime fun meant cannonballing off the whale's two-story tail or swooshing down the waterslide on its pectoral fin.

Pass through Tulsa and continue west to **Arcadia** for another of the oddities that make driving the old road such a treat. The **Round Barn** *(107 E. Hwy. 66. 405-396-0824. www.arcadiaroundbarn.com),* which was built in 1898 with the idea that its circular design would render it tornado-proof, soon transcended its lowly agricultural roots when the soaring loft became a site for weekly dances. Arcadia is also home to **Pops Restaurant** *(660 W. Hwy. 66. 405-928-7677. www.route66.com),* an ultramodern take on the classic diner. The real attraction here, however, is the attached "soda ranch" that offers more than 500 different hard-to-find varieties of soda pop.

For a look at the highway in its heyday, continue on to **Clinton's Oklahoma Route 66 Museum** *(2229 Gary Blvd. 580-323-7866. www.route66.org),* which features a decade-by-decade look at the Mother Road's history and even has its own "drive-in style" movie theater. After that, all that awaits you is the Texas border and the quasi ghost town of **Texola**. The town's lack of active businesses is more than made up for by its highly photogenic abandoned gas stations, cafés, and motor courts. Each one attests to the glory days of Oklahoma's portion of historic Route 66.

ARKANSAS
Arkansas 7

Hot Springs to Harrison on Arkansas 7

- 160 miles - 1 day - Spring through fall. Peak fall foliage times vary; check locally.

Over forested hills and through friendly mountain towns, Ark. 7 curves and rolls south to north in the rugged highlands of western Arkansas. Along the way, the road passes fine rural scenery, a national park, two national forests, several state parks, and a national river. In addition to these, expect to find plenty of down-home hospitality in the cafés and craft shops that line the roads.

The drive begins in **Hot Springs,** the boyhood home of former President Bill Clinton. As it cuts through town, Ark. 7 becomes Central Avenue and passes a block of lush landscaping that graces a row of elegant bathhouses dating back to the 1890s. The Spanish Renaissance-style Fordyce Bathhouse (1915) now serves as the visitor center for **Hot Springs National Park** *(501-624-2701. www.nps.gov/hosp).* Established in 1832 by President Andrew Jackson as a special national reservation, the park considers itself the oldest holding in the National Park System.

The city of Hot Springs itself, built into high limestone bluffs, encompasses part of the park.

For a grand view of the city and surroundings, turn right on Fountain Street and drive up twisting Hot Springs Mountain Drive to **Hot Springs Mountain Tower** *(501-623-6035. Adm. fee).* Returning to Ark. 7, note the numerous Victorian houses that line the street, among them the historic 1910

Arkansas Ozarks

classic revival building at 150 Central Ave. Today it serves as the **Mountain Valley Water Visitor Center** *(800-828-0836. www.mountainvalleyspring.com.)*

After leaving the hot water scene behind, the highway travels up a tree-lined valley that heralds the natural beauty to come. At mile 7 turn left at the small town of Fountain Lake and continue on Ark. 7 another 6 miles to Mountain Valley, the town where the famous springwater is bottled. North of Hot Springs Village 1 mile, take Ark. 192 6 miles to Ark. 227 where you'll find **Lake Ouachita State Park** *(501-767-9366. www.arkansasstateparks.com/lakeouachita),* nestled at the edge of Arkansas's largest man-made lake. Its 975-mile shoreline encompasses 48,000 acres.

North again on Ark. 7, you can make an 8.5-mile detour to crystal mines by turning left on Ark. 298. You can rummage around yourself in these mines for the sparkling stones. After the tiny town of Jessieville, Ark. 7 enters **Ouachita National Forest**, 1.6 million acres in the east-west-running Ouachita Mountains. The **ranger station** *(501-984-5313)* on the left has exhibits, information, and a short interpretive trail.

The road now begins winding up and down hills, presenting glorious views of low mountains and deep hollows. For the next 15 almost uninhabited miles you see gentle slopes of pines and hardwoods, steep rock walls, and the worn **Ouachita Mountains,** which look their finest in the dazzling hues of autumn. At mile 42, cross the **Fourche La Fave River** and turn left into **Quarry Cove Park** to see impressive **Nimrod Dam** and **Lake.** Completed in 1942 for flood control, the 97-foot-high dam stretches 1,012 feet across the lake's east end. The resulting miles of shoreline offer excellent opportunities for fishing, swimming, and waterskiing.

The limpid, undammed waters of the Buffalo National River have long attracted canoeists and anglers.

Beyond here, Ark. 7 weaves uphill from the river and soon opens to views of Nimrod Lake and the surrounding hills. By the time you reach Ola, the woods alternate with soothing pastures and green farm fields.

For the next few miles the air is redolent of pine woods and cured hams. In addition to hams, numerous wayside shops sell handmade quilts, pottery, honey, jams, and furniture. In the small town of Centerville you can detour 16 miles east on Ark. 154 to **Petit Jean State Park** *(501-727-5441. www.petitjeanstatepark.com),* which features dramatic overlooks, 95-foot-high Cedar Falls, and a lodge. After returning to Centerville, follow the byway past wide fields of soybean and grain that extend to the distant, gently rolling mountains.

In 8 miles you reach the historic river port of Dardanelle. Take a left at the sign for Dardanelle Powerhouse and Riverview Park, a worthwhile 1.5-mile digression that leads to excellent views of the mighty **Arkansas River** and **Lake Dardanelle Dam** with its towering spillways. **Lake**

Fordyce Bathhouse, Hot Springs National Park

Dardanelle State Park *(479-967-5516. www.arkansas stateparks.com/lakedardanelle)* lies just to the northwest of town on Ark. 22. A 7-mile excursion west on Ark. 155 takes you up a zigzagging mountain road to **Mount Nebo State Park** *(479-229-3655. www .arkansasstateparks.com/mountnebo)*, where you'll be rewarded with wonderful views of the **Arkansas River Valley.**

As you cross the Arkansas River at the north end of Dardanelle, you'll see on the north shore the prominent grain elevators at the **Port of Dardanelle,** where barges dock to load shipments of locally grown soybeans and grains. North of here, the byway passes through fast-paced Russellville and its bedroom communities.

Five miles beyond Dover, the drive enters **Ozark National Forest** *(479-964-7200. www.fs.usda.gov/ osfnf)*, whose steep-flanked mountains offer a more

North Arkansas's Buffalo River

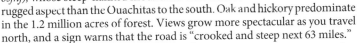

rugged aspect than the Ouachitas to the south. Oak and hickory predominate in the 1.2 million acres of forest. Views grow more spectacular as you travel north, and a sign warns that the road is "crooked and steep next 63 miles."

Bending through a gently sloping forest, you pass signs announcing **Booger Hollow,** a tongue-in-cheek hillbilly trading post. Along with cheap souvenirs, it sells real crafts, sorghum, smoked ham, and other backwoods wares hawked by area shops.

About 10 miles farther on, you pass through the village of **Pelsor,** whose family-run general store has been around since 1922. Just north the forest opens to marvelous views in all directions. Stop at one of the pullouts or at the access to the 165-mile-long **Ozark Highlands Trail,** a mile beyond Pelsor.

After 9 miles you come to the quaint highland village of **Cowell,** with its little church and pond. Past this area, the drive offers more fabulous views of the valley and rumpled ridge to the west.

Three miles north of Cowell, you can divert a mile west on Ark. 16, then northwest on Cty. Rd. NE28 (gravel) 3 miles to **Alum Cove Natural Bridge,** a fascinating 130-foot-long rock span.

Back on Ark. 7, for the next several miles you twist along the side of **Judea Mountain,** through meadows, hollows, and coves. If you want to savor the spectacular scenery and some country cooking, stop at **Cliff House Inn** *(870-446-2292. www.cliffhouseinnar.com)*, which hangs over the edge of the Ozarks' deepest canyon—the Arkansas Grand Canyon.

Just north, the byway enters **Jasper,** a gateway to the Buffalo National River. The town has craft shops, cafés, motels, and river outfitters. Just north of Jasper the **Hilary Jones Wildlife Museum** *(870-446-6180)* provides information on the Arkansas elk herds including the one that can frequently be spotted at dawn or dusk along Ark. 74. Back on Ark 7 as you cross the **Little Buffalo River** on the way out of Jasper, notice the exposed limestone and sandstone walls. The road continues through the **Boston Mountains** (part of the Ozarks) before descending once again, this time down to the **Buffalo National River.**

Before crossing the bridge here, stop for information at **Pruitt Ranger Station** *(870-446-5373. March-Sept., call for hours)*. A national river since 1972, this wilderness protects such animals as bobcats, mink, and bears.

269

After passing **Mystic Caverns,** where you can tour two mountain caves, the road begins to smooth out somewhat, the hills flattening into green pastures where horses and cattle graze beside barns.

Soon you come to the drive's end in the resort town of **Harrison,** "crossroads of the Ozarks." Here, next to the local high school, a little-known piece of the past survives: **Baker Prairie,** a remnant of the vanishing tallgrass prairie that once blanketed much of the country's midsection. For information, visit the **Harrison Tourist Information Center** *(870-741-3343)* on US 65 north.

The Levee

Loop from Lake Chicot State Park on Arkansas 257, 144, County Road 59, and the levee

■ 30 miles ■ 1 hour ■ All year. Best in early morning and late afternoon. About half the drive is on a one-lane gravel-topped levee that limits speeds to 25 mph.

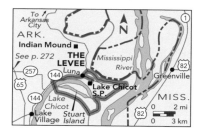

See p. 272

Following the Mississippi River, this adventurous loop travels the levees and back roads of southeastern Arkansas. Along the way, you have views of fertile farmlands, swamps, streams, abundant waterbirds, and other wildlife.

Start at **Lake Chicot State Park** *(870-265-5480. www.arkansasstateparks.com/lakechicot),* situated on Arkansas's largest natural lake. The 20-mile-long oxbow lake is thought to have formed about 500 years ago when the Mississippi River changed course. From here head north on Ark. 257, then left on Ark. 144. Turn right after 1.3 miles by the grain bins at the intersection of unmarked Luna Road, which leads to the levee.

Drive up onto the gravel-topped levee and turn right. Running 640 miles along the Arkansas and Mississippi Rivers, this ranks among the world's longest continuous levees. After a flood in 1927 broke through the former levee, construction on the present one began. Although the levee follows the Mississippi, views of the river are limited.

At mile 3.6, you pass the site of Columbia, a bygone county seat that was flooded in 1855, then burned by Union troops in 1864. Along here too, on the left, the sloughs and borrow pits from which soil was taken to build the levee harbor a wonderful variety of birds, including cattle egrets, great blue herons, and sometimes ducks. Birds and beavers feed among the willows and cypress knees at the edges of these pits.

After about 6 miles the levee turns abruptly southwest; continue for another 1.5 miles to **Leland Chute,** a side channel of the river, where unusual paddlefish are sometimes caught. Farms stretching into

Pink smartweed

the distance on the other side of the levee grow cotton, soybeans, milo, winter wheat, and rice.

Continuing on the levee 3 more miles, you can glimpse the northeastern end of Lake Chicot. In late summer the woods and shore here explode with the chatter of migrating ibis, herons, egrets, and endangered wood storks. After 2 more miles, you can cross the cattle guards and head west

On the Mississippi levee

on pavement. Or you can continue exploring the levee to the south, and in 4.3 miles you'll arrive at the grand **Mississippi River.**

If you choose to take the paved road west, in a couple of miles you'll see the 1898 **Hyner Cemetery,** resting place for Italian immigrants who came to work the area plantations and frequently died of malaria. Two miles farther on, the road passes **Whiskey Chute** and **Stuart Island** *(on the right),* headquarters for a band of early 19th-century river pirates. Then you cross the dam over crescent-shaped Lake Chicot and intersect Ark. 144. From here you can take a 3-mile detour left and visit **Lake Village.** Settled in the mid-1800s, it is now an upscale resort town of nice houses and lakeside docks that are in striking contrast to some of the humbler dwellings in the rest of the county. Or continue the tour by turning right and then left *(in 0.2 miles)* onto unmarked Cty. Rd. 59.

Just beyond this turn stands the lovely old Georgian manor house *(private)* that was once the centerpiece of 10,400-acre **Yellow Bayou Plantation** (circa 1850). After 4.5 more miles past farmlands and banks colored by seasonal wildflowers, you reach the **Chicot Pumping Station.** The three-story facility, built by the Army Corps of Engineers, diverts muddy waters to the Mississippi. A **visitor center** details the project.

If you take the levee 14 miles north, you arrive in **Arkansas City,** historic seat of Desha County. The views along the way are excellent, but there are few turnoffs and no facilities.

To continue the loop, turn toward the pumping plant and head south on the levee. In 2 miles you see to the left the **Panther Forest Crevasse,** created by a 1912 break in the levee that flooded Lake Village. Anhingas and ducks favor the deep water here.

A half mile farther along, notice on your right the earth mound at the field's edge. It was constructed by Native Americans about 600 years ago. Continue 3.7 miles south on the levee past more views of fields and backwaters to the turnoff at Luna. In a half mile the loop ends back at Ark. 144.

Great River Road (Arkansas)

Blytheville to Eudora on US 61, 70, 79, 165, 65, Arkansas 77, 147, 38, 44, 20, 318, 316, 1, 4, Lee County Road 221, and Phillips County Roads 217, 239

■ 362 miles ■ 1½ days ■ All year. Summers can be very hot.

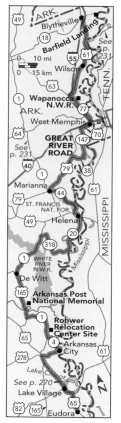

The "great river" of this road is, of course, the Mississippi, the force that shaped the landscape along the route. Often called the Delta, this geographic region is more accurately known as the Mississippi River Alluvial Plain. Whatever you call it, the land is flat, the soil is rich, and the great forests that once flourished here were long ago displaced by agriculture. Arkansas's section of the Great River Road connects with similarly themed routes in Missouri and Louisiana.

The 1924 arch over US 61 marks the Arkansas-Missouri line a few miles north of Blytheville. As you travel south you'll roughly parallel the Mississippi, though views of the river will be rare. To get a good look at the working side of the Mississippi, take a side trip east about 10 miles on Ark. 18 to Barfield Landing, where barges dock to service nearby steel mills.

Cotton is no longer king of crops as it once was, but many fields still gleam white with cotton bolls in late summer along the northern portion of the route. Wilson was named by and for a wealthy 19th-century planter; note the oddly out-of-place English Tudor architecture around the town square. **Hampson Archeological Museum State Park** (*US 61 & Lake Dr. 870-655-8622. www.arkansasstateparks.com/hampsonmuseum. Closed Mon.; adm. fee*) exhibits collections from the Nodena site, a village of a farming-based Native American civilization that thrived from A.D. 1400 to 1650.

Shortly after the junction with Ark. 77, **Wapanocca National Wildlife Refuge** (*870-343-2595. www.fws.gov/wapanocca*) offers a fine opportunity to see a remnant of the bottomland forest that once covered this region. Bald eagles and waterfowl frequent the refuge in winter.

The route to and beyond West Memphis, following US 70, Ark. 147, and US 79, leads through cropland to Marianna, a small town on Crowley's Ridge. This geological anomaly—a narrow strip of high ground running through northeastern Arkansas up into Missouri—comprises the only "uplands" along this route, 150 feet or so above the surrounding delta. Ark. 44 leads south into **St. Francis National Forest** (*479-968-2354. www.fs.usda.gov/osfnf*). Planning is under way for a new **Mississippi River State Park** (*870-295-4040. www.arkansasstateparks.com/mississippiriver*) to take over management of the recreational lakes and trails in this small but scenic area.

Helena (*Phillips County Chamber of Commerce, 111 Hickory Hill Dr. 870-338-8327. www.phillipscountychamber.org*) once was a major port on the Mississippi River (Mark Twain wrote that it "occupies one of the prettiest situations on the river"), and boasts a number of historic buildings and sites connected with an important Civil War battle on July 4, 1863. The **1891 Helena Library and Museum** *(623 Pecan St. 870-338-7790. Tues.-Fri., 1st and 3rd Sat.)* provides an overview of local history. The **Delta Cultural Center** *(141 Cherry St. 870-338-4350. www.deltaculturalcenter.com. Tues.-Sat.)* interprets the area's heritage, especially its influential blues connections.

The route makes a southward bend through agricultural areas along Ark. 44, 20, 318, 316, and 1, to reach **White River National Wildlife Refuge** *(870-282-8200. www.fws.gov/whiteriver),* a wild expanse of woods, bayous, and lakes that is home to black bears, bald eagles, swallow-tailed kites, and hundreds of others species of the bottomland hardwood forest, including the largest concentration of wintering mallard ducks in the Mississippi flyway. A **visitor center** just off Ark. 1 at St. Charles provides a good introduction to the area, and offers a short interpretive trail.

At DeWitt, US 165 leads past **Arkansas Post National Memorial** *(870-548-2207. www.nps.gov/arpo),* which commemorates the first semipermanent French settlement in the lower Mississippi River Valley. A museum explores nearly 300 years of human occupation, and 2 miles of trails wind through the historic townsite (of which almost nothing is left). Set on a peninsula bordered by the Arkansas River and two backwaters, Arkansas Post is one of the most reliable places to see alligators in the state.

After crossing the Arkansas River, the highway winds through extensive flat cropland. Take Ark. 1 and 4 to pass two very different historic sites. The **Rohwer Relocation Center Site** *(9 miles south of Watson)* was home to more than 8,000 Japanese Americans interned during World War II. A national historic landmark, the site features monuments to residents and to Japanese Americans who served in the armed forces during the war. The small town of **Arkansas City** offers a walking tour of several downtown structures on the National Register of Historic Places, including the 1900 Romanesque Revival courthouse. Arkansas City was a thriving steamboat landing as early as 1834, and survives today as one of the few remaining examples of an old Mississippi River port town in Arkansas.

Lake Village sits on the shore of Lake Chicot, a 20-mile-long Mississippi River oxbow that is the largest natural lake in Arkansas. **Lake Chicot State Park** *(Ark. 144 8 miles northeast of Lake Village. 870-265-5480. www.arkansas stateparks.com/lakechicot)* offers cabins, hiking trails, lake and levee tours, and fishing for crappie, bass, bream, and catfish (see p. 270).

273

Visitors viewing Louisiana Purchase Monument

WYOMING

NEBRASKA

Cheyenne ✦

Trail Ridge Road/
Beaver Meadow Road
p. 338

Colorado River
adwaters Byway
p. 336

Granby

Fort Collins

Peak to Peak Scenic Byway
p. 335

Boulder

Denver

Lariat Loop Scenic
& Historic Byway
p. 342

Top of the Rockies
National Scenic Byway
p. 340

rand Mesa
Scenic and
Historic Byway
p. 335

Colorado Springs

COLORADO

Gold Belt Tour
Scenic and Historic Byway
p. 332

weep-Tabeguache
ic Byway
29

Pueblo

Alpine Loop
Detour
p. 326

Frontier
Pathways
Scenic and
Historic Byway
p. 331

San Juan
Skyway
p. 325

Enchanted
Circle
p. 319

Santa Fe
Trail
p. 322

OKLA.

KANS.

El Camino
Real
p. 314

High Road
to Taos
p. 318

Jemez
Mountain
Trail
p. 321

Santa Fe

Turquoise Trail p. 317

Albuquerque

Historic Route 66
p. 297

Amarillo

El Malpais
p. 316

NEW MEXICO

onimo Trail
nic Byway
p. 312

Billy the
Kid Trail
p. 314

El Camino
Real
p. 314

Lubbock

TEXAS

d of the
untain Spirits
nic Byway
10

Heart of
the Sands
p. 313

Las Cruces

El Paso

UTAH
Logan Canyon Scenic Byway

Logan to Bear Lake on US 89

- 41 miles ▪ 1 hour ▪ Spring through fall

This scenic route in northern Utah through Wasatch-Cache National Forest's Logan Canyon is part of US 89, which runs most of the way between the Mexican and Canadian borders. Along the way it passes many of the West's great sights, including the Grand Canyon, the Great Salt Lake, and Grand Teton, Yellowstone, and Glacier National Parks. Here the highway slips between towering limestone walls and shadows the Logan River. After a 3,000-foot climb, the road opens up to spectacular views of Bear Lake, shining jewel-like turquoise. Moose, elk, and deer are abundant in Logan's forests, and you can often spot them along the drive.

Outside of **Logan,** US 89 shoots straight into **Logan Canyon,** passing a **Forest Service information center** *(Logan Ranger Dist. 435-755-3620. www.fs.usda.gov/uwcnf)* on the right. Beyond the building to the right, the gently sloping terraces are embankments left over from ancient Lake Bonneville, which once covered 19,500 square miles of northwestern Utah. The first 4 miles pass three small dams, popular with fly fishermen. At the **Spring Hollow Campground Area,** the pleasant, 1-mile interpretive **Riverside Nature Trail** skirts the Logan River's rich riparian habitat; you can see beavers and their lodges. For spectacular views, skilled hikers can head up the precipitous, 4-mile **Crimson Trail** to the top of the limestone cliffs.

Continue along US 89 about 15 miles to a good side trip. It begins on Tony Grove Road and winds up nearly 7 miles through aspen groves to **Tony Grove Lake** at 8,100 feet. The tranquil, pristine 25-acre lake nestles against steep rock cliffs—a glacial basin formed more than 10,000 years ago.

Back on US 89, the route continues to climb, passing the **Beaver Mountain Ski Resort** *(1351 E. 700 N. 435-753-0921. www.skithebeav.com),* until it reaches 7,800-foot **Bear Lake Summit** and then drops down to an overlook

Midgley Bridge spans the Oak Creek Canyon near Sedona, AZ

for **Bear Lake.** The 20-mile-long lake sparkles a blue-green reminiscent of the tropics. Some 8,000 years ago, earthquakes isolated the lake from the Bear River, creating an unusual water chemistry and eventually nurturing four unique fish species.

Down by the lake, **Garden City** contains a marina and numerous shacks selling local raspberry jam and delicious raspberry shakes. Wide, sandy swimming beaches line the lake along the road southeast to Laketown.

Flaming Gorge–
Uintas Scenic Byway

Vernal to Manila on US 191, Utah 44, and Forest Road 218

▪ 95 miles ▪ 3 hours ▪ All year

Tucked into the northeastern corner of Utah, this route climbs across high desert country into lush evergreen-aspen forests as it traverses the eastern flank of the rugged Uinta Mountains, one of the few chains that run east-west in the hemisphere. Highlights include rim views of Flaming Gorge and the rock maze of Sheep Creek Canyon as you travel a portion of the Flaming Gorge–Uintas Scenic Byway.

Before beginning the drive, stop in **Vernal** to see the **Utah Field House of Natural History State Park Museum and Dinosaur Gardens** *(496 E. Main St. 435-789-3799. www.utah.com/ stateparks/field_house.htm. Adm. fee)* for a good overview of area wildlife, geology, and Fremont Indian prehistory, including a room full of fluorescent rocks and a garden with full-size dinosaur reproductions. On US 191 geologic signs plot the route as it progresses steadily back through time from the Cretaceous, about 80 million years ago, to the Precambrian, about a billion years ago. After nearly 6 miles the dry desertscape of juniper and sagebrush gives way to **Steinaker State Park** *(4335 N. Hwy. 191. 435-789-4432. www.stateparks.utah.gov/parks/steinaker. Adm. fee),*

Flaming Gorge National Recreation Area

a 780-acre lake that offers good trout and bass fishing. Three miles farther is **Red Fleet State Park** *(435-789-4432. www.utah.com/stateparks/red_fleet .htm. Adm. fee).* Ask for directions to the Jurassic dinosaur footprints across the lake.

After Red Fleet the road switchbacks uphill, passing the gray gravel detritus of a large open-pit phosphate mine. Used for fertilizer, the phosphate-rich rock originated from the decomposition of billions of microscopic marine organisms some 225 million years ago. About 17 miles from Vernal, **Windy Point** offers good views of the **Ashley Valley** and reservoirs below. The road leaves the juniper-covered terrain, crosses high rolling grassland—a favorite wintering area for elk—and enters **Ashley National Forest** (*355 N. Vernal Ave. 435-789-1181. www.fs.usda.gov/ashley*). Four miles later the Red Cloud–Dry Fork drive (see sidebar) heads off to the left.

Fourteen miles from the Red Cloud turnoff, a side trip on US 191 descends northeast for 6 miles to the **Flaming Gorge Dam** and **Visitor Center** (*435-885-3135. www.utah.com/nationalsites/flaming_gorge.htm. Visitor center Mem. Day–Labor Day, weekends in winter*), site of the Green River dam that created the 91-mile-long Flaming Gorge Reservoir. Take a self-guided, 20-minute tour to the power plant. In summer watch for ospreys on islands in the reservoir.

While the official byway does continue north on US 191 to Dutch John and the Wyoming border, the other byway option returns to Utah 44 where, after nearly 4 miles, the turnoff for the **Red Canyon Overlook** appears on the right. The forested, 1.5-mile drive little prepares the visitor for one of Utah's most unforgettable vistas. The breathtaking vertical red-rock cliffs of **Flaming Gorge** plummet more than 1,300 feet to the reservoir below. A rim trail leads along the edge for incredible views of the **Green River**. Farther down the road, the **visitor center** (*435-889-3713. Mem. Day–Labor Day*) hangs precariously on the cliff's edge.

Back on Utah 44, look for milepost 14. **Sheep Creek Canyon**, a must-see 13-mile side trip (*closed in winter*), splits off to the west on FR 218. After nearly 7 miles the road passes Palisades Campground and enters **Sheep Creek Canyon Geological Area**, where upthrusts and erosion have created strange rock sculptures. Almost 8 miles later, the craggy rock walls narrow as the road passes **Big Spring** (*camping prohibited June-Oct. because of danger of flash floods*). Bighorn sheep were recently reintroduced into this area. The road widens to reveal the dirty white cliffs of

Red Cloud–Dry Fork

Forest Road 018

■ 45 miles ■ 2 hours ■ Summer. Higher elevations snow covered from late fall to mid-spring; partly dirt route is usually closed in winter. Passage not recommended in wet weather. See map p. 278.

Seventeen miles north of Vernal on US 191, this partly dirt road penetrates the Uinta (*you-INTA*) Mountains' deep canyons and high-elevation forests laced with trout streams.

From inside the **Ashley National Forest** (*435-789-1181*) boundary off US 191, FR 018 cuts west across open grassland toward forests of lodgepole pine. Near the FR 018 turnoff, there's a place to park for the 32.5-mile round-trip **East Park Loop** bike trail. At 3 miles FR 018 (Red Cloud Loop Road) turns left, while the paved road leads north to the **East Park Reservoir**.

For the next 24 miles, FR 018 passes through groves of aspens, open meadows, and pine forests, offering some breathtaking views of Uinta peaks, including 12,240-foot **Marsh Peak**, one of the range's highest. Mule deer and elk are common; bobcat, coyote, mountain lion, and bear are also present, though they are rarely seen.

The road continues past Dry Fork Overlook, with a spectacular view of Brownie Canyon far below. From here, the road drops 2,000 feet in 10 miles, descending into Dry Fork Canyon, with picnic and camping sites. At about mile 43 the road passes Dry Fork, site of a thriving community in early frontier days. A wall of prehistoric petroglyphs of the Fremont culture is visible 1.5 miles south of Dry Fork on the Sadie McConkie Ranch (*donation*).

Navajo sandstone from the Jurassic period, when dinosaurs roamed here, and then at the junction with Utah 44 it passes picnic sites beneath cottonwoods. It's worthwhile to backtrack 4.5 miles east on Utah 44 to the **Flaming Gorge Overlook,** whose sweeping vistas of red, yellow, and green rock cliffs caused explorer Maj. John Wesley Powell to dub it a "flaming, brilliant red gorge." The rest of the route passes over desertscape to the town of **Manila.**

Nebo Loop Byway

Utah 132 east of Nephi to Payson on Forest Road 015

■ 37 miles ■ 1 hour ■ Spring through fall. Closed in winter

Though not far from the traffic of I-15, this central Utah route leaves civilization behind, climbing quickly into the quiet forests and far-reaching vistas of the Wasatch Range. Gently rising and falling over aspen-clad ridges and hills, the road passes under the nose of Mount Nebo and by a passel of peaceful mountain lakes. Mule deer and elk abound.

Begin the route 6 miles east of **Nephi** on FR 015. You'll head into the southernmost section of the **Uinta National Forest** *(435-755-3620. www.fs.usda.gov/uwcnf),* rising into the **Wasatch Range.** The road skirts gray, fingerlike rock outcroppings and passes Pole Canyon Road, which pushes northeast into groves of quaking aspen until it reaches **Bear Canyon.** Turn off at the **Ponderosa** and **Bear Canyon Campgrounds;** these peaceful sites, beneath a canopy of mixed conifers, rustle with animals. The **Nebo Bench Trail** leaves from here, climbing up into the 28,170-acre **Mount Nebo Wilderness** and eventually reaching the mountain's summit.

Back on the road, you'll switchback up the broad-backed mountains, through aspen and evergreen forests, to the **Devils Kitchen Geologic Interest Site.** A short walk takes you to an observation deck, passing informative signs about the vegetation. The natural rock amphitheater below features a strange

Dawn along Forest Road 015, Mount Nebo Wilderness

landscape of knob-shaped pinnacles of red sandstone and conglomerate known as hoodoos.

Continue along the road for about 2 miles to the **Mount Nebo Overlook.** Like gnomes with pointy hats, white firs cling to the steep sides of the mountain, at 11,877 feet the tallest peak in the Wasatch Range. Long swathes on the mountain's flanks remain clear of vegetation, either because of thin soil, landslides, or avalanches. Early Mormon settlers named Mount Nebo after a mountain in Palestine; the name comes from a word meaning "sentinel of God." The road continues past FR 014, which shoots down **Santaquin Canyon** along a trout stream to I-15.

Just beyond the turnoff, **Utah Lake Overlook** offers stunning views of the turquoise waters of **Utah Lake** to the north and the flat desert beyond. The picturesque **Payson Lakes** at mile 24 lure rainbow trout fishermen in droves. Heading off the mountain toward **Payson,** the road curves down into a narrow canyon, past maples that flash brilliant red in fall.

Dinosaur Diamond
Prehistoric Highway

Loop through western Colorado and eastern Utah on I-70, US 40, 191, Utah 128, Colorado 139 and 64

▪ 480 miles ▪ 3 to 4 days ▪ Spring through fall. Some side trips are on unpaved roads that can be impassable after rain or snow; check locally before proceeding.

Traces of prehistoric "thunder lizards" highlight the route through an expanse of Utah and Colorado. Dinosaur fossils and footprints date from 150 million years ago, when conditions were right for preserving the bones of huge plant-eaters and those of the fierce carnivores that preyed on them. As you drive this loop, you'll pass rugged red-rock canyons, spectacular geological formations, and cottonwood-lined rivers flowing through rolling, arid, high-plains terrain.

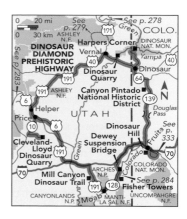

Before visiting **Dinosaur National Monument** *(435-781-7700. www.nps.gov/dino. Adm. fee),* begin your trip just over the Colorado state line near the town of **Dinosaur.** A 31-mile scenic drive starts at the park visitor center and winds north to Harpers Corner, near where the Green and Yampa Rivers meet.

You may want to head straight for the national monument's **Dinosaur Quarry** north of Jensen, Utah. At the visitor center here you can see thousands of fossils of many species of dinosaurs.

Newspaper Rock,
Canyonlands NP, Utah

Then follow US 40 west to **Vernal**. In the **Dinosaur Garden** outside the **Utah Field House of Natural History State Park Museum** *(496 E. Main St. 435-789-3799. www.utah.com/stateparks/field_house.htm. Adm. fee)*, are 18 life-size models, including the predator called Utahraptor, discovered in 1991. The museum itself is full of dinosaur skeletons and exhibits.

Vernal is also the headquarters for the **Ashley National Forest** *(435-789-1181. www.fs.usda.gov/ashley)*, through which the route passes as US 191 heads west and south into Indian Canyon. Cliffs rise steeply beside the road as it climbs into coniferous forest at 9,100-foot Indian Creek Pass and then heads down to the small town of Helper. The **Western Mining and Railroad Museum** *(294 S. Main St. 435-472-3009. www.wmrrm.org. Closed Sun., Sun.-Mon. in winter)* has exhibits on coal mining and railroads.

The route follows the Price River to Price—another must stop for dinosaur buffs. The **College of Eastern Utah Prehistoric Museum** *(155 E. Main St. 435-613-5060 or 800-817-9949. www.ceu.edu/museum. Closed Sun. in winter; adm. fee)* displays fossil dinosaurs and a cast of a mammoth skeleton.

For more dinosaurs, take a short side trip off the main loop. From Price drive south on Utah 10 for 12 miles to Utah 155 and turn east to Elmo and Cleveland. Follow signs to **Cleveland-Lloyd Dinosaur Quarry** *(435-636-3600. www.blm.gov/ut/st/en/fo/price/recreation/quarry.html. Daily in summer, call for schedule rest of year; adm. fee)*, which has the most concentrated collection of Jurassic-era dinosaur bones known anywhere.

Back in Price, the loop heads southeast for 60 miles through rolling terrain and washes to meet I-70. Go east 25 miles and continue south on US 191. In about 15 miles, turn west on Mill Canyon Road *(impassable after rain)* to reach the **Mill Canyon Dinosaur Trail** *(435-259-2100. www.utah.com/playgrounds/mill_canyon.htm)*. Your next side trip off US 191 might be on Utah 313 to the Needles section of **Canyonlands National Park** *(435-719-2313. www.nps.gov/cany. Adm. fee)* where you can catch a glimpse of the Green River before it joins the Colorado.

Just before you reach Moab on 191, you'll find **Arches National Park** *(435-719-2299. www.nps.gov/arch. Adm. fee)*, the premier showcase of the rock formations that have made this region famous. More than 2,000 natural arches are here, as well as buttes, spires, and a vast variety of other shapes. Many formations can be seen from park roads, especially in the **Windows** area.

After Arches you can visit **Moab** *(Information center, Main & Center Sts. 800-635-6622. www.discovermoab.com)*, famed as a center of outdoor activities in this red-rock country, or pick up the **Colorado River Scenic Byway** (see pp. 284-285) and follow it to the historic **Dewey Suspension Bridge**, built in 1916. Over the state line, stop in Fruita to visit the **Dinosaur Journey Museum** *(550 Jurassic Ct. 970-858-7282. www.dinosaurjourney.org. Adm. fee)*, full of robotic dinosaur models, fossils, interactive displays, and dino-themed exhibits. After your museum visit, drive to **Dinosaur Hill** *(1 mile south on Colo. 340)* and view past excavations of several important dinosaur finds.

Fruita is the western gateway to **Colorado National Monument** *(970-858-3617. www.nps.gov/colm. Adm. fee)*, with its gorges and monoliths. Get an overview of the park along 23-mile **Rim Rock Drive,** a paved road with overlooks and interpretive areas offering far-reaching panoramas.

The loop returns to its start along Colo. 139, which climbs to excellent views at 8,240-foot Douglas Pass. The highway passes through **Canyon Pintado National Historic District,** a "painted canyon" with more then 200 Native American pictograph and petroglyph sites. Roadside signs identify several of these sites as you drive north to Rangely.

The Energy Loop: Huntington & Eccles Canyons Scenic Byway

Huntington to Colton on Utah 31, 264, and 96

▪ 86 miles ▪ 1 day ▪ Summer and fall

The Energy Loop winds through attractive central Utah high-elevation scenery on the Wasatch Plateau, climbing up through a canyon past several reservoirs and curving north to end at a ghost town. The "energy" part of the name comes primarily from the heritage of coal mining in these mountains, as well as power plants and reservoirs.

The loop begins at the junction of Utah 10 and 31 at **Huntington,** heading up Huntington Canyon along the latter highway. The route borders Huntington Creek as it enters **Manti-La Sal National Forest** *(435-637-2817. www.fs.usda.gov/mantilasal)*, which provides campsites and trailheads along the way. In fall, groves of aspen can glow brilliant yellow against the dark green of pines.

About 20 miles up the canyon stands the **Stuart Historic Guard Station,** a 1930s ranger station that now serves as a seasonal *(Mem. Day–Labor Day)* visitor center. As the road climbs to and beyond Electric and Huntington Reservoirs at elevations over 9,800 feet, the views get better and better, encompassing mountain ranges up to 100 miles away. At the **Sanpete Valley Overlook** you'll have a view of the Fairview Lakes on one side of the road and the western edge of the Wasatch Plateau dropping to the valley far below on the other.

The route follows Utah 31 down out of the mountains to Fairview and the **Fairview Museum of History and Art** *(85 N. 100 East St. 435-427-9216)*, perhaps best known for its life-size reproduction of the skeleton of a 10,000-year-old mammoth found during construction of Huntington Reservoir.

The loop backtracks east on Utah 31 to Utah 264, where the region's legacy of coal extraction can be seen as the highway returns to Upper Huntington Canyon, passes Burnout Canyon, then climbs a ridge to descend into Eccles Canyon. **Scofield,** once a thriving mining town (the largest in aptly named Carbon County), has shrunk to only a few dozen permanent residents. On May 1, 1900, the town suffered a terrible blow when an explosion in the local coal mine killed more than a hundred men. Row after row of markers in the cemetery testify to the tragedy.

The picture is nicer at **Scofield State Park** *(435-448-9449. www.stateparks .utah.gov/parks/scofield. Adm. fee),* popular for boating and fishing for rainbow and cutthroat trout. Cold weather doesn't end the quest, by any means: **Scofield Reservoir** is one of the Utah's most popular ice-fishing spots. The drive ends in Colton, where little remains of the small railroad town that once stood here.

Colorado River Scenic Byway

Moab to I-70 on US 191 and Utah 128

▪ 44 miles ▪ 2 hours ▪ All year

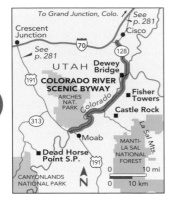

Hugging the southeast side of the Colorado River as it winds below sheer cliffs of Wingate sandstone, this route passes isolated side canyons and the spectacular pinnacles known as Fisher Towers. Rafters and kayakers ply the muddy rapids, and sand beaches line the water's edge.

The lively town of **Moab** is a base for river runners, mountain bikers, four-wheel-drive enthusiasts, and rock climbers *(Moab Information Center, Main & Center Sts. 800-635-6622. www.discovermoab.com).* Five miles to the north lies **Arches National Park** *(435-719-2299. www .nps.gov/arch. Adm. fee).* Also nearby are the red-rock canyons of **Canyonlands National Park** *(435-719-2313. www.nps.gov/cany. Adm. fee).*

Drive 2 miles north of Moab on US 191, then turn right on Utah 128 for the Colorado River Scenic Byway. Roadside vegetation provides a lovely counterpoint to the red and orange hues of the sandstone cliffs.

Three miles in, the road passes **Negro Bill Canyon,** named after an early settler. A 2-mile hike up the canyon leads to views of **Morning Glory Natural Bridge.** High across the river from the trailhead lie thousand-year-old Pueblo granaries.

The **Big Bend Recreation Area** offers a rest spot and sand beaches as the river makes a sweeping U-turn. Above Big Bend the Colorado picks up speed. Several miles later, the canyon widens, and the road leaves the river. At about mile 15, Castle Valley Road heads east, winding up through knolls to **Castle Valley** and views of the high **La Sal Mountains.**

Colorado River with La Sal Mountains

Continuing north on Utah 128 for several more miles, you'll see to the south **Castle Rock,** site of several car commercials. At about mile 21, a 2.2-mile, graded dirt road turns right off Utah 128 toward **Fisher Towers Recreation Site.** The 900-foot-high **Titan** and other pinnacles are remnants of an ancient floodplain. A 2-mile hike crosses to the foot of the spires, ducks through narrow canyons, crosses a steel ladder, and passes convoluted rock formations. The hike ends with spectacular views of adjacent **Onion Creek Canyon.** Five miles beyond Fisher Towers, the road crosses the river near the 1916 **Dewey Suspension Bridge** and heads through desert to I-70 near Cisco.

Bicentennial Highway

Hanksville to Blanding on Utah 95

- 133 miles - ¹/₂ day - Spring and fall

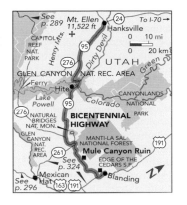

Miles of southeastern Utah's desert little prepare you for the panoramic views of sparkling Lake Powell against the sheer red-rock cliffs of the Glen Canyon National Recreation Area. From Lake Powell the route continues southeast through sheer red-rock canyons, passing world-famous natural bridges as well as numerous ancestral Puebloan ruins. Finished in the bicentennial year of 1976, this route samples an extraordinary range of scenery, history, and geologic wonders.

285

From **Hanksville,** Utah 95 sweeps south through miles of open desert, with the imposing **Henry Mountains** to the west. Rugged and remote, these mountains support mountain lions and a herd of nearly 400 bison. After about 10 miles an unimproved road heads west up to **Bull Creek Pass,** where a 4-mile trail near Lonesome Beaver Campground leads to the summit of 11,522-foot **Mount Ellen** and sweeping Utah views. Some 11 miles from the turnoff, the **Little Egypt Geologic Site** offers views of sphinxlike formations eroded from the Entrada sandstone.

About 9 miles farther along, the route descends into the red rock of **North Wash Canyon** and passes **Hog Springs Picnic Grounds,** where a trail over a bridge leads past walls of Wingate and Kayenta sandstone eroded over the past 100 million years. Six miles later the road enters the **Glen Canyon National Recreation Area** *(928-608-6200. www.nps.gov/glca. Adm. fee),* then, after another 5 miles, arrives at the **Hite Overlook.** From atop the mesa the views of **Lake Powell** are extraordinary. Clear bands of brown and red sediments form cakelike layers in the eroding mesas. Look for **Hite Marina** in the far distance across the lake. This is the northernmost area of Lake Powell, a huge reservoir created by the Glen Canyon Dam on the Colorado River some 190 miles to the southwest. The road weaves down the cliff, crossing a bridge over the deep canyon of the **Dirty Devil River,** then

Arches are created by wind and rain and appear on the skyline, while natural bridges are carved by stream erosion and lie deep in canyons.

Cathedral Valley

Utah 24 near Caineville to I-70 at Fremont Junction

■ 56 miles ■ 1 day ■ Spring through fall. High-clearance vehicles only. Not advisable in wet weather. Check conditions at visitor center (435-425-3791).

This maintained dirt road into the northern end of **Capitol Reef National Park** *(435-425-3791. www.nps.gov/care. Adm. fee)* crosses a desertscape of twisting canyons and upthrust rock to Upper Cathedral Valley and its 500-foot monoliths.

Follow Utah 24 east of the park visitor center for 11 miles. Turn off at the marked **Fremont River Ford**. *(If river is too high, go to Caineville to access valley.)* The road follows the **Hartnet**, a region of low cliffs, canyons, and sandy valleys. At mile 14, a 1.2-mile side road cuts west to a steep drop-off and the **Lower South Desert Overlook,** with views of the contorted terrain of the **Waterpocket Fold.** Some 17 miles beyond the ford, the road passes the **Lower Cathedral Valley Overlook.** Take the easy 1-mile walk to the rim to see the pinnacles known as **Temple of the Sun** and **Temple of the Moon.** The road continues to the Upper Cathedral Valley Overlook spur road. Turn right in just under a half mile for splendid views. After a series of steep switchbacks, you'll be treated to more views of the **Upper Cathedral Valley.** Soon the road goes north, paralleling a volcanic dike, into the **Last Chance Desert.** As you head toward I-70, to the west will be the **Thousand Lake Plateau,** and to the east the **San Rafael Swell** badlands.

another over the **Narrow Canyon** of the **Colorado River.**

Shortly after crossing the Colorado, a road heads west to **Hite Marina Campground** *(435-684-2457)*, a primitive campground and one of Lake Powell's four marinas. Nearby ruins suggest that prehistoric peoples used Hite as a point to ford the Colorado. Just past Hite, several access roads lead down to small side canyons flooded by Lake Powell. Utah 95 continues southeast through **White Canyon,** past the rock formations of **Jacob's Chair** and **Cheesebox Butte.**

Rising to 6,000-foot **Cedar Mesa,** the route enters a pinyon juniper forest and reaches the entrance to **Natural Bridges National Monument** *(435-692-1234. www.nps.gov/nabr. Adm. fee).* Continue 4 miles to the visitor center for a guide to the 9-mile loop-drive. Over eons, streams have cut deep into the white sandstone of **White** and **Armstrong Canyons** and left three spectacular natural bridges, each bearing a Hopi name: **Sipapu, Kachina,** and **Owachomo.** At each stop, trails lead down to the bridges on the floor of the canyon. The easy, 0.6-mile round-trip **Horsecollar Ruin Overlook Trail** winds around a cliff face to a dramatic view of ancestral Puebloan ruins far below.

Back on Utah 95, you can see an ancestral Puebloan habitation with below-ground structures at the **Mule Canyon Ruin.** Archaeologists stabilized a 700-year-old tower and kiva, or ceremonial chamber. One mile southeast of here lies **Cave Towers,** reachable by foot on a road east of the entrance to Mule Canyon Ruin. At the head of precipitous **Mule Canyon** sit seven towers more than 900 years old. Other structures are visible halfway up in the cliff walls.

Utah 95 continues east from the ruins, then jogs north across **Comb Wash** and up through a passage cut out of **Comb Ridge.** Extending 80 miles from the Abajo Mountains south to Kayenta, Arizona, this steeply eroded monocline—a bend in the Earth's crust—long hindered travel in Utah's southeastern corner. Just ahead, **Butler Wash Rest Stop,** another cliffside ruin, is reached by a 1-mile round-trip trail. Cross smooth rock, or slickrock, to an overlook of cliff dwellings above a dead-end canyon.

Continue on to **Blanding** for a visit to the **Edge of the Cedars State Park** *(435-678-2238. Follow signs to northwest edge of town. www.state parks.utah.gov/parks/edge-of-the-cedars. Closed Sun.; adm. fee),* the site of a small ancestral Puebloan village and a museum with a large collection of objects, some of them rare. If this tweaks an interest in North America's early cultures, continue on the **Trail of the Ancients National Scenic Byway** (see pp. 323-325).

Temples of the Sun and Moon, Cathedral Valley

Scenic Byway 12

287

Panguitch through Bryce Canyon and Capitol Reef National Parks on Utah 12, 63, and 24

▪ 122 miles ▪ At least ½ day ▪ Spring and fall. Be sure to check road and weather conditions before taking any unpaved side routes. Adm. fee to parks.

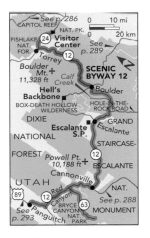

Some of Utah's most outstanding high desert scenery unfolds along this All-American Road, which begins near the pale orange spires of Bryce Canyon and ends amid the immense sandstone domes of Capitol Reef. Between these two national parks, this remote highway snakes along narrow ridgetops, carves through red-rock canyons past prehistoric Native American ruins, and ascends 11,000-foot Boulder Mountain for breathtaking views. Only paved in its entirety since 1985, Utah 12 serves as the roadhead for many small but scenic side roads offering unparalleled opportunities to delve into one of continental America's last explored frontiers.

The route begins at the county seat of **Panguitch,** an Old West town dotted with redbrick houses full of Mormon history, and heads southeast toward Bryce Canyon. About 2 miles past the intersection with US 89, Utah 12 enters **Dixie National Forest** *(435-865-3700. www.fs.usda.gov/dixie)* and rolls through **Red Canyon,** a fairy-like world of curiously sculptured limestone formations colored brilliant red

Cottonwood Canyon Road

Cannonville to US 89 east of Paria Ranger Station

■ 46 miles ■ 2 hours ■ Spring through fall. Southern part of route is graded dirt, which is impassable when wet and hard to navigate when too dry.

The paved portion of this southern Utah road—originally planned as a route between Bryce Canyon and Lake Powell—shoots 7 miles south of **Cannonville** to the entrance of the **Kodachrome Basin State Park** *(435-679-8562. www.stateparks.utah.gov/parks/koda chrome. Adm. fee),* a name suggested by 1940s visitors from the National Geographic Society.

Monolithic spires known as chimneys tower up from the valley floor. Once the area had springs and geysers, which gradually filled up with sediment and solidified. The soft Entrada sandstone eroded, leaving these odd desert spires. The road leads to **Chimney Rock;** from there a 1.5-mile round-trip trail takes you to a formation known as **Ballerina Slipper** and to a sandstone arch.

Continue along the route for 10 miles to where a short side road leads to **Grosvenor Arch,** which is named for Gilbert H. Grosvenor, the first full-time editor of the *National Geographic* magazine. The magnificent sandstone buttress actually contains two arches.

The road then passes into **Cottonwood Canyon,** through a slickrock desertscape of colorful red and white eroded rock. The road continues to US 89, paralleling the **Paria River** and affording views of the **Cockscomb,** a jagged upthrust of the Earth's crust.

by iron oxides and accented by large ponderosa pines. Outlaw Butch Cassidy often hid out here. At 9 miles, the national forest's **Red Canyon Campground** *(435-676-8815. Mid-May–mid Sept.)* offers full camping facilities. The orange-tinted cliffs and spires of Bryce Canyon appear to the southeast as the road ascends to the flats of the **Paunsaugunt Plateau.** Twelve miles from US 89, Utah 63 branches off to the south, passing **Ruby's Inn** *(435-834-5341. www.rubysinn.com),* a descendant of the original "Tourist Rest" located near Bryce Canyon's rim. Some 2 miles beyond, this road enters **Bryce Canyon National Park** *(435-834-5322. www.nps.gov/brca. Adm. fee).* The road along the rim skirts 12 huge amphitheaters that drop 1,000 feet. The single-lane—in places no-shoulder—road through the dense, mixed-conifer forest can become crowded, especially on weekends.

Half a mile from the excellent visitor center, a short loop-road heads east to the rim at **Sunset Point,** a vantage point for the 6-square-mile **Bryce Amphitheater,** the scenic heart of the park. **Sunrise Point** offers superb views of the many-spired **Queen's Garden,** rock formations suggesting a queen facing her court, and of **Powell Plateau** in the distance. **Queen's Garden Trail** descends into the formations, known as hoodoos. Other hikes from Sunrise Point descend to the formations known as **Thor's Hammer** and **Wall Street.** The road continues to the rustic, remodeled 1920s **Bryce Canyon Lodge** *(435-834-5361. www.brycecanyon forever.com. April-Oct.).* Well worth taking is a horse or mule ride *(call lodge for information)* that begins at the lodge and descends to the canyon floor through a surreal landscape of tortured bristlecone pine and red rock.

From the visitor center continue 2 miles along the park road to a left turn for **Inspiration** and **Bryce Points,** where the half-mile **Rim Trail** begins. From here, **Silent City**

See p. 287

looks like a congregation frozen in its seats. Bryce's many freeze-thaw cycles—about 200 a year—help nature sculpture these spires and spindles. The park road continues for 14 more miles, passing other lookouts, canyons, and an arch before ending at **Rainbow** and **Yovimpa Points** for views up to 200 miles to **Navajo Mountain** and the **Kaibab Plateau** in Arizona.

Retrace the park road to rejoin Utah 12 running along the northern edge of the park. Follow it eastward into **Water Canyon. Mossy Cave** has a 1-mile round-trip trail that goes to a small cave and waterfall. From the park, the road drops south through the

Waterpocket Fold, Capitol Reef NP

small towns of Tropic and Cannonville, the roadhead for the **Cottonwood Canyon Road** (see sidebar p. 288).

About 13 miles past Tropic, stop at a pullout for stunning views of the salmon-colored cliffs of 10,188-foot **Powell Point,** an early landmark in Maj. John Wesley Powell's survey of the Southwest. The road continues toward Escalante across the high pastures of the **Table Cliff Plateau.** Seventeen miles beyond the pullout, another one provides views of a Fremont granary built high in the cliff face. Primarily hunter-gatherers, the Fremont Indians occupied the area between A.D. 1050 and 1200.

A mile west of Escalante is the **Escalante State Park** (*435-826-4466.*

Burr Trail

Boulder to Utah 276

■ 66 miles ■ ¹/₂ day ■ Spring and fall. Check road conditions at visitor center (435-425-3791).

This spectacular, partly dirt byway cuts across the rugged canyonland of southeastern Utah, descending precipitously to the giant Waterpocket Fold at the southern end of **Capitol Reef National Park** (see p. 291).

Heading southeast out of Boulder, the route weaves around domes and buttes of Navajo sandstone before crossing **Deer Creek** and coming to a primitive campground after 6 miles.

The road descends into the narrow confines of **Long Canyon,** its fractured sandstone walls shooting hundreds of feet above the road. After 12 miles the **Long Canyon Overlook** affords sweeping views of **Circle Cliffs Basin.**

Just before a series of switchbacks continue descending steeply into the **Waterpocket Fold,** a giant monocline, or fold in the Earth's surface, a spur road *(four-wheel drive needed)* heads 3 miles north into **Upper Muley Twist Canyon,** past several arches.

At the end, a short hike leads to the **Strike Valley Overlook,** with breathtaking views of the Waterpocket Fold. Crossing the fold, the Burr Trail drops 1,000 feet in a mile.

Take Notom-Bullfrog Road south 30 miles to Utah 276. A left turn will lead you to the **Bicentennial Highway** (see pp. 285–287). A right turn will take you to the **Glen Canyon National Recreation Area** *(928-608-6200. www.nps .gov/glca. Adm. fee).*

www.stateparks.utah.gov/parks/
escalante. Adm. fee). **Wide Hollow
Reservoir** offers trout fishing, while a
1-mile nature trail leads to a petrified
forest, with brightly colored rock
logs and a view of the early Mormon
town of **Escalante.** Hell's Backbone,
a spine-tingling, high-mountain,
dirt-and-gravel road accessible in
good weather, heads north from
Escalante and overlooks **Box-Death
Hollow Wilderness** area. The gravel-
and-dirt Hole-in-the-Rock Road
cuts south from Escalante 18 miles
to the twisted slickrock desertscape
of **Devil's Garden.** The side road ends
at the **Hole-in-the Rock,** a spot where
in 1879-1880 some 200 Mormon
pioneers with 83 wagons and 1,200
head of livestock penetrated a notch
in the canyon wall 2,000 feet above
the Colorado River.

The 29 miles between Escalante
and Boulder are quite dramatic.
The road crosses **Calf Creek** near the
Calf Creek Campground (*435-826-
5499*), where a 5.5-mile trail leads
to 126-foot **Calf Creek Falls.** In this
area, known as the **Hogback,** the road
twists along the crest of a narrow
ridge with spectacular views of Calf
Creek far below. Continue on 6 miles
to **Boulder,** where **Anasazi State Park
Museum** (*435-335-7308. www.state
parks.utah.gov/parks/anasazi. Adm.
fee*) offers a close-up view of the
ancestral Pueblo people, who, along
with the Fremont Indians, occupied
this region in prehistoric times. University of Utah archaeologists uncovered an 87-room village here in the
1950s, one of the largest ancestral
Puebloan communities west of the
Colorado River. The state park has
recreated a six-room dwelling and
museum. From Boulder, the **Burr
Trail** (see sidebar p. 289) leads southeast to Lake Powell and the Glen
Canyon National Recreation Area.

Utah 12 heads north from Boulder and enters a landscape of sagebrush and pinyon pine. It ascends

Kimberly–
Big John Road

*Junction to I-70 near Fremont Indian
State Park on Utah 153 and Forest Road
123 and 113*

■ 40 miles ■ 3 hours ■ Summer and
fall. Generally passable by high-
clearance vehicles, but dangerous
in wet weather. Closed winter
and spring.

At altitudes ranging from 6,000 to 11,500
feet, this southwestern Utah dirt road
explores a corner of the **Fishlake National
Forest** (*435-438-2436 or 435-896-9233.
www.fs.usda.gov/fishlake*), ascending the
naked slopes of the **Tushar Mountains**
and passing an old mining town.

From the town of **Junction** on
US 89, head west on Utah 153 into the
national forest, passing **Puffer Lake** and
Elk Meadows, with its downhill ski area.

Near **Beaver Canyon,** take FR 123
north to the **Big John Flat,** ascending
the **Tushar Mountains.** Three peaks
soar above 12,000 feet, and a half
dozen others top 11,000 feet. On their
flanks, high mountain meadows burst
with wildflowers in late summer.

Their open summits provide
sweeping views of south and central
Utah. At the northern and eastern
flanks of the mountains, the road joins
FR 113 and passes **Kimberly,** a turn-of-
the-20th-century gold-mining boomtown. The road continues on to I-70.

Bryce Canyon National Park at sunrise

the broad flanks of **Boulder Mountain,** which sits on the **Aquarius Plateau,** one of the continent's highest timbered plateaus. In fall, stands of fire yellow aspen play against the evergreens. Views from several overlooks, such as **Point Lookout,** are exceptional. The tangled canyons and colored sandstone cliffs of **Capitol Reef** lie in the foreground, while the imposing **Henry Mountains** and **Navajo Mountain** dominate the horizon. The road descends to the junction with Utah 24 near Torrey and the official terminus of Utah 12 Scenic Byway.

Turn right onto Utah 24 and enter **Capitol Reef National Park** *(435-425-3791. www.nps.gov/care. Adm. fee),* which preserves a portion of the **Waterpocket Fold,** a great wrinkle in the Earth's crust—known to geologists as a monocline—that reveals its raw colors and layers. For 100 miles the fold's parallel ridges rise from the desert like the swells of giant waves. Exposed edges of the uplift have eroded into a dramatic slickrock wilderness of massive domes, cliffs, and a maze of twisted canyons. Stop at the **visitor center** to plan your park visit. To take the **Cathedral Valley** drive (see sidebar p. 286) into the isolated northern end of the park, continue on Utah 24 to the departure point 11 miles beyond the visitor center.

Zion National Park Scenic Byway

I-15 to Mount Carmel Junction on Utah 9

■ 54 miles ■ ½ day ■ April through October. Adm. fee to park.

This route penetrates some of Utah's most dramatic scenery: the confines of Zion Canyon, where massive sandstone cliffs shoot 2,000 to 3,000 feet overhead. From the canyon floor the road climbs through two narrow tunnels to high slickrock plateaus, an undulating moonscape of petrified sand dunes smoothed and then cracked over time. Each minute of the day presents a changing array of color.

From **St. George** take I-15 north for 8 miles and go east on Utah 9 toward Zion. You'll pass the **Quail Creek State Park** *(435-879-2378. www.stateparks .utah.gov/parks/quail-creek. Adm. fee).* From the fast-growing town of Hurricane, the road climbs **Hurricane Cliff,** where views of the **Pine Valley Mountains** unfold. Paralleling the northern banks of the **Virgin River,** the road skirts the base of **Hurricane Mesa, Smithsonian Butte,** and the **Eagle Crags** before arriving at the quaint western town of **Springdale,** just before the entrance to **Zion National Park** *(435-772-3256. www.nps.gov/zion. Adm. fee).*

The new **Zion Canyon Visitor Center** lies just inside the park and offers a film and an excellent bookstore. After 2 miles **Zion Canyon Scenic Drive** goes north, while Utah 9 heads east up Pine Creek. First take the must-see 7-mile scenic drive *(by free shuttle only late March–Nov.),* which follows the bubbling waters of the **North Fork Virgin River.** Zion Canyon has an average width of half a mile, with walls 2,000 to 3,000 feet high.

Desert varnish—oxidized iron and manganese—colors the towering walls of the **Beehives** and the **Sentinel** to the west. **Zion Lodge** *(435-772-7700. www.zionlodge.com)* operates cabins and motel rooms year-round. Horse and mule rides are available from March through November *(435-772-3810. Fee).* Across the road near the lodge is the parking lot for the **Emerald Pools.** A stroll on a well-maintained trail takes you to a series of pools, ledges, and waterfalls at the base of the cliffs.

Back on the road, a half mile ahead, is the **Grotto Picnic Area,** the trailhead for 5,990-foot **Angels Landing,** reached via 22 dizzying switchbacks. It's not for people who fear heights, but the views of the canyon are superb. The canyon road continues to **Weeping Rock,** where a pull-off offers excellent views of the sandstone behemoth called the **Great White Throne,** rising some 2,500 feet above the Virgin River.

The Zion Canyon Scenic Drive ends where the canyon narrows at the **Temple of Sinawava,** an immense natural amphitheater named for the Spirit Coyote of the Paiute Indians. The **Riverside Walk,** 2 miles round-trip, begins here and winds north along the river; hanging wildflowers adorn the canyon walls in season. Here and elsewhere in the park look out for the tiny denizens of this realm, including canyon tree frogs, pocket gophers, and more than 270 bird species.

Back at the beginning of the scenic drive, Utah 9 splits off east along **Pine Creek,** switchbacking up to the **Zion–Mount Carmel Tunnel,** a monumental engineering feat when bored out of the rock mountain in 1930. *(Large vehicles escorted through tunnel for fee.)* As it climbs to the high eastern plateaus, the narrow roadway passes several open windows that look off into the canyon. After the tunnel Utah 9 becomes the Zion–Mount Carmel Highway. A small parking area to the right is the trailhead for the **Canyon Overlook Trail.** Fences enclose much

The West Temple after a spring snowstorm, Zion National Park

of the half-mile trail as it threads a narrow course along the lip of a canyon. The trail ends at a sheer drop-off and excellent views of Pine Creek and lower Zion Canyon.

Back on Utah 9, the upper eastern plateaus seem a world apart from Zion Canyon. Ancient sand dunes roll upward to sheer cliff faces. Frequent pull-offs offer opportunities to explore the slickrock. A mile before the park's East Entrance, stop at the pull-off for views of **Checkerboard Mesa,** whose weathered sandstone beds have been uniformly cracked by freezing and thawing cycles. From the park entrance, the highway continues past high pastures to **Mount Carmel Junction.**

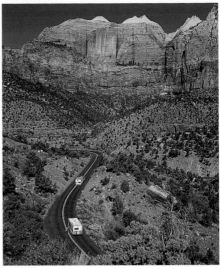

Zion–Mount Carmel Highway

Scenic Byway 143— Utah's Patchwork Parkway

Parowan to Panguitch, Utah, on Utah 143

- 51 miles ▪ 2 hours to 1 day ▪ All year

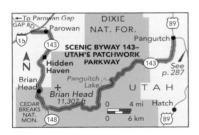

Even by the standards of Utah's superlative scenery, the Patchwork Parkway—Scenic Byway 143—is something special. The unusual nickname commemorates a group of settlers who were forced to put down quilts to cross the deep snow that separated their starving families in Panguitch from supplies in Parowan during the brutal winter of 1864. The name also hints at the variety of the terrain along the route. Climbing to elevations of more than 10,000 feet, the road travels amid lush forests, clear mountain lakes, barren lava flows, eroded redrock, and more.

Don't forget that high altitudes lower the oxygen content of the air you're breathing. Practically speaking, that means you'll want to take it easy and drink lots of water when hiking or biking until you're sure about how the altitude affects you.

The route starts at exit 75 off I-15 at the small town of **Parowan,** which in 1851 became the first Mormon settlement in southern Utah. History buffs may want to make time to check out several local museums, including the distinctive **Old Rock Church Museum** *(90 S. Main St.),* where you can see photographs and other artifacts that document the early days of what was originally called the City of the Little Salt Lake.

Before you set off on the route itself, however, stop at the **Parowan Visitors Center** *(73 N. Main St. 435-477-8190. Closed Sun.)* to get directions to the **Parowan Gap.** This off-the-beaten-track natural cleft, formed by an ancient river about ten miles northwest of town, has earned a spot on the National Register of Historic Places for the large number of intricate abstract and representational petroglyphs created by Native Americans who frequented this area for thousands of years before European settlers arrived.

Back in town, you'll follow Utah 143 up through Parowan Canyon. Between mile markers 8 and 9, you can stop to get a little exercise at a spot they call **Hidden Haven,** where the one-mile trail follows a stream to a pleasant 20-foot waterfall.

From here, the route continues to climb toward the town of **Brian Head** *(435-677-2810. www.brianheadchamber.com),* which, at 9,800 feet above sea level, has the distinction of being the state's highest community as well as Utah's southernmost ski resort. You'll find a range of outdoor recreation opportunities, including an extensive trail network that makes the area a hot spot for mountain bikers, skiers, and snowmobiling enthusiasts.

Several local outfitters offer equipment rentals year-round, including **Georg's Ski Shop** *(612 S. Hwy. 143. 435-677-2013. www.georgsskishop.com).* Local markets also stock everything you'll need for an impromptu picnic at one of the many scenic spots down the road.

You'll find a prime example as you head south out of town and follow the sign pointing you to the turnoff for the road to the top of 11,307-foot **Brian Head Peak.** At the end of the passenger car–friendly, 2½-mile, unpaved track, you'll be rewarded with broad vistas that reach as far as Arizona and Nevada on a clear day.

Petroglyphs at Parowan Gap, UT

Even if you choose to skip this side trip, continuing to follow Utah 143 will still earn you bragging rights as it soon crests at over 10,568 feet. Be sure to pull over a few miles down the road at the **Cedar Breaks National Monument** *(435-586-0787. www .nps.gov/cebr)* overlook to take in spectacular views of a convoluted landscape of redrock ridges and pinnacles sculpted by 30 million years of wind and water.

Farther on, you'll come to **Mammoth Creek** at mile 29, where you can see the starkly barren remnants of ancient lava flows. If you picked up picnic supplies earlier, this is a great spot to break them out.

Ten or so miles down the road, you'll come to **Panguitch Lake,** located at an elevation of 8,400 feet and surrounded by lava flows and ponderosa pine forests. Here you can rent a boat and pick up tackle at **Panguitch Lake Adventure Resort** *(791 S. Lakeshore Dr. 435-676-2864. www.rvfish.com),* if you feel like trying your luck at hooking a few of the lake's sizable rainbow trout.

From here, the road follows Panguitch Creek 18 miles northeast to the town of **Panguitch** itself. While you're in town, pick up a walking tour brochure at City Hall *(25 S. 200 E. 435-676-8585. www.panguitch.org. Closed Sat.-Sun.)* to learn about the many 19th-century brick buildings that have

Cedar Breaks National Monument, UT

put virtually the entire town on the National Register of Historic Places. Then, stop off at **Scoops From the Past** *(105 N. Main St. 435-676-8885. www .scoopsfromthepast.com. Closed Sun.)*, a local ice cream parlor serving hand made ice cream in the lobby of the historic Gem Theatre.

ARIZONA
Kaibab Plateau–North Rim Parkway

Jacob Lake to Grand Canyon North Rim on Arizona 67

▪ 42 miles ▪ 1 day ▪ Late spring through fall. Weather can be unpredictable. North Rim of Grand Canyon National Park is closed late October to early May.

Only about 10 percent of the visitors to **Grand Canyon National Park** *(2 Albright Ave. 928-638-7888. www.nps.gov/ grca. Adm. fee)* travel to the North Rim, visible from the popular sites along the South Rim but requiring a drive of more than 200 miles. While seeing it is by no means a solitary trek, a visit does take you away from the crowds of the south side.

From the crossroads of **Jacob Lake,** Ariz. 67 runs south through **Kaibab National Forest** *(928-635-8200 or 643-7395. www.fs.usda.gov/kaibab)*, which provides campgrounds (including Jacob Lake and DeMotte, at the park boundary) and trails, some of which lead into the **Saddle Mountain Wilderness,** east of Ariz. 67. The Forest Service's **Kaibab Plateau Visitor Center** *(928-643-7298)* at Jacob Lake is open seasonally.

North Rim view

Once you've passed the park entrance, you wind through forests of ponderosa pine, spruce, Douglas-fir, and aspen to reach the **North Rim Visitor Center** *(928-638-7864. www.grandcanyonforever .com),* with a bookstore and information to aid your visit. The **Grand Canyon Lodge** *(303-297-2757 or 888-297-2757)* is famed for its stunning views of **Bright Angel Canyon.** Trails here vary from easy to challenging, but you don't have to walk far to experience the heart-stopping magnificence that is the **Grand Canyon.** Remember, though, that the North Rim is over 8,000 feet in elevation (1,000 feet higher than the South Rim), and that climbing up is much harder than going down.

Three miles back along the entrance road is the turnoff to **Point Imperial** and **Cape Royal,** both offering fabulous vistas of **Granite Gorge** and other areas in the eastern part of the park. The former overlook, at 8,803 feet, is the highest viewpoint anywhere on the canyon rim, with views far eastward over the Colorado River and into the Navajo Nation Reservation.

296

Monument Valley

Kayenta to Mexican Hat on US 163 and County Road 42B

▪ 26 miles ▪ 2 hours ▪ All year

Few thrills compare with driving north on US 163 across the endless sagebrush and red sand desertscape of northern Arizona and coming upon Monument Valley. Immense mesas, buttes, and pinnacles of raw sandstone rise like phantom ships on a silent sea. Swirled slickrock, precarious spires, and domed formations hardly seem of this world, a mélange of reds, oranges, and yellows against a brilliant blue sky.

The drive begins just south of **Kayenta,** a Navajo town established as a trading post in 1910 by archaeologist John Wetherill. US 163 shoots past a 7,096-foot rock monolith named **Agathla,** or "piles of wool," by the Navajo. Just after 6 miles, an overlook on the right offers good views of Agathla and its neighbor across the highway, **Owl Rock**—a red sandstone formation with protruding "ears." At mile 15 the large formations of Monument Valley come suddenly into view. A million and a half years of weathering have worn away huge amounts of soft rock, leaving these monoliths with their erosion-resistant caps of DeChelly sandstone.

After crossing the Utah border at mile 21, a side road (Cty. Rd. 42B) leads 4 miles east to the **Monument Valley Navajo Tribal Park** *(www.navajonationparks .org/htm/monumentvalley.htm. Adm. fee).* At this intersection Native Americans sell jewelry, pots, and samples of Navajo fry bread. After a mile the side road dips back into Arizona, passing vendors offering horseback trips, and comes to the valley **visitor center,** site of a small museum, campground, gift shop, and the roadhead for a 17-mile, dirt

Monument Valley buttes

loop-trail into the formations. Jeep tour operators sell off-road excursions from the parking lot, but you can also guide yourself with a booklet from the visitor center. The ride is rough, and recommended for high-clearance vehicles only. **John Ford Point,** 3.5 miles along the drive, celebrates the director who filmed such Westerns as *Stagecoach* here. Three miles later you'll see the figures of **Totem Pole** and **Yei-Bi-Chei,** thin pinnacles that seem far too fragile to be rock.

Heading back west and crossing US 163, Cty. Rd. 42B continues to Goulding's Lodge *(435-727-3231. www.gouldings.com).* Established as a small trading post in 1920, Goulding's grew world famous as a haunt of Ford and John Wayne when they were filming here. A museum *(donation)* contains film memorabilia, as well as photographs and ancestral Puebloan artifacts. Return to US 163 and go 5 miles north to the drive's end at **Mexican Hat,** a town on the San Juan River named for a balanced rock formation reminiscent of a large sombrero.

Historic Route 66
(New Mexico and Arizona)

Glenrio, New Mexico, to Topock, Arizona, on I-40, US 84, Route 66, New Mexico 313, 333, 124, 117, 122, 118, and County Road 10

▪ 974 miles including alternative routes ▪ 3 to 4 days ▪ All year. Snow can affect roads at higher elevations.

Route 66, famously called "the mother road" by John Steinbeck, has meant many things to thousands of different people. To some, it meant escape from the poverty of the midwestern Dust Bowl of the 1930s. To others, it was the road to the sunshine, glamour, and opportunity of Los Angeles. To families in the 1950s and '60s, it was the route to summer vacation fun.

Inaugurated in 1926, running 2,440 miles from Chicago, Illinois, to Santa Monica, California, Route 66 was known as "America's Main Street." It gave a major boost to the country's automobile culture: the world of motels, diners, gas stations, roadside attractions, and the promise of something new just over the next hill. Interstate highways have eliminated

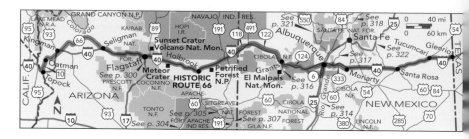

many segments of the old Route 66, but there are still stretches of the original road awaiting exploration (see also Historic Route 66–Illinois pp. 189-190). Here and there vintage diners and motels still stand alongside the concrete ribbon that once linked the Great Lakes with the Pacific Ocean. Be prepared to get on and off I-40 if you want to experience the history and nostalgia of Route 66.

Beginning at the Texas state line, you can follow the original Route 66 westward through arid grassland 40 miles to **Tucumcari** (*Chamber of Commerce, 404 W. Route 66. 575-461-1694 or 888-664-7255. www.tucumcarinm .com*), a town that's taken its Route 66 heritage to heart. Scattered along the old highway through Tucumcari, neon signs greet you—signs that have been restored to their fabulous fifties-era dazzle, such as the TeePee Curio Shop and La Cita restaurant.

As you continue west through Montoya and Santa Rosa, you'll find segments of the original Route 66 mixed with stretches of I-40. Sixteen miles west of Santa Rosa, US 84 heads northwest, following the pre-1938 Route 66 to **Santa Fe** (*201 W. Marcy St. Convention & Visitors Bureau. 505-955-6200 or 800-777-2489. www.santafe.org*). For information on attractions along this route, such as **Las Vegas National Wildlife Refuge, Pecos National Historical Park,** and Santa Fe itself, see the **Santa Fe Trail** byway (pp. 321-323). After 1938, Route 66 took a direct path west from Santa Rosa, now followed by I-40. At Moriarty, exit the interstate and take N. Mex. 333 (historic 66) west into **Albuquerque** (*Convention & Visitors Bureau, 20 First Plaza N.W., Suite 601. 800-284-2282. www.itsatrip.org*). For information on Albuquerque attractions, see **El Camino Real** byway (pp. 314-331).

Route 66 followed Albuquerque's Central Avenue (N. Mex. 333), and as you drive that urban thoroughfare today you'll see many sites from the highway's glory days, such as the 1927 Pueblo-style **KiMo Theatre** (*423 Central Ave. N.W. 505-768-3544. www.cabq .gov/kimo*). To follow the pre-1938 Route 66, take N. Mex. 314, 47, and 6 to loop south of Albuquerque, and then back northwest to join I-40. Otherwise, take I-40 to Laguna and then follow N. Mex. 124, 117, 122, and 118, which allow you to follow historic 66 all the way to Arizona. Along the way, the town of Grants is the gateway to **El Malpais National Monument** (*505-783-4774. www.nps.gov/elma*), a badlands of lava flows, cinder cones, lava tubes, and other volcanic formations. (See El Malpais pp. 316-317.)

In eastern Arizona, most drivable segments of old Route 66 are now simply frontage roads for I-40; many travelers will choose to take the

In Tucumcari, NM, look for 17 Route 66–themed murals and, on the western edge of town, a sculpture entitled "Roadside Attraction," an homage to Route 66 featuring massive taillights that shine red at night.

interstate. Don't miss the side trip through **Petrified Forest National Park** *(928-524-6228. www.nps.gov/pefo. Adm. fee),* showcase for colorful rock formations and hundreds of impressive petrified logs dating from 225 million years ago. The **Blue Mesa** and **Long Logs Trails** reward brief hikes with stunning landscapes.

In **Holbrook,** a detour onto the I-40 business route takes you past the **Wigwam Motel** *(811 W. Hopi Dr. 928-524 3048. www.wigwammotel .com),* which, as its name plainly states, is a collection of 16 concrete "wigwam" rooms; it's surely one of the most wonderful reminders of the vintage days of Route 66. Make the side trip south of I-40 to see **Meteor Crater** *(exit 233. 928-289-5898 or 800-289-5898. www .meteorcrater.com. Adm. fee),* the enormous (4,000 feet across) impact mark of a meteor that hit the Earth 50,000 years ago with the power of 20 million tons of TNT.

At **Flagstaff,** you can follow historic Route 66 by leaving I-40 and taking US 180 and US 89 through town; this stretch has numerous vintage motels. Just 15 miles northeast of town, **Sunset Crater Volcano National Monument** *(928-526-0502. www.nps.gov/sucr. Adm. fee)* makes for a fascinating side trip. Active as recently as 900 years ago, the volcano here has left a harsh landscape of lava and ash, dominated by a 1,000-foot-high symmetrical cone, colored by oxidized cinders that gave it its "sunset" name. In Flagstaff, the **Museum of Northern Arizona** *(3101 N. Ft. Valley Rd. 928-774-5213. www.musnaz.org. Adm. fee)* is an excellent place to learn about the region's geology, natural history, and Native American people who lived (and still live) nearby.

From the ponderosa pine forest of Flagstaff at 7,000 feet, I-40 continues west, dropping in elevation into a drier landscape. Just beyond Ash Fork *(at exit 139),* you'll leave the interstate for the longest remaining stretch of the original Route 66. The old railroad town of **Seligman** is the first of several small towns you'll travel through, many of which preserve fifties-style motels, drive-ins, and shops. **Seligman's Route 66 Gift Shop and Visitor Center** *(217 E. Route 66. 928-422-3352. www.route66giftshop.com)* is full of memorabilia and information on the route to the California state line.

The terrain is increasingly desertlike as you reach **Kingman,** where the **Powerhouse Visitor Center** *(120 W. Route 66. 928-753-6106. www.kingmantourism.org)* features local tourism information and the **Historic Route 66 Museum** *(928-753-9889. Adm. fee).* Exhibits here recall travel along the route from Native American paths through stagecoach days, the Dust Bowl era, and the "Main Street America" period of automobile travel.

Historic Route 66 continues as Cty. Rd. 10 out of Kingman, twisting through tight switchbacks over 3,652-foot Sitgreaves Pass to the Western-themed town of **Oatman,** known for mock gunfights and semi-tame burros wandering the streets. You're in real desert now, as you wind down to meet I-40 and the Colorado River at Topock.

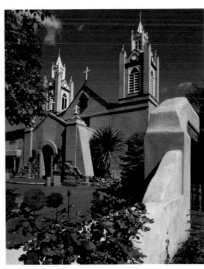

Historic Old Town, Albuquerque

Oak Creek Canyon Drive

Flagstaff to Sedona on US 89A

- 27 miles - 2 hours - All year. Can be very congested in summer. Best in fall when cottonwoods turn yellow and crowds thin out.

On the southern edge of the great Colorado Plateau that produced such marvels as Grand, Zion, and Bryce Canyons lies an equally stunning, but far more intimate spot—Oak Creek Canyon. For the past three million years, Oak Creek has carved a 12-mile-long, 2,000-foot-deep slice along the fault line into the ancient geologic past. From the ponderosa pines of Flagstaff to the red-rock desertscape of Sedona, the Oak Creek Canyon Drive reveals layers of red sandstone, tan limestone, purple siltstone, all eroded into curious shapes. Shady cottonwoods and a year-round water source attract a wide variety of animals, and the Forest Service has established numerous camping and picnic grounds along the short route.

US 89A leaves the bustle of **Flagstaff,** a former lumber town in the shadows of the rugged **San Francisco Peaks,** and travels through the thick ponderosa pines of the **Coconino National Forest** *(928-527-3600. www.fs.usda.gov/coconino).* After 3 miles the road passes the small **Lindbergh Spring Roadside Park,** a good spot for a close-up look at ponderosas. Their clusters of three long needles distinguish them from other pine species.

After 8 miles atop the plateau, the road comes to the **Oak Creek Overlook** on the left, at the lip of a great escarpment known as the **Mogollon Rim.** Thirty million years ago, seismic forces thrust this section of Earth's crust thousands of feet above the surrounding land.

A short loop-trail, where Native Americans sell crafts, brings you to the edge of a sheer drop. From this 6,400-foot vantage point, you'll see a diversity of plant life resulting from the dramatic elevation changes and relative abundance of water. Douglas-fir and white fir cling to the cliff walls. Water-loving trees, such as alder, willow, oak, and walnut, thrive along the creek. Dense brush dominates

Oak Creek, Coconino National Forest

the dry hillsides. Where the canyon widens, desert plants appear.

From the overlook, the road—which began as a cattle trail and was later adapted to wagons—switchbacks precipitously downward for 2 miles to the Pumphouse Wash Bridge. About 17 miles south of Flagstaff, a day-use area leads to the canyon's most popular hike, the **West Fork Trail,** a moderate 3-mile walk into **West Fork Canyon,** past fern forests and sandy beaches under sheer walls.

The road continues, passing campsites and picnic grounds along **Oak Creek.** Above, layers of sedimentary rock mark the rock walls. In age and composition they are like the rocks in the top third of the Grand Canyon.

Halfway through the canyon drive, **Slide Rock State Park** *(928-282-3034. www.azstateparks.com. Adm. fee)* appears on the right. Beyond the orchard and down some steps, a path leads to the site of the park's most popular activity. Here, the creek bubbles through a shoot of smooth Coconino sandstone, and the air fills with shouts as people ride the natural slide. *(Bring water socks and jeans—ride can be bumpy.)* In summer you must arrive before 11 a.m. to park. Not far beyond Slide Rock is Oak Creek's other popular swim spot, **Grasshopper Swim Area,** with deep pools and soaring cliffs.

Just after this swim area, a pull-off on the north side of Midgely Bridge serves as the trailhead for the **Wilson Mountain Trail,** which pushes west into the **Red Rocks–Secret Mountain Wilderness.** Though strenuous—the trail rises 2,300 feet in 5.6 miles—the spectacular views extend several hundred miles and encompass **Verde Valley, Sedona,** and **Oak Creek Canyon.** An equally strenuous alternative is the **North Wilson Trail,** which starts north of the Encinoso Picnic Area and joins the **Wilson Mountain**

Red Rock Scenic Byway

Along Arizona 179 southeast of Sedona

■ **7.5 miles** ■ **1 hour** ■ **All year**

The town of **Sedona** *(928-282-7722 or 800-288-7336. www.visitsedona.com)* lies at the edge of the Colorado Plateau, an accident of geography. Beautiful canyons have been eroded back into the plateau, showing stunning colors among the rugged rock formations.

Sand laid down about 300 million years ago became sandstone, which has been eroded and tinted red by the presence of iron, then shaped by water and wind into endlessly varied shapes with names such as Chimney Rock, Rabbit Ears, and Cathedral Rock.

This short but highly scenic drive passes in large part through **Coconino National Forest** *(928-527-3600. www.fs.usda.gov/coconino),* which offers campgrounds and hiking trails.

The byway officially begins just north of I-17. Ariz. 179 soon crosses Dry Beaver Creek. As you pass through the village of **Oak Creek,** you won't have any doubt that the butte in front of you is **Bell Rock,** one of the most famous landmarks around. To see it and nearby **Courthouse Butte** close up, go to the Bell Rock Vista trailhead just north of the village to park. The trailhead here offers options for short strolls or longer hikes.

Just a mile farther, the **Little Horse Trailhead** offers views of more formations, including **Cathedral Rock** to the west. The byway

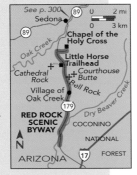

officially ends at the **Chapel of the Holy Cross,** a striking building tucked into a red-rock canyon east of the highway.

301

Trail. Two miles from Midgely Bridge, the road passes out of the canyon and into **Sedona** *(Chamber of Commerce, 331 Forest Rd. 928-282-7722 or 800-288-7336. www.visitsedona.com),* an arts community set among spectacular red-rock formations.

Apache Trail

Apache Junction to Tonto National Monument on Arizona 88

■ 46 miles ■ 3 hours ■ Fall through spring. The 25-mile Tortilla Flat—Roosevelt Dam section is dirt—avoid in wet weather, if bothered by heights, or if driving an RV; best driven south to north to stay on inside lane near cliff wall.

Shadowing the ancient footpaths of Apache Indians, this partly unpaved route claims an abundance of switchbacks and dazzling views as it skirts the craggy Superstition Mountains just east of Phoenix, plunges into the sheer rock canyons of the Salt River, and encounters blue desert lakes. Along the spine-tingling section between Tortilla Flat and Theodore Roosevelt Dam, the road drops 1,500 feet in several miles.

From **Apache Junction** take Ariz. 88 for 5 miles to **Lost Dutchman State Park** *(480-982-4485. www .azstateparks.com. Adm. fee),* which offers an introduction to the native Sonoran Desert scrub-plant community on its **Native Plant Trail.** Other paths, such as the **Siphon Draw Trail,** lead up the sheer escarpment of **Superstition Mountain.** Of the legends that give the mountain its name, none is more famous than the story of Jacob "The Dutchman" Waltz, who allegedly discovered a mine and hid a cache of gold here in the 1870s. It remains undiscovered. Gold seekers continue to visit 4,553-foot **Weaver's Needle,** a volcanic plug visible north of the park at the **Needle Vista Viewpoint.**

Now inside the nearly 3-million-acre **Tonto National Forest** *(602-225-5200. www.fs.usda.gov/tonto. Day-use fee),* the road curves up through saguaro cactuses to a view of 10-mile-long **Canyon Lake,** azure blue against a desertscape of steep brown cliffs. Four lakes—**Saguaro** to the west, **Canyon, Apache,** and **Theodore Roosevelt**—were created in the early 20th century by damming the **Salt River** for irrigation and flood control. At Canyon Lake's edge, the **Acacia Picnic Area** offers swimming, **Palo Verde Recreation Site** contains a boating ramp, and **Boulder Recreation Area** has a fishing ramp and pavilion. **Canyon Lake Marina** *(480-288-9233. www.canyonlakemarina.com)* features the **Lakeside Restaurant and Cantina** and offers lake cruises on *The Dolly (Arizona Steamboat Cruises. 480-827-9144. www.dollysteamboat.com. Fare).*

The road winds around the lake for several miles, climbs again, and descends into **Tortilla Flat,** an old stagecoach stop and the only town along the Apache Trail. The ramshackle stores are right out of a Hollywood set, and the bar has saddles for seats and prickly pear ice cream. Beyond Mesquite Flat, the dirt road begins, heading to **Fish Creek Hill,** the highlight of the drive. A short trail leads cliffside for panoramic views of sheer-walled **Fish Creek Canyon.** From here, the road descends precipitously 800 feet in the next mile, with sharp switchbacks narrowing in places to a car's width, before crossing a one-lane bridge over **Fish Creek.** A small pull-off after the bridge is the trailhead for a trail up the creek.

The road winds along Fish Creek and other small streams until it descends to views of 17-mile-long Apache Lake, flush against the eroded, multilayered desert rock face known as the **Painted Cliffs of the Mazatzal Mountains.** From one of the overlooks a road drops a mile down to **Apache Lake Marina and Resort** *(928-467-2511. www.apachelake.com),* which has a marina, boat ramp, restaurant, and campground.

For the remaining 10 miles the road snakes along the narrow waters of Apache Lake, pushing between tall hills past the **Burnt Corral Recreation Site** to **Theodore Roosevelt Dam.** When built between 1903 and 1911, it was the world's largest masonry dam at 280 feet high and 723 feet long. Beyond the dam, 23-mile-long Theodore Roosevelt Lake spreads into the surrounding desert. Continue east to the **Roosevelt Lake Visitor Center** *(928-467-3200)* for displays and an observation deck.

Though the official Apache Trail ends here, it's worth continuing 5 miles east on Ariz. 88 to **Tonto National Monument** *(928-467-2241. www.nps.gov/ tont. Adm. fee)* for a peek at the prehistoric Salado people. From the visitor

303

Agave and yucca in the Superstition Mountains, Tonto National Forest

center a lovely trail winds up 350 feet to cliff dwellings, one of the nation's best preserved Salado sites. In the 14th century, population pressures forced the Salado up into caves, where they built a 19-room community. Call in advance for a guided 3-hour (round-trip) hike to the even more spectacular 40-room **Upper Ruin.**

Globe to Show Low

US 60

▪ 87 miles ▪ 2 to 3 hours ▪ All year. Temperatures can vary greatly from canyon to rim, especially in winter.

Well-traveled and well-built, US 60 runs across the transition zone that connects Arizona's arid southern desert lands with the cool forested mountains of the Colorado Plateau. As it gains nearly 3,000 feet in elevation, the road passes the mesa and buttes of the San Carlos Apache Reservation, plunges more than 2,000 feet into the Salt River Canyon, and races up the Mogollon Rim to the edge of the White Mountains. It begins in semidesert and ends in the nation's largest contiguous stand of ponderosa pine. When snowmelt engorges the Salt River, water rushes over the Mogollon Rim and through beautiful canyons—excellent for white water rafting and kayaking (*for outfitters, call Globe Ranger District. 928-425-7189*).

See p. 305

Before embarking on the drive, stop at the **Besh-Ba-Gowah Archaeological Park** (*Jesse Hayes Rd. 928-425-0320. www.historicgilacounty.com/besh_ba_gowah.shtml. Adm. fee*), a site 1 mile southeast of Globe that in the 13th and 14th centuries was a Salado pueblo with more than 200 rooms. Shell and turquoise jewelry and polychrome pottery were traded here.

Leaving Globe, a former silver- and copper-mining town, US 60 climbs through the southeastern corner of the **Tonto National Forest** (*928-225-5200. www.fs.usda.gov/tonto*), a sea of desert shrub, semidesert grasslands, and mesquite-choked washes. **Apache Peaks, Chrome Butte,** and **Rockinstraw Mountain** rise in the distance. After more than 16 miles, the road passes the **Jones Water Campground** on the right, a shady oasis of oak trees amid the hills.

An 1873 boomtown, Globe may have gotten its name when someone found a hunk of silver with cracks that resembled continent boundaries.

As the road climbs toward the crest of nearly 6,000-foot **Timber Camp Mountain,** the vegetation becomes pinyon pine and juniper and then ponderosa pine.

Continuing along US 60, the route enters the **San Carlos Apache Reservation,** once home to the Apache leader Geronimo, and drops down to cattail-fringed **Seneca Lake** on the left. If you walk around the lake to the right, you'll see dramatic **Seneca Falls.**

From Seneca Lake the road continues to drop, opening up to breathtaking views of the **Salt River Canyon,** with its colorful sedimentary and basaltic rock faces and plunging cliff sides. The best pull-off, **Hieroglyphic Point,** provides an extraordinary view of geologic history from cliffs that descend 2,000 feet. Before gawking at the chasm, search out the thousand-year-old petroglyphs in the rocks near the foot of the stairs.

Great winding switchbacks weave down the cliff face to a bridge, rest area, and trails down to the bubbling **Salt River,** so named by the Pima Indians and early Europeans for its salty composition. The river drains

2,500 square miles and drops more than 10,000 feet, offering excellent white-water rafting. Some of the best begins here at the bridge and extends 52 miles to Theodore Roosevelt Lake. Across the bridge lies the **White Mountain Apache Reservation** (*White Mountain Apache Game and Fish Dept. 928-338-4385. www.wmatoutdoors.org*) and a small store where hiking and fishing permits are available. A dirt road leads some 3 miles west along the Salt River to **Cibecue Creek.** A rugged, mile-long scramble northeast along the creek ends at a spectacular **Cibecue Falls.** Stop at the store

Cibecue Falls

before starting out to check on road conditions and pick up required permits.

US 60 climbs out of the Salt River Canyon; at several pull-offs you can scan far below for the rusted hulks of old cars. From the main canyon the road passes over rounded mountains and offers views of the massive **White Mountains** to the northeast. It climbs the **Mogollon Rim,** the sharply defined southern edge of the upthrust Colorado Plateau. Atop the rim and higher, the road enters deep ponderosa pine forests. At 6,331 feet it reaches Show Low, a frontier town whose ownership was once decided in a poker game.

White Mountains Drive

Alpine to Hon Dah on Forest Road 249, Arizona 273, 261, and 260

▪ 68 miles ▪ 3 to 4 hours ▪ Spring through fall. Parts of drive are closed in winter.

This route in central Arizona near the New Mexico border penetrates the remote forests of the White Mountains, passing Big Lake and skirting Mount Baldy, a sacred Apache site and one of Arizona's highest peaks. The eastern portion of the route falls within the Apache-Sitgreaves National Forests; the western half is under the jurisdiction of the White Mountain Apache Reservation.

This route begins off the **Coronado Trail** (see pp. 307-308), 1.5 miles northwest of **Alpine,** and heads west on well-maintained gravel FR 249, arriving at the open meadows of **Williams Valley** after 4.5 miles. Especially popular in winter, the area has 5 miles of gentle trails and a toboggan run.

Five miles from here, the road passes a small lake and picks up the meandering **Black River,** following it to **Three Forks,** the pretty confluence of three streams. The grasslands offer excellent opportunities to spot elk and mule deer. One mile later is the turnoff to **Big Lake** and the **Big Lake Visitor Center** *(spring-summer).* A Forest Service pamphlet serves as an excellent guide to the short **Big Lake Nature Trail** that loops behind the center. The access road continues on to the dock, where you can rent a boat or buy fishing equipment.

Go north on Ariz. 273. The route passes **Crescent Lake** and picks up Ariz. 261, entering large tracts of treeless grassland interrupted only by volcanic rocks. Twelve miles from Big Lake, the road passes peaceful, 164-acre **Mexican Hay Lake,** packed with mallard, teal, buffleheads, and other ducks in fall. The route descends from the **White Mountains** to the plateau and joins Ariz. 260 west of Springerville.

> Mexican Hay is a small, weedy lake, thus the name—but fly fishermen have landed 15-inchers there.

Head west past grasslands, where pronghorn often graze. Ancient volcanic cinder cones rise to the right. About 7.5 miles from the turnoff, the highway passes a 5-mile side road (Ariz. 373) to the small resort town of **Greer,** which lies in a pretty canyon near the **East** and **West Forks Little Colorado River.**

Along the side road are the short **Butler Canyon Nature Trail,** several campgrounds, and a cross-country ski area.

Wetlands along Arizona 273, Apache-Sitgreaves National Forests

Ariz. 260 continues west into the **White Mountain Apache Reservation** *(hiking and fishing permits. 928-338-4385. www.wmatoutdoors.org)* after 7 miles and crosses the turnoff to Ariz. 273, which leads south to Sunrise Lake and Sheep's Crossing, where trails head into the **Mount Baldy Wilderness** and to 11,590-foot **Mount Baldy.** The trail to Baldy stops short of the summit. Back on Ariz. 260, continue on to the casino town of **Hon Dah,** past a handful of mountain lakes.

Coronado Trail Scenic Byway

Clifton to Springerville on US 191

- 123 miles ▪ 4 to 6 hours ▪ All year, but plowed weekdays only during snow season. Includes sharp curves and steep drop-offs.

Some 450 years ago Francisco Vásquez de Coronado passed near this route on his expedition to find the fabled Seven Cities of Cíbola. Paralleling the border with New Mexico, this route—which follows almost exactly the official Coronado Trail Scenic Byway—skirts the eastern edge of the Apache-Sitgreaves National Forests, passes one of the nation's largest open-pit copper mines, then switchbacks up (427 curves between Clifton and Alpine) to cross the ragged edge of the Mogollon Rim. In its first 60 miles the highway climbs 5,000 feet, passing from the Upper Sonoran Desert to high alpine meadows and crossing as many life zones as you'd find from Mexico to Canada.

The route begins in **Clifton**, an early copper-mining town tucked into a canyon hewn by the **San Francisco River.** US 191 twists and curves over mine tailings, passes a copper concentrator at about 5 miles, and edges along the lip of an immense pit. At nearly 10 miles an observation point affords views of the Phelps Dodge Mine and the tiny-looking trucks that haul out 125,000 tons of copper each day.

The route continues for another 5 miles along the mine, past piles of rubble with rocks containing copper ore. Suddenly the road follows a little creek bed up into rocky **Chase Canyon.** Slow down to 10 miles per hour for the next 5 miles. The road squeezes between colorful rock faces and dramatic drops, crossing from one side of the ridge to the other for about 15 miles, until the terrain flattens out to grassland and juniper-pinyon forest.

The route continues over ridgelines and mountainsides for another 18 miles, then passes a small parking area where you can take a half-mile hike up to a watchtower atop 8,786-foot **Rose Peak.** Some 17 miles farther, after passing the **Stray Horse Campground,** US 191 ascends the **Mogollon Rim,** the southernmost edge of the Colorado Plateau, and comes to 9,346-foot **Blue Vista.** Outstanding views open to the southeast and west, a tangle of peaks and canyons enveloped in soft blue haze.

After Blue Vista the highway winds through thick, "aspect sensitive" forests: North-facing ridges bear spruce, fir, and aspen, while those facing south support oak and ponderosa pines. Seven miles later the road passes **Hannagan Meadow,** with a lodge and store; it's a good point of departure for cross-country skiing.

For the next 23 miles, the route curves along the eastern edge of the **White Mountains,** past thick aspen groves and alpine meadows alive with Indian paintbrush, columbine, and lupine in late July and August. In the small town of **Alpine** you can find good hiking information at the Alpine Ranger District *(928-339-4384)* of the **Apache-Sitgreaves National Forests** *(928-333-4301. www.fs.usda.gov/asnf).* The White Mountains Drive (see pp. 305-306), begins 1.5 miles north of Alpine on FR 249. From Alpine, US 191 gently rises and falls over wide-flanked mountains past Arizona's third highest

307

Apache-Sitgreaves National Forests

peak, 10,912-foot **Escudilla Mountain,** an old volcano inside the **Escudilla Wilderness Area.** The 3-mile hike on the **Escudilla National Recreational Trail** traverses an area burned by fire more than 40 years ago and ends at the Forest Service's fire tower for spectacular views. After crossing a wide, grassy valley, the road passes the **Nelson Reservoir,** a thin, mile-long lake with ducks, ospreys, and migratory birds in season. Seven miles from the reservoir, the route descends to flatlands and the town of **Springerville.**

Sky Island Scenic Byway

Coronado National Forest to Mount Lemmon on Catalina Highway

■ 60 miles ■ 3 hours ■ All year. Summer weekends can be crowded.

In 25 miles of hairpin and blind turns, this drive, following much of the official Sky Island Scenic Byway, climbs more than 6,300 feet, winding up the southern flank of the Santa Catalina Mountains to 9,157-foot Mount Lemmon. Beginning in the saguaro cactus forests of the arid Sonoran Desert, it passes through five distinct life zones, ending in a cool mixed conifer forest more reminiscent of Canada than southern Arizona.

Seventeen miles northeast of Tucson, the Catalina Highway crosses into the **Coronado National Forest** *(520-388-8300. www.fs.usda.gov/coronado. Day-use fee)* and heads across canyons guarded by saguaro cactuses to the **Babat Duag Viewpoint** at 2.5 miles; the **Tucson Basin** and the **Rincon Mountains** to the southeast. After 3 miles the road enters narrow **Molino Canyon.** You can get a good look at it from the **Molino Canyon Overlook.** Beyond the canyon lies 4,200-foot **Molino Basin,** site of a campground and trailhead and the transition zone from desert scrub to oak tree vegetation.

As you climb, the trees change from oak to juniper in **Bear Canyon** to cypress, sycamore, pine, and walnut in upper Bear Canyon. After 14 miles, at 6,400-foot **Windy Point,** come the drive's most sweeping views: the **Tucson Basin, Santa Rita, Huachuca,** and **Patagonia Mountains,** and occasionally the **Sierra de San Antonio** of Mexico, to the south. A half mile later, **Geology Vista** offers interpretive information.

The road continues up through ponderosa pine forests to 7,400-foot **San Pedro Vista,** with views looking north to the San Pedro River Valley. A couple of miles after the vista, the **Palisade Information Station** (*Santa Catalina Ranger District 520-749-8700. Thurs.-Mon. in summer. Parking fee*) has ecological exhibits. It is the trailhead for the **Butterfly** and **Crystal Springs** hiking trails. Just before reaching Summerhaven, the end of the road, a 2-mile spur road leads to the **Mount Lemmon Ski Valley** (*520-885-1181. www.skithelemmon.com*), one of the country's southernmost ski resorts. An unmarked, mile-long trail takes you from beyond the ski area through a quiet forest to near Mount Lemmon's summit.

Flowering saguaro

Tucson Mountains Drive

Tucson Mountain Park to Saguaro National Park on Gates Pass, Kinney, and Golden Gate Roads

■ 22 miles ■ 2 hours ■ All year. Partly graded dirt and gravel; fine for passenger cars.

In minutes this road leaves the sprawl of Tucson and enters a magical forest of immense saguaro cactuses. On the way it passes a desert museum.

At the edge of the **Tucson Mountain Regional Park,** the road winds past saguaros to Gates Pass for views of the Tucson Mountains. After a mile, a road veers left toward **Old Tucson Studios** (*520-883-0100. Check calendar on www.oldtucson.com. Adm. fee*), a Wild West theme park and movie set. About 1.5 miles north of the turnoff you will find the **Arizona–Sonora Desert Museum** (*520-883-2702. www.desertmuseum.org. Adm. fee*), a feast of outdoor exhibits about the varied and surprising life-forms found in the Sonoran desert, including mountain lions, rattle-

snakes, hummingbirds, and peccaries. Exhibits tell about the saguaro cactus, which can grow 60 feet high and live 150 years. A mile past the museum, the road enters **Saguaro National Park** (*www.nps.gov/sagu. Parking fee*) and comes to the **Red Hills Information Center** (*520-733-5158*), with the **Cactus Garden Trail** and park information. The **Bajada Loop Drive** passes rocks with Hohokam culture petroglyphs at the **Signal Hill Picnic Area.** Trails lead into saguaro forests and explore the ridges of the Tucson Mountains.

309

NEW MEXICO
Trail of the
Mountain Spirits Scenic Byway

Loop from Silver City on New Mexico 15, 35, and 152 and US 180

- 110 miles ▪ 3 to 8 hours ▪ All year. Many curves make driving slow. Some sections are not recommended for RVs and trailers. Trail to cliff dwellings closes at 4 p.m.

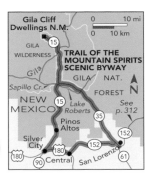

Within the high desert forests of Gila National Forest, this southwestern New Mexico route penetrates some of the nation's largest and most remote tracts of wilderness. It passes a couple of Old West towns, winds to ancient cliff dwellings, and bypasses an immense open-pit copper mine. Make sure to leave time to visit the cliff dwellings.

The route begins at **Silver City,** a mining town that boomed in the 1870s when silver was discovered behind the present-day Grant County courthouse. The town's colorful history is told at the **Silver City Museum** *(312 W. Broadway. 575-538-5921. www.silvercitymuseum.com. Closed Mon.).*

From town, the route climbs north on N. Mex. 15 for 6 miles into the **Pinos Altos Range** and reaches the town of **Pinos Altos,** or "tall pines," which hugs the Continental Divide at 7,840 feet. After a brief gold boom in the late 19th century, the town went bust. The famous bar at the **Buckhorn Saloon** *(575-538-9911. www.buckhornsaloonand operahouse.com. Closed Sun.),* along with its fine restaurant, keep the sleepy town alive.

After Pinos Altos the road loses its center line and narrows considerably as it winds through the Pinos Altos Range, heading up **Cherry Creek** past a couple of rustic picnic areas shaded by ponderosa pines and cottonwoods. Eighteen miles after Pinos Altos,

West Fork of the Gila River, Gila Cliff Dwellings NM

the route drops steeply to **Sapillo Creek**. At the creek, N. Mex. 15 intersects with N. Mex. 35, but continue north for 17 miles to the Gila Cliff Dwellings National Monument. On its way up to the cliff dwellings, the road

Gila Cliff Dwellings National Monument

climbs steeply through a series of switchbacks, passing the **Senator Clinton P. Anderson Scenic Overlook** after almost 7 miles. The **Gila River Canyon** lies 2,000 feet below, while spectacular vistas of the **Gila Wilderness** spread to the horizon. After the overlook, N. Mex. 15 crosses a level ridge with open views and then descends sharply to a bridge across the **Gila River** and a primitive camping site.

Four miles later, the road reaches **Gila Cliff Dwellings National Monument** *(575-536-9461. www.nps.gov/gicl. Adm. fee).* Drive straight ahead to the **visitor center,** which offers good displays and information about the peoples who inhabited this remote area for a millennium or more. Be sure to pick up the informative guide. The road to the dwellings passes the **Lower Scorpion Campground,** which features a 0.25-mile trail leading to a small cave dwelling. (The short paved path to the right ends at a series of ancient red pictographs painted with hematite.) The parking area for the major cliff dwellings lies just beyond the campground. A 1-mile loop climbs 175 feet to the dwellings on the southeast-facing cliff. Five caves contain a remarkable series of 42 rooms connected by passageways. Some 40 to 50 Pueblo Indians lived in these dwellings in the late 13th century.

Ruins of circular pit houses show that people known as the Mogollon inhabited the Gila area at least 14 centuries ago.

Retrace the route to Sapillo Creek and take N. Mex. 35 southeast for 4 miles to **Lake Roberts,** a pretty lake surrounded by pines. As the road winds around the lake, it passes **Vista Village,** an archaeological site undergoing excavation. It's believed that prehistoric people occupied an 18- to 25-room pueblo here. The road continues up a wide valley and again crests the Continental Divide before reaching the **Mimbres River Valley** and coming on the **Mimbres Ranger District** *(505-536-2250)* outside the town of Mimbres.

At the town of San Lorenzo, the route intersects N. Mex. 152, which heads west 8.5 miles to the overlook of the **Phelps Dodge Santa Rita Copper Mine,** an immense hole in the earth. Continue on to Central, where US 180 takes you back to Silver City.

Geronimo Trail Scenic Byway

San Lorenzo to Gila National Forest's Beaverhead Work Center on New Mexico 152, 52, 59, and I-25

■ 154 miles ■ 1 day ■ Spring through fall. Mountain roads may close temporarily after snowfall.

Traversing the homeland of the Apache warrior Geronimo, who was born just to the west, this byway ranges from high mountains to the flat valley of the Rio Grande.

The route begins at the junction of N. Mex. 61 and 152 at the Mimbres River, near the town of San Lorenzo. The latter highway will climb 2,500 feet in the next 20 miles as it ascends into the **Black Range.** About 10 miles along the way, look back west to a volcanic rock formation called the **Kneeling Nun** and the scar of the **Santa Rita Mine,** the world's largest open-pit copper mine. From 8,178-foot Emory Pass a panorama of peaks is presented to the east, with the Caballo Reservoir and the Sierra Caballo beyond.

The drive quickly reaches tiny **Kingston,** the first of several ghost or near-ghost towns you'll encounter on the byway. An 1882 silver strike brought Kingston a population of 7,000, three newspapers, a brewery, and a brothel located on Virtue Avenue. Much the same story applies to **Hillsboro,** 9 miles down the road, where 19th-century buildings still line the streets. The route drops to the valley of the Rio Grande, impounded here as **Caballo Reservoir,** a popular recreational lake.

North on I-25, the byway reaches **Truth or Consequences** *(www.torcnm .org),* which was called Palomas Hot Springs until changing its name in 1950. "T or C" still has its natural hot springs, which legend says made this neutral ground where American Indian tribes met in peace to enjoy the mineral waters. **Geronimo Springs Museum** *(211 Main St. 505-894-6600. www.geronimo springsmuseum.com. Adm. fee)* has exhibits on local fossils, Native Americans, Hispanic heritage, and a real miner's log cabin brought from the Black Range to the west. That's where the byway heads next, following N. Mex. 52

up past pecan orchards, through Cuchillo to the old mining town of **Winston.** Take a side trip to the almost-ghost town of **Chloride** and the **Pioneer Store Museum** *(575-743-2736. www.pioneerstore museum.com).*

Finally, the byway takes N. Mex. 59 west, crosses the Continental Divide in the **Gila National Forest** *(575-388-8201. www.fs.usda.gov/gila. Adm. fee),* and ends at the Forest Service's Beaverhead Work Station.

Sunflowers in almost-ghost town of Chloride

Heart of the Sands

White Sands National Monument

▪ 16 miles ▪ 1 hour ▪ Fall through winter

Waves of brilliant white sand dunes ringed by distant towering peaks make this southwestern New Mexico drive one of the most unusual in the Southwest. Ever shifting, the gypsum dunes can reach up to 60 feet high and move 12 to 16 feet per year. Enclosed by the White Sands Missile Range, White Sands National

Monument closes occasionally for an hour or two for missile testing. Hikers should exercise caution: It's easy to lose one's bearing in this trackless desert, especially during sandstorms.

At the beginning of the route, the visitor center of **White Sands National Monument** *(575-479-6124. www.nps.gov/whsa. Adm. fee)* offers interpretive information on this unusual geologic feature. The sun evaporates water from nearby Lake Lucero and alkali flats, leaving a thin crust of tiny gypsum crystals, which the wind blows into dunes. In this harsh, dry environment, a species of mice, lizards, snakes, and scorpions have adapted light coloration to survive.

313

Rabbitbrush, White Sands National Monument

For about 3 miles the road skirts the edge of the dunes, where saltbush comes right up to the road. Fine, snowlike sand blows across the road and the parking lot for the **Big Dune Trail** on the left. This 1-hour nature hike climbs up a 60-foot dune past gnarled cottonwoods and provides many chances to follow animal tracks.

As the road pushes farther into the dunes, vegetation gradually disappears, though you see an occasional yucca plant whose roots stretch down as far as 30 to 40 feet. In the heart of the dunes, swirling sand prevents plants from taking root (and the absence of plants causes the sand to swirl). At the end of the 8-mile road, the **Alkali Flat Trail** leads 2.3 miles through the dunes. Wide parking lots offer ample opportunity to park and hike or sand surf some of the steep dune faces.

Billy the Kid Trail

Loop from Ruidoso on US 70, 380, and New Mexico 48

- 84 miles ▪ 3 hours ▪ All year

This mountain-ringed loop in south-central New Mexico is named for William H. Bonney, better known as the gunfighter Billy the Kid.

On US 70 at Ruidoso Downs, the **Byway Interpretive Center** *(575-378-5318. www.billybyway .com/bywaycenter.html)* provides information about attractions along the route. Next door, the **Hubbard Museum of the American West** *(575-378-4142. www.hubbardmuseum.org. Adm. fee)* features horse-related items, Native American artifacts, stagecoaches, firearms, and other historic pieces.

Driving west past the **Ruidoso Downs Race Track** *(575-378-4431. www.race ruidoso.com),* home of the All American Futurity, the richest quarter-horse race in the world, you take N. Mex. 48 north to **Ruidoso** *(575-257-7395. www .ruidosonow.com).* Named for the Ruidoso ("noisy") River, the town offers dining, lodging, and entertainment.

As N. Mex. 48 heads north, you'll be just minutes from the boundary of **Lincoln National Forest** *(575-434-7200. www.fs.usda.gov/lincoln),* with easily accessible campgrounds and trails. The tiny town of Lincoln is now mostly preserved as **Lincoln State Monument** *(575-653-4372. www.nmstatemonuments .org. Adm. fee),* where 11 adobe and stone buildings remain much as they were in the late 19th century, including the **Old Lincoln County Courthouse,** where Billy the Kid was jailed (and from which he escaped before he was shot in 1881).

El Camino Real

Texas–New Mexico state line to San Juan Pueblo on I-25 and connecting roads

- 299 miles ▪ 1 day ▪ All year. Portions of northern part of route can be hazardous after winter snow. Observe proper etiquette and be respectful when visiting pueblos.

The heritage of "The Royal Road" makes it one of the most important routes in the history of North America. Following Native American trade paths paralleling the Rio Grande, 16th-century Spanish settlers made their way northward from Mexico City across the desert to establish colonies as part of Spain's New World empire. Commercial, religious, and military use made this the

Sandhill crane pair in marsh

major road in the region, connecting Mexico City with Santa Fe, which since 1600 has been the capital of New Mexico. Today's El Camino Real byway runs from the Texas–New Mexico border to San Juan Pueblo, north of Santa Fe. History, diverse cultures, and nature combine to make this a most rewarding trip.

Las Cruces *(Convention & Visitors Bureau, 211 N. Water St. 575-541-2444. www.lascrucescvb.org)* is thought to have been named "the crosses" for grave markers of travelers who died on El Camino Real, in the days when the trek across the desert was a dangerous undertaking. **Mesilla** *(south on Avenida de Mesilla. 575-524-3262, ext. 117. www.oldmesilla.org)* was a thriving community and a major stop on the Butterfield Overland Mail stagecoach line until the railroad passed it by. Today it features traditional adobe buildings and a national historic landmark plaza. The **New Mexico Farm and Ranch Heritage Museum** *(4100 Dripping Springs Rd. 575-522-4100. www.nmfarmandranchmuseum.org. Adm. fee)* tells the story of regional agriculture from the days of Native Americans to the present.

Fifteen miles north at Radium Springs, **Fort Selden State Monument** *(575-526-8911. www.nmmonuments .org. Closed Tues.; adm. fee)* preserves the adobe walls of a post built in 1865 to protect settlers and travelers. The **visitor center** has exhibits on 19th-century frontier life.

Bosque del Apache National Wildlife Refuge *(575-835-1828. www.fws.gov/southwest/refuges/newmex/ bosque. Adm. fee)* offers wildlife-watching rewards anytime of year but especially in winter, when massive flocks of sandhill cranes, geese, and ducks arrive. The crane flocks are the focus of a popular annual festival in mid-November *(contact refuge or www.friendsofthebosque.org/crane).*

The best place to learn about The Royal Road is **El Camino Real International Heritage Center** *(300 E. County Rd. 575-854-3600. www.caminoreal heritage.org. Closed Mon.-Tues.; adm. fee),* a state monument, set in a building in a desert landscape.

Native American lands are scattered along El Camino Real, such as **Pueblo of Isleta** *(www.isletapueblo.com).* Some pueblos offer interpretive centers, dining, and shopping. Each pueblo or reservation is an independent nation and has rules on such matters as photography, behavior, and trespassing. Always check with tribal authorities.

Albuquerque *(Convention & Visitors Bureau, 20 First Plaza N.W., Suite 601. 800-284-2282. www.itsatrip.org),* as New Mexico's largest city, offers entertainment and a number of museums. The **Indian Pueblo Cultural Center** *(2401 12th St. NW. 575-843-7270. www.indianpueblo.org. Adm. fee)* introduces Pueblo Indian history and art. Stop here first before visiting a pueblo. The **New Mexico Museum of Natural History and Science** *(1801 Mountain Rd. N.W. 575-841-2800. www.nmnaturalhistory.org. Adm. fee)* provides a look at the state's past, from the first life on Earth through dinosaur days to the recent ice ages. The city's **Old Town** *(San Felipe south of Mountain Rd.)* is

315

an entertainment and shopping area with many historic buildings, centered on a traditional plaza and the San Felipe de Neri church.

At **Coronado State Monument** *(485 Kuaua Rd. 575-867-5351. www .nmmonuments.org. Adm. fee)* near Bernalillo, visit the partially reconstructed ruins of the Pueblo of Kuaua, abandoned by its inhabitants around 1600.

The route now heads toward **Santa Fe** *(Convention & Visitors Bureau. 505-955-6200 or 800-777-2489. www.santafe.org).* The meeting point of El Camino Real and the Santa Fe Trail made this a commercial center, and a major travel destination today (see Santa Fe Trail, pp. 321-323).

El Malpais

I-40 east of Grants to Quemado on New Mexico 117 and 36

- 78 miles ▪ 2 to 3 hours ▪ All year

As recently as a couple of thousand years ago, massive volcanic eruptions poured rivers of molten lava into a remote valley in the high desert of west-central New Mexico. The route explores this bizarre world, winding between the flow's eastern edge and a series of high sandstone cliffs. In addition to the unforgettable fields of tortured black rock, views include a giant sandstone arch and distant cinder cones and craters.

As you begin your drive south from I-40, you see the lava flows immediately to the west. After 9 miles, N. Mex. 117 passes the ranger station for the **El Malpais National Monument and Conservation Area** *(505-783-4774. www.nps.gov/elma),* with displays on the region's culture. A mile later the route goes by a side road to the **Sandstone Bluffs Overlook,** a 1.5-mile drive to

a picnic area atop yellow sandstone bluffs. Here you'll get the area's best views of El Malpais, the "bad country" in Spanish. Across the valley are the **Zuni Mountains;** to the north near Grants, sits 11,301-foot **Mount Taylor,** a volcano that blew 3 million to 1.5 million years ago.

Five miles later the **Zuni-Acoma Trail** offers an opportunity to examine different forms of lava rock up close. The 7.5-mile footpath follows an old Indian route connecting the pueblos of Acoma and Zuni. Be careful: The rock is rough on shoes, the hike is hot during the summer, and the cairns marking the trail are sometimes difficult to follow.

An easier walk begins 3 miles farther at the **La Ventana Natural Arch,** one of New Mexico's largest arches, carved by wind and water out of Zuni sandstone. Just after the arch, the road comes to the **Narrows,** where lava flowed close

View from Sandstone Bluffs Overlook

to the 500-foot-high sandstone cliffs. A picnic area loops around to the cliff face. About 3 miles beyond, the road crosses a grassland where cinder cone volcanoes appear on the distant horizon.

Not far past Rte. 41, the **Chain of Craters Back Country Byway** (Rte. 42) heads north on a gravel road that follows a line of volcanic cinder cones along the Continental Divide. The 36-mile route is generally passable in high-clearance vehicles, but may not be in rain or snow.

N. Mex. 117 continues across desolate stretches of the North Plains, where pronghorn often cavort, and climbs into pinyon pine forests. At N. Mex. 36, head south to the small town of **Quemado** on US 60.

Turquoise Trail

Tijeras to I-25 south of Santa Fe on New Mexico 14 and 536

- 76 miles (includes 28-mile round-trip to Sandia Crest) - ½ day
- All year. In winter bundle up for Sandia Crest.

A pleasant alternative to I-25, the Turquoise Trail connects Albuquerque and Santa Fe, passing through several small mining towns that retain the charm of the Old West. The road to the Sandia Crest, off the main trail, is a highlight. It shoots up nearly 4,000 feet through Cibola National Forest to the top of 10,678-foot Sandia Crest for spectacular views of Albuquerque. In its 14-mile length, the side road curves through four life zones, the equivalent of driving from New Mexico to Canada's Hudson Bay.

317

The route begins in **Tijeras,** a small town that's home to a ranger station of the **Cibola National Forest** (*11776 N. Mex. 337. 505-281-3304. www.fs.usda .gov/cibola*) and an interpretive walk through the archaeological site of the **Tijeras Pueblo,** where several hundred people lived 600 years ago. N. Mex. 14 ascends from Tijeras across a flank of the **Sandia Mountains** and through ponderosa pines to busy **Cedar Crest,** a suburb of Albuquerque.

After nearly 4 miles, N. Mex. 536 (**Sandia Crest National Scenic Byway**) leads northwest to Sandia Crest. About a mile up, the byway passes the **Tinkertown Museum** (*505-281-5233. www.tinkertown.com. April-Oct.; adm. fee*), a private museum with a western town and miniature circus in a building made from 55,000 bottles. For the next 6.5 miles the road curves past several rest stops and the **Sandia Peak Ski Area** (*505-242-9052. www.sandiapeak .com*), developed by the Civilian Conservation Corps in 1938. At 8,651 feet, the **Balsam Glade Picnic Ground** has tables beneath a stand of ponderosa pines. Here, dirt-and-gravel N. Mex. 165 descends 5 miles into **Las Huertas Canyon** to the trailhead for **Sandia Cave.** A gentle, 1-mile trail leads to the cave, site of famous archaeological excavations that revealed human occupation some 12,000 years ago.

Back on N. Mex. 536, the road continues to climb to Sandia Crest, where an observation deck affords spectacular views of **Albuquerque,** the **Rio Grande,** and distant **Mount Taylor.** In addition to a restaurant, the peak offers several good hikes, including the **Peak Nature Trail,** an easy half-mile loop along the limestone ledge and through stands of spruce and fir. Retrace the route back to the Turquoise Trail.

The Turquoise Trail winds for another 44 miles through a rolling desert of stunted pinyon pine and juniper, passing the dusty former boomtowns of **Golden; Madrid,** with its craft shops and New Age artists; and **Cerrillos,** once boasting 21 saloons and four hotels catering to prospectors. The towns along the trail now draw Hollywood film crews. The Turquoise Trail ends at I-25, just south of the lively, historic state capital, **Santa Fe.**

High Road to Taos

Española to Ranchos de Taos on New Mexico 76, 75, and 518

- 54 miles ■ 3 to 4 hours ■ All year

Pressing into the Sangre de Cristo Mountains past 13,000-foot peaks, this route is the most scenic between Santa Fe and Taos. The small, isolated mountain towns sprinkled along the way retain the flavor of the early Spanish settlers who came here four centuries ago.

From Española on US 84, N. Mex. 76 cuts east about 9 miles to **Chimayó.** Its adobe **Plaza del Cerro** is probably the Spanish Southwest's only surviving fortified plaza. Just north of the plaza, **Ortega's Weaving Shop** *(505-351-4215. www.ortegasweaving .com. Closed Sun.)* carries the beautiful wool products of a family that has been weaving for eight generations. Pilgrims travel from all over the Southwest to visit the **Santuario de Chimayó** *(505-351-4889. www.elsantuariodechimayo.us. Adm. fee),* legendary as a center for curing the sick. The sanctuary has five colorful sacred paintings on wood, while a room off the sacristy features a hole from which cure seekers pull handfuls of earth to rub on their bodies. Don't miss **Rancho de Chimayó** *(505-351-4444. www.ranchodechimayo.com. Closed Mon. Nov.-April),* a restaurant in a 19th-century hacienda-style building.

From Chimayó, N. Mex. 518 climbs into forest past **Cordova.** A road curves south to the tiny hillside town; signs invite you to visit artisans who carve figures from aspen and cedar. After climbing nearly 7 more miles, the route cuts through **Truchas,** once a Spanish outpost high on a mesa beneath 13,102-foot **Truchas Peak.** With views of the **Rio Grande Valley,** Truchas was the setting for Robert Redford's film *The Milagro Beanfield War.* As you enter town, the adobe building with the cross serves as the meeting place for the Brotherhood of the Penitentes, a secret religious society famous for their self-flagellation rites.

From Truchas the High Road to Taos enters the **Carson National Forest** and, for the last 35 miles, winds up and down through forests, past several small towns. The highlight of this leg is the tiny town of **Trampas,** about 8 miles northeast of Truchas. The **San José de Gracia Church,** built in the late 1700s, remains one of the most beautiful of colonial-era churches. At Peñasco follow N. Mex. 75 to N. Mex. 518. The end of the High Road is

318

Santuario de Chimayó, Chimayó

Ranchos de Taos, where you can visit **San Francisco de Asis** *(575-758-2754),* the 18th-century mission church that captivated painter Georgia O'Keeffe. You can complete the drive by taking N. Mex. 68 to Taos, an artist colony with a square surrounded by adobe buildings.

319

Enchanted Circle

Loop from Taos on US 64 and New Mexico 38 and 522

■ 85 miles ■ 4 to 5 hours ■ All year. Ski areas draw crowds to the route over winter weekends.

In moments, this northern New Mexico route leaves the bustle of Taos and climbs into a remote, high-altitude world of cool forests, crystal lakes, windswept valleys, and tiny towns filled with Wild West history. It encircles 13,161-foot Wheeler Peak, the state's highest mountain, and passes some of the nation's most popular ski areas.

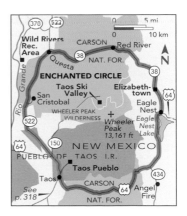

Head east out of **Taos** on US 64. The route climbs through **Taos Canyon's** thick ever-green forests, passing several campgrounds and picnic spots. After 18 winding miles through the **Carson National Forest** *(575-758-6200. www.fs.usda.gov/carson),* the road curves over a 9,101-foot pass, then descends to grasslands and the ski town of **Angel Fire** *(Chamber of Commerce. 575-377-6661 or 800-446-8117. www.angelfirechamber .org),* 3 miles down N. Mex. 434. A mile beyond the Angel Fire turnoff, you'll see the sail-like chapel of the **Vietnam Veterans Memorial** *(575-377-6900. www .vietnamveteransmemorial.org)* occupying a windblown hill on the left. In

Indian woman at Taos Pueblo

another 5 miles, **Eagle Nest Lake** emerges on the right. To the west, across the **Moreno Valley,** rises **Wheeler Peak,** contained within the **Wheeler Peak Wilderness** *(Questa Ranger District. 575-586-0520),* an area laced with hiking trails. At the town of Eagle Nest, US 64, now a side road, heads around the north end of the lake to quiet **Cimarron Canyon State Park** *(575-377-6271. www.emnrd.state.nm.us/SPD/cimarroncanyonstatepark.html. Adm. fee),* with campsites and good fly-fishing on the **Cimarron River.**

From Eagle Nest take N. Mex. 38 for several miles to the ruins of **Elizabethtown,** a gold-boom site in the mid-1860s. The route continues across the valley, climbing up to 9,820-foot **Bobcat Pass** and back into Carson National Forest before descending into the resort town of **Red River** *(Chamber of Commerce. 575-754-2366. www.redrivernewmex.com),* once a mining camp and now a center for outdoor activities. Several miles after Red River the road passes a molybdenite mine, then slips through towering rock cliffs. At the village of Questa, detour north about 3 miles on N. Mex. 522, then turn left on N. Mex. 378 for a worthwhile 13-mile side trip to the **Wild Rivers Recreation Area** *(575-758-8851. www.nm.blm.gov/recreation/taos/wild_rivers_rec_area .htm. Adm. fee),* which skirts the edge of the **Rio Grande Gorge.**

The drive continues south from Questa on N. Mex. 522, passing the turnoff for the **D. H. Lawrence Memorial** *(575-776-2245. www.dhlsna.com)* at San Cristobal, where the writer lived in the early 1920s. Soon you'll run into the intersection of US 64 and N. Mex. 150 with N. Mex. 522. From here, detour west on US 64 for 8 miles to the **Rio Grande Gorge Bridge.** To reach the world-famous **Taos Ski Valley** *(575-776-2291. www.skitaos.org),* head northeast on N. Mex. 150. Just past the intersection, look for tiny Museum Road on the right to reach the **Millicent Rogers Museum** *(575-758-2462. www.millicentrogers.org. Closed Mon. Nov.-March; adm. fee),* an excellent gallery devoted to Native American and Hispanic art. Two miles down N. Mex. 522, you pass signs for **Taos Pueblo** *(575-758-1028. www .taospueblo.com. Daily spring-fall except for certain tribal rituals, call for winter schedule; adm. fee),* one of the country's largest multi-storied pueblos. The drive ends back in Taos.

Jemez Mountain Trail

Loop from Bandelier National Monument on New Mexico 4, 501, 126, and US 550

■ 163 miles ■ 1 day ■ Summer and fall. A section of N. Mex. 126 is unpaved and requires caution in bad weather; it is closed in winter.

Native American culture and splendid scenery combine in this drive through the mountains of north-central New Mexico.

The route begins on the Rio Grande at **Bandelier National Monument** *(575-672-3861. www.nps.gov/band. Adm. fee),* which protects thousands of archaeological sites scattered across a terrain of rugged canyons and hills. The best known are the cliff dwellings and other structures in Frijoles Canyon, reached by a short walk from the visitor center.

Take a side trip from N. Mex. 4 on N. Mex. 501 to **Los Alamos,** the town that gave birth to the atomic bomb in World War II. Back on N. Mex. 4, you'll head west across the Jemez Mountains, the remains of a huge volcano that erupted more than one million years ago. The caldera (collapsed crater) lies to the north of the route, a grassland 14 miles across that is now **Valles Caldera National Preserve** *(505-661-3333. www.vallescaldera.gov. Daily summer, weekends winter. Adm. fee. Access is controlled; contact the preserve for information).* As you drive, watch on the south side of N. Mex. 4 for the turn to Jemez Falls, a picnic area within **Santa Fe National Forest** *(505-438-5300. www.fs.fed.us/r3/sfe).*

With 11,254-foot **Redondo Peak** (part of the caldera rim) to the north, the drive continues west on N. Mex. 126 *(closed in winter)* through coniferous forest and reaching elevations over 8,800 feet. At Cuba, US 550 runs south for 40 miles through arid terrain along Rio Puerco to **San Isidro,** where there's a pretty little restored adobe church as you turn north on N. Mex. 4. You can learn about the history, culture, and art of the **Jemez Pueblo** and its people at the **Walatowa Visitor Center** *(505-834-7235. www .jemezpueblo.org).* For the 21 miles back north to the N. Mex. 126 junction, the drive passes through a red-rock canyon, then ascends under cliffs along the Jemez River. A number of sites are along the road, including the **Jemez Springs Bathhouse** *(505-829-3303. www.jemezspringsbathhouse.com. Adm. fee),* which dates from the 1870s.

A few miles north is the striking formation called **Battleship Rock,** and just beyond is the parking area for **Spence Hot Springs,** a natural rock pool where many bathers see no need for swimsuits.

Santa Fe Trail

Santa Fe, New Mexico, to Colorado-Kansas state line or to Clayton, New Mexico, on I-25, New Mexico 518, 161, 21, 453, 406, and US 64, 56, 350, and 50

▪ 565 miles ▪ 3 to 4 days ▪ Spring through fall. When following I-25, using frontage roads where possible allows more leisurely driving. Trinidad Pass near Raton, New Mexico, occasionally closed after snowfall.

For six decades, the Santa Fe Trail was one of the continent's most important trade routes, opening commerce between the United States and Mexico. When Mexico gained independence from Spain in 1821, previously banned

commerce was allowed, thus starting a stream of traders, military troops, gold seekers, and immigrants, in covered wagons or on horseback, between Missouri and Santa Fe. The coming of the railroad in 1880 made the old route obsolete, but its heritage and romance have endured to the present day, as have scattered sections of the original trail with the ruts of wagon wheels still visible on the plains.

The drive begins in **Santa Fe** (*Convention & Visitors Bureau. 505-955-6200 or 800-777-2489. www.santafe.org*), the capital of New Mexico and a blend of Native American, Hispanic, and European culture. The meeting point of **El Camino Real** (see pp. 314-316) and the Santa Fe Trail made a commercial center of what formerly had been a remote colonial post. Historic sites include the central **Plaza** with the **Palace of the Governors** (*100 Palace Ave. 505-476-5100. www.palaceofthegovernors.org. Adm. fee*), now a history museum, and the adjacent **Museum of Fine Arts** (*107 W. Palace Ave. 505-476-5072. www.nmartmuseum.org. Closed Mon.; adm. fee*), with works by Georgia O'Keeffe and Ansel Adams. **San Miguel Mission** (*401 Old Santa Fe Trail. www.missionsanmiguel.org*) is one of the oldest churches in North America.

Heading east on I-25, you're following the exact path of the historic Santa Fe Trail through juniper-dotted hills where the Civil War Battle of Glorieta Pass occurred. At **Pecos National Historical Park** (*N. Mex. 63, just north of I-25. 505-757-6414. www.nps.gov/peco. Adm. fee*) you can see the ruins of a 14th-century pueblo and two 17th-century Spanish missions. Where I-25 turns north, the prominent hill to the south, known as **Starvation Peak,** was a landmark and campsite for travelers on the Santa Fe Trail.

Las Vegas National Wildlife Refuge (*east of I-25 off N. Mex. 104. 505-425-3581. www.fws.gov/southwest/refuges/newmex/lasvegas*) lies where the foothills of the Sangre de Cristos have given way to the Great Plains. The 8-mile auto tour passes ponds, marshes, and cottonwood groves.

Northwest of Watrous, **Fort Union National Monument** (*N. Mex. 161. 505-425-8025. www.nps.gov/foun. Adm. fee*) encompasses the adobe ruins of a military post that once was the largest in the American Southwest.

In this area, two paths of the Santa Fe Trail met (or diverged, for those heading east). The **Mountain Branch** continued north into what is now Colorado before turning east to Missouri, while the **Cimarron Cutoff** took a more direct northeast path. The latter was shorter but more dangerous because of stretches without reliable water and the danger of Indian attacks.

In Springer, the **Santa Fe Trail Museum** (*614 Maxwell Ave. 575-483-2682. www.santafetrailnm.org/site58.html.*)

Fort Union National Monument, New Mexico

Mem. Day–Labor Day. Adm. fee), housed in the 1881 former Colfax County Courthouse, displays exhibits and artifacts.

To follow the **Cimarron Route** of the trail, from Springer take US 56 east 54 miles to N. Mex. 453. (The actual trail route lies to the north.) Take N. Mex. 453 north to US 64, then turn east 27 miles to Clayton. Here, take N. Mex. 370 north to **Clayton Lake State Park** *(505-374-8808. www.emnrd.state .nm.us/prd/clayton.htm. Adm. fee).* Along the way you'll see several landmarks for Santa Fe Trail travelers, including **Mount Dora** *(north of US 64),* nearby **Round Mound,** and **Rabbit Ear Mountain** *(east of N. Mex. 370).* The park is best known for its dinosaur footprints. Taking N. Mex. 406 north of Clayton, you can access **McNees Crossing,** a campsite at Corrumpa Creek, and 3 miles of the original Santa Fe Trail on the **Kiowa National Grasslands** *(505-374-9652. www.fs.usda.gov/cibola).*

Back in Springer, the drive following the **Mountain Branch** of the Santa Fe Trail heads west on N. Mex. 21 to US 64, where a side trip takes you to **Cimarron Canyon State Park** *(505-476-3355. www.emnrd.state.nm.us/prd/ cimarroncanyon.htm),* known for its trout fishing and granite columns rising by the river. The byway continues east on US 64 to I-25, crossing 7,834-foot **Raton Pass** into Colorado. In **Trinidad,** you'll find the **Trinidad History Museum** *(312 E. Main St. 719-846-7217. http://www.historycolorado .org/museums/trinidad-history-museum-0. May-Sept.; adm. fee).*

The route follows US 350 northeast into the gently rolling shortgrass prairie of the Great Plains. About 8 miles after crossing into Otero County, take Cty. Rd. 9 south 1 mile to the **Iron Springs Historic Area,** a water hole and a stagecoach stop for early travelers. Fourteen miles farther, take Colo. 71 north a half mile to the **Sierra Vista Overlook,** where you'll see the Rocky Mountains in the distance, once a journey milestone.

Ten miles past La Junta, where the trail follows US 50 and the Arkansas River, you'll reach **Bent's Old Fort National Historic Site** *(719-383-5010. www.nps.gov/beol. Adm. fee).* Here, in 1833, a trading post was built, now reconstructed, that for most of its existence was the major white settlement on the Santa Fe Trail between Missouri and the route's end point.

The drive continues east on US 50 through irrigated cropland, past Lamar, to end at the Kansas state line.

Colorado
Trail of the Ancients

Loop through southwestern Colorado and southeastern Utah, beginning at Mesa Verde National Park

▪ 480 miles ▪ 2 days ▪ Spring through fall. Some roads are unpaved and little traveled; be sure your vehicle is in good condition and drive with caution.

Scattered throughout this southwestern region of juniper, sagebrush, and red rock are some of the most fascinating and important archaeological sites in North America. On the Trail of the Ancients you learn about the culture and lifeways of Native American people while enjoying landscapes

323

of striking beauty in the Four Corners area where Colorado, Utah, Arizona, and New Mexico meet.

Mesa Verde National Park *(970-529-4465. www.nps.gov/meve. Adm. fee)* protects extensive ruins of a people who lived here from about A.D. 600

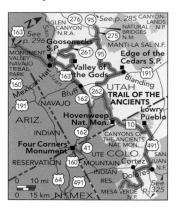

to 1300. These people once were commonly called the Anasazi, but today are more often referred to as ancestral Puebloan. The park, a World Heritage site, is best known for extensive and well-preserved stone cliff dwellings of amazing complexity. A visit to the **Chapin Mesa Museum** is a must, followed by tours at **Balcony House, Cliff Palace, Spruce Tree House,** or **Long House,** depending on the time you have. There are interpretive exhibits all along parks roads, as well as some wonderful vistas from overlooks at the mesa rim.

Leaving the park west on US 160, take Colo. 145 and 184 to Dolores and the **Anasazi Heritage Center** *(27501 Colo. 184. 970-882-5600. www.co.blm.gov/ahc. Adm. fee),* a museum dedicated to the ancestral Puebloan people and to the archaeological studies that have revealed their history. Many exhibits are hands-on, allowing you to weave cloth, grind corn, or touch genuine artifacts. On the museum grounds are two 12th-century pueblos, accessible by short trails.

The center is also the contact point for visiting **Canyons of the Ancients National Monument** *(www.co.blm.gov/canm),* a huge tract that protects about 6,000 ruins and archaeological sites in southwestern Colorado. Many simply resemble mounds of rocks, while some are more intact. To see one of the best, drive west on Colo. 184 to US 491, drive northwest to Pleasant View, turn west on Cty. Rd. CC, and go 9 miles to **Lowry Pueblo,** a thousand-year-old ancestral Puebloan village that features standing walls, 40 rooms, and several kivas (ceremonial rooms), as well as interpretive signs.

Return east on Cty. Rd. CC 3 miles to Cty. Rd. 10 and take it south and southwest about 20 miles into Utah. (Unpaved road can be in bad condition after rain; check locally.) You'll reach **Hovenweep National Monument** *(970-562-4282. www.nps.gov/hove. Adm. fee),* which administers six prehistoric ancestral Puebloan villages scattered over 20 miles. Near the visitor center is the **Square Tower Group,** which includes the three-story-high tower and several kivas. This is the only site within the monument accessible by paved road.

Continuing west on county roads from Hovenweep to Utah 262 and on to US 191, drive north 15 miles to Blanding and **Edge of the Cedars State Park** *(435-678-2238. http://stateparks.utah.gov/parks/edge-of-the-cedars. Adm. fee),* a small park that includes an ancestral Puebloan village and a museum with the largest collection of prehistoric Pueblo pottery in the Four Corners region. Return south on US 191 and drive west on Utah 95 through starkly rugged red-rock country. Watch for more ruins along the road, such as at Butler Wash and Mule Canyon. Thirty-five miles west of Blanding, take Utah 275 north to **Natural Bridges National Monument** *(435-692-1234. www.nps.gov/nabr. Adm. fee),* where a scenic drive leads past three natural bridges formed where streams eroded sandstone canyon walls (see Bicentennial Highway pp. 285-287).

Return east on Utah 95 and turn south on Utah 261. In about 25 miles a road on the east leads down into the **Valley of the Gods,** a grand landscape of eroded buttes, mesas, and other sculpted rock formations accessed by a 17-mile unpaved drive *(ask locally about road conditions).* The road ends at US 163; turn west here to **Mexican Hat,** named for a rock formation northeast of town shaped like an upside-down sombrero. Drive north on Utah 261 a few miles and turn west to **Goosenecks State Park** *(435-678-2238. http://stateparks.utah.gov/parks/goosenecks),* where the **San Juan River** has cut a 1,000-foot-deep chasm into the rock strata, resembling a smaller-scale Grand Canyon winding in a series of loops.

Cliff dwellings at Mesa Verde, Colorado

Back in Mexican Hat, a 24-mile drive southwest on US 163 leads to famed **Monument Valley Navajo Tribal Park** *(435-727-5874. www.navajo nationparks.org/htm/monumentvalley.htm. Adm. fee).* Rock towers and buttes stand hundreds of feet high, including **The Mittens,** familiar worldwide through photographs and as movie locations. You can take a Navajo-guided tour through the valley, accessing areas not visible from public roads or the visitor center (see Monument Valley drive pp. 296-297).

Return to Mexican Hat and follow US 163 to Bluff, continuing on Utah 163, 262, and Colo. 41 to US 160. Turn southwest here a few miles to a spot geographically unique in the United States: **Four Corners Monument** *(www.navajonationparks.org/htm/fourcorners.htm. Adm. fee).* This is the only place in the country where four states come together. In the small flag plaza here, countless people have had their photos taken while standing on the spot where Colorado, Utah, Arizona, and New Mexico meet.

San Juan Skyway

Loop from Ridgway through Ouray, Silverton, Durango, Cortez, Dolores, Telluride, and Placerville

- 233 miles - 1 to 2 days - All year. Mountain passes sometimes closed in winter.

As its fanciful name implies, the San Juan Skyway flirts with the heights, climbing to more than 10,000 feet three times as it charts a ragged loop through the mountains and high deserts of southwestern Colorado. Starting at Ridgway, this spectacular route heads south over the crest of the San Juan Mountains and passes through the historic mining towns of Ouray and Silverton.

325

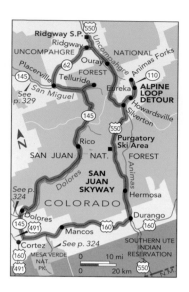

The byway drops into red-rock canyons near Durango and sails west across the desert to Mesa Verde National Park, where you can walk through 800-year-old ancient Pueblo cliff dwellings. Returning north, the road climbs back into the heart of the San Juans, pausing at Telluride before descending again to Ridgway.

Begin 4 miles north of town at **Ridgway State Park** (*970-626-5822. www.parks.state .co.us/parks/ridgway. Vehicle fee*); US 550 tops a dry hill and the southern skyline suddenly fills with the jagged crest of the **San Juan Mountains.** Carved by glaciers, these bony peaks are a mass of overlapping flows of lava and ash that spewed through layers of sedimentary rock beginning 40 million years ago.

Cross the valley floor to **Ridgway,** an 1891 railroad and ranching town at the base of 14,150-foot **Mount Sneffels,** then continue

south along the **Uncompahgre River** toward a deep cleft in the mountain front. The valley narrows under peaks rising at least 6,000 feet above the river, and the road caroms between red-rock cliffs and foothills covered with scrub oak, aspen, juniper, and pinyon pine.

An abundance of hot springs and large herds of elk and deer once made this valley a favorite winter camp for the Ute. The elk and deer still winter here, but the Ute were forced out of the San Juans during the 1870s after prospectors found rich lodes of gold and silver.

At **Ouray,** named for a Ute chief, multicolored cliffs squeeze the valley against the base of 14,000-foot peaks. **Ouray Hot Springs** (*970-325-7073. Adm. fee*), a municipal pool, steams at the north end of town. Drive through the historic district of ornate 1880s buildings, turn right, and follow the gravel road to **Box Canyon Falls** (*Adm. fee May-Sept.*), a thunderous plume

plunging over smooth walls of dark limestone.

From Ouray, US 550 switchbacks up into the mountains, offering splendid vistas back down to Ridgway. Waterfalls and creeks spill from the high cliffs and side canyons into **Uncompahgre Gorge,** the deep gash to your right. **Abrams Mountain,** 12,801 feet, looms over the head of the canyon.

There's no bracing yourself for what comes next. Just drive up the

Telluride beneath the San Juan Mountains

Cliff Palace, Mesa Verde National Park

short series of hairpin turns, top the rim of the gorge, and let your spirit soar. Vivid red peaks burst into view, with broad smears of orange and red gravel streaming down their flanks into the dark surrounding evergreens. It's an astonishing, surreal sight, and yet the peaks carry the mundane labels of **Red Mountain No. 1, No. 2,** and **No. 3.** The road curves beneath these amazing peaks, running through a wide meadow and passing the debris of an active mining history: shacks, mills, heaps of gravel.

You climb nearly to tree line before arriving at 11,075-foot **Red Mountain Pass,** and then the road begins its 10-mile, 1,700-foot descent into Silverton. Look for deer and elk as you pass through the U-shaped valley framing 12,987-foot **Bear Mountain.** Soon, the road drops, curves left, and runs across the wide floor of the **Animas River Valley** toward 13,338-foot **Kendall Mountain.**

Go left at the junction with Colo. 110 and drive into **Silverton.**

Incorporated in 1876 and spared the fires that wiped out other old mining towns, Silverton retains its rickety historic look. Brush up on the region's past at the **San Juan County Historical Museum** (*970-387-5838. www.sjmuseum.org. Mem. Day–mid-Oct.; adm. fee*). Then consider a side trip to the ghost town of **Animas Forks** (see sidebar p. 328). While you knock around town, the **Durango & Silverton Narrow Gauge Railroad** (*970-247-2733. www.durangotrain.com. Fare*) might come chuffing up the valley. This coal-fired steam train runs several times a day between Silverton and Durango.

From Silverton, head south on US 550 and climb Sultan Mountain to **Molas Pass,** with its fine view of the **West Needle Mountains,** the **Grenadier Range,** and other peaks rising over tiny **Molas Lake.**

The road winds for 7 miles to **Coal Bank Pass,** then tilts downward, leaving the mountains behind and heading for the plateau and canyon country around Durango. With a 4,000-foot drop in elevation, the forests change from spruce and fir to ponderosa pine and Gambel oak. As you descend, you'll see the condos and trails of **Durango Mountain Resort** (*970-247-9000. www.durangomountainresort.com*); then pass under the **Hermosa Cliffs,** a long band of high sedimentary rocks.

The **Animas River** runs through the forested gorge to the left. Soon, the gorge widens into a broad, flat-floored canyon with red-rock walls rising over the trees. In **Hermosa** the lush canyon floor of grass and hayfields is fast yielding to vacation houses and golf courses.

The red-rock cliffs give out before you arrive in **Durango**, an 1880s railroad town that boomed with the San Juan mines. Elegant brick and stone Victorian buildings line its downtown streets. At the end of Main Street, you'll find the yellow 1882 train depot, a historic landmark and starting point for the narrow-gauge railroad to Silverton.

From Durango, follow US 160 west through a rolling terrain of minor canyons and mesas. The **La Plata Mountains** rise to the north over a dark forest of low-growing trees. After about 23 miles the broad dome of **Sleeping Ute Mountain** appears on the western horizon. **Mesa Verde** stands to the left. You pass Mancos and drive about 8 miles across a flat, grassy plain to **Mesa Verde National Park** *(970-529-4465. www.nps.gov/meve. Adm. fee).* (See also Trail of the Ancients pp. 323-325.) The park protects the ruins of ancient Puebloan villages and dwellings built here between A.D. 550 and 1270. Roads cross the top of the mesa, where the ancestral Puebloans grew crops, and wind along the rims of side canyons, where you see the

Silverton stagecoach

dwellings under overhanging cliffs. Rangers lead tours of the major dwellings, including **Cliff Palace** and **Balcony House** *(free tour tickets at visitor center).* Views from the mesa are extraordinary.

Continue along US 160 toward Cortez, then follow Colo. 145 north 7.5 miles and turn left at the junction with Colo. 184 to visit the **Anasazi Heritage Center** *(27501 Colo. 184. 970-882-5600.*

Alpine Loop Detour

Silverton to Animas Forks on Colorado 110

■ 12 miles ■ ½ day ■ Early summer through fall. Gravel road. Closed in winter. See map p. 326.

This jolting, backcountry road connects Silverton with Animas Forks, a weather-beaten ghost town high in the San Juan Mountains. The route winds through spectacular forested canyons crowded with 13,000-foot peaks and passes the remains of several other abandoned mining camps and mills.

At the northern edge of **Silverton**, turn right on Colo. 110 and follow the **Animas River** over its flat gravel bed toward a narrow canyon in the mountains ahead. At the **Mayflower Mill**, idle since 1991, look for ore buckets dangling overhead from an aerial cableway that spans the canyon and rises to a glacially carved cirque. Below the cirque, **Arrastra Creek** tumbles down the canyon.

The canyon widens at **Howardsville**, a tiny cluster of shacks, cabins, and industrial buildings where miners have toiled sporadically since the 1870s. To gain some appreciation for their work, consider an underground tour of the **Old Hundred Gold Mine** *(970-387-5444. www.minetour .com. Mid-May–mid-Oct.; adm. fee).*

At **Eureka** the road passes a mill foundation, narrows to one lane with turnouts, and hugs the chasm walls. The reddish peak straight ahead is **Cinnamon Mountain.** Waterfalls spill from **Niagara Peak.**

At nearly tree line you bump to a halt in **Animas Forks.** Laid out in 1877, it once thrived as a busy mining town. Today, its collapsed houses rot amid wildflower meadows. An astounding crest of naked gray rock, **Niagara Peak,** looms down the valley.

www.co.blm.gov/ ahc. Adm. fee), which depicts the evolution of the ancestral Puebloans. Self-guided trails lead to two sets of ruins.

Once again on Colo. 145, you follow the **Dolores River** back into the San Juan Mountains. As the road gains elevation, it cuts through layers of sedimentary rock that bulged upward as magma rose through the Earth's crust and formed the mountains above Rico.

About 10 miles from Rico, you'll see 13,113-foot **Lizard Head Peak** off to the left—an isolated column of rock jutting from a broad, rounded mountaintop. A couple of miles farther, pull over at **Lizard Head Pass,** 10,222 feet, for another incredible view of the toothy San Juan crest, which soars 3,000 feet above the road. From right to left, these are **Sheep Mountain, Yellow Mountain,** and the **Ophir Needles.** You glide down over a meadow toward the Ophir Needles, pass **Trout Lake,** and then plunge down the mountainside. Huge, glaciated valleys open up to the right under broad amphitheaters of 13,000-foot peaks.

Then the road stops at a T-intersection. Turn right and drive toward the booming ski town of **Telluride.** Founded as a mining town during the late 1870s, Telluride boasts a magnificent downtown district of Victorian buildings, including a bank Butch Cassidy robbed in 1889. **Bridal Veil Falls** drops 365 feet from the cliffs behind town. Skiing resurrected Telluride, a near ghost town for decades.

From Telluride, Colo. 145 and the **San Miguel River** burrow down through sedimentary layers into a canyon lined by vermilion sandstone cliffs. At **Placerville** turn right on Colo. 62 and climb 11 miles to the **Dallas Divide.** As you top the pass, a spine of naked rock heaves into view, slicing upward from gentle foothills. Most peaks exceed 12,000 feet. From the divide, you glide back down to Ridgway.

329

Unaweep–Tabeguache Scenic Byway

Whitewater to Placerville on Colorado 141 and 145

- 133 miles - 5 hours - All year

West of Colorado's mountain ranges lies a vast, arid region of plateaus and mesas and deep river canyon, that snake through smooth walls of vivid red stone. At the heart of this beautiful land stands the Uncompahgre Plateau, a huge, flat mass of rock extending for 100 miles between Grand Junction and Telluride.

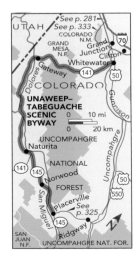

This drive crosses the plateau through Unaweep Canyon, a 1,000-foot gorge, then skirts the plateau's southwestern flank, following red-rock canyons carved by the Dolores and San Miguel Rivers. Toward the end of the drive, the road climbs over a mesa offering terrific views of the San Juan Mountains.

The route starts on Colo. 141 at **Whitewater,** south of Grand Junction. Across the arid **Gunnison River Valley** stands the **Uncompahgre Plateau,** known to the Ute as Tabeguache—"where the snow melts first." The plateau rose twice: first as a mountain range that eroded down to its roots of Precambrian granite and gneiss, then again carrying its present load of sedimentary rock.

Soon you enter **Unaweep Canyon,** its floor a jumble of boulders, gravel, and sandy soils dotted with juniper and pinyon pines. Geologists think the canyon was cut by the ancestral Gunnison River, which shifted to its present course as the plateau rose the second time.

Hawks, eagles—even peregrine falcons—nest among Unaweep Canyon's cliffs, while mountain lions and bobcats prowl the side canyons for deer and rabbits.

Stop at **Grand Valley Overlook** for a long, backward view, then continue 6 miles to Divide Road and turn left. By now, the canyon resembles a broad trough. Its wide, grassy floor runs between palisades of gray granite capped by forested red-rock cliffs.

Divide Road climbs 2 miles to a cattle guard. Park there and walk to the edge of the bluff for an excellent view of the canyon and of the **Great Unconformity**—the distinct line between gray Precambrian granite and vivid red Triassic sandstone that represents a gap in the geologic record of roughly 2.2 billion years.

Return to Colo. 141 and go 4.5 miles to **Unaweep Divide.** Here, **East Creek** and **West Creek** flow in opposite directions. This topographic oddity named the canyon: In Ute, Unaweep means "canyon with two mouths." You pass the ruins of **Driggs Mansion** (a sign explains its history) and, after about 12 miles, the canyon suddenly narrows. In this tight chasm, stop at **West Creek Picnic Area,** a lovely shaded swimming hole.

Just 1.4 miles beyond, the road punches out of the chasm into a broad red-rock gorge. You just crossed the **Uncompahgre Fault** and are now on the west side of the Uncompahgre Plateau.

Dolores River, San Juan National Forest

After a few miles you arrive in Gateway and enter the **Dolores River Canyon.** Broad walls of vermilion rock soar 1,500 feet above rustling cottonwoods along the river. Here, the new **Gateway Auto Museum** (*43200 Hwy. 141. 970-931-2895. www.gatewayautomuseum.com. Adm. fee*) provides a physical time line of the American car, including its design, engineering, and social impact.

From here the road climbs along the Dolores and San Miguel Rivers through all those sedimentary layers. Continue driving for about 30 miles along the banks of the Dolores, then climb 300 feet to an overlook for **Hanging Flume.** Miners bolted this 7-mile-long wooden trough to the canyon wall in 1889 to carry water to a placer gold mine. Soon you pick up the **San Miguel River** and pass some uranium tailings ponds. Across the river a defunct mill marks the site of a uranium company town.

You go through Naturita, then climb out of the canyon on Colo. 145 and cross the broad back of **Wright's Mesa.** Ahead rise the jagged peaks of the **San Juan Mountains;** to the north, the flat Uncompahgre Plateau.

Beyond Norwood the road dives again to the San Miguel River, where you'll find a mix of trees reflecting the shift between desert and mountain: juniper, Gambel oak, willow, Douglas-fir, ponderosa pine, blue spruce, aspen—all grown in compelling contrast to the brilliant red cliffs. At **Placerville** you can pick up the San Juan Skyway (see pp. 325-329).

Frontier Pathways
Scenic and Historic Byway

Pueblo to Westcliffe on Colorado 96, with a side route to Colorado City on Colorado 165

- 103 miles ▪ 4 hours ▪ Summer and fall

Climbing from the Colorado plains to the Rockies, travelers on this byway enjoy expansive vistas as they encounter traces of the region's rich history.

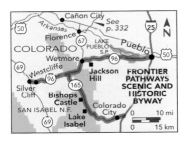

Beginning in **Pueblo** *(Greater Pueblo Chamber, 302 N. Santa Fe Ave. 719-542-1704 or 800-233-3446. www.pueblochamber.org),* take time to visit **El Pueblo History Museum** *(301 N. Union St. 719-583-0453. www.historycolorado.org/ museums/el-pueblo-history-museum-0. Tues.- Sat.; adm. fee).* It interprets the traditions of the region's cultural and ethnic groups, from Plains Indians to Mexican settlers to European traders and miners.

Heading west on Colo. 96, you quickly reach **Lake Pueblo State Park** *(719-561-9320. www.parks.state.co.us. Adm. fee),* with recreational opportunities ranging from boating to hiking. Here, and along the highway as you continue west, you pass through shortgrass prairie with rugged bluffs dotted with junipers and pinyon pine. Twenty miles past the park you reach Jackson Hill; turn right on the road at the top to see a stage stop from the late 19th century *(private),* where coaches got fresh horses.

Past the little town of Wetmore, the byway ascends in Hardscrabble Canyon and enters the **Wet Mountains** and **San Isabel National Forest** *(719-553-1400. www.fs.usda.gov/psicc),* which administers campgrounds and picnic sites such as **Lake Isabel** *(18 miles south on Colo. 165. Adm. fee).*

Farm and fog at foot of Sangre de Cristo Mountains near Westcliffe, Colorado

Now you're in coniferous forests, mixed with meadows and ranches. After you've passed 9,300-foot Hardscrabble Divide, you descend into the **Wet Mountain Valley** and the towns of Silver Cliff and Westcliffe. Before you is the panorama of the **Sangre de Cristo Mountains,** with 14,294-foot Crestone Peak the high point.

A side trip of the Frontier Pathways byway heads southeast on Colo. 165 10 miles west of Wetmore, through the San Isabel National Forest and on to Colorado City on I-25. Here, **Bishop's Castle** *(719-485-3040. www .bishopcastle.org. Donation),* 12 miles south of Colo. 96, is the eccentric creation of one man, who has been building the monumental structure by himself since 1969. He has his own way of doing things, and it's worth a visit to see just what they are.

332

Gold Belt Tour
Scenic and Historic Byway

Loop between Florissant and Florence on Teller County Road 1, Phantom Canyon Road, Shelf Road, High Park Road, US 50, and Colorado 67, 9, and 120

■ 135 miles ■ 1 day ■ Summer and fall. Shelf and Phantom Canyon roads may require caution after rain or snow; inquire locally.

Travelers on this central Colorado mountain route will enjoy the awesome sight of Royal Gorge and the rich legacy of a mining-boom era. To begin, though, the history on display dates back much further than pioneer days.

Just south of the town of Florissant, **Florissant Fossil Beds National Monument** *(719-748-3253. www.nps.gov/ flfo. Adm. fee)* protects one of the world's richest fossil deposits: mostly ancient insects and plants, including massive sequoias that are among the largest known petrified trees. A sampling is readily accessible in the park **visitor center** and along interpretive trails such as the easy, half-mile **Walk through Time.** The fossils here were preserved by a volcanic eruption 35 million years ago and subsequent burial by lake sediments.

Teller Cty. Rd. 1 continues south though ranch country to **Cripple Creek** *(www.visitcripplecreek.com)* and nearby **Victor** *(www.victorcolorado.com).* In the 1890s, these two towns attracted thousands of prospectors thanks to some of the largest gold strikes in history. Although casino gambling has become the main attraction in Cripple Creek, the past is still visible in historic buildings and museums. The **Mollie Kathleen Gold Mine** *(719-689-2466. www.goldminetours.com. May-Oct.; adm. fee)* offers underground tours of a mine discovered in 1891, complete with displays.

The road from Cripple Creek to Victor reveals much evidence of mining both historic and modern. Stop at the bridge overlook at **Arequa Gulch** for a vista of the Sangre de Cristo Mountains before continuing south on unpaved **Phantom Canyon Road,** which drops in elevation from 9,500 to 5,500 feet before it reaches the Arkansas River valley at Florence. A few miles west is **Cañon City,** best known as the gateway to **Royal Gorge Bridge and Park** *(719-275-7507 or 888-333-5597. www.royalgorgebridge.com. Adm. fee),* where the world's highest suspension bridge crosses the spectacular 1,053-foot-deep granite canyon of the **Arkansas River.** Here, too, are a tramway across the gorge and an incline railway to the bottom.

From Cañon City you have two options back north to Florissant. You can drive northwest on US 50 and Colo. 9 to **High Park Road,** a paved route through mountainous ranching country. Or, if you have a four-wheel-drive vehicle and are feeling adventurous, you can take Field Avenue north to unpaved **Shelf Road,** so-called because its narrow, winding route was blasted out of sheer limestone cliffs. Along the way you'll pass **Red Canyon Park** (the road is paved to this point), a 600-acre park with hiking trails through beautiful, rugged red-rock formations and pinyon-juniper woods. Farther north, the cliffs of **Shelf Road Recreation Area** include popular technical rock-climbing routes, but are for experts only.

333

Colorado National Monument

Rim Rock Drive

■ 23 miles ■ 1 hour ■ All year. Adm. fee.

Colorado National Monument, near the Utah border in west-central Colorado, lies along the northeastern edge of the Uncompahgre Plateau. This huge chunk of the Earth's surface rises more than 2,000 feet above the Grand Valley of the Colorado River. **Rim Rock Drive** hugs the plateau's edge and offers a tour of soul-aching beauty among juniper-pinyon highlands, red-rock cliffs, and deep side canyons.

Take Colo. 340 from Grand Junction to Monument Road and the **East Entrance** *(970-858-3617. www.nps.gov/colm. Adm. fee),* where you start the long, switchbacking drive to the top of the plateau. As you climb, you pass through 200 million years of accumulated sedimentary rock—tilted in great slabs, standing as isolated columns, crumbled over steep boulder fields, and curving sensuously overhead in continuous, smooth cliffs.

At the top, pull into **Cold Shivers Point,** which overlooks the deep, narrow trough of **Columbus Canyon** and offers a stunning view across the **Grand Valley.** The plateau's core has risen twice, first as the base of a mountain range that eroded away. Then, after layers of rock reburied the core, it rose again while the valley floor sank.

At **Red Canyon Overlook,** about 2.5 miles up the road, parallel walls of red stone rise 500 feet over a broad, relatively flat canyon floor. White-throated swifts flit through the void, and along the rim, pinyon jays hop among the pine branches. You might see a coyote or a yellowheaded collared lizard, but most of the monument's wildlife is hard to spot. Bighorn sheep and bobcats do live here, though.

Interpretive signs at the next three overlooks (**Ute Canyon, Fallen Rock,** and **Upper Ute Canyon**) offer a quick geology lesson on how erosion forms the many side canyons spilling from the edge of the plateau. Farther along the rim, stop at **Highland View,** where you have a vista across the Grand Valley to the distant badlands of the **Book Cliffs,** which rise about 1,200 feet above the **Colorado River.**

Drive another mile to **Artists Point,** where an eroded ridge of rock juts into the canyon and ends in a descending series of stone pinnacles the color of sunset. Around the corner you'll find the **Coke Ovens Trail,** a half-mile path to a spectacular overlook at the tip of the **Coke Ovens.** These are massive columns of red stone roughly 400 feet high and rounded at their tops like kilns or coke ovens. Other formations crowd **Monument Canyon** and help fill digital camera memory cards.

The overlook at **Grand View** is one of the best spots in the park to see how the core of the plateau rose beneath its overlying layers of sedimentary stone. From the railing, look north across the canyon and trace the red cliffs as they curve downward to the right. The dark gray knobs of coarse rock beneath the cliffs are gneiss and schist, the 1.5-billion-year-old core of the plateau. The overlying layers tilted, warped, and sometimes broke as

Monument Canyon

the core was heaved upward and the valley floor fell.

Continue on Rim Rock Drive to the **visitor center** *(970-858-3617)* for an overview of the park's geology, plants, and animals. Nearby, you'll find picnic tables and a campground. If you have time, stroll one of the nature trails: **Alcove** (through the pinyon pines) and **Window Rock** (to the rim).

You get your last high-altitude view from the plateau at **Distant View,** then the road switchbacks to the valley floor through **Fruita Canyon.** Stop at **Balanced Rock View** to admire the 600-ton boulder perched on a pedestal of red sandstone, and at **Redlands View** to trace the meandering fault line between the fallen valley floor and the risen block of the plateau.

Grand Mesa
Scenic and Historic Byway

*I-70 at Mesa to Cedaredge on Colorado 65, with a spur on
Land's End Road*

- 63 miles ▪ 2 hours ▪ Summer and fall. Land's End Road
closed October to June.

Superb mountain scenery and an abundance
of lakes for camping, picnicking, and fishing
highlight this short drive across what has
been called the largest flat-topped mountain
in the world.

Beginning at I-70 where Plateau Creek
enters the Colorado River, the byway heads
up the canyon of the latter stream under
steep bluffs for about 10 miles before rising
to the mesa for which the drive is named.
After passing **Powderhorn Resort** ski area *(970-268-5700. www.powderhorn
.com)*, you'll reach the first of several scenic overlooks along the route. You're
entering **Grand Mesa National Forest** *(970-874-6600. www.fs.usda.gov/gmug)*,
which provides a number of recreational opportunities, such as the trails
and campgrounds at **Mesa Lakes** (where there's also a privately run lodge).

Turn west at Land's End Road (FR 100) for an 11-mile side trip on a
gravel road to **Land's End Observatory,** where the stunning vista takes in
mountains 80 miles west in Utah. Along the way, the **Raber Cow Camp**
features restored cabins from the days when ranchers brought their herds
to the top of Grand Mesa in summer.

Back on Colo. 65, the **Land O Lakes Overlook** provides another fine
panorama of some of the 300 lakes that dot the landscape. A short distance
beyond is the **Grand Mesa Visitor Center** *(970-856-4153. May-Oct.)*, with
exhibits and hiking trails, set among some of the mesa's prettiest lakes.

Continuing south off the mesa, you reach the town of Cedaredge and
the **Cedaredge Welcome Center** *(970-856-7554)*, which provides information on the byway and local attractions. Part of the center is **Pioneer Town**
(www.pioneertown.org. Adm. fee), which preserves several historic buildings,
including three distinctive wooden silos from the Bar I Ranch, established
in the early 1880s.

335

Peak to Peak Scenic Byway

Central City to Estes Park on Colorado 119, 72, and 7

- 55 miles ▪ 2 hours ▪ All year

This high mountain drive traverses the eastern flank of Colorado's Front
Range, seesawing over forested ridges and running crosswise to almost every
major valley between Central City and Estes Park. Sights include historic
towns, 13,000-foot peaks, and portions of Rocky Mountain National Park.

Begin the drive on Colo. 119 at the mining, now casino, towns of **Central City** and **Black Hawk.** A gold strike here in 1859 kicked off Colorado's first gold rush and helped pay for the towns' elaborate Victorian buildings. Nine miles beyond Central City, turn into **Golden Gate Canyon State Park** *(303-582-3707. www.parks.state.co.us. Adm. fee)* for the 100-mile vista. From Colo. 119, you descend toward Nederland through hilly lodgepole forests. Turn left on Colo. 72 and after a few miles look for the **Indian Peaks** to the northwest. Summits exceed 13,000 feet and lie within the popular **Indian Peaks Wilderness.** At the junction with Colo. 7, turn left and go 2.5 miles to an overlook for your first good view of Trail Ridge Road (see pp. 337-340). The great domed summit to the north is **Mount Meeker,** 13,911 feet. As you continue north, the forest opens up, and you begin to move through

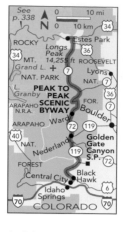

meadows peppered with stands of ponderosa pine typical of the park's east side. Look for elk, deer, and coyotes.

About 3 miles beyond Meeker Park, pull over at the **Enos Mills Memorial** *(970-586-4706. www.enosmills.com. Thurs.-Fri. in summer; adm. fee).* Mills was an innkeeper and naturalist who lobbied for the creation of the national park and spoke at its 1915 dedication. His homestead cabin stands at the eastern edge of a meadow. Here you also get the best view of **Longs Peak.** Soaring 14,255 feet, it towers a mile above the valley floor. Every year some 10,000 people attempt its summit.

Head north about 2 miles to Rocky Mountain National Park and have a look over the rim of **Fish Creek Canyon.** Then continue on Colo. 7 as it drops 1,300 feet down the north wall of the canyon to the town of **Estes Park,** which sprawls among rolling meadows.

Hiking to Long Lake, Indian Peaks Wilderness

Colorado River Headwaters Byway

Grand Lake to State Bridge on US 34, 40 and County Road 1

■ 69 miles ■ 3 hours ■ Summer and fall. The road between Kremmling and State Bridge is gravel, but passable by ordinary vehicles.

This route following a segment of the upper Colorado River begins in the resort town of **Grand Lake** *(970-627-3402. www.grandlakechamber.com),* which serves as the western gateway to the scenery and wildlife of **Rocky Mountain National Park** *(970-586-1206. www.nps.gov/romo. Adm. fee).* The park's **Kawuneeche Visitor Center** *(970-586-1513),* a mile north of town, can provide information on the wealth of things to see and do in the area.

Expansive lakes in the surrounding region, including **Grand, Shadow Mountain,** and **Granby** (see p. 339), offer all sorts of recreational opportunities, from camping and picnicking to fishing and boating. A range of facilities is offered by **Arapaho National Recreation Area** *(970-887-4100. Adm. fee),* which covers 36,000 acres around the lakes.

After skirting the western edges of Shadow Mountain and Granby Lakes, the byway crosses the Colorado River, heads west along the broad valley, and leaves the Rockies in the rearview mirror. At Granby, it follows US 40 west and re-crosses the river to its north bank at a spot called Windy Gap.

Anglers should note that the next 20 miles of the river are managed as a Colorado Gold Medal trout stream, in recognition of high-quality habitat and large fish. Get a close look at the river at **Pioneer Park** in the small resort town of **Hot Sulphur Springs;** turn right on Park Street and left on Grand Avenue to reach the park, where you can picnic, hike, bike, or fish.

The Colorado meanders and the valley widens through a landscape of sagebrush and juniper as you approach Kremmling. Take Colo. 9 south

and, 0.3 mile after crossing the river, turn west on Cty. Rd. 1.

The byway diverges from the river through arid terrain, but in about 8 miles approaches the stream again near **Gore Canyon,** where the Colorado has cut a spectacularly deep gorge. You can see the river from an overlook reached by a county road west off the main route about 10 miles from Kremmling. The rapids below are rated at Class V by whitewater rafters and kayakers, and are considered among the most difficult and dangerous in Colorado.

The remainder of the byway winds through rugged low hills and ravines, dropping down into the Colorado River canyon to parallel railroad tracks to its terminus at Colo. 131.

Trail Ridge Road/ Beaver Meadow Road

Estes Park to Granby on US 34 through Rocky Mountain National Park

- 55 miles - ¹/₂ to 1 day - Open from about Mem. Day to mid-October. Be prepared for crowds between mid-June and mid-August. Adm. fee to park.

Trail Ridge Road crosses the broad back of Colorado's Front Range through Rocky Mountain National Park. It rises to 12,183 feet, well above tree line, and rolls along over a gentle landscape akin to the world's Arctic regions. Tremendous views open up of peaks, deep valleys, and, often, the churning violence of approaching thunderstorms. Expect to be pelted by hail one moment, baked by sunshine the next. But you get more than stunning top-of-the-world vistas on this drive. You skirt wide meadows where bighorn

337

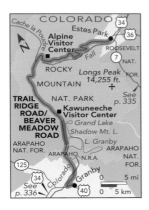

sheep, elk, and deer browse. You follow streams and rivers—including the meek headwaters of the Colorado—and plunge through subalpine forests.

Start in **Estes Park,** a growing resort town in a wide basin first homesteaded in 1860 by Joel Estes. At nearly every turn, the flat summit of **Longs Peak** (14,255 feet) and its companion peaks loom over the rooftops. Follow US 34 past the 1909 **Stanley Hotel** *(970-586-3371. www.stanleyhotel.com),* built by the inventor of the Stanley Steamer automobile.

The road winds along **Fall River,** squeezing between high forested ridges studded with immense domes of exposed granite. Pick up a map for **Rocky Mountain National Park** *(970-586-1206. www.nps.gov/romo. Adm. fee)* at the **Fall River Entrance Station** and drive 1.7 miles to **Sheep Lakes** in **Horseshoe Park,** a meadow at the foot of the **Mummy Range.** Salty soils here draw bighorn sheep, but also look for mule deer and, especially in fall, elk.

Follow Trail Ridge Road through Horseshoe Park and up the slope to **Deer Ridge Junction,** where you'll turn right. Park first, though, and stroll to the edge of the hill overlooking **Moraine Park** and Longs Peak. This parkland, or mountain meadow dotted with stands of ponderosa pine, is typical of much of the national park's east side.

You leave the parkland behind as the road begins to rise into the forest of Engelmann spruce, subalpine fir, and limber pine. About 2 miles from Deer Ridge Junction, stop at the **Beaver Ponds,** where a self-guided nature trail leads through an active beaver colony.

At **Many Parks Curve,** 9,640 feet, a boardwalk offers an expansive view of Moraine Park, Horseshoe Park, and other long, glaciated basins carved out during the Ice Age. **Estes Valley,** just visible beyond **Deer Mountain,** looks glaciated but wasn't. Four miles and 1,200 vertical feet up the road, stop at **Rainbow Curve,** the last turnout before tree line. Here, the stresses of an increasingly harsh climate show in the trees. Some windblasted trunks grow branches only to leeward, and hundred-year-old, sapling-size dwarfs

Fogbound Trail Ridge Road near the Continental Divide

grow horizontally, protected by boulders. The trees give out completely as the road traverses a knife-edged ridgeline, and soon you've arrived in the wide, rolling meadows of the alpine tundra. A deep canyon drops off to the left toward an incredible panorama of the park's major peaks.

Stop at **Forest Canyon Overlook,** 11,716 feet, and take the footpath down to the platform. A peaks-finder chart identifies the summits, which run across your field of vision for 20 miles. Glaciers carved the bowls and basins, spires and ridges that make this ragged mass of gneiss and granite such a pleasure to look at. A valley glacier also gouged out **Forest Canyon,** 2,500 feet below.

The road parallels the summits for 2 miles to **Rock Cut** at 12,110 feet, where a steep, self-guided, 1-mile round-trip nature trail climbs a hill. Worth every gasping breath, it offers more than views of mountains rising over colorful wildflower meadows. You'll also learn about the adaptations plants and animals make to survive a very short growing season, wind speeds of 150 miles an hour, and intense sunlight.

Fall aspen leaf on lichen

US 34 reaches its highest point between the **Lava Cliffs** and **Gore Range** turnoffs. Stop at the **Alpine Visitor Center** *(June-Sept.)* for more about the alpine tundra. If you've brought binoculars, you can usually see a dozen or more elk in a glacial amphitheater beneath the center's viewing platform. The road descends quickly to **Medicine Bow Curve,** a hairpin with a view of the **Medicine Bow Mountains,** 20 miles north. It also overlooks the headwaters of the **Cache la Poudre River,** a silver thread meandering over the treeless floor of a long valley.

You slant down through a subalpine forest and soon approach a small lake, **Poudre Lake.** At its far end lies **Milner Pass,** where you can plant a foot on either side of the **Continental Divide.**

Continue your descent through the forest 2 miles to **Farview Curve,** with its impressive view of the **Never Summer Mountains** across the wide **Kawuneeche Valley.** That timid little stream winding across the valley is the **Colorado River. Grand Ditch,** the faint diagonal line cutting across the Never Summers, intercepts meltwater for farmers near Fort Collins.

Follow the switchbacks down to the valley floor and drive about 14 miles along enormous meadows. Stop at the parking area for **Never Summer Ranch,** a preserved, 1920s-era dude ranch nestled in the forest. A half-mile walk leads to the cluster of ranch buildings erected by John Holzwarth after Prohibition shut down his Denver saloon.

The "parks" here are mountain meadows created when Ice Age glaciers melted, leaving lakes that eventually silted up and drained.

Displays at the **Kawuneeche Visitor Center** *(970-586-1513),* about 8 miles from the ranch, focus on animals and plants that live on the colder, wetter west side of the park. Historic **Grand Lake Lodge** *(970-627-3967. www.grandlakelodge.com. Late May-Oct.)* perches on a slope overlooking Grand and Shadow Mountain Lakes. You'll enjoy sitting on its veranda for a drink or a meal. **Grand Lake**—a jewel surrounded by mountains and enormous glacial troughs—is Colorado's largest natural lake.

The road continues south along **Shadow Mountain Lake,** which, like **Lake Granby** a little farther along, is a huge reservoir impounding the Colorado

River. Water is carried by tunnel through the mountains for use on the east slopes. You'll find picnic areas, campgrounds, and boat ramps along the lake's perimeter, most of which is in the **Arapaho National Recreation Area** *(970-887-4100. Adm. fee).* The mountains to the southeast are part of the **Indian Peaks Wilderness,** a backpacking area accessible from the Arapaho Bay campground on Lake Granby.

The road continues for about 5 miles over rolling hills to **Granby.**

Top of the Rockies
National Scenic Byway

I-70 to Leadville on Colorado 91, on to Aspen on US 24 and Colorado 82, returning through Leadville to Minturn on US 24

■ 130 miles ■ 4 hours ■ Summer and fall. Roads are well maintained and regularly cleared of snow; winter driving can be beautiful if caution is used. Drink plenty of water and avoid alcohol until accustomed to the high altitude.

Spectacular Rocky Mountain scenery and the historic mining town of Leadville highlight this central Colorado byway. "Top of the Rockies" is an appropriate name, since you reach altitudes of more than 2 miles above sea level and pass near Colorado's highest peak.

The drive leaves I-70 on Colo. 91 with the imposing summits of the **Tenmile Range** to the east and the ski resort of **Copper Mountain** *(866-841-2481. www.coppercolorado.com)* to the west. The resort offers summer hiking, biking, and other activities as well as winter skiing. You're heading into mining country now, with tailings (waste materials) from abandoned operations obvious along the road. Thriving towns such as Kokomo once occupied this valley, but long ago disappeared as mines shut down.

The road climbs to reach the **Continental Divide** at 11,318-foot **Fremont Pass,** where, despite the fact that you're traveling generally southwest, you're actually moving from the western continental drainage to the eastern. The town of **Climax** here once had a population of 3,000 connected with the world's largest molybdenum mine. The operation closed in the 1980s, but reopened in 2012.

The byway descends through the valley of the **East Fork Arkansas River** to **Leadville** *(Leadville-Lake County Chamber of Commerce, 809 Harrison Ave. 719-486-3900 or 888-532-3845. www.leadvilleusa.com),* at 10,152 feet the highest incorporated town in the nation. Leadville arguably is Colorado's most historic town, too—or at least the one with the most colorful past, having seen the likes of Buffalo Bill Cody, Oscar Wilde, John Phillip Sousa, Susan B. Anthony, Doc Holliday, and Horace "Silver Dollar" Tabor, who gained and lost a huge fortune in the silver mines that made Leadville a boomtown in the 1880s. Seventy square blocks of town compose a national historic landmark district. Start learning about Leadville history at the **Heritage Museum** *(9th St. & Harrison Ave. 719-486-1878. www.visitleadvilleco.com/history_tours. May-Oct.; adm. fee),* recounting the town's past, and the **National Mining Hall of Fame and Museum** *(120 W. 9th St. 719-486-1229. www.mining halloffame.org. Closed Sun. in winter; adm. fee).* Housed in the 1899 former Leadville High School building, the latter museum recounts the history of the mining industry in America and displays a dazzling collection of gems and minerals. Don't miss the **1879 Tabor Opera House** *(308 Har-rison Ave. 719-486-8409. www*

Skiing at Copper Mountain Resort, Colorado

.taboroperahouse.net. June-Sept., closed Sun.; adm. fee), once the grandest structure of its type between St. Louis and San Francisco.

US 24 leads south through the valley of the Arkansas River with massive mountains in the distance, including **Mount Elbert,** at 14,433 feet the highest peak in the state. A turn west on Colo. 82 leads to **Twin Lakes,** a thriving mountain resort in the 1880s, now a small village with a few historic buildings, including the now abandoned 1879 **Interlaken Hotel.**

Fifteen miles west of Twin Lakes, enter the glacially carved **Independence Pass** *(www.independencepass.org. Mem. Day–early Nov.),* elevation 12,095 feet, for a summit overview of the **Roaring Fork Valley** and three mountain ranges (**Collegiate Range** to the southwest, **Sawatch Range** to the north, and **West Elk Range** to the northwest).

Just beyond the pass, park the car for a difficult 8.8-mile, out-and-back hike beginning at **Upper Lost Man Trailhead** *(Mem. Day–early Nov.).* Bring a buddy for safety during this high-altitude exercise.

The once booming **Independence Ghost Town** *(www.heritageaspen.org/indep .html)* at mile 57 offers a glimpse into 1880s mining life. Before Aspen's milder climate lured away workers, they extracted $190,000 of gold in one year alone.

The world's first trail for the blind, **Braille Trail,** built in 1961, and its sister trail, **Discovery,** at mile 54, let hikers with or without disabilities experience nature by touch, taste, scent, and sound. Call ahead to grab headphones from the **Aspen District Forest Service Office** *(970-925-3445 or 970-945-2521. www.topoftherockiesbyway.org/map guide. Mem. Day–early Nov.).*

In **Aspen** *(Chamber of Commerce, 425 Rio Grande Pl. 970-925-1940 or 800-670-0792. www.aspenchamber.org),* snow-sport at **Aspen Mountain Ski Area** *(800-525-6200. www.aspensnowmass.com)* from Thanksgiving to April or try year-round summer sports, including horseback riding, kayaking, paintballing, and biking.

Learn about silver refinement at **Aspen's Holden/Marolt Mining and Ranching Museum** *(40180 Hwy. 82. 970-925-3721. www.aspenhistorysociety .com/holdenmuseum.html. Mid-June–early Oct.; adm. fee).* Opened as an 1891 processing plant, the mill went bust in 1893 when Congress repealed the Sherman Silver Act, which had mandated federal purchase of silver.

341

Backtrack through Independence Pass and Twin Lakes to Balltown. The byway route returns north on US 24 through Leadville, back across the Continental Divide at 10,424-foot **Tennessee Pass**. The **Ski Cooper** area *(719-486-3684 or 800-707-6114. www.skicooper.com. Mid-Dec.–mid-April)* was used for training in World War II by troops at nearby Camp Hale who were being sent to fight in the Alps. The camp, deactivated in 1965, was located 5 miles down the highway where the Eagle River Valley broadens into a flat plain.

Lariat Loop Scenic & Historic Byway

Loop from Golden, Colorado, on Colorado 470, 74, and 40

■ 40 miles ■ ½ to 1 day ■ April to October

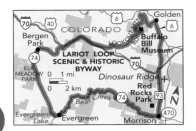

Laid out in 1912—which incidentally makes it one of the nation's earliest scenic byways—this 40-mile circular route through the foothills of the Rocky Mountains was designed specifically to flaunt the breathtaking landscapes and fascinating natural history of the area.

The fact that the Lariat Loop and Scenic Byway begins just minutes from downtown Denver adds convenience to its appeal. From the Mile High City, the byway rises another 2,000 feet; the elevation change makes it important to pace yourself and drink plenty of water to help minimize the effects of altitude.

Start your drive from the Denver suburb of Golden by following US 40 south toward **Dinosaur Ridge** *(16831 W. Alameda. 303-697-3466. www.dinoridge.org)*. Hike the 1½-mile trail, from which you can ogle hundreds of remarkably distinct dinosaur footprints and touch the fossilized bones of Jurassic-era giants like stegosaurus and apatosaurus still embedded in the 150-million-year-old rock.

From here, continue south to **Red Rocks Park** *(18300 W. Alameda Pkwy. 303-697-4939. www.redrocksonline.com)*. Widely known as a world-class outdoor concert venue that's played host to big names from Bruce Springsteen to Willie Nelson, the 640-acre park also offers quiet hiking trails with postcard views of the impressive sandstone formations that give it its name.

The Colorado Railroad Museum

Unlike other scenic byways, the Lariat Loop blends a distinct off-the-beaten-path feel with the up-to-the-minute hipness of reborn mining towns full of sophisticated eateries and boutiques. Follow the road south and you'll come to the quaint Victorian mining town of **Morrison** *(303-697-8749. http://town.morrison.co.us)*. While the entire town has been designated as a National Historic District, the main attraction here is the

342

The Red Rocks Amphitheatre in Red Rocks Park

Morrison Natural History Museum *(501 Hwy. 8. 303-697-1873. www.mnhm .org. Adm. fee)*, which features an extensive collection of prehistoric remains large and small, from baby dinosaur tracks to a life-size cast of a *T. rex* skull.

Leaving town, the scenic byway turns west on Colo. 74 as it winds below the granite cliffs of Bear Creek Canyon. Continue on and you'll reach the upscale mountain community of **Evergreen** *(www.downtownevergreen.com)*, which makes a great place to do a little window shopping or grab a bite to eat.

Just outside town is the **HiWan Homestead Museum** *(4208 S. Timbervale Dr. 720-497-7650)*, a grand 1890s-era lodge complete with some original furnishings, Apache baskets, Navajo blankets, and Pueblo pottery. If the day's become a bit too warm, consider stopping off at nearby **Evergreen Lake** *(www.evergreenrecreation.com)*, where you can drift along in a rented canoe or wet a line in search of rainbow trout.

When you're feeling sufficiently refreshed and ready to hit the road again, follow Colo. 74 northwest through Elk Meadow Park. Just ahead, you'll leave the two-lane behind for a brief stretch of eastbound I-70. Jump off the freeway at exit 254 for a good look at a local bison herd on land owned by the Denver park system before continuing east on US 40.

From there, Lookout Mountain Road winds northeast toward the park of the same name. Along the way, you'll find the **Buffalo Bill Museum and Grave** *(303-526-0744. www.buffalobill.org)*, where you can gain insight into the legendary showman who, more than anyone else, created the image of the American West that's still celebrated around the world today.

As you approach the end of the route, the road drops 2,000 feet in less than five miles on its way to the former territorial capital of **Golden**. Topping the list of must-see attractions here is the **Coors Brewery** *(303-277-2337. www.millercoors.com)*, where you'll get a look at brewing and bottling operations and a sample of some of the freshest beer you're ever likely to taste. Those looking for something more family friendly can plan a visit to the **Colorado Railroad Museum** *(17155 W. 44th Ave. 303-279-4591. www .coloradorailroadmuseum.org; adm. fee)*, where kids of all ages can enjoy everything from elaborate model railroad layouts to a ride aboard the rare half-truck/half-train contraption known as a Galloping Goose *(only on Saturdays; additional charge)*.

CANADA

International
Selkirk Loop
p. 376

3A

6

Going-to-the-
Sun Road
p. 347

2

95

20

Sandpoint

Pend Oreille
Scenic Byway
p. 375

Kalispell

89

15

MONTA

2

Spokane

Coeur
d'Alene

200

93

Great Falls

US 89
p. 350

90

Lake
Coeur
d'Alene
p. 374

90

Missoula

Helena

89

W A S H .

95

Moscow

Butte

90

12

12

Lewiston

Northwest
Passage
Scenic Byway
p. 373

93

15

Bozeman

Bearto
High
p.

Walla Walla

Grangeville

Salmon River
Scenic Route
p. 370

Lewis and Clark
Drive
p. 372

O R E G O N

New
Meadows

Payette River
Scenic Byway
p. 369

20

Mesa Falls
Scenic Byway
p. 365

Teton Park
Drive
p. 362

84

95

93

I D A H O

15

Jackson

55

Sawtooth Drive
p. 366

Big Hole
Mountains Drive
p. 364

Centennia
Scenic
Bywa
p.

Boise

Idaho Falls

26

89

Western Heritage
Historic Byway
p. 368

84

Pocatello

86

34

30

Twin
Falls

Pioneer
Historic Byway
p. 363

30

93

84

N E V A D A

89

15

30

Great
Salt
Lake

80

Ogden

80

Salt Lake City

U T A H

Snake

Columbia

0   50   100 miles
0   50   100   150 kilometers

2

Missouri

NORTH DAKOTA

94

Miles City

94

Billings

90

2

SOUTH DAKOTA

Sheridan

Black Hills
p. 219

Big Horn Mountains Scenic Byway
p. 357

14

North Fork
f the Shoshone
. 330

Buffalo

Gillette

90

Rapid City

26

Casper

25

WYOMING

NEBR.

Rock Springs

80

130

Snowy Range
Road
p. 358

Laramie

Cheyenne

80

25

COLORADO

Fort Collins

76

MONTANA
Going-to-the-Sun Road

St. Mary to Apgar through Glacier National Park

▪ 50 miles ▪ 2 hours ▪ Late spring through fall. Closed October to early June. Best driven in the morning. Good chance of wildlife sightings. Adm. fee to park.

High in the mountains of northwest Montana, Glacier National Park sprawls over a magnificent landscape of jagged peaks, deep mountain lakes, and steep-sided valleys. Crossing the park's backbone from east to west, Going-to-the-Sun Road climbs from the fringe of the Great Plains to the Continental Divide, then drops into the lush rain forests of the McDonald Valley. The route passes ribbon-like waterfalls, vibrant wildflower meadows, and turquoise streams.

347

From the town of **St. Mary** head a mile west to the entrance to **Glacier National Park** *(406-888-7800. www.nps.gov/glac. Adm. fee).* The drive begins at the east end of **St. Mary Lake.** Ten miles long, the lake occupies a trough gouged by a huge glacier thousands of years

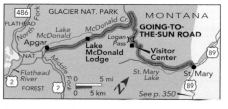

ago. Along its upper end, peaks of sedimentary rock sweep up 4,500 feet.

From here, the road curves through meadows colored by wildflowers and bordered by aspen and lodgepole pine. The haunts of elk and deer, these meadowlands also provide homes for mice, voles, gophers, and squirrels. Look for hawks circling above, on the prowl for lunch.

Continue past the Rising Sun Campground to **Wild Goose Island Turnout,** with its famous view of an islet dwarfed by mammoth peaks. Three miles up the road at **Sun Point,** a short path climbs to a fine lake overlook, where a peaks-finder chart identifies the major summits. All of them suffered the glorious vandalism of the Ice Age. Cirques, knife-edged crests, horns, and broad U-shaped valleys track the flow of glaciers inching down from high summits to fill valleys like this one.

Within a mile of Sun Point, the road begins to climb through a massive layer of vermilion mudstone. On the left, a 1.5-mile trail leads to **St. Mary Falls,** one of the loveliest cascades in the park. Across the lake, look for **Virginia Falls** dropping through the forest.

Avalanche Creek, Going-to-the-Sun Road, Glacier National Park

At the **Jackson Glacier Turnout** a sign explains how the glacier, barely visible over the treetops, has shrunk to just a quarter of the size it was in the mid-19th century. Black bears thrive in these deep subalpine forests of Engelmann spruce and fir, as do weasels, red squirrels, porcupines, and great horned owls.

After another mile the road breaks out of the forest and into a broad, open slope rimmed by mountains. Stop at the hairpin turn and crane your neck to see 10,014-foot Mount Siyeh standing over the apex of the curve, with 9,642-foot Going-to-the-Sun Mountain to the right and Cataract and Piegan Mountains on the left. Grizzly bears roam the scrubby amphitheater enclosed by the peaks, and bighorn sheep and mountain goats browse along the upper slopes.

> Going-to-the-Sun Road opened in 1933 after years of arduous construction. Every spring it takes about two months to clear the road of snow.

As you drive toward Logan Pass, the road edges along the nearly vertical cliffs of Piegan Mountain, and a waterfall thunders right onto the pavement. At 6,646 feet, Logan Pass is one of the best areas in the park to spot mountain goats. You might see them crossing the road, but if you don't, stop at the visitor center *(June-Sept.)* and hike to the **Hidden Lake Overlook.** The 1.5-mile boardwalk trail rises through a wide basin of rock terraces overgrown with wildflowers, ending at the brink of a spectacular hanging valley. Even if you don't see goats, you won't be disappointed.

From Logan Pass, you descend along the broad face of the **Garden Wall,** a knife-edged crest stretching along the Continental Divide. In Glacier, the divide not only separates Pacific and Atlantic watersheds, but it also forms a climatic divide. Tree species typical of the northern Rockies grow

St. Mary Lake and Wild Goose Island

Monkey flower, arnica, and Indian paintbrush

on the cooler, drier east side, while the west side fosters cedars, hemlocks, and other trees found in Northwest rain forests.

After about 5 miles you come to **Bird Woman Falls Overlook,** with views of a white ribbon of water cascading off a hanging valley enclosed by (left to right) Mounts Oberlin, Clements, and Cannon. The turnout also overlooks deep, glaciated **McDonald Valley.**

For the next 4.5 miles the road slants down through an area still recovering from a 1967 lightning fire. Silver trunks of dead trees stand like ships' masts over a lush carpet of fireweed, black cottonwood, mountain maple, young lodgepole pine, and a variety of berry bushes.

Soon the road makes a sharp turn to the left and glides down through the forest to the floor of the valley. Here, you pick up **McDonald Creek,** a rippling sheet of glacier blue water that races over a bed of red and green pebbles. Its waters draw white-tailed deer and moose.

Pull over at the **Avalanche Exhibit** for a neck-crimping view of Mount Cannon and its avalanche chutes, then drive 3 miles to an unmarked turnout on the right side. Short paths through cedars and hemlocks lead to **Red Rock Point,** where McDonald Creek zigzags between tilted blocks of red mudstone and rests in murmuring turquoise pools.

Just a mile down the road, the **Trail of the Cedars** makes a short loop through a forest of cedar and hemlock. The trail also passes the mouth of **Avalanche Creek,** where sapphire waters swirl over bloodred rock.

It's hard to get enough of McDonald Creek. A footbridge and trail at **Sacred Dancing Cascade** follows the creek past a series of rapids and falls. There's also a turnout at **McDonald Falls.**

349

Soon, though, the road pulls away from the creek and bores through a dense forest of cedar, hemlock, larch, white pine, and birch, emerging at **Lake McDonald Lodge** *(406-756-2444. www .glacierparkinc.com/lodging.php. Late May-Sept.),* a fine rustic structure with an immense lobby of stone and timber and a public dining room. **Lake McDonald** itself occupies a deep trench 10 miles long, 1.25 miles wide, and 472 feet deep. Views of it from the road are limited because of an intervening strip of thick forest, but you'll find dozens of turnouts with paths leading through the trees to wide pebble beaches. The beaches seem made for picnics, the red and green pebbles for skipping across the water.

Going-to-the-Sun Road near Logan Pass

At the southwest end of the lake, follow signs to the village of **Apgar,** where the drive ends with a sweeping view up Lake McDonald to the mountains above Logan Pass.

US 89

Yellowstone National Park to Glacier National Park

▪ 377 miles ▪ 2 days ▪ All year

This lightly traveled route between Yellowstone and Glacier National Parks crosses Montana through an epic western landscape that sprawls along the base of the northern Rockies. It traces the sinuous course of the Yellowstone River to Livingston, then cruises through wide intermontane basins full of sagebrush and pronghorn. North of White Sulphur Springs, the road climbs over a gentle, forested range of mountains, scrambles around in gullies and canyons, then breaks out onto the Great Plains, crossing the Missouri River at Great Falls. Rollicking through the foothills of the awesome Rocky Mountain Front, it finally drops into the St. Mary Valley at the eastern edge of Glacier National Park.

From **Gardiner,** follow the **Yellowstone River** northwest through a semiarid valley of steep, gravelly hills thinly covered by grass and sagebrush. Across the river you can see two prominent summits: 9,652-foot **Sepulcher Mountain** on the left and 10,992-foot **Electric Peak** to the right.

Broad, deep, and swift, the Yellowstone rushes between stony banks and coasts past narrow sand beaches shaded by gnarled juniper trees and rustling willow thickets. Twice a year, the river corridor acts as a migratory funnel, guiding thousands of elk, deer, pronghorn, bighorn sheep, and bison between their summer and winter feeding grounds. It's the largest migration of wildlife in the lower 48 states, and you can learn more about it at the **Wildlife Viewing Area,** 5 miles from Gardiner. Here you can also see **Devil's Slide,** a vertical band of red sedimentary rock across the valley at the base of Cinnabar Mountain.

US 89 continues 8 more miles through this broad canyon before the hills crimp down into **Yankee Jim Canyon,** a narrow gorge the Yellowstone has cut through Precambrian metamorphic rock.

Soon the road exits the gorge and heads across the expansive, undulating floor of **Paradise Valley,** spreading between the **Gallatin** and the **Absaroka** (Ab-SORE-kuh) **Ranges.** Above the river rise black basalt cliffs, which give out

Mule deer

as you pass a rest area. Suddenly, the entire Absaroka massif stands before you—a grand alignment of peaks bulking up more than 4,500 feet above the valley and forming a backdrop to Livingston.

Absaroka Range near Livingston

Seven miles beyond the rest area, you'll pass the turnoff for **Chico Hot Springs** *(406-333-4933. www.chicohotsprings.com. Adm. fee),* one of Montana's finest commercial soaking grounds, with a saloon and two restaurants to match.

In the midst of the sun, sweat, and dust of summer, the shaded banks and cool waters of the Yellowstone River are always inviting. One of the best sites on the river lies 10 miles past Chico: **Mallard's Rest Fishing Access** occupies a flat bench of sand and gravel under huge cottonwoods. Here, you can let the broad, dimpled sheet of the Yellowstone run across your toes while you gaze into the glacially carved high country of the **Absaroka-Beartooth Wilderness.**

Twelve miles north the road enters **Livingston,** an 1880s railroad town with a colorful historic district. Its **Depot Center** *(200 W. Park St. 406-222-2300. www.livingstondepot.org. Adm. fee),* a 1902 Northern Pacific train depot designed by the architectural firm that did New York City's Grand Central Station, now houses a railroad museum. Across the street stands another town landmark—**Dan Bailey's Fly Shop** *(406-222-1673. www.dan-bailey.com),* legendary among fly-fishing enthusiasts.

From Livingston US 89 joins I-90 briefly, rounds the northern spur of the Absaroka Range, and heads north. Crossing the Yellowstone for the last time, it enters **Crazy Mountain Basin,** a broad, rumpled floor of grass and sagebrush that extends from Livingston nearly to White Sulphur Springs. The **Bridger Range** rises to the west, and the jagged crest of the **Crazy Mountains** cuts into the eastern sky. Below them, the **Shields River** meanders across dry ranch fields, sometimes pooling into backwater sloughs and ponds rimmed with cattails, reeds, and cottonwoods. Deer, owls, kingfishers, woodpeckers, beavers, mink, and muskrat live in the wetland areas. Out on the flats pronghorn are everywhere, while hawks, coyotes, and badgers are on the prowl for gophers and other rodents.

Aspen grove, Two Medicine Valley

As the Crazy Mountains sink from view, the **Castle Mountains** rise straight ahead like a forested granite dome. On the western horizon, the **Big Belt Mountains** replace the Bridger Range. As you enter **White Sulphur Springs,** look for the impressive Victorian mansion standing atop the highest hill in town: **The Castle** *(406-547-2324. www.russell .visitmt.com/listings/102.htm. Mid-May–mid-Sept.; adm. fee).* It was built of hand-hewn granite in 1892 by a local rancher and mine owner; today, it's a house museum.

From White Sulphur Springs, the road crosses the **Little Belt Mountains,** which look like big swells on a prairie-grass sea. As you climb higher, a forest thickens around you, but the trees open often into meadows where you're likely to see elk and deer in the evening. The road tops out at 7,393-foot **Kings Hill Pass,** then drifts down through the forest along **Belt Creek.** As you descend to drier elevations, the trees shift from lodgepole pine and Engelmann spruce to drought-resistant ponderosa pine.

At Monarch the road breaks away from Belt Creek to avoid a major chasm of 1,000-foot cliffs, then climbs over the open backs of the surrounding hills to a scenic turnout. From here you can see the cliffs plunging down to Belt Creek. **Sluice Boxes State Park** *(406-444-3750. http://stateparks.mt.gov/ sluice-boxes/default.html. Adm. fee)* occupies part of the chasm *(follow signs at bottom of hill).*

US 89 continues to follow Belt Creek and its ribbon of trees and shrubs through a wide, dry canyon to the junction with US 87/Mont. 200. Turn left to continue on US 89 and cross 15 miles of rolling prairie to the outskirts of

Cattle drive along US 89

Great Falls, which straddles a gorge cut by the Missouri River. When the Lewis and Clark expedition encountered this gorge in 1805, they were forced to spend nearly two weeks portaging around it. A series of five dams has extinguished some of the grand cascades that once thundered here, but the road along the river is worth driving for its views of the Missouri.

To reach the river, turn right on the US 87 bypass. Stop first at the **Lewis and Clark National Historic Trail Interpretive Center** *(4201 Giant Springs Rd. 406-727-8733. Daily May-Sept., Oct.-April closed Sun.; adm. fee),* which details the expedition from beginning to end. **Giant Springs Heritage State Park** *(406-454-5840. www.stateparks.com/giant_springs_ heritage_state_park_in_montana.html. Adm. fee)* on the river is just up the road; catch up on the area's plants and animals at the park **visitor center**

(Mon.-Fri.). Continue to Giant Springs, a small pond of crystalline water welling up through a bed of lush aquatic plants. Huge trout glide around in a display tank at a fish hatchery beside the springs.

Abundant on the prairie along US 89, pronghorn can cruise about as fast as cars, clocking in at speeds above 55 mph.

Return to the US 87 bypass and follow the river into town. Turn left on 14th Street to reach the **C. M. Russell Museum** *(400 13th St. N. 406-727-8787. www .cmrussell.org. Adm. fee),* home of the world's most extensive collection of paintings, sculptures, and drawings by the cowboy artist Charles M. Russell.

From Great Falls, follow I-15 to the Vaughn exit and continue on US 89 across a corner of the **Great Plains** toward the **Rocky Mountain Front.** This seemingly endless barricade of high serrated peaks slid out onto the prairie about 70 million years ago—the leading edge of an overthrust belt of mountains that now extends from Helena north into Canada and west to Kalispell. It's a vast tract of wildland that gathers Glacier National Park, three contiguous wilderness areas, and several national forests into an ecosystem that is larger than the states of Delaware and Rhode Island combined.

Just north of Fairfield, **Freezeout Lake** spreads across the prairie with the mountains as a distant backdrop. Freezeout is a major stopover for migrating waterfowl, and its skies explode each spring and autumn with flocks of gabbling snow geese and tundra swans.

About 10 miles farther along, the drive passes the small town of **Choteau.** At the north end of town, you can stop at the **Old Trail Museum Complex** *(406-466-5332. www.oldtrailmuseum.org. Mem. Day-Labor Day; adm. fee).* More than simply an interesting pioneer museum, the complex also sponsors excursions to local dinosaur fossil sites between May and September.

From Choteau to Browning the highway bobs along over prairie swells as it heads toward the Rocky Mountain Front. During the 19th century, the Blackfeet Indians controlled the buffalo country east of the mountains here, though they were occasionally challenged by the Kootenai and Flathead tribes who lived to the west.

In Browning, the heart of the Blackfeet Indian Reservation, stop at the **Museum of the Plains Indian** *(406-338-2230. www.browningmontana .com/museum.html. Closed weekends Oct.-May; adm. fee June-Sept.),* which celebrates the traditional life of the northern Plains tribes with exhibits of clothing, weapons, tools, and ceremonial gear.

Beyond Browning, the highway swings toward the mountains, bounding over lateral moraines left by glaciers that mauled the peaks and plowed their way down to the plains about 10,000 years ago. Before long, you climb into the foothills and then descend the northeastern flank of **Divide Mountain** into the **St. Mary Valley.**

Wooden church, Ringling

353

The drive ends at the eastern entrance to **Glacier National Park** (see Going-to-the-Sun Road, pp. 347-349), where you have a stunning view of the massive mountains that characterize the park's terrain.

Beartooth Highway

Red Lodge to Yellowstone National Park on US 212 via Wyoming

- 68.7 miles ■ 2 to 3 hours ■ Late spring to fall. Aspens glorious in late September. Generally closed mid-October to Memorial Day. Major switchbacks.

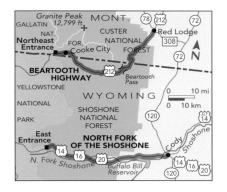

From the rarefied heights of Montana's alpine tundra to the thirsty soils of Wyoming's High Plains desert, this spectacular drive winds through some of the most beautiful and varied landscapes in the Yellowstone region.

As you come into Red Lodge from the north on US 212, the **Beartooth Plateau** looms over the surrounding prairie foothills as a hulking mass of black, rounded mountains. The plateau, an immense block of metamorphic rock, was heaved up through the Earth's crust about 50 million years ago. Much later, an enormous ice cap smoothed its surface and flowed down into the plateau's side canyons, hollowing them into spacious U-shaped valleys.

Red Lodge is an 1880s coal-mining and ranching town lined with turn-of-the-20th-century redbrick storefronts and hotels catering mainly to skiers and visitors to Yellowstone. Here you can visit the **Yellowstone Wildlife Sanctuary** *(north end of Red Lodge. 406-446-1133. www .beartoothnaturecenter.org. Adm. fee),* which exhibits native wildlife. The road follows **Rock Creek**, winding through grassy hills that soon give way to heavily forested mountains. Rocky outcrops interrupt evergreen forests, and an occasional spire juts over the trees. About 13 miles from Red Lodge, the road climbs away from the creek, and suddenly the vista opens up toward the 1,800-foot cliffs that bend around the head of the valley in a tight semicircle.

After 5 miles of dramatic switchbacks, stop at the **Vista Point** scenic overlook. Here, at 9,200 feet, a short path leads to the tip of a promontory with phenomenal views across **Rock Creek Canyon** to the high, rolling country of the Beartooth Plateau. Signs brief you on the geology, plants, and animals of the area.

As you continue on US 212, the trees give out entirely and you begin crossing a landscape of low, rounded hills covered with

Angler on Beartooth Lake

grasses, sedges, and lavish summer wildflowers. Soon the road cuts back to the rim of the canyon, and from the narrow turnouts you can see a chain of glacial lakes, including **Twin Lakes,** 1,000 feet below. Even in July, enough snow accumulates against the headwall here to draw skiers.

View of Twin Lakes from Beartooth Pass

As you pass by the ski lift, the **Absaroka Range** breaks over the southwest horizon in a row of jagged volcanic peaks. Wildflower meadows lead to the west summit of **Beartooth Pass,** at an exalted 10,947 feet.

The brutal climate at this elevation—frigid, wind hammered, dry— deters the growth of trees and shrubs, and the plants that do grow here have adapted in remarkable ways. Some convert sunlight to heat, and many conserve water the way desert plants do.

Only marmots, squirrels, pikas, and mountain goats live here year-round. The goats frequent the cliffs called **Quintuple Peaks,** to your immediate right. Grizzlies passing through dig up the meadows for roots and for squirrels, and bighorn sheep summer among the boulder fields. If you scan the sky, you may see hawks, eagles, or falcons sweeping the high country in search of rodents.

From the pass, you descend to a landscape where scattered islands of pine and spruce eke out a living amid knobs of granite and fields of wildflowers. Hundreds of tiny ponds and several small lakes shimmer in glaciated depressions.

As you approach the turnoff for **Island Lake Campground,** two prominent spires of the Absaroka Range swing into view: 11,708-foot **Pilot Peak** and 11,313-foot **Index Peak.** Beyond here, you descend through a forest of lodgepole and whitebark pines toward 10,514-foot **Beartooth Butte.** Soon you pass **Beartooth Lake,** a great picnic spot nestled against the butte's 1,500-foot cliffs.

When the road breaks out of the trees, look to the left across a deep canyon to see **Beartooth Falls** cascading through the forest. In another mile follow the gravel road to **Clay Butte Lookout,** a fire tower with a smashing view of some of Montana's highest mountains.

Watch for deer, moose, and elk in the meadows as the road moves down the flank of the plateau to the **Pilot and Index Overlook.** You're looking at the northeastern edge of the Absaroka Range, an eroded mass of lava, ash, and mudflows that began forming 50 million years ago.

Continue 5.5 miles to an unmarked bridge over **Lake Creek** and take the short path back to a powerful waterfall thundering through a narrow chasm. A completely different sort of cascade fans out over a broad ramp of granite in the trees above **Crazy Creek Campground,** 2.5 miles farther.

From here the road picks up the **Clarks Fork River** and follows it through what is left of a centuries-old forest, much of which fell victim to the great Yellowstone fires of 1988. Soon the road passes through the tiny tourist crossroads of **Cooke City,** begun as a 19th-century mining camp. In 1877 the Nez Perce retreated through this area on their way to Canada. Four miles beyond, the drive ends at the northeast entrance to **Yellowstone National Park** *(307-344-7381. www.nps.gov/yell. Adm. fee).*

Lake Creek, Shoshone National Forest

WYOMING
North Fork of the Shoshone

East entrance of Yellowstone National Park to Cody on US 14/16/20

▪ 52 miles ▪ 2 hours ▪ Spring through fall. Yellowstone's east entrance is closed in winter. *See map p. 354.*

From Yellowstone's east entrance, the drive descends through dense evergreen forests into the high, semiarid country surrounding Cody and its famous Western museum.

Beginning at the east edge of Yellowstone, US 14/16/20 follows the shallow waters of **Middle Creek** to **Pahaska Tepee** *(307-527-7701. www .pahaska.com. Mid-May–mid-Oct.),* a modern dude ranch built around one of Buffalo Bill Cody's hunting lodges. Behind a roadside curio shop, the rustic lodge holds mounted elk heads, a big fireplace, and burl furniture. After the lodge, you pick up the **North Fork Shoshone River.**

As you descend through the forest, cliffs and narrow columns of bulbous rock carved by water begin to rise through the trees. These formations, including **Chimney Rock,** are the remains of ancient volcanic mudflows. Soon, the forest thins to a peppering of juniper scattered along the canyon cliffs. The **Wapiti Ranger Station** *(307-527-6921. http://wyoshpo.state .wy.us)* here in the canyon was built in 1903 as headquarters for **Shoshone National Forest** *(www .fs.usda.gov/shoshone).*

Following the curves of the river beneath red rock, you coast out of the canyon into a wide valley, hugging the shore of **Buffalo Bill Reservoir** and **Buffalo Bill State Park** *(307-587-9227. http://wyoparks .state.wy.us/Site/SiteInfo.aspx?siteID=3. May-Sept.; adm. fee).* If you stop at the **Buffalo Bill Dam Visitor Center** *(307-527-6076. www.bbdvc.com),* you can gaze down into **Shoshone Canyon,** an impressively

Colter's Hell hot springs, Shoshone River

deep gorge between Cedar and Rattlesnake Mountains. A roadside exhibit partway down the gorge explains the geology of Rattlesnake Mountain.

As the road emerges from the gorge onto the desert floor of the **Big Horn Basin,** you'll see isolated **Heart Mountain** off to the northeast. It slid off the Beartooth Plateau and came to rest north of Cody. Entering **Cody** from the west, look for **Trail Town** *(307-587-5302. www.nezperce.com/trltown.html. Mid-May–Sept.; adm. fee).* A mix of replicated and authentic frontier buildings, it offers shops, eateries, and period exhibits. Drive downtown to see Cody's **Buffalo Bill Historical Center** *(720 Sheridan Ave. 307-587-4771. www.bbhc.org. May-Oct. 1; adm. fee).* Perhaps the best Western museum in the northern Rockies, it has a fine collection of Western painting and sculpture, a Plains Indian museum, a world-renowned collection of firearms, and a treasure trove of Buffalo Bill memorabilia.

357

Big Horn Mountains Scenic Byway

Dayton to Shell on US 14

- 60 miles - 2 hours - Late spring through fall. Pass is occasionally closed in winter.

This splendid drive over the broad back of the Big Horn Mountains rises from the Tongue River Valley, booms across meadows, then dives into a dazzling gorge on the range's west side.

From **Dayton,** US 14 leaves the shaded banks of the **Tongue River** and winds through rolling prairie foothills toward the dark eastern front of the **Big Horn Mountains.** The range formed 60 million years ago, when a section of

Precambrian "basement" rocks—some of them 2.9 billion years old—was forced through the surface. The Precambrian rock carried with it a cap of mostly eroded sedimentary rock.

Big Horn Mountains

About 10 miles from Dayton, stop at the **Sand Turn Pullout** on the flank of the mountains. Here, a sign identifies Buffalo Tongue Rock, one of the sedimentary rock layers that tilted as the Big Horns rose. Within a mile, the road begins traversing the north wall of **Little Tongue River Canyon.** Pull over at the turnout for **Fallen City,** a steep field of huge limestone chunks that tumbled from the ridgeline across the canyon.

After this stop, the road switchbacks up through a deep lodgepole pine forest that slowly gives way to expansive subalpine meadows, typical of the Big Horn crest.

At Burgess Junction, an hour detour on US 14A will bring you to **Medicine Wheel,** an ancient stone circle sacred to Native Americans. Back on US 14, you'll soon reach **Granite Pass,** elevation 9,033 feet, whose vast, grassy meadows attract elk and deer. As you descend to **Shell Canyon,** stop at **Shell Falls Interpretive Site,** where a self-guided nature trail hugs the rim of a granite-lined chasm overlooking the falls. Exhibits cover canyon geology, plants, and animals.

Below the falls, the drive gets even better. You pass two roadside exhibits showing where bighorn sheep tend to congregate during winter. Then the canyon narrows and you plunge into a slender gap that curves between high walls of smooth, colorful rock. Cliffs of pink, orange, beige, and reddish brown rise hundreds of feet from the swift waters of **Shell Creek.** Savor the view because it lasts only about a mile before the road punches out of the western flank of the Big Horns and heads across the desert floor to the town of **Shell** and the drive's end.

Pebbling a barren plateau high in the Big Horn Mountains, the Medicine Wheel is an enigmatic message from a people long gone.

Snowy Range Road

Laramie to Saratoga on Wyoming 130 and 230

▪ 85 miles ▪ 3 hours ▪ Late spring through fall. Closed in winter

Easily one of the most spectacular drives in Wyoming, the Snowy Range Road crosses the Medicine Bow Mountains in southern Wyoming, passing expansive wildflower meadows, tiny alpine lakes, and high glaciated cliffs before descending to the plains. It's the sort of drive that makes you want to stop the car, get out, amble around, and smell the lousewort.

From **Laramie** take Wyo. 130 west across a broad, grassy flat toward the **Medicine Bow Mountains.** A dark band across the western horizon, they were raised along a fault roughly 65 million years ago. Look for coyotes, pronghorn, and hawks as you drive the 27 miles to **Centennial,** a small town founded in 1876 in hopes of gold that never panned out.

From Centennial, you climb into a forest of lodgepole pine, aspen, subalpine fir, and Engelmann spruce. As you gain elevation, wide meadows covered with thick mats of grass and summer wildflowers dot the forest, frequented by deer, elk, and moose. About 10 miles from Centennial, the high peaks of the **Snowy Range,** part of the Medicine Bow Mountains, burst into view. This impressive crest of 1,000-foot cliffs is composed of glaciated quartzite two billion years old. From the plains, the grayish white quartzite looks like snow during the dry hot months, when the ground cover is gone.

Weaving through high mountain country and past alpine lakes, this drive is a welcome relief from the dry Wyoming flatlands.

For a closer look, drive 3 miles to the **Sugarloaf Recreation Area** and rumble a mile down a rough road of glacial gravel to the picnic area. Here, you'll find two tiny alpine lakes nestled among wildflower meadows at the foot of **Sugarloaf Mountain.**

Return to the main road and drive a mile to the **Libby Flats Observation Point,** at the summit of a 10,847-foot pass. A stone turret here overlooks a landscape dotted with boulders and dwarf subalpine fir. On clear days, you can see as far south as Rocky Mountain National Park in Colorado. A peaks-finder chart points out **Medicine Bow Peak,** at 12,013 feet the Snowy Range's highest.

Summit of the Snowy Range Road

Making a 26-mile descent through arid foothills, across a sagebrush plain, and over the **North Platte River,** the drive reaches the junction with Wyo. 230. Turn right and go 7.5 miles to **Saratoga,** which offers a public hot springs and the **Wolf Hotel** (*101 E. Bridge St. 307-326-5525. www.wolfhotel .com*), built in the 1890s as a stage stop.

Centennial Scenic Byway

Dubois to Pinedale on US 26 and US 189/191

■ 162 miles ■ 1 day ■ All year. Pass is occasionally closed in winter.

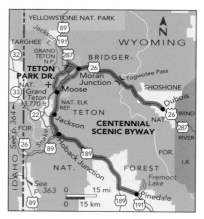

One of the finest drives in the Rockies, the Centennial Scenic Byway charts a long, doglegging course through the mountains and river valleys of northwest Wyoming. Along the way, it passes nearly every major sight in the region—the Wind River Range, the Tetons, the Snake River, and the Green River Valley. Get an early start to catch the morning light on the Tetons and still make Pinedale to watch the sun set on the Winds.

The byway begins at **Dubois** (DOO-boyce), in a portion of the **Wind River Valley** where the surrounding terrain shifts from colorful arid badlands to densely forested mountain slopes. Before leaving town, stop at the innovative **National Bighorn Sheep Interpretive Center** (*907 W. Ramshorn. 307-455-3429. www.bighorn.org. Adm. fee*). Next door you'll find the **Wind River Historical Center/Dubois Museum** (*307-455-2284. www.duboismuseum.org. Summer daily, winter closed Sun.-Mon.; donation*), a good pioneer, archaeology, and natural history museum.

US 26 climbs from town between layer-cake badlands and the gentle eastern flank of the Wind River Range. To the northeast rears 11,920-foot Ramshorn Peak, part of the volcanic Absaroka Range. Beside the road, the **Wind River** curves over beds of cobblestone, sliding past evergreens and aspens, washing through thickets of willows, and sometimes wetting the feet of moose, elk, and fishermen.

About 17 miles from town, pull over at the **Tie Hack Memorial,** which venerates the tough, mostly Scandinavian lumberjacks who hacked railroad ties from these forests until the 1930s. Within a few miles, the crenellated battlements of the **Breccia Cliffs** and then **Pinnacle Buttes** burst over the treetops. Stop at **Falls Campground** to stroll the rim of the waterfall. Nearby, FR 515 leads to historic **Brooks Lake Lodge** (*307-455-2121. www.brookslake.com. June-Sept. & late Dec.–mid-March*) at the foot of soaring Pinnacle Buttes.

US 26 rises steadily through a forest of rough-barked Engelmann spruce, silvery-barked subalpine fir, and towering lodgepole pine. In meadows rife with wildflowers, be on the lookout for moose, elk, deer, even bear. Soon, you cross **Togwotee** (TOE-guh-dee) **Pass,** elevation 9,544 feet, and descend to **Teton Range Overlook,** with its view of Wyoming's best known mountains. A peaks-finder chart identifies summits, including the Grand Teton.

Drive out of the mountains onto the floodplain of the Buffalo Fork River, and you're soon in **Grand Teton National Park** (*307-739-3600. www.nps.gov/grte. Adm. fee*). From **Moran Junction,** Yellowstone National Park lies 27 miles north. At Moran you can also pick up the Teton Park Drive (see p. 362).

US 26 turns south, however, and passes through a wetland area. Look for moose, elk, and bison along here. Continue south over gently rolling terrain to the **Snake River Overlook,** perched above a wide bend of the river with one of the classic views of "The Grand" and its attendant peaks. Bald eagles and ospreys sometimes glide over the river. From here, the drive heads south through **Jackson Hole** to **Moose Junction**, where you'll find the main park visitor center and the chuckwagon tepee of legendary **Dornan's** *(307-733-2522. www.dornans.com)* with fine views of the Tetons. About 6 miles south of Moose, a fence encloses the **National Elk Refuge** *(307-733-9212. www.fws.gov/nationalelkrefuge. Adm. fee),* where more than 10,000 elk gather every winter. Sleigh rides among the elk start from refuge headquarters. Nearby, take a sharp left turn into the **Jackson National Fish Hatchery** *(307-733-2510)* to see cutthroat trout bred for Wyoming and other states. Back on US 26, the **National Museum of Wildlife Art** *(307-733-5771. www .wildlifeart.com. Adm. fee),* a mile beyond, displays works by fine wildlife artists.

A bull moose in rut is a belligerent animal, known to charge anything that annoys it—other bulls, people with cameras, cars, and even locomotives.

Soon you arrive in **Jackson,** a former ranch town turned tourist mecca. If you want to avoid the traffic cruising past its boutiques, art galleries, restaurants, bars, and outfitters, take the truck route and follow US 189/191 south. Seven miles from Jackson you hit the **Snake River** and follow it to **Hoback Junction.** Here, the **Hoback River** joins the Snake, and their combined waters rush into the **Grand Canyon of the Snake River.**

The byway, though, follows US 189/191 up **Hoback Canyon,** through winter range for deer, elk, moose, and bighorn sheep. The Hoback River, a good trout stream, sweeps by campgrounds and picnic areas. For soaking in a hot spring, turn left on the Granite Creek Road 11 miles south of Hoback Junction and drive up the side canyon to a commercial pool.

Southeast of Bondurant, the road drops out of the mountains onto the sagebrush flats of the **Green River Valley.** Bursting over the eastern foothills, the crest of the **Wind River Range** rises more than 13,000 feet and includes Wyoming's highest summit, 13,804-foot Gannet Peak. A heavily glaciated mass of Precambrian rock, the Winds were formed 55 million to 60 million years ago.

The wide Green River Valley lay at the heart of the 19th-century fur trade. Trappers roaming the West rendezvoused here summers to trade their "plews" for goods caravanned from Missouri. Their brief tenure, 1824-1840, is celebrated at the **Museum of the Mountain Man** *(US 189/191. 307-367-4101. www.museumofthemountain man.com. Daily May-Sept., Mon.-Fri. Oct.; adm. fee).*

End your tour by following Fremont Lake Road to **Fremont Lake,** which stretches beneath the Winds.

Nez Perce Peak in the Tetons

361

Teton Park Drive

*Moran Junction to Moose Junction on Teton Park and
Jenny Lake Loop Roads*

■ 25 miles ■ 2 hours ■ Closed late October to early May.
Adm. fee to park. *See map p. 360.*

Bull elk in velvet

This drive swings through the scenic heart of a preserve built around one of Earth's most dramatic geologic statements.

From US 26/287, turn right at **Moran Junction**, pick up a map for **Grand Teton National Park** *(307-739-3600. www.nps.gov/grte)* at the entrance station and drive about 3 miles to the **Oxbow Bend Turnout**. Here you get a classic view of **Mount Moran** towering above a bend in the **Snake River**. This unforgettable fang of Precambrian rock, along with its companion peaks, soars some 6,000 feet above the flat floor of Jackson Hole. Below the turnout, ponds formed by river meanders attract moose, otters, swans, bald eagles, and herons.

The **Tetons,** young mountains that are still growing, began rising from the earth just 5 million to 10 million years ago, but they are composed of rocks 2.5 billion years old. As the mountains rose, the valley floor sank, creating the spectacular landscape of today. At **Jackson Lake Junction,** turn left and drive along Jackson Lake to **Signal Mountain Road,** which climbs to the summit of Signal Mountain and offers a grandstand vista of Jackson Lake, the Tetons, and the other ranges that ring Jackson Hole.

Return to the main park road, then turn right at **North Jenny Lake Junction** and follow the one-way loop road into the scenic center of the Tetons. Load your camera for the **Cathedral Group Turnout**, with its tremendous close-up views of **Mount Owen, Teewinot Mountain,** and the nearly vertical north face of the **Grand Teton**. From the picnic area at **String Lake,** take the short trail to **Leigh Lake,** with its unrivaled views of Mount Moran. The **Jenny Lake Turnout** offers a stunning vista of the Tetons.

Continue on the main park road to the **South Jenny Lake** area. Take the 3-mile trail around the lake or pay for the boat ride. On the other side, a trail of less than a mile leads to **Hidden Falls** and **Inspiration Point**—the most popular short hike in the park.

Back on the park road, the **Menor-Noble Historic District** features a restored 1890s homestead and cable ferry across the Snake. The park's nearby **Moose Visitor Center** has exhibits on the natural history of the area. The drive ends just beyond, at the junction with US 26.

Officially, a local man named W. O. Owen is recognized as the first to climb the Grand Teton in 1898, but a U.S. Geological Survey team claims to have gotten there before him in 1872.

362

IDAHO

Pioneer Historic Byway

Franklin to the Wyoming state line on US 91 and Idaho 34

- 127 miles ▪ 3 hours ▪ Spring through fall

History, geology, and striking scenery combine along this byway that runs through the farmland and mountains of southeastern Idaho.

The route begins in **Franklin** *(208-646-2300. www .franklinidaho.org)*, the oldest permanent settlement in Idaho. Founded in 1860 by Mormon pioneers moving north from Salt Lake City, the community's historic district includes the 1872 Hatch House, the quaint old city hall, and a boulder used to mark an early stagecoach route to Yellowstone National Park.

The first segment of this byway passes mostly through agricultural land of grains and cattle, as well as through grassland and sagebrush with distant mountains. In **Preston** *(208-852-2403. www.preston idaho.org)*, the most evocative reminder of the past is the 1890s **Oneida Stake Academy** in Benson Park. Once a Mormon academy, the grand Romanesque stone building, topped with an octagonal bell tower, is undergoing restoration.

363

Just outside of Preston the byway follows Idaho 34 to the north through low hills to first cross the Bear River. Three miles before the town of Grace, a quick detour east on Ice Cave Road will bring you to **Niter Ice Cave,** where flowing volcanic material created a lava tube, used by early pioneers as a refrigerator. In Grace, turn west on Center Street and drive 1 mile to see **Black Canyon Gorge,** where the Bear River has cut down into basalt layers to create a rugged canyon.

Six miles beyond where Idaho 34 joins US 30 and turns east, you reach **Soda Springs** *(208-547-2600. www.sodachamber.com)*, called Beer Springs by early settlers for its fizzy water. Soda Springs boasts the only "captive" geyser in the world, a shoot of water accidentally tapped by drilling in 1937. Now capped and controlled by a timer, it erupts 100 feet high once an hour. To sample some of the local sparkling soda water, turn west to **Hooper Spring** from Idaho 34, 2 miles north of town. (By the way, the decidedly nonscenic landscape in this area is caused by phosphate

Old wooden barn in the Caribou Mountains

mining.) Eight miles farther on Idaho 34, look west to see the volcanic formations called **China Hat** and **China Cap.** In the tiny town of Henry, note the **Chester Country Store,** which dates from 1908.

The landscape quickly becomes more rugged as Idaho 34 once again turns eastward for its last 30 miles, entering the **Caribou-Targhee National Forest** *(208-524-7500. www.fs.usda.gov/ctnf).* This stretch of the byway is by far the most scenic, as the road winds through conifer forests of the Caribou Range, then descends through Tincup Creek Canyon into the heavily agricultural watershed of the Salt River in Wyoming.

Big Hole Mountains Drive

Swan Valley to Victor on US 26 and Idaho 31

■ 21 miles ■ ¹/₂ hour ■ Spring through fall. *See map opposite.*

This short drive over eastern Idaho's Big Hole Mountains rises from the banks of the Snake River, winds along the rim of a narrow gorge, and tops a lovely mountain pass overlooking Wyoming's Teton Range.

Start 3.5 miles west of the town of **Swan Valley,** where US 26 crosses the **Snake River,** southern Idaho's principal waterway and a major tributary of the Columbia. Here the river sweeps north around a high, arid hill, then enters a deep canyon cut into basaltic lava and hardened volcanic ash. For a quick side trip follow the signs 1.5 miles to **Fall Creek Falls,** a 60-foot cascade over travertine outcroppings.

Return to US 26 and continue to the town of Swan Valley, where you turn left onto Idaho 31. Gliding over rolling fields of wheat and barley, the road runs toward the forested slopes of the **Big Hole Mountains,** then climbs to the rim of **Pine Creek Canyon.** A couple of turnouts offer good views of this narrow cleft in black basalt that flowed as lava onto the floor of Swan Valley almost two million years ago.

Blue columbine

Within a mile or so the gorge ends, and the road runs along the floor of a small valley. **Pine Creek,** a good fishing spot for cutthroat and rainbow trout, meanders through thickets of willow and dogwood. Moose, elk, and deer browse the bottomlands.

After several miles, you begin climbing through another, longer canyon to the top of 6,764-foot **Pine Creek Pass.** From here, a 4-mile round-trip on **Rainy Creek Road** rambles through wildflower meadows with great views of the Teton Valley and the sea of broad-backed mountains to the southwest.

Coming off the pass, Idaho 31 winds down out of the forests and onto the wide, flat floor of the **Teton Basin,** where you get a sweeping view of the gentle western slopes of the **Tetons,** including the **Grand Teton**—that distinctive prong of gray rock jutting over the foothills.

The drive ends in **Victor,** fast becoming a bedroom community for Jackson, Wyoming, which is just over the Teton Range to the east.

Mesa Falls Scenic Byway

Ashton to US 20 on Idaho 47

- 28 miles ▪ 1 hour ▪ Spring through fall

In all of Idaho, there remain just two undisturbed waterfalls of any real consequence. Both thunder through a narrow chasm carved by the Henrys Fork River in eastern Idaho, near Yellowstone National Park. The Mesa Falls Scenic Byway visits both of them, offers good views of the Teton Range, and passes through forests and meadows frequented by deer, elk, and moose.

From **Ashton,** drive east on Idaho 47 toward the toothy skyline of the **Teton Range,** which thrusts up 7,000 feet. Keep an eye out to the north for **Big Bend Ridge,** the western flank of a volcano that erupted 1.3 million years ago.

365

The road soon curves to the north and drops to the floor of a forested gorge. Stop near the **Warm River Bridge** to look for trout and for the ospreys, bald eagles, and river otters that feed on them. Driving out of the gorge, you come to a narrow ridge separating **Warm River Canyon** *(right)* from the **Henrys Fork Canyon** *(left).* Dense forests hide canyon vistas, but an overlook offers a glimpse of the Tetons and a bend of the Warm River. A turnoff 3 miles beyond leads to **Lower Mesa Falls.** Along the paved trail to its rim, the sound of thunder rises from the canyon, as far below the river squeezes between columns of basalt, then plunges 65 feet.

Return to the byway, drive a mile to the turnoff for **Upper Mesa Falls,** and follow the road down the canyon wall to a large parking area. A footpath here skirts the ruins of a turn-of-the-20th-century log lodge, then leads to viewing platforms of the 114-foot falls. One platform stands at the very edge of the cataract. (In 1981 the hydroelectric industry proposed to dam both upper and lower falls. Fortunately, the plans were thwarted.)

The road continues past a dozen heavily logged miles of Targhee National Forest *(208-652-7442. www.fs.usda.gov/ctnf),* then joins US 20.

Upper Mesa Falls

Sawtooth Drive

Boise to Shoshone on Idaho 21 and 75

■ 246 miles ■ 2 days ■ All year. Occasionally closed in winter

Starting from the desert floor at Boise, this drive climbs into central Idaho's spectacular Sawtooth Range then winds down through Sun Valley to the volcanic desert floor.

Built in a rare spot of shade along the edge of Idaho's southern desert, **Boise** took root as a mining center and military post during the Idaho gold rush of the 1860s. As befits a state capital, Boise offers several museums. For state history, visit the **Idaho Historical Museum** *(Julia Davis Park. 208-334-2120. www.history.idaho.gov. Tues.-Sun. May-Sept., Tues.-Sat. Oct.-April; adm. fee)*; for a look at a living stream, stop at the **Morrison Knudsen Nature Center** *(600 S. Walnut Ave. 208-334-2225. Call first; donation)*; for rare birds, go to the **World Center for Birds of Prey** *(5668 W. Flying Hawk Ln. 208-362-8687. www.peregrinefund.org/world-center. Adm. fee)*.

From downtown Boise take Warm Springs Avenue as it curves through the city's outskirts and connects to Idaho 21. This route follows the Boise River into a shallow canyon. In 7 miles, you pass the turnoff for **Sandy Point** *(208-334-2342. parksandrecreation.idaho.gov/parks/lucky-peak. Adm. fee)*, a lovely bathing area beneath the high wall of Lucky Peak Dam.

As you climb into the swollen brown hills above Boise, expansive views open up behind you of the **Snake River Plain**—a vast sheet of basaltic lava flows

> A chaotic mass of splintering crags, knife-edged ridges, and jagged rock towers, the Sawtooth Range punctuates the horizon for miles.

capping thousands of feet of volcanic ash. Scrambling upward, the road follows a twisting side canyon into ever cooler and moister surroundings. Grass thickens, ponderosa pines begin to sift in among the gullies and ravines, and soon you find yourself driving through a proper forest.

Approaching **Idaho City**, the terrain flattens, and heaps of cobblestones appear on the forest floor among the trees—the leavings of placer miners who swarmed here after gold was discovered in 1862. Soon, Idaho City grew into a mining town of 20,000. Many original buildings survive, including the 1864 territorial penitentiary, where period graffiti includes "Judge Bears is a sun of a bich [sic] and everybody knows it." To learn more, stop by the **Boise Basin Museum** *(Montgomery & Wall Sts. 208-392-4550. www.visitidaho.org. Daily Mem. Day–Labor Day, weekends May, Sept.; adm. fee)*.

Continuing north along Idaho 21 takes you over **Mores Creek Summit**, 6,117 feet, and, 10 miles beyond, into the **Lowman Burn**. For the next 24 miles exhibits explain the forest fires of 1989 and their aftermath. Four miles past Lowman, one of the signs overlooks **Kirkham Hot Springs**, where the **South Fork Payette River** flows through a chasm of white granite. Along the South Fork, the road runs through a forest of towering ponderosa pines.

After the turnoff for **Grandjean** (hot springs and lodge), it winds up through lodgepole pines and Douglas-firs to 7,056-foot **Banner Summit.** Here, you start driving through broad meadows ringed by forest—likely areas to see elk, deer, coyotes, and hawks. This is the northern fringe of the **Sawtooth National Recreation Area** *(208-727-5013. www.fs.usda.gov/ sawtooth)*—756,000 acres that encompass four mountain ranges, several large lakes, lush evergreen forests, the source of the Salmon River, and such uncommon wildlife as mountain goats and bighorn sheep.

Suddenly, the shattered crest of the **Sawtooth Range** bursts over the treetops. Stop at the **Park Creek Overlook,** 18 miles from Banner Summit, for a terrific view of the peaks rising over a wetland meadow frequented by elk and deer. Continue 6.5 miles to **Stanley,** a mining town turned ranching town now catering to fishermen, hunters, backpackers, and white-water boaters. At Idaho 75, you can begin the Salmon River Scenic Route (see pp. 370-372) by turning left. This drive turns right, following the **Salmon River** south through **Sawtooth Valley.**

The core of the Sawtooths is made of pink granite that rose from the Earth's crust 50 million years ago. Glaciers draped the peaks several times, gouging out cirques and ridges and piling up the large moraines that still dam the lakes. The high peaks, many over 10,000 feet, lie within the **Sawtooth Wilderness,** an enticing landscape for day hikes and backpacking trips. Pick up information at the **Stanley Ranger Station** *(208-774-3000. www.stanleycc .org/sleeping/camping. Mon.-Fri.),* 3 miles south of town.

Follow the signs to **Redfish Lake Visitor Center** *(208-774-3376. www .visitidaho.org. Mid-June–Labor Day),* overlooking the biggest lake in the recreation area. The stunning sheet of turquoise water, ringed with beaches and lodgepole pine forests, is nearly overwhelmed by a mass of peaks so close they seem to overhang the lake. From **Redfish Lake Lodge** *(208-774-3536. Mem. Day–Labor Day; fee for boat)* an excursion boat crosses to a wilderness hiking trail. Return to Idaho 75 and stop at the **Sawtooth Hatchery** *(208-774- 3684. www.fws.gov/lsnakecomplan/hatcheries/sawtooth.html. Tours Mem. Day–Labor Day),* 1.5 miles south. From there, the road continues past the

Born Lakes in the White Cloud Mountains, Sawtooth National Recreation Area

sites of **Sawtooth City** and **Vienna** (1870s mining towns), then up a broad hillside to the **Galena Overlook;** 2,000 feet above the valley floor, you gaze upon the Sawtooth Range. That squiggle of willows traces the headwaters of the **Salmon River.**

Soon you top 8,701-foot **Galena Summit** and drop into the forested **Big Wood River Valley.** The colorful **Boulder Mountains** rise to your left. As you drive south, the valley opens up into rolling hills and benchlands. The

Wildflowers in meadow near Stanley

Big Wood River winds toward **Ketchum,** a popular ski town. Turn left on Sun Valley Road and follow the signs to **Sun Valley** (*Visitors Bureau. 208-726-3423 or 800-634-3347. www.visitsunvalley.com*), with its historic 1936 lodge and upscale vacation houses. Along the bike path east of town, the **Hemingway Memorial,** a bust of the writer, is tucked among the cottonwoods alongside Trail Creek.

Return to Ketchum and head south on Idaho 75 to **Hailey** to drive past poet Ezra Pound's boyhood home *(private)* at 314 Second Avenue S. Beyond Hailey, pull over at the sign for **Magic Dam,** where you can get an idea of the vastness of the **Snake River Plain.** A mile beyond at **Shoshone Ice Caves** (*208-886-2058. www.roadsideamerica.com/story/2503. May-Sept.; adm. fee*), guided tours lead through a lava tube partially filled with ice. Eight miles south, you tour **Mammoth Cave** (*208-886-7072. www.idahosmammothcave .com. May-Sept.; adm. fee*) at your own pace. The byway ends 12 miles south in **Shoshone,** whose older buildings are made of lava blocks.

Western Heritage Historic Byway

Meridian to the Snake River on Idaho 69 and Swan Falls Road

▪ 40 miles ▪ 2 hours ▪ All year. Birds of prey nest March through June.

The spectacularly rugged canyon of the Snake River awaits travelers on this short drive south of I-84 in western Idaho, along with the chance to see a variety of hawks and other birds of prey.

The first several miles of the drive lead through suburbs and agricultural land to **Kuna,** where a small **visitor center** (*123 Swan Falls Rd. 208-922-9254*) has information on the area. Continue south for 3 miles, and you reach the **Snake River Birds of Prey National Conservation Area** (*208-384-3300*), a 600,000-acre tract set aside to protect the densest concentration of nesting birds of prey in North America, including golden eagles, prairie falcons, ferruginous hawks, and 13 other species.

Eight miles south of Kuna, the small volcanic cone to the east is **Initial Point,** the spot from which, beginning in 1867, surveyors mapped the entire state of Idaho. A short trails leads to the top for good views of the surroundings, including the imposing **Owyhee Mountains** to the south. Watch for hawks on power lines as you drive the next 7 miles across sagebrush flats to **Dedication Point,** a lookout over the amazing **Snake River Canyon.** Miles of steep cliffs here provide excellent nesting sites for hawks and eagles. There's another designated overlook shortly before the road winds down into the canyon to **Swan Falls Dam,** built in 1901 and no longer in service.

To get the most from your visit to the conservation area, consider a side trip to the nearby **World Center for Birds of Prey** *(208-362-8687. www .peregrinefund.org. Adm fee).* On your return to I-84, drive east to the South Cole Road exit and go south 6 miles to the visitor center, which explores the world of raptors through interactive displays, multi-media shows, and close-up views of a wide variety of birds of prey.

Payette River Scenic Byway

Eagle to New Meadows on Idaho 55

▪ 112 miles ▪ 3 hours ▪ All year. Winter weather can occasionally be severe.

One of Idaho's most popular recreational streams serves as the centerpiece for most of this drive, which departs from the Boise area to explore white-water rapids, conifer forests, pastoral valleys, and resort towns.

Heading north from the suburbs of **Eagle,** the drive winds through high-desert grassland before reaching the aptly named town of **Horseshoe Bend,** where the **Payette River** makes a loop as its flow changes from southward to westward. For the next 80 miles, the byway will travel upstream along the Payette. Soon, you'll probably begin seeing rafters and kayakers, as this stretch is one of Idaho's favorite float streams. Outfitters along the way can arrange trips from beginner-friendly half-day floats to serious white-water adventure.

As you climb in elevation, pines and other conifers slowly begin to replace the roadside grasses and shrubs, mountains close in on both sides of the river, and the rapids get more continuous in the Payette. Thirty-three winding miles north of Horseshoe Bend, the valley opens out a bit at the village of Smith's Ferry, where a ferry once shuttled cattle across the river. Just a couple of miles farther, Idaho 55 crosses the Payette on the striking **Rainbow Bridge,** a concrete arch built in 1933. Its engineering and style have earned it a place on the National Register of Historic Places.

The byway leaves the river to run through agricultural land before reaching the town of Cascade, set where the Payette has been dammed to create **Lake Cascade,** popular with anglers for rainbow trout, coho salmon, smallmouth bass, and perch.

Beyond the lake, the route once again passes along the broad floor of the Long Valley to arrive at **McCall** *(Chamber of Commerce, 102 N. 3rd.*

369

Spawning kokanee salmon

208-634-7631 or 800-260-5130. *www.mccallchamber.org.)*, a resort town well stocked with restaurants, shopping, and lodging options. McCall sits at the edge of **Payette Lake,** formed where the Payette River fills an ancient volcanic crater. The town has a winter carnival *(late Jan.)* with music, sleigh rides, various sports events, and a snow-sculpture contest.

On the northern edge of McCall, explore the environment in **Ponderosa State Park** *(208-634-2164. www.idahoparks.org/parks/ponderosa.aspx. Adm. fee),* which occupies a peninsula jutting 2.5 miles into Payette Lake. The overlook at **Osprey Point** views the lake, and nature trails wind through grand western trees. McCall is virtually surrounded by the **Payette National Forest** *(208-634-0700. www.fs.usda.gov/payette)*—more than 2.3 million acres—that offers campgrounds and hiking trails of varying difficulty.

The byway continues westward over a ridge of Granite Mountain, to end in the Meadows Valley and the farming community of New Meadows.

Salmon River Scenic Route

Stanley, Idaho, to Darby, Montana, on Idaho 75 and US 93

- 184 miles ▪ 5 hours ▪ Spring through fall

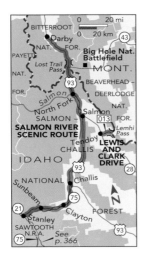

This scenic route follows central Idaho's largest river north from its headwaters in the Sawtooth Range through desert canyons to the tiny town of North Fork, where the waters swerve suddenly to the west and leave all roads far behind. The drive then heads back into the mountains, following the path of Lewis and Clark over Lost Trail Pass and down into the Bitterroot Valley. It's a gorgeous drive and one that touches on the themes of exploration, fur trapping, mining, settlement, and Native American conflicts.

The route begins in Stanley, on the floor of Stanley Basin and in view of Idaho's most spectacular peaks, the **Sawtooth Range.** Follow Idaho 75 east to the **Stanley Museum** *(208-774-3517. www.visitidaho .org/attraction/museums/stanley-museum. Mem. Day–Labor Day),* which summarizes the area's mining and ranching past in a small, historic ranger station.

Paralleling the **Salmon River,** the road soon slants down into a forested gorge lined with granite outcroppings. The river—clean, cold, and swift—drops 15 feet a mile, charging through turbulent rapids and sweeping past several hot spring pools.

Sunbeam Hot Springs, the best known and most obvious of the springs, trickles down a rocky slope about 11 miles from Stanley. Less than a mile beyond the springs, the river stalls out in deep pools of emerald green and turquoise at the crossroads town of **Sunbeam.** The dynamited remains of the only dam ever built on the Salmon River stand below an overlook.

If you detour about 10 miles up Yankee Fork Road, you'll find the ghost towns of **Bonanza** and **Custer,** built during the area's 1870s gold rush. The **Yankee Fork Gold Dredge,** still standing here, operated from 1940 to 1952.

As it rushes across central Idaho, the Salmon River cuts one of the deepest gorges on the continent.

Follow the river 2.5 miles east of Sunbeam to **Indian Riffles,** which overlooks spawning beds for chinook salmon. Years ago, chinook and sockeye salmon migrated through here in such numbers that locals said you could almost walk across the river on the backs of spawning fish. No longer. Hydroelectric dams on the Columbia and Snake Rivers have endangered both species. In 1994 only 96 chinook and just one sockeye returned to spawn.

The road continues along the Salmon River through small canyons that get wider and drier as you descend. Beyond Clayton, the river bends to the northeast and runs through a valley surrounded by high desert hills. This eroded volcanic landscape was carved from ash and lava that spread across the region 50 million years ago from calderas lying northwest of Challis.

Approaching the junction with US 93, you pass under a towering cliff of rust-colored rock. Bighorn sheep frequent the area, and so did bison in earlier times. At the **Bison Jump Archaeological Site,** a sign describes how Native Americans drove small herds of the animals over the cliff.

At the junction of Idaho 75 and US 93 stop at the **Land of the Yankee Fork Visitor Center** *(208-879-5244. www.parksandrecreation.idaho.gov/parks/land-yankee-fork)* to see exhibits on area geology, history, and mining methods—from pick-and-shovel to shaft mines.

371

As you head north from **Challis,** founded in 1878 to supply the mining camps, look for pronghorn on the desert floor and hawks wheeling overhead. To the southeast rise the gravelly, colorful ramparts of the **Lost River Range.**

Soon you cross the **Pahsimeroi River** and then round the northern

Salmon River and the Sawtooth Range

flank of the **Lemhi Range.** About 18 miles past Challis, both road and river punch through a narrow gorge that widens into a spectacular canyon. The walls soar hundreds of feet above the river to cliffs that cut a gap-toothed silhouette across the sky. Just south of Salmon, you begin to cross the **Lemhi Valley.** On the far side are the Beaverhead Mountains, a massive block of Precambrian sedimentary rock that slid east during the general uplift of the Rockies some 70 million years ago.

Follow US 93 to **Salmon,** an 1860s mining town and now a center for ranchers, loggers, and river runners. Here, you can pick up the Lewis and Clark Drive (see sidebar), tracing the explorers' route over Lemhi Pass.

Heading north, the road runs through yet another canyon carved by the Salmon. Look for great blue herons, cliff swallows, deer, pronghorn, and maybe even river otters.

At North Fork the river plunges west into the **Salmon River Canyon,** one of the continent's deepest gorges. Rushing across the vast wilderness of central Idaho, the river is no less forbidding today than it was when early explorers named it the River of No Return.

US 93 tunnels through dense forests to **Lost Trail Pass,** 7,014 feet, named in 1805 by the bewildered northbound party of Lewis and Clark. In 1877, during their epic flight for freedom, the Nez Perce also crossed east through these mountains into the Big Hole Valley. At the **Big Hole National Battlefield** *(15 miles east on Idaho 43. 406-689-3155. www.nps.gov/biho),* you can walk over the ground where the Nez Perce beat back the army.

From the pass, you descend into the **Bitterroot Valley,** a region heavily dependent on logging. Stop at the **Indian Trees Campground** to admire stands of mature ponderosa pines, whose reddish, plate-like bark can smell like vanilla.

South of **Darby,** the high peaks you'll see to the left are the Bitterroots; the low-lying mountains to the right are the Sapphires, which once overlay the Bitterroots. As the Bitterroots rose, the Sapphire Mountains slid 50 miles to their present location.

372

Lewis and Clark Drive

Tendoy to Lemhi Pass on Idaho 28 and Forest Road 013

■ 1 mile ■ 1 hour ■ Late spring through fall. See map p. 370.

This steep gravel road climbs through the arid hills of the Bitterroot Range to Lemhi Pass on the Continental Divide. Here you'll find, as Lewis and Clark did, one of the headwaters of the Missouri River.

From Idaho 28, turn east at Tendoy and south at the T-junction immediately beyond, picking up FR 013, as it follows along beside Agency Creek.

The road climbs a wooded crease between the hills, lush with willows, alders, and cottonwoods. After almost 10 miles, you reach **Lemhi Pass,** elevation 7,373 feet.

From the buck-rail fence that marks the Continental Divide and the border between Montana and Idaho, you can look west over humpbacked hills to the **Lemhi Range** and east to the **Horse Prairie Valley.**

Signs here commemorate Lewis and Clark's crossing of the pass, but the commemorative plaques say little about the Lemhi Shoshone, Nez Perce, and Blackfeet who had beaten this path so thoroughly that the white explorers called it a "highway."

Turn right beyond the signs and follow the short road to the **Sacajawea Historical Area,** which honors the Lemhi Shoshone woman who helped Lewis and Clark in their explorations. At the historical area, you'll find a shady campground, and, just north of it, one of the sources of the **Missouri River** welling from a hillside.

When Meriwether Lewis arrived here in 1805, he wrote, "I had accomplished one of those great objects on which my mind had been unalterably fixed for many years; judge then the pleasure I felt in allaying my thirst with this pure and ice-cold water."

Northwest Passage Scenic Byway

Lewiston to Lola Pass on US 12 and Idaho 13

- 202 miles - 6 hours - Spring through fall

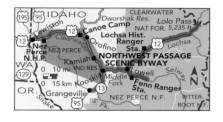

Follow part of Lewis and Clark's route through what is now central Idaho. This history-oriented byway also provides a look at the heritage and culture of the Nez Perce people. The route passes through their homeland on its way to the Montana border at Lolo Pass. Along the way you'll have gorgeous views of the Clearwater and Lochsa Rivers.

The byway begins in Lewiston, where the Clearwater and Snake Rivers meet. Get oriented at the **Lewis and Clark Discovery Center** inside **Hells Gate State Park** *(4 miles south via Snake River Ave. 208-799-5015. www.idahoparks .org/parks/hellsgate.aspx. Adm. fee)* with exhibits and a film on the explorers. While you're here you can also take a boat trip upriver into spectacular **Hells Canyon**, one of the deepest gorges in North America.

Eight miles east of Lewiston, cross the Clearwater south on US 95 to the **Spalding Visitor Center** of **Nez Perce National Historical Park** *(208-843-7001. www.nps.gov/nepe),* one of 38 park sites in Washington, Oregon, Idaho, and Montana. The Nez Perce lived seasonally at this site for thousands of years before European settlement. Displays introduce you to Nez Perce (who call themselves, Nimi'ipuu) history and culture. For the next 60 miles you'll be in their reservation *(www.nezperce.org).*

US 12 clings closely to the banks of the **Clearwater River** as it winds eastward, along grassy rolling hills dotted with ponderosa pine. Watch for the sign at **Canoe Camp,** where Lewis and Clark stopped in September 1805. With the help of the Nez Perce, they made the canoes they would take to the Pacific Ocean. Beyond Orofino, bluffs rise steeply along the Clearwater and the byway, making for an especially scenic stretch. Along the road at Kamiah and just beyond, look for interpretive displays on Lewis and Clark's **Long Camp,** where the Corps of Discovery waited for winter snows to melt before they could continue east in late

Camas Prairie wheat field

spring 1806. Two miles from Kamiah is a rock formation called **Heart of the Monster,** site of an important Nez Perce creation story.

At Kooskia, the byway splits. One section leads south on Idaho 13 along the South Fork Clearwater to **Grangeville.** The town **visitor center** *(US 95 at Pine St. 208-983-0460. www.grangevilleidaho.com)* displays a reproduction mammoth skeleton like the ones accidentally found at nearby Tolo Lake in 1994. Nearby you will find several stops that are part of the Nez Perce National Historical Park, including **Camas Prairie** and **White Bird Battlefield.**

Back on US 12, for the 22 miles beyond Kooskia the byway follows the **Middle Fork Clearwater,** one of the stretches of the river noted for white-water rafting and kayaking. Local outfitters can provide guidance and arrange trips of different lengths.

If you feel adventurous, leave the byway temporarily at Lowell—the confluence of the Lochsa, Selway, and Middle Fork Clearwater Rivers—and drive 5 miles to the historic **Fenn Ranger Station** built by the Civilian Conservation Corps in the 1930s. Continue on a gravel road along the Selway for 20 miles for out-of-the-way picnic spots and scenic views.

The main route along US 12 now makes its constantly winding way along the nationally designated wild and scenic Lochsa through **Clearwater National Forest** *(208-476-4541. www.fs.fed.us/r1/clearwater).* Look for **Lochsa Historical Ranger Station,** a 1920s backcountry ranger station with displays that interpret the daily life of rangers who worked in remote national forest lands. Volunteers staff the station in summer.

The byway is now roughly paralleling the route that Lewis and Clark followed on their historic journey, though they took a route slightly to the north of the present US 12 (the exact path is not known). They followed trails that Native Americans, including the Nez Perce, had used for hunting and travel for centuries. The explorers crossed the Bitterroot Range at 5,233-foot **Lolo Pass,** where the Forest Service operates a **visitor center** *(208-942-1234. www.nps.gov/partnerships/lolo_pass_nez_perce.htm. Mid-May–Oct., schedule varies rest of year).*

Lake Coeur d'Alene

Coeur d'Alene to Potlatch on Idaho 97, 3, and 6

■ 92 miles ■ 2 hours ■ Spring through fall

Sunset on Lake Coeur d'Alene

This trip through the forested mountains of Idaho's panhandle skirts the shoreline of Lake Coeur d'Alene, then bounds over hilly terrain all the way to Potlatch. Along the way, forests of ponderosa pine, cedar, hemlock, and larch alternate with open farmland and marshy river bottoms.

East of the town of Coeur d'Alene, take the Idaho 97 exit from I-90 and head south. The road runs along **Wolf Lodge Bay,** an arm of **Lake Coeur d'Alene** stretching beneath high cliffs. Fall salmon runs draw about 60 bald eagles to the bay every year. Follow Idaho 97 for 4.5 miles as it hugs the shoreline of the bay, then switchbacks up a cliff to a rest area. Here, a short gravel trail leads to a platform overlooking Wolf Lodge Bay and **Beauty Bay.** This is about as panoramic a view of the lake as you'll find along this road, because the forests are too thick and the lake too serpentine to afford more than quick glimpses.

In 23 miles, you will come to **Harrison,** a timber town that boomed from 1890 to 1917, when a huge fire wiped out the dominant lumber company.

A mile south of town, a geology exhibit describes how Lake Coeur d'Alene formed in the **St. Joe River Valley.** Geologists now think the glaciers that dammed the river date back 70,000 to 130,000 years.

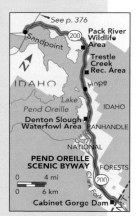

Turn right at the junction of Idaho 97 and 3, and drive through farmland beside the St. Joe River to **St. Maries,** where the **Hughes Historical House** *(538 Main Ave. 208-245-3563. www .stmarieschamber.org/hhm.html. Mem. Day–Labor Day Wed.-Sun.)* has exhibits on the town's timbering heritage. Then head south 15 miles on Idaho 3 and make a right on Idaho 6.

Beyond **Emida,** Idaho 6 runs for about 10 miles through dense forests of hemlock, cedar, larch, and white pine. At the **Giant White Pine Campground,** the namesake pine, a soaring column of gray scaly bark 6 feet in diameter, approaches 200 feet in height and has lived for more than 400 years. At the turn of the 20th century, loggers felled thousands of these giants, mainly to make matches.

From here, the road continues west, dropping from the forest to the farmland around **Potlatch,** a company town established in 1905 by Potlatch Lumber.

Pend Oreille Scenic Byway

Sandpoint to the Montana state line on Idaho 200

■ 33 miles ■ 2 hours ■ Spring through fall

Northern Idaho's **Lake Pend Oreille** (pronounced pond-er-AY) shows the effects of the biggest of the ice age floods that shaped the continent. Pend Oreille, at 1,150 feet, is the fifth deepest lake in the nation. It is so deep, in fact, that the U.S. Navy uses it as a research base to test sonar. But depth isn't the lake's only impressive dimension. A kayaker would need a week to paddle its 111 miles of coastline.

In about 7 miles after leaving Sandpoint, Idaho 200 reaches the **Pack River Wildlife Area,** where you may see moose, bald eagles, waterfowl, and other wildlife. Stretching to the southeast is a 10-mile vista of the lake, and to the east rise the Cabinet Mountains with several peaks over 7,000 feet.

Look for the **Trestle Creek Recreation Area,** a good place for long-distance views, and for the **Pend Oreille Geologic Site,** which explains how prehistoric Lake Missoula repeatedly broke through a huge ice dam to cause massive flooding in the Pacific Northwest.

Past the small town of Hope is the **Denton Slough Waterfowl Area,** an excellent birding site. The byway ends just beyond the Cabinet Gorge Dam, under the bluffs of the canyon through which the **Clark Fork River** flows.

See p. 376

375

International Selkirk Loop

Loop from Sandpoint, Idaho, to Creston, British Columbia, on US 95, Idaho 1, and British Columbia 21; to Nelson, British Columbia, on British Columbia 3A; to Washington State on British Columbia 6 and Washington 31 and 20; returning to Sandpoint on US 2

■ 280 miles ■ 2 days ■ Spring through fall. Photo ID or passport is required for border crossings, which close from late evening to morning (check for individual stop closing times).

Rare among America's scenic byways, this route crosses an international border, stitching together regions of the United States and Canada. The Selkirk Mountains, a range of the Rockies, stretch north-south for 200 miles from British Columbia into Washington and Idaho.

Starting in **Sandpoint** (*Sandpoint Visitor Center, 900 N. 5th. 208-263-0887 or 800-800-2106. www.visitsandpoint.info),* you have a view of **Lake Pend Oreille** (see p. 375). On the north edge of town, **Schweitzer Mountain Resort** (*800-831-8810. www.schweitzer.com. Fee)* offers a chairlift ride to the top of its 6,400-foot peak, with views of Lake Pend Oreille and the Selkirks and other ranges north into Canada.

As you drive US 95, you're on the Wild Horse Trail, which saw thousands pouring north when gold was discovered in Wild Horse Creek in Canada in 1863. The route passes through farmland with the Selkirks on the west, arriving in 15 miles at **McArthur Lake Wildlife Management Area.**

Just before Bonners Ferry, the landscape opens in the **Kootenai River Valley,** where the rich soil is used for pasture and grain crops. Wildlife-watchers can make the 5-mile detour west to visit **Kootenai National Wildlife Refuge** (*208-267-3888. www.fws.gov/kootenai),* home to moose, elk, black bears, mule and white-tailed deer, bald eagles, ospreys, and ruffed grouse.

In the last ice age, a lobe of ice reached through this region, creating a glacially carved valley called the Purcell Trench extending north into British Columbia and as far south as Lake Coeur d'Alene. The Selkirks on the west and the Purcells to the east offer easy access to hundreds of miles of trails, lakes, and public lands. Check with the **Panhandle National Forest Bonners Ferry Ranger District** (*208-267-5561. www.fs.fed.us/ipnf/bonnersferry)* about appropriate trails within the forest or with the **Bonners Ferry Visitor Center** (*US 95. 208-267-5922. www.visitidaho.org/attraction/visitor-centers/bonners-ferry-visitor-center)* on local outdoor activities.

From Bonners Ferry it's only 30 miles to the border of British Columbia. Seven miles west of Creston on Brit. Col. 3A is the **Creston Valley Wildlife Management Area** (*250-402-6900. www.crestonwildlife.ca)* with an interpretive center open from late April to mid-October.

Since the 1960s, Brit. Col. 3A runs right along the shore of narrow **Kootenay Lake,** famed for clear, clean water. For a change of pace, stop in **Boswell** at The Glass House *(250-223-8372. May 1–mid-Oct. Adm. fee),* built of more than a half million embalming fluid bottles.

At Kootenay Bay, Brit. Col. 3A continues across Kootenay Lake on a ferry; the 35-minute trip makes it the world's longest free ferry ride. Just 5 minutes southwest of Blafour is **Kokanee Creek Provincial Park** *(Hwy. 3A. 250-825-4212. www.britishcolumbia.com/parks/?id=79)* offering an interpretive center, trails, and beaches. You'll continue along the north shore of the lake's west arm, crossing to **Nelson** *(Chamber of Commerce, 225 Hall St. 250-352-3433. www.discovernelson.com),* a city known for its historic architecture and its arts community. From Nelson, Brit. Col. 6 winds south through the old mining towns of Ymir and Salmo, along the Salmo River to the U.S. border. The loop, now Wash. 31, winds into the valley of the **Pend Oreille River,** the major thoroughfare for this region before railroads and highways. After passing the old mining and lumber communities of Metaline Falls, Metaline, and Ione, note Tiger's **Tiger Historical Center** *(509-442-0288. www.tigerhistoricalmuseum.org. May-Sept. daily, Oct. weekends),* an old country story made into a visitor center. Around the small town of **Cusick,** watch for bald eagles and ospreys nesting along the river.

As you enter the town of **Newport,** turn north on Warren Avenue 1 mile to reach the two short **Lower Wolf Trails.** It's worthwhile to visit the **Pend Oreille County Museum** *(402 S. Washington Ave. 509-447-5388. www.pocmuseum.org. Donation),* a complex that includes a 1908 rail depot, reconstructed log cabins, and a steam-driven sawmill engine. US 2 crosses the Pend Oreille back into Idaho at **Oldtown.** Turn north on LeClerc Road 2 miles to Pioneer Park and the **Heritage Trail,** which interprets the history and culture of the Kalispel people. Return to US 2 and continue east as the route follows the shore of the Pend Oreille past historic Priest River. Nestled in the heart of the Selkirks is **Priest Lake,** a 19 mile detour on Idaho 75.

Moose in pond in Kootenai National Wildlife Refuge, Idaho

ALASKA

Fairbanks

Glenn
Highway
p. 384

George Parks
Highway
p. 381

Richardson
Highway
p. 386

Haines Highway
p. 391

Anchorage

Seward Highway
p. 389

Alaska's
Marine Highway
p. 393

Haines

Juneau

Alaska's
Marine Highway
p. 393

Bellingha

Strait of Juan de Fuca
Highway
p. 411

Port
Angeles

Olympic Peninsula
p. 408

Seat

Tacóma

Olympia

White P
Scenic Byw
p. 3

Astoria

Vancouver

Portland

Troutdale

Northern
Oregon Coast
p. 421

Salem

Central
Oregon Coast
p. 422

West Cascade
Scenic Byway
p. 43

Eugene

Rogue-Umpqua
Scenic Byway
p. 426

Volcanic Legacy
Scenic Byway
p. 428

Southern
Oregon Coast
p. 424

Medford

CALIFO

PACIFIC
OCEAN

0   200   400 miles
0   200 400 600 kilometers

0   50   100 miles
0   50   100   150 kilometers

CANADA

Mount Baker Scenic Byway
p. 398

Sherman Pass
Scenic Byway
p. 403

International
Selkirk Loop
p. 376

North Cascades
Highway
p. 401

Stevens Pass
Greenway
p. 406

W A S H I N G T O N

Spokane

Coulee Corridor
Scenic Byway
p. 404

Mountains to Sound
Greenway
p. 407

Naches

Chinook
Scenic Byway
p. 416

Yakima

Mount Adams
Drive
p. 412

ount St. Helens
414

Kennewick

Historic Columbia
River Highway
p. 417

Columbia

Mount Hood
Scenic Byway
p. 419

La Grande

Hells Canyon
Scenic Byway
p. 438

Baker City

McKenzie-Santiam
Scenic Byway
p. 430

Elkhorn Drive
p. 435

O R E G O N

IDAHO

Bend

Cascade Lakes
Scenic Byway
p. 433

Outback
Scenic Byway
p. 436

math Falls

N E V A D A

A

ALASKA
George Parks Highway

Wasilla to Fairbanks on Alaska 3

■ 323 miles ■ 1½ days ■ June to mid-September. Summer days offer as much as 21 hours of daylight, but by early September heavy snow can fall in Fairbanks. Distances are designated by mileposts.

Linking the state's two largest cities—Anchorage and Fairbanks—with Denali National Park and Preserve, this highway travels through the kind of scenery that defines the Alaskan interior: tundra and muskeg, the continent's highest peaks, glaciers, forests, wild rivers, and lonely expanses inhabited only by moose, grizzlies, foxes, wolves, and a wealth of birds.

381

The George Parks Highway begins at its junction with the Glenn Highway (see pp. 384-385) in the **Matanuska-Susitna Valley,** 35 miles northeast of Anchorage. Alaska's breadbasket, the Mat-Su stretches in a long fertile swath between the Chugach and Talkeetna Ranges.

Vintage buildings at the **Wasilla Historic Town Site** *(mile 42.2. 907-373-9071. www.cityofwasilla.com/museum. Tues.-Fri. in summer, call for winter hours; adm. fee)* testify to the isolation and self sufficiency of the area's old-time bush communities in the days before the Parks was built. (The highway dates back only to 1971.) Wasilla's original log community hall houses the **Dorothy G. Page Museum** *(323 Main St. 907-373-9071. April-Sept. Mon.-Sat., call for winter hours; adm. fee),* an evocative collection of personal artifacts. The nearby **Iditarod Museum** *(22 Knik Goose Bay Rd. 907-376-5155. Daily in summer, Mon.-Fri. fall-spring)* displays pictures and videos of Alaska's world-famous Iditarod Trail Sled Dog Race, which covers the 1,150 miles from Anchorage to Nome. At Wasilla's sprawling outdoor **Museum of Alaska Transportation and Industry** *(mile 46.7 exit at Rocky Ridge Rd., follow signs. 907-376-1211. www.museumofalaska .org. May-Sept.; adm. fee),* hybrid planes, trains, and other conveyances celebrate sourdough ingenuity with Alaska's weather, terrain, and size.

Leaving Wasilla, the highway soon picks up the **Little Susitna River** *(mile 57.1),* thronged by migrating salmon in

Bandon Beach, southern Oregon coast

Mount McKinley, Denali National Park and Preserve

late spring and midsummer. At mile 67.2, the **Nancy Lake State Recreation Area** *(Mile 1.3 Nancy Lake Pkwy. 907-495-6273. http://dnr.alaska.gov/parks. Vehicle fee)* also features similar wetlands, as well as several lakes and a canoe trail.

A couple of miles farther on, you will see the turbid **Susitna River** conveying its gritty cargo of silt rasped by glaciers sliding past Alaska Range peaks. The Willow Creek Parkway at mile 70.8 offers access to riverside wetlands flanking the Susitna's **Delta Islands.** The Hatcher Pass Junction Road at mile 71.2 leads to the **Willow Creek State Recreation Area** *(70.8 Parks Hwy. 907-269-8400. http://dnr.alaska.gov/parks. Vehicle fee),* noted for its profusion of wildflowers.

Weather permitting, northbound views of 20,320-foot **Mount McKinley,** highest peak in North America, begin about mile 76. Also called Denali—meaning the "high one" in an Athabaskan dialect—the peak rises 15,000 feet above the surrounding terrain.

For a taste of bush-community life, exit at mile 98.7 and follow the 14.5-mile road to **Talkeetna** (population 450), at the meeting of the Susitna, **Chulitna,** and **Talkeetna Rivers.** Established as a riverboat station in 1910, Talkeetna is now a popular staging area for climbing expeditions to Mount McKinley.

Northbound from the Talkeetna turnoff, the Parks crosses the Susitna *(mile 104.3)* and traverses a boggy region favored by harvesters of edible fiddlehead ferns. Some of the finest stands of white birch in Alaska can be seen for several miles on both sides of the river. About 28 miles beyond,

> **A wide-open, sparsely timbered tundra basin humped with moraines and flanked by soaring ridges, Broad Pass exudes a profound solitude that affects many travelers.**

you enter **Denali State Park** *(907-745-3975. http://dnr.alaska.gov/parks. Closed mid-Oct.–mid-May; vehicle fee).* This primitive 325,240-acre state preserve shares the natural wonders but not the crowds of the adjoining national park.

Few McKinley views match the one from the turnout at mile 135.2, where signs identify various **Alaska Range** landmarks. In another 20 miles you will be able to see the rugged **Eldridge Glacier,** just 6 miles west of the road. Turnouts along here lead to creeks, beaver ponds, and good fishing spots. Near **Little Coal Creek** *(mile 163.8),* you see the imposing **Kesugi Ridge** rising steeply to the east.

At mile 174, the road crosses the bridge above 260-foot-deep **Hurricane Gulch,** then continues north to **Broad Pass** *(mile 201.3),* whose summit marks a watershed divide: From here, north-flowing streams drain into the Yukon River and south-flowing into the Cook Inlet. Descending toward the **Jack River,** the highway rides the crest of a long hill running parallel with similar ridges, with **Summit Lake** in between. These are drumlins, carved by glaciers moving parallel to their lengths.

The Denali Highway *(closed Oct.–mid-May)* intersects at sleepy **Cantwell,** an Alaska Railroad flag stop. North of town, the road skirts the **Reindeer Hills** and joins the **Nenana River,** popular with canoeists and kayakers. River and road cross at mile 215.7 beside 5,778-foot **Panorama Mountain.** Toward evening, sunlight and shadows on 4,476-foot **Mount Fellows** *(mile 234)* can be gorgeous.

Traffic builds near the entrance to **Denali National Park and Preserve** *(mile 237.3. 907-683-2294. www.nps.gov/dena. Park open all year, services May-Sept., depending on weather; adm. fee).* Only the first 15 miles of the interior park road are open to private vehicles; shuttles provide further access. Reservations on the shuttle are a must. The park's renowned beauty and wildlife attract heavy summer crowds. The **visitor center,** 0.7 mile from the highway, has information.

North of the park entrance, the highway negotiates the steep **Nenana River Canyon.** Its luminous slopes are rich in phyllite, a lustrous rock containing small particles of mica. Scan the heights above **Moody Bridge** *(mile 242.9)* for Dall sheep.

383

This region is rich in coal, and between miles 247 and 251 dark seams stripe the eastern bluffs. The Usibelli Coal Mine, east of Healy, is Alaska's top producer. Between Healy and the **Rex Bridge** *(mile 279.8),* the highway follows the Nenana over boggy terrain, then veers east away from the river.

In the town of **Nenana** *(mile 304.5)* the highway rejoins the Nenana River at its confluence with the 440-mile-long **Tanana River,** which is one of Alaska's few commercially navigable inland waterways.

Denali shuttle bus yielding to a grizzly

Between Nenana and Fairbanks, far horizons suggest the scale of Alaskan terrain. The plain extending west from mile 318 includes **Minto Flats State Game Refuge** *(907-459-7213),* a primordially pristine wildlife sanctuary. Look south for a wide perspective on the circuitous Tanana.

The Parks ends near downtown **Fairbanks,** at the junction with Alas. 2. Don't miss the **University of Alaska Museum of the North** *(907-474-7505. www.uaf.edu/museum. Adm. fee),* the state's premier cultural, historical, and scientific showcase. The nature walk through fields and woods at 1,800-acre **Creamer's Field Migratory Waterfowl Refuge** *(1300 College Rd. 907-459-7307. www.creamersfield.org. Visitors center Sat.)* offers glimpses of moose, fox, and snowshoe hare.

Glenn Highway

Anchorage to Glennallen on Alaska 1

- 135 miles ▪ 4 hours ▪ June to mid-September. Be aware of heavy traffic, winter frost heaves and bumps, and narrow stretches. Distances designated by mileposts.

Angling across south-central Alaska, this drive begins at Cook Inlet and follows glacially carved river valleys between the towering peaks of the Chugach and Talkeetna Mountains to the foot of the wild Wrangell Mountains.

Leaving Anchorage, the highway skirts **Knik Arm,** a fjord off Cook Inlet, and the western reach of the **Chugach Mountains.** Great views and the possibility of seeing moose, bear, and Dall sheep justify a 13-mile side trip to **Chugach State Park Visitor Center** *(Eagle River exit at mile 13.4. 907-345-5014. http://dnr.alaska.gov/parks. May–Labor Day; adm. fee).*

Alaska's Athabaskan and Russian heritage live on at the **Eklutna Historical Park** *(mile 26 exit. 907-688-6026. www.eklutnahistoricalpark.org. Mid-May–Sept.; adm. fee),* where Orthodox churches and colorful cemetery "spirit houses" combine Russian-Slavic and Deda'ina Athabaskan design.

Take the Old Glenn Highway from mile 29.6 and loop 18.6 miles through the **Matanuska Valley Colony,** a Depression-era agricultural project that relocated some 200 impoverished Great Lakes farm families. The old and new routes rejoin in **Palmer,** a pleasant town of 3,000 in the **Matanuska Valley.**

About 17 miles from Palmer on the spur road, the **Independence Mine State Historical Park** *(mile 49.5 exit onto Hatcher Pass Rd. 907-745-3975. http://dnr .alaska.gov/parks. Daily June–Labor Day; adm. fee)* is a relic from the region's gold-mining past. Back on the Glenn about a mile farther on, the **Musk Ox Farm** *(907-745-4151. www.muskoxfarm.org. May-Sept.; adm. fee)* breeds the hoofed, shaggy Ice Age survivors that were hunted nearly to extinction in the 19th century. Their ultralight underwool, called qiviut, is worked by an Eskimo knitting cooperative.

Heading east, the Glenn Highway follows the **Matanuska River** between the northerly **Talkeetna Mountains** and the southerly Chugach. Aspen and cottonwood color autumn along here, and there's an impressive view of 4,541-foot **Pinnacle Mountain** at mile 66.5, where the transparent **Kings River** joins the muddy Matanuska. Turnouts at miles 70.6 and 71 offer river access.

Matanuska River Glacier

At mile 93 you can see **Monument Glacier,** a rock glacier formed from the stony debris carried by an ice glacier. Trails from **Matanuska Glacier State Recreation Site** *(mile 101)* lead to unobstructed views of 1,000-foot-thick **Matanuska Glacier**

Moose crossing Glenn Highway

(access to its base is by private road from mile 102. 907-745-2534. May-Oct., by reservation in winter; adm. fee). Striated by broken rock, the glacier flows 27 miles from 13,000-foot-high Chugach ice fields. It once reached Knik Arm, flowing through what is now the Matanuska Valley. Turnouts at mile 102.8 and 107.8 offer photogenic perspectives. Between mile 107 and 118, look for Dall sheep on 6,300-foot **Sheep Mountain** to the north. Wildflowers bloom along this stretch, including pink fireweed (named for its quick reappearance after fires) and yellow-eyed, blue-petaled alpine forget-me-not, the state flower.

Around 3,000-foot **Tahneta Pass** *(mile 122),* sparse stands of stunted black spruce struggle to survive in sodden muskeg. The views are splendid from 3,322-foot **Eureka Summit** *(mile 129.3),* the Glenn's loftiest

Road crews take advantage of short Alaskan summers, so expect gravel, dust, or mud.

pass and the divide of the Matanuska, Susitna, and Copper River systems. Looking east from mile 131 you'll see the **Wrangell Range,** which reaches elevations exceeding 16,000 feet. This is caribou country, and in autumn you may spot migrating herds.

Tazlina Glacier and 20-mile long **Tazlina Lake** appear near mile 156. Abundant meltwater keeps hundreds of lakes and ponds brimming. A 20-mile side road at mile 159.8 leads to **Lake Louise,** a good spot for fishing and boating.

The falling-down "drunken forests" seen in this area are the result of trees growing in soil too soggy to hold them upright. At mile 176.6, a turnout affords a fine view east across **Copper River Valley** to the Wrangells. An interpretive sign identifies 14,163-foot **Mount Wrangell,** a steaming, semidormant volcano. The Wrangell peaks, among the highest in mammoth Wrangell–St. Elias National Park and Preserve, dominate easterly vistas as you approach Glennallen and the junction with Alas. 4, the Richardson Highway (see pp. 386-388).

Richardson Highway

Glennallen to Valdez on Alaska 4

- 115 miles - ½ day - June to mid-September. Mileposts record mileages in reverse, from Valdez to Glennallen.

The Richardson Highway got its start as a treacherous gold rush trail heading to the Klondike. This portion of the historic route travels through south-central Alaska, skirting volcano country, passing through tundra and forest, and arcing over barren ridges where glaciers slide from ice fields.

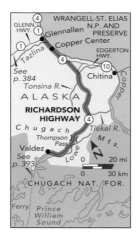

Begin east of **Glennallen** by heading south on the Richardson Highway from its junction with the Glenn Highway (see pp. 384-385). Stop at the viewpoint near mile 112 for a long vista across the **Copper River** to a quartet of snowcapped peaks, highest of the **Wrangell Mountains**. The tallest two, **Mount Sanford** and **Mount Blackburn,** exceed 16,000 feet. Near mile 111 you'll cross the **Tazlina River,** where there is an ideal picnic spot. The Tazlina—"swift river" in Athabaskan—flows from Tazlina Glacier, north of Valdez, into the Copper River at Glennallen.

At mile 106 a 6.5-mile loop road leads to **Copper Center** on the western edge of Wrangell–St. Elias, an 1896 gold rush-era refuge for snowbound tenderfeet. The vintage log **Copper Center Lodge** *(907-822-3245)* offers rustic rooms and sourdough-style fare. Two adjoining old log bunkhouses con-

tain the **George Ashby Memorial Museum** *(June-Sept.; donation),* an eclectic display of artifacts that include items from Russian settlements.

At the **Wrangell–St. Elias National Park and Preserve Visitor Center** *(mile 105 between Copper Center loop-road turnoffs. 907-822-5234. www.nps.gov/wrst. Daily May-Sept., Mon.-Fri. rest of year),* you can obtain information on this 13.2-million-acre area, America's largest national park.

Fishing from a floatplane, Willow Lake

Heading south from here, you'll cross rolling hills of paper birch, black spruce, and willow trees, a region favored by homesteaders earlier in this century. The **Willow Lake Turnoff** *(mile 87.7)* offers an excellent view of the ice fields of the Wrangell Mountains, and a mile farther on you come to the roaring Trans-Alaska Pipeline System's **Pump Station 11.** Signs explain how two or three pumps move about 1.8 million barrels of oil a day 800 miles from Prudhoe Bay to Port Valdez.

The Edgerton Highway *(mile 82.6)* permits an easy 33-mile side trip to **Chitina** (pop. 49), a former railroad stop and supply center on the Copper River. In the summer, hordes of dip-netters gather here for the annual salmon runs.

Fisherman on the Little Tonsina River

Back on the Richardson, opposite Tonsina Lodge *(mile 79)* you'll see layers of silt, sediments, and cobbles dropped by melting icebergs, evidence that a deep glacial lake once covered the area. As you travel the **Tiekel River Valley,** watch for grazing moose along the 20-mile stretch beginning at the **Little Tonsina River State Recreation Area** *(mile 65.1. 907-269-8400. Mem. Day–Labor Day; parking fee).* Nearby **Pump Station 12** also has an interpretive viewpoint.

Silence reigns again along the **Tiekel River,** where, beginning around mile 60, you'll see beaver dams and lodges. In summer, deep red dwarf fireweed and blue arctic lupine decorate the roadside. The riverside rest area at mile 47.9 looks up at 7,217-foot **Mount Billy Mitchell,** and a couple of miles beyond, grassy **Stuart Creek** attracts nesting trumpeter swans in spring and summer.

As the highway angles through the **Tsina River Valley,** the sheer cliffs rising from the moraines were worn smooth by passing glaciers. When the valley narrows, stop to savor the soothing murmur of rushing streams and take in the nearly 360-degree panorama of soaring peaks. From here the highway climbs to **Worthington Glacier** *(mile 28.7).*

From Valdez, a day-long ferry voyage across Prince William Sound to Seward sets up a lovely drive north on the Seward Highway back to Anchorage.

Continue on to barren 2,678-foot **Thompson Pass** *(mile 26),* which holds Alaska's seasonal snowfall record (81 feet). Snow patches on the pass often last through summer. Push your hand into one: Its density suggests how the weight of accumulating snow layers compacts the underlayers into ice so dense its crystals absorb all but the blue spectrum of light, thus giving glaciers their distinctive blue color.

The stone ramparts of the **Chugach Mountains** loom as you descend to **Heiden Canyon** and the **Blueberry Lake State Recreation Site** *(mile 25 off Richardson Hwy. 907-269-8400. Mem. Day–Labor Day; parking fee),* considered one of Alaska's most idyllic alpine settings. Around mile 16, you'll enter precipitous **Keystone Canyon.** Whitewater enthusiasts relish the challenges of the **Lowe River,** which tumbles through the gorge. Look above the highway for terraced remnants of the original **Valdez-Eagle Trail,** built for horse-drawn sleds and wagons. Violent feuds among competing early railroaders left the roadside tunnel *(mile 14.9)* unfinished. Along this stretch, waterfalls cascade into the canyon.

387

Mount Drum, Wrangell Mountains

You'll emerge from Keystone Canyon beside the gravel plain of the **Lowe River Delta** and cross the moraine of **Valdez Glacier** *(mile 0.9)*. **Valdez Arm,** an 11-mile-long fjord, is America's northernmost ice-free harbor. The old Valdez townsite was abandoned after its waterfront was submerged during the devastating 1964 earthquake.

As you approach Valdez, watch for **Duck Flat,** a migratory waterfowl sanctuary, and nearby **Crooked Creek,** where spawning salmon converge in midsummer and fall. An observation platform permits a close look at the fish. This and other local phenomena are superbly explained at the downtown **Valdez Museum** *(907-835-2764. www.valdezmuseum.org. Daily in summer, Tues.-Fri. fall-spring; adm. fee),* which celebrates the region's dramatic human and geologic history. Once in Valdez, stop by the **Alyeska Pipeline Visitor Center** *(Tatitlek St. 907-835-2686)* for details and information about the pipeline's history and construction.

Seward Highway

Anchorage to Seward on Alaska 1 and 9

- 127 miles (one way) ▪ 1 day ▪ June to mid-September.
Mileposts record mileages in reverse, from Seward to Anchorage.
Currently there is no ferry service from Seward so you must
drive this road round-trip.

A remarkably compact sampler of Alaska's trademark natural phenomena, this national forest scenic byway in south-central Alaska includes fjords, glaciers, mountain ranges, alpine lakes and meadows, evergreen forests, and wildlife-rich wetlands.

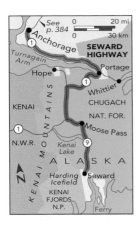

From Anchorage take either the New or Old Seward Highway south. They merge as Alas. 1 near **Turnagain Arm,** an easterly extension of **Cook Inlet** gouged by Ice Age glaciers. At the **Anchorage Coastal Wildlife Refuge** *(mile 117. 907-267-2342. www.travelalaska.com)* you'll gain a sense of Alaska's dramatic geology: Looking 75 miles west, you can see 11,070-foot **Mount Spurr,** an active volcano looming above the **Alaska Range,** one of North America's highest mountain systems. Easterly views are dominated by the jagged ridges of the **Chugach Mountains,** lifted to over 13,000 feet by colliding continental plates, then crushed by ancient glaciers. Across Turnagain Arm the spires of the **Kenai Mountains** crown the spruce and hemlock wilderness of the **Chugach National Forest** *(907-743-9500. www.fs.usda.gov/chugach).*

Around mile 117 you'll see **Potter Marsh,** a watery expanse of sedges and willows. Stroll across the wetland on the elevated boardwalk; if you're here in spring and summer, look for pairs of trumpeter swans, Canada geese, mallard, and pintail. From mid-July to mid-August the wetland teems with fish, including chinook salmon that average 3 feet and 40 pounds.

Two miles farther on, Alas. 1 passes the **Potter Section House,** a camp for crews who maintained the railroad in this area during the age of steam. The site now serves as **Chugach State Park Headquarters** *(907-345-5021. http://dnr.alaska.gov/parks. Closed weekends).*

For the next 36 miles the highway follows Turnagain's north shore. The phenomenal bore tides here, with ranges of 40 feet, occur about 2.25 hours after low tide in Anchorage and are seen best from turnouts between miles 95 and 90. Don't venture onto these flats, whose deep quicksands have proved fatal. Stop at **Beluga Point** near mile 110 for a sweeping panorama of Turnagain Arm and the possibility of seeing the white whales for which the point is named.

As you continue south on Alas. 1, near mile 80 you'll see what remains of **Portage,** a village abandoned after the 1964 earthquake dropped the site onto a tidal plain. At the motor vehicle–loading area for the **Alaska Railroad**

389

Brown bear roams the shoreline

(907-265-2494 or 265-2343. www.alaskarailroad.com. Fare), you can drive onto flatcars for a half-hour run over wetlands and through pitch black tunnels to **Whittier.** Here, the ferries of the **Alaska's Ferry Adventures** (800-382-9229. www.ferryalaska.com. Mon.-Sat.; fare; see pp. 393-397) head across **Prince William Sound,** passing mammoth Columbia Glacier on their way to Valdez and Cordova.

Aurora borealis lighting the Alaskan wilderness

Back on Alas. 1, you soon see **Portage Glacier,** which offers a superb opportunity to gauge the colossal power of Alaska's fabled mountain-crushing rivers of ice. Drive 5.2 miles, past **Explorer** and **Middle Glaciers,** to the **Begich Boggs Visitor Center** (907-783-2326. Daily in summer, closed winter; adm. fee). Stroll the gravel beach of milky **Portage Lake,** where icebergs calved by the glaciers melt into graceful shapes. During August and September nearby **Williwaw Creek** churns with spawning salmon.

Near mile 78 you'll hook around the end of Turnagain Arm and cross the broad **Placer River Delta.** The river's silty gray waters flow from nearby ice masses. The ascent to 988-foot **Turnagain Pass** follows the steep **Ingram Creek Canyon** to alpine meadows that in summer are as green as billiard tables and decorated with wildflowers. Stands of hemlock, spruce, and cottonwood quiver in summer breezes, and the cottonwood flash tawny yellow in autumn. Above tree line are slopes of glinting stone polished by long-gone glaciers. At the pass near mile 68 you'll see low mounds on the flats south of the rest stop. These are moraines—gravel terraces deposited by retreating glaciers. The scars on the mountainside east of the road mark avalanche paths.

The mudflats of Turnagain Arm are flooded daily by a fast-moving bore tide whose 40-foot range ranks it as one of the greatest in the world.

Near mile 56 you'll come to the Hope Highway, a 17.7-mile route north and west to the historic gold-mining community of **Hope** on Turnagain's south shore. Bear left to stay on the byway and follow Canyon Creek to **Summit Lake Lodge** (mile 45.5. 907-244-2031. www.summit lakelodge.com. Closed Nov.-March). The handsome, peeled-log lakeside inn is an excellent place to stop and sample hearty Alaskan cuisine.

At mile 37 bear left onto Alas. 9 for Seward. Nearby **Tern Lake** is a noted bird-watching site deep in the **Kenai Mountains.** You might also want to check out the local sourdough color in **Moose Pass,** a spunky hamlet in the crook of Y-shaped **Upper Trail Lake.**

Starting around mile 24 you'll skirt the southern reach of **Kenai Lake,** whose 24-mile-long bed was gouged by glaciers. Farther on, placid **Snow River** backwaters flank the highway. Patrolled by beavers and grazed by moose, these pools are thick in summer with yellow pond lilies that resemble golden teacups on floating saucers of jade. Stop at **Grayling Lake Trailhead** *(mile 13)* for a view east up the pristine **Snow River Valley.** Near mile 4, a good 9-mile road leads to **Exit Glacier** in **Kenai Fjords National Park** *(907-224-2132 or 907-224-2125. www.nps.gov/kefj).* An easy half-mile trail ends at the glacier's 150-foot-high seracs, spires of broken blue ice at its base. An arduous 3.5-mile trail leads to the **Harding Ice Field,** third largest on the continent.

Lily pond in Chugach National Forest

When you arrive in **Seward** *(Chamber of Commerce, 2001 Seward Hwy. 907-224-8051. www.sewardchamber.org),* take a leisurely walking tour of the town. This ruggedly hospitable sportfishing center on **Resurrection Bay** has been the Kenai Peninsula's principal port since 1903.

Haines Highway

Haines, Alaska, to Haines Junction, Yukon Territory, on Alaska 7 (the Haines Highway)

■ 44 miles ■ 1 hour ■ Year-round (but check the weather conditions)

Linking the southeastern Alaskan port of Haines to Canada's Yukon Territory, this highway (named a scenic byway in 2009) is a frequent starting point for drivers who ferry their cars up from the Lower 48 intending to drive a section of the Alaska Highway after crossing the Yukon. But, at just 44 miles in length, the highway also makes a fine up-and-back day trip for visitors to **Haines.**

Few roads pack in as much as the Haines Highway does in its 44 miles. The Haines Highway provides a link to the history of the Chilkat Indians and immerses visitors in the culture of the Tlingit people. It follows the horse trail used during the Klondike gold rush. Between October and February, it rewards travelers with one of the world's largest gatherings of bald eagles. And a drive along the Haines Highway offers a taste of classic road food: The historic 33 Mile Roadhouse toward the end of the byway serves up some of the best (and biggest) burgers and pie slices in Alaska.

Keep cameras at the ready during the drive: The Chilkat River, a constant companion throughout the drive, and surrounding woodland give a wide variety of wildlife reason to stick around. Bears, moose, beavers, and

Bald eagle

more may be part of the day's sightings. Last but far from least, keep in mind that while it's important to check weather conditions frequently during any season when driving in Alaska, it's essential during the fall and winter months, when roads can become treacherous in no time. For the latest weather conditions, visit 511.Alaska.gov or 511yukon.ca.

Anchor the drive in knowledge of the area. Start at the **Convention and Visitors Bureau** *(122 2nd Ave. 907-766-2234. www.haines.ak.us. Closed weekends Oct.–mid-May)* in Haines for maps or other last-minute information. Then pop into the nearby **Hammer Museum** *(108 Main St. 907-766-2374. www.hammermuseum.org. Open weekdays May-Sept.).* What at first seems merely quirky quickly becomes memorable. The museum's extensive collection of namesake objects spotlights the tool's place throughout history. Before the visit is over, the owner will have even the most tool-apathetic reconsidering his or her interest level.

Just steps away (so no need to move the car), the **Sheldon Museum and Cultural Center** *(Main St. & 1st Ave. 907-766-2366. www.sheldonmuseum.org. Closed Sun. mid-Sept.–mid-May; adm. fee)* returns visitors to the task at hand: learning about the region's history, its people, and their close link to nature. The museum sits on a fjord, the **Lynn Canal.**

Then head down Second Avenue to explore the historic buildings at **Fort William H. Seward.** See demonstrations of traditional arts, including totem pole carving and printmaking, at **Alaska Indian Arts** *(907-766-2160. www.alaskaindianarts.com. Closed weekends & winter).* The artisans also sell their work through the center.

Drive a few blocks back up Second Avenue and turn left onto the Haines Highway. About a mile from town, the **Charlie Anway Cabin** *(under renovation at publication time)* offers a glimpse at homesteading life in the early 1900s. A few minutes later, at miles 9 and 10, pull off to see fish wheels on the Chilkat River. The modern-day devices, used to catch salmon as they make their way up the Chilkat, are based on technology developed by the Tlingit.

At mile 9.4, the rural highway passes through one of the drive's great delights: the **Alaska Chilkat Bald Eagle Preserve** *(http://dnr.alaska.gov/parks/units/eagleprv.htm).* While some 400 bald eagles live year-round in the 48,000-acre preserve, it simply teems with eagles from fall into winter when the waters get thick with salmon. This is the last salmon run in the entire state—and the eagles are drawn by the good feeding. The best spots for eagle viewing are along the flats from miles 18 to 24. Don't walk onto the flats, though, as this disturbs the eagles.

In the midst of the preserve, at mile 18.7, sits **Kluktoo**—or rather, the site that was Kluktoo. Just after a shaman had a vision of the village's destruction and persuaded its Tlingit residents to move a few miles away to **Klukwan,** a landslide wiped out the former village site in 1919.

At mile 21.5, don't turn toward Klukwan itself; instead, visit the **Jilkaat Kwaan Cultural Heritage Center** *(www.visitklukwan.com)*. Run by residents of Klukwan, the cultural center gives visitors an in-depth look at the Tlingit way of life. In the craft shed, master artisans teach local teens how to carve totem poles, hand-build boats, and more. The **Bentwood Box Gift Store** stocks crafts by local artisans, many of whom are working to revive traditional Tlingit arts.

Before Haines was established in 1878, the area's original inhabitants, the Chilkat Indians, called it Dei Shu or "End of the Trail."

Then it's time for those burgers and that pie. At mile 33, the aptly named and kid-friendly **33 Mile Roadhouse** *(907-767-5510. www.33mileroadhouse.com)* serves top-notch road food. Vegetarians can indulge, too: The restaurant does serve a veggie burger. There are also rental cabins for those who want to stretch out their drive experience. Be sure to gas up adequately before hitting the road: The Roadhouse's gas tends toward the pricier side.

The road winds along the river for another 11 miles before ending at the **U.S./Canada border.** From there, you can get out your passports and start a **Yukon** adventure.

Alaska's Marine Highway

Bellingham, Washington, to Unalaska/Dutch Harbor, Alaska, on regularly scheduled ferries

■ 3,500 miles ■ One-day excursions to several weeks for extensive travel along coast ■ Late spring through fall. Check for winter ferry schedules.

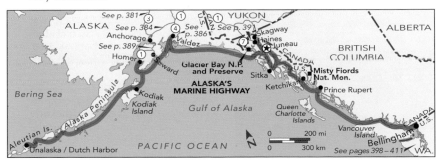

Uniquely among all America's byways, Alaska's Marine Highway carries travelers from point to point entirely by water. This is unusual for a "highway" system, of course—but Alaska is an unusual state. With only a little more than half a million people in an area one-fifth the size of the lower 48 states, Alaska is a place of rugged terrain, few roads, and scattered towns and cities, where the best way to get around is often by airplane or boat.

The **Alaska Marine Highway Ferry System** *(800-382-9229. Mon.-Sat. www.dot.state.ak.us/amhs/pubs)* is an official arm of the state's Department of Transportation and Public Facilities. Its operation is vital to many communities along the coasts of the Pacific Ocean and Gulf of Alaska, providing the major means of transport for both people and goods. (Even though there are roads in and around towns, many towns are not connected by highway to "the rest of the world.") Connecting with the Marine Highway system and serving a smaller area in the state's southeast corner is the **Inter-Island Ferry Authority** *(866-308-4848. www.interislandferry.com).*

On an Alaska marine ferry, you'll be in the company of both tourists on extended vacation and locals traveling short distances for work or personal reasons. Ferries accommodate buses, recreational vehicles, automobiles, motorcycles, bicycles, and "walk-ons." Overnight travelers can book a private cabin, although some simply sleep in a lounge chair, roll out a sleeping bag on deck, or even pitch a tent. Individual vessels differ in their amenities and food options, ranging from dining rooms to cafeteria-style meals to vending machines. It's always best to check the ferry system website for fares and details on the exact route you're considering. Ferry schedules make possible an almost limitless range of possible itineraries. In any case, for most people, a trip on the ferry is unlike any journey they've experienced before.

What's in store along the way? Astonishing scenery every mile, including coastal fjords, glaciers, volcanoes, mountains, and rain forests. Whales, sea otters, sea lions, seals, bald eagles, and a great variety of seabirds can be spotted regularly. On summer trips, interpreters from the Forest Service and the Fish and Wildlife Service are often on board to talk about wildlife and the coastal environment. In addition to the dramatic vistas and wildlife, your fellow passengers will always include a range of interesting people, reflecting those who are drawn to visit Alaska as well as those who choose to live in this often demanding state on the edge of the frontier.

Two ports of the Marine Highway are located outside Alaska: Travelers can board a ferry at Bellingham, Washington, or Prince Rupert, British Columbia. The southern part of the Marine Highway is known as the **Inside Passage,** where the route winds among islands (around 1,500 are found

along this section of the coast) covered in temperate rain forest of Sitka spruce, western hemlock, and cedar. Humpback whales, sea lions, harbor seals, killer whales, and Dall's porpoises swim in the cold waters.

At the Alaska border, the route nears **Misty Fiords National Monument,** administered by Tongass National Forest *(907-225-3101. www.fs.fed.us/r10/tongass).* Travelers who want to explore Alaska's wild places need good advice, careful planning, and plenty of respect for its remoteness, its challenges, and its wildlife. In **Ketchikan** *(Visitors Bureau, 131 Front St. 907-225-6166 or 800-770-3300. www.visit-ketchikan.com),* the major port in extreme southern Alaska, you can visit the **Southeast Alaska Discovery Center** *(50 Main St. 907-228-6220. Closed Sun.-Mon. Oct.-May; adm. fee)* to learn about the possibilities. The **Totem Heritage Center** *(601 Deermount St. 907-225-5900. Closed weekends Oct.-May;*

Totem pole, Sitka, AK

Sea otters resting on icebergs

adm. fee) displays historic and re-created totems of the Tlingit and Haida who lived nearby in the 19th century.

Sitka *(Convention & Visitors Bureau. 907-747-5940. www.sitka.org)* was home to Tlingit Indians before Russian fur traders moved in and made it the capital of Russian America. When Russia sold Alaska to the United States for 7.2 million dollars in 1867, the transfer ceremony took place here; Sitka then served as capital of Alaska Territory until 1906. Set on Baranof Island, Sitka still preserves aspects of Tlingit and Russian cultures. Visit **Sitka National Historical Park** *(106 Metlakatla St. 907-747-0110. www.nps.gov/sitk. Adm. fee)* for an overview of local history, including Haida and Tlingit totem poles, Tlingit and Russian artifacts, the site of a Tlingit fort, the 1843 Russian bishop's house (one of the last surviving examples of Russian colonial architecture in North America), and the **Southeast Alaska Indian Cultural Center** *(907-747-8061. Donation),* where Tlingit artists work and interpret their cultures for visitors. The **Sheldon Jackson Museum** *(104 College Dr. 907-747-8981. www.museums.state.ak.us. Closed Sun.-Mon. in winter; adm. fee)* houses a fine collection of Native artifacts and cultural displays.

Alaska's capital city, **Juneau** *(Convention & Visitors Bureau, 1 Sealaska Plaza. 907-586-1737 or 800-587-2201. www.traveljuneau.com),* a popular cruise-ship stop, has many attractions, one of which is the region's most visited glacier. The visitor center of **Mendenhall Glacier** *(907-789-0097. Adm. fee),* located 13 miles from downtown, is operated by the Forest Service and features interpreters and several trails that approach the glacier. The **Alaska State Museum** *(395 Whittier St. 907-465-2901. www.museums.state.ak.us. Closed Mon. late Sept.–mid-May; adm. fee)* displays clothing, weapons, tools, and ceremonial objects from Native peoples, icons from the Russian period, and natural history exhibits including a life-size eagle nest.

A side route of the Marine Highway leads to **Haines** *(Convention & Visitors Bureau. 907-766-2234 or 800-458-3579. www.haines.ak.us),* where many people offload vehicles to connect with the Alaska Highway, 153 miles north in Canada's Yukon. The town is best known for the **Chilkat Bald Eagle Preserve** *(Haines Ranger Station. 907-766-2292. http://dnr.alaska.gov/parks)*

on the Chilkat River north of town, where hundreds of eagles gather from October through February. This segment of the route also accesses **Skagway** *(Convention & Visitors Bureau. 907-983-2854. www.skagway.com),* offering another road connection to the Alaska Highway. Skagway was the gateway to the Klondike during the world-famous gold rush of 1898, when thousands of would-be millionaires made the difficult trek northward after gathering supplies in Seattle. The best place to learn about those rough-and-tumble years is the **Klondike Gold Rush National Historical Park** *(291 2nd Ave. 907-983-9200. www.nps.gov/klgo. May-Sept.),* which preserves 15 buildings in the town's historic district; park rangers lead interpretive walks.

Fireweed and glacier

Continuing north, the Marine Highway passes **Glacier Bay National Park and Preserve** *(907-697-2661. www.nps.gov/glba).* Ferries provide no access to it, although commercial cruise ships and tours do. Wildlife species in these waters include humpback whales (which summer here after wintering near Hawaii and Baja California), minke whales, killer whales, harbor and Dall's porpoises, Steller sea lions, harbor seals, and sea otters.

Valdez *(Convention & Visitors Bureau, 200 Fairbanks St. 907-835-4636. www.valdezalaska.org)* gained fame as the southern terminus of the trans-Alaska oil pipeline, but its history goes back to its days as a port for prospectors in the 1898 gold rush. Devastated by an earthquake in 1964, Valdez attracts anglers, river rafters, skiers, and visitors who explore nearby glaciers and mountains by trail or flightseeing.

The small town of **Homer** *(Visitor Information Center, 201 Sterling Hwy. 907-235-7740. www.homeralaska .org)* is known as an arts community, as well as for the boating and fishing services available along the 5-mile Homer Spit, where a boardwalk leads past galleries, shops, and cafes. Homer is headquarters for the **Alaska Maritime National Wildlife Refuge** *(907-235-6546. http://alaskamaritime.fws.gov),* which administers a vast area of ocean and islands, home to marine mammals, seabirds, and countless other species. Visit the **Alaska Islands and Ocean Visitor Center** *(95 Sterling Hwy. 907-235-6961. www.islandsandocean.org)* to take a virtual trip to a remote seabird colony and enjoy the "One Big Ocean" exhibit on sea ecology.

Many misjudge Alaska's temperatures. Consider that during January 1936 Homer had 11 consecutive days when the temperature did not fall below 40 degrees.

Crossing Kennedy Entrance to Cook Inlet, the route reaches **Kodiak Island** (*Convention & Visitors Bureau. 100 E. Marine Way, #200. 907-486-4782 or 800-789-4782. www.kodiak.org*), a major commercial fishing port, but most notable as home for the huge Kodiak brown bear. (It's also the second largest island in the United States, after the main island of Hawaii.) Kodiak Island has long been home to the Alutiiq, who maintain their traditions through dances, songs, and other arts. In the town of Kodiak, the **Alutiiq Museum** (*215 Mission Rd. 907-486-7004. www.alutiiqmuseum.org. Closed Tues. June-Aug., Sun.-Mon. Sept.-May; adm. fee*) preserves local culture with educational exhibits and programs.

Many people visit Kodiak Island to see the famed brown bears, which number close to 3,000. Companies offer a variety of tours for bear viewing, ranging from half-day trips by plane to lengthy stays at remote wilderness lodges. **Kodiak National Wildlife Refuge** (*1390 Buskin River Rd. 907-487-2600. www.fws.gov/refuge/kodiak*), established in 1941 to protect the bears' habitat, covers the southern two-thirds of the island.

From Kodiak, the Marine Highway now begins a long, long journey westward, visiting ports in the Aleutian Islands. (The route extends only partway across the Aleutians, which stretch across 1,100 miles, separating the Pacific Ocean from the Bering Sea.) Service is suspended because of severe weather in winter. Ferries dock at several small fishing towns, reaching the end of the Marine Highway at **Unalaska/Dutch Harbor** (*Convention & Visitors Bureau. 5 Broadway Ave. 907-581-2612 or 877-581-2612. www.unalaska.info*), the largest community in the Aleutians. **Unalaska** is the nation's highest volume fishing port and seafood-processing center. Most travelers come for the fishing (halibut and salmon are most popular), but Unalaska also attracts a small but steady stream of bird-watchers. The rare whiskered auklet, a small seabird, nests only in the Aleutians, and birders hoping to add it to their life lists take charter trips to its nesting grounds on the eastern end of Unalaska Island and the nearby Baby Islands.

The **Church of the Holy Ascension** (*contact the Convention & Visitors Bureau for details on visiting*), dating from the mid-1890s, features two Russian-style onion domes and artifacts. The **Museum of the Aleutians** (*314 Salmon Way. 907-581-5150. www.aleutians.org. Closed Mon., and also Sun. in winter; adm. fee*) presents exhibits on the culture and history of the Aleutians and Pribilof Islands, including grass baskets, sculpture, tools, masks, and weapons. The **Aleutian World War II National Historical Park** (*907-581-9944. www.nps.gov/aleu. Permit and fee*) interprets the role of the Aleutian Islands and the native Unangan people during World War II. The **visitor center** (*Thurs.-Sun.*) near the Unalaska dock has exhibits, and the park preserves structures that had been deteriorating in the harsh Aleutian weather.

Orca "spy-hopping"

Washington
Mount Baker Scenic Byway

Glacier to Artist Point on Washington 542

▪ 24 miles ▪ 1 hour ▪ Summer to early fall. Final portion to Artist Point is closed in winter.

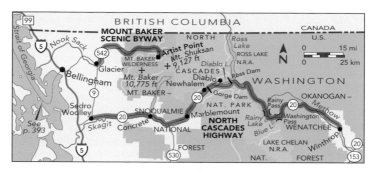

Embraced by the Mount Baker Wilderness, this spur road takes you deep into the kind of rugged high country usually seen only by backpackers. For the last 10 miles the switchbacking drive gains 3,200 feet in elevation, affording you panoramic views of the Cascade Range.

Start by picking up information at the Forest Service's **Glacier Public Service Center** *(360-599-2714. www.nps.gov/noca. June-Sept., call for winter hours).*

Mount Baker Scenic Byway

From here the scenic byway follows the **North Fork Nooksack River** through a forest of old-growth and second-growth evergreens. After about 7 miles, Wells Creek Road leads south less than a mile to **Nooksack Falls,** a stunning 175-foot-high waterfall. Back on the byway, you soon pass several turnouts with views of a thrashing, white-water stretch of the river hundreds of feet below.

After 13 miles, you pass the **Silver Fir Campground.** Here, through a forest of big trees, you begin to glimpse the burly, glacier-clad mountains ahead. Within a couple of miles the high country comes into full view as the road leaves the dense forests and snakes steeply up the exposed sides of the mountains. Plentiful turnouts allow you to stop and savor the view.

In another 7 miles you enter **Heather Meadows,** where the ground is dominated by eponymous heather and the sky is dominated by 9,127-foot **Mount Shuksan,** a massive patriarch ornamented with rock outcroppings, jagged ridges, and hanging glaciers. A half mile farther, aptly named **Picture Lake** reflects Mount

Shuksan in its placid waters. On the other side of the lake, you'll come to the **Mount Baker Ski Area** *(360-734-6771. www.mtbaker.us. To accommodate skiers, road to this point open all year).* On summer weekends, guided nature walks leave from the **Heather Meadows Visitor Center,** a mile farther up the road.

From the visitor center the road climbs past sobering rock slides and stunted conifers until it reaches the sublime alpine, where earth and sky blur into one. For the last couple of miles, the byway seems suspended in air as it twists skyward, passing a number of trails along the way. The drive makes a stunning finish at 5,140-foot **Artist Point,** where the easy, mile-long **Artist Ridge Trail** puts 10,775-foot **Mount Baker** in your lap.

White Pass Scenic Byway

Marys Corner to Naches, Washington, on US 12

▪ 124 miles ▪ 3 to 6 hours ▪ All year

Stick to the White Pass Scenic Byway without detours or side trips and the route delivers a satisfying day's worth of exploration that includes two national forests, lake-dotted scenery, and small towns ready-made for lazy wandering. But devoting a few extra days to the trip brings outsized rewards: The byway offers easy access to Mount Rainier National Park and Mount St. Helens National Volcanic Monument. White Pass itself cuts across the Cascade Mountains, so—skiers take note—there's serious powder to play with in the area.

Outdoor enthusiasts and photographers will likely find themselves planning return trips to White Pass

to take in its seasonal changes. Fall hikes through foliage ablaze with brilliant reds and oranges give way to winter snowshoeing over snow-covered mountains. In spring and summer, the local farm stands' bounty is reason enough to make the drive: The berries are divine.

Turn off I-5, Washington's main north–south highway, at exit 68 (about 40 miles south of Olympia) onto US 12 east. Almost immediately, there are signs for the first of the White Pass Scenic Byway's treats. Turn right onto Jackson Highway and drive 1.5 miles to **Lewis and Clark State Park** *(712-423-2829. www.parks.wa.gov/parks),* which borders the highway to the south. The 621-acre park—which offers campsites both rustic and with RV services—protects one of the state's largest remaining ancient forests, mostly of Douglas fir and red cedar.

Back on US 12, continue along the tree-lined highway past Mayfield Lake, home to an eponymous state park and **Lake Mayfield Resort and Marina** *(www.lakemayfield.com),* both of which offer boating, camping, and fishing. Along the way, haphazard natural growth patterns give way to gridlike Christmas tree farms. Near the wonderfully named town of **Mossyrock** are a blueberry farm and a tulip farm. If lunch is on your mind, pick up

Emmons Glacier and the volcanic peak
of Mount Rainier

sandwiches in town at the **Country Lunch Box** *(120 E. State St. 360-983-8090)* for a lakeside picnic.

Just after Mossyrock, detour off US 12 to the lunch spot: **Riffe Lake,** a favorite of fishermen and boaters. The 13-mile reservoir abounds with kokanee, three kinds of trout, landlocked salmon, bass, crappie, perch, and more. The lake is bookended by Mossyrock Dam on its western end and Cowlitz Falls Dam to the east, just south of the town of Glenoma.

Back on 12, just before Morton, **Hopkins Hill Viewpoint** looks out on Mount St. Helens's crater. The surrounding landscape, nowhere near as green as the rest of the area, showcases nature's slow return after the 1980 volcanic eruption. (If you get to the town of Morton without the photo op, go back. There's a good chance this is the photo that will be pulled out the most to show to friends back home.)

For those with time to spare, one of several tempting add-ons—if there's time for only one, this is the one—is a trip up to **Mount Rainier National Park** *(360-569-2211. www.nps.gov/mora).* Take a left at Morton onto Wash. 7 and drive 16.5 miles; a section of Gifford Pinchot National Forest borders the road on the left. Make a right at the town of Elbe onto Wash. 706. (This route is especially important to keep in mind if exploring during colder months, because Mount Rainier's other entrances close for winter.)

The town of Ashford is the last stop for gas or cell phone service before the park gates, 23 miles away. If staying the night, Ashford offers several lodging options. But if there's a room open at either of Mount Rainier's two full-service, scenery-drenched hotels, the **National Park Inn** or the **Paradise Inn** *(both 360-569-2275. www.mtrainierguestservices .com),* stay in the park and bask in its wonders.

Before its infamous 1980 eruption, Mount St. Helens was the fifth highest peak in Washington and was known for its remarkably symmetrical summit cone.

The next day, follow Wash. 706 back to Wash. 7 and US 12 to continue east along the scenic byway. (Drivers can also return to 12 by continuing east on 706 and making a right onto Wash. 123—though the road does close for the winter and, at times, through spring.) At Randle, the road again skirts Gifford Pinchot National Forest, home of the Mount St. Helens National Volcanic Monument. To visit, drive south on Wash. 131. When the road forks, continue on National Forest road (NF) 25 and, finally, NF-99. At the end of the road, you'll reach Windy Ridge, with a view of the volcano and an interpretive site about the eruption. After exploring the area, continue back to US 12.

After stopping at the town of **Packwood** (hikers might want to stay and hike the nine-mile Tatoosh Mountain Lookout Trail; the trailhead is on NF-5270, about ten miles northwest of town), continue on to the byway's namesake: **White Pass.** This Cascades ski area averages 350 inches of snow each year. Ten miles later, stop by **Rimrock Lake**—also a favorite of local fishermen. If traveling through in September when the dam is released (and if you have an adventurous streak), set aside several hours for a whitewater rafting trip on the **Tieton River.**

Near the byway's end, drivers pass through **Oak Creek Wildlife Area** *(www.wdfw.wa.gov/lands/wildlife_areas/oak_creek).* Managed by the Washington Department of Fish and Wildlife, the 47,200-acre area offers wintertime visitors the chance to watch elk herds feeding.

Continue on to Naches and the end of the White Pass Scenic Byway. Still ahead is one of Washington's great agricultural areas. Drive on to explore farms, vineyards, and much more.

North Cascades Highway

Sedro Woolley to Winthrop on Washington 20

■ 128 miles ■ 4 hours ■ Late spring to early fall. Road closed from Ross Dam east through Washington Pass November to April. No major services for the 86 miles from Marblemount to Winthrop. *See map p. 398.*

This highway travels from the verdant pastureland of Washington's rainy west to the sagebrush ranching country of the eastern hills and valleys. In between, it weaves past the high peaks and dense forests of North Cascades National Park and surrounding national forest lands.

Begin in **Sedro Woolley** with a stop at the **North Cascades National Park/ Mount Baker Ranger District USGS/North Cascades Institute Information Office** *(On Wash. 20. 360-856-5700).* From here Wash. 20 rolls east through the lower **Skagit River Valley**—a mosaic of farms, orchards, and small ranches edged by low mountains covered in evergreens.

After some 24 miles, you'll enter the town of **Concrete,** named for the material it produced from the 1930s to the 1950s, when it functioned as a company town. Most of its public buildings are still made of concrete.

401

Ross Lake National Recreation Area

East of Concrete, the valley narrows as the mountains grow higher, closing in on the **Skagit River,** a federally designated Wild and Scenic River. During the winter, keep an eye out along the river for bald eagles.

An old store facade in Winthrop, WA

The Skagit chum salmon run then attracts hundreds of the birds, making this one of the largest gatherings of eagles outside Alaska.

About 18 miles farther on, the road enters **Marblemount,** entrance to the "American Alps," as the northern Cascades are called.

Six miles east of Marblemount, you cross **Bacon Creek** and enter the **Ross Lake National Recreation Area,** which is part of **North Cascades National Park** *(360-856-5700. www.nps.gov/noca).* Husky mountains lean in and force the road to cling tightly to the thin ribbon of flatland along the Skagit. In places the river roars through rocky gorges.

A turnoff 9 miles beyond leads to the **North Cascades Visitor Center** *(206-386-4495. May-Oct.),* where fine exhibits explain the natural history of the region. A half mile farther, Wash. 20 passes through **Newhalem,** a little company town built by Seattle City Light to house the workers who operate the three dams on the Skagit.

The first of these, **Gorge Dam,** plugs the river about 3 miles east of Newhalem. Just past it, a high bridge arches above slender, 242-foot **Gorge Creek Falls.** About 3 miles beyond the falls, a turnoff leads to **Diablo.** Here, **Seattle City Light's Tour Center** *(360-854-2589. www.seattle.gov/light/tours/skagit)* offers boat and powerhouse tours *(fare).*

After the Diablo turnoff, the highway skirts dammed reservoirs; turnouts provide sweeping views of these bodies of water and the surrounding mountains. At the **Diablo Lake Overlook,** interpretive signs explain that the green-blue color of the water is the result of rock flour. These suspended particles of fine glacial sediments are washed down from the high country.

Curving along **Diablo Lake** for another 2.5 miles, Wash. 20 passes a turnout for the **Happy Creek Forest Walk,** a 0.3-mile boardwalk that leads through a forest of venerable Douglas-firs towering above their younger offspring. The older firs survived a fire long ago and provided the seeds for the regeneration of the grove.

On its way from Canada to Mexico, the 2,600-mile-long Pacific Crest Trail wanders through the spectacular North Cascades high country, crossing the road in some places.

About 4 miles beyond, the road enters **Okanogan-Wenatchee National Forest** *(509-548-5807. www.fs.usda.gov/okawen. Trailer & camping fees).* Climbing southeast along **Granite Creek,** you drive through splendid raw mountains, past turnouts that provide good views and trails that lead into the backcountry.

After 20 miles, you crest 4,860-foot **Rainy Pass,** where a mile-long, paved path leads to mountain-ringed **Rainy Lake.**

About 4 miles east, the **Blue Lake Trail** ascends 2 miles through forests and meadows, with superb views to the east of 7,720-foot **Liberty Bell Mountain** and the 7,807-foot **Early Winters Spires. Blue Lake** lies in a gorgeous alpine bowl, whose steep slopes are popular with mountain goats.

Two miles farther on, the road tops 5,477-foot **Washington Pass,** the highest point on the highway. From here, a panorama of peaks lies before you. For the next 15 miles the road descends sharply between big mountains and big trees until it levels out in the **Methow Valley.** Here, dense forests give way to open ponderosa pine woodlands and ranchlands on the drier east side of the northern Cascades. The highway signs warning drivers to watch for horseback riders and cattle define the character of the valley.

The drive ends in **Winthrop,** a re-created frontier town with Old West facades, wooden sidewalks, and the **Shafer Museum** *(285 Castle Ave. 509-996-2712. Mem. Day–Labor Day; donation),* with exhibits on turn-of-the-20th-century mining, logging, and farming in the area.

Sherman Pass Scenic Byway

Republic to US 395 on Washington 20

▪ 37 miles ▪ 1½ hours ▪ Late spring to early fall

Traveling through the sprawling ranch country east of the Cascades, this drive offers a taste of classic sagebrush-covered western hill country.

The scenic byway begins about 3 miles east of **Republic** on Wash. 20. After angling 5 miles through rolling ranchland edged by stands of ponderosa pine, western larch, and Douglas-fir, you cross into the **Colville National Forest** *(509-684-7000. www.fs.usda.gov/colville).*

Climbing 4 miles, the road traverses a burned landscape created by the 1988 White Mountain fire, which blazed through some 20,000 acres. Big trees survived the fire while the underbrush burned, opening up space for new growth. Amid the lush grass and wildflowers now growing, you might spy deer or the flash of a bluebird.

A 3-mile climb through both burned and unburned forests brings you to 5,575-foot **Sherman Pass.** The **Kettle Crest National Recreation Trail** here leads north to wildflower meadows, and a 0.25-mile spur ascends to a fine vantage point atop **Columbia Mountain,** with panoramic 100-mile views that include **Sherman Peak** to the south and **Wapaloosie Mountain** to the

Western larch in autumn

north. At **Sherman Overlook,** about a mile down the byway, a short interpretive trail with generous vistas provides information on plant life and the area's fire history.

As the highway travels through the dense forests along **Sherman Creek,** look for the occasional beaver dam and the prominent summit of 5,838-foot **Paradise Peak** on the southern horizon.

At about mile 30, an interpretive trail explains early logging in the area. From here, the byway descends to enormous **Franklin Roosevelt Lake,** a portion of the **Columbia River** now harnessed as a reservoir by Grand Coulee Dam, some 90 miles downstream. After edging the reservoir for several miles, the byway ends at the junction with US 395, 3 miles west of Kettle Falls.

Coulee Corridor Scenic Byway

Othello to Omak on Washington 17, US 2, and Washington 155

▪ 150 miles ▪ 4 hours ▪ All year

Lying in the rain shadow of the Cascade Mountains, this region of eastern Washington receives only about 8 inches of rain a year, resulting in a shrub-steppe environment of sparse grasses and other arid-country vegetation. Yet water has played a major role in shaping the landscape, carving canyons locally called coulees, many of them spectacular in their scale.

Heading north on Wash. 17 from Othello, the byway traverses heavily irrigated fields. A short side trip west leads to a more natural environment at **Columbia National Wildlife Refuge** *(509-488-2668. www.fws.gov/columbia),* set in the Channeled Scablands, an area of canyons, rocky buttes, and cliffs. Watch here for waterfowl, raptors, beavers, yellow-bellied marmots, and mule deer. After the byway crosses I-90, stop in Moses Lake at the **Moses Lake Museum and Art Center** *(401 S. Balsam St. 509-764-3830.*

404

Abandoned schoolhouse near Coulee City

Grand Coulee Dam on the Columbia River

www.moseslakemuseum.com. Closed Sun.), which offers exhibits on the shrub-steppe habitat as well as local history from the Native American period to the present. Crossing a semidesert terrain, you'll reach **Soap Lake,** known for its mineral-rich water and mud that were once highly valued for their healing properties.

405

Soap Lake marks the southern end of Grand Coulee, a great canyon carved during the Ice Age by massive floods caused when ice dams repeatedly formed and collapsed, sending walls of water 1,000 feet high down the ancient bed of the Columbia River. The massive cliffs before you testify to the incredible power of the surging floodwater. On the east side of the highway is the trailhead to the **Lake Lenore Caves,** seven shallow caves set into the cliff and once used by American Indians as shelters. Farther north, **Sun Lakes–Dry Falls State Park** *(509-632-5583. www .parks.wa.gov)* is most noted for the 400-foot-high, 3.5-mile-long cliff of **Dry Falls,** the site of a prehistoric waterfall ten times the size of Niagara.

At one point in 1937 during the Depression, 8,000 people were employed on the Grand Coulee Dam project.

A short jog east on US 2 takes you to Wash. 155, which runs north along the east shore of **Banks Lake,** now filling the great canyon of the upper Grand Coulee. In 18 miles you'll pass **Steamboat Rock,** an impressive geologic feature of volcanic basalt.

Where the byway meets the Columbia River, **Grand Coulee Dam** *(509-633-9265. www.usbr.gov/pn/grandcoulee)* stands 550 feet high, the largest concrete structure in the United States. A laser light show is presented on the dam face in summer and tours are offered, subject to security conditions; call for information.

Across the dam in the town of **Coulee Dam,** the **Colville Tribal Museum** *(512 Mead Way. 509-633-0751)* has exhibits on the history of the 12 tribes that make up the Colville Confederated Tribes. The remainder of the byway passes through the **Colville Indian Reservation.**

At the small town of **Nespelem,** a memorial to Chief Joseph, the legendary 19th-century leader of the Nez Perce, stands near the highway. The Nez Perce ask that travelers *not* visit his grave in a local cemetery.

Stevens Pass Greenway

Everett to Wenatchee on US 2

- 89 miles ▪ 2 hours ▪ Summer and fall. Stevens Pass is open through winter but road conditions sometimes require caution.

Following a trail blazed by the Great Northern Railway, Stevens Pass Greenway runs from northwestern Washington's Puget Sound over the beautiful Cascade Range to the eastern slope. Rivers, trails, mountain peaks, waterfalls, and historic towns highlight the route.

On US 2 in Everett, you're only minutes from the **Future of Flight Aviation Center and Boeing Tour** *(360-756-0086 or 800-464-1476. www.boeing.com/companyoffices/aboutus/tours. Adm. fee).* Here visit the world's largest building (nearly half a billion cubic feet) and see how airliners are assembled.

Snohomish *(Visitor Information Center, 1301 1st St. 360-862-9609. www.snohomishvic.org)* dates from an 1859 ferry crossing of the Snohomish River. Today the town calls itself the "antique capital of the Northwest," and has more than 400 dealers—many of them in the 26-block area of downtown on the National Register of Historic Places.

The greenway continues east alongside the Skykomish River, soon entering **Mount Baker–Snoqualmie National Forest** *(425-783-6000. www.fs.usda.gov/mbs),* with Mount Index rising to the south. Watch for the turn south to **Sunset Falls** on the South Fork Skykomish.

In the historic railroad town of **Skykomish**, the national forest **ranger station** *(US 2. 360-677-2414)* offers information and maps on nearby trails, campgrounds, and picnic areas. Eight miles east, an easy trail leads to **Deception Falls**.

Stevens Pass, at 4,061 feet, is home to a modern ski resort, but its early railroad period earned its designation as a historic district. The **Bygone Byways Interpretive Trail** tells the story of transportation through this area of the Cascades. You're now following Nason Creek east through **Okanogan-Wenatchee National Forest** *(509-664-9200. www.fs.usda.gov/okawen).* The gorge gets even narrower when you reach **Tumwater Canyon** on the Wenatchee River.

At the end of the gorge you'll reach **Leavenworth** *(Chamber of Commerce, 940 US 2. 509-548-5807. www.leavenworth.org),* which styles itself as a

Stevens Pass in the North Cascades

Bavarian village in architecture, festivals (including Oktoberfest, of course), food, shopping, and general atmosphere.

In **Cashmere,** visit the **Cashmere Museum and Pioneer Village** *(600 Cotlets Way. 509-782-3230. Closed Nov.-March; adm. fee),* which includes 20 structures dating back to the 1880s, as well as pioneer artifacts and exhibits on Native Americans and natural history.

You're in the heart of Washington's apple country now, and in **Wenatchee** *(Chamber of Commerce, 2 S. Mission St. 509-662-2116. www.wenatchee.org. Mon.-Fri.),* the **Washington Apple Commission Visitor Center** *(2900 Euclid Ave. 509-663-9600. www.bestapples.com)* will tell you everything about apple growing in the state that provides more than half the fresh apples eaten in America. Located north of town above the Columbia River, **Ohme Gardens County Park** *(3327 Ohme Rd. 509-662-5785. www.ohmegardens.com. Mid-April–mid-Oct.; adm. fee)* was begun as a private garden in 1929 and now ranks as one of the most popular gardens in the Northwest. Trails wind through acres of lawn, trees, flowers, waterfalls, and ponds, with views of the surrounding eastern Cascades landscape.

Mountains to Sound Greenway

Seattle to Thorp on I-90

- 100 miles ▪ 3 hours ▪ Summer and fall. Snoqualmie Pass is rarely closed in winter, but snow conditions at the pass regularly require use of chains or other traction devices.

Citizens of Seattle and the rest of Washington have saved the section of I-90 called the Mountains to Sound Greenway from development. Much of it lies within national forests, and it runs from Puget Sound over the Cascades to the edge of central Washington's semidesert landscape.

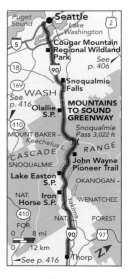

The western terminus of I-90 in **Seattle** *(Convention & Visitors Bureau, 701 Pike St. 206-461-5840. www.scvscattle .org)* is within the shadows of the city's sports stadiums. To the north is **Pike Place Market,** the nation's oldest continually working farmers' market, with dozens of restaurants, food stores, craftspeople and artists, shops, and bars. The nearby **Seattle Aquarium** *(Pier 59. 206-386-4320. www.seattle aquarium.org. Adm. fee)* houses creatures from the local waters and a Pacific coral reef. And, of course, few visit Seattle without enjoying the spectacular view from the **Space Needle** *(400 Broad St. 206-905-2111. www.spaceneedle .com. Adm. fee),* 520 feet above the city streets.

The greenway crosses Lake Washington and in just minutes passes alongside **Cougar Mountain Regional Wildland Park** *(exit 13, south 3 miles),* where more than 3,000 acres encompass 36 miles of trails in the **Issaquah Alps.** In the park are waterfalls, wetlands, meadows, mountaintop vistas, and forests.

Waterfalls highlight the drive's next section. Just north of I-90 between Snoqualmie and Fall City, 270-foot-high **Snoqualmie Falls** can be viewed from above or below. Eastward, **Olallie State Park** *(www.parks.wa.gov)*

features **Twin Falls** and **Weeks Falls.** As the drive approaches 3,022-foot Snoqualmie Pass, you're in **Mount Baker–Snoqualmie National Forest** *(425-783-6000. www.fs.usda.gov/mbs).* At several locations *(including Olallie State Park and Hyak at exit 54)* you can access the **John Wayne Pioneer Trail** *(509-656-2586),* an abandoned railroad bed con-

verted to a long-distance hiking-biking trail. More than 60 miles of the trail are managed as **Iron Horse State Park** *(www.parks.wa.gov),* including a 2.3-mile rail tunnel.

Beyond the pass you briefly traverse **Okanogan-Wenatchee National Forest** *(509-664-9200. www.fs.usda.gov/okawen),* pass alongside Keechelus Lake, and descend the valley of the Yakima River. **Lake Easton State Park** *(509-656-2230. www.parks.wa.gov)* offers access to the river, Lake Easton, and the John Wayne Pioneer Trail.

The drive reaches **Thorp,** which began as an 1895 depot on the Northern Pacific Railroad. Today it's best known for the 1882 **Thorp Grist Mill** *(11640 N. Thorp Hwy. 509-964-9640. www.thorp.org. Tours Jun.-Aug., Thurs.-Sun.; donation).*

Pike Place Market in Seattle

Olympic Peninsula

Aberdeen to Hoodsport on US 101, Washington 109, the Moclips Highway, and the Dungeness Scenic Loop

■ 278 miles ■ 1 day ■ Spring through fall

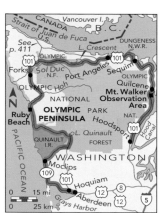

Following the perimeter of the Olympic Peninsula, this drive rambles through fern-clad rain forests and alpine meadows, past wild remote beaches, and into classic logging towns. Above it all rise the glacier-streaked Olympic Mountains.

Start in downtown **Aberdeen,** with a visit to the **Grays Harbor Historical Seaport** *(360-532-8611. www.historicalseaport.org. Fee for tours).* The seaport's centerpiece, the *Lady Washington,* is a full-size reproduction of the tall ship that sailed into these Northwest waters in 1788—the first American vessel to land in the region.

Heading west on US 101, you pass the **Polson Museum** *(1611 Riverside Ave. 360-533-5862. www.polsonmuseum.org. Closed Mon.-Tues.; adm. fee),* about 3 miles outside town. Once the home of lumber baron Arnold Polson, the 26-room mansion now has exhibits on logging and shipping.

Less than a quarter mile farther on, you cross the **Hoquiam River** and enter downtown **Hoquiam.** US 101 turns north here, but you take

Wash. 109 west. As you pass through town, keep an eye out for **Hoquiam's Castle** *(515 Chenault Ave. 360-533-2005. www.hoquiamcastle.com. Tours by appt.),* the meticulously restored Victorian fantasy of yet another lumber baron. Outside Hoquiam, the road skirts **Bowerman Basin,** part of which is protected as the **Grays Harbor National Wildlife Refuge** *(360-753-9467. www.fws.gov/graysharbor).* The basin and its mudflats host half a million migrating shorebirds every spring.

The highway skirts **Grays Harbor** for 2 miles, then veers into a forest of young trees that were planted to repair the wounds of clear-cutting. In a dozen miles, the road meets the ocean and turns north, following the shoreline for about the next 15 miles. Along this stretch, you'll pass small towns, ocean-front homes, tourist facilities, Sitka spruce forests, and broad sandy beaches.

Just past Moclips, you'll enter the **Quinault Indian Reservation.** Turn east onto the Moclips Highway, part of which is unpaved but usually well graded. After winding 20 miles through forests of young and middle-aged Douglas-fir and western hemlock, you rejoin US 101.

As you head north, you'll notice that the clear-cuts and young trees give way to some respectably tall timber. You're now in the **Olympic National Forest** *(360-956-2400. www.fs.usda.gov/olympic. Day-use fee).* About 5 miles into the forest, you begin passing stands of old-growth Douglas-fir and Sitka spruce. If you detour about a mile down South Shore Road, you'll find the 0.25-mile **Rain Forest Nature Trail** leading through a forest, dripping with hanging moss, made unbelievably lush by some 140 inches of rain a year. Another minute down the road brings you to deep, clear **Lake Quinault** and the lovely old **Lake Quinault Lodge** *(360-288-2900).* If you continue 10 miles farther east, South Shore Road

409

Ruby Beach, Olympic National Park

enters the interior portion of spectacular 922,626-acre **Olympic National Park** *(360-565-3100. www.nps.gov/olym. Adm. fee).*

Back on US 101, you curve for the next 28 miles through a forested landscape that runs the gamut from inspiring old-growth to one of the largest clear-cuts you'll ever see.

Olympic National Park

US 101 reaches the **Pacific Ocean** at the southern end of a 57-mile sweep of seashore that represents a coastal segment of Olympic National Park. For 10 miles you follow virtually undeveloped shorelines. About 1.5 miles after entering the park you'll come to the pullout for **Beach No. 1.** The trail here tunnels through Sitka spruce, ending abruptly at the rim of a 100-foot-high cliff, with views of wild sandy beaches.

At rocky **Ruby Beach,** 9 miles farther on, waves pound sea stacks and shorebirds skitter around the edges of tide pools that teem with sea stars, sea urchins, mussels, and hermit crabs.

After this, the highway turns inland, leaves the park, and parallels the **Hoh River** for about 10 miles before crossing it and heading north. Along the way, you pass **Den's Wood Den** *(360-374-5079),* featuring chain-saw sculpture that ranges from toadstools to panthers.

Ten miles north, US 101 enters **Forks,** a quintessential Pacific Northwest logging town, where locals favor "hickory" shirts and pickup trucks. At its south end, look for the **visitor center** *(1411 S. Forks Ave. 800-443-6757. www .forkswa.com)* and the **Forks Timber Museum** *(360-374-9663. April-Oct. Tues.-Sat., tours by appt. all year; donation),* displaying antique logging equipment and photographs of pioneer loggers.

For about the next 30 miles, you head north along the **Sol Duc River,** then east up the **Sol Duc Valley.** When the highway again reenters Olympic National Park, the trees and mountains return, and you soon see the western tip of **Lake Crescent,** a beautiful dark-blue glacial lake framed by thick fir forests.

Clinging tightly to the southern shore of the lake for the next 10 miles, the road passes numerous viewpoints, interpretive signs, and turnouts. About 7 miles from the western tip of the lake, a short road leads to the historic 1916 **Lake Crescent Lodge** *(360-928-3211. May-Oct.),* with its wonderful view of the lake. A mile-long trail here winds through a forest of Douglas-fir to 90-foot-high **Marymere Falls.**

After Lake Crescent, the highway leaves the park and picks up the shoreline of **Lake Sutherland,** then **Indian Creek,** and finally **Lake Aldwell.** At this point you can look out across the **Strait of Juan de Fuca** to Vancouver Island in Canada.

About 5 miles farther on, **Port Angeles** faces toward the ocean. Teeming with activity, its waterfront docks berth ferries going to and from nearby Victoria (British Columbia) and ships loaded with timber, bound for ports around the world.

The 20-some miles of US 101 east of Port Angeles constitute the route's most developed stretch. To avoid some of this, turn left about 12 miles from Port Angeles onto the Dungeness Scenic Loop. Signs lead the way as the route twists and turns through pastoral **Dungeness Valley,** noted for its berry farms and unexpectedly sunny climate; in the rain shadow of the **Olympic Mountains,** it gets an average 17 inches of rain a year.

Tiger lilies

About 3 miles from US 101 you'll come to the **Dungeness National Wildlife Refuge** *(360-457-8451. www.fws.gov/washingtonmaritime/dungeness. Adm. fee).* Its principal feature is the **Dungeness Spit,** a finger of sand that hooks into the strait. Hiking to the lighthouse, you may spot harbor seals and many birds.

From the refuge, the loop curves along the edge of the strait, then heads inland to **Sequim** (pronounced SKWIM). Here, you rejoin US 101 before turning south through wooded hills, scattered farms and ranches, and small towns. About 30 miles beyond Sequim, the famous oyster-producing town of **Quilcene** sits beside **Quilcene Bay,** an arm of the Hood Canal.

For a grand view of the bay and canal continue 5.5 miles south to FR 2730 and go 4 miles to the 2,804-foot **Mount Walker Observation Area.**

Just south of the road to Mount Walker, US 101 comes to the **Hood Canal** and follows its western shore. You'll pass marshes speckled with birds, oyster farms, waterfront homes, and small towns sporting seafood cafés. The drive finishes near the south end of the Hood Canal in **Hoodsport.**

411

Strait of Juan de Fuca Highway

Elwha River to Makah Indian Reservation on Washington 112

■ 61 miles ■ 4 hours ■ All year. Summer traffic congestion requires attentive driving.

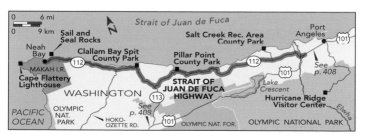

Just 60 miles as the raven flies from downtown Seattle, this drive along the Strait of Juan de Fuca provides fine scenery and wildlife viewing at the northwestern extremity of the Washington coastline. The strait—actually a glacial fjord—connects Puget Sound with the Pacific Ocean; its beaches, cliffs, lakes, and rivers make it an appealing destination any time of year.

The drive officially begins where Wash. 112 crosses the **Elwha River,** but you should stop in nearby Port Angeles at the **visitor center** for **Olympic National Park** *(360-565-3130. www.nps.gov/olym. Adm. fee)* for information about the park and maps (see pp. 408-411).

Makah Reservation, Olympic Peninsula

Back at the Elwha, check out the river overlook just off Wash. 112; a mile past the bridge, turn north on Elwha River Road to reach the old wooden bridge for good views of the rushing water. In another 5 miles, turn north on Camp Hayden Road to reach **Salt Creek Recreation Area County Park** *(360-928-3441. www.clallam.net/Parks/saltcreek.html),* where you can explore beaches and tide pools and enjoy views of the strait, Crescent Bay, and, to the north, Vancouver Island.

Wash. 112 continues west, alternately leaving and hugging the coast. **Pillar Point** *(22 miles west of Salt Creek)* and **Clallam Bay Spit** *(10 miles farther)* are two more county parks offering beach access. A detour on Hoko-Ozette Road takes you to the Lake Ozette section of Olympic National Park and provides an opportunity to hike to the Pacific Ocean at road's end.

Back on Wash. 112, just before you reach the town of Neah Bay, look north to the small islets called **Sail** and **Seal Rocks,** where you might see harbor seals, puffins, or, in nearby waters, gray whales.

The route ends in **Neah Bay** at the **Makah Indian Reservation** *(360-645-2201. www.makah.com),* but you may want to continue to the **Cape Flattery Trail** *(permit required from Makah Nation; available locally),* a 0.75-mile path to viewpoints of **Tatoosh Island** (the northwesternmost point of the contiguous United States) and the historic **Cape Flattery Lighthouse.**

Mount Adams Drive

Randle to Packwood on Washington 131, Cispus Road, and Forest Roads 23, 2329, 56, 2160, and 21

■ 67 miles ■ 2 hours ■ Summer to early fall. Gravel roads require slow speeds but can be negotiated by ordinary passenger cars.

This drive in southern Washington feels almost like a hike, as it follows a series of paved and unpaved roads deep into the Gifford Pinchot National Forest. Along the way, it passes lakes, rivers and creeks, old-growth forests, and memorable mountain views.

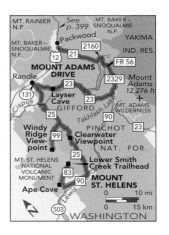

From **Randle,** turn south on Wash. 131. After going 2 miles, make a left turn onto Cispus Road. You'll pass a bucolic blend of small ranches, farms, and orchards for several miles until you cross into the **Gifford Pinchot National Forest** *(Cowlitz Valley Ranger District. 360-497-1100. www.fs.usda .gov/giffordpinchot).* At this point the road designation changes to FR 23.

Once in the national forest, the drive tunnels through a classic western Cascades old-growth forest that is anchored by massive Douglas-firs. To truly appreciate their size, walk up to one of these evergreen skyscrapers. You'll probably find that its trunk is bigger around than you are tall, and its tip towers some 250 to 300 feet above your head.

Cruising 3 miles through the big trees, you come to a narrow, steep gravel logging road on the left that climbs almost 2 miles to **Layser Cave.** You can walk through the 0.25-mile-long cave, which was inhabited seasonally by prehistoric peoples for 3,500 years, archaeologists tell us.

Back on FR 23, keep an eye out for wildlife. The undergrowth limits visibility, but birds and small mammals are common and you may even spot deer and elk. You may also encounter logging trucks roaring down this paved section of the loop, so be on the lookout.

A number of trails branch off FR 23 along this stretch, and even a short hike, like the 0.25-mile **Camp Creek Falls Trail** 7 or 8 miles from the Layser Cave turnoff, yields many discoveries. **Camp Creek Falls** itself plunges 30 feet over a rocky ledge, and if you move slowly along the trail, you might see a 6-inch banana slug chomping on leaves or a newt stepping in slow motion across the forest floor.

From here, the road enters a shaded corridor overarched by the forest and soon picks up the **Cispus River.** For the next 15 miles, you stay with the river as it meanders down the valley.

Deer and elk roam the broad river valley and adjacent coniferous forest, most of it still vaunting old growth. Ridge after ridge of mountains, many of them striped with avalanche chutes, rim the horizon. If you're here in the fall, the roadside trees burn in tones of bronze and gold in the autumn sunlight.

After about 10 miles, you'll see a snow-draped peak in the east—**Mount Adams,** the 12,276-foot volcano for which this route is named. At about the same point, the old-growth forest becomes interspersed with clear-cuts and younger stands.

Many of the trees seem to have sprouted whiskers: A pale green lichen, called old man's beard, hangs in profusion from the trunks as well as from the branches.

Mount Adams and Takhlakh Lake

A couple of miles farther on, you leave FR 23 and turn left onto FR 2329, which soon brings you to **Takhlakh Lake.** The large, tree-lined lake is exquisitely backdropped by Mount Adams. Picnic tables and campsites take full advantage of the view, and a mile-long trail leads around the lake. An interpretive sign explains that Mount Adams lacks the single point of a classic volcano, because it comprises several cones. In the 1930s people mined sulfur from the mountain.

FR 2329 follows along the northern edge of the **Mount Adams Wilderness,** passing through young and old forests, pocket meadows that in spring and summer are radiant with wildflowers, and ancient lava flows spewed out from the mountain.

Along the way, Mount Adams frequently punctuates the southern sky, while 14,410-foot **Mount Rainier** rises far to the north. Shimmering ribbons of icy, clear water flow from the nearby mountainsides, giving rise to lovely little gardens of wildflowers and bright green mosses.

Some 10 miles past Takhlakh Lake, turn right onto FR 56 and follow it along the Cispus River for about a mile, then turn left on FR 2160. After 2 miles, turn right on FR 21. Passing several more groves of enormous Douglas-fir, the road tightropes along a mountainside high above **Johnson Creek** for several miles before it ends at the junction with US 12, just south of **Packwood.**

Mount St. Helens

Randle to Lower Smith Creek Trailhead on Washington 131 and Forest Roads 25, 99, 90, and 83

▪ 103 miles ▪ 4 hours ▪ Late spring to early fall. This route provides a less traveled alternative to more accessible western side of the Mount St. Helens National Volcanic Monument. *See map p. 413.*

This drive winds through a landscape that is testament to both the destructive forces of nature and its regenerative ability.

From US 12 in **Randle,** take Wash. 131 south past grassy fields, ranches,

Through Mount St. Helens NVM

and the **Cowlitz River.** After 2 miles Wash. 131 forks right, and in another mile the bucolic scenery gives way to forests as you enter the **Gifford Pinchot National Forest** *(Cowlitz Valley Ranger District 360-497-1100. www.fs.usda.gov/ giffordpinchot),* and the road becomes FR 25.

For the next 17 miles the drive angles through a mix of old-growth and second-growth coniferous forests with hiking trails and picnic areas. Turn right on FR 99, a 17-mile spur road that penetrates deep into the heart of **Mount St. Helens National Volcanic Monument** *(360-247-3900. www.fs.usda.gov/mountsthelens).* Established in 1982, the monument protects the awesome terrain created by the eruption of Mount St. Helens. One in a string of Cascades volcanoes, it exploded at 8:32 a.m. on May 18, 1980, spewing out rock,

View of Mount Adams sunrise from Mount St. Helens National Volcanic Monument

ash, and gas at a speed of 200 miles per hour. The heat of the blast melted glaciers that in turn caused mudflows and floods, wreaking further destruction on the region. Today, the area is slowly recovering its former beauty.

Climbing through a handsome forest of Douglas-fir, FR 99 gives you a good look at a before-the-cataclysm picture. After about 8 miles on this road, a turnout will provide you with your first good look at an after-the-cataclysm picture. Here, the nearest trees still standing have been reduced to bare gray sticks, and more distant trees, those closer to the volcano, have been slammed flat to the ground by the blast. Hunching into the sky 10 miles away is the beheaded volcano itself. Behind you, however, a surprisingly sharp division exists between the unaffected forest and the ravaged one.

A mile farther, the 0.4-mile-long **Meta Lake Trail** offers a glimpse of the resiliency of life: Saplings poke through pumice; birds flit through shrubs; fish and frogs inhabit lakes; and you might glimpse elk and deer.

For its final 8 miles the winding, sometimes precipitous road runs through the carnage. Along the way turnouts have interpretive signs explaining this volcanic terrain, and several trails enable you to walk out into the blast area—otherwise off-limits to hikers. Now and then, you might also catch glimpses of the glaciated crown of **Mount Adams** on the eastern horizon.

The landscape of this national monument was formed in a moment, when the top 1,300 feet of Mount St. Helens blew off, devastating 200 square miles.

The road ends at the **Windy Ridge Viewpoint.** Here, less than 5 miles from Mount St. Helens, you can look across into the gaping crater created when the northeast flank of the mountain blew out, leaving a chasm 1.2 miles wide and 2.4 miles long. Forest Service interpreters and interpretive signs provide details.

Retrace your route along FR 99, then turn south on FR 25. The mosaic of forests here survived the blast, though they were coated by gritty ash that covered the land, even as far away as western Montana. Occasionally you'll catch fine views of Mount St. Helens and the monument area, notably from the **Clearwater Viewpoint,** about 8 miles from the FR 25/99 junction.

Sixteen miles beyond, drive west on FR 90 along the north side of **Swift Reservoir.** Making one last sally into the monument, the drive turns north 11.5 miles farther on at FR 83 and heads through a beautiful forest of spruce and fir. Two miles on FR 83 brings you to a short side road up to **Ape Cave,** actually two lava tubes—an upper one 1.5 miles long and a lower one half as long. You can hike through both, but you'll need a flashlight.

The next 5 to 6 miles along FR 83 offer close-up views of the looming, unexploded south side of Mount St. Helens. After crossing a lahar, a broad floodplain formed by a river of hot mud and ash, the drive ends a few miles farther on at the **Lower Smith Creek Trailhead,** where you can hike along a mudflow-scoured canyon.

Chinook Scenic Byway

Enumclaw to Naches on Washington 410

▪ 85 miles ▪ 4 hours ▪ Summer and fall. Central portion of byway and much of Mount Rainier National Park are closed in winter.

See p. 399

The beauty and adventure of Mount Rainier National Park highlight this byway through the Cascade Range in south-central Washington. Rainier dominates the route figuratively and literally, with its snowy peak visible for much of the way.

Heading east from **Enumclaw,** the byway runs alongside the White River to reach **Federation Forest State Park** *(360-902-8844. www.parks.wa.gov/parks),* an excellent place to start learning about the Cascades' environment. Three interpretive trails wind through old-growth forest of cedar, Douglas-fir, hemlock, Sitka spruce, and maple, sampling five ecological zones in a small area. Beyond Greenwater, as you enter **Mount Baker–Snoqualmie National Forest** *(425-783-6000. www.fs.usda.gov/mbs),* you'll have great views of Mount Rainier.

Known to Native Americans as Tahoma ("great mountain"), Rainier is indeed massive. When you reach the boundary of **Mount Rainier National Park** *(360-569-2211. www.nps.gov/mora. Adm. fee)* on Wash. 410 at 2,749 feet, the 14,411-foot summit is more than 2 miles higher. Turn into the park to reach the **White River Wilderness Information Center** *(360-569-6670. May-Oct.)* for advice on what to do in this 235,625-acre park. An active volcano, Rainier is also known for the greatest assemblage of glaciers in the United States outside Alaska. Continue to the **Sunrise Visitor Center** *(360-663-2425. July–mid-Sept.),* at 6,400 feet the highest point in the park accessible by car.

Back on Wash. 410 at 5,430-foot Chinook Pass, note the log bridge over the road, built for hikers on the **Pacific Crest National Scenic Trail** *(www.pcta .org),* which runs 2,650 miles from Mexico to Canada through California, Oregon, and Washington. Take time to walk at least part of the trail at **Tipsoo Lake.** From this point you descend the eastern slope of the Cascade Range through **Okanogan-Wenatchee National Forest** *(509-664-9200. www.fs.usda*

.gov/okawen), where dramatic basalt columns, reminders of past volcanic activity, are prominent.

Watch for the turn to **Boulder Cave** *(Naches Ranger District. 509-653-1401. Closed Nov.-April)*, where a 1.5-mile trail leads through a 200-foot-long natural cave formed by weathering of lava deposits. The last section of the byway continues east to the town of Naches under arid, shrub-dotted cliffs, far different from the lush forests of the eastern slope of the Cascades.

Pika in Mount Rainier National Park

OREGON

Historic Columbia River Highway

Troutdale, Oregon, to Maryhill Museum of Art, Washington, on Historic Columbia River Highway, I-84, and Washington 14

- 90 miles ▪ 3 hours ▪ Early spring to late fall. *See map p. 419.*

417

Historic Columbia River Highway

The drive travels the length of the dramatic Columbia River Gorge National Scenic Area, whose natural beauty is complemented by ample civilized pleasures. This route follows a portion of the Historic Columbia River All-American Road, before crossing the river into Washington. You can dine elegantly, raft down a wild river, or hike in an old-growth forest.

Start in downtown **Troutdale,** just off I-84, where 257th Avenue intersects the Historic Columbia Highway. In about a mile you'll cross the **Sandy River** before reaching the 292,500-acre **Columbia River Gorge National Scenic Area** *(541-308-1700. www .fs.usda.gov/crgnsa. Parking fee).* For the next 8 miles the drive passes houses, parks, farms, produce stands, and small towns.

A pullout at the **Portland Women's Forum State Park** will give you your first look at the gorge itself. Extending far upriver, the view includes the broad **Columbia River** and some of the brown-black columnar basaltic cliffs, covered with dense green vegetation, for which the gorge is famous. This cleft in the earth was carved by water over millions of years. Floods at the end of the last ice age swept down the ancestral Columbia River, scouring the gorge.

Construction on the highway began in 1913. Now, few stretches of the older original road are still drivable. The 25-mile section beginning in Troutdale is the longest original portion remaining.

Vista House, Columbia River Gorge

Leaving the pullout, you soon reach the drive's high point: the **Vista House** *(503-695-2230. March-Nov.)*, a lovely stone building perched atop a 733-foot promontory overlooking the river. Inside, you'll find displays on the natural history of the gorge and the crafting of the highway.

After Vista House, the narrow, winding highway slips down through deep forests to the river's edge. About 2 miles past Vista House, **Latourell Falls** signals the beginning of the many waterfalls you'll encounter. Tallest of them all is 620-foot **Multnomah Falls,** viewable from a short, steep paved trail about 8 miles farther on.

Of special interest is **Oneonta Gorge.** This deep, narrow slash in basaltic cliffs rises hundreds of feet above your head, while the **Oneonta Creek** squeezes down to just a few yards as it courses through. The perpetually cool, moist, shaded conditions here nurture a profusion of ferns, mosses, lichens, and other plants, some found nowhere else.

When the historic highway ends, you have to tolerate about 9 miles of traveling east on I-84. Five miles down this stretch, you may want to stop for a tour of the **Bonneville Dam** *(541-374-8820. Self-guided tours daily)* or for a hike. Four miles past the dam, exit at Cascade Locks to visit **Cascade Locks Marine Park.** Here you can tour the **Cascade Locks Historical Museum** *(541-374-8535. www.portofcascadelocks.org/museum.htm. May-Oct.; donation)* or cruise the Columbia River aboard the stern-wheeler *Columbia Gorge (800-643-1354. www.portlandspirit.com. May-Oct.; fare).*

From Cascade Locks, the soaring **Bridge of the Gods** *(toll)* crosses the river into Washington, where you pick up Wash. 14. Head east on Wash. 14 and in about a mile take a left on Rock Creek Drive to visit the **Columbia Gorge Interpretive Center** *(509-427-8211. www.columbiagorge.org. Adm. fee),* which features displays on the gorge's human and natural history.

Begun in 1913, the old historic highway has been called a "poem in stone," its intricate stonework and graceful bridges blending with the natural surroundings.

Continuing along the river in the shadow of forested mountains, the road passes bird-rich wetlands and a couple of small towns. Leaving the wet west slopes of the **Cascade Range,** you move into the drier eastern side. For the next 40 miles, the annual rainfall decreases about an inch a mile.

At Hood River you can recross the Columbia to Oregon and pick up the officially designated Historic Columbia River Highway that runs along US 30, or you can choose to remain on the Washington side. You'll probably see fishing boats and enormous grain barges loaded down with wheat on either side.

You might also see windsurfers, because the gorge attracts these sports enthusiasts from throughout the world. They come here because of the vigorous wind that constantly funnels through what is the only sea level corridor in the Cascade Range.

After some 20 miles, the road on the north shore of the Columbia River enters serious ranching, farming, and orchard country. Towns become fewer and smaller, broad-shouldered plateaus are silhouetted against the sky, and red-tailed hawks ride the thermals that rise from basaltic cliffs. In some places, notably around **Murdock,** you'll get great views of **Mount Hood,** across the river in Oregon.

About 3 miles past Murdock, **Columbia Hills State Park** *(509-767-1159. www.parks.wa.gov. April-Oct., mile-long rock art trail accessible only by guided tour Fri.-Sat.)* boasts wonderful Native American petroglyphs and pictographs.

For the last 18 miles of the drive, you cruise atop grassy open tableland, often far above the river. A mile after the road leaves the Columbia River Gorge National Scenic Area, you'll find the **Maryhill Museum of Art** *(509-773-3733. www.maryhillmuseum.org. Mid-March–mid-Nov.; adm. fee).* Built in the 1920s as the private residence of famed railroad man and social visionary, Sam Hill, this edifice on the bluffs above the Columbia is now a respected art museum.

Mount Hood Scenic Byway

Troutdale to Hood River on US 26 and Oregon 35

■ 105 miles ■ 3 hours ■ Late spring to early fall. April is blooming season for Hood River Valley orchards.

Making a half circle around Oregon's highest peak—volcanic, snow-mantled Mount Hood—the drive then cruises through the rich orchard country of the Hood River Valley, following much of the Mount Hood Scenic Byway.

From Troutdale travel on Ore. 35 to the town of **Sandy,** "gateway to Mount Hood," where the classic cone of the 11,235-foot volcano dominates the eastern sky. As you head east on US 26, you move into a forested landscape. After about 15 miles, you come to the **Mount Hood Information Center** *(503-622-4822),* which offers regional information. Half a mile past the center, the aptly named **Wildwood Recreation Site** *(503-622-3696. www.blm.gov/or. March-Nov. Parking fee)* contains forests of Douglas-fir, red alder, and bigleaf maple, threaded by hiking trails beside the **Salmon River.**

In 2 miles you reach the **Zig Zag Ranger Station** *(503-622-3191)* for the **Mount Hood National Forest** *(503-668-1700. www.fs.usda.gov/mthood).* The ranger station features the **Wy'East Rhododendron Gardens,** showcasing the plants that create a lush understory in these Oregon forests.

Heading into the national forest, the highway curves past some sizable trees and along the sides of some strapping mountains. The stark, rocky southwest flank of **Mount Hood** can be seen from time to time through the

419

Mount Hood NF

trees. Many trails lead into the forest from the highway; the **Mirror Lake Trail,** about 10 miles from the Zig Zag Ranger Station, is a justifiably popular 1.4-mile hike to a lovely lake. The trail continues up **Tom, Dick, and Harry Mountain.**

A mile or two past the Mirror Lake trailhead, you may want to turn north onto Timberline Road and proceed 6 miles up to **Timberline Lodge** (*27500 E. Timberline Rd. 503-272-3311. www.timberlinelodge.com*). A 1930s WPA project, the finely crafted timber-and-stone lodge sits above tree line, high on the side of Mount Hood. Besides its breathtaking views, it has a perpetual snowfield that attracts skiers year-round.

Back on US 26, go 2 miles to the junction with Oreg. 35 and head north toward the town of Hood River. Almost immediately you come to the intersection with FR 3531, which leads to a pioneer woman's grave. If you're curious about what crossing these mountains in a covered wagon was like, take the 1-mile trail from here to **Barlow Pass** along a remnant of the **Barlow Road.** Built in the 1840s, this dirt track was the first road across the Cascades.

For the next 20 miles you descend through a forest of Douglas-fir, hemlock, and pine, catching glimpses of Mount Hood as you play tag with the **East Fork Hood River.** Finally you emerge into the **Hood River Valley,** Oregon's premier fruit-growing district. Stands along the road here sell pears, apples, cherries, nectarines, marionberries, peaches, and apricots, often ladling out free homemade cider as well.

The drive ends in the town of **Hood River,** where the **Hood River** and its 25-mile-long valley run into the **Columbia River.** Get a different perspective on the valley by taking the tourist train operated by the **Mount Hood Railroad** (*541-386-3556 or 800-872-4661. www.mthoodrr.com. April-Dec., call for schedule; fare*).

Mount Hood reflected in Trillium Lake

Northern Oregon Coast
(Northern section of Pacific Coast Scenic Byway)

Astoria to Pacific City on local roads and US 101

- 104 miles - 3 hours - All year

Bob Straub State Park,
Pacific City

A microcosm of the entire Oregon coast, this portion of the Pacific Coast Scenic Byway offers beaches stitched with driftwood, misty capes blanketed by thick rain forests, and tiny towns where almost every café has an ocean view.

The byway starts in **Astoria** *(Chamber of Commerce, 111 W. Marine Dr. 503-325-6311 or 800-875-6807. www.oldoregon.com),* founded in 1811 as a fur-trading post and named for financier John Jacob Astor. Drive up to the **Astoria Column,** on a hill south of downtown, for a great view of the city and surrounding rivers, bay, and Pacific Ocean. The **Columbia River Maritime Museum** *(1792 Marine Dr. 503-325-2323. www.crmm.org. Adm. fee)* contains interactive exhibits on vessels and water travel from the days of dugout canoes and sailing ships to the present. The film *The Great River of the West* recounts life and commerce on the river that runs just outside.

The byway starts on US 101 and heads south. At Warrenton, **Fort Clatsop National Memorial Park** is now part of **Lewis and Clark National Historical Park** *(503-861-2471. www.nps.gov/lewi. Adm. fee).* The main attraction is a reconstruction of the small fort where the Corps of Discovery spent the rainy winter of 1805 to 1806; costumed interpreters conduct programs in the summer.

Beyond this point is a series of state parks, many with access to the ocean. Where Lewis and Clark arrived on the Pacific shore to study a beached whale in 1806, you'll find **Ecola State Park** *(503-436-2844. www.oregonstateparks.org/park_188.php).* A mile offshore, the lighthouse on Tillamook Rock was in use from 1881 to 1957. Southward, **Hug Point State Recreation Site** and **Oswald West State Park** *(800-551-6949. www.oregonstateparks.org/park_195.php)* are two beach access points. At the former, you can walk to see the trail carved into the point *(watch for incoming tide)* by stagecoaches when the beach was the only way to travel along the coast.

Manhattan Beach State Recreation Site is another beautiful stretch of sandy shore that's perfect for beachcombing, lazy strolls, picnics, bird-watching, or whale-watching *(March & Oct. are best for migrating gray whales).*

The byway approaches **Tillamook** alongside Tillamook Bay. Tillamook and its dairy farms have made the town famous for cheddar cheese. The largest manufacturer, **Tillamook County Creamery Association** *(4185 US 101 N. 503-815-1300. www.tillamook.com)* allows self-guided tours. The

421

See p. 422

Cape Kiwanda

county's **Pioneer Museum** *(2106 2nd St. 503-842-4553. www.tcpm.org. Closed Mon.; adm. fee)* houses a natural history collection and historical artifacts.

Beyond, on Cape Meares Loop Road, you reach **Cape Meares State Scenic Viewpoint** on the open ocean. Stop to see the 1890s lighthouse and the Octopus Tree, a Sitka spruce with a 50-foot circumference. You'll also have a view of a large colony of nesting common murres (puffin-like birds) and other seabirds working the tidal flats.

Just before the small community of **Oceanside,** stop at the bluff on the north edge of town to scan **Three Arch Rocks National Wildlife Refuge,** islets less than a mile off-shore teeming with birds and sea lions. **Cape Lookout State Park** *(800-551-6949. www.oregonstateparks.org/park_186.php)* provides trails leading through the lush rain forest to the tip of the cape, with 40-mile views up and down the coast. Look for sea lions resting on sandbars.

This drive ends in **Pacific City** where the dunes and beaches of **Bob Straub State Park** *(800-551-6949. www.oregonstateparks.org/park_183.php)* offer both beauty and solitude. Just to the north, you see the radiant red-and-yellow sandstone cliffs of **Cape Kiwanda State Natural Area,** standing against the fury of the Pacific. Sand Lake Road runs along the coast before heading inland. To continue along the coast, see the Central Oregon Coast (see below) and Southern Oregon Coast drives (see pp. 424-426).

Central Oregon Coast
(Central section of the Pacific Coast Scenic Byway)

Cascade Head to Bandon on US 101

▪ 160 miles ▪ 6 hours ▪ All year

The northern portion of this section of the Pacific Coast Scenic Byway is a vintage Oregon coast blend of seashore and forest, while the southern section skirts the incomparable Oregon dunes.

Picking up from the Northern Oregon Coast drive (see above), continue on US 101 for miles past state parks, and appreciate the wildlife as well as the head-turning views—the threatened silverspot butterfly at the **Cascade Head Preserve,** seals and brown pelicans near **Siletz Bay,** and gray whales off the coast near **Yaquina Head.**

To the south lies **Newport** *(Chamber of Commerce. 555 SW Coast Hwy. 541-265-8801 or 800-262-7844. www.newportchamber.org)* located on the Yaquina River. Side by side on the bay's south shore are two premier institutions for teaching the general public about the coast and ocean: the **Oregon Coast Aquarium** *(2820 S.E. Ferry Slip Rd. 541-867-3474. www.aquarium.org. Adm. fee)* and the **Hatfield Marine Science Center** *(2030 S. Marine Science Dr. 541-867-0100. http://hmsc.oregonstate.edu. Closed Tues.-Wed. & Labor Day–Mem. Day, after Mem. Day daily; donation).* Here in Newport you will also

See p. 421
Cascade Head Preserve (18)
Siletz Bay — SIUSLAW
PACIFIC
OCEAN (101)
Yaquina Head
Newport (20)
CENTRAL Yaquina
OREGON
COAST NATIONAL
Cape Perpetua (34)
Scenic Area Yachats
Heceta Head
Lighthouse Sea Lion
State Scenic Caves
Viewpoint
Darlingtonia FOREST
State Wayside (126)
Florence Siuslaw
Siltcoos
Rec. Corridor
OREGON DUNES Gardiner
N.R.A.
Winchester (38)
Bay Umpqua
Reedsport
(101)
North Bend OREGON
Coos Bay
N
0 10 mi
Bandon (42) 0 15 km
See p. 424

find one (some say the most beautiful in America) of the 11 remaining lighthouses along the coast. The **Yaquina Head Lighthouse** is still in use, but you can visit it for a nominal charge.

In **Yachats** (yah-HOTS), a small but charming coastal town, the US 101 bridge takes you over the **Yachats River.** Go south a mile and you enter the **Cape Perpetua Scenic Area** *(Visitor Information Center. 541-547-3289. Mem. Day–Labor Day, scenic area all year; adm. fee).* Here, at the **Devils Churn,** waves rumble up a narrow channel and explode against massive rocks. Just beyond, a side road climbs 2 miles to the **Cape Perpetua Overlook.** Highest point on the Oregon coast, it offers views of the **Pacific,** the coast, and the towering **Coast Range.**

The **Cape Perpetua Visitor Center** *(closed Nov.-April)* on US 101 is the access point for numerous trails that fan out to tide pools, old-growth forests, and Native American shell middens.

For the next 23 miles, state parks and waysides hold the delights of rocky shores and sandy beaches, where sandpipers scamper at the edge of the surf and harbor seals loll. In the area's deep forests, you might see elk browsing. At **Heceta Head Lighthouse**

423

State Scenic Viewpoint *(near mile 172. 541-547-3696. Lighthouse tours; parking fee),* you can visit the lighthouse and a mile farther on the **Sea Lion Caves** *(541-547-3111. Adm. fee).* The vast cavern houses a raucous colony of Steller sea lions. Five miles beyond at the little **Darlingtonia State Wayside,** a boardwalk leads through bogs thick with carnivorous cobra lilies.

Just south of here, US 101 quits the coast, leveling out as it enters the fast-growing town of **Florence.** The **Old Town** waterfront has a pleasant mix of galleries, cafés, and shops.

Across the **Siuslaw River,** you enter the **Oregon Dunes National Recreation Area** *(541-271-3611. www.oregonstateparks.org/park_124.php),* its 31,500 acres stretching along 40-some miles of coastline. Right away you see dunes, but they're mostly covered by forest. In fact, the Oregon dunes are not a sea of pure sand but a blend of open dunes, tree islands, wetlands, forests, and lakes.

About 6 miles inside the recreation area, you'll come to a side road for the **Siltcoos Recreation Corridor.** The recreation area has a broad sandy beach fronting the ocean and a trail that follows a wildlife-rich estuary of the **Siltcoos River.** Farther along US 101, turn

Sunset over Heceta Head Lighthouse State Scenic Viewpoint

Pacific rhododendron,
Oregon Dunes NRA

right at the Carter Lake Campground and walk the half-mile **Taylor Dune Trail.**

About a mile down US 101, you can look across waves of sand that reach heights of several hundred feet at the **Oregon Dunes Overlook.** From here, the road continues south past forests and lakes until it hits civilization at **Gardiner,** on the **Umpqua River.** This tiny town was named after the owner of the brigantine *Bostonian,* which went down off the coast in 1850. Salvage was used to build the town.

Across the Umpqua, in the larger town of **Reedsport,** the **Oregon Dunes Headquarters** *(541-271-3611. Closed weekends)* has brochures, displays, and a film on the dunes. Four miles farther, the drive passes the town of **Winchester Bay.** A brief detour into town will bring you to a marina, the **Umpqua Lighthouse,** a nice park, and some savory clam chowder.

After Winchester Bay, US 101 once again passes by forested dunes and lakes as it returns to the east side of the Oregon dunes. After about 9 miles you can hike into the **Umpqua Dunes** via a 0.25-mile trail out of the **North Eel Campground.** Reaching heights of 400 feet, the Umpqua Dunes are among the highest in the recreation area. From North Eel, you pass through a familiar landscape of forests and lakes for another 11 miles. The drive continues through the coastal towns of **North Bend** and **Coos Bay** *(Bay Area Chamber of Commerce, 145 Central Ave. 541-269-0215 or 800-824-8486. www.oregonsbayareachamber.com)* before ending 30 miles later in **Bandon.**

Southern Oregon Coast
(Southern section of the Pacific Coast Scenic Byway)

Bandon to Brookings on US 101

▪ 81 miles ▪ 3 hours ▪ All year

See p. 422

This segment of the Pacific Coast Scenic Byway showcases the Oregon coast's rough side, where stalwart cliffs and sea stacks stand against the Pacific's relentless assault. But away from the coast, the drive takes on a tamer tone as it passes through pleasant little towns and farmlands.

Start in **Bandon,** a small seaside town with a surprising variety of activities. You can bird-watch at **Bandon Marsh National Wildlife Refuge** *(541-867-4550. www.fws.gov/oregoncoast/bandon marsh),* relish the huge winter waves that pound the coast, or shop in **Old Town.** At **Cranberry Sweets** *(1005 Newmark Ave. 541-347-9475. www.cranberrysweets.com)* courageous visitors may want to try a local favorite—cheddar cheese fudge.

As you leave Bandon on US 101 south, you quickly enter farmland. After 3 miles you'll see the first of many cranberry bogs, as cranberries are the major crop around here. During the fall you may also spot farmers in their hip waders out harvesting these tart berries. In 3 more miles you encounter another of this area's distinctive products: carved myrtlewood. At several roadside factories along the route, you can tour the facilities and buy items carved of this beautiful hardwood.

For the next 25 miles or so, US 101 stays inland, passing sheep ranches, forests, little towns, jam-and-honey stands, and more cranberry bogs. When you rejoin the Pacific at **Port Orford,** a detour of a couple of blocks in the middle of town will give you a generous ocean view. At the town's **Battle Rock Park,** a beach and picnic area are placid memorials to the fierce 1851 battle fought here between Native Americans and the first pioneers, who came by sea to build a settlement.

From Port Orford the road rapidly climbs into the **Coast Range,** edging along high above the sea and providing views limited only by the curve of the Earth. Hundreds of feet below, waves hammer the shore. This landscape continues as you cross the boundary into **Humbug Mountain State Park** *(541-332-6774. www.oregonstateparks .org/park_56.php. Parking fee).* Even more spectacular vistas await at the top of **Humbug Mountain;** a 3-mile trail leads to its 1,756-foot summit.

> **Oceanside bluffs serve as box seats where you can sit and watch hulking Pacific waves break against the rocks.**

After veering inland for a few miles to get around Humbug Mountain, the road once again slithers along the mountainsides right above the ocean. As it comes down to sea level, you have access to miles of virtually deserted sand beaches ornamented by twisted pieces of driftwood.

When the road enters the **Rogue River Valley,** it travels through the more settled lower reaches of the **Rogue River,** one of the nation's premier wild and scenic rivers. To see the wilder side of the river, take one of the jet-boat trips offered by local outfitters. These excursions go as far as 52 miles upriver. Across the river in **Gold Beach,** you can also take a look around the **Rogue**

River Museum *(at Jerry's Rogue Jets. 800-451 3645. www.roguejets.com/ gift-shop).* The museum details the history of boating and settlement along the Rogue River.

After Gold Beach, the drive climbs out of the Rogue River Valley and back into the Coast Range. About 8 miles south of the Rogue River, a short side road leads up to the top of **Cape Sebastian** and a panoramic view of the mountains and ocean. From here the road drops to the shore, passing by 3 or 4 miles of beaches backed by low dunes.

A few miles beyond, US 101 ascends to new heights, literally and figuratively; this final 14-mile stretch of coast is stunning, especially at **Samuel H. Boardman State Park** *(541-469-2021. www .oregonstateparks.org/park_77.php).*

Samuel H. Boardman State Park

425

Extending along the coast for nearly 10 miles, the park consists of forests and clifftops poised dramatically between US 101 and the ocean. For the most part, you can't see the ocean from the highway, but a number of overlooks, side roads, waysides, and trails provide plenty of vistas.

You might want to stop and admire the scenery from the **Oregon Coast Trail.** This 3-foot-wide trail traverses a steep slope with views of sea cliffs, pocket coves, wind-twisted trees, sea stacks, and the sweep of the Pacific. Descending through a spruce forest to some dunes, you cross the open sand above the crashing surf and climb up to a path that cuts through a dense blanket of waist-high coastal scrub. In spring and winter you're likely to spot migrating gray whales. Similar scenes of this monumental meeting between land and sea can be savored from dozens of other vantage points.

Beyond the park, the drive continues a couple of miles to its terminus in the fishing town of **Brookings.**

Rogue–Umpqua Scenic Byway

Roseburg to Prospect on Oregon 138, 230, and 62

■ 120 miles ■ ½ day ■ Late spring through fall

This byway in southwest Oregon offers the rare opportunity to drive alongside two of the country's stellar wild and scenic waterways—the North Umpqua and Rogue Rivers—both a feast of rapids, waterfalls, gorges, storied fishing holes, and serene stretches of cold, clear mountain water.

From the quiet town of **Roseburg,** head east on Oreg. 138. For the next 16 miles the road passes through farmland on its way to the **North Umpqua River,** which stages a dramatic entrance in the town of Glide. Below the town's **Colliding Rivers Viewpoint,** the North Umpqua and **Little River** meet.

Leaving Glide, the road follows the North Umpqua up into the forests of the **Cascade Range.** The river narrows into impressive rapids at several points, particularly at the pullout at mile 21.5. Stop a half mile later at **Swiftwater Park,** where a viewing platform has interpretive signs explaining the North Umpqua's renowned salmon and steelhead runs. The 79-mile **North Umpqua Trail** begins across the river here.

Among fly-fishing enthusiasts the next 30 miles of the North Umpqua are world famous for summer steelhead runs. Much of this stretch is framed by the towering basaltic cliffs of the **North Umpqua River Canyon.**

About 9 miles past Swiftwater Park you enter the **Umpqua National Forest** *(541-957-3200. www.fs.usda.gov/umpqua. Parking fee).* Trails are plentiful here, often leading to waterfalls. Near the Toketee (TOE-ke-tee) Ranger Station, the gorgeous half-mile trail to 120-foot-high **Toketee Falls** winds above a narrow, rocky gorge resounding with the North Umpqua's turbulence. The trail ends at a viewing platform high above the falls. Another half-mile trail to one of southern Oregon's highest waterfalls, 272-foot **Watson Falls,** starts a mile up Oreg. 138.

Toketee Falls

About 18 miles farther on, a short jaunt on FR 4795 takes you to capacious **Diamond Lake,** backdropped by thick coniferous forests and the snow-covered peaks of the Cascades, including 8,363-foot **Mount Bailey** and 9,182-foot **Mount Thielsen.** A side trip of about 5 miles on Oreg. 138 leads to **Crater Lake National Park** *(541-594-3000. www.nps .gov/crla. This entrance closed in winter; adm. fee).* The ink blue waters of Crater Lake fill the caldera of dormant Mount Mazama (see Volcanic Legacy Scenic Byway p. 428-430).

To continue on the drive, head right on Oreg. 230. Three miles farther, you'll enter the **Rogue River–Siskiyou National Forest** *(541-618-2200. www.fs.usda.gov/rogue-siskiyou),* where the **Rogue River** emerges from underground lava tubes. Stop at the **Crater Rim Viewpoint,** a couple of miles into the national forest, to see the peaks and ridges around Crater Lake,

For about the next 20 miles, Oreg. 230 descends past trees and occasional lava flows almost two million years old. As you get lower, lodgepole pines give way to mostly old-growth forest. Dropping into the Rogue's canyon, the road meanders alongside the river.

Oreg. 230 soon ends, and you join Oreg. 62 south. In 1.5 miles you'll come to **Union Creek,** an historic Civilian Conservation Corps center that is now a tiny hamlet. On the north end of Union Creek, you can hike the **Rogue Gorge Trail.** The short, paved path leads to an observation platform overlooking the 25-foot-wide, 40-foot-deep chasm—a collapsed basalt lava tube now occupied by the river.

At **Natural Bridge,** a mile south of Union Creek, a short interpretive trail offers more great views of the Rogue. At one point here, the river actually disappears as it travels underground for some 200 feet through another ancient lava tube, forming a natural land bridge.

Continuing 4 more miles through stands of looming sugar pines, ponderosa pines, and Douglas-firs, the drive passes **Mammoth Pines Nature Trail.** This 0.25-mile interpretive loop leads through an old-growth coniferous forest.

This drive ends about 6 miles farther on, when it emerges from Rogue River National Forest and enters the small logging town of **Prospect,** but the America's Byway Rogue-Umpqua Scenic Byway continues to **Gold Hill.**

427

Bridge over the Rogue River

Volcanic Legacy Scenic Byway
(Oregon)

Crater Lake National Park to California state line on Oregon 138, 232, 62, and 140, US 97, and local roads

- 140 miles ▪ 1 to 2 days ▪ All year, but some portions of route are subject to weather-related closures in winter.

Much of the landscape of the Pacific Northwest was shaped by volcanic activity, and this two-state byway offers the chance to experience some of the most dramatic evidence of that fiery heritage, including magnificent craters, cinder cones, geothermal vents, lava flows, and lava caves. Anchored at its northern end by Crater Lake National Park, the route passes through desert, conifer woodland, and national wildlife refuge wetlands that offer excellent wildlife viewing. The Oregon portion of the route links with a continuation south into California (see California segment pp. 461-463), through Lassen Volcanic National Park.

In the warm seasons, the byway enters **Crater Lake National Park** *(541-594-3100. www.nps.gov/crla. Adm. fee)* from Oreg. 138 in the north, with the distinctive pointed peak of 9,182-foot **Mount Thielsen** behind and 8,926-foot **Mount Scott** (the highest point in the park) ahead. This north entrance to the park is closed in winter, but you can reach the park's south and west entrances via Oreg. 62.

As you drive south, the moonscape of the **Pumice Desert** lies all around you, the result of the massive eruption of Mount Mazama about 7,700 years ago. So much material was ejected from the volcanic crater that it collapsed, forming a huge caldera that is today's **Crater Lake.** You ascend to reach 33-mile **Rim Drive,** which circles the 21-square-mile lake, offering fabulous views of its intense blue. The color, by the way, indicates the extreme purity and clarity of Crater Lake's water. Rim Road vistas undoubtedly rank with the most spectacular in the entire National Park System—for example, the cinder cone of **Wizard Island** floating magically in the lake below, its peak rising nearly 800 feet above the water.

Crater Lake, first called "Deep Blue Lake" by John W. Hillman in 1853, has also been known as Mysterious Lake, Lake Majesty, and Lake Mystery.

Pines, fir, and hemlock cloak the volcanic slopes, dotted with wildflower meadows, which can be explored on a variety of hiking trails from easy strolls to strenuous treks. The **Castle Crest Wildflower Garden Trail** is an easy half-mile loop known for floral displays in mid- to late summer. The only safe and legal way to reach the lakeshore is the **Cleetwood Cove Trail** (which requires a 2-mile round-trip). It drops and climbs 700 feet and is recommended only for those in good physical condition. South of Crater Lake in the southwest corner of the park stands **Union Peak,** frequently a target of lightning. An 11-mile hike offers a breathtaking 360-degree view.

The route continues through pastureland to the small town of **Fort Klamath**. The original fort was built in 1863 to protect wagon trains; the old guardhouse is now the **Fort Klamath Museum** *(Oreg. 62. 541-381-2230. www.discoverklamath.com/attractions/museums.asp. June-Sept. Thurs.-Mon.; donation)*. The Modoc Indian chief known as Captain Jack, a leader in the Modoc Wars of the 1870s, was hanged here and is buried nearby.

About 12 miles beyond Fort Klamath by West Side Road you reach Upper Klamath National Wildlife Refuge, part of Klamath Basin National Wildlife Refuges Complex *(530-667-2231. www.fws.gov/klamathbasin refuges)*. These areas spanning the Oregon-California border constitute a paradise for bird-watchers. Depending on the season, you can see white pelicans, raptors, geese, ducks, shorebirds, and other species in astounding numbers. From December through February, the Klamath area hosts the largest concentration of bald eagles in the lower 48 states, with more than a thousand present some winters. Upper Klamath is best explored by boat; canoes can be rented nearby at **Rocky Point Resort** *(28121 Rocky Point Rd. 541-356-2287. http://rockypointoregon.com)*. There is a marked 9.5-mile canoe trail through a marsh. By car, the best bet for wildlife observation is Lower Klamath refuge (see below).

The byway, on Oreg. 140, skirts the western side of **Upper Klamath Lake,** the largest U.S. freshwater lake west of the Rockies, occasionally rising to views of wide-open pastures and farmland, arid juniper-sagebrush grasslands, and surrounding distant mountains.

Klamath Falls *(Klamath Visitor Center, 205 Riverside Dr. 800-445-6728. www.discoverklamath.com)* is home to the **Favell Museum** *(125 W. Main. 541-882-9996. www.favellmuseum.org. Closed Sun.-Mon.; adm. fee)*, with an extensive collection of Native American and Western artifacts and art.

429

Crater Lake

The **Baldwin Hotel Museum** *(31 Main St. 541-883-4207. www.co.klamath .or.us/museum/index.htm. June-Sept. Wed.-Sun.; adm. fee)* houses historic photographs and memorabilia. If you want to stretch your legs, the **OC&E Woods Line State Trail** *(503-986-0707. www.oregonstateparks.org/park_230 .php)* follows an old railbed eastward for 100 miles.

On the southern outskirts of Klamath Falls, the byway enters **Lower Klamath National Wildlife Refuge,** part of the Klamath Basin complex.

This 46,900-acre tract was the nation's first refuge set aside for waterfowl, established by President Theodore Roosevelt in 1908. A 10-mile auto tour route *(fee)* is accessed by taking Calif. 161 east just beyond the California state line. In spring and summer, expect to see white pelicans, waders such as egrets and herons, grebes, and shorebirds such as avocets and stilts. In migration and winter, look for swans, bald eagles, geese, and ducks.

Just at the state line the byway crosses the route of the **Applegate National Historic Trail,** first used by immigrants in covered wagons traveling to Oregon in 1846 and thereafter followed by thousands more. The route was blazed by brothers named Applegate in honor of family members who drowned in the Columbia River while heading west on the Oregon Trail. Their route was intended to be a safer alternative.

McKenzie–Santiam Scenic Byway

Loop from Sisters on Oregon 242 and 126

- 82 miles ▪ 2 to 5 hours ▪ Late summer to early fall. Oregon 242 closed in winter. Not recommended for RVs or trailers.

Nature began working on the scenery in this region some three million years ago, when volcanic activity first gave rise to the High Cascades. In the shadow of 10,000-foot volcanoes, this America's Byways **McKenzie Pass–Santiam Pass Scenic Byway** passes lava flows, lakes, old-growth forests, a wild river, and bounteous waterfalls.

Start in **Sisters** at the junction of Oreg. 126 and Oreg. 242. Head southwest on Oreg. 242, a narrow highway that within minutes leads into the ponderosa pines of the **Deschutes National Forest** *(541-383-5300. www.fs.usda.gov/centraloregon. Parking fee).* Stop at **Windy Point,** at mile 11.5, for a clear look at the Cascades' volcanic nature. From this 4,909-foot viewpoint, you look out over a sprawling lava flow, with snow-topped **Mount Washington** in the background.

Several pullouts provide opportunities to stop and explore, and 3 miles past Windy Point the road travels right through a flow. The Forest Service has made this 75-square-mile sea of rock quite inviting. Right next to the highway is the **Dee Wright Observatory,** which perches atop the 5,324-foot crest of **McKenzie Pass.** Built from lava blocks in the 1930s by the Civilian Conservation Corps, the observatory provides a 360-degree view of the lava field, the craters from which the molten rock poured, and several high volcanic cones. The half-mile **Lava River Trail** leads onto a flow, with interpretive signs on the natural history of the area.

From the observatory, the drive passes into the **Willamette National Forest** *(541-225-6300. www.fs.usda.gov/willamette. Parking fee)* and continues through the lava jumble for another 2 or 3 miles. Then you reenter lush, wet forests typical of the west side of the Cascades. During the next 11 miles you'll encounter a few small lava flows topped with trees that are windswept and stunted. As you descend, brawny Douglas-firs stretch heavenward and vine maples, brilliant gold during autumn, ensnare the understory. The road is tortuous and slow, which is just as well as it gives you time to spot the

Fall color along Oregon 126

poorly marked trailhead for **Proxy Falls.** This short trail weaves through old-growth forest, taking in two beautiful waterfalls along the way.

Back on the highway, you'll drive another 9 miles through forests so thick that they sometimes make a virtual tunnel of the road. When Oreg. 242 ends at Oreg. 126, you head north on this straighter, more heavily trafficked, but still scenic road. For the next 20 miles you'll be traveling against the flow of the **McKenzie River** as it rushes downstream past fine old-growth forests, pleasant lakes, and lava flows.

The **McKenzie River National Recreation Trail** runs mostly along the west side of the river, and at several points you can pick up the 26-mile-long footpath. After about 13 miles on Oreg. 126, you pass **Koosah Falls** and a half mile beyond, **Sahalie Falls.** Both falls, 70 and 100 feet high respectively, gush from the mouth of the forest and thunder into misty pools surrounded by green moss and grass. A mile beyond the turnoff for Sahalie Falls is **Clear Lake,** the headwaters of the McKenzie River. About 4 miles farther, you leave McKenzie River country and continue east on Oreg. 126, a major trans-Cascades route.

After climbing to 4,817-foot **Santiam Pass,** the road slowly descends through forests, with some exhilarating views of **Mount Washington.** Passing lakes, lava flows, and old-growth forests, you're soon back in Sisters.

431

Willamette National Forest

West Cascades Scenic Byway

Estacada to Oakridge on Oregon 224, Forest Road 46, Oregon 22 and 126, and Forest Road 19

■ 220 miles ■ 1 day ■ Late spring through fall. Forest Roads 46 and 19 are usually closed by snow from mid-November to May. Forest Service permits (fee) are needed to park at most trailheads; available at ranger stations and sometimes on-site.

Lush conifer forests and swirling white-water rivers make this byway a joy for outdoors enthusiasts of all types—whether hikers, paddlers, or those who enjoy scenic views during a relaxing drive. Set along the western slope of Oregon's Cascade Range, the route passes waterfalls and lakes and at times offers views of mountain peaks to the east.

Beginning only a short distance from the Portland metropolitan area, the byway leaves **Estacada** to follow the **Clackamas River** upstream for nearly 50 miles. This section of the river is popular for white-water rafting, with spring Class IV rapids and easier running in summer. You'll quickly enter **Mount Hood National Forest** *(503-668-1700. www.fs.usda.gov/mthood),* where you'll find several roadside campgrounds, picnic areas, and trails. Take time to walk at least a bit of the **Riverside National Recreation Trail,** which runs alongside the Clackamas. Very nice old-growth woods are located about a mile south of the Rainbow Campground.

Where the byway meets Oreg. 22, **Detroit Lake State Park** *(503-854-3346. www.oregon stateparks.org/park_93.php. Adm. fee)* provides access to 9-mile-long reservoir, popular for water sports and fishing for rainbow trout and salmon. To the east rises 10,497-foot Mount Jefferson, one of the snowcapped peaks of the Cascade crest. You're now following the Santiam River through **Willamette National Forest** *(541-225-6300. www.fs.usda .gov/willamette. Parking fee),* with **Mount Jefferson Wilderness Area** sprawling in the mountains to the east. At **Marion Forks Fish Hatchery** *(503-845-3522. www.dfw.state.or.us/ fish/hatchery)* you can see rainbow and cutthroat trout and chinook being raised for release in nearby rivers and lakes.

After the byway joins Oreg. 126, parallel-ing the McKenzie River, you'll pass **Sahalie Falls** and **Koosah Falls,** two stunning cascades connected by a loop-trail. Here, too, is one of the access points for the **McKenzie River National Recreation Trail,** which runs 26.5 miles along the stream, providing wonderful opportunities to experience its beauty.

Totem pole in the Cascades

432

West of McKenzie Bridge, the byway follows FR 19 south. Immediately after crossing the river, turn west to reach the **Delta Nature Trail**, an easy interpretive trail that winds among old-growth trees more than 200 feet tall. The remainder of the byway follows rushing, trout-filled rivers, tributaries of the McKenzie and the Willamette, as it passes through canyons to its end at **Oakridge**. Just west is the small town of **Westfir** and the 1944 **Westfir covered bridge**, at 180 feet the longest covered bridge in Oregon.

Cascade Lakes Scenic Byway

Bend to Sunriver on Oregon 372, and County Roads 46 and 42

■ 83 miles ■ 3 hours ■ Summer through fall. Portions of route are closed in winter.

Weaving through a classic Cascades landscape, the highway passes massive volcanoes, murmuring streams, forests of awesome evergreens, lava flows, glittering lakes, and meadows full of wildflowers.

Head southwest out of **Bend** on Oreg. 372, following the signs to Cascade Lakes and Mount Bachelor. Almost immediately, you start climbing into ponderosa pine forests characteristic of the drier east side of the Cascades as you cross into the **Deschutes National Forest** *(541-383-5300. www.fs.usda.gov/centraloregon)*. After 5 miles, you'll see an immense swath of the eastern Cascades, including some extensive lava flows.

As you continue climbing, the forest becomes a dense mix of pine, fir, hemlock, and spruce. About 7 miles past the viewpoint, you round a bend and **Bachelor Butte** suddenly fills the horizon. After about 5 miles a turnoff leads up to the **Mount Bachelor Ski and Summer Resort** *(541-382-2607. www.mtbachelor.com. Lift open July–Labor Day, Fri.-Sun.; fare)*; a chairlift ascends to the 9,065-foot summit of this volcano. On clear days, the view here takes in the surrounding peaks.

Back on the drive, now called Cty. Rd. 46, you have more dramatic views of other volcanoes and mountains, with **Broken Top** hulking in the foreground. A side road a mile or so past the ski-area turnoff leads a half mile to a short trail with great views of **Todd Lake** and the snow-crowned mountains that rear above it. Fringed by spruce and fir forests, Todd Lake is favored by American dippers, which dive into it with abandon. This is the first of many beautiful mountain lakes along the drive; most were formed when ancient lava flows dammed or redirected rivers.

Forging on between Bachelor Butte and Broken Top, the road

Running the Upper Deschutes

433

Cascade Lakes Highway

skirts the marshy north end of **Sparks Lake.** Then it curves around **Devils Hill,** a jumble of dark lava boulders.

You can get a close-up look at this fascinating area by parking at **Devils Lake** and walking back along the highway to Devils Hill. At its base lie a lovely little pond and a meadow that is sprinkled with wildflowers during the summer.

As Cty. Rd. 46 swings south, it edges the 283,402-acre **Three Sisters Wilderness** *(hiking permits available at most trailheads).* Here, you pass more lakes and lava formations and more views of Mount Bachelor and other towering Cascades giants. Opportunities for hiking, fishing, boating, and picnicking abound, particularly if you make a stop at **Elk Lake,** where there's even a sandy beach.

Six or seven miles past this lake, the highway pulls alongside the **Deschutes River.** From its source in nearby **Little Lava Lake,** it begins its journey to the Columbia River. For the next few miles you follow the river, only 25 feet wide at this stage. After river and road part company, you continue for several miles along a wild natural boulevard lined with pines, firs, and hemlocks; watch the forest edge for deer. For more wildlife, turn off at the **Osprey Point** and **Crane Prairie Reservoir.** Here, a short trail through the forest opens onto the reservoir, where dead trees cradle the nests of a variety of birds, including ospreys. From Osprey Point itself, you may also spot geese, ducks, river otters, great blue herons, and sandhill cranes.

About 3 miles past Osprey Point, this route separates from the America's Byway official Cascade Lakes Scenic Byway and turns east onto Cty. Rd. 42 where it passes groves of ponderosa pines. About 3 miles from the junction, the Deschutes River reappears. If you stop at the observation platform overlooking the river, you may spot kokanee, a landlocked species of salmon.

For the next 15 miles or so the drive leads through a mix of pristine and cut-over pine forests. Soon houses begin to reappear, heralding a return to civilization and the end of the drive in the town of **Sunriver,** a resort community catering to summer vacationers and winter skiers. To visit Sunriver, turn left on South Century Drive.

Elkhorn Drive

Loop from Baker on Oregon 7 and 410, County Roads 24 and 1146, Forest Road 73, and US 30

- 106 miles ■ 4 hours ■ Summer to early fall. Road between Sumpter and Anthony Lakes is frequently closed due to snow.

This national forest scenic byway circles through a pretty parcel of the Elkhorn Mountains, laden with ghost towns, hulking gold dredges, abandoned mines, and other remnants of the 1860s gold boom.

Begin in historic **Baker** by picking up information at the **Wallowa-Whitman National Forest Reception Office** *(3285 11th St. 541-523-6391. www.fs.usda.gov/wallowa-whitman. Mon.-Fri.).*

The drive heads south out of town on Oreg. 7, following the **Powder River** through ranch country. After 13 miles you enter the **Wallowa-Whitman National Forest** and grasslands cede to ponderosa pine forests. Watch for elk, deer, ducks, and geese for the next 10 miles, especially at the **Mowich Loop** picnic site. Three miles past the loop, the depot for the **Sumpter Valley Railroad** *(541-894-2268. www.sumptervalleyrailroad.org. Mem. Day–Sept. weekends & holidays; fare)* offers a vintage, steam-train tour of the valley, which still shelters a fair amount of wildlife.

About 2 miles past the depot, turn north onto Oreg. 410 and follow the Powder River another couple of miles to **Sumpter.** Once a 15-saloon boomtown of 3,500, Sumpter is now home to only about 175 people. A historic gold dredge still stands in the **Sumpter Valley Dredge State Heritage Area** *(south end of town. 541-894-2486. Check schedule on www.sumptervalleyrailroad.org).*

Countryside near Baker

From Sumpter you'll climb into the **Elkhorns** on Cty. Rd. 24, with some fine views of the mountains. About 16 miles out of town, the road enters **Granite,** an old mining center that's now a virtual ghost town. As you continue, the road becomes FR 73.

About 6 miles past Granite, you'll drive alongside **Crane Flats,** an

extensive series of meadows favored by elk and deer. After crossing the **North Fork of the John Day,** a designated Wild and Scenic River famed for its salmon and trout, turn right and follow the river. After 5 miles, you leave the river and climb about 9 miles to 7,392-foot **Elkhorn Summit,** with its vistas of the **Blue Mountains** and beyond. Just past the summit lie several pocket lakes, where you can hike, swim, canoe, picnic, or camp.

For the next 10 miles the road descends through evergreen forests to the **Baker Valley.** Cutting south

Local stop, Sumpter

through this beautiful pastoral setting, follow Cty. Rd. 1146 to Haines, then pick up US 30 to return to Baker.

Outback Scenic Byway

La Pine to California state line on Oregon 31 and US 395

■ 170 miles ■ 1 day ■ Spring through fall. Services are lacking over sections of route; make sure you have enough fuel.

The wide-open spaces and isolation implicit in the word "outback" are certainly apparent to drivers on this byway through south-central Oregon. The pines of higher elevations give way to stark, scrubby high-desert vegetation that stretches for miles in all directions—forbidding to some, but inviting to those who feel compelled to explore, to see what's around the next curve. Much of the area is administered by national forests or the Bureau of Land Management, meaning that travelers are largely free to wander where they will, through terrain that was shaped by volcanic activity and still shows the scars of fiery eruptions and lava flows.

The byway begins near La Pine in **Deschutes National Forest** *(541-383-5300. www.fs.usda.gov/central oregon)* in woods of ponderosa and lodgepole pine, soon giving way to sagebrush flats. Here in the rain shadow of the Cascade Range, meager precipitation is reflected in the arid environment and sparse plant life.

About 25 miles from US 97, the volcanic explosion crater called **Hole-in-the-Ground** lies a little over a mile north of Oreg. 31. Four miles farther, turn east on Cty. Rd. 5-10 to reach

Fort Rock State Natural Area *(1 mile north of Fort Rock. 541-388-6055. www .oregonstateparks.org/park_40.php)*, an amazing near-circle of rock that's actually an ancient volcanic crater ring of lava and tuff (solidified ash). One side of the crater wall was broken down by an ancient sea, allowing easy access to the interior. Wave-cut rock benches are apparent on the crater walls.

Fort Rock Cave *(541-388-6055. www.oregonstateparks.org/park_249 .php. April-Nov., accessible by guided tours only)* shows evidence of occupation by Native Americans dating back 9,000 to 13,000 years. Watch for white-throated swifts, prairie falcons, and canyon wrens around the rock, and for pronghorn in the fields. The local historical society operates the nearby **Fort Rock Valley Historical Homestead Museum** *(541-576-2251. www .fortrockoregon.com. Mem. Day–Labor Day Fri.-Sun.)*, which has gathered a number of historic buildings, including cabins, houses, a land office, a church, and a school.

Back on Oreg. 31, about 9 miles south, watch on the west for **Oatman Flat,** an irrigated area where mule deer often gather in numbers from fall through spring. Just past the small town of Silver Lake, **Paulina Marsh** lies to the north of the highway, home to herons, raptors, sandhill cranes, and shorebirds. The actual **Silver Lake,** just south, is a dry basin that rarely collects rain as a shallow body of water.

Soon the road climbs to 4,830-foot **Picture Rock Pass,** named for Native American petroglyphs (incised rock markings) found a short walk from the highway along **Medicine Man Trail.** From the pass you can spot the Three Sisters volcanoes in the Cascades, 90 miles to the northwest.

In 10 miles, you'll reach **Summer Lake Wildlife Area** *(541-943-3152. www .dfw.state.or.us/resources/visitors/summer_lake_wildlife_area.asp. Parking permit)*, one of the best places in Oregon to see Spring migrant swans, geese, ducks, and other waterbirds. An 8.3-mile auto tour route *(closed in hunting season)* offers viewing opportunities. Around Paisley, anglers will have the chance to cast for trout in the Chewaucan River, while birders can scan the nearby seasonal marshes.

The landscape gets more rugged as the byway joins US 395, and the view to the east is dominated by the massive wall of **Abert Rim,** the largest geological fault in North America. The western edge of a great tilted fault block, Abert Rim rises more than 2,000 feet above the valley below and stretches more than 30 miles. The cliff edge and other nearby peaks are so popular with hang gliders that the town of **Lakeview** *(Lake County Chamber of Commerce, 126 North E St. 541-947-6040. www.lakecountychamber .org)* calls itself "the hang-gliding capital of the West."

Lakeview is best known for Oregon's only geyser. "Old Perpetual" typically shoots 200-degree water 60 feet into the air every 30 seconds. The geyser is located within a resort complex called **Hunter's Hot Springs** *(1 mile north of Lakeview. 800-858-8266)*.

Avocet in Summer Lake Wildlife Area

Hells Canyon Scenic Byway

La Grande to Baker City on Oregon 82 and 86 and Forest Road 39

- 218 miles ▪ 1 to 2 days ▪ Late spring through fall. Forest Road 39 between Joseph and Oregon 86 is closed in winter because of snow.

Forming a backward C beginning and ending on I-84, Hells Canyon Scenic Byway traverses mountain forests, river canyons, valleys, farmland, and ranches, and touches the edge of the massive gorge for which it is named. The route makes a semicircle around the Wallowa Mountains, which rise more than 9,000 feet as a near-constant presence along the way.

The byway begins in **La Grande** *(Union County Tourism, 207 Depot St. 800-848-9969. www.visitlagrande.com),* which lies within a geological formation called the Grande Ronde Valley, a vast circular valley bordered by the **Blue** and **Wallowa Mountains.** As you travel Oreg. 82 north, you'll pass through agricultural fields (including canola, mint, garbanzo beans, and turf grass) until you reach **Elgin,** known for its nicely restored 1912 brick **opera house** *(104 N. 8th St. 541-663-6324. www.elginoperahouse .com).* The rivers in this region—the **Grande Ronde, Minam,** and **Wallowa**—are renowned for trout fishing and river rafting. As the route bends to the southeast along the Wallowa River, the canyon opens into a broad valley and the summits of the Wallowa Mountains, snowcapped most of the year, rise ahead.

From spring through fall, check the schedule for the Eagle Cap Excursion Train *(541-963-9000 or 800-323-7330. www.eaglecaptrain.com. Fare),* a volunteer-operated train that runs on 63 miles of track in the **Wallowa Valley.** You can sit back in the Pullman and dining cars and watch the scenery pass, from mountains and rivers to ranches and towns. The options include meals and occasional side trips to nearby attractions.

The town of **Wallowa** is a place whose residents wear cowboy hats and boots and a sign in someone's front yard reads, "Will buy or trade deer or elk skins." Eighteen miles farther, a hilltop outside Enterprise is home to the **Wallowa Mountains Visitor Center** *(541-426-4978),* a ranger district office of the **Wallowa-Whitman National Forest** *(541-523-6391. www.fs.usda.gov/wallowa-whitman).*

Gunsight Mountain and Anthony Lake, Wallowa-Whitman National Forest

438

Stop here to learn of the many recreational opportunities you can find in the mountains, from picnics and short hikes to adventures in the **Eagle Cap Wilderness**. South of town, look for huge black Clydesdale horses raised on ranches along the highway.

The small town of **Joseph** has become an arts community, stemming in large part from the presence of one of the nation's finest bronze foundries: **Valley Bronze** *(18 S. Main St. 541-432-7445. www.valleybronze.com. May-Dec., tours by appt.; adm. fee)*. You can visit the sculpture gallery or take a tour of the foundry, which casts works by both regional and national artists.

From here, take Oreg. 350 east for 9 miles and then turn south on FR 39, also known as the Wallowa Mountain Loop Road *(this section of byway closed in winter)*. You leave the farmlands behind quickly now, as the road climbs and winds into the national forest. You'll note signs of a 1989 forest fire for a while, and then continue into more mature woods of large ponderosa pines.

Twenty-some twisting miles after you entered the national forest, turn east on FR 3965 and drive 3 miles to the **Hells Canyon Overlook**. From here, you can see down into the deepest canyon in North America. Measuring 10 miles from rim to rim and 8,043 feet at its deepest point, this wild gorge was carved over eons by the Snake River's relentless erosion. Back on the Wallowa Mountain Loop, continue to Oreg. 86, where you can make a 6-mile side trip east to another view of **Hells Canyon**, this time from the river's edge.

Heading west, Oreg. 86 ascends Pine Creek to the old mining town of **Halfway**, and then crosses into the Powder River Valley. A few miles past Richland, you'll reach the site of the **Hole in the Wall slide**, where a 1984 landslide temporarily dammed the river and covered the old highway, causing it to be rerouted. Eventually the gulches open up into a broader valley, and the road climbs into arid, sagebrush-covered hills.

Where the byway intersects the route of the Oregon Trail, visit the **National Historic Oregon Trail Interpretive Center** *(541-523-1843. www.blm.gov/or/oregontrail. Adm. fee)*, an excellent facility with exhibits on American Indians, mountain men, pioneer life, and natural history. Interpretive walking paths lead to a well-preserved section of the original **Oregon Trail**, complete with wagon ruts. Regularly scheduled living history presentations take place both inside the center and outside.

The byway ends at **Baker City** *(490 Campbell St. 541-523-5855 or 888-523-5855. www.visitbaker.com)*, which in 1900 was the largest community between Salt Lake City, Utah, and Portland, Oregon. Thanks to a gold rush in the nearby hills, the town boasted fancy hotels, an opera house, and trolleys. Today, Baker City has

Hells Canyon Overlook

the second largest number of structures on the National Register of Historic Places of any city in Oregon. Walk **Main Street** downtown to admire the restored buildings, including the 1889 **Geiser Grand Hotel** *(1996 Main St. 541-523-1889 or 888 434-7374. www.geisergrand.com)*, with its clock tower, beautiful woodwork, and stained glass.

439

OREGON

5
Medford

97

139

395

Volcanic Legacy
Scenic Byway
p. 461

Eureka

299

Redding

44

Pyramid Lake
Scenic Byway
p. 444

Lost Coast
p. 464

Avenue of
the Giants
p. 465

36

Lassen Park
Road
p. 463

395

101

1

5

Lake Tahoe-
East Shore Drive
p. 459

Reno

Fallon

California 1
North
p. 466

Silverado Trail
p. 469

80

Carson
City

505

Sacramento

50

95

Ebbetts Pass
Scenic Byway
p. 458

101

80

5

Marin County
p. 468

San Francisco

Oakland

4

120

Lee Vining

June Lake
Loop
p. 457

280

San
Jose

Tioga Pass/
Big Oak Flat Road
p. 756

6

1

CALIFORNIA

Kings Canyon
Scenic Byway
p. 454

17-Mile
Drive
p. 474

Monterey

Fresno

180

101

5

99

Route 1
p. 471

Bakersfield

PACIFIC
OCEAN

Arroyo Seco
Historic Parkway
p. 451

Los Angeles

Kalanianaole
Highway
p. 475

O'ahu

Hana
Highway
p. 477

Honolulu

Hamakua
Coast
p. 479

HAWAI'I

Maui

Crater Rim Drive
p. 481

Hawai'i

Chain of Craters
Road
p. 481

0   50   100 miles
0 50 100 150 kilometers

0   50   100 miles
0   50   100   150 kilometer

IDAHO

Twin
Falls

WYO.

86

84

15

80

Evanston

Great
Salt
Lake

Ogden

80

93

Elko

Salt
Lake
City

Provo

Lamoille Canyon
Scenic Byway
p. 443

80

15

NEVADA

50

UTAH

Ely

6

50

70

6

93

15

95

St. George

Moapa
Valley
Drive
p. 445

Red Rock Canyon
Loop Drive
p. 449

190

Colorado

Death Valley
Scenic Byway
p. 452

Las Vegas

127

Las Vegas
Strip
p. 446

Las Vegas Boulevard
State Scenic Byway
p. 447

15

95

93

40

Flagstaff

ARIZONA

Rim of the World
Scenic Byway
p. 449

40

17

10

10

Phoenix

5

15

San Diego

8

8

Yuma

10

MEXICO

Tucson

19

NEVADA

Lamoille Canyon Scenic Byway

Into the Ruby Mountains on Forest Road 660

- 24 miles round-trip ▪ 2 hours ▪ Spring through fall.
  Closed in winter

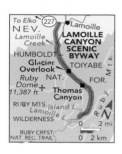

Called the Yosemite of Nevada, Lamoille Canyon in northeastern Nevada is a deep, glaciated trough that descends in one long, gentle curve from the subalpine forests of the Ruby Mountains to the high desert plains southeast of Elko. Dozens of waterfalls spill from the cliffs. Bighorn sheep and mountain goats amble the high country. Hawks and eagles soar overhead.

To get there, follow Nev. 227 east of **Elko** for 20 miles to the well-marked start of the byway. The **Ruby Mountains**—a magnificent crest of broad, serrated peaks—seem to burst from the flat valley floor. About 10 miles wide and 100 miles long, the range is composed of a mass of metamorphic and igneous rocks faulted upward about ten million years ago.

FR 660 leads through **Humboldt-Toiyabe National Forest** *(775-331-6444. www.fs.usda.gov/htnf)* and dead-ends in **Lamoille Canyon,** a deep cleft in the mountains straight ahead. To the right of the canyon bulks 11,387-foot **Ruby Dome,** mauled by glaciers. Almost immediately you cross **Lamoille Creek,** a lush corridor of cottonwoods, willows, and aspens that zigzags up the canyon from the **Powerhouse Picnic Area** beneath the road. For a quick orientation on the historical and recreational features of the canyon, stop at the interpretive exhibit above the picnic area. A number of the peaks you see ahead top 10,000 feet.

Six miles up the road at **Glacier Overlook,** another exhibit explains the glaciers that moved through here during the Ice Age and identifies the spot where the tongues of ice converged. The U-shaped walls of Lamoille Canyon trace the glaciers' paths. Here, too, you may see bighorn sheep on cliffs across the canyon. Continue 2 miles to **Thomas Canyon Campground,** at the mouth of another glacial side canyon. A difficult trail wanders a couple of miles up the broad floor of **Thomas Canyon** to wildflower meadows and limber and whitebark pine forests.

Take the time to stroll the **Changing Canyon Nature Trail,** which starts 1.5 miles up the road at the pull-off for **Hanging Valley.** The short loop-trail and its accompanying brochure describe the canyon's formation and offer a primer of common plants and animals.

The **Terraces Picnic Area** is a quiet, off-road spot where you can admire a 1,500-foot cliff of metamorphic rock swirled with light-colored granite that curves for miles along the canyon's east wall. From here, the road coasts over nearly flat meadows, rich with grasses, sedges, and wildflowers. Willow thickets cloak Lamoille Creek's meandering course. Within 2 miles you arrive at **Road's End,** a trailhead beneath an astounding ring of peaks that rise from a forest—and the end of the byway. The elevation here is 8,800 feet, some 2,700 feet above the byway's start.

The **Ruby Crest National Recreation Trail** begins here. It leads into the **Ruby Mountains Wilderness,** a 90,000-acre tract of lakes, forests, meadows, and glacial peaks where bighorn sheep, mountain goats, and eagles live. But you don't have to hike far to see the backcountry.

Island Lake lies just 2 miles away in a glacial cirque. And you can fish for brookies at **Lamoille Lake,** 2 miles up Ruby Crest.

To return, retrace the route.

Ruby Mountains

Pyramid Lake Scenic Byway

Nevada 445 northeast of Reno to Wadsworth on Nevada 447

▪ 30 miles ▪ 1 hour ▪ All year. Weather can be extreme in both summer and winter. Day-use permit (fee) from Paiute tribal authorities is needed when camping, swimming, fishing, hiking, picnicking, or driving off-road; available at several locations around lake.

A high-desert, mountain-ringed lake lies at the heart of this national byway, the only one entirely contained within a tribal reservation. Located a short distance from Reno, Pyramid Lake is administered by the **Pyramid Lake Paiute Tribe** *(775-476-1155. www.plpt.nsn.us).*

Approaching Pyramid Lake from Reno on Nev. 445, you climb slowly to **Mullen Pass,** beyond which is a vista of the lake—including the 400-foot-high, pyramid-shaped rock formation that gave it its name. The water of the lake can, depending on the light, seem blue, green, or some combination.

For part of the year, the surrounding mountains are capped with snow. The 525-acre island in the distance is **Anaho Island National Wildlife Refuge**

(775-423-5128. www.fws.gov/refuges), established to protect nesting colonies of white pelicans, cormorants, and other birds. The refuge is closed to public access, and boating is prohibited within 500 feet of the island.

Pyramid Lake is popular for boating, swimming, and other water sports, and the segment of Nev. 445 north to Sutcliffe and beyond provides access to some of the lake's many beaches. The main byway route heads south on Nev. 446 toward the town of **Nixon,** where you'll find the **Pyramid Lake Museum and Visitor Center** *(709 State St. 775-574-1088. www.pyramidlake .us/pyramid-lake-visitor-center.html. Mem. Day–Labor Day Wed.-Sun., Mon.- Fri. off-season),* with displays on Paiute tribal history and culture, as well as information on lake activities. Around 15,000 years ago, Pyramid Lake was part of much larger Lake Lahontan, which sprawled across much of the Great Basin.

Take Nev. 447 south toward Wadsworth. You'll see a marker that interprets two battles in May and June 1860 between Paiutes and white militias. The clashes were short-lived; a cease-fire resulted later in the year.

Moapa Valley Drive

Overton through the Valley of Fire on Nevada 169

■ 32 miles ■ 2 to 3 hours ■ Spring and fall. Summer temperatures frequently exceed 100°F.

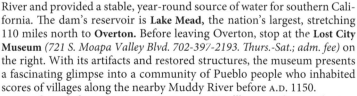

445

The first glimpse of Lake Mead as the highway heads south from Overton is startling—it's as though a piece of sky had fallen to earth amid the seared desertscape of southeastern Nevada's Mojave Desert. Along Lake Mead's western shores, the route passes a museum on area prehistory, gives access to marinas and sandy beaches, and takes you through a land of tortured red rock known as the Valley of Fire.

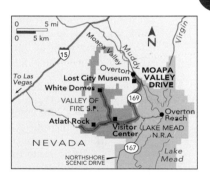

Completed in 1936, the Hoover Dam near Boulder City tamed the Colorado River and provided a stable, year-round source of water for southern California. The dam's reservoir is **Lake Mead,** the nation's largest, stretching 110 miles north to **Overton.** Before leaving Overton, stop at the **Lost City Museum** *(721 S. Moapa Valley Blvd. 702-397-2193. Thurs.-Sat.; adm. fee)* on the right. With its artifacts and restored structures, the museum presents a fascinating glimpse into a community of Pueblo people who inhabited scores of villages along the nearby Muddy River before A.D. 1150.

Head south from Overton on Nev. 169. You'll pass a silica sand mine, and soon, across the stark desertscape, you'll see Lake Mead to the east. About 9 miles farther, Nev. 169 turns off to the west toward the Valley of Fire. First turn east and take a side road almost 3 miles down to **Overton Beach** for a close-up of Lake Mead.

Return to Nev. 169 and head west into the **Valley of Fire State Park** *(702-397-2088. http://parks.nv. gov/valley-of-fire-state-park. Adm. fee).* The park road takes you through the 7-mile valley—a land of tortured sandstone turned red from oxidized iron and eroded into curious shapes. In 5 miles the road passes **Elephant Rock,** the **Seven Sisters** formations, and a short trail leading to petrified logs before arriving at the informative **visitor center.** From here, a road leads north to the **Petroglyph Canyon Trail,** a half-mile path through canyon walls decorated with petroglyphs. Continue on this road for 2 miles to **Rainbow Vista,** offering a spectacular view of canyons, domes, towers, ridges, and valleys in an amazing range of color. The road ends after 5.5 miles at the **White Domes,** immense blocks of white sandstone. Return to the visitor center and head west. You'll find a campground, more formations, and **Atlatl Rock,** where 84 steel steps lead up to a well-preserved wall of petroglyphs. As you exit the park, head east then south on **Northshore Scenic Drive** through the **Lake Mead National Recreation Area** *(702-293-8990. www.nps.gov/lame)* or go west toward I-15.

Las Vegas Strip

Las Vegas Boulevard

- 4.5 miles - 1 hour - All year

Las Vegas Paris Hotel

On the Strip, hundreds of signs blink, whirl, and transform in an infinitude of colors. The goal of all this near-hallucinogenic ornamentation is to get people to book a room, eat a meal, have a drink, see a show, and perhaps place a bet or two. There has been a "Strip" for decades, of course, with hotels, casinos, and golf courses along Las Vegas Boulevard, but the boom in megaresorts with exotic themes—ancient Egypt and Greece, European cities, pirate ships, and volcanoes—has occurred mostly since the 1980s.

The official All-American Road (as designated by the U.S. Department of Transportation) begins at the famous **"Welcome to Fabulous Las Vegas Nevada" sign,** featured in countless movies and photographs. Over the next 4.5 miles, the Strip runs past some of the most famous hotel-casinos in the world, including the **Bellagio** *(www.bellagio.com),* **Caesars Palace** *(www.caesarspalace.com),* the **Luxor** *(www.luxor.com),* **New York New York** *(www.newyorknewyork.com),* **Mandalay Bay** *(www.mandalaybay.com),* the **MGM Grand** *(www.mgmgrand.com),* **Paris** *(www.parislasvegas.com),* the **Venetian** *(www.venetian.com),* and the **Wynn** *(www.wynnlasvegas.com).* Kids often like the arcade-like **Circus Circus** *(www.circuscircus.com)* and **Excalibur** *(www.excalibur.com)* hotels, but for a high-end treat for two, stay at the brand-new **Cosmopolitan** *(www.cosmopolitanlasvegas.com)* or **Aria** *(www.arialasvegas.com).*

About 120,000 couples get married here every year. All you need is $55 and proof that you're over 18. There's no blood test or waiting period, and "chapels" along the Strip are waiting to conduct the ceremony.

The **Las Vegas Visitor Information Center** *(3150 Paradise Rd. 702-892-0711 or 877-847-4858. www.visitlasvegas.com)* is located just a block east of the northern end of the Strip. The All-American Road officially ends at Sahara Avenue, but the adventure continues inside the **World's Largest Gift Shop** *(702-385-7359. www.worldslargestgiftshop.com)* across the street. Drop in for a gag gift or a light-up Las Vegas sign to commemorate your time on the Strip.

Las Vegas Boulevard State Scenic Byway

Las Vegas Boulevard from Washington Avenue to Sahara Avenue

▪ 3.4 miles ▪ 1 hour ▪ All year

If you're searching for proof of the old adage that everything that falls out of fashion eventually becomes hip again, look no further than the Las Vegas Boulevard Scenic Byway.

Unlike the city's Las Vegas Strip (see p. 446), where both overflow crowds and over-the-top spectacles are thick, this section of Las Vegas Boulevard, which runs through downtown, feels much less contrived. Gritty elements like tattoo parlors and bail bond offices mix with vintage Vegas neon and cutting-edge outdoor light shows to create a cool, old-school Rat Pack vibe.

Put it all together and you have one of the few scenic byways that's just as entertaining—maybe more so—after the sun goes down. The fact that many Vegas visitors don't even know it exists only adds to the appeal.

Start your drive at the corner of Washington Avenue and Las Vegas Boulevard. There are several museums in this area, the first of which sits right at the intersection of these two streets and offers a perfect introduction to Las Vegas history. The **Old Las Vegas Mormon Fort** *(702-486-3511.*

Las Vegas Boulevard's Neon Museum and Boneyard

http://parks.nv.gov/parks/old-las-vegas-mormon-fort. Closed Sun.-Mon.; adm. fee) is the site of the first permanent Las Vegas valley settlement, built in 1885 to support the Mormons who came to irrigate crops with fresh water from a nearby creek. Today the creek is gone—vanished after the city of Las Vegas's water needs cannibalized the water supply. But you can still feel out the lifestyle of the people who were first inspired to call this oasis in the desert *las vegas* ("the meadows").

After gaining historical context, head southwest on the byway toward a fun attraction, the **Neon Museum and Boneyard** *(702-387-6366. www.neon museum.org. Under construction, tours by appt. only),* a two-acre park filled with classic neon signs, some dating back to the 1930s. This is where Las Vegas's marquees have come to die. Each of the roughly 150 signs comes from a local hotel, casino, or business, though none of them light up anymore and only part of the "boneyard" is tourable. While you're there, pick up a map of the many refurbished signs installed along the byway, including one of a whimsical horse and rider that for decades welcomed guests to the now-defunct Hacienda Hotel.

Cross the bridge over I-515 and continue past City Hall to the **Fremont Street Experience** *(www.vegasexperience.com).* This five-block area of vintage hotels and casinos, once known as Glitter Gulch, has been transformed into a pedestrian mall covered by a 90-foot-high barrel-vaulted shade canopy that doubles as the backdrop for an audio/video extravaganza propelled by a 555,000-watt sound system and 12 million tiny LED lights. Live entertainment and **Flightlinez** *(425 Fremont St. 702-410-7999. www.flightlinezfremont .com)* zip-line rides under the canopy help keep things interesting. If you're looking for slot machines that still use and dispense buckets of clanking quarters, the old-time casinos on Fremont Street are your safest bet.

Old Las Vegas Mormon Fort State Park, NV

As Vegas attractions go, the **Graceland Wedding Chapel** *(619 Las Vegas Blvd. S. 702-382-0091. www.gracelandchapel .com)* is as kitsch as they come. If you're feeling romantic, you can tie the knot (or renew your vows) with a choice of Elvis impersonators to walk the bride down the aisle—he may even wrap up the ceremony with a rousing chorus of "Viva Las Vegas!"

At the intersection of the byway and Charleston Boulevard begins the **18b Arts District.** Named for the 18 blocks the district encompasses, here art lovers can dive into galleries, antique shops, and restaurants.

Before the byway ends at Sahara Avenue, you'll come to the 1,149-foot **Stratosphere** *(2000 Las Vegas Blvd. S. 702-380-7777. www.stratospherehotel .com/tower. Adm. fee),* the tallest freestanding observation tower in the United States. Skip the casino below and head up top. Here, you can get a meal while watching daredevils jump from the 108th floor on some of the highest thrill rides anywhere. A floor below, step outside onto the observation deck to get one of the best full views of the Strip anywhere.

Red Rock Canyon Loop Drive

From Red Rock Canyon National Conservation Area to Nevada 159

■ 13 miles on a one-way road ■ 1 to 2 hours ■ All year. Open during daylight hours. Summer temperatures soar into the 100s, so exercise caution.

Less than 20 miles from the glitter of Las Vegas, this route enters a world of sheer sandstone cliffs, deep canyons, and rugged vistas. With temperatures cooler than the surrounding desert and natural springs, this desert basin and deep canyon provide havens for wild burros, bighorn sheep, foxes, and coyotes.

Stop first at the Bureau of Land Management's **visitor center** at **Red Rock Canyon National Conservation Area** *(702-515-5350. www.blm.gov/nv. Adm. fee)* for informative displays. From here, the drive climbs toward the **Calico Hills,** sandstone domes cut by deep canyons. At the end of the hills, a moderate 1.25-mile hike from the **Sandstone Quarry** leads to the **Calico Tanks,** holes in the rock that collect rainwater and attract wildlife.

Back on the road, view the **Wilson Cliffs,** high sandstone walls that reveal the **Keystone Thrust Fault.** About 65 million years ago, two of Earth's crustal plates collided and thrust up gray limestone. After 6.5 miles, a mile-long side road to **Willow Spring Picnic Area** penetrates **Red Rock Canyon,** with Native American art on the canyon walls. The main route continues past **Ice Box Canyon** to the **Pine Creek Canyon Overlook.** The ponderosa pines are probably relics from the last ice age. The loop ends at Nev. 159.

449

CALIFORNIA
Rim of the World Scenic Byway

Mormon Rocks Fire Station to Mill Creek Ranger Station on California 138, 18, and 38

■ 107 miles ■ 4 hours ■ All year. Traffic is thick on summer weekends, and winter brings throngs of skiers.

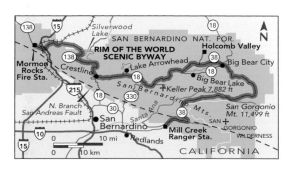

This ride through the San Bernardino Mountains traces some routes used by Native Americans, Mormon pioneers, and miners.

Your drive begins on Calif. 138 at the **Mormon Rocks Fire Station,** where you can walk a half-mile trail through coastal sage scrub and desert. It leads

Big Bear Lake

to views of **Mormon Rocks,** uptilted beds of pinkish sandstone. In 1851 Mormons passed here, then settled what became San Bernardino.

Drive 5 miles east to the **Cajon Pass Overlook,** the conduit for the Old Spanish Trail (1830), the Santa Fe–Salt Lake Trail (1849), John Brown's Toll Road (1861), and the Santa Fe Railroad (1885), whose tracks are just ahead of you, with the Southern Pacific tracks beyond. Continue into **Horsethief Canyon,** through which Ute Indians moved stolen horses out of southern California during the 1830s and 1840s.

Calif. 138 climbs past stands of California junipers toward the **Silverwood Lake Overlook** *(6 miles from Cajon Pass Overlook).* The lake doubles as a recreational site and reservoir for southern California farms and communities. Below you lies the basin of the **West Fork Mojave River,** filled with chaparral. After driving another 6 miles or so you enter a forest of pine, Douglas-fir, incense cedar, and black oak, whose leaves turn bronze in autumn.

Go 11 miles to **Crestline,** a hub of subdivision development that began in the 1920s, and turn onto Calif. 18 heading east. If the day is clear, pull into a turnout and enjoy the view over the vast **San Bernardino Valley.** The **Santa Ana Mountains** rise to the southwest, the **San Jacintos** to the southeast.

About 10 miles farther, a side trip on Calif. 173 leads 2 miles to the resort community of **Lake Arrowhead** *(Chamber of Commerce. 909-337-3715. http:// lakearrowhead.net).* The picturesque, private lake is edged with white firs, sugar pines, and dogwoods. Return to Calif. 18 and continue east. To learn the names of the trees in the **San Bernardino National Forest** *(909-382-2600. www.fs.usda.gov/sbnf),* continue 2.5 miles to the **Heaps Peak Arboretum** and walk its 0.7-mile, self-guided trail.

Another side trip, on Keller Peak Road 5.5 miles ahead, takes you to the **Keller Peak Fire Lookout** *(www.nationalforestassociation.org/keller.php. May-Nov.),* a tower with a view of the 53,000 acres burned during the 1970 Bear Fire, and to the **National Children's Forest,** where replanting was partly financed by schoolchildren.

Two miles beyond the Snow Valley ski area on Calif. 18, a divide separates the mountains' drainage toward the Pacific Ocean and the Great Basin.

Continuing on Calif. 18 about 20 miles takes you to **Big Bear Dam** and the communities along **Big Bear Lake** *(Big Bear Resort Assoc. 909-866-7000.*

www.citybigbearlake.com). The scenic byway itself turns left at the dam onto Calif. 38, following the north shore. Past Fawnskin, look for the **Big Bear Solar Observatory** *(909-866-5791. www.bbso.njit.edu. July–Labor Day. No tours while under construction).* Stay on Calif. 38 as it turns south through Big Bear City; continue to **Onyx Summit,** at 8,443 feet the byway's highest point. Next, descend to **Barton Flats** where the **visitor center** *(May-Oct.)* has information on the 58,969-acre **San Gorgonio Wilderness** *(permit required; available at Mill Creek Ranger Station).* Follow **Mill Creek Canyon** 7.5 miles as it descends. **Vista Point** turnout, 4 miles later, lies on the North Branch of the San Andreas Fault. Go past the Edison Mill Creek Powerhouse to the **Mill Creek Ranger Station** *(909-382-2882).*

Arroyo Seco Historic Parkway

Downtown Los Angeles to downtown Pasadena on California 110

▪ 9 miles ▪ 3 hours ▪ All year. Avoid morning and afternoon rush hours.

A.k.a. the "Pasadena Freeway" this historic parkway begins at the Four-level Interchange in **Los Angeles** *(http://discoverlosangeles.com)* and travels through the Arroyo Seco region.

LA's Chinatown lies just south of the Figueroa Street Tunnels. A walk on Broadway north from Ord Street will take you into an area filled with shops, restaurants, and galleries. Farther north, west of the Parkway, the **Southwest Museum** *(234 Museum Dr. 323-221-2164. www.theautry.org. Sat. only)* has a collection representing Native American cultures.

Within Los Angeles the 300-acre **Audubon Center at Debs Park** *(4700 North Griffith Ave. 323-221-2255. www.ca.audubon.org/audubon-center-debs-park. Closed Sun.-Tues.)* offers nature trails among the native landscape. The Arroyo Seco Parkway ends and becomes a city street, Arroyo Parkway, in **Pasadena** *(Pasadena Convention and Visitors Bureau. 300 E. Green St. 626-795-9311 or 800-307-7977. www.visitpasadena.com),* home to the **Gamble House** *(4 Westmoreland Pl. 626-793-3334. www.gamblehouse.org),* an outstanding example of American Arts & Crafts style architecture. Just west of the northern terminus at Colorado Blvd., **Old Pasadena** *(between Del Mar Blvd. and Walnut St.)* has shopping, restaurants, and clubs.

451

Oak trees in vineyard

Death Valley Scenic Byway

Olancha to Death Valley Junction on California 190

- 130 miles ▪ 3 hours, plus side trips ▪ All year, but summer is extremely hot. Carry drinking water and set out with a full tank of gas. Adm. fee to park.

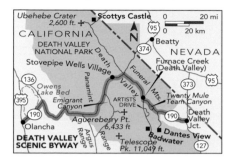

This southeastern California drive takes you into one of the world's great desert realms, Death Valley. This kingdom of extremes has the hemisphere's lowest elevation and highest temperatures (record high: 134°F). Facing its heat, mountains, and vast emptiness, a motorist sympathizes with the pioneers who crossed the 130-mile-long valley en route to California in 1849. "[It was] always the same," one wrote. "Hunger and thirst and an awful silence."

This drive, slightly longer than the America's Byways officially designated Death Valley Scenic Byway, starts west of Death Valley in nondescript **Olancha**. After skirting the dry **Owens Lake Bed** for about 15 miles, Calif. 190 jogs southeast, then climbs through the **Argus Range** past 5,000 feet and enters **Death Valley National Park** *(760-786-3200. www.nps.gov/deva. Adm. fee)*. Then it descends into the **Panamint Valley**, where you may see low-flying military jets scream past on training runs. Geologically, this is basin-and-range country, from the **Sierra Nevada** range, towering behind you, eastward into Nevada.

Soon you climb into the **Panamint Range**. At Emigrant Campground turn right for a trip up **Emigrant Canyon**; after a dozen miles, an unpaved 6.5-mile road leads past the site of Harrisburg, a vanished boomtown, and the Eureka Mine shaft to **Aguereberry Point** (6,433 feet), with a dizzying view into **Death Valley**.

Back on the highway, drive into Death Valley and the tiny resort of **Stovepipe Wells Village**. There a 2.3-mile side trip leads to the mouth of **Mosaic Canyon** and a walk through halls of breccia and white marble, carved by water. Return to the drive and continue about 2 miles to sand dunes, that cover 14 square miles; hikers may see the tracks of creatures from stinkbugs to coyotes. Kangaroo rats eat the seeds of mesquite trees, one of the most common of 900 plant species in this "barren" valley.

Drive on to the junction where Calif. 190 turns south. A side trip to the north leads 36 miles to **Scottys Castle** *(760-786-2392. Adm. fee)*, a mansion of Mediterranean style with a 270-foot swimming pool, built in the 1920s. Then drive about 9 miles west to **Ubehebe Crater**, a volcanic steam explosion pit with dark cinders atop lighter colored alluvial deposits.

Return south to the junction with Calif. 190 and take that road some 4 miles to the turnoff for **Salt Creek**. Along a short nature trail you'll see tiny

When a pioneer party crested the Panamint Range and gazed back at the place that had nearly been their cemetery, one woman exclaimed, "Goodbye, Death Valley." The name stuck.

452

desert pupfish whose ancestors swam in vanished Lake Manly 12,000 years ago. Drive on to the **Furnace Creek** area, where natural springs gush with more than 600 gallons a minute, supporting trees (tamarisk, date palms) and visitor accommodations (even a golf course!). The park **visitor center** has geology and wildlife exhibits. At the foot of the **Funeral Mountains,** the mission-style **Furnace Creek Inn** *(760-786-2345. www.furnacecreekresort .com)* made Death Valley a stylish winter resort in 1927. Built of adobe bricks and local travertine stone, the elegant oasis has a swimming pool fed by warm springs and a dramatic view of the valley.

From Furnace Creek take a side trip south on Badwater Road. After about 2 miles, pause for a walk up **Golden Canyon,** whose walls and mud hills seem to glow like gold at sunset. About 9 miles farther, turn right to

Rocky hills of Death Valley

the **Devils Golf Course,** a sharp jumble of rock-hard salt pinnacles created by evaporated brine risen from a deeper layer of mud. Then drive on to **Badwater** (279 feet below sea level), whose pools are saltier than the ocean. The hemisphere's lowest spot is several miles west, at minus 282 feet.

On the return drive north, take a side jaunt on one-way **Artists Drive,** which winds some 10 miles through terrain streaked with iron oxides (yellow, red, pink) and volcanic minerals (green, purple), then through canyons cut into alluvial fans, common in the valley.

On rejoining Badwater Road, drive to Calif. 190 and turn right 4.5 miles to **Zabriskie Point,** where a stroll takes you to an overlook of badlands created from ancient lake beds, tilted and eroded. Drive on about a mile to a side trip on a one-way gravel road through **Twenty Mule Team Canyon,** part of the badlands seen from Zabriskie Point. After this road rejoins the highway, drive on to the turnoff for a 13-mile side trip to **Dantes View,** which shows you the essential Death Valley—alluvial fans, salt flats (with Badwater right below you), and the Panamint Range, topped by 11,049-foot **Telescope Peak,** across the three-million-year-old valley. Return to Calif. 190 and turn right; the drive ends in 18 miles at **Death Valley Junction.**

Kings Canyon Scenic Byway

Sequoia National Forest boundary to Copper Creek and return on California 180

- 100 miles round-trip ▪ 4 hours ▪ Late spring through fall. Route is closed east of Hume Lake Road from early November to mid-April.

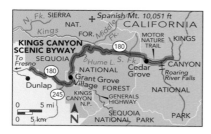

Along this drive you'll gaze up at giant sequoias and down into Kings Canyon, which is deeper than the Grand Canyon. The road has its ups and downs, too: It climbs 4,000 feet up the western slope of the Sierra Nevada, then drops 3,700 feet into the geological wonderland of the canyon depths.

Once you've entered the oak-studded hills of **Sequoia National Forest** *(Hume Lake Ranger District. 559-338-2251. www.fs.fed.us/r5/sequoia),* watch for colorful hang gliders taking off from the ridge about 2,000 feet above the highway and gliding to earth 1,000 feet below in **Dunlap Valley.**

Continue to the Big Stump Entrance Station to **Kings Canyon National Park** *(559-565-3341. www.nps.gov/seki. Adm. fee).* Here you'll see giant sequoias, a species that can grow more than 270 feet high and survive more than 3,000 years; they occur naturally only on the western slope of the Sierra Nevada. Loggers rampaged here between 1860 and 1890, and the **Big Stump Trail** loops for a mile among stumps, logs, and downed trees—reminders of the sequoia logging days. The living trees are young, second-growth sequoias.

Grant Grove Village has tourist facilities and a park visitor center. Just ahead, turn west on the side road to **General Grant Grove,** where a 0.3-mile trail leads to the world's third largest sequoia, the **General Grant Tree.** Standing 267 feet high, with a diameter of more than 40 feet, this 2,000-year-old giant is honored as the nation's Christmas tree.

Return to Calif. 180 and perhaps cross to take the narrow 2.6-mile side road to **Panoramic Point** (7,700 feet), where the view reaches from the Sierra Nevada's peaks to the canyons of the **Middle** and **South Forks Kings River.** Back on the highway, you'll leave the national park and reenter the national forest, and soon reach **Cherry Gap** (6,804 feet) and the **McGee Burn Overlook;** damage from a 1955 forest fire still shows. Two great granite ridges, **McKenzie** and **Verplank,** stretch toward the west.

Now the road descends into **Indian Basin.** About 1.5 miles from Cherry Gap a side road leads into **Converse Basin,** where some 8,000 sequoias were logged at the turn of the 20th century. A mile-long trail takes you to the **Boole Tree,** at 269 feet tall the largest tree in a U.S. national forest.

Return to the highway. Just over a mile ahead is the side road to **Hume Lake,** offering sandy beaches and trout fishing. Or continue on the main route, which descends through cedars and pines until suddenly the view explodes to take in the impressive canyons of the Middle and South Forks Kings River. Ahead, **Junction Overlook** shows you the two forks flowing together against a backdrop of towering peaks. Look northward, lovers of

General Grant Tree

superlatives: The 7,800-foot drop from **Spanish Mountain** (10,051 feet) to the river creates one of North America's deepest gorges.

Follow the South Fork's canyon to **Yucca Point**, where a 2.5-mile trail descends more than 1,000 feet to the confluence of the roaring river forks. Just ahead at **Horseshoe Bend**, where the canyon narrows to a cleft less than 200 feet across, the river has cut a curve through weak layers in the folded metamorphic rock.

In another 2 miles you reach the riverbank. You can tour **Boyden Cave** *(adm. fee)*, hollowed from a marble formation by the slow forces of water. Drive on about 5.5 miles to **Grizzly Falls**, which tumbles down granite cliffs; the base is a good spot to picnic. Next the road ascends and reenters Kings Canyon National Park. All at once the V-shaped canyon changes to a U-shaped valley—evidence that this section was carved in the granite not by a river but by a broad mass of glacial ice. Naturalist John Muir termed the result "a rival to the Yosemite."

After crossing the South Fork Kings River, you reach **Cedar Grove**, a beautiful, mile-deep valley named for its incense cedars; there are abundant hiking trails and a ranger station. Drive a mile to **Canyon View**, a turnout with an unobstructed picture of the gorge. On the sandy flats below, red-barked manzanita defy drought. Ahead 2 miles, look for the quarter-mile trail to **Roaring River Falls**, which leaps through a granite slot to a pool 80 feet below.

In autumn the highway is edged with chokecherries (bitter and inedible), actually members of the rose family.

In another 0.3 mile, note the turnoff for the **Motor Nature Trail**, a rough dirt road leading 3.5 miles back to Cedar Grove; it's a one-way route, so drive it on the return trip *(at trailhead, pick up pamphlet on area geology)*. For now, continue eastward as the road slices through ridges of rocky rubble—actually terminal moraines created when glaciers retreated, leaving their debris behind.

South Fork Kings River

Soon you reach peaceful **Zumwalt Meadow,** formed when a glacial lake slowly filled with silt. In the shelter of granite walls, a mile-long nature trail takes in the river, mixed conifers, and meadow and bog vegetation, including Venus's-flytrap.

To the north, glacial abrasion scarred granite **North Dome** (8,717 feet). Drive half a mile to the viewpoint looking southeast toward **Grand Sentinel,** a mass of stone towers whose similarly angled summits indicate parallel fracture zones in the granite. The road ends just ahead at **Copper Creek;** trails link with the Pacific Crest Trail and lead into the high country of Kings Canyon.

The return trip offers fresh perspectives on all you have seen.

Tioga Road/Big Oak Flat Road

Yosemite National Park's Big Oak Flat Entrance Station to US 395 at Mono Lake on California 120

▪ 66 miles ▪ 4 hours ▪ Late spring through fall. Closed late October to Memorial Day. Adm. fee to park.

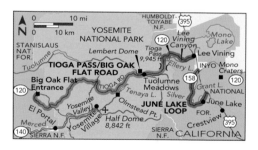

Here is a chance to see Yosemite's backcountry—the granite peaks of the Sierra Nevada, shimmering lakes, glacial valleys, and wildflower meadows. You'll drive over the highest automobile pass in California before descending rocky, dramatic Lee Vining Canyon to Mono Lake. The route—slightly longer than the Tioga Road/Big Oak Flat Road America's Byway—is less crowded than the road through Yosemite Valley.

Drive into **Yosemite National Park** *(209-372-0200. www.nps.gov/yose. Adm. fee)* at the **Big Oak Flat Entrance Station** and go east 8 miles on Calif. 120 (Big Oak Flat Road). Then turn left, following Calif. 120 as it becomes **Tioga Road,** whose points of interest will be handily marked with numbered "T signs."

You begin a climb through mixed evergreen forests, but after about 14 miles the trees begin clearing and views broaden to the high country as you reach the vista point (T11) for **Mount Clark** (11,522 feet) and **Mount Hoffman** (10,850 feet). At **Yosemite Creek** (T15) a granite canyon resembling a trough conducts snowmelt 7 miles downstream to Yosemite Falls. To learn to recognize trees along Tioga Road, stop ahead at a nature trail (T18) that identifies pines (Jeffrey, western white, lodge-pole) and firs (red and white).

Also stop at **Olmsted Point** (T24) and stroll 0.25 mile for a look down **Tenaya Canyon** at **Half Dome**, the world-famous granite monolith rising nearly a mile above Yosemite Valley's floor.

You can picnic on the sandy beach at mile-long **Tenaya Lake**. The rock formations girding the lake exhibit glacier polish that prompted the Yosemite Indians to name it Py-wi-ack—"lake of the shining rocks." Then drive on, past the polished granite knob of **Fairview Dome** (T28).

Much loved **Tuolumne Meadows** (8,600 feet) is the largest subalpine meadow in the Sierra Nevada. During the Ice Age this region lay buried under 2,000 feet of ice, and all the features you see—ponds, domes, horned peaks—were carved by glaciers. Today, meandering creeks and the **Tuolumne River** help flood the meadows in June. By July there are blossoms of wildflowers, such as Indian paintbrush and cinquefoil. Stop in at the **Tuolumne Meadows Visitor Center** (209-372-0200 ext. 3, then 5. Mem. Day–late-Sept.), a hub from which hiking trails radiate into the high country.

As you leave, look northward to **Lembert Dome** (T32), another piece of glacial sculpture. After 2 miles the road parallels the boulder-strewn **Dana Fork Tuolumne River** (T34). At T36 you have a clear view of **Mount Dana** (13,053 feet) and **Mount Gibbs** (12,764 feet), whose metamorphic rocks are often tinged with colorful alpenglow in the evenings.

At **Tioga Pass** (9,945 feet) the road crests the state's highest auto pass, and you leave Yosemite National Park. Continue on Calif. 120 past glacially carved **Ellery Lake**. Now the road begins a plunge down **Lee Vining Canyon**. Six miles along, the road runs between moraines—ridges of rocky

June Lake Loop

California 158

■ 15 miles ■ 1 hour ■ Late spring through fall. Roads closed with first big snowfall (usually November) and reopens late April. See map p. 456.

On this drive *(Inyo National Forest: 760-647-3044; Mono Basin Scenic Area Ranger Station and Visitor Center: 760-873-2400)* you'll see five lakes and fascinating evidence of the passage of glaciers. This part of the eastern Sierra, having been raked by glacial ice, appears raw and rocky, but its aspect is softened when spring brings wild irises, and in late September the aspens turn gold.

Turn west from US 395 onto Calif. 158 at the southern access point for the June Lake Loop. You climb a glacial moraine to its summit, called **Oh! Ridge** for its exclamation-inducing view of **June Lake** and **Carson Peak** (10,909 feet).

Take the campground road to the right for a side trip to the sandy swimming beach at June Lake.

Now continue to June Lake village, where on your right rest two glacial erratics. These 30-ton boulders, amazingly balanced one atop the other, were left by retreating glaciers.

Soon you glimpse **Gull Lake,** offering good trout fishing. Next the highway flanks the geologically unusual **Reversed Creek**; glacial debris blocked its course and made it reverse direction.

On your right, aspens hide **Silver Lake** until it edges the road. The vegetation starts thinning as you reach **Grant Lake**, where you may see great blue herons.

Leaving the lake, you drive over another glacial moraine and descend toward **Mono Lake**. On your right rise the **Mono Craters**, plug-dome volcanoes formed of pumice and obsidian.

Rejoin US 395 at the northern entrance to the June Lake Loop.

Tenaya Lake, Yosemite National Park

debris left by passing glaciers—that stand as high as 700 feet. Stop for information at the **Inyo National Forest Ranger Station** *(760-647-3044. Daily in summer, call for winter schedule).* The route ends in just over a mile at US 395 and **Mono Lake,** a haunting body of water that is 700,000 years old and studded with spires of white tufa.

Ebbetts Pass Scenic Byway

Arnold to Markleeville on California 4 and 89

■ 61 miles ■ 4 hours ■ Summer and fall. Higher elevations closed in winter; at any time of year, use caution on this often steep, narrow, and winding road. Oversize vehicles not recommended.

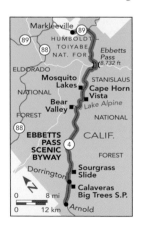

Following an ancient American Indian trade route across California's Sierra Nevadas, this route up and over Ebbetts Pass packs magnificent scenery into its 61 miles: volcanic peaks, glacier-sculpted valleys, alpine lakes, rocky rivers, and awe-inspiring forests of huge trees.

At **Arnold,** the ascent to the pass begins in a mixed forest of ponderosa and sugar pine, white fir, incense cedar, and oak; in spring, look for blooming dogwoods along streams. After just 4 miles along Calif. 4 you arrive at **Calaveras Big Tree State Park** *(209-795-2334. www.parks .ca.gov. Vehicle fee),* which protects two major groves of Sierra redwoods (also known as giant sequoias), the Earth's largest living things. The biggest tree in the park towers 250 feet high, with a diameter of 25 feet.

About 3 miles east of Dorrington, look for the **Sourgrass Slide,** where a quarter-million tons of earth slipped in a gigantic landslide in 1997. See lupine, fireweed, penstemon, and many other species of wildflowers in summer. Oaks and bigleaf maples can blaze with color in fall as the road climbs toward the ski complex at **Bear Valley** *(209-753-2301. www.bearvalley.com),* along the way passing several stunning vistas of peaks and valleys.

You're traversing the **Stanislaus National Forest** *(209-532-3671. www .fs.usda.gov/stanislaus)*, which offers a range of recreational activities from easy hikes to wilderness backpacking to white-water floating on the **North Fork Stanislaus River**. Or you can simply stop to enjoy beautiful mountain sites such as **Lake Alpine**—be sure to pull over at **Cape Horn Vista,** just beyond, for a spectacular panorama—and **Mosquito Lakes.** The narrow road here has no striping. Use caution as you drive. This segment of the route is not recommended for large vehicles.

Ebbetts Pass

As you approach 8,732-foot **Ebbetts Pass,** the environment changes from subalpine vegetation such as mountain hemlock and limber pine to true alpine habitat of stunted shrubs, mosses, and lichens. Beyond the pass, the road descends steeply along hairpin turns through beautiful **Silver Creek Canyon.** You pass lovely aspen groves into a drier area of pinyon pine, juniper, and sagebrush. Where Calif. 4 meets Calif. 89, Silver Creek flows into the **East Fork** of the **Carson River,** offering more opportunity for white-water thrills as well as renowned trout fishing.

459

Lake Tahoe–East Shore Drive

Loop from South Lake Tahoe on California 89, California 28 and along Nevada's Lake Tahoe–East Shore Drive, Nevada 28, and US 50

▪ 72 miles ▪ 3 hours ▪ All year. Tahoe can be jammed during summer weekends and August. Winter weekends are also crowded.

This route traces the perimeter of a majestic alpine lake 6,225 feet above sea level, ringed by the peaks of the Sierra Nevada and its Carson Range. The sparkling water, whose color varies from pale aquamarine near shore to deep sapphire, is so clear that you can see an object more than 75 feet down. The area's scenery is stunning: The lake was created by faulting, then during the last ice age, glaciers created bays, U-shaped valleys, and jagged peaks, all offering outdoor recreation. For indoor recreation, gaming (casinos no longer call it gambling) is legal on the Nevada side of the state line. This line runs north-south through the 22-mile-long lake.

Set off from the city of **South Lake Tahoe** *(Visitors Bureau. 530-544-5050 or 800-288-2463. www.visitinglaketahoe.com),* taking Calif. 89 northwest from US 50. Stop in at the **U.S. Forest Service Visitor Center** *(530-543-2674.*

Mid-June–Oct. daily, Nov.-late June weekends) after about a mile. It maintains natural history trails through a conifer forest and a chamber on **Taylor Creek** for observing the fall salmon run. Adjacent **Tallac Historic Site** *(530-541-5227. www .tahoeheritage.org. Grounds open all year, estates open spring-fall; fee for weekend tours)* showcases luxury estates of the 1890s and early 1900s, when Lake Tahoe became a retreat for San Francisco's wealthy elite.

As you continue farther on Calif. 89, look southwest toward **Mount Tallac** (9,735 feet), where a cross of snow appears on the east face most of the year. Continue on until the road threads a dramatic ridge, with **Cascade Lake** to your left

Cave Rock State Park at sunset

and fabled **Emerald Bay** to your right. Pull off just ahead at **Inspiration Point** for a fine view of this bay and of Lake Tahoe's only island, **Fannette**. The island is topped with a stone teahouse, built in 1929 by heiress Lora Knight along with her 38-room **Vikingsholm** *(530-525-7232. www.vikingsholm.org. Mem. Day–Labor Day; adm. fee)*, a mansion in the style of a Scandinavian castle. At the head of the bay, the house can be reached only by boat or steep footpath, which local wags say goes "1 mile down and 2 miles back up."

As you drive along the north side of Emerald Bay, look across the lake to the granite peaks of the **Carson Range**. Continue to **D. L. Bliss State Park** *(530-525-7232. www.parks.ca.gov/?page_id=505. Adm. fee)*, named for a lumber baron who once owned 75 percent of Tahoe's lakefront property. The 957-acre preserve (1,830 acres for D. L. Bliss and Emerald Bay) has beaches, an early 19th-century wooden lighthouse, and rock formations such as Turk in Turban and the 130-ton Balancing Rock. On the park's northern edge, off **Rubicon Point,** the lake floor drops to 1,411 feet, the deepest point along the shore.

Lake Tahoe contains more than 37 trillion gallons of water— enough to cover a flat area the size of California to a depth of 14 inches.

Past **Meeks Bay,** whose mile-long beach was once a Native American fishing camp, you enter **Ed Z'berg Sugar Pine Point State Park** *(530-525-7232. www.parks .ca.gov/?page_id=510. Adm. fee)* and its 2,000 acres of shore and forest, including sugar and Jeffrey pines, incense cedars, and black cottonwoods. Take a look at **Phipps Cabin,** built by trapper and fisherman William Phipps in 1872, and the lavish 1902 **Hellman-Ehrman Mansion** *(530-525-7232. June–Labor Day);* on its lakeside lawn you can enjoy a picnic and a million-dollar view.

Continue 9 miles to **Tahoe City** *(Visitors Bureau. 530-581-6900 or 800-824-6348. www.visittahoecity.org)*, a winter skiing hub for nearby Squaw Valley and Alpine Meadows. Summer attractions include the Native American and pioneer artifacts at the **Gatekeeper's Museum** *(530-583-1762. May-Oct., closed Tues.; adm. fee)* and the 1909 **Watson Cabin** *(530-583-1762. www.northtahoemuseums.org. Mid-June–Labor Day, closed Tues.; donation)*.

Leaving town on Calif./Nev. 28, follow the developed shoreline 9 miles to **Kings Beach,** a long and often crowded strand. After you cross the Nevada line into Crystal Bay, casinos appear.

Soon comes **Ponderosa Ranch** *(private),* where television's *Bonanza* was filmed, and then you begin Nevada's **Lake Tahoe–East Shore Drive.** The first stop along the America's Byway is at **Lake Tahoe–Nevada State Park** where **Sand Harbor** *(775-831-0494. www.aboutlaketahoe.com/beaches. Adm. fee)* provides a delightful picnic spot. About 5 miles after Nev. 28 merges into US 50, a sign at **Logan Vista Point** explains that, after the virgin pine forests were felled in the mid-1800s to build towns, fir thickets replaced them.

Continue to **Cave Rock,** part of a volcanic rock in which caves were carved by waves. Then come **Zephyr Cove's** beach and facilities and the gambling hub of **Stateline.** Cross into California, and soon you're back in South Lake Tahoe, tying your drive into a neat circle. For the big picture, drive south on Ski Run Boulevard to the **Heavenly Mountain Resort** *(775-586-7000. www.skiheavenly.com),* where a new gondola *(fare)* ascends 2,800 feet up the slopes for a superb view of Lake Tahoe and surroundings.

Volcanic Legacy Scenic Byway
(California)

Oregon state line to Lake Almanor on California 161, 89, 44, 36, 147, US 97, and I-5

▪ 360 miles ▪ 2 days ▪ All year, but some portions of the route are subject to weather-related closures in winter.

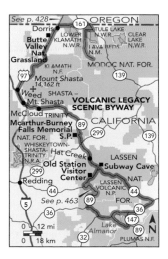

This two-state byway, anchored at each end by volcano-centered national parks, lets drivers see tall craters covered in conifer woods, ash fields, geothermal features, and lava caves. The Oregon portion (see p. 428) begins at Crater Lake National Park. This California segment ends near Lassen Volcanic National Park.

Taking Calif. 161 east from US 97 leads past Lower Klamath National Wildlife Refuge (see p. 399) to Tule Lake National Wildlife Refuge, part of **Klamath Basin National Wildlife Refuges Complex** *(530-667-2231. www.fws.gov/klamath basinrefuges).* Its lakes, marshes, and fields spans the Oregon-California border. Famed among bird-watchers, Tule Lake hosts a diversity of bird species in great numbers. Begin at the visitor center, then drive the 10-mile auto tour route *(fee).*

One of the highlights of the byway is found just a few miles south of Tule Lake. At **Lava Beds National Monument** *(530-667-8100. www.nps.gov/labe. Adm. fee)* a half million years of volcanic eruptions have created a rugged landscape of cinder cones, lava flows, spatter cones, lava-tube caves, and craters. In addition, the park protects historic Native American rock art (painted pictographs and

Horseback riding at Drakesbad Guest Ranch, Lassen Volcanic National Park

carved or pecked petroglyphs) dating back as much as 1,500 years. Drive to **Mammoth Crater** and walk the short trail to the top to see the volcano that created most of this terrain, flowing as recently as 30,000 years ago. The **Big Nasty Trail** passes through rough and rugged lava. In the Modoc War of 1872-1873, Modoc Indians led by a chief known as Captain Jack used the lava fields of what is now the park to evade Army units for 5 months; interpretive exhibits tell their story.

Back on US 97, just south of Dorris you'll enter **Butte Valley National Grasslands** *(Ranger District. 530-398-4391),* an expanse of wetlands, sagebrush flats, and farmland. In the distance, 14,162-foot **Mount Shasta** *(Shasta-Trinity National Forest. 530-226-2500. www.fs.usda.gov/stnf)* dominates the horizon. A volcano with a history of fairly regular eruptions, Shasta is still considered active, and scientists expect more activity, possibly in the next few hundred years.

The towns of Weed, Mount Shasta, and McCloud offer access to an array of recreational pursuits including skiing, river rafting, and hiking *(Mount Shasta Visitors Bureau. 800-926-4865. www.visitmtshasta.com).* Anglers come for trout in the **Upper Klamath, McCloud,** and **Sacramento Rivers** and for salmon in the **Klamath River.**

Waterfalls dominate the next stretch of the byway. Five miles east of McCloud, leave Calif. 89 to Lower Falls of the McCloud River waterfalls. By road or trail you can continue eastward through ponderosa pine forest to see Middle Falls (the best of the three) or Upper Falls. Forty miles farther along the byway, **McArthur-Burney Falls Memorial State Park** *(530-335-2777. www.parks.ca.gov. Adm. fee)* protects 129-foot-tall Burney Falls, which many consider to be the most beautiful waterfall in California.

Continuing southeast, the byway enters **Lassen National Forest** *(530-257-2151. www.fs.usda.gov/lassen)* and the Hat Creek area. At the junction of Calif. 89 and 44, stop at the **Old Station Visitor Center** *(530-335-7517)* to learn about recreational opportunities, including a visit to **Subway Cave** *(adjacent to Calif. 89, near Cave Campground. Closed in winter),* where you can walk 1,300 feet through a lava-tube cave.

It's just a short distance now to **Lassen Volcanic National Park** *(530-595-4444. www.nps.gov/lavo. Most roads closed in winter; adm. fee),* whose character is revealed by place names such as Devastated Area, Bumpass

Hell, Sulphur Works, Chaos Jumbles, and Cold Boiling Lake. Hundreds of thousands of years ago, a volcanic peak called Mount Tehama rose here, 11,500 feet high. Geologic activity caused it to collapse, leaving smaller volcanoes around its rim. One of them, **Lassen Peak,** rises 10,457 feet as the park's centerpiece. The main park road (see below) provides access to many thermal features, as well as grasslands and conifer forests. The 3-mile round-trip walk to **Bumpass Hell** *(surrounding terrain can be dangerous; stay on trail)* leads past mud pots and boiling springs. In the northeast part of the park, reached off Calif. 44, you can climb a cinder cone, a symmetrical mound of lava. To reach the summit requires an ascent of 800 feet.

The byway continues south to circle **Lake Almanor** *(Almanor Ranger District. 530-258-2141. www.fs.usda.gov/lassen),* popular for swimming, boating, and fishing.

Lassen Park Road

Manzanita Lake Entrance to Southwest Entrance of Lassen Volcanic National Park

■ 30 miles ■ 1½ hours ■ Open June through October. Adm. fee to park.

On this scenic drive through 106,000-acre **Lassen Volcanic National Park** *(530-595-4444. www.nps.gov/lavo),* you'll see nature's beauty—and power. The chain of volcanic activity has been unbroken for over two million years, with the most recent activity in 1914-1915.

Nearly every rock in the park was born of a volcano, and every hydrothermal feature on Earth (except geysers) appears here.

Enter the park at the **Manzanita Lake Entrance** and stop at the **Loomis Museum** *(530-595-4444, ext. 5180. Late-May–late-Sept.; adm. fee).* Exhibits explain the area's volcanic history.

Adjacent **Manzanita Lake** is a fall stopover for wood ducks and Canada geese. Continue to **Chaos Jumbles,** a 2-square-mile boulder field left 300 years ago during a rockfall from nearby plug-dome volcanoes, the **Chaos Crags.**

At Noble Pass the 1850s **Old Emigrant Trail** wends through. Ahead lies the **Hot Rock**—not a heisted diamond, but a 300-ton chunk of lava. It rode a mudflow from Lassen Peak, 5 miles away, during the May 19, 1915, eruption. Drive on 2 miles to the **Devastated**

Sunset over Manzanita Lake and Lassen Peak

Area, where that mudflow swept through. As an encore, on May 22nd Lassen Peak spewed gas and volcanic debris 25,000 feet into the sky.

On the ascent to **Summit Lake** the road is edged by stands of quaking aspen and red fir. Past the lake, continue to the serene meadow at **Kings Creek.** Then go on to **Lassen Peak** (10,457 feet), where a 2.5-mile trail climbs the rocky slopes to the summit. Keep going about a mile to **Bumpass Hell,** a major hydrothermal area with hot springs, mud pots, and steam vents that you reach on a 3-mile round-trip hike. You can view the same features about 5 miles ahead on a short loop-trail at the **Sulphur Works,** the surviving vent system of ancient Mount Tehama, an 11,500-foot-high volcano that was 11 miles across at its base. Nearby **Brokeoff Mountain** (9,235 feet) is a remnant. You'll see sputtering mud pots and sniff clouds of reeking steam whose smell derives from hydrogen sulfide. This chemical dissolves in water to form sulfuric acid, which is decomposing the lava.

Go a mile to the **Southwest Entrance Station** and the drive's end.

Lost Coast

Ferndale to South Fork on Mattole Road

- 65 miles ▪ 2 hours ▪ All year. For the best views as you descend toward the Pacific Ocean, drive north to south.

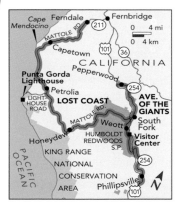

This little-traveled road climbs and dips through forests and windy ranchlands to one of the westernmost points in the contiguous 48 states, Cape Mendocino, with stops at two friendly settlements.

Begin in the Eel River Valley at **Ferndale** *(Chamber of Commerce. 707-786-4477. www .ferndalechamber.com),* an 1852 town that grew rich from creameries and enjoyed a boom in Victorian houses and commercial false-front architecture.

Follow Mattole Road out of town, zig-zagging up slopes wooded with maples and evergreens. After 4 miles a wide view opens across forested valleys; then grassy hills appear. This stretch is called **Wildcat Ridge,** but the animals you're likely to see are hawks and windblown cows. The road descends to the **Bear River** and a ranch at **Capetown,** a former stage stop. A precipitous stretch continues on to **Cape Mendocino,** site of many shipwrecks. Here three large tectonic plates grind together just off the coast, creating one of the continent's most active earthquake zones. For some 5 miles you drive beside a tidal zone that rose about 4 feet during the April 1992 earthquake, giving the appearance of perpetual low tide. Most of the land is private, with limited beach access.

At **Petrolia** the state's first commercial oil wells were drilled in 1865. Ahead, a 5-mile detour on Lighthouse Road leads to the shore; a 3.5-mile trail then leads to an old lighthouse. This is the northern margin of the **King Range National Conservation Area** *(707-986-5400.*

Mendocino Bay

www.blm.gov/ca/arcata/kingrange). Steep terrain includes 4,088-foot **King Peak,** defying highway engineers.

Return to Mattole Road and drive on to **Honeydew,** no more than a store yawning in the shade. This is the local hangout, so sit on the porch and gab. The road climbs, crossing the Mattole River and then **Panther Gap** (2,744 feet) as you enter **Humboldt Redwoods State Park** *(707-946-2409. www.parks .ca.gov)* and **Rockefeller Forest,** which holds many of the world's remaining old-growth redwoods. Stop at **Giant Tree** and marvel at the champion coast redwood, soaring 363 feet. Ahead in **South Fork,** the road joins the Avenue of the Giants (see below) and US 101.

Avenue of the Giants

Phillipsville to Pepperwood on California 254

■ 31 miles ■ 1½ hours ■ All year. Autumn colors are vibrant. *See map opposite.*

465

For visitors to 53,000-acre **Humboldt Redwoods State Park** *(707-946-2409. http://humboldtredwoods.org),* this is a quiet alternative to US 101, which it more or less parallels. You'll see ancient redwoods soaring from the alluvial flats of the Eel River and enjoy miles of hiking trails. Interspersed are woodsy hamlets, as well as tourist bait. (If you wish to buy a bear carved from a tree

Humboldt Redwoods State Park

stump with a chain saw, this is the place.) Heading north on US 101, take the **Phillipsville** exit and pick up a free auto tour pamphlet from the roadside box. On your left are views of the **South Fork Eel River.** Ahead, get a good look at redwoods from the short loop-trail through **F. K. Lane Grove.** About 6 miles farther, you enter a stretch of bigleaf maples, black cottonwoods, and other trees that share space with the redwoods and ferns. Ahead, **Williams Grove** offers river access for fishing *(mid-Oct.–Feb.),* and the park **visitor center** *(707-946-2263)* has exhibits on wildlife and local history.

Proceed 1.5 miles beyond Burlington Campground to **Weott,** a town that vanished under 33 feet of water during the 1964 Eel River flood; a pole on the right side of the road shows the high-water mark. Continue to the **California Federation of Women's Clubs Grove,** with its four-sided fireplace by architect Julia Morgan. Ahead, take the South Fork turnoff for **Founders Grove** and its trail to the 362-foot **Dyerville Giant,** the champion coast redwood, estimated to have weighed more than a million pounds, until it fell in 1991.

Return to the Avenue of the Giants. About a mile north, the Mattole Road to Honeydew cuts off to the left (see Lost Coast drive, pp. 464-465). Continue 7.5 miles to the **Drury-Chaney Groves** and walk one of the park's prettiest trails. The drive ends in 2 or 3 miles at Pepperwood on US 101.

California 1 North

Jenner to Mendocino

■ 87 miles ■ 3 hours ■ All year. Try to drive northbound (in the lane farthest from the sheer drops), and avoid darkness and heavy fog.

On this wild northern California coast, the blue Pacific pounds itself white on mighty headlands. The skies shift from haunting fog to glorious sunshine, changing your mood in synchrony. Small towns alternate with state parks. Begin in **Jenner,** a charming, don't-blink-or-you-missed-it settlement near the mouth of the **Russian River.** Where the river slips into the sea at **Goat Rock Beach,** look down at the colony of harbor seals *(pupping season: March-May).* In the estuary you'll see ospreys, and **Penny Island** is home to several hundred species of birds.

The portion of Calif. 1 (known locally as Highway 1) that switchbacks along the cliffs north of Jenner was originally built in the 19th century. After about 4 miles stop at the **Vista Trail,** a 1-mile loop with amazing coastal views. Heading north, look for broken shale and sandstone in the road cuts near the mouth of Timber Gulch; here the earth-shaking **San Andreas Fault** crosses the coastline and vanishes northward on its circuitous coastal journey. As you proceed, the woods part to reveal the palisades of **Fort Ross State Historic Park** *(707-847-3286. www.parks.ca.gov/?page_id=449. Vehicle fee).* The 1812 fort, built by Russians to hunt sea otters and grow food for their Alaska outposts, has a reconstructed chapel and residences.

Fort Ross SHP

Continuing north, you enter 6,000-acre **Salt Point State Park** *(707-847-3221. www.parks .ca.gov/?page_id=453. Adm. fee),* where Native Americans once searched for salt to preserve seafood and tan hides. If you scuba dive or snorkel here at **Gerstle Cove,** a wet suit is a must; water temperatures average 52°F.

In another few miles you reach **Kruse Rhododendron State Reserve** *(707-847-3221. www .parks.ca.gov/?page_id=448),* whose 317 forested acres are splashed with blossoms in spring. Then Calif. 1 edges one of the coast's numerous marine terraces, formed by tectonic uplift and fluctuating sea levels that carved platforms and bluffs into the land. Next comes **Sea Ranch,** a 5,000-acre development among meadows, trees, and cliffs. You can decide whether the geometric boxes and angled roofs blend into the landscape as planned. Five marked trails allow public beach access.

Driftwood hunters should stop at **Gualala** (wa-LA-la) **Point County Park** to comb the strand. Farther north, near **Anchor Bay,** geologists found pebbles eroded from rocks that were originally deposited near Santa Barbara—350 miles south. They were carried along as the land west of the San Andreas Fault moved northward over some 20 million years.

After the town of Point Arena, turn left on Lighthouse Road and drive about 2 miles to **Point Arena Light Station and Museum** *(707-882-2777 or 877-725-4448. www.pointarenalighthouse.com. Adm. fee.).* A replacement of the 1870 lighthouse, it has the original Fresnel lens. The 115-foot tower is a good perch for spying gray whales from December through April. If you want to experience the loneliness of a lighthouse keeper, rent a bungalow overnight.

Return to Calif. 1, which soon crosses the wide **Garcia River plain,** where white whistling swans arrive for the winter from Siberia and the Arctic. Continue to the beaches and dunes of **Manchester State Park** *(707-882-2463. www.parks .ca.gov/?page_id=437. Adm. fee).*

Two miles offshore, **Arena Rock** is a submerged, 10-acre pinnacle where snorkelers and divers observe sea creatures such as the tiger rockfish. At the park's north end, near Alder Creek, the San Andreas Fault slashes out to sea.

After passing the town of Elk and the **Navarro** and **Albion Rivers,** you reach **Van Damme State Park** *(707-937-5804. www.parks.ca.gov/?page_ id=433. Adm. fee),* a spot for snorkelers to gather abalone *(April-Nov., except July).* Brown "heads" bobbing in the ocean are often mistaken for sea otters, which no longer live here; they are air-filled bulbs of kelp. Tide pools hold sea stars and anemones. The park runs inland, too, along the fern-draped canyon of the **Little River.**

Take Airport Road off Calif. 1 to the **Pygmy Forest Discovery Trail,** where nature practices

467

Mendocino coastline

Cow parsnip along California 1

bonsai on pine and cypress trees. About 2 miles north of Little River is the Victorian village of **Mendocino.** An art colony since the 1950s, the town features highlights such as the **Mendocino Art Center** *(45200 Lake St. 707-937-5818. www.mendocinoartcenter.org),* gabled **MacCallum House** *(Inn & restaurant. 45020 Albion St. 707-937-0289 or 800-609-0492. www.maccallumhouse.com),* and **Kelley House Museum** *(45007 Albion St. 707-937-5791. www.kelleyhouse museum.org. Oct.-May Fri.-Mon., June-Sept. closed Wed.; donation).*

The **Ford House Visitor Center and Museum** *(735 Main St. 707-937-5397. Donation)* displays a model of the town from the 1890s, when it had a 12-seat outhouse. Trails wind across **Mendocino Headlands State Park** *(707-937-5804. www.parks.ca.gov/?page_id=442),* which surrounds the village on three sides. The park epitomizes the north coast—bluffs, grasslands, tide pools, wave-carved tunnels, blue waters, gray whales, and views to expand the spirit.

Marin County

Golden Gate Bridge to Point Reyes National Seashore (with 8-mile round-trip up Mount Tamalpais) on US 101, California 1, and Panoramic Highway

■ 34 miles ■ 2 hours ■ All year

This drive has all the classic sights of northern California. After crossing the **Golden Gate Bridge** northbound on US 101/Calif. 1, pass Sausalito and exit onto Calif. 1 just north of Marin City. Drive 3 miles and turn right onto the Panoramic Highway, then, less than a mile ahead, turn left on Muir Woods Road to **Muir Woods National Monument** *(415-388-2596. www.nps.gov/muwo. Adm. fee).*

These 560 acres embrace the Bay Area's only virgin redwood forest, with trees as high as 252 feet and at least a thousand years old. Trails loop around Redwood Creek, beyond the visitor center.

Return to the Panoramic Highway, turn left, and continue to the Pan Toll Road. Turn right to ascend the east peak of **Mount Tamalpais** (2,571 feet), the mountain biking center of Marin County. A startling panorama takes in San Francisco, the bay, and the Pacific Ocean.

Drive back to the Panoramic Highway, turn right, and zigzag 4 miles downhill among grassy hills and forests of redwood and California bay to reach Calif. 1. Here **Stinson Beach** lies on a sandspit in front of **Bolinas Lagoon,** where great blue herons and snowy egrets fish. The road follows the shoreline and, 3.5 miles north of Stinson Beach, birds nest in the reserve at **Audubon Canyon Ranch** *(415-868-9244. www.egret.org. Mid-March–mid-July weekends & holidays; donation).*

As Calif. 1 unwinds northward through the **Olema Valley,** its center line virtually traces the dreaded **San Andreas Fault.** On your left lies the **Point Reyes Peninsula,** which during the 1906 San Francisco earthquake jolted as much as 18 feet northwest, pulling roads and trees asunder. To walk an interpretive trail along the fault line, continue just north of Olema and turn left on Bear Valley Road to the visitor center for **Point Reyes National Seashore** *(415-464-5100. www.nps.gov/pore).* This preserve embraces forests, grasslands, coastal wetlands, and seashore. Migrating gray whales are easy to spy in winter from **Point Reyes Lighthouse.** The 71,000 acre preserve also shelters tule elk, marine mammals, and more than 430 species of birds. Nearly half the continent's bird species have been spotted here.

Point Reyes National Seashore

On the return drive, stay on Calif. 1, stopping at the **Muir Beach Overlook** for a view of the coastline and the fabled Golden Gate Bridge.

Continue to US 101, which you can take back to the bridge.

469

Silverado Trail

Napa to Calistoga

■ 29 miles ■ 1 hour ■ Spring through fall. In spring mustard flowers carpet the Napa Valley. Summer is hot and crowded. Fall is grape harvesttime. Winter brings 70 percent of the year's rainfall.

The Silverado Trail runs parallel to Calif. 29, the main (and often clogged) traffic artery through the Napa Valley. This quieter back road offers glimpses of the nation's foremost wine region, about an hour northeast of San Francisco, as it was perhaps 30 years ago. Because the roadway dips and curves along the foothills, it offers gorgeous views of vineyards and mountains.

Along the way you can stop in at small wineries for tours and tastings; most of the larger ones are along Calif. 29. The Silverado Trail was established in 1852, when floods swamped the valley's main road. By the late 1800s it was the wagon route from the cinnabar mines at the valley's north end to the docks of San Pablo Bay to the south.

To begin the drive, go north on Calif. 29 through the city of **Napa** to Trancas Street; turn right, drive less than 2 miles, then turn left on the Silverado Trail. As you proceed, most of the grapevines surrounding you are Chardonnay, but when you reach the Yountville Cross Road after 8 miles, Cabernet Sauvignon begins its reign. Turn left at this crossroads—one of many east-west links between the trail and Calif. 29—and go about a mile to the **Napa River Ecological Reserve**. This is a rare public access point to the river. The 73-acre riparian habitat reveals what the area looked like 150 years ago. A path winds among oaks, California bays, and willows; 150 bird species have been catalogued here.

Drive another mile on the crossroad for a side trip to **Yountville,** a cozy tourist town named for George Yount, who planted the valley's first grapes in 1838. Back on the Silverado Trail north, the valley opens up and allows you to grasp the picture of local geography. The mountains rising 1,500 to 2,000 feet on both sides of the valley are part of the Coast Range. Those that form the valley's western wall are covered in chaparral and Douglas-fir, while the less lofty, drier mountains to the east are generally cloaked in oaks and manzanitas. The mountains were created when sedimentary rocks buckled upward under great pressure, then were covered with volcanic lava and ash. Alluvial deposits made the rich soil that's perfect for wine grapes.

Vineyard along the Silverado Trail

Continue to Rutherford Hill Road, passing countless vines and serene wineries; a right turn leads a half mile to the **Auberge du Soleil** *(707-963-1211. www.aubergedusoleil.com).* The renowned restaurant's outdoor deck seems to hang over the valley like a hot-air balloon.

A mile north on the trail brings you to Zinfandel Lane. For a side trip to **St. Helena,** a principal town of the Napa Valley, turn left and go about a mile to Calif. 29, then turn right. Highlights include the old-fashioned main street, and the **Robert Louis Stevenson Silverado Museum** *(1490 Library La. 707-963-3757. www.silveradomuseum.org. Closed Sun.-Mon.; donation),* devoted to the noted Scot.

Continuing north on the Silverado Trail to Taplin Road, notice one of the valley's original 60 or 70 stone bridges; another picturesque example stands a bit farther at Pope Street. About 10 miles farther, your drive ends upon turning left on Lincoln Avenue into **Calistoga,** settled in 1859. The mineral spas and hot mud baths of this resort town represent the last gasps of the volcanic activity that helped shape the Napa Valley. Another geothermal remnant, the **Old Faithful Geyser** *(707-942-6463. Adm. fee)* gushes 60 feet every 40 minutes. There's a large model of the early resort at the **Sharpsteen Museum** *(1311 Washington St. 707-942-5911. www.sharpsteen-museum.org. Donation).*

Above town looms 4,343-foot **Mount St. Helena,** formed when manifold ridges were covered with hundreds of feet of volcanic materials. A brief silver boom erupted here in the early 1870s; Silverado City boasted 1,500 people, several saloons, and a hotel. The boom went bust by the time Robert Louis Stevenson spent his honeymoon in a cabin there in 1880. Today Mount St. Helena is preserved as 4,747-acre **Robert Louis Stevenson State Park** *(8 miles north of Calistoga on Calif. 29. 707-942-4575. www.parks.ca.gov/?page_id=472).* A rough trail ascends past the old Silverado Mine and Stevenson's cabin site to dramatic views over the Napa Valley.

Route 1

Monterey to Morro Bay

- 123 miles - 6 hours - All year

This drive encompasses both Big Sur Coast Highway and the San Luis Obispo North Coast Byway. The drive starts in historic Monterey, visits the art colony of Carmel, and threads through Big Sur, where mountains plunge into the Pacific. Farther south, the landscape mellows to oak-studded hills as the road passes Hearst Castle on its way to Morro Bay.

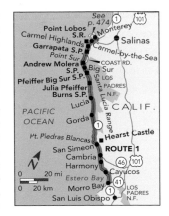

Join Calif. 1 in **Monterey** *(Monterey County Convention & Visitors Bureau. 831-657-6400. www .seemonterey.com).* The town served as California's capital under Spanish, Mexican, and American flags, and by the early 1900s boasted an important sardine industry. Surviving sites include the **Royal Presidio Chapel, Monterey State Historic Park, Custom House, Casa Soberanes, Larkin House,** and other adobe buildings, as well as touristy **Fisherman's Wharf** and **Cannery Row,** home of the celebrated **Monterey Bay Aquarium**. After enjoying your visit here, drive 3 miles south on Calif. 1 to **Carmel-by-the-Sea** *(Carmel Visitors Center, San Carlos St. 831-624-2522 or 800-550-4333.*

www.carmelcalifornia .org), an upscale village of quaint colorful cottages, restaurants, inns, shops, and art galleries fronted by a broad beach fringed with Monterey pines. Among the highlights are **Mission San Carlos Borromeo del Rio Carmelo,** second of the California missions, founded by Padre Junipero Serra in 1770; **Tor House,** the 1919 home of poet Robinson Jeffers; and mile-long **Carmel River State Beach,** with its pelicans and kingfishers.

From Carmel drive 3.5 miles south to **Point Lobos State Reserve** *(831-624-4909. www.point lobos.org. Vehicle fee),* a 550-acre park encompassing coves, head-

Big Sur coastline

lands, meadows, tide pools, and the nation's first undersea ecological reserve, covering 770 acres, with kelp forests 80 feet high. Trails lead past Monterey cypresses, which grow naturally only here and on the 17-Mile Drive (see pp. 474-475). The park's 250 species of birds and mammals include black-tailed deer, gray foxes, sea otters, and sea lions. Migrating gray whales pass by from December through April.

Onetime resident writer Henry Miller called Big Sur "the face of the earth as the creator intended it to look."

After driving through **Carmel Highlands,** where impressive houses perch on granite cliffs above the sea, you reach the start of **Big Sur,** which extends 90 miles south to San Simeon. On this fabled coastline, redwood groves reach skyward, the **Santa Lucia Range** plunges into the sea, and waves are beaten to froth on ragged rocks. It's a place of elemental power that can make human affairs seem inconsequential.

Sea otter

Route 1, opened in 1937, climbs as high as 1,000 feet above the sea. One of the few easy-to-reach beaches is at **Garrapata State Park** *(831-667-2315. www.parks .ca.gov/?page_id=579),* about 2 miles south of Carmel Highlands. From **Soberanes Point** watch for sea otters, which are protected along the entire coast.

En route to Bixby Creek Bridge, 7 miles farther, you can choose to leave Calif. 1 and drive the 12-mile old Coast Road, which climbs through remote forests and canyons and offers silent ocean views before ending at

Andrew Molera State Park (see below). The unpaved road is tortuous and impassable when it rains.

Much photographed **Bixby Creek Bridge** is a single-span concrete arch more than 260 feet high and 700 feet long. Park at turnouts near either end to gawk or take pictures. Ahead, the highway passes **Hurricane Point,** a place of big winds and big views, and the mouth of the **Little Sur River.** Looking inland, you'll see 3,710-foot-high **Pico Blanco,** distinguishable by its lime deposits. Toward the sea, sand dunes soon appear, rolling toward the 1889 **Point Sur Light Station** *(831-625-4419. www.pointsur.org. Tours Sat.-Sun., call for additional days April-Oct.; adm. fee),* a state historic park. In 3 miles you reach 4,800-acre **Andrew Molera State Park** *(831-667-2315. www .parks.ca.gov/?page_id=582. Adm. fee),* whose broad beach, oak and redwood forests, and stretch of the Big Sur River are accessible only by foot.

Pass through the settlement of **Big Sur,** which offers food and lodging, and head for **Pfeiffer Big Sur State Park** *(831-667-2315. www.parks .ca.gov/?page_id=570. Adm. fee),* where the **Big Sur River** runs through 964 acres of redwoods, maples, sycamores, bay laurel, and ferns. Then go 1.5 miles south and turn right on the 2-mile road down **Sycamore Canyon** to the white sands of **Pfeiffer Beach,** where the surf roars through arched rocks.

Nearly 2 miles farther on the highway you come to **Nepenthe** *(831-667-2345),* an indoor-outdoor restaurant perched 800 feet above the sea and famous for its views. About half a mile south, on the left, look for the **Henry Miller Memorial Library** *(831-667-2574. www.henrymiller.org. Closed Tues. in summer),* perched among towering redwoods. It displays books and memorabilia of the novelist who spent 18 years in Big Sur. Also stop 8 miles farther

at **Julia Pfeiffer Burns State Park** *(831-667-2315. www.parks.ca.gov/?page_id=578. Adm. fee),* whose terrain ranges from 3,000-foot-high ridges to an underwater preserve. Do walk the short trail along the seaside bluff to see **McWay Falls** pour 80 feet into a picturesque cove.

Ahead of you lies the southern stretch of Big Sur. The road clings to a precipitous coastline, and the only settlements in the next 35 miles are Lucia, Pacific Valley, Gorda, and Ragged Point. From here onward are hills and pastureland. You'll spy the **Piedras Blancas Light Station** on a point supposedly named in 1542 by Spanish explorer Juan Rodríguez Cabrillo for its white rocks (so tinted by bird droppings).

After a spell away from the Pacific, the road reaches the town of **San Simeon,** a staging area for the 5-mile bus ride to

California 1 near Big Sur

Hearst Castle *(805-927-2020 or 800-444-4445. www.hearstcastle.org. Tours only, call for reservations; adm. fee),* begun in 1919 by newspaperman William Randolph Hearst. Perched in the Santa Lucia Range, the 127-acre estate features the 115-room main house and guesthouses, which mix classical and Mediterranean Revival styles, using European architectural elements, antiques, and artwork collected by Hearst.

Continue 7 miles to **Cambria,** nestled against hills where Monterey pines thrive in porous soil of decomposed sandstone. On the ocean side of the highway, at Moonstone Beach, look for moonstones and California jade. Drive on 6 miles to the colony of **Harmony,** where you can watch artists at work. Ahead on **Estero Bay,** small **Cayucos** dates from the coastal schooner era of the 1860s; the pier has good fishing for rockfish and perch, plus views of pelicans and cormorants.

The end of your route is **Morro Bay** *(Morro Bay Chamber of Commerce. 805-772-4467. www.morrobay.org),* easily identified by its landmark **Morro Rock.** A turban-shaped, extinct volcanic cone perhaps 50 million years old, it is 576 feet high and linked to the mainland by a 2,000-foot-long sandbar.

Mission San Carlos, Carmel

Peregrine falcons live here. To learn about local wildlife, visit the **Morro Bay State Park Museum of Natural History** *(805-772-2694. www .mbspmuseum.org. Adm. fee).* Around Morro Bay you'll see great blue herons and, from October to March, monarch butterflies in eucalyptus trees.

474

17-Mile Drive

Loop from California 1 Gate, midway between Monterey and Carmel-by-the-Sea.

▪ 17 miles ▪ 1 hour ▪ All year. Adm. fee.

On this drive around the Monterey Peninsula, about 2.5 hours south of San Francisco, you'll see a series of marvels. Some are natural (a ragged, romantic shoreline, offshore rocks swarming with seals and seabirds, the 5,300-acre **Del Monte Forest** and its windswept cypresses); some are man-made (elegant houses, world-famous golf courses). To enter the drive, you can use four additional gates: Carmel *(off N. San Antonio Dr.),* Morse *(off Calif. 68),* Pacific Grove *(off Sunset Dr.),* and Country Club *(off Congress Ave. in Pacific Grove).* Your entrance fee includes a guide map with numbered stops, and there are plenty of directional signs.

You'll start on the inland portion of the route. Drive about a mile from the **Calif. 1 Gate** to the **Shepherd's Knoll Vista Point** to see the long, white arc of **Monterey Bay.** Now the road climbs to **Huckleberry Hill,** where you look over the **Monterey Peninsula,** a vast projection of the Santa Lucia Range. After threading your way downhill among luxury houses in a forest of Monterey and bishop pines, you pass a golf resort and reach the coast at **Spanish Bay.** At this spot Spanish explorer Gaspar de Portolá camped in 1769 while trying to find Monterey Bay; today you can picnic on the white-sand beach.

Continue to **Point Joe,** where the sea surges perpetually due to submerged rocks (although one theory says that ocean currents collide here). The area is a graveyard of ships that mistook Point Joe for the entrance to Monterey Bay.

To see tide pools, drive on to the 3-mile **Coastal Bluff Walking Trail.** Farther ahead, your nose will know when you're near **Seal** and **Bird Rocks,** the home of countless squealing gulls and cormorants. The barks of hundreds of harbor seals and California sea lions also fill the air. Continue to **Fanshell Beach,** a white crescent where harbor seals bear their pups each spring.

The drive's best view of the Pacific coastline is from the **Cypress Point Lookout;** the view sometimes stretches 20 miles down the coast to the **Point Sur Lighthouse.** Drive another mile to 13-acre **Crocker Grove,** a wildlife preserve with the oldest and largest Monterey cypress. The next stop is the wind-ravaged **Lone Cypress,** venerable symbol of the Monterey coast, on its rocky knob. The road then loops out to **Pescadero Point,** the northern tip of Carmel Bay, then passes the famous Pebble Beach golf resort opened in 1919.

Lone Cypress

475

Conclude your drive at the Carmel Gate or back at the Calif. 1 Gate.

HAWAII
Kalanianaole Highway, Oahu

Lunalilo Freeway (H1) to Hawaii 61 on Hawaii 72

- 20 miles ▪ 1 hour ▪ All year

Here's a handy escape route from Honolulu's Waikiki Beach. Replacing the madness and crowds is a quieter side of Oahu—the tropical fish of Hanauma Bay, sandy beaches and expert bodysurfing waters, and the forested back side of the **Koolau Range** *(Hawaii Visitors Bureau. 808-923-1811).*

The route begins where H1 becomes Hawaii 72, northeast of Diamond Head. From Waikiki you can reach H1 via a scenic shoreline route: Drive east on Kalakaua Avenue to Diamond Head Road, which soon becomes Kahala Avenue and passes through elegant oceanfront estates. Turn left on Hunakai Street, then right on Kilauea Avenue. Follow the signs to H1 east.

Pali Highway through the Koolau Range with Honolulu in the distance

You'll drive the length of 6-mile-long **Maunalua Bay.** Then, ahead of you, rise 1,208-foot **Koko Crater** *(on the left)* and 646-foot **Koko Head** *(right).* Continue to **Hanauma Bay State Underwater Park** *(www.hawaiiforvisitors .com. closed Tues.; adm. fee),* the island's most popular snorkeling spot. (Visit early to beat the crowds.) Hanauma began taking shape 35,000 years ago, when a volcanic explosion under the sea pushed up a cone of ash, silicate, basalt boulders, and limestone. Some 7,000 years ago the ocean eroded through the cone's wall, creating the bay. On the palm-fringed sand grows *pohuehue,* or beach morning glory. Caution: The rock ledges and turbulent outer zones are dangerous.

Within the next 2 miles you reach the **Molokai Island Viewpoint** (the island of **Lanai** is also visible) and then the **Halona Blowhole,** where water rushes into an undersea tunnel and up through a crevice, spewing into the air; the effect is best during rough surf. Almost immediately past that is the brown-sugar-colored strand of **Sandy Beach Park,** where bodysurfing championships are held in the often treacherous surf.

Hawaii 72 climbs away from the sea, then passes **Makapuu Point,** the easternmost spot on Oahu. (Look for the lighthouse.) You reach the coast again at **Makapuu Beach Park,** where bodysurfers ride waves as high as 12 feet and hang gliders soar from cliffs. Not far offshore lie **Rabbit Island,** an old volcanic crater occupied by wild rabbits and wedge-tailed shearwaters, and smaller Turtle Island. Across the road is **Sea Life Park** *(808-259-7933. www.sealifeparkhawaii .com. Adm. fee),* offering performances by whales and dolphins, as well as a 300,000-gallon reef tank full of sharks and tropical fish.

Hanauma Bay's turquoise waters and coral reefs are home to sea turtles and schools of angelfish, parrot fish, and other finned creatures so tame they'll eat from your hand.

Proceed 2.5 miles to **Waimanalo Beach Park,** with white sand and good swimming. Then comes the gate to **Bellows Air Force Station,** where a good "local secret" beach opens to the public on weekends and holidays only.

To your left rises the rugged green Koolau Range, the island's dominant mountain chain. About 4 miles past the ethnically Hawaiian town of **Waimanalo,** the route ends at Hawaii 61. You can turn right to visit the bedroom community of **Kailua** (windsurfing at Kailua Beach Park, swimming at Lanikai Beach). Or turn left to take the scenic **Pali Highway** (Hawaii 61) over the Koolau Range, stopping at windy **Nuuanu Pali Lookout** for a view of windward **Oahu,** then descending into Honolulu. Or simply return to Honolulu the way you came.

Hana Highway, Maui

Kahului to Hana on Hawaii 36 and 360

■ 100 miles round-trip ■ 6 hours ■ All year. Since there are 54 bridges and more than 600 curves, don't drive this route if you are in a hurry or suffer from motion sickness.

477

Known as one of Hawaii's most scenic routes, the Hana Highway winds along the coast past waterfalls and rocky streams, through rain forests, and among tropical blossoms and fruit trees. The twisting "highway," built in 1927 by convict labor, is well paved but narrow, with many stops while oncoming traffic crosses one-lane bridges. Set out early in the day, pull over for restless drivers behind you, and take it easy. It's the trip that counts here, not the destination.

Hawaii 36 begins in **Kahului.** A surf-laced coastline and sugarcane fields appear alongside you on the 7 miles to **Paia,** the last place before Hana to fill your gas tank and picnic basket. Once a busy sugar plantation town, Paia has become a laid back colony of hippies, craftspeople, and windsurfers, who show their stuff at **Hookipa Beach Park,** near the 9 mile marker past town.

The road climbs away from the coast through an area of increased rainfall that supports pineapple fields. Just past the 16-mile marker, the road is renumbered as Hawaii 360, and mile markers go back to zero. This is the start of the "real" Hana Highway. Gardens and mailboxes sprout up when you reach tiny **Kailua,** where many residents work on the ditches that carry rainwater from the wet uplands to the dry cane fields of central Maui. Along this stretch, guava trees and mountain apple

Keanae Peninsula

Wailua Falls, near Kipahulu

478

trees are common. On the way out of town notice Norfolk pine, rainbow eucalyptus, and bamboo.

Past the 9-mile marker, stop at the short **Waikamoi Ridge Trail** to stroll among tall eucalyptus trees, their trunks twined with South American taro vines.

On the road just ahead are **Waikamoi Falls** and **Puohokamoa Falls,** the latter a fine picnic spot surrounded by kukui nut trees, heliconias, and impatiens, with pools to swim in. Then continue just over a mile to **Kaumahina State Wayside Park** and its expansive view over the coastline.

The road runs along several hundred feet above the sea, then skirts U-shaped **Honomanu Bay** *(entrance just past mile 14).* The bay encloses a rocky, black-sand beach and rough water, while the verdant gulch behind it is home to African tulip trees with fiery red blossoms.

After you climb the bay's far side, there is a small pull-off with a stunning view back over the bay. In about 2 miles you reach the **Keanae Arboretum,** where trails lead to native and introduced plants (taro, breadfruit, banana, bamboo, ti, ginger). Just ahead is the road down to the **Keanae Peninsula,** an extension of land created by rough lava that spilled down from **Haleakala,** the dormant volcano that dominates eastern Maui. Down in quiet **Keanae** village, whose residents are mainly native Hawaiians, there is a restored 1860 stone church and cultivated patches of taro, the source of poi. You can get a good view of the peninsula from the small, unmarked **Keanae Overlook,** just past mile 17.

Now comes a stretch where the road climbs high above the ocean. Above this region, Haleakala's slopes receive an average 390 inches (and sometimes as much as 500 inches) of rain yearly, which accounts for the many waterfalls throughout this area. One of the prettiest is beyond mile 22 at the wayside park of **Puaa Kaa.** Here, you will welcome the picnic tables beside a stream among tree ferns, guavas, and gingers as a wonderful place to rest and contemplate.

Just after the Hana Gardenland nursery, you can take a side trip to the left on the rutted, muddy Ulaino road leading to **Piilanihale Heiau,** a large temple of fitted lava rocks built by a 14th-century chief.

Back on Hawaii 360, stop at **Waianapanapa State Park,** which offers a black-sand beach and caves formed of collapsed lava tubes. (The water inside sometimes turns red—some say because of clouds of small shrimp, while others cite the legend of a slain Hawaiian princess whose blood tinges the water.) Sweet-smelling plumeria blooms in the park, and you may see black noddy terns flying near the sea.

Within a few miles you reach the pastoral town of **Hana,** which is quiet and unspectacular, though its setting between **Hana Bay** and the green hills

The 54 bridges along the Hana road have Hawaiian names with such poetic translations as Whirling Waters, Open Laughter, First Ruffled Waters, Prayer Blossoms, and Heavenly Mist.

is lovely and its mood timeless. The main businesses are ranching and the **Hotel Hana-Maui** *(808-248-8211)*, started in 1946. Do see the Hawaiian artifacts and crafts on display at the **Hana Cultural Center** *(808-248-8622. www .hanaculturalcenter.org. Mon.-Thurs.; adm. fee)* and visit the 1838 **Wananalua Church,** built of lava rock.

The drive ends in Hana, but the road continues as Hawaii 31 to **Oheo Gulch,** part of **Haleakala National Park** *(808-572-4400. www.nps.gov/hale. Adm. fee),* where pools form in **Palikea Stream** as it descends from Haleakala.

In the nearby village of **Kipahulu,** you'll find the grave of aviator Charles Lindbergh at the **Palapala Hoomau Church cemetery.** Return to Kahului over the same route you came.

Hamakua Coast, Hawaii

Hilo to the Waipio Valley on Hawaii 19 and 240

- 51 miles ■ 2 hours ■ All year

This rugged coast—edged with cliffs, crossed by streams, lush with foliage and waterfalls—represents a real departure from the island's highly developed Kona and Kohala coasts. Begin your drive in **Hilo** *(Visitors Bureau, 250 Keawe St. 808-961-5797. Mon.-Fri.),* a tropical town whose warm weather and annual 137 inches of rain make it a garden and orchid-growing center *(largest number of orchid blooms Feb.-April).* The **Lyman House Memorial Museum** *(276 Haili St. 808-935-5021. Closed Sun.; adm. fee)* focuses on Hawaiian life and artifacts.

In the weathered, turn-of-the-20th-century downtown district, Hawaii 19 fronts **Hilo Bay;** take this route north. From a scenic point between miles 3 and 4, you can look back at the crescent of Hilo Bay. Bananas and wild sugarcane grow in this lush area.

Between miles 7 and 8, turn right on the **Onomea Bay Scenic Route,** which parallels Hawaii 19 for 4 miles, passing through an area that matches most people's idea of the "real Hawaii." The road is lined with Alexandra palms, mango trees, and red-blooming African tulip trees. Narrow stone bridges cross streams. Below a bluff you'll see the black rocks and crashing waves of **Onomea Bay,** where sea turtles swim. Along this route

Along the Hamakua coast drive

you can visit the **Hawaii Tropical Botanical Garden** *(808-964-5233. http://htbg.com. Adm. fee),* which preserves a seaside rain forest and displays more than 2,000 species of flowers and plants from around the world. Shorebirds and sea turtles inhabit this garden.

After you rejoin Hawaii 19, continue past mile 13 and turn then left on Hawaii 220 for a 3-mile side trip to a state park—**Akaka Falls State Park** *(808-587-0300. www.hawaiistateparks.org. Adm. fee).* There, a half-mile loop leads you among bamboo groves, red ginger, impatiens, hanging orchids, and other rain forest plants to reach the falls, which plunge more than 440 feet down a volcanic cliff. After returning to the main road, drive north about half a mile to **Kolekole Beach Park.** Here **Kolekole Stream** (from Akaka Falls) meets the sea at a black-sand beach. The surf is dangerous, but the stream has pools for swimming, and this is a nice picnic spot.

You can also stop ahead at **Laupahoehoe Beach Park,** a grassy patch on a lava peninsula pounded by surf. Then continue 12 miles and take a 3-mile side trip to little-used **Kalopa State Park,** a rain forest on the lower slopes of **Mauna Kea,** with a 0.7-mile nature trail. Back on the main road, continue to the former sugar-mill town of **Honokaa,** a quiet, multicultural hamlet, and turn onto Hawaii 240, traveling about 9 miles to road's end at the **Waipio Valley Overlook.**

Some people believe the ghosts of ancient Hawaiian nobility walk the Waipio Valley and you can hear their chants and see their torches.

Kayaker on Waipio River, Big Island

From here you gaze over a fertile, mile-wide valley enclosed by pali (cliffs) as high as 2,000 feet. Far below you'll see taro patches and fishponds, fruit trees (coconut, mango, guava, banana), waterfalls, and a black-sand beach split by **Waipio Stream.**

The valley, inhabited for a thousand years, was in ancient times a hub of Hawaii's political and religious life, a home of chiefs. Although 2,500 people once lived here, that number dwindled drastically in the 1800s, and after a disastrous 1946 tsunami, most people moved topside.

If you want to visit, the hourly **Waipio Valley Shuttle** *(808-775-7121. Closed Sun.; fare)* plies the steep, treacherous road *(suitable only for four-wheel-drive vehicles),* or you can walk a mile down. (And up!)

Return to Hilo the way you came.

Chain of Craters Road, Hawaii

Hawaii Volcanoes National Park

- 46 miles round-trip ▪ 6 hours
- All year. Adm. fee.

Lava-flow tour

From southeast **Crater Rim Drive,** Chain of Craters Road descends 3,700 feet until it ends sharply at a lava flow. From there it's usually a short walk to see flowing, red-hot lava. On the way you drive among the vast flows that spilled from the shield vent called **Maunu Ulu;** the lava expelled here from 1969 to 1974 would pave a highway around the Equator. (The smooth lava is *pahoehoe,* the jagged is *aa.*)

After 17 miles, a 2-mile trail leads to the **Puu Loa Petroglyphs,** some 15,000 figures and symbols carved in lava by early Hawaiians. Drive 2.5 miles to where the road meets the ocean at the **Holei Sea Arch,** eroded by waves in the sea cliffs. Swimming is unsafe. The current route ends near here, where lava has swamped the road. Since 1983, lava flows have buried more than 13 miles of highway, destroyed 10,000 acres of trees and plants, and added more than 500 acres of new land to the island.

Despite all the road changes, you still might see sizzling hot (2100°F) lava flows entering the water off the coast. Be sure to follow the guidance of park rangers as to where you can safely go.

Crater Rim Drive, Hawaii

Hawaii Volcanoes National Park

- 11 miles ▪ 2 hours ▪ All year. Adm. fee to park.

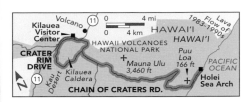

At **Hawaii Volcanoes National Park** *(808-985-6000. www.nps.gov/havo. Adm. fee)* you can actually witness the force that continues to build the Big Island of Hawaii—volcano power. Kilauea is one of the world's most active volcanoes. Steam rises from its caldera, and the terrain is a surreal moonscape of craters, cinder cones, and congealed lava flows. You'll circle Kilauea's rim, see a rain forest and a desert, and enter the realm of Pele, Hawaii's volcano goddess.

Begin with the natural history displays at the **Kilauea Visitor Center,** then cross the road to see the **Volcano House** *(Call sister hotel*

Hapuu tree ferns and ohia forest on Kilauea

Naniloa Volcanoes Resort for more info. 808-969-3333), a historic hotel perched on the rim of the caldera. From its parking lot, walk the 0.3-mile **Earthquake Trail** for a view of **Kilauea Caldera** (2 miles across, 500 feet at its deepest) and **Mauna Loa,** the world's most massive mountain, rising 32,000 feet from seafloor to peak. Mauna Loa erupted in 1984, spewing forth a million cubic yards of lava per hour and ultimately covering almost 12,000 acres of land.

The east rift zone of Kilauea has been flowing since 1983, so you may be able to see rivers of red molten rock, which reaches 2100°F.

Now you'll drive clockwise around Kilauea's rim, soon entering a rain forest of ferns and red-blossomed ohia trees. Stop at the **Kilauea Iki** ("little Kilauea") **Crater,** which in 1959 was a lake of boiling lava with fountains 1,900 feet high; now you see a steaming black crust. Continue to the **Thurston Lava Tube** (0.3-mile loop-trail) to walk through a former conduit for molten rock. Among the nearby ohia trees and tree ferns you may see the apapane, a bright red honeycreeper that feeds on nectar and insects.

Ahead stop at **Puu Puai Overlook,** where a 0.4-mile paved walkway leads along the **Devastation Trail.** (A member of your party can drive 0.7 mile ahead to the Devastation parking area to pick you up at trail's end.) This former rain forest area was obliterated by pumice and cinders from Kilauea Iki's 1959 eruption, but is being recolonized by both native and non-native plants. Ahead, impressively steaming **Halemaumau Crater** is said to be the home of Pele Honua Mea (Sacred Earth Person). Hawaiians still come to pay homage with dances on the crater's edge. Above the crater look for white-tailed tropic birds.

After this, you cross old lava flows, see the **Kau Desert** (created by natural acid rain), and view the **Southwest Rift Zone** (fractures in the weakened side of the volcano). Stop at the **Jaggar Museum** *(808-985-6000. www.nps .gov/havo)* to look at diverse types of lava and bits of volcanic glass called Pele's tears. Then you pass the vents of **Steaming Bluff** and the volcanic gases and colorful rocks of the **Sulfur Banks.** Your circle concludes back at the visitor center.

Amaumau ferns on the edge of Kilauea Caldera

Lava from Kilauea sizzling into the Pacific Ocean

State Tourism Offices

Alabama Tourism Dept.
401 Adams Ave., Ste. 126
Montgomery, AL 36103-4927
334-242-4169 or 800-252-2262
www.alabama.travel

Alaska Travel Industry
  Association
2600 Cordova St., Ste. 201
Anchorage, AK 99503
800-478-1255
www.travelalaska.com

Arizona Office of Tourism
1110 W Washington St., Ste. 155
Phoenix, AZ 85007
866-275-5816
www.arizonaguide.com

Arkansas Dept. of Parks
  & Tourism
1 Capitol Mall, Dept. 7701
Little Rock, AK 72201
501-682-777 or 800-628-8725
www.arkansas.com

California Tourism
P.O. Box 1499
Sacramento, CA 95812-1499
916-444-4429 or 800-862-2543
www.visitcalifornia.com

Colorado Tourism Office
1625 Broadway, Ste. 1700
Denver, CO 80202
800-265-6723
www.colorado.com

Connecticut Office of Tourism
755 Main St.
Hartford, CT 06103
888-288-4748
www.ctvisit.com

Delaware Tourism Office
99 Kings Highway
Dover, DE 19901-7305
302-739-4271 or 866-284-7483
www.visitdelaware.com

Visit Florida
661 E Jefferson St., Ste. 300
Tallahassee, FL 32301
850-488-5607 Ext. 320
www.visitflorida.com

Georgia Dept. of Economic Dev.
75 Fifth St., NW, Ste. 1200
Atlanta, GA 30308
404-962-4079
www.georgia.org

Hawaii Visitors & Convention
  Bureau
2270 Kalakaua Ave., Ste. 801
Honolulu, HI 96815
800-923-1811
www.gohawaii.com

Idaho Division of Tourism Dev.
700 W State St.
Boise, ID 83720-0093
208-334-2470 or 800-847-4843
www.visitidaho.org

Illinois Bureau of Tourism
100 W Randolph St., Ste. 3-400
Chicago, IL 60601
800-226-6632
www.enjoyillinois.com

Indiana Office of Tourism Dev.
One North Capitol #600
Indianapolis, IN 46204-2288
317-232-8860 or 800-677-9800
www.in.gov/visitindiana

Iowa Division of Tourism
200 E Grand Ave.
Des Moines, IA 50309
515-242-4705 or 888-472-6035
www.traveliowa.com

Kansas Travel & Tourism
1020 S Kansas Ave., #200
Topeka, KS 66612
800-252-6727
www.travelks.com

Kentucky Dept. of Travel
500 Mero St., 22nd Floor
Frankfort, KY 40601
502-564-4930 or 800-225-8747
www.kentuckytourism.com

Louisiana Office of Tourism
PO Box 94291
Baton Rouge, LA 70804-9291
800-994-8626
www.louisianatravel.com

Maine Office of Tourism
#59 State House Station
Augusta, ME 04333-0059
888-624-6345
www.visitmaine.com

Maryland Office of Tourism
401 E Pratt St., 14th Floor
Baltimore, MD 21202
866-639-3526
www.mdisfun.org

Massachusetts Office of Travel
  & Tourism
10 Park Plaza, Ste. 4510
Boston, MA 02116
617-973-8500 or 800-227-6277
www.massvacation.com

Michigan Economic Dev.
  & Travel
300 N Washington Sq., 2nd Fl.
Lansing, MI 48913
888-784-7328
www.michigan.org

Explore Minnesota Tourism
121 7th Place E., Ste. 100
St. Paul, MN 55101
651-296-5029 or 888-868-7476
www.exploreminnesota.com

Mississippi Division of
  Tourism
PO Box 849
Jackson, MS 39205
866-733-6477
www.visitmississippi.org

Missouri Division of Tourism
PO Box 1055
Jefferson City, MO 65102
573-751-4133 or 800-519-2100
www.visitmo.com

Travel Montana
PO Box 200533
Helena, MT 59620-0133
406-841-2870 or 800-847-4868
www.visitmt.com

Nebraska Div. of Travel &
  Tourism
PO Box 98907
Lincoln, NE 68509-8907
888-444-1867
www.visitnebraska.gov

Nevada Commission on
  Tourism
401 N Carson St.
Carson City, NV 89701
775-687-4322 or 800-638-2328
www.travelnevada.com

New Hampshire Div. of Travel
  & Tourism Dev.
PO Box 1856
Concord, NH 03302-1856
603-271-2665 or 800-386-4664
www.visitnh.gov

New Jersey Tourism
Commission
P.O. Box 460
Trenton, NJ 08625-0820
609-599-6540
www.visitnj.org

New Mexico Dept.
of Tourism
491 Old Santa Fe Trail
Santa Fe, NM 87501
505-827-7400
www.newmexico.org

New York State Tourism
Empire State Dev., 8th Floor
Albany, NY 12245
800-225-5697
www.iloveny.com

North Carolina Tourism
Division
301 N. Wilmington
Raleigh, NC 27699-4324
919-733-8372 or 800-847-4862
www.visitnc.com

North Dakota Tourism
Division
1600 E. Century Ave., Ste. 2
Bismarck, ND 58503-0657
701-328-2525 or 800-435-5663
www.ndtourism.com

Ohio Division of Travel
& Tourism
PO Box 1001
Columbus, OH 43216-1001
800-282-5393
www.consumer.discover
ohio.com

Oklahoma Tourism &
Recreation Dept.
PO Box 52002
Oklahoma City, OK 73152-2002
800-652-6552
www.travelok.com

Oregon Tourism Commission
670 Hawthorne Ave. SE, Ste. 240
Salem, OR 97301
503-378-8850 or 800-547-7842
www.traveloregon.com

Pennsylvania Tourism Office
400 North St., 4th Floor
Harrisburg, PA 17120-0225
800-847-4872
www.visitpa.com

Rhode Island Tourism
Division
315 Iron Horse Way, Ste. 101
Providence, RI 02903

800-556-2484
www.visitrhodeisland.com

South Carolina Dept. of
Tourism
1205 Pendleton St.
Columbia, SC 29201
803-734-1700 or 866-224-9339
www.discoversouth
carolina.com

South Dakota Office of
Tourism
711 E Wells Ave.
Pierre, SD 57501-5070
605-773-3301
www.travelsd.com

Tennessee Dept. of Tourist
Development
312 Rosa Parks Ave. N, 25th
Floor
Nashville, TN 37243
615-741-2159
www.tnvacation.com

Texas Tourism
PO Box 141009
Austin, TX 78714-1009
800-452-9292
www.traveltex.com

Utah Office of Tourism
300 North St.
Salt Lake City, UT 84114-7420
801-538-1030 or 800-200-1160
travel.utah.gov

Vermont Dept. of Tourism &
Marketing
One National Life Dr.,
6th Floor, Drawer 20
Montpelier, VT 05620-0501
802-828-3237 or 800-837-6668
www.vermontvacation.com

Virginia Tourism
Corporation
901 E Byrd St.
Richmond, VA 23219
800-847-4882
www.virginia.org

Washington State Dept. of
Tourism
PO Box 42525
Olympia, WA 98504-2525
866-964-8913
www.experiencewa.com

West Virginia Division of
Tourism
90 MacCorkle Ave. SW
South Charleston, WV 25303

304-558-2200
www.WVtourism.com

Wisconsin Dept. of Tourism
PO Box 8690
Madison, WI 53702-8690
608-266-2161 or 800-432-8747
www.TravelWisconsin.com

Wyoming Travel & Tourism
1520 Etchepare Circle
Cheyenne, WY 82002
307-777-7777 or 800-225-5996
www.WyomingTourism.org

485

Dairy farm outside Dover, Delaware

America's Byways

www.byways.org

ALABAMA
Alabama Coastal Connection
Natchez Trace Parkway
Selma to Montgomery March
Byway
Talladega Scenic Drive

ALASKA
Alaska's Marine Highway
George Parks Highway
Scenic Byway
Glenn Highway
Haines Highway
Seward Highway

ARIZONA
Coronado Trail Scenic Byway
Historic Route 66
Kaibab Plateau-North Rim
Parkway
Red Rock Scenic Byway
Sky Island Scenic Byway

ARKANSAS
Crowley's Ridge Parkway
Great River Road
Talimena Scenic Drive

CALIFORNIA
Arroyo Seco Historic Parkway–
Route 110
Death Valley Scenic Byway
Ebbetts Pass Scenic Byway
Route 1–Big Sur Coast Highway
Route 1–San Luis Obispo North
Coast Byway
Tioga Road/Big Oak Flat Road
Volcanic Legacy Scenic Byway

COLORADO
Colorado River Headwaters
Byway
Dinosaur Diamond Prehistoric
Highway
Frontier Pathways Scenic
and Historic Byway
Gold Belt Tour Scenic and
Historic Byway
Grand Mesa Scenic and
Historic Byway
Lariat Loop Scenic and Historic
Byway
San Juan Skyway
Santa Fe Trail Scenic and
Historic Byway
Top of the Rockies
Trail of the Ancients
Trail Ridge Road/Beaver
Meadow Road

CONNECTICUT
Connecticut State Route 169
Merritt Parkway

DELAWARE
Brandywine Valley Scenic Byway

FLORIDA
A1A Scenic & Historic Coastal
Byway
Big Bend Scenic Byway
Florida Black Bear Scenic Byway
Florida Keys Scenic Highway
Indian River Lagoon Scenic
Highway
Ormand Scenic Loop and Trail

GEORGIA
Russell-Brasstown National
Scenic Byway

IDAHO
International Selkirk Loop
Northwest Passage Scenic Byway
Payette River Scenic Byway
Pend Oreille Scenic Byway
Pioneer Historic Byway
Western Heritage Historic
Byway

ILLINOIS
Great River Road
Historic National Road
Historic Route 66
Illinois River Road: Route of
the Voyageurs
Lincoln Highway
Meeting of the Great Rivers
Scenic Route
Ohio River Scenic Byway

INDIANA
Historic National Road
Indiana's Historic Pathways
Ohio River Scenic Byway

IOWA
Great River Road
Loess Hills Scenic Byway

KANSAS
Flint Hills Scenic Byway
Wetlands and Wildlife Scenic
Byway

KENTUCKY
Country Music Highway
Great River Road
Lincoln Heritage Scenic
Highway
Red River Gorge Scenic Byway
Wilderness Road Heritage
Highway
Woodland Trace

LOUISIANA
Creole Nature Trail
Great River Road

MAINE
Acadia All-American Byway
Old Canada Road Scenic Byway
Rangeley Lakes Scenic Byway
Schoodic Scenic Byway

MARYLAND
Baltimore's Historic Charles
Street
Catoctin Mountain Scenic
Byway
Chesapeake Country Scenic
Byway
Harriet Tubman Underground
Railroad Byway
Historic National Road
Journey Through the Hallowed
Ground Byway
Religious Freedom Byway

MASSACHUSETTS
Connecticut River Byway

Red Canyon, east of Panguitch

486

Black bear cub

MICHIGAN
Copper Country Trail
River Road Scenic Byway
Woodward Avenue (M-1)

MINNESOTA
Edge of the Wilderness
Grand Rounds Scenic Byway
Great River Road
Gunflint Trail Scenic Byway
Historic Bluff Country Scenic
    Byway
Minnesota River Valley Scenic
    Byway
North Shore Scenic Drive
Paul Bunyan Scenic Byway

MISSISSIPPI
Lower Mississippi Great
    River Road
Natchez Trace Parkway

MISSOURI
Crowley's Ridge Parkway
Little Dixie Highway of the
    Great River Road

MONTANA
Beartooth Highway

NEVADA
City of Las Vegas Boulevard
Lake Tahoe–Eastshore Drive
Las Vegas Strip
Pyramid Lake Scenic Byway

NEW HAMPSHIRE
Connecticut River Byway
Kancamagus Scenic Byway
White Mountain Trail

NEW JERSEY
Delaware River Scenic Byway
Millstone Valley

NEW MEXICO
Billy the Kid Trail
El Camino Real

Geronimo Trail Scenic
    Byway
Historic Route 66
Jemez Mountain Trail
Santa Fe Trail
Trail of the Mountain Spirits
    Scenic Byway
Turquoise Trail

NEW YORK
Great Lakes Seaway Trail
Lakes to Locks Passage
Mohawk Towpath Byway

NORTH CAROLINA
Blue Ridge Parkway
Cherohala Skyway
Forest Heritage National
    Scenic Byway
Outer Banks Scenic Byway

NORTH DAKOTA
Native American Scenic
    Byway
Sheyenne River Valley
    Scenic Byway

OHIO
Amish Country Byway
Historic National Road
Lake Erie Coastal Ohio
    Trail
Ohio & Erie Canalway
Ohio River Scenic Byway

OKLAHOMA
Cherokee Hills Byway
Historic Route 66
Talimena Scenic Drive
Wichita Mountains

OREGON
Cascade Lakes Scenic Byway
Hells Canyon Scenic Byway
Historic Columbia River
    Highway
McKenzie Pass-Santiam Pass
    Scenic Byway
Mt. Hood Scenic Byway
Outback Scenic Byway
Pacific Coast Scenic Byway
Rogue–Umpqua Scenic Byway
Volcanic Legacy Scenic Byway
West Cascades Scenic Byway

PENNSYLVANIA
Great Lakes Seaway Trail
Historic National Road
Journey Through the
    Hallowed Ground Byway

SOUTH CAROLINA
Ashley River Road
Cherokee Foothills Scenic
    Highway

Edisto Island National Scenic
    Byway
Savannah River Scenic Byway

SOUTH DAKOTA
Native American Scenic Byway
Peter Norbeck Scenic Byway

TENNESSEE
Cherohala Skyway
East Tennessee Crossing
Great River Road
Natchez Trace Parkway
Woodland Trace

UTAH
Dinosaur Diamond Prehistoric
    Highway
Energy Loop: Huntington &
    Eccles Canyons Scenic Byway
Flaming Gorge–Uintas Scenic
    Byway
Logan Canyon Scenic Byway
Nebo Loop Scenic Byway
Scenic Byway 12
Scenic Byway 143—Utah's
    Patchwork Parkway
Trail of the Ancients

VERMONT
Connecticut River Byway

VIRGINIA
Blue Ridge Parkway
Colonial Parkway
George Washington Memorial
    Parkway
Journey Through the Hallowed
    Ground Byway
Skyline Drive

WASHINGTON
Chinook Scenic Byway
Coulee Corridor Scenic Byway
International Selkirk Loop
Mountains to Sound
    Greenway–I-90
Stevens Pass Greenway
Strait of Juan de Fuca
    Highway–SR 112
White Pass Scenic Byway

WEST VIRGINIA
Coal Heritage Trail
Highland Scenic Highway
Historic National Road
Midland Trail
Staunton-Parkersburg Turnpike
Washington Heritage Trail

WISCONSIN
Great River Road

WYOMING
Beartooth Highway

487

Illustrations Credits

Index

Picture Library Ltd/Alamy; 401, Jeff Gnass; 402, Kevin Schafer/Alamy; 403, John Marshall; 404, Mike Dobel/Alamy; 405, Danita Delimont/Alamy; 406, Chuck Pefley/Alamy; 408, Tom Mareschal/Alamy; 409, John Marshall; 410, Susan G. Drinker/Drinker Durrance Graphics; 411, Ralph Lee Hopkins; 412, Brad Mitchell/Alamy; 413, Harley Soltes; 414, Jake Rajs; 415, Harley Soltes; 417 (UP), Brad Mitchell/Alamy; 417 (LO), Rick Schafer Photography, LLC; 418, Jon Gnass/Gnass Photo Images; 420 (UP), Steve Terrill; 420 (LO), John Marshall; 421, Bob Pool; 422, Charles Gurche; 423, Rick Schafer Photography, LLC; 424, Steve Terrill; 425, Rick Schafer Photography, LLC; 427 (UP), Bob Devine; 427 (LO), Steve Terrill; 429, ImageState/Alamy; 431 (UP & LO), Phil Schermeister; 432, Craig Lovell/Eagle Visions Photography/Alamy; 433, Bob Pool; 434, Rick Schafer Photography, LLC; 435 & 436, Phil Schermeister; 437, Darrell Gulin/Corbis; 438, Steve Terrill; 439, Bob Devine; 442, Michael Wa/Lonely Planet Images/Getty Images; 444, Muench Photography; 446, Enigma/Alamy; 447, James Schaedig/Alamy; 448, John Elk III/Alamy; 450, Larry Ulrich Stock; 451, Thomas Hallstein/Alamy; 453, Robert Llewellyn; 455 & 456, Muench Photography; 458, Carr Clifton; 459, Robert Holmes/Corbis; 460, J.C. Leacock; 462, Thomas Hallstein/Alamy; 463, Bob Clemenz; 465 (UP), Steven Folino/Alamy; 465 (LO), James Randklev; 467 (UP), Larry Ulrich Stock; 467 (LO), Muench Photography; 468, Larry Ulrich Stock; 469, Dewitt Jones; 470, James A. Sugar; 472 (UP), Muench Photography; 472 (LO), Jeff Foott; 473, West Light/Charles O'Rear/Corbis; 474, James Randklev; 475, Dick Dietrick/Dietrick Leis Stock Photo; 476, Chris Johns, NGS; 477, Jeff Gnass; 478, Fred Hirschmann; 479, Photo Resource Hawaii/Alamy; 480, Muench Photography; 481 (UP), Scott Barrow; 481 (LO), Jeff Gnass; 482, James Randklev; 483, Roger Ressmeyer/Corbis; 485, Jake Rajs; 486, James Kay; 487, Tom & Pat Leeson.

A

A1A Scenic & Historic Coastal Byway, Fla. 149–150
Acadia All-American Road, Me. 18–19
Adams, Mount, Wash. 412–414
The Adirondacks, N.Y. (drive) 61–63
Akron, Ohio 171–172
Alabama 132–136
   Alabama's Coastal Connection 134–136
   Natchez Trace Parkway 127–131
   Selma to Montgomery March Byway 132–133
   Talladega Scenic Drive 133–134
Alaska 381–397
   Alaska's Marine Highway 393–397
   George Parks Highway 381–383
   Glenn Highway 384–385
   Haines Highway 391–393
   Richardson Highway 386–388
   Seward Highway 388–391
Albuquerque, N.Mex. 298, 315–316
Alpine Loop Detour, Colo. 328
Amish Country Byway, Ohio 172–173
Amish Culture and Crafts Route, Ind. 178–179
Anchorage, Alas. 388–389
Apache Trail, Ariz. 302–303
Apostle Islands Country, Wis. (drive) 197–198
Arches N.P., Utah 282, 284
Arizona 295–309
   Apache Trail 302–303
   Coronado Trail Scenic Byway 307–308
   Globe to Show Low 304–305
   Historic Route 66 297–299
   Kaibab Plateau–North Rim Parkway 295–296
   Monument Valley 296–297
   Oak Creek Canyon Drive 300–302
   Red Rock Scenic Byway 301
   Sky Island Scenic Byway 308–309
   Tucson Mountains Drive 309
   White Mountains Drive 305–306
Arkansas 267–273
   Arkansas 7 267–270
   Crowley's Ridge Parkway 231–233
   Great River Road 272–273
   The Levee 270–271
   Talimena Scenic Drive 262–264
Arroyo Seco Historic Parkway, Calif. 451
Ashley N.F., Utah 279, 282
Ashley River Road, S.C. 136–137
Astoria, Oreg. 421
Avenue of the Giants, Calif. 465–466

B

Badlands, S.Dak. (drive) 226–227
Baker, Mount, Wash. 398–399
Baltimore, Md. 83, 87
Beartooth Highway, Mont.-Wyo. 354–356
Bicentennial Highway, Utah 285–287, 289
Big Bend N.P., Tex. 255–256
Big Bend Scenic Byway, Fla. 147–149

Big Hole Mountains Drive, Idaho 364–365
Big Horn Mountains Scenic Byway, Wyo. 357–358
Big Sur, Me. (drive) 15–18
Big Sur Coast Highway, Calif. 471–474
Billy the Kid Trail, N.Mex. 314
Black Hills, S.Dak.-Wyo. (drive) 219–222
Blue Ridge Parkway, N.C.-Va. 102–105
Boise, Idaho 366
Brandywine Valley Scenic Byway, Del.-Pa. 76
Bryce Canyon N.P., Utah 287–289
Buffalo, N.Y. 64
Buffalo Gap Natl. Grassland, S.Dak. 225
Burr Trail, Utah 289

C

Cades Cove Loop Drive, Tenn. 117
Cahokia Mounds S.H.S., Ill. 177
California 449–475
   Arroyo Seco Historic Parkway 451
   Avenue of the Giants 465–466
   California 1 (Jenner to Mendocino) 466–468
   California 1 (Monterey to Morro Bay) 471–474
   Death Valley Scenic Byway 452–453
   Ebbetts Pass Scenic Byway 458–459
   June Lake Loop 457
   Kings Canyon Scenic Byway 454–456
   Lake Tahoe–East Shore Drive 459–461
   Lassen Park Road 462–464
   Lost Coast 464–465
   Marin County 468–469
   Rim of the World Scenic Byway 449–451
   17-Mile Drive 474–475
   Silverado Trail 469–471
   Tioga Road/Big Oak Flat Road 456–458
   Volcanic Legacy Scenic Byway 461–463
Canaan Valley Byway, W.Va. 91–92
Canyon Sweep, Tex. (drive) 259–260
Canyonlands N.P., Utah 282, 284
Cape Ann Ramble, Mass. 43–45
Cape Hatteras Natl. Seashore, N.C. 109–111
Capitol Reef N.P., Utah 29, 286, 287, 289
Carmel-by-the-Sea, Calif. 471–472
Cascade Lakes Scenic Byway, Oreg. 433–434
Cathedral Valley, Utah (drive) 286
Catoctin Mountain Scenic Byway, Md. 81
Catskill Mountains, N.Y. (drive) 71–72
Cayuga Lake, N.Y. (drive) 70–71
Centennial Scenic Byway, Wyo. 360–361

INDEX

Central Oregon Coast (drive)
422–424
Chain of Craters Road, Hawaii
(drive) 481
Champlain Islands, Vt. (drive) 36–38
Charles St., Baltimore, Md. 87
Charleston, S.C. 136–137
Cherohala Skyway, N.C.-Tenn. 118
Cherokee Foothills Scenic Highway,
S.C. 137–139
Cherokee Hills Byway, Okla.
264–265
Cherry Orchards Drive, Mich.
166–168
Chesapeake Bay Bridge-Tunnel,
Va. 98
Chesapeake Country, Md. (drive)
88–89
Chicago, Ill. 189
Chimayó, N.Mex. 317–318
Chinook Scenic Byway, Wash.
416–417
Chippewa N.F., Minn. 203
Cibola N.F., N.Mex. 317
Cimarron Canyon S.P., N.Mex. 318,
320, 323
Cincinnati, Ohio 181–182
Cleveland, Ohio 170, 171
Coal Heritage Trail, W.Va. 96–97
Coastal Connection Scenic Byway,
Ala. 134–136
Coconino N.F., Ariz. 300–301
Cod, Cape, Mass. 45–47
Coeur d'Alene, Lake, Idaho 374–375
Colonial Williamsburg, Va. 98
Colorado 323–343
Alpine Loop Detour 328
Colorado N.M. 333–334
Colorado River Headwaters Byway
336–337
Dinosaur Diamond Prehistoric
Highway 281–283
Frontier Pathways Scenic and His-
toric Byway 331–332
Gold Belt Tour Scenic and Historic
Byway 332–333
Grand Mesa Scenic and Historic
Byway 335
Lariat Loop Scenic & Historic
Byway 342–343
Peak to Peak Scenic Byway
335–336
San Juan Skyway 325–329
Santa Fe Trail 321–323
Top of the Rockies Natl. Scenic
Byway 340–342
Trail of the Ancients 323–325
Trail Ridge Road/Beaver Meadow
Road 337–340
Unaweep-Tabeguache Scenic
Byway 329–331
Colorado River Scenic Byway, Utah
284–285
Columbia River Gorge Natl. Scenic
Area, Oreg. 417–419
Columbus, Ohio 176
Colville N.F., Wash. 403
Connecticut 50–57
Connecticut State Route 169 50–52
Litchfield 54–55
Lower Connecticut River Valley
52–54
Merritt Parkway 53

Connecticut River Byway, N.H.-Vt.
30–31
Connecticut State Route 169 50–52
Copper Country Trail, Mich.
163–164
Coronado N.F., Ariz. 308–309
Coronado Trail Scenic Byway, Ariz.
307–308
Cottonwood Canyon Road, Utah
288
Coulee Corridor Scenic Byway,
Wash. 404–405
Country Music Highway, Ky. 121
Covered Bridge Scenic Byway, Ohio
173–174
Crater Lake N.P., Oreg. 427, 428
Crater Rim Drive, Hawaii 481–482
Crazy Horse Memorial, S.Dak. 222
Creole Nature Trail, La. 249–250
Cripple Creek, Colo. 333
Crowley's Ridge Parkway, Ark.-Mo.
231–233
Cullasaja River Gorge, N.C. (drive)
114–115
Cumberland Gap N.H.P., Ky. 120,
123
Custer Scenic Byway, S.Dak. 224
Cuyahoga Valley N.P., Ohio 171

D

Davis Mountains Loop, Tex.
258–259
Death Valley Scenic Byway, Calif.
452–453
Deer Isle Drive, Me. 19–20
Delaware 75–76
Brandywine Valley Scenic Byway
76
Mouth of the Delaware 75–76
Delaware Valley Scenic Byway, N.J.
73–74
Denali N.P. and Preserve, Alas.
382, 383
Detroit, Mich. 169
Devil's Backbone, Tex. (drive) 254
Devils Tower N.M., Wyo. 219–220
Dinosaur Diamond Prehistoric High-
way, Colo.-Utah 281–283
Dismal Swamp Canal, N.C.-Va.
111–112
Duluth, Minn. 200
Dungeness Scenic Loop, Wash. 411

E

East Tennessee Crossing, Tenn.
120–121
Ebbetts Pass Scenic Byway, Calif.
458–459
Edge of the Wilderness, Minn.
(drive) 203
Edisto Island Natl. Scenic Byway, S.C.
139–141
El Camino del Rio, Tex. 256–257
El Camino Real, N.Mex. 314–316
El Malpais, N.Mex. (drive)
316–317
Elkhorn Drive, Oreg. 435–436
Enchanted Circle, N.Mex. 319–320
The Energy Loop: Huntington &
Eccles Canyons Scenic Byway,
Utah 283–284
Equinox Skyline Drive, Vt. 33
Erie, Lake 63–64, 169–170

Estes Park, Colo. 336, 338
Everglades N.P., Fla. 155–157

F

Fairbanks, Alas. 383
Flagstaff, Ariz. 299, 300
Flaming Gorge–Uintas Scenic Byway,
Utah 278–280
Flint Hills Scenic Byway, Kans.
229–230
Florida 146–159
A1A Scenic & Historic Coastal
Byway 149–150
Big Bend Scenic Byway 147–149
Florida Black Bear Scenic Byway
151–152
Florida Keys 157–159
Indian River Lagoon Scenic High-
way 153–155
Ormond Scenic Loop and Trail
152–153
Panhandle Scenic Drive 146–147
Southern Everglades 155–157
Tamiami Trail Scenic Highway 156
Florissant Fossil Beds N.M., Colo. 332
Forest Heritage Scenic Byway, N.C.
113–114
Frontier Pathways Scenic and His-
toric Byway, Colo. 331–332

G

George Parks Highway, Alas.
381–383
George W. Perkins Memorial Drive,
N.Y. 72–73
George Washington Memorial Park-
way, Va. 99–100
Georgia 142–145
Russell–Brasstown Natl. Scenic
Byway 142–143
Sea Islands 143–145
Geronimo Trail Scenic Byway,
N.Mex. 312
Gettysburg, Pa. 80–81
Gifford Pinchot N.F., Wash. 413, 414
Gila Cliff Dwellings N.M., N.Mex.
310–311
Gila N.F., N.Mex. 310, 312
Glacier Bay N.P. and Preserve,
Alas. 396
Glacier N.P., Mont. 347–349, 353
Glade Top Trail, Mo. 232
Glen Canyon N.R.A., Utah 285–286,
289, 290
Glenn Highway, Alas. 384–385
Globe to Show Low, Ariz. (drive)
304–305
Gloucester, Mass. 43, 44–45
Going-to-the-Sun Road, Mont.
347–349
Gold Belt Tour Scenic and Historic
Byway, Colo. 332–333
Grand Army of the Republic High-
way, Pa. 78
Grand Canyon N.P., Ariz. 295
Grand Lake, Colo. 336, 339
Grand Mesa Scenic and Historic
Byway, Colo. 335
Grand Portage Bay, Minn. 201
Grand Rounds Scenic Byway, Minn.
204
Grand Teton N.P., Wyo. 360, 362
Great Falls, Mont. 352

490

Great Lakes Seaway Trail, N.Y.-Pa. 63–66
Great River Road
    Arkansas 272–273
    Illinois 186–188
    Iowa 239–241
    Kentucky 127
    Louisiana 245–246
    Minnesota 202–205
    Mississippi 129
    Missouri 235
    Tennessee 118–120
    Wisconsin 196–197
Great Smoky Mountains N.P., N.C.-Tenn. 115–117
Green Mountains, Vt. 32, 33, 35, 37
Gulf Island Natl. Seashore, Fla. 146
Gunflint Trail Scenic Byway, Minn. 199

H
Haines, Alas. 391–392, 395–396
Haines Highway, Alas. 391–393
Hamakua Coast, Hawaii (drive) 479–480
Hana Highway, Maui, Hawaii 477–479
Harpers Ferry N.H.P., W.Va. 90
Harriet Tubman Underground Railroad Byway, Md. 89–90
Hatteras, Cape, N.C. 109–111
Hawaii 475–482
    Chain of Craters Road, Hawaii 481
    Crater Rim Drive, Hawaii 481–482
    Hamakua Coast, Hawaii 479–480
    Hana Highway, Maui 477–479
    Kalanianaole Highway, Oahu 475–477
Heart of the Sands, N.Mex. (drive) 313
Hells Canyon Scenic Byway, Oreg. 438–439
High Road to Taos, N.Mex. 318–319
Highland Scenic Highway, W.Va. 94–95
Hill Country, Tex. 252–255
Hilo, Hawaii 479
Historic Bluff Country Scenic Byway, Minn. 206–208
Historic Columbia River Highway, Oreg. 417–419
Historic Natl. Road
    Maryland-Pennsylvania-West Virginia 83–84
    Ohio-Indiana-Illinois 174–177
Historic Route 66
    Illinois 189–190
    New Mexico-Arizona 297–299
    Oklahoma 265–266
Holmes County, Ohio 172–173
Hood, Mount, Oreg. 419–420
Hospitality Highway, Miss. 131–132
Hot Springs, Ark. 267–268
Humboldt Redwoods S.P., Calif. 465–466
Humboldt-Toiyabe N.F., Nev. 443
Huntington Canyon, Utah 283–284

I
Idaho 363–377
    Big Hole Mountains Drive 364–365
    International Selkirk Loop 376–377

Lake Coeur d'Alene 374–375
Lewis and Clark Drive 372
Mesa Falls Scenic Byway 365
Northwest Passage Scenic Byway 373–374
Payette River Scenic Byway 369–370
Pend Oreille Scenic Byway 375
Pioneer Historic Byway 363–364
Salmon River Scenic Route 367
Sawtooth Drive 366–368
Western Heritage Historic Byway 368–369
Illinois 185–192
    Great River Road 186–188
    Historic Natl. Road 174–177
    Historic Route 66 189–190
    Illinois River Road: Route of the Voyageurs 190–191
    Lincoln Highway 191–192
    Meeting of the Great Rivers Scenic Route 188–189
    Ohio River Scenic Byway 180–183
    Shawnee Hills 185–186
Indian River Lagoon Scenic Highway, Fla. 153–155
Indiana 174–185
    Amish Culture and Crafts Route 178–179
    Historic Natl. Road 174–177
    Indiana's Historic Pathways 183–185
    Lincoln Hills Scenic Drive 179–180
    Ohio River Scenic Byway 180–183
Indianapolis, Ind. 177
International Selkirk Loop, Idaho-B.C.-Wash. 376–377
Inyo N.F., Calif. 457, 458
Iowa 237–241
    Great River Road 239–241
    Loess Hills Scenic Byway 238–239
    Woodlands Scenic Byway 237–238
Itasca S.P., Minn. 202

J
Jekyll Island, Ga. 143–144
Jemez Mountain Trail, N.Mex. 320–321
Johnson City, Tex. 252
Jonesboro, Ark. 232
Journey through Hallowed Ground, Pa.-Md.-Va. 80–82
June Lake Loop, Calif. 457
Juneau, Alas. 395

K
Kaibab Plateau–North Rim Parkway, Ariz. 295–296
Kalanianaole Highway, Oahu, Hawaii 475–477
Kancamagus Scenic Byway, N.H. 24, 26–28
Kansas 229–231
    Flint Hills 229–230
    Wetlands and Wildlife Scenic Byway 230–231
Kentucky 121–127
    Country Music Highway 121
    Great River Road 127
    Kentucky Heartland Drive 124
    Lincoln Heritage Scenic Highway 125–126
    Red River Gorge Scenic Byway 122

Wilderness Road Heritage Highway 123
Woodlands Trace 126
Kettle Moraine Scenic Drive, Wis. 192–194
Keweenaw N.H.P., Mich. 163–164
Key West, Fla. 157, 158, 159
Kimberly–Big John Road, Utah 290
Kings Canyon Scenic Byway, Calif. 454–456
Kisatchie N.F., La. 250–251
Klamath Basin N.W.R. Complex, Calif.-Oreg. 429–430, 461
Kodiak Island, Alas. 397

L
Lake Chicot S.P., Ark. 270–271, 273
Lake Coeur d'Alene, Idaho (drive) 374–375
Lake Erie Coastal Ohio Trail, Ohio 169–170
Lake Tahoe–East Shore Drive, Calif.-Nev. 459–461
Lakes to Locks Passage, N.Y. 67–70
Lamoille Canyon Scenic Byway, Nev. 443–444
Lancaster County Drive, Pa. 77
Lariat Loop Scenic & Historic Byway, Colo. 342–343
Las Vegas Boulevard State Scenic Byway, Nev. 447–448
Las Vegas Strip, Nev. 446–447
Lassen Park Road, Calif. 462–464
Laurel Highlands, Pa. (drive) 80
Lava Beds N.M., Calif. 461–462
Leadville, Colo. 340–341
The Levee, Ark. (drive) 270–271
Lewis and Clark Drive, Idaho 372
Lincoln Heritage Scenic Highway, Ky. 125–126
Lincoln Highway, Ill. 191–192
Lincoln Hills Scenic Drive, Ind. 179–180
Litchfield Hills, Conn. (drive) 54–57
Little Compton, R.I. 49–50
Little Dixie Highway of the Great River Road, Mo. 235
Loess Hills Scenic Byway, Iowa 238–239
Logan Canyon Scenic Byway, Utah 277–278
Longhouse Scenic Byway, Pa. 79
Longleaf Trail Scenic Byway, La. 250–251
Los Angeles, Calif. 451
Lost Coast, Calif. (drive) 464–465
Lost Dutchman S.P., Ariz. 302
Louisiana 245–251
    Creole Nature Trail 249–250
    Great River Road 245–246
    Longleaf Trail Scenic Byway 250–251
    Old Spanish Trail 247–248
Lower Connecticut River Valley, Conn. (drive) 52–54
Lower Mississippi Great River Road, Miss. 129

M
Maine 15–22
    Acadia All-American Road 18–19
    Deer Isle Drive 19–20
    Maine's Big Sur 15–18

Old Canada Road Scenic Byway 21–22
Rangeley Lakes Scenic Byway 20–21
Manti-La Sal N.F., Utah 283
Marin County, Calif. (drive) 468–469
Marine Highway, Alas. 393–397
Mark Twain N.F., Mo. 232, 233–234
Maryland 80–90
  Baltimore's Historic Charles Street 87
  Chesapeake Country 88–89
  Harriet Tubman Underground Railroad Byway 89–90
  Historic Natl. Road 83–84
  Journey through Hallowed Ground 80–82
  Religious Freedom Byway 85–86
Massachusetts 40–47
  Cape Ann Ramble 43–45
  Mohawk Trail Drive 40–42
  Old King's Highway 45–47
  Tyringham Valley 42–43
McKenzie–Santiam Scenic Byway, Oreg. 430–431
McKinley, Mount, Alas. 382
Mead, Lake, Ariz.-Nev. 445, 446
Meeting of the Great Rivers Scenic Route, Ill. 188–189
Memphis, Tenn. 119–120
Merritt Parkway, Conn. 53
Mesa Falls Scenic Byway, Idaho 365
Mesa Verde N.P., Colo. 324, 326, 328
Michigan 163–169
  Cherry Orchards Drive 166–168
  Copper Country Trail 163–164
  Pierce Stocking Scenic Drive 167
  River Road Scenic Byway 168
  Whitefish Bay Scenic Byway 164–165
  Woodward Avenue 169
Midland Trail, W.Va. 95–96
Millstone Valley Scenic Byway, N.J. 74–75
Minneapolis, Minn. 204
Minnesota 199–209
  Edge of the Wilderness 203
  Grand Rounds Scenic Byway 204
  Great River Road 202–205
  Gunflint Trail Scenic Byway 199
  Historic Bluff Country Scenic Byway 206–208
  Minnesota River Valley Scenic Byway 208–209
  North Shore Scenic Drive 200–201
  Paul Bunyan Scenic Byway 205–206
Mississippi 127–132
  Hospitality Highway 131–132
  Lower Mississippi Great River Road 129
  Natchez Trace Parkway 127–131
Mississippi River, U.S. see Great River Road
Missouri 231–237
  Crowley's Ridge Parkway 231–233
  Glade Top Trail 232
  Little Dixie Highway of the Great River Road 235
  Missouri Ozarks 233–234
  Missouri Valley Wine Country 234–237

Moab, Utah 284
Moapa Valley Drive, Nev. 445–446
Mogollon Rim, Ariz. 300, 304, 305
Mohawk Towpath Scenic Byway, N.Y. 68
Mohawk Trail Drive, Mass. 40–42
Monongahela N.F., W.Va. 93, 94–95
Montana 347–356
  Beartooth Highway 354–356
  Going-to-the-Sun Road 347–349
  Salmon River Scenic Route 367, 370–372
  US 89 350–353
Monterey, Calif. 471
Monterey Peninsula, Calif. 474–475
Montgomery, Ala. 132–133
Monument Valley, Ariz. (drive) 296–297
Moosehorn N.W.R., Me. 17, 18
Mount Adams Drive, Wash. 412–414
Mount Baker Scenic Byway, Wash. 398–399
Mount Hood Scenic Byway, Oreg. 419–420
Mount Rainier N.P., Wash. 400, 414, 416
Mount Rushmore Natl. Memorial, S.Dak. 223–224
Mount St. Helens, Wash. (drive) 414–416
Mount Vernon, Va. 99
Mount Washington Auto Road, N.H. 25
Mountains to Sound Greenway, Wash. 407–408
Mouth of the Delaware (drive) 75–76

N

Napa Valley, Calif. 469–471
Natchez Trace Parkway, Ala.-Miss.-Tenn. 127–131
National Road. see Historic Natl. Road
Native American Scenic Byway, N.Dak-S.Dak. 214–215
Natural Bridges N.M., Utah 286, 324
Nebo Loop Scenic Byway, Utah 280–281
Nebraska 227–229
  Nebraska 29 228
  Pine Ridge Country 227–229
Nevada 443–449
  Lake Tahoe–East Shore Drive 459–461
  Lamoille Canyon Scenic Byway 443–444
  Las Vegas Boulevard State Scenic Byway 447–448
  Las Vegas Strip 446–447
  Moapa Valley Drive 445–446
  Pyramid Lake Scenic Byway 444–445
  Red Rock Canyon Loop Drive 449
New Hampshire 22–31
  Connecticut River Byway 30–31
  Kancamagus Scenic Byway 26–28
  Mount Washington Auto Road 25
  New Hampshire 153 29–30
  North Road 23
  Sandwich Notch Road 28
  Three Rivers Scenic Drive 22–24
  White Mountain Trail 24–26

New Jersey 73–75
  Delaware Valley Scenic Byway 73–74
  Millstone Valley Scenic Byway 74–75
New Mexico 310–323
  Billy the Kid Trail 314
  El Camino Real 314–316
  El Malpais 316–317
  Enchanted Circle 319–320
  Geronimo Trail Scenic Byway 312
  Heart of the Sands 313
  High Road to Taos 318–319
  Historic Route 66 297–299
  Jemez Mountain Trail 320–321
  Santa Fe Trail 321–323
  Trail of the Mountain Spirits Scenic Byway 310–311
  Turquoise Trail 317–318
New York 61–73
  The Adirondacks 61–63
  Catskill Mountains 71–72
  Cayuga Lake 70–71
  George W. Perkins Memorial Drive 72–73
  Great Lakes Seaway Trail 63–66
  Lakes to Locks Passage 67–70
  Mohawk Towpath Scenic Byway 68
  River Road 69
  Whiteface Mountain Memorial Highway 62
Newfound Gap Road, N.C.-Tenn. 115–117
Newport, Oreg. 422–423
Newport, R.I. 49
Nez Perce N.H.P., Idaho 373, 374
Niagara Falls 63, 64–65
North Carolina 102–105, 109–115
  Blue Ridge Parkway 102–105
  Cherohala Skyway 118
  Cullasaja River Gorge 114–115
  Forest Heritage Scenic Byway 113–114
  Newfound Gap Road 115–117
  Outer Banks Scenic Byway 109–111
  The Tidewater 111–113
North Cascades Highway, Wash. 401–403
North Dakota 213–219
  Native American Scenic Byway 214–215
  North Dakota 22 217–218
  Oxbow Overlook Scenic Drive 218–219
  Sakakawea Trail 215–217
  Sheyenne River Valley Scenic Byway 213–214
North Fork of the Shoshone, Wyo. (drive) 356–357
North Road, N.H. 23
North Shore Scenic Drive, Minn. 200–201
North Umpqua River, Oreg. 426–427
Northern Oregon Coast (drive) 421–422
Northwest Passage Scenic Byway, Idaho 373–374

O

Oak Creek Canyon Drive, Ariz. 300–302
Ocean Drive, Newport, R.I. 49

Ohio 169–177
Amish Country Byway 172–173
Covered Bridge Scenic Byway
173–174
Historic Natl. Road 174–177
Lake Erie Coastal Ohio Trail
169–170
Ohio & Erie Canalway 171–172
Ohio River Scenic Byway 180–183
Oklahoma 260–266
Cherokee Hills Byway 264–265
Historic Route 66 265–266
Quartz Mountains 260
Talimena Scenic Drive 262–264
Wichita Mountains Byway 261–262
Old Canada Road Scenic Byway,
Me. 21–22
Old King's Highway, Mass. 45–47
Old Spanish Trail, La. 247–248
Olympic Peninsula, Wash. (drive)
408–411
Onomea Bay Scenic Route, Hawaii
479–480
Ontario, Lake 63, 65
Oregon 417–439
Cascade Lakes Scenic Byway
433–434
Central Oregon Coast 422–424
Elkhorn Byway 435–436
Hells Canyon Scenic Byway 438–439
Historic Columbia River Highway
417–419
McKenzie–Santiam Scenic Byway
430–431
Mount Hood Scenic Byway 419–420
Northern Oregon Coast 421–422
Outback Scenic Byway 436–437
Pacific Coast Scenic Byway
421–426
Rogue–Umpqua Scenic Byway
426–427
Southern Oregon Coast 424–426
Volcanic Legacy Scenic Byway
428–430
West Cascades Scenic Byway
432–433
Oregon Coast 421–426
Oregon Dunes N.R.A., Oreg. 423–424
Ormond Scenic Loop and Trail, Fla.
152–153
Ouachita N.F., Ark.-Okla. 263, 268
Outback Scenic Byway, Oreg.
436–437
Outer Banks Scenic Byway, N.C.
109–111
Oxbow Overlook Scenic Drive,
N.Dak. 218–219
Ozark N.F., Ark. 269
Ozark Plateau, Mo. 232, 233–234

P
Pacific Coast Scenic Byway, Oreg.
421–426
Palo Duro Canyon, Tex. 259–260
Panhandle Scenic Drive, Fla. 146–147
Panoramic Highway, Calif. 468–469
Parowan, Utah 293–294
Pasadena, Calif. 451
Patchwork Parkway, Utah 293–295
Paul Bunyan Scenic Byway, Minn.
205–206
Payette River Scenic Byway, Idaho
369–370

Peak to Peak Scenic Byway, Colo.
335–336
Pend Oreille Scenic Byway, Idaho 375
Pennsylvania 77–82
Grand Army of the Republic
Highway 78
Great Lakes Seaway Trail 63–66
Historic Natl. Road 83–84
Journey through Hallowed Ground
80–82
Lancaster County Drive 77
Laurel Highlands 80
Longhouse Scenic Byway 79
Timber, Oil, and Coal Country
Drive 78–79
Pensacola, Fla. 146
Peter Norbeck Scenic Byway, S.Dak.
222–224
Pierce Stocking Scenic Drive, Mich.
167
Pine Ridge Country, Nebr. (drive)
227–229
Pine Ridge Indian Res., S.Dak.
225, 226
Pioneer Historic Byway, Idaho
363–364
Pisgah N.F., N.C. 113–114
Powell, Lake, Utah 285–286
Presque Isle, Pa. 63–64
Pyramid Lake Scenic Byway, Nev.
444–445

Q
Quartz Mountains, Okla. (drive) 260

R
Rangeley Lakes Scenic Byway, Me.
20–21
Red Cloud–Dry Fork, Utah (drive)
279
Red River Gorge Scenic Byway,
Ky. 122
Red Rock Canyon Loop Drive,
Nev. 449
Red Rock Scenic Byway, Ariz. 301
Religious Freedom Byway, Md. 85–86
Rhode Island 48–50
Ocean Drive 49
Rhode Island 77 48–50
Richardson Highway, Alas. 386–388
Rim of the World Scenic Byway,
Calif. 449–451
River Road, N.Y. 69
River Road Scenic Byway, Mich. 168
Rochester, N.Y. 65
Rocky Gorge Scenic Area, N.H. 28
Rocky Mountain N.P., Colo. 336–339
Rogue–Umpqua Scenic Byway, Oreg.
426–427
Ross Maxwell Scenic Drive, Tex.
255–256
Route 66. see Historic Route 66
Ruby Mountains, Nev. 443–444
Russell–Brasstown Natl. Scenic
Byway, Ga. 142–143

S
St. Augustine, Fla. 150
St. Helens, Mount, Wash. (drive)
414–416
St. Lawrence River 63, 66
St. Paul, Minn. 204
Sakakawea Trail, N.Dak. 215–217

Salem, Mass. 45
Salmon River Scenic Route, Idaho-
Mont. 367, 370–372
Salt River, Ariz. 302, 304–305
San Juan Skyway, Colo. 325–329
Sandia Crest Natl. Scenic Byway,
N.Mex. 317
Sandwich Notch Road, N.H. 28
Santa Fe, N.Mex. 316, 322
Santa Fe Trail, Colo.-N.Mex. 321–323
Saratoga N.H.P., N.Y. 67
Savannah River Scenic Byway, S.C.
141–142
Sawtooth Drive, Idaho 366–368
Scenic Byway 12, Utah 287–291
Scenic Byway 143–Utah's Patchwork
Parkway 293–295
Schoodic Scenic Byway, Me. 15–18
Sea Islands, Ga. (drive) 143–145
Seattle, Wash. 407
Sedona, Ariz. 300, 301, 302
Selkirk Mountains, Canada-U.S.
376–377
Selma to Montgomery March Byway,
Ala. 132–133
Sequoia N.F., Calif. 454
17-Mile Drive, Calif. 474–475
Seward Highway, Alas. 388–391
Shawnee Hills, Ill. 185–186
Shenandoah N.P., Va. 100–102
Sherman Pass Scenic Byway, Wash.
403–404
Sheyenne River Valley Scenic Byway,
N.Dak. 213–214
Silverado Trail, Calif. 469–471
Silverton, Colo. 327, 328
Sioux City, Iowa 238–239
Sky Island Scenic Byway, Ariz.
308–309
Skyline Drive, Va. 100–102
Sleeping Bear Dunes Natl. Lakeshore,
Mich. 167
Smugglers Notch, Vt. (drive) 34
Snowy Range Road, Wyo. 358–359
South Carolina 136–142
Ashley River Road 136–137
Cherokee Foothills Scenic High-
way 137–139
Edisto Island Natl. Scenic Byway
139–141
Savannah River Scenic Byway
141–142
South Carolina 107 138
South Dakota 219–227
Badlands 226–227
Black Hills 219–222
Custer Scenic Byway 224
Native American Scenic Byway
214–215
Peter Norbeck Scenic Byway
222–224
South Dakota 44 225–226
Southern Everglades, Fla. (drive)
155–157
Southern Oregon Coast (drive)
424–426
Staunton-Parkersburg Turnpike,
W.Va. 93
Stevens Pass Greenway, Wash.
406–407
Stowe, Vt. 34–35
Strait of Juan de Fuca Highway,
Wash. 411–412

493

INDEX

Superior, Lake 163–165, 200–201
Superior N.F., Minn. 201

T

Tahoe, Lake, Calif.-Nev. 459–461
Talimena Scenic Drive, Okla.-Ark.
 262–264
Talladega Scenic Drive, Ala. 133–134
Tamiami Trail Scenic Highway,
 Fla. 156
Taos, N.Mex. 318–319
Taughannock Falls S.P., N.Y. 70
Tennessee 115–121
 Cades Cove Loop Drive 117
 Cherohala Skyway 118
 East Tennessee Crossing 120–121
 Great River Road 118–120
 Natchez Trace Parkway 127–131
 Newfound Gap Road 115–117
 Woodlands Trace 126
Teton Park Drive, Wyo. 362
Texas 252–260
 Canyon Sweep 259–260
 Davis Mountains Loop 258–259
 Devil's Backbone 254
 El Camino del Rio 256–257
 Ross Maxwell Scenic Drive 255–256
 Texas Hill Country 252–255
Theodore Roosevelt N.P., N.Dak.
 218–219
Three Rivers Scenic Drive, N.H.
 22–24
Three Sisters Wilderness, Oreg. 434
The Tidewater, N.C. (drive) 111–113
Tillamook, Oreg. 421–422
Timber, Oil, and Coal Country Drive,
 Pa. 78–79
Tioga Road/Big Oak Flat Road, Calif.
 456–458
Tonto N.F., Ariz. 302–303, 304
Top of the Rockies Natl. Scenic
 Byway, Colo. 340–342
Trail of the Ancients, Colo.-Utah
 323–325
Trail of the Mountain Spirits Scenic
 Byway, N.Mex. 310–311
Trail Ridge Road/Beaver Meadow
 Road, Colo. 337–340
Tubman, Harriet 89–90
Tucson Mountains Drive, Ariz. 309
Turquoise Trail, N.Mex. 317–318
Tyringham Valley, Mass. (drive)
 42–43

U

Uinta N.F., Utah 280
Umpqua N.F., Oreg. 426–427
Unaweep–Tabeguache Scenic Byway,
 Colo. 329–331
US 66. see Historic Route 66
US 89, Mont. 350–353
Utah 277–295
 Bicentennial Highway 285–287, 289
 Burr Trail 289
 Cathedral Valley 286
 Colorado River Scenic Byway
  284–285
 Cottonwood Canyon Road 288
 Dinosaur Diamond Prehistoric
  Highway 281–283
 The Energy Loop: Huntington &
  Eccles Canyons Scenic Byway
  283–284

Flaming Gorge–Uintas Scenic
 Byway 278–280
 Kimberly–Big John Road 290
 Logan Canyon Scenic Byway
  277–278
 Nebo Loop Scenic Byway 280–281
 Red Cloud–Dry Fork 279
 Scenic Byway 12 287–291
 Scenic Byway 143–Utah's Patch-
  work Parkway 293–295
 Trail of the Ancients 323–325
 Zion N.P. Scenic Byway 291–293

V

Valley of Fire S.P., Nev. 445–446
Vermont 30–40
 Champlain Islands 36–38
 Connecticut River Byway 30–31
 Equinox Skyline Drive 33
 Smugglers Notch 34
 Vermont 100 31–35
 Vermont 22A 38–40
 Victory Basin Drive 35–36
Victory Basin Drive, Vt. 35–36
Virginia 97–105
 Blue Ridge Parkway 102–105
 Chesapeake Bay Bridge-Tunnel 98
 Colonial Parkway 97–98
 George Washington Memorial
  Parkway 99–100
 Journey through Hallowed Ground
  80–82
 Skyline Drive 100–102
Volcanic Legacy Scenic Byway, Calif.-
 Oreg. 428–430, 461–463

W

Waipio Valley, Hawaii 480
Wallowa-Whitman N.F., Oreg. 435,
 438–439
Wasatch-Cache N.F., Utah 277–279
Washington 398–417
 Chinook Scenic Byway 416–417
 Coulee Corridor Scenic Byway
  404–405
 International Selkirk Loop
  376–377
 Mount Adams Drive 412–414
 Mount Baker Scenic Byway
  398–399
 Mount St. Helens 414–416
 Mountains to Sound Greenway
  407–408
 North Cascades Highway 401–403
 Olympic Peninsula 408–411
 Sherman Pass Scenic Byway
  403–404
 Stevens Pass Greenway 406–407
 Strait of Juan de Fuca Highway
  411–412
 White Pass Scenic Byway 399–401
Washington Heritage Trail, W.Va.
 90–91
West Cascades Scenic Byway, Oreg.
 432–433
West Virginia 90–97
 Canaan Valley Byway 91–92
 Coal Heritage Trail 96–97
 Highland Scenic Highway 94–95
 Historic Natl. Road 83–84
 Midland Trail 95–96
 Staunton-Parkersburg Turnpike 93
 Washington Heritage Trail 90–91

Western Heritage Historic Byway,
 Idaho 368–369
Wetlands and Wildlife Scenic Byway,
 Kans. 230–231
White Mountain Apache Reserva-
 tion, Ariz. 305, 306
White Mountain Trail, N.H. 24–26
White Mountains Drive, Ariz.
 305–306
White Pass Scenic Byway, Wash.
 399–401
White Sands N.M., N.Mex. 313
Whiteface Mountain Memorial High-
 way, N.Y. 62
Whitefish Bay Scenic Byway, Mich.
 164–165
Wichita Mountains Byway, Okla.
 261–262
Wilderness Road Heritage Highway,
 Ky. 123
Willamette N.F., Oreg. 430–431, 432
Williamsburg, Va. 98
Wind River Range, Wyo. 360, 361,
 362
Wisconsin 192–198
 Apostle Islands Country 197–198
 Great River Road 196–197
 Kettle Moraine Scenic Drive
  192–194
 Wisconsin River Scenic Drive
  194–195
Woodlands Scenic Byway, Iowa
 237–238
Woodlands Trace, Ky.-Tenn. 126
Woodward Avenue, Mich. 169
Wrangell–St. Elias N.P. and Preserve,
 Alas. 385, 386
Wyoming 356–362
 Beartooth Highway 354–356
 Big Horn Mountains Scenic Byway
  357–358
 Black Hills 219–222
 Centennial Scenic Byway 360–361
 North Fork of the Shoshone
  356–357
 Snowy Range Road 358–359
 Teton Park Drive 362

Y

Yellowstone N.P., Idaho-Mont.-Wyo.
 350–353, 354–355
Yosemite N.P., Calif. 456–458

Z

Zion N.P. Scenic Byway, Utah
 291–293

Acknowledgments

National Geographic Books
warmly thanks the staff
of the Federal Highway
Administration, National
Scenic Byways Program,
for its support and assistance,
especially Rob Draper,
Director, and Patricia
McNally, Marketing
Communications Director.

National Geographic Guide to Scenic Highways & Byways Fourth Edition

Published by the National Geographic Society

John M. Fahey, *Chairman of the Board and Chief Executive Officer*

Timothy T. Kelly, *President*

Declan Moore, *Executive Vice President; President, Publishing and Digital Media*

Melina Gerosa Bellows, *Executive Vice President; Chief Creative Officer, Books, Kids, and Family*

Lynn Cutter, *Executive Vice President, Travel*

Keith Bellows, *Senior Vice President and Editor-in-Chief, National Geographic Travel Media*

Prepared by the Book Division

Hector Sierra, *Senior Vice President and General Manager*

Jonathan Halling, *Design Director, Books and Children's Publishing*

Marianne R. Koszorus, *Design Director, Books*

Barbara A. Noe, *Senior Editor, National Geographic Travel Books*

R. Gary Colbert, *Production Director*

Jennifer A. Thornton, *Director of Managing Editorial*

Susan S. Blair, *Director of Photography*

Meredith C. Wilcox, *Director, Administration and Rights Clearance*

Staff for the Fourth Edition

Lawrence M. Porges, *Project Editor*

Leslie Allen, *Text Editor*

Sanaa Akkach, *Art Director*

Rob Waymouth, *Illustrations Editor*

Ruthie Thompson, *Designer*

Carl Mehler, *Director of Maps*

Sven M. Dolling, Martin S. Walz, Michael McNey, *Map Research and Production*

Sarah Alban, Karen Carmichael, Justin Kavanagh, Christine O'Toole, Alan Rider, Jenna Schnuer, *Contributing Writers*

Marshall Kiker, Michael O'Connor, *Associate Managing Editors*

Judith Klein, *Production Editor*

Mike Horenstein, *Production Manager*

Galen Young, *Rights Clearance Specialist*

Katie Olsen, *Production Design Assistant*

Danielle Fisher, Jane Plegge, Erin Stone, *Contributors*

Manufacturing and Quality Management

Phillip L. Schlosser, *Senior Vice President*

Chris Brown, *Vice President, NG Book Manufacturing*

George Bounelis, *Vice President, Production Services*

Nicole Elliott, *Manager*

Rachel Faulise, *Manager*

Robert L. Barr, *Manager*

CELEBRATING

◄125►

YEARS

The National Geographic Society is one of the world's largest nonprofit scientific and educational organizations. Founded in 1888 to "increase and diffuse geographic knowledge," the Society's mission is to inspire people to care about the planet. It reaches more than 400 million people worldwide each month through its official journal, *National Geographic,* and other magazines; National Geographic Channel; television documentaries; music; radio; films; books; DVDs; maps; exhibitions; live events; school publishing programs; interactive media; and merchandise. National Geographic has funded more than 10,000 scientific research, conservation and exploration projects and supports an education program promoting geographic literacy. For more information, visit www.nationalgeographic.com.

For more information, please call 1-800-NGS LINE (647-5463) or write to the following address:
National Geographic Society
1145 17th Street N.W.
Washington, D.C. 20036-4688 U.S.A.

For information about special discounts for bulk purchases, please contact National Geographic Books Special Sales: ngspecsales@ngs.org

For rights or permissions inquiries, please contact National Geographic Books Subsidiary Rights: ngbookrights@ngs.org

ISBN: 978-1-4262-1014-3

The Library of Congress has cataloged the first edition as follows:

National geographic guide to scenic highways and byways.
   p. cm.
   Includes index.
   ISBN 0-7922-7468-7 (revised)
   1. United States—Tours. 2. Automobile travel—United States—Guidebooks.
   I. National Geographic Society (U.S.).
   Book Division.
E158.N263 1995
917.304'929—dc20   95-16166

Printed in China
15/PPS/2

The information in this book has been carefully checked and to the best of our knowledge is accurate. However, details can change, and the National Geographic Society cannot be responsible for such changes, or for errors or omissions.